JEWISH CEMETERIES

OF
FIVE COUNTIES
OF CONNECTICUT

THE
COHEN/GOLDFARB COLLECTION

VOLUME 2

Rabbi Edward A. Cohen
and
Lewis Goldfarb

HERITAGE BOOKS
2015

HERITAGE BOOKS

AN IMPRINT OF HERITAGE BOOKS, INC.

Books, CDs, and more—Worldwide

For our listing of thousands of titles see our website
at
www.HeritageBooks.com

Published 2015 by
HERITAGE BOOKS, INC.
Publishing Division
5810 Ruatan Street
Berwyn Heights, Md. 20740

Heritage Books by the authors:

Jewish Cemeteries of Hartford, Connecticut: The Cohen/Goldfarb Collection, Volume 1
Jewish Cemeteries of Five Counties of Connecticut. The Cohen/Goldfarb Collection, Volume 2

International Standard Book Numbers
Paperbound: 978-0-7884-0997-4
Clothbound: 978-0-7884-6108-8

DEDICATION

A project like this cannot be done alone. Although I have spent more than 1000 hours on this project and have worked until the wee hours of the night, I would like to thank my family, and especially my mother. It was her encouragement and understanding that helped me find and reach my goal in becoming a Rabbi, and to find my place in life.

Rabbi Edward A Cohen
25 Stoneham Drive
West Hartford, Ct 06117

I dedicate this volume to Weslie, my wife, who has encouraged me to keep up my lonely task. She has also provided an extra pair of eyes in editing both books. Her understanding and helpfulness has helped to make the first two volumes possible. I would also like to mention Beau, my faithful pet, who sacrificed may hours of playtime.

Lewis Goldfarb
22 Marilyn Road
South Windsor, Ct 06074

INTRODUCTION

Tombstones are very helpful in researching family and family history. The Jewish tombstone offers the following sources of information, although not every stone has all these elements:

1   Name, English and Hebrew, sometimes nickname

2   Death date, sometimes both Hebrew and English

3   Birth date, not traditional to give birth date but stones often give age at death

4   Fathers Name, if done with Hebrew inscription

5   Mothers name which is rare

6   Tribal affiliation if Levite or Cohan (descendent of Aaron, Moses's brother)

7   Inscription either personal or biblical

8   Pictures i.e.. picture of deceased, broken tree for early death, water pitcher for Levite, divided hands for Cohan

9   Sometimes the stone will give place of birth

10 Spouse

We have attempted to capture elements 1,2,3,4,5, 10. In addition, we are attempting to find each grave and give its location. The letter and number attempt to show row and grave from left side of cemetery. Although we have tried to be accurate we can not attest that errors may exist such as guessing spouse (grave next door) or difficulty reading weather-worn inscriptions. We have attempted to translate Hebrew in some instances in order to establish name and death date. We generally did not translate the Hebrew when English inscriptions were available. Therefore, at some later time, the stones will have to be reread to get the father's name when possible.

HISTORY

Even before the Association of Jewish Genealogical Societies attempted to have each chapter prepare a cemetery and tombstone list, I had plans to start such a project. Death dates find obituaries and obituaries give family connections. I have been asked to look up relatives and when I do I generally go to the Connecticut State Library on Capitol Avenue across from the State Capitol and look through City Directories, Obituaries and the State tombstone collection circa 1934 called "The Hale Collection".

Object #1 Instead of going to the state library, make copies of the state tombstone collection of the Jewish Cemeteries, index the collection alphabetically and by cemetery.

Object #2 The Hale Collection had several points of error which had to be addressed. The tombstone readers were generally of Irish in origin, could not read Hebrew, were not knowledgeable of Jewish customs, copied headstones and missed footstones, were unaware that by Jewish law tombstones are unveiled one year after a person's death (did not read grave markers). By far the worst situation existed if the cemetery name was written in Hebrew. They called the cemetery "Jewish Cemetery", New Jewish Cemetery", "Old Jewish Cemetery", "Hebrew Cemetery". The Hale Collection did not give location of the cemetery except for the town and did not attempt to give grave locations.

Object #3 Bring the Collection up to date. This means 60 plus years more of additional stones.

How to use the Cohen/Goldfarb Collection

If you are trying to find relatives who are buried in Connecticut, our collection will be of great assistance in helping you to locate the graves, find obituaries and death certificates. As was stated in our first volume, Jewish Cememteries of Hartford, Connecticut, Connecticut is a closed state and only members of recognized genealogical societies of Connecticut may look through death and birth certificates. Those that cannot do their own searches because they can not show proof of belonging to a recognized society must have the clerks do the search. They limit the search usually to 3 years before and after the guessed date. The guess work has now been eliminated.

If you know that your relative was buried in Hartford, he or she , in most cases, can be found in Volume 1. However, if they were buried outside of Hartford, this volume can be of help. It covers Hartford county, Litchfield county, Middlesex county, Tolland county, and New London county. New Haven county and Fairfield county are not complete, and, as of now, we have found no Jewish cemeteries in Windham county.

If you are looking for family plots, or possible relatives, we would suggest looking at the maps available from the authors. Perhaps the location of your relative may give a hint if the person next door is kin. Maps were only done for the Hartford cemeteries and not the others. However, the authors can provide information on individual cemeteries and in any sequence. All our data is stored on our computers using data base software. Thus we are able to extract and manipulate the data any way we wish.

When you look at the files, you will see several columns that may help you locate the grave or provide information. These might help you interpret what they mean.

Cem	Cemetery number - See Appendix A and it will tell you the name of the cemetery and the city or town and county where it is located.
Row	The letter represents the row, measured from the front end of the cemetery, while the number is the placement in the row.
Maiden Name	In most cases, Maiden Name is exactly what it appears. However, it is also used for other bits of information. Place of birth is sometimes shown, as well as age (if there is no date of death). An "*" after a date signifies that the year was Gregorian while the month was by the Jewish date. When the month (Tevet) and day were converted, There were two possible dates.
DOD	Date of Death - When left blank it could mean that it was not readable. NDD means no death date.
DOB	Date of Birth - If only the year is given, the stone only had the age. Blank could mean that it was not readable or not present.
Parents	The name in parenthesis is the mother's surname.

Good Luck,

Rabbi Edward A. Cohen and Lew Goldfarb

Cem	Row	Name	Maiden Name	DOD	DOB	Parents	Spouse
446	C73	A. P.					
102	AJ138	AARON, ABRAHAM H		2 JUN 1958	1897		
102	AF33	AARON, ANNE	GOLDENBERG	3 DEC 1990	4 JUL 1889		
391	GG 5	AARON, JOSHUA					
127	T	AARON, YUSIN		26 NOV 1982	14 JUL 1901		
125	D 68	ABBOT, LILLIAN	KOLODNEY	19 MAY 1984	1894		
447	L 8	ABEL, BERTHA	GORDON	25 NOV 1981	15 MAY 1899	YALE & JENNIE	
447	S22	ABEL, FRANK		4 JAN 1974	25 DEC 1892		GRACE
114	D17	ABEL, GERALD DAVID		1985	1946		
447	S23	ABEL, GRACE		22 NOV 1957	28 AUG 1893		FRANK
125	K 63	ABEL, ISRAEL ISAAC					
125	I 71	ABEL, JOSEPH		25 JAN 1914	1848		
125	M102	ABEL, MORRIS		11 MAR 1929	1856	ABRAHAM & FEIGE	REBECCA
125	M101	ABEL, REBECCA		31 JUL 1926	1854		MORRIS
125	K 62	ABEL, SAMUEL E		18 DEC 1913	1880		
125	M100	ABEL, SARAH		3 JUN 1935	1852		
104	N43	ABEL, SIDNEY H		17 MAY 1967	24 NOV 1920		
392	F23	ABELEVSKY, ISAAC		31 JAN 1926	1870	AARON	
392	I50	ABELMAN, LESTER H		15 NOV 1993	8 OCT 1928	OSCAR	
392	G50	ABELMAN, OSCAR		10 OCT 1991	1906	ABRAHAM	
125	J 63	ABELSON, FANNIE B		30 MAR 1903	1868		JACOB
103	E20	ABKOWICZ, LEON		21 SEP 1973	1919		ROSE
103	E19	ABKOWICZ, ROSE		22 AUG 1990			LEON
370	S46	ABKOWITZ, ABRAHAM		29 OCT 1961	1895		
370	P 5	ABLEMAN, ABRAHAM		11 APR 1952	1872		ANNIE
370	P 6	ABLEMAN, ANNIE		3 MAY 1967	1878		ABRAHAM
370	P 7	ABLEMAN, BURTON		24 JAN 1990	23 JUN 1903	ABRAHAM & ANNIE	
370	S35	ABLEMAN, SADIE	MAPSIK	21 OCT 1984	6 AUG 1904		SAMUEL
370	S36	ABLEMAN, SAMUEL		19 SEP 1978	4 NOV 1897	ABRAHAM & ANNIE	SADIE
374	G15	ABLETZ, NISAN		16 SEP 1916			
750	A21	ABRAHAMS, JOSEPH LOUIS		22 JUL 1965	29 APR 1932		
125		ABRAHAMSON, (BABY)		2 APR 1921	11 MAR 1921	JULIUS & FANNIE	
102	AJ34	ABRAHAMSON, ABRAHAM		17 OCT 1941	21 JUN 1879		MARY
125		ABRAHAMSON, DAVID		31 JAN 1925	1923	JULIUS & FANNIE	
125	Y183	ABRAHAMSON, FANNY	TEMKEIN	30 MAY 1984	28 MAR 1896		JULIUS
125	L161	ABRAHAMSON, GERTRUDE		4 SEP 1957	1907		
125	X177	ABRAHAMSON, JULIA		1991	1911		LOUIS
125	N142	ABRAHAMSON, JULIUS		6 MAR 1951	1893		FANNY
125	X176	ABRAHAMSON, LOUIS		25 DEC 1981	1901		JULIA
102	AJ33	ABRAHAMSON, MARY		23 MAR 1967	8 MAY 1881		ABRAHAM
125	W189	ABRAHAMSON, MAX		18 DEC 1979	1906		
125	I103	ABRAHAMSON, RACHEL		28 NOV 1943	1868	HYMAN & SARAH	SAMUEL
125	I104	ABRAHAMSON, SAMUEL		12 NOV 1928	1865	ABRAHAM & CHANA	RACHEL
125	K 46	ABRAHAMSON, SARAH		18 SEP 1912	1862		
103	E18	ABRAMOVICH, MARK	ANIKIN	1987	1937		
370	F14	ABRAMOWITZ, GUSSIE	SADINSKY	22 NOV 1963	1886		
248	F68	ABRAMS, BEN F		16 APR 1978	2 OCT 1914		
111	6	ABRAMS, BENJAMIN J		9 APR 1969	4 JUL 1896		IDA
125	G136	ABRAMS, BERTHA		7 APR 1974	1894		MAX
125	G137	ABRAMS, DOROTHY		5 MAY 1994		MAX & BERTHA	
447	R38	ABRAMS, HARRY		13 NOV 1974	1887		NELLIE
111	6	ABRAMS, IDA	STONE	1 JUL 1976	19 JAN 1891		BENJAMIN
377	O 7	ABRAMS, JANE S		1988	1893		MAX
125	G135	ABRAMS, MAX I		4 JUN 1967	1882		BERTHA
377	O 6	ABRAMS, MAX N		1945	1883		JANE
447	R37	ABRAMS, NELLIE		4 MAY 1962	1893		HARRY
391	O34	ABRAMS, RACHEL		22 JAN 1909		JOSEPH SHMARYAHU	
102	BH23	ABRAMS, SYDNEY L		7 OCT 1991	25 MAR 1913		
107	I21	ABRAMSKY, MORRIS		1980	1918		
102	C25	ABRAMSON, BENJAMIN		13 AUG 1972	1898	MORRIS & SONIA (RICKMAN)	
370	L15	ABRAMSON, BENJAMIN		14 JAN 1942	1870		ROSE
370	D 1	ABRAMSON, HYMAN A		19 OCT 1932	3 JUN 1872		SARAH
102	C34	ABRAMSON, LEO MYRON		13 JAN 1949	29 JAN 1896	MORRIS & SONIA (RICKMAN)	ROSE
330	G55	ABRAMSON, LILLIAN GOLDIE		23 APR 1929	1903		
102	CA27	ABRAMSON, LOUIS		5 NOV 1990	1911		ROSE

Cem	Row	Name	Maiden Name	DOD	DOB	Parents	Spouse
119	B55	ABRAMSON, MAX		27 MAY 1985	9 SEP 1913		
102	A34	ABRAMSON, MORRIS	OF POLTAVA	3 OCT 1936	1870		
391	G27	ABRAMSON, RACHEL		4 SEP 1961	1881	PHALIK	SONIA
102	CA26	ABRAMSON, ROSE		16 AUG 1968	1902		SAMUEL
102	C35	ABRAMSON, ROSE	WELINSKY	2 NOV 1986	21 JUN 1897		LOUIS
370	L14	ABRAMSON, ROSE		27 NOV 1957	1871		LEO
391	F 9	ABRAMSON, SAMUEL		5 NOV 1935	1880	ABRAHAM	BENJAMIN
102	C24	ABRAMSON, SARAH		16 NOV 1946	10 MAR 1893	MORRIS & SONIA (RICKMAN)	RACHEL
370	K 1	ABRAMSON, SARAH RACHEL		2 MAR 1952	22 FEB 1884		
102	C23	ABRAMSON, SIDNEY		8 APR 1955	3 SEP 1900	MORRIS & SONIA (RICKMAN)	HYMAN
102	A33	ABRAMSON, SONIA	RICKMAN	25 JUN 1952	1874		MORRIS
119	B56	ABRAMSON, SYLVIA		2 MAY 1990	19 DEC 1915		
375	D17	ABRASKIN, SAM		10 AUG 1984	1910		
102	BE 9	ABRETTER, BARBARA	ROTH	1988	1938		GERALD
102	AA29	ABUZA, BLANCHE MARIE		26 JAN 1966	8 FEB 1902		MOSES
222	G 6	ABUZA, HELEN		28 JUN 1979	28 APR 1915	HENRY W	
102	S13	ABUZA, LEAH	ZWILLINGER	7 FEB 1973	27 AUG 1887		PHILIP
102	AA28	ABUZA, MOSES CHARLES		27 FEB 1978	6 NOV 1889	CHARLES P & JENNIE (LENZ)	BLANCHE
102	S12	ABUZA, PHILIP		9 MAY 1945	5 JAN 1885	CHARLES P & JENNIE (LENZ)	LEAH
112	B26	ACKERMAN, HANS		18 FEB 1989	16 NOV 1907		HELMA
112	B27	ACKERMAN, HELMA		15 JUN 1989	18 MAY 1908		HANS
392	B 6	ADEL, LILLIAN		29 OCT 1967	1898		PHILIP
392	B12	ADEL, MAX		1943	1871		
392	B 7	ADEL, PHILIP		31 MAR 1965	1896	MAX	LILLIAN
125	N 80	ADELMAN, CLARA		31 MAR 1922	1867		
374	D46	ADELMAN, ETHEL		11 OCT 1960			MEYER
377	T44	ADELMAN, MARTIN		9 JUL 1989	16 JUL 1914	ISAAC	
374	D45	ADELMAN, MYER		13 FEB 1961			ETHEL
392	E38	ADELMAN, NATHAN		21 DEC 1946	1911	ISAAC	
377	U47	ADELMAN, PETER DAVID		23 JUN 1986	17 JUN 1945	NECHEMYA	
391	W79	ADELMAN, REBECCA		10 JUN 1981	1905	RUBEN	
105	I22	ADELSON, MAX		9 APR 1985	7 DEC 1895		
116	V 9	ADELSON, SIDNEY		6 MAR 1987	2 NOV 1918		
105	AA25	ADELSTEIN, FERN E		14 APR 1985	8 NOV 1945		
330	AA30	ADLER, BENJAMIN		29 AUG 1985	24 SEP 1916		
433	B 9	ADLER, ELEANOR	SANDER	27 DEC 1976	1940	SAMUEL & GERTRUDE	
113	L74	ADLER, ESTHER		11 MAY 1977	14 OCT 1907		MEYER
330	G64	ADLER, ETHEL		15 DEC 1938	1860		JACOB
433	F14	ADLER, GERTRUDE		2 JUN 1969	23 MAY 1906	MORDECHAI	SAMUEL
330	H32	ADLER, HENRY		4 APR 1950	7 JUL 1901	JACOB & ETHEL	
125	I186	ADLER, HERMAN		26 DEC 1968	1884		LENA
330	F31	ADLER, JACOB		2 DEC 1938	1846		ETHEL
330	H37	ADLER, JOSEPH		24 SEP 1946	25 DEC 1928		
125	I185	ADLER, LENA	ABRAHAMSON	31 OCT 1980	1895		HERMAN
330	C28	ADLER, LENA		12 APR 1965			WILLIAM
330	H36	ADLER, LEVI		9 APR 1947			
125	N104	ADLER, MARY	KASMAN	29 MAY 1927	1882	SHLOMO	NATHAN
113	L73	ADLER, MEYER		28 OCT 1976	28 APR 1903		ESTHER
125	T164	ADLER, NATHAN		5 APR 1940	1878		MARY
447	S34	ADLER, RALPH MICKEY		1987	1904		
433	F13	ADLER, SAMUEL		16 DEC 1955	1898	JACOB	GERTRUDE
330	C27	ADLER, WILLIAM		22 JUN 1959			LENA
392	B37	AFSMAN, RAISAL		10 AUG 1937			
114	C 7	AGDISH, MOLLIE B		2 AUG 1985	12 APR 1910		
391	O39	AGEN, ANNIE		2 MAR 1940	1892	MEYER	MORRIS
391	E34	AGEN, KATIE		1918	1916	MORRIS & ANNIE	
391	F 2	AGEN, MORRIS		25 NOV 1943	1878	ABARAHAM	ANNIE
392	J 4	AGRAN, BABIES		JUN 1968			
372	I14	AGRANOVITCH, ABRAHAM J		1951	1890		ROSE
371	J30	AGRANOVITCH, ANNA	ELGART	4 JUN 1986	2 DEC 1899		SAUL
391	N27	AGRANOVITCH, ISSAC		17 SEP 1915	1859	NAFTALI	
330	C12	AGRANOVITCH, JOSEPH		12 JAN 1973	15 MAR 1891		RAYZEL
372	I15	AGRANOVITCH, PAUL J		1944	1921	ABRAHAM & ROSE	
330	C11	AGRANOVITCH, RAYZEL		5 JUL 1967	4 JUL 1884		JOSEPH
372	I13	AGRANOVITCH, ROSE	CRUMB	1960	1890		ABRAHAM
371	J29	AGRANOVITCH, SAUL		14 JAN 1975	25 MAR 1893		ANNA

Cem	Row	Name	Maiden Name	DOD	DOB	Parents	Spouse
377	D27	AGRIN, AARON		16 FEB 1963	8 NOV 1894	LEV	ROSE
377	D28	AGRIN, ROSE		25 DEC 1976	1 FEB 1893	BENJAMIN	AARON
391	Q32	AGRONOVITCH, CAROL		19 NOV 1920		JOSEPH	
391	ZD55	AIGENSON, SADIE	LANN	23 OCT 1976	18 APR 1892	ISAAC	
125	H 72	AISENBERG, ABRAHAM K		11 AUG 1919	1867	MORDECHAI	BERTHA
125	H 73	AISENBERG, ADA		1916	1899	ABRAHAM & BERTHA	
125	G 71	AISENBERG, BERTHA		19 MAR 1954	1869		ABRAHAM
370	I24	AISENBERG, GITEL RAZZA		1 JAN 1929			ISAAC
370	A 3	AISENBERG, ISAAC		23 AUG 1928		YESHAI	GITEL
125	G 73	AISENBERG, WILLIAM D		23 MAR 1971	1904	ABRAHAM & BERTHA	
103	D17	AKERMAN, BRINA		28 JUN 1984	1 DEC 1949		
102	AB19	ALBERT, ANNIE		10 AUG 1976	1890		HARRIS
751	B14	ALBERT, CELIA		12 NOV 1990	3 NOV 1914	LOUIS & FANNIE	
447	H40	ALBERT, DEWEY		1988	1904		SADIE
751	B15	ALBERT, FANNIE		19 JUL 1983	1888		LOUIS
751	A35	ALBERT, HANNAH		14 DEC 1924	1857		
751	K37	ALBERT, ISRAEL		5 FEB 1954	1861		
751	B16	ALBERT, LOUIS		4 NOV 1963	1886	HANNAH	FANNIE
391	J36	ALBERT, MARTHA	GREENBERG	4 DEC 1990	1902	BENJAMIN	
751	K21	ALBERT, MAX		1 SEP 1933			
330	G60	ALBERT, MINNIE		3 JUN 1935	1876		
447	H39	ALBERT, SADIE		NDD	1906		DEWEY
106	A7	ALBERT, YANCI BETH		24 AUG 1989	4 FEB 1970		
222	AM 8	ALBOM, MILTON J		9 APR 1959	29 DEC 1915		
106	A38	ALBOUKREK, CORINA		10 NOV 1977	1906		JACOBO
106	A39	ALBOUKREK, JACOBO		17 FEB 1976	1902		CORINA
101	G22	ALBRECHT, ABRAHAM		12 JUN 1979	29 SEP 1895		
222	I 3	ALDERMAN, RAE		7 NOV 1991	6 MAY 1909		
125	R155	ALEX, HARRY		21 JUN 1943	1873	ABRAHAM	MINNIE
125	R156	ALEX, MINNIE	GREENBERG	21 AUG 1959	1881		HARRIS
370	J39	ALEXANDER, ABRAHAM R		1953	1880		UDES
372	A 1	ALEXANDER, BELLA		7 AUG 1883			LOAB
371	AR 3	ALEXANDER, ETHEL		29 OCT 1961			
119	L33	ALEXANDER, EVA		1988	1900		
119	L34	ALEXANDER, JOSEPH		1987	1895		
249	E30	ALEXANDER, MAURICE L		26 MAR 1962	18 JUL 1919		
102	CA38	ALEXANDER, MINNIE		8 JUN 1978	7 APR 1900		SAMUEL
112	D 3	ALEXANDER, NATHAN		1979	1890		
371	AR 4	ALEXANDER, ROSALIND		20 JUL 1974			
371	AR 1	ALEXANDER, RUBIN		21 JAN 1960			TESSIE
102	CA39	ALEXANDER, SAMUEL		21 AUG 1961	1897		MINNIE
447	T34	ALEXANDER, STANLEY J		4 JUN 1976	11 JUL 1906		
371	AR 2	ALEXANDER, TESSIE		31 OCT 1955			RUBEN
370	J40	ALEXANDER, UDES		1946	1880		ABRAHAM
102	AB 1	ALLEN, BELLE	COHEN	18 JUL 1972	20 APR 1909		
222	AP19	ALLEN, HARRY		14 SEP 1968	1885		
371	AN14	ALLEN, LENA KREIGER	8 JAN 1977*	28 DEC 1977*	1904		MANDELL
392	H37	ALLEN, LILLIAN	RIBCHINSKY	16 APR 1980	16 OCT 1913	ABRAHAM & ANNA (BLUM)	MYER
372	K 6	ALLEN, LOUIS		1984	1905		
371	AN13	ALLEN, MANDELL H		9 DEC 1978	1903		LENA
372	K 7	ALLEN, MARTHA	ROSENTHAL	1986	1907	JOSEPH & CHARLOTTE	
371	AI25	ALLEN, MYER		19 DEC 1973	1901	CHAIM	LILLIAN
371	AI26	ALLEN, SAMUEL		1 JUN 1969	1899	CHAIM	
249	C34	ALLEN, SAMUEL		15 APR 1984	6 SEP 1916		
370	Q31	ALLEN, TILLIE		1946	1878		
370	C25	ALOFSIN, ARI DAVID				CHAIM	
370	O27	ALOFSIN, BENJAMIN		16 OCT 1905	1869		
370	A48	ALOFSIN, BESSIE		14 NOV 1953	14 JUN 1889		
370	W13	ALOFSIN, ELIAS H		21 NOV 1924	1889		
370	O28	ALOFSIN, ELLIS		1936	1844		
370	I32	ALOFSIN, ETTA B		22 AUG 1915	28 OCT 1879		J B
370	O31	ALOFSIN, FANNIE		24 FEB 1913			SAUL
370	O29	ALOFSIN, HARRY		11 NOV 1939			
370	W15	ALOFSIN, HENRY A		28 AUG 1895	1881	HERMAN	
370	W12	ALOFSIN, HERMAN		12 SEP 1927	1857		
370	W11	ALOFSIN, LOUIS M DR		1 JUN 1939	1884		

Cem	Row	Name	Maiden Name	DOD	DOB	Parents	Spouse
370	W14	ALOFSIN, MAX J		2 NOV 1923	1886	HERMAN	
370	O30	ALOFSIN, SAUL		23 APR 1955		HERMAN	
370	T23	ALOFSIN, SOPHIA		16 DEC 1937			FANNIE
103	B36	ALPERIN, ANN		17 NOV 1988	15 MAY 1911		
103	B35	ALPERIN, SOPHIE		8 SEP 1990	26 OCT 1899		
101	F39	ALPEROWITZ, ALEX		3 MAR 1990	6 JAN 1895		
329	C 1	ALPERT, ABRAHAM		20 FEB 1967	15 JUN 1888		IDA
125	F 87	ALPERT, FRANCES	SCHUPACK	18 OCT 1972	1893		
102	AB20	ALPERT, HARRIS		7 AUG 1960	1890		ANNIE
330	AH18	ALPERT, HYMAN ISIDORE		24 OCT 1972	27 FEB 1907	MINNIE	
329	C 2	ALPERT, IDA		26 FEB 1964	22 AUG 1886		ABRAHAM
125	Q180	ALPERT, ISADORE		26 JUL 1982	1888		MINNIE
125	F140	ALPERT, LEWIS BERNARD		21 NOV 1965	8 DEC 1901		MURIEL
125	Q181	ALPERT, MINNIE	KING	2 JUL 1961	1889		ISADORE
125	F141	ALPERT, MURIEL DANA	BERKOWITZ	11 DEC 1977	23 FEB 1906	SAMUEL & JENNIE (WELINSKY)	LEWIS
119	C31	ALPORT, HERMAN J		6 AUG 1985	4 OCT 1908		
392	D44	ALTER, CLARA		9 JUN 1959	15 DEC 1898	ELIYAHU	DAVID
392	G17	ALTER, DAVID N		31 OCT 1942	15 AUG 1888	YECHEZKEL	CLARA
392	A 4	ALTER, HENRIETTA		12 MAR 1994	28 OCT 1921		
103	C48	ALTERMAN, FEIGA		15 JUN 1991	1 DEC 1905		
119	F66	ALTMAN, MAX		2 MAR 1978	16 NOV 1910		
751	C 4	ALTSCHULER, HARRY		7 OCT 1961	1897		YETTA
751	C 3	ALTSCHULER, YETTA		5 JUL 1967	1904		HARRY
248	E67	AMDUR, MILLARD JASON MD		15 MAR 1984	23 AUG 1937		
110	E23	ANDELMAN, FRANCES		9 JAN 1989	22 SEP 1899		
249	J 6	ANDERT, CELIA		11 DEC 1961	29 APR 1878		
104	F27	ANDORSKY, I FRED		9 NOV 1980	5 JAN 1913		
446	A40	ANENBERG, TOBIAS		1924	1924	J & R	
113	O36	ANGEL, ESTHER		21 JUN 1987	24 DEC 1900		MICHAEL
113	O37	ANGEL, MICHAEL		9 MAR 1960	6 JUL 1896		ESTHER
330	F34	ANGERT, ISRAEL		11 JAN 1916	1859		
125	N 83	ANOLICK, SYLVIA		24 FEB 1923	14 DEC 1922	SAUL & MOLLIE	
329	B36	ANSHEL, ABRAHAM		13 JUN 1943	1873		
329	B35	ANSHEL, ESTHER		8 JUL 1966			
329	D51	ANSHEL, HARRY		8 MAY 1972	16 APR 1915		
329	D52	ANSHEL, JOSEPH		15 JAN 1974	14 OCT 1902		
329	C49	ANSHEL, WILLIAM		28 FEB 1964			
102	AC159	ANTARSH, BETTY	ZITSER	3 OCT 1981	10 OCT 1913		LEON
103	B31	ANTARSH, ISADORE		10 JUN 1984	8 NOV 1901		
102	AC158	ANTARSH, LEON		22 MAR 1962	6 MAR 1908		BETTY
370	I30	ANTOKOL, IDA GERTRUDE		1960	1887		MEYER
370	L16	ANTOKOL, MEYER E		1942	1882		IDA
370	L17	ANTOKOL, NORMAN J		1943	1918	MEYER & IDA	
370	L19	ANTOKOL, SAMUEL		1944	1884		
105	O49	ANTONOVSKY, BORIS		16 DEC 1959	1893		SOPHIE
105	O50	ANTONOVSKY, SOPHIE		4 MAR 1972	1892		BORIS
101	K25	ANTONSKY, LENA		8 DEC 1937	1899		
116	T21	ANTOVIL, ABRAHAM		15 MAY 1981	1910		BEATRICE
116	T22	ANTOVIL, BEATRICE		4 SEP 1984	13 JUN 1917		ABRAHAM
102	AH206	APATOW, M MOLLY		11 OCT 1972	10 MAR 1902		
391	G13	APELBAUM, IDA		31 DEC 1922	1852	DAVID HIRSH	
102	C27	APPELBAUM, FRANCES M	GOLDBERG	12 APR 1971	9 JUN 1900		MICHAEL
102	C26	APPELBAUM, MICHAEL		13 MAY 1965	1896	BERNARD & GOLDIE	FRANCES
125	E 69	APPELL, ABE		1990	1911		
125	H 66	APPELL, DAVID		25 JUN 1945	1870	ABRAHAM & FRAIDA	SARAH
125	I 32	APPELL, ELIZABETH		26 DEC 1925	1 AUG 1861		
125	H151	APPELL, FREDERICA	WALLACE	15 MAY 1963	1907		HARRY
125	K 61	APPELL, FREIDA		20 MAY 1913	1833		ABRAHAM
125	D 69	APPELL, HARRY		30 MAR 1992	1906		
125	G152	APPELL, HARRY S		19 NOV 1965	1896		FREDERICA
377	W14	APPELL, JACK		1960	1902		
125	F 63	APPELL, MOLLY		6 DEC 1962	1889		MORRIS
125	F 64	APPELL, MORRIS		22 SEP 1941	1877	ALEXANDER	MOLLY
125	J 47	APPELL, PAULINE		19 NOV 1895	1882		
125	F 65	APPELL, SARAH		18 OCT 1918	1877		
125	H 65	APPELL, SARAH		22 DEC 1954	1872		DAVID

Cem	Row	Name	Maiden Name	DOD	DOB	Parents	Spouse
125	J 32	APPELL, SOLOMON		16 FEB 1914	20 NOV 1858	ABRAHAM	
119	H54	APPLEBAUM, CELIA	BROWN	6 FEB 1988	23 APR 1914		
493	B20	APPLEBAUM, MORTON		28 SEP 1983	21 MAR 1913		
119	L47	APPLEMAN, BESSIE		21 JUN 1982	2 JUL 1911		
119	L46	APPLEMAN, GEORGE		14 APR 1912	19 JUL 1911		
248	N80	APTER, BERTHA		26 SEP 1975	3 JUN 1880		
102	R27	APTER, BESSIE	HORWITZ	9 SEP 1943	1903		MORRIS
109	E10	APTER, MARVIN		4 NOV 1975	3 JUN 1917		ROSALIND
102	R26	APTER, MORRIS		21 JUN 1956	1889		BESSIE
113	J65	APTER, SAYDE		26 OCT 1978	19 AUG 1911		
125	DA41	ARBACH, EDITH		3 SEP 1972	1900		
102	BE10	ARBETTER, GERALD A		3 JUN 1992			BARBARA
101	M17	ARBITMAN, HANNAH		2 DEC 1900	1848		
121	E18	ARCHAMBAULT, ROSE	COHEN	6 JAN 1976	7 APR 1912		
371	L26	ARENBERG, ABRAHAM E		1962	1893		ROSE
371	L25	ARENBERG, ROSE		1978	1896		ABRAHAM
102	D43	ARENSON, ETTA H	HERSH	27 AUG 1978	16 APR 1905		HARRY
102	D44	ARENSON, HARRY L		17 MAY 1952	5 SEP 1905	MORRIS J & MARCIA (LUBROW)	ETTA
374	B46	ARIEWITZ, DINAH		11 JUN 1946	1870		
374	B44	ARIEWITZ, SAMUEL H		24 SEP 1966	1893	DINAH	SARAH
374	B45	ARIEWITZ, SARAH		30 MAY 1954	1891		SAMUEL
371	N21	ARIKER, LOUIS		21 APR 1963	30 JAN 1904		RAE
371	N20	ARIKER, RAE		24 JUL 1981	22 OCT 1900		LOUIS
391	ZA80	ARITZIS, SARAH	SLADE	20 JUL 1982	14 JAN 1907	JOSEPH	
371	K13	ARKAVA, BESSIE	YALEN	7 NOV 1988	4 JUL 1902		WOLF
391	V53	ARKAVA, MOLLIE		9 FEB 1954		JOSHUA	SIMON
370	C 4	ARKAVA, MOSES L		16 MAY 1927			
391	V54	ARKAVA, SIMON ISAAC		15 OCT 1966		ARYEH	MOLLIE
371	AQ22	ARKAVA, SOLOMON		6 JUN 1965	9 AUG 1906		
371	K12	ARKAVA, WOLF		1967	1901		BESSIE
125	D 39	ARKIN, IDA SARAH		17 SEP 1950	1893		LOUIS
125		ARKIN, JACOB AARON		21 JUL 1921	1871	AARON & ANNA	
125	D 38	ARKIN, LOUIS N		27 FEB 1970	1898	JACOB	IDA
391	D40	ARKOW, CHANA CHAYA		23 JUN 1922		ISAAC SIMON	
446	B40	ARNDT, BERNARD		1946	1874		FLORENCE
446	B41	ARNDT, FLORENCE B		1959	1891		BERNARD
370	C 3	ARNOWITZ, AARON		10 FEB 1927			
116	J13	ARON, FRED J		29 JUL 1991	7 MAR 1914		
112	C 8	ARON, OSCAR		5 OCT 1982	1 DEC 1901		
107	D15	ARONOWITZ, CHARLOTTE	LUTWACK	29 MAY 1986	7 AUG 1912		EDWARD
107	D16	ARONOWITZ, EDWARD		12 FEB 1972	1904		CHARLOTTE
105	J41	ARONOWITZ, PAUL		29 DEC 1956	1901		
102	BA 9	ARONS, MILTON R		6 AUG 1990	11 AUG 1903		
123		ARONSON, ABRAHAM A		11 AUG 1947	1900		
102	Z29	ARONSON, ANNIE	ABUZA	29 SEP 1960	25 MAR 1892	CHARLES & JENNIE (LENZ)	JULIUS
113	N30	ARONSON, BARBARA	MANDEL	28 MAR 1976	13 JUL 1926		
123		ARONSON, EDWARD		9 MAR 1945			
377	N11	ARONSON, ELI		14 MAY 1986	12 MAR 1902		
123		ARONSON, IRVING		15 JAN 1945	1919		
102	Z28	ARONSON, JULIUS		5 OCT 1970	7 NOV 1894		ANNIE
123		ARONSON, NATHAN		4 JUN 1956	1890		
125	N163	ARRICK, EVA		3 JUL 1951	1871		
376	C 8	ARUNDELL, PHILIP F		1 SEP 1988	3 SEP 1936		
222	AE14	ASBEL, CHARLES		16 JAN 1957	1895	CHASHE	RACHEL
222	AE15	ASBEL, CHASHE (FEMALE)		12 MAR 1924	1856		
222	AE13	ASBEL, RACHEL		20 OCT 1967	1900		CHARLES
104	K13	ASCHER, ELEANOR	EVAL	4 AUG 1988			
372	F 4	ASHER, SARAH I		1946	1860		
370	I46	ASHKENASY, AARON I		28 SEP 1925	1857		FRUME
370	I47	ASHKENASY, FRUME ESTHER		19 JUN 1929	1857		AARON
370	X16	ASHKINASY, ANNIE		4 SEP 1936		AARON & FRUME	
110	B26	ASIA, ESTHER		29 MAR 1937	1880		
102	AC 5	ASKINAS, MARY	NETUPSKY	13 NOV 1984	25 MAR 1898		
123		ASTON, MORRIS		22 DEC 1939	1894		
249	D35	ASTOR, ABRAHAM I		8 OCT 1990	15 MAY 1905		
433	F23	ASTROVE, BELLA		28 OCT 1957	1886		

Cem	Row	Name	Maiden Name	DOD	DOB	Parents	Spouse
370	G21	ATKIND, JENNIE R		19 FEB 1958	1882		
370	G20	ATKIND, LOUIS		4 AUG 1973	1882		LOUIS
119	K41	ATTAS, HELEN		24 AUG 1988	3 JUN 1916		JENNIE
121	D18	ATTAS, MYRON		1983	1918		
447	U 9	AUERBACH, MOLLIE L		11 DEC 1961	1891		
493	E34	AUERBACH, PHILIP		OCT 1985	OCT 1920		SAMUEL
248	I72	AUERBACH, SAMUEL		25 MAR 1922	1881		
447	U10	AUERBACH, SAMUEL		8 OCT 1961	1886		MOLLIE
372	G13	AUGENBLICK, BERTHA	GREENBERGER	1917	1891		HARRY A
372	G14	AUGENBLICK, BETTY		1922	1917	HARRY & BERTHA	
107	B10	AURBACH, LILLIAN M		18 FEB 1988	1918		
447	R12	AUSTER, DAVID		21 MAY 1982	18 FEB 1926		
433	K 2	AUSTER, LENA		23 JUL 1948	1889	YEHUDA	PHILIP
433	J 2	AUSTER, MARY P		14 SEP 1962	1918	PHILIP & LENA	
447	Y 8	AUSTER, MORRIS		17 DEC 1967	28 APR 1914		
433	K 1	AUSTER, PHILIP		16 JUL 1955	1890	MEYER ZALMAN	LENA
114	B18	AUSTIN, MILTON J		24 OCT 1991	30 APR 1929	MEYER	
433	D26	AXELROD, ANNA E		29 APR 1982	1905		SAMUEL
248	I59	AXELROD, ANNIE		4 JUN 1914	1905	LAZAR	
249	Q 2	AXELROD, BARUCH AVRAHAM					
376	A 6	AXELROD, BENJAMIN		NDD	15 OCT 1903		MARY
249	I 3	AXELROD, ITAH		20 MAR 1955	1880		YACOV
433	G21	AXELROD, JOSEPH		19 MAY 1953	1871	JACOB	
249	C18	AXELROD, LOUIS		8 SEP 1980	2 JAN 1914		
376	A 7	AXELROD, MARY F		25 FEB 1991	6 APR 1895		BENJAMIN
125	D 59	AXELROD, MORRIS A		6 MAY 1947	21 MAR 1891	NACHUM & SARAH	
102	BC22	AXELROD, RUTH	FRANCIS	21 JUN 1992	19 MAR 1929		
433	D25	AXELROD, SAMUEL		21 AUG 1958	1894	JOSEPH	ANNA
125	K138	AXELROD, SARAH		6 MAR 1932	1848		NACHUM
249	I 4	AXELROD, YACOV MOSHE		13 MAR 1960	1872		ITAH
110	D23	AZIA, ABRAHAM		4 FEB 1973	15 AUG 1879		
110	C16	AZIA, ESTHER		1 SEP 1962	1886		
119	K30	BACHRACH, LEVI MONTAGUE		21 NOV 1982	20 JUN 1896		
119	K32	BACHRACK, BEVERLY N	POLLACK	26 MAR 1986	24 SEP 1933	SAMUEL	
447	V24	BACHUS, MASHARNA		25 OCT 1935	1860		
119	C 6	BACKER, NATHAN L		24 APR 1991	3 NOV 1917		
112	D 4	BACKER, STELLA	PICK	30 NOV 1983	19 NOV 1901		
446	C37	BAER, HEINIE		1914	1913		
112	C 3	BAER, JULIUS		5 OCT 1983	22 MAR 1907		
102	AG 3	BAGGISH, BLUMA	WHITE	22 MAY 1956	1874		NATHAN
102	AG 4	BAGGISH, NATHAN		22 MAY 1940	1873	PINCUS M & PESHE (ROSENBERG)	BLUMA
102	AD 8	BAILEY, JAMES R		1990	1907		
102	W 2	BAILYN, CHARLES M		26 JAN 1946	15 MAY 1888		ESTHER
102	W 1	BAILYN, ESTHER	SCHLOSS	19 SEP 1964	1 JAN 1894		CHARLES
751	O 8	BAKER, AARON		1978	1895		
248	J23	BAKER, ALEXANDER		15 SEP 1912			
751	O 7	BAKER, ANNA		1986	1904		
370	T 4	BAKER, ARNOLD B		2 APR 1988	13 MAR 1917		BEATRICE
370	T 5	BAKER, BEATRICE R		21 OCT 1976	31 MAY 1918		ARNOLD
751	C24	BAKER, BESSIE		28 MAY 1964	1886		ELLIS
751	K25	BAKER, ELIAS M		8 JUN 1928	1876		
751	C25	BAKER, ELLIS D		15 JUN 1955	1876		BESSIE
751	K12	BAKER, ETHEL		25 OCT 1936	1849		
751	O 6	BAKER, HARRY		1988	1904		
751	D35	BAKER, HETTY		1920	1900		
751	B23	BAKER, ISRAEL		3 DEC 1985	2 FEB 1909		
751	O 5	BAKER, JEAN	SILVER	1989	1908		
377	V42	BAKER, KENNETH ALLEN		7 NOV 1986	11 DEC 1947	WOLF & CHANA	
125	M179	BAKER, MORRIS		28 MAY 1968	1912		
329	E 2	BALABAN, BERTHA		28 FEB 1991	1898		JACK
329	E 3	BALABAN, IDA		15 OCT 1984	1926	JACK & BERTHA	
329	E 1	BALABAN, JACK		13 JAN 1981	1896		BERTHA
329	F 1	BALABAN, JULIUS		16 MAR 1989	2 NOV 1930	JACK & BERTHA	
101	M22	BALACHOVSKY, ANNIE		15 JUL 1911	13 MAY 1887		
374	C 3	BALESON, YETTA		17 MAR 1922	12 DEC 1909		
377	D32	BALINE, BENJAMIN		12 MAY 1953	1880	MOSHE	NETTIE

Cem	Row	Name	Maiden Name	DOD	DOB	Parents	Spouse
391	D41	BALINE, LEONARD		23 OCT 1925	10 OCT 1925	BENJAMIN & NETTIE	
377	D30	BALINE, MILTON P		3 DEC 1966	1917	BENJAMIN & NETTIE	
377	D31	BALINE, NETTIE R		21 JUL 1951	1886	MOSHE	
116	AV 5	BALKAN, LOUISE HARRIET		30 SEP 1962	23 APR 1920		BENJAMIN
377	N 8	BALKANSKY, ROSE		1958	1899		SIMON
377	N 9	BALKANSKY, SIMON		1953	1897		ROSE
248	H62	BALLON, BENJAMIN		7 SEP 1958	1871		EMMA
248	H58	BALLON, DORA	STOTZ	14 FEB 1926	1890		SAMUEL
248	H63	BALLON, EMMA		4 JAN 1966	1880		BENJAMIN
371	AM11	BALLON, EVELYN HILDA	BOKOFF	11 APR 1972	1923		
371	AJ21	BALLON, JULIAN		1986	1922		
248	I55	BALLON, LAWRENCE		8 MAR 1915	22 AUG 1912	S & D	
248	I56	BALLON, RACHEL				S & P	
248	H64	BALLON, SAMUEL		29 MAR 1966	1881		
222	AT 4	BALLOT, GERTRUDE		24 OCT 1953	15 JAN 1885		LOUIS
222	AT 3	BALLOT, LENA G		12 JUL 1960	24 DEC 1911		
222	AT 5	BALLOT, LOUIS		13 OCT 1952	2 SEP 1877	LOUIS & GERTRUDE	GERTRUDE
125	T170	BALOGH, JOSEPH		31 MAR 1988	24 OCT 1922		
446	C21	BALTER, ROSIE R		2 FEB 1920	1860		
447	M15	BALTIMORE, HARRY		20 JAN 1940	1897		
447	M21	BALTIMORE, JACOB		24 DEC 1983	1 OCT 1888		SADIE
447	M20	BALTIMORE, SADIE		26 JUL 1941	18 JUL 1893		JACOB
392	J18	BALTINSKY, ROSE		1943	1882		
447	U23	BANDER, PAULINE		12 MAR 1936	15 DEC 1919		
222	L 8	BANEMAN, DOROTHY		14 MAY 1981	2 FEB 1902		
222	L11	BANEMAN, RHODA		9 FEB 1955			
110	E12	BANK, GALE LESLIE		17 JAN 1979	18 JAN 1954	HARRY	
102	AE53	BANKS, CECELIA	YESSNER	27 SEP 1986	4 SEP 1903		GOODMAN
102	S 6	BANKS, CHARLES H		15 JAN 1985	6 AUG 1897		ELIZABETH
102	S 5	BANKS, ELIZABETH W		5 JUN 1989	8 JUN 1899		CHARLES
102	AE101	BANKS, FANNIE	SAVITSKY	17 AUG 1953	1883		HARRY
102	AE54	BANKS, GOODMAN		1 MAY 1973	21 SEP 1902		CECELIA
102	AE100	BANKS, HARRY		20 FEB 1965	1878		FANNIE
102	AF98	BANKS, JACOB J		1 NOV 1977	11 DEC 1915		ROSE
102	AF96	BANKS, ROSE	GAYLOR	19 JUN 1979	14 JUN 1913		JACOB
249	F36	BANNER, JULIUS		14 OCT 1977	29 APR 1914		MARY
249	F35	BANNER, MARY		20 JUL 1991	9 DEC 1913		JULIUS
433	I 2	BANNER, ROSE		5 JUN 1948	1888	YOEL	SAMUEL
433	I 1	BANNER, SAMUEL		1968	1880	SAMUEL	ROSE
395	B 9	BARASCH, EUGENE		26 MAR 1890	19 JUN 1874	ABRAHAM	
127	Q	BARASH, LUCAS SCOTT		23 JUN 1984	25 NOV 1974		
391	I31	BARATZ, GERTRUDE		1 DEC 1939	1868	SHLOM ZALMAN	MAX
377	B 1	BARATZ, JOHN		17 MAY 1972	30 SEP 1887		SOPHIE
377	B 3	BARATZ, LEW	SHERRY	1976	1894		JOHN
377	B 5	BARATZ, LYDIA	SACHS	4 APR 1972	26 AUG 1897		MOSS
391	I30	BARATZ, MAX		20 JUN 1921	1864	MOSHE	GERTRUDE
377	B 6	BARATZ, MOSS		27 NOV 1956	9 OCT 1889		LYDIA
377	B 2	BARATZ, SOPHIE	ROSEN	1957	1892		JOHN
377	A 1	BARATZ, WILBUR S		17 AUG 1972	2 APR 1917		
370	Y12	BARBER, MAX HERMAN		18 AUG 1957	1902		ROSE
370	Y13	BARBER, ROSE	BERNSTEIN	6 SEP 1973	1905		MAX
119	E21	BARENBAUM, JACOB		20 JAN 1975	20 MAR 1904		
751	L39	BARENKRANTZ, HARRY		5 NOV 1931	JAN 1931		
391	GL 5	BARNET, TUWIE L		10 DEC 1930	1858		
377	R33	BARNETT, ANNE F		1969	1910		
391	P54	BARNETT, DAVID		22 APR 1953	11 APR 1898	JOSEPH	LILLIAN
391	P56	BARNETT, IDA		11 DEC 1953	1861	DAVID & LILLIAN	
391	P57	BARNETT, JOAN		31 MAY 1980	24 MAY 1926	DOV BER	
391	Q27	BARNETT, JOSEPH T		17 JAN 1914	1843	BARUCH YECSKEL	
391	C12	BARNETT, JULIUS		21 JUN 1947	1884	JOSEPH	
391	P55	BARNETT, LILLIAN		10 JUL 1973	6 FEB 1898	HIRSH	DAVID
433	I18	BARON, BUNIE		7 DEC 1927	1854	ZALMAN	HYMAN
433	H16	BARON, HARRY		23 OCT 1939	1874	HYMAN & BUNIE	
104	I 1	BARON, HYMAN		27 JUL 1962	1878		SARAH
433	I17	BARON, HYMAN B		2 MAR 1931	1852	ISRAEL TZVI	BUNIE
433	K13	BARON, IDA S		10 APR 1970	2 APR 1894	SHLOMO	ISADORE

Cem	Row	Name	Maiden Name	DOD	DOB	Parents	Spouse
433	K14	BARON, ISADORE		19 NOV 1989	10 APR 1891	HYMAN & BUNIE	IDA
433	J18	BARON, MELVIN		4 JUN 1944	6 MAY 1944	ISADORE & IDA	
750	C20	BARON, MILTON		25 NOV 1969	26 SEP 1910		SYLVIA
104	I 2	BARON, SARAH		26 DEC 1959	1883		HYMAN
433	I16	BARON, SIDNEY		18 MAY 1928	6 SEP 1921	HYMAN & BUNIE	
750	C19	BARON, SYLVIA		3 FEB 1988	22 MAR 1908		MILTON
125	F 27	BAROWSKY, MAE (MOLLY)	SHAEFER	5 JUL 1921	1894	SIMON & ROSE	
119	H42	BARR, ALBERT P		1977	1925		
102	BC25	BARSHAY, SHARON	LUFTGLAS	17 JUL 1987	16 JAN 1955		
446	B32	BARSHOP, MENACHEM MENDEL		5 JAN 1894			
102	AD207	BARSON, NATALIE		13 MAR 1992			SAMUEL
102	AD206	BARSON, SAMUEL		18 MAY 1986	6 OCT 1906		NATALIE
119	D27	BARTH, ANNETTA		26 FEB 1980			
119	D28	BARTH, JACOB		7 NOV 1981			
119	C12	BARTH, MORRIS H		1987	1911		
374	F20	BARTKOWSKI, ITZIG HIRSH		1936	1923		
102	CB59	BARTON, SAUL S		1 FEB 1989	21 APR 1911		
395	A 4	BARUCH, ADOLPH		1944	1863		ANNIE
395	A 5	BARUCH, ANNIE		1936	1865		ADOLPH
102	T47	BASCH, CHARLES		11 NOV 1979	15 SEP 1888		ROSE
116	A 8	BASCH, JERROLD LEE		6 SEP 1983	14 AUG 1955		
102	T48	BASCH, ROSE F		26 DEC 1977	3 APR 1895		CHARLES
102	K17	BASCH, SIDNEY		2 APR 1989	24 JUN 1910		SYLVIA
102	K14	BASCH, SILVIA B		16 MAY 1968	15 JAN 1916		SIDNEY
116	U17	BASCHE, MALCOLM		25 JUN 1975	20 NOV 1926		
102	A10	BASHNER, JENNIE		6 DEC 1942	1864		LOUIS
102	A 9	BASHNER, LOUIS		9 JUL 1931	1861		JENNIE
111	4	BASKIN, ABRAHAM H MD		24 NOV 1981	8 JUN 1907		
102	AA152	BASKIND, GERTRUDE		31 JAN 1987	5 APR 1904		JACOB
102	AA153	BASKIND, JACOB P		29 SEP 1972	16 AUG 1907		GERTRUDE
125	K123	BASON, HARRY		5 JUL 1933	1865		
102	L 5	BASOW, EDITH RAPHAEL		30 APR 1948	1873		HENRY
102	L 4	BASOW, HENRY		15 DEC 1941	1872		EDITH
102	L 6	BASOW, JOSEPH E		9 MAR 1971	1895	HENRY & EDITH	
371	A35	BASS, ABRAHAM		22 MAR 1955	14 FEB 1896		ROSE
101	L35	BASS, BESSIE		1 APR 1956	1889		
119	H44	BASS, CLARA	TULIN	1 SEP 1976	6 SEP 1912		
371	A33	BASS, HARRY DR		1975	1907		LENA
106	A33	BASS, IDA	ALTERMAN	26 FEB 1979	23 DEC 1904		HARRY
371	A34	BASS, LENA S		27 MAR 1970			HARRY
370	B35	BASS, MORRIS		18 FEB 1946			
125	N170	BASS, NOAH NATHAN		16 NOV 1981	1891		SIPERA
371	A36	BASS, ROSE ELLA		19 OCT 1950			ABRAHAM
125	Z177	BASS, SAUL J		28 SEP 1986	8 JUL 1914		
125	N171	BASS, SIPERA PAULINE		1965	1889		NOAH
102	AI68	BASSEVITCH, BLUMA	JACOBS	30 APR 1989	28 SEP 1908		ISADORE
102	AH67	BASSEVITCH, ISADORE L		12 JAN 1981	15 AUG 1895	JULIUS & SARAH (GLOTZER)	BLUMA
102	AH70	BASSEVITCH, JULIUS	OF PINSK	17 JUN 1951	1870		SARAH
102	AH69	BASSEVITCH, SARAH	GLOTZER	15 DEC 1949	1870		JULIUS
102	CB17	BASSOCK, BEATRICE	ARMOUR	5 APR 1982	24 SEP 1906		MAXWELL
102	CB16	BASSOCK, MAXWELL		16 DEC 1981	1 MAY 1898		BEATRICE
102	AJ193	BASSOK, BENNIE		2 JAN 1983	22 SEP 1900		SARAH
102	AJ192	BASSOK, SARAH		3 DEC 1973	23 SEP 1900		BENNIE
391	GB 3	BASSON, FLORENCE		20 JAN 1961	13 APR 1881	MOSHE	MAX
374	I44	BASSON, HAROLD		28 FEB 1993	11 NOV 1912		VIOLA
391	G20	BASSON, HAYDA		8 JUN 1922	1859	YESHIYAHU ZELIG	
391	GN 6	BASSON, MAX		9 NOV 1928	10 APR 1882	ZALMAN & HAYDA	FLORENCE
374	I43	BASSON, VIOLA		12 JUN 1976	11 JUL 1915		HAROLD
447	P38	BATTALIN, HENRY MD		21 MAY 1961	1870		RACHEL
447	P37	BATTALIN, RACHEL R		17 JUL 1965	1873		HENRY
102	AA16	BATTALION, EDYTHE		24 JUN 1989	13 APR 1914		JOSEPH
102	AA17	BATTALION, JOSEPH M		18 DEC 1982	5 DEC 1911		EDYTHE
125	W196	BAUER, M LEONARD		12 MAY 1991			MARCIA
125	W195	BAUER, MARCIA	WEXLER	28 FEB 1980			LEONARD
102	AI175	BAUM, FRED A		16 DEC 1982			
446	A13	BAUM, HINDA		9 JUL 1965	1877		MAX

Cem	Row	Name	Maiden Name	DOD	DOB	Parents	Spouse
446	A12	BAUM, MAX		5 MAY 1925	1871		HINDA
127	C	BAUM, ROSE	FOSTER	14 APR 1976	4 JUL 1902		ROSE
127	C	BAUM, SAMUEL		8 AUG 1977	25 JUN 1904		SAMUEL
446	A17	BAUMSTEIN, CHARLES		20 JAN 1924	1883		
102	AF55	BAUMSTEIN, DORA	ITZKOVITZ	29 SEP 1957	19 NOV 1891		SOLOMON
102	AF53	BAUMSTEIN, HAROLD L		16 NOV 1943	14 AUG 1922	SOLOMON & DORA (ITZKOVITZ)	
104	C28	BAUMSTEIN, MAY		23 AUG 1992	19 MAR 1900		SAMUEL
104	C29	BAUMSTEIN, SAMUEL		1969	1893		MAY
102	AF52	BAUMSTEIN, SAMUEL A		8 JAN 1929	30 MAR 1913	ISRAEL & ANNA (LEADES)	
102	AF54	BAUMSTEIN, SOLOMON	OF SLONIM	12 DEC 1969	5 DEC 1885	ISRAEL & ANNA (LEADES)	DORA
103	A14	BAYER, ARNOLD E		4 DEC 1983	29 SEP 1937	JACK	JUDITH
113	H32	BAYER, BESSIE		2 JAN 1964	10 JAN 1888		LOUIS
125	AA119	BAYER, DORA		1991	1900		ESRAEL
125	AA118	BAYER, ESRAEL		1989	1894		DORA
125	O162	BAYER, ETTA		25 MAR 1962	1883		
125	O104	BAYER, EVA		22 APR 1927			
103	A15	BAYER, JACK		6 FEB 1988	1 JAN 1900		
113	H31	BAYER, LOUIS		30 NOV 1958	4 JUL 1887		BESSIE
125	O161	BAYER, MORRIS		17 JAN 1950	1867	MOSHE	RACHEL
113	H33	BAYER, PHILIP		12 JUL 1977	26 AUG 1916	LOUIS & BESSIE	RUTH
125	J136	BAYER, RACHEL	MILLER	19 MAR 1935	1871	MILLER	MORRIS
113	H30	BAYER, RUTH K		21 MAY 1990	29 APR 1913		PHILIP
107	C21	BAZAN, MAXINE	SPECTOR	11 MAR 1974	22 OCT 1924		
116	W23	BAZER, ROBERT		24 SEP 1978	12 JAN 1936		
751	C14	BAZIL, BERTHA	FAGERSON	1966	1883		ISRAEL
751	C15	BAZIL, ISRAEL		1953	1883		BERTHA
102	BA 1	BAZILLIAN, JOSEPH		22 OCT 1989	12 JUN 1902		
105	A13	BEATMAN, BESSIE		29 JAN 1957	1896		
102	F44	BEATMAN, CAROLINE	KRAUSS	5 APR 1985	29 APR 1902		
102	M33	BEATMAN, ETHEL	KLEINMAN	11 FEB 1986	5 JUL 1905		ESTHER
102	Q 6	BEATMAN, EVELYN	ZEMAN	7 SEP 1948	9 MAR 1903		JOSEPH
102	M32	BEATMAN, ISRAEL MD		30 NOV 1960	7 APR 1900		ETHEL
102	Q 3	BEATMAN, JOSEPH W		2 NOV 1965	21 SEP 1901	WALTER & ROSE (BORDON)	EVELYN
105	B14	BEATMAN, MORRIS		1 JUN 1949	1888		
377	R23	BEATMAN, NORMA BELLE		18 DEC 1982	14 FEB 1930		
125	S195	BEATMAN, RACHEL	BESSOFF	6 JAN 1963	11 DEC 1898		RAYMOND
125	S196	BEATMAN, RAYMOND DAVID		27 OCT 1958	4 JUL 1896	ISRAEL	RACHEL
102	Q 4	BEATMAN, ROSE	BORDON	27 MAY 1961	27 MAR 1880		WALTER
102	M34	BEATMAN, SYLVIA ANN		5 MAY 1941	13 SEP 1937	ISRAEL & ETHEL	
102	Q 5	BEATMAN, WALTER	OF PIATER	21 MAR 1929	2 MAY 1879	JOSEPH & LIBBY	ROSE
125	M191	BECAL, DIANA	COHEN	15 AUG 1969			
102	CA14	BECK, DOROTHY		17 OCT 1975			
102	A89	BECK, DOROTHY J		25 APR 1986	1905		HARRY
102	AB18	BECK, ESTHER K		18 MAY 1987	12 SEP 1921		
102	A82	BECK, HARRY		7 JUN 1944	1900		
102	E15	BECK, LOUIS A		17 MAR 1990	28 AUG 1909		
102	AA220	BECK, MARIE MITZI C		6 OCT 1989	26 OCT 1910		ROBERT
102	CA15	BECK, PAULINE RIKA		9 JUL 1960			
102	AA219	BECK, ROBERT		1982	1911		MARY
102	AJ160	BECK, SALLY		31 MAR 1966	13 JUN 1895		HARRY
123		BECKENSTEIN, DAVID		21 JUN 1971	1912		
370	U16	BECKENSTEIN, HERMAN		1928	1922	ISSAC & TILLIE	
370	U17	BECKENSTEIN, ISAAC		15 AUG 1940			TILLIE
391	Z53	BECKENSTEIN, LOUIS		19 DEC 1963	1894	MORDECHAI	SOPHIE
116	BL42	BECKENSTEIN, LOUIS M		11 MAR 1977	20 JUN 1908		ROSE
116	BL37	BECKENSTEIN, REUBEN		13 JUN 1962	3 MAR 1915		
116	BL43	BECKENSTEIN, ROSE W		30 JAN 1985	16 SEP 1907		LOUIS
370	U19	BECKENSTEIN, SAMUEL DR		14 DEC 1974	9 DEC 1912	ISAAC & TILLIE	
391	Z54	BECKENSTEIN, SOPHIE		25 FEB 1979	1903	MORDECHAI	LOUIS
370	U18	BECKENSTEIN, TILLIE		6 JUN 1970			ISAAC
330	AA 3	BECKER, BERTHA		1 JUL 1978	6 JAN 1887		BERTHA
375	D 9	BECKER, CHARLES		7 AUG 1990	4 JAN 1910		ETHEL
391	X69	BECKER, ELIYAHU		28 OCT 1971	1898	SHLOMO DAVID	JEAN
375	D10	BECKER, ETHEL		19 JAN 1992	9 AUG 1911		CHARLES
371	O13	BECKER, FRANK		27 AUG 1965	1892		ROSE
371	O12	BECKER, HAROLD M		5 APR 1993	31 MAR 1919	FRANK & ROSE	

Cem	Row	Name	Maiden Name	DOD	DOB	Parents	Spouse
330	F35	BECKER, HARRY		12 JUN 1917	1897		
102	AF73	BECKER, HARRY L		1985	1895		HARRY
102	AB75	BECKER, IDA SARAH		7 JUL 1832	14 MAR 1866		JACOB
391	Y66	BECKER, ISADORE		28 FEB 1983	4 NOV 1896	SAMUEL	
102	AB7	BECKER, JACOB		15 SEP 1956	28 JUN 1866		IDA
391	X68	BECKER, JEAN L		30 SEP 1971	1901	NACHEM	ELIYAHU
374	C 1	BECKER, JEANETTE		15 NOV 1913	MAR 1913		
374	A12	BECKER, JOSEPH		9 MAY 1913	1896		
391	T54	BECKER, JOSEPH		1977	1905	SAMUEL	PEARL
391	G15	BECKER, LENA		29 OCT 1933	10 JUL 1870	ISRAEL	SAMUEL
102	BA15	BECKER, LIBBY		23 JAN 1986	3 MAY 1893		
375	D 7	BECKER, LILLIAN			14 MAY 1906	MEYER	WILLIAM
370	L27	BECKER, MICHAEL S		1947	1947		
391	T55	BECKER, PEARL		1987	1904	ZENDEL	JOSEPH
371	O14	BECKER, ROSE		6 SEP 1954	1896		FRANK
391	F20	BECKER, SAMUEL		6 NOV 1929	1872	ZEV	LENA
391	G19	BECKER, SARA		3 JAN 1925	1899	SAMUEL & LENA	
375	D 8	BECKER, WILLIAM H		15 MAY 1983	17 OCT 1902	SOLOMON	LILLIAN
127	R	BECKERMAN, ELLEN	MILLER	23 SEP 1990	5 JUL 1900		
125	M153	BECKWITH, HARRY	BERKOWITZ	21 JUN 1972	1895		
248	M65	BEIN, IRVING		20 DEC 1992			
248	L64	BEIN, MICHAEL MAX		28 MAY 1964	20 JAN 1908		
374	E17	BEIT, ABE SAMUEL		14 NOV 1964	1895	MINNIE	SADIE
374	E19	BEIT, ALFRED E		23 FEB 1990	2 NOV 1923		
374	E41	BEIT, ANNA		5 MAR 1954	1892		
377	Y13	BEIT, ETHEL MAUDE		6 DEC 1987		SHALOM	MAX
374	F15	BEIT, JACOB		7 AUG 1921	1 JUL 1920		
371	AG10	BEIT, LOUIS ABRAHAM		26 MAR 1964	1893		MATTIE
371	AG 9	BEIT, MATTIE	CLARK	10 JUN 1963	1898		LOUIS
377	Y14	BEIT, MAX		1970	1900	SIMON MEYER	ETHEL
374	E16	BEIT, MINNIE		28 MAY 1935	1866		
374	E14	BEIT, MIRIAM N		10 AUG 1986	28 SEP 1901		NATHAN
374	E15	BEIT, NATHAN		4 APR 1958	6 OCT 1897	MINNIE	MIRIAM
374	E18	BEIT, SADIE		12 NOV 1975	1896		ABE
374	F16	BEIT, SAMUEL		29 JAN 1921	1866		
447	Z 6	BEIT, SANFORD I		1974	1922		
101	K 2	BEIZER, BELLA	LEIBEL	7 JAN 1969	1901		HYMAN
102	AA161	BEIZER, BENJAMIN J		6 JAN 1986	12 FEB 1898		
102	N13	BEIZER, EDMUND MD		25 OCT 1976	25 APR 1903	MORRIS & ROSE	
101	J 7	BEIZER, HYMAN		4 FEB 1961	1889		BELLA
102	AC153	BEIZER, IDA		21 JUN 1983	18 FEB 1896		
102	N10	BEIZER, LAWRENCE IRVING		26 OCT 1930	12 MAR 1920	MORRIS & ROSE	
102	N12	BEIZER, MORRIS		12 JAN 1945	24 JAN 1878		ROSE
121	D42	BEIZER, MORRIS G		25 MAR 1989	11 AUG 1905		
102	AC152	BEIZER, ROSE		26 DEC 1981	25 DEC 1895		
102	N11	BEIZER, ROSE	ABEL	17 JAN 1951	25 JAN 1885		MORRIS
104	H11	BEIZER, ROSE N		24 AUG 1982	12 OCT 1894		
125	O137	BELDING, JANET	SOCHRIN	6 MAR 1976	1922		
392	E21	BELGRADE, BARNEY		9 SEP 1951	1889		ROSE
392	J 7	BELGRADE, LILLIAN		12 MAR 1925	21 APR 1907	DAVID	
377	Q 3	BELGRADE, LOUIS		6 MAR 1975	22 MAR 1909		
375	G16	BELGRADE, MAX		11 JAN 1966	1915		
392	A56	BELGRADE, MOLLIE		1967	10 APR 1886		SAMUEL
392	E20	BELGRADE, ROSE		23 MAY 1969	1891	DOV BEAR	BARNEY
377	S 6	BELGRADE, RUTH		15 DEC 1967	29 SEP 1912		
392	A55	BELGRADE, SAMUEL		1961	1 JAN 1886		MOLLIE
392	A10	BELGROD, ESTHER C		1991	1908		ISADORE
392	C24	BELGROD, ETHEL		6 AUG 1950	1865		LOUIS
392	A 9	BELGROD, ISADORE J		1977	1903		ESTHER
392	G30	BELGROD, LOUIS		13 OCT 1926	5 SEP 1862	MORDECHAI	ETHEL
392	F32	BELGROD, SADIE		15 NOV 1915	1904	DAVID & BRACHA	
125	E128	BELKIN, GERTRUDE		14 APR 1959	1867		
125	Q150	BELKIN, HERMAN		25 NOV 1944	11 SEP 1864	DOV WOLF & LEAH	
125	I175	BELKIN, IDA	LEVY	15 JAN 1978			MAX
125	W170	BELKIN, LEWIS		18 FEB 1978	1898		
125	J 46	BELKIN, LOUIS		7 FEB 1897	1870	YECHESKEL ELCHANON	

Cem	Row	Name	Maiden Name	DOD	DOB	Parents	Spouse
125	I174	BELKIN, MAX		19 AUG 1972			IDA
125	N140	BELKIN, MICHAEL A		4 AUG 1950	1893		
125	E127	BELKIN, MITCHEL I		5 FEB 1955	1896		
125	E129	BELKIN, ROSE		1988	1889		
125	Y191	BELKIN, WILLIAM J		10 NOV 1984	1927		
125	E 94	BELL, ABRAHAM		1990	1908		
125	EL26	BELL, HERBERT		26 JAN 1944	11 FEB 1943	ABRAHAM	
125	F 93	BELL, IDA		11 DEC 1942	1883		LOUIS
125	F 94	BELL, LOUIS		21 AUG 1960	1879		IDA
125	B144	BELLACH, HARRY MD		7 JAN 1992	8 AUG 1908		
248	B34	BELLER, ABRAHAM		1976	1889		LENA
371	AI10	BELLER, BRUCE IRA		9 MAR 1955	1951	SIDNEY	
248	B33	BELLER, LENA		1977	1895		ABRAHAM
371	AI11	BELLER, SIDNEY		21 AUG 1988	1919		
107	A16	BELLOW, CAROLONE	KRAMER	9 DEC 1985	26 JUL 1917		
125	N114	BELMAN, BENJAMIN		21 AUG 1939	1884	ABRAHAM	
447	K 7	BELMAN, ISAAC		1932	1883		
116	BJ140	BELMAN, PERCIVAL		22 APR 1969	5 NOV 1910		
377	L28	BELOFF, GEORGE A		5 OCT 1963	24 JUL 1889	ABRAHAM	
101	B37	BEN ESHRIM, MORDECHAI		27 MAR 1934			
117	I10	BEN KIKI, MEYER		31 MAR 1991	13 SEP 1928		
116	BI54	BENANAV, JONATHAN		10 OCT 1989	5 MAR 1956		
371	K30	BENDELL, BESSE		30 SEP 1986	25 DEC 1903		
123		BENDELL, GERTURDE	BIRNBAUM	4 AUG 1967	4 AUG 1901		GERTRUDE
123		BENDELL, HARRY		28 NOV 1980	9 MAR 1897		
392	J37	BENDER, MOSHE		14 NOV 1914			
370	M36	BENDETT, BENJAMIN		24 JUL 1976	26 JAN 1893		CLARA
391	GD 7	BENDETT, CELIA	HOLZER	29 MAY 1941	1886	DAVID	
370	M35	BENDETT, CLARA M		13 SEP 1975	14 FEB 1894		BENJAMIN
370	F 9	BENDETT, DAVID		1921	1890		
370	M 5	BENDETT, DAVID MILTON		16 JUL 1944	1922		
370	R17	BENDETT, EVA		1970	1877		WILLIAM
370	R14	BENDETT, GUSSIE		26 NOV 1951	1869		WILLIAM
370	S21	BENDETT, HANNAH		5 JUN 1909	1845		REUBEN
370	P38	BENDETT, HARRY		30 MAR 1940	1871		
370	A18	BENDETT, JACOB		28 APR 1904			ROSA
371	AA 2	BENDETT, JAMIE S		2 FEB 1986	27 NOV 1956		
370	H24	BENDETT, JENNIE		27 JUN 1909	15 JUL 1877		MICHAEL
391	G10	BENDETT, KATE		29 DEC 1933	1868	MEYER	
370	M41	BENDETT, LOUIS		1970	1879		PAULINE
370	R13	BENDETT, MAURICE H		22 SEP 1938	2 JAN 1895	WILLIAM & GUSSIE	
370	P37	BENDETT, MAX		1934	1873		
370	F32	BENDETT, MICHAEL		24 DEC 1951	1879		JENNIE
391	R51	BENDETT, NATHAN		11 JAN 1955	1863	REUBEN MOSHE	
370	M42	BENDETT, PAULINE		1976	1897		LOUIS
370	S20	BENDETT, REUBEN MOSES		26 JUL 1914	1841		HANNAH
370	M34	BENDETT, RODMAN		29 SEP 1981	6 MAY 1929		
370	H31	BENDETT, ROSA		3 APR 1913			DAVID
370	K30	BENDETT, ROSE K		1943	1892		
371	K11	BENDETT, TILLIE G		1982	1895		
370	R15	BENDETT, WILLIAM		4 FEB 1952	1868		GUSSIE
370	R16	BENDETT, WILLIAM		1931	1869		EVA
102	I46	BENJAMIN, JOSEPH		24 JAN 1947	19 NOV 1891		YETTA
102	I45	BENJAMIN, YETTA		1 JUN 1956	18 JUN 1895		JOSEPH
113	O24	BENNETT, ELLIOTT		14 MAY 1977	23 NOV 1904		JEANNETTE
113	O25	BENNETT, JEANNETTE D		28 NOV 1990	13 FEB 1909		ELLIOTT
446	B15	BENOVITS, LESTER		1963	1907		
373	F 5	BENOWITZ, BERTHA		1982	1903		LOUIS
373	F 4	BENOWITZ, LOUIS		1971	1905		BERTHA
102	D15	BENSON, LOUIS D		11 APR 1970	15 JUN 1899	YEHUDA LEIB & MOLLIE (GOLUB)	SARAH
102	D16	BENSON, ROSALYN S		1 APR 1978	13 AUG 1922	LOUIS & SARAH	
102	D14	BENSON, SARAH N	NELEBER	25 FEB 1986	29 MAR 1902		LOUIS
370	C26	BENSON, SIMON JACOB					
329	F22	BENVENISTE, MALCA		27 DEC 1978			
370	F27	BERBITSKY, ISAAC					
102	AD50	BERCHNER, META	SANDER	8 MAR 1990	11 JUL 1896		

Cem	Row	Name	Maiden Name	DOD	DOB	Parents	Spouse
121	K 9	BERCOWETZ, REBECCA	DOIGAN	23 JUL 1973	1886		
102	AJ24	BERCOWITZ, KALMAN		23 JUL 1970	1882		
102	AJ23	BERCOWITZ, REBECCA		5 DEC 1942	1890		REBECCA
433	H 3	BERELOWITZ, RACHEL		13 SEP 1938	1853	BERLITZ	KALMON
118	D11	BERELSON, YALE		22 MAR 1987			
103	E6	BERENBAUM, CELIA	NEIKRE	28 MAR 1986	15 NOV 1901		
248	E43	BERENS, BESSIE		4 JUL 1944	1906		
119	E39	BERENS, MICHAEL		26 FEB 1979	3 MAR 1911		
125	EL24	BERENSTEIN, DAVID ALLEN		25 OCT 1942	5 SEP 1942		
391	V50	BERESOWICH, CHAYE ESTHER		19 MAY 1951	1867	ASHER	
101	B 4	BEREZOVITZ, CHARLES		3 MAY 1915	1836		
330	E 2	BERG, ANNA		27 JUN 1946	1856		
125	O185	BERG, MORRIS		11 NOV 1964	1889		
102	J 9	BERGEN, BERTHA D		1981	1908		HERMAN
102	J10	BERGEN, HERMAN S		1974	1907		BERTHA
101	B23	BERGEN, ISAAC H		23 NOV 1938	1865		JENNIE
101	C21	BERGEN, JACOB D		29 APR 1947	1893	ISAAC & JENNIE	
101	B22	BERGEN, JENNIE		18 JUN 1943	1868		ISAAC
105	E28	BERGEN, LEONARD		6 DEC 1974	1890		
370	P17	BERGER, ANNA		1949	1860		
330	AC13	BERGER, CHARLES LOUIS		23 DEC 1966	7 NOV 1899		
750	E20	BERGER, HARRY		10 OCT 1878			
330	F21	BERGER, MAX		3 JAN 1910	1853		
391	Q45	BERGMAN, BENJAMIN		9 MAR 1944	1886	GEMALYA	SARAH
377	S15	BERGMAN, FRANK		1937	1896		
395	C 6	BERGMAN, HENRY A		12 NOV 1924			SOPHIE
391	GL 3	BERGMAN, JOSEPH		17 JUN 1946	1880	BAER GAMLIEL	
391	Q46	BERGMAN, SARAH ZELDA		9 JUL 1974	1893	ISAAC	BENJAMIN
330	F10	BERGMAN, SOLOMON		8 FEB 1929	1847		
395	C 7	BERGMAN, SOPHIE	EISENBERG	NDD			HENRY
391	ZA54	BERGWEIN, JOSEPH		17 NOV 1962	1896	SAMUEL	
374	I51	BERK, JACK		1974	1910	LOUIS & LENA BERKOWITZ	
374	J50	BERK, JULIUS		16 FEB 1976	8 FEB 1924		
107	E7	BERKAL, RUTH		1992	1914		
330	B44	BERKLEY, DAVID PHILIP		21 DEC 1957	30 SEP 1895		
370	Q43	BERKMAN, ANNE		26 FEB 1962	7 APR 1911		SAMUEL
370	Q40	BERKMAN, BARNEY		13 MAY 1967	6 JUN 1901	BESSIE	
370	Q39	BERKMAN, BESSIE		22 FEB 1933	1 MAR 1877		
102	AH 5	BERKMAN, HARRY		16 JAN 1940	1867		SARAH
370	Q41	BERKMAN, ISIDORE		5 AUG 1980	10 MAR 1900	BESSIE	
248	E18	BERKMAN, JOSEPH		20 APR 1967	1888		MINNIE
248	E17	BERKMAN, MINNIE		6 MAY 1961	1888		JOSEPH
370	Q44	BERKMAN, SAMUEL		1 JUN 1987	16 MAY 1901	BESSIE	ANNE
248	E16	BERKMAN, SAMUEL A		13 NOV 1967	1913	JOSEPH & MINNIE	
102	AH 4	BERKMAN, SARAH	HERTZMAN	20 APR 1948	1866		HARRY
103	E13	BERKON, DAVID L		12 JAN 1989	14 DEC 1940		
103	D12	BERKON, MORRIS J		8 DEC 1985	15 AUG 1903		
248	N68	BERKOVITZ, ANNA		4 NOV 1927	1896		
104	F26	BERKOVITZ, ROSA		21 MAY 1990			
101	L14	BERKOVSKY, IDA		11 JAN 1914	1830		
125		BERKOWITZ, (CHILD/STILL BOR		APR 1923	APR 1923	BENJAMIN & BESSIE (LEVINE)	
125	J 33	BERKOWITZ, ABRAHAM		5 NOV 1911	1875		
125	P153	BERKOWITZ, ABRAHAM		6 APR 1948	27 DEC 1867	HILLEL	CELIA
125	W185	BERKOWITZ, ABRAHAM G		20 JUN 1979	1907	LOUIS & YETTA (GORFAIN)	ALICE
125	E137	BERKOWITZ, ALICE		NDD			MORRIS
125	W186	BERKOWITZ, ALICE		1993	1907		ABRAHAM
249	D41	BERKOWITZ, ARCHIE		12 NOV 1965	15 OCT 1899		BELLA
249	D42	BERKOWITZ, BELLA		31 OCT 1960	18 MAR 1903		ARCHIE
125	H167	BERKOWITZ, BENJAMIN		29 APR 1952	1896		
125	S167	BERKOWITZ, BENJAMIN		6 DEC 1941	1883	MORRIS & ESTHER (GREENSTEIN)	
125	I107	BERKOWITZ, BERNARD		25 JAN 1930	1873	LEVI	
392	A54	BERKOWITZ, BESS		1974	1914		
125	V188	BERKOWITZ, BESSIE	LEVINE	18 AUG 1977	1889		
125	P152	BERKOWITZ, CEILIA		29 SEP 1948	1865		ABRAHAM
248	H55	BERKOWITZ, CHANA SARAH		9 OCT 1931	1859		
372	B 3	BERKOWITZ, CLARA		15 DEC 1978	1 JAN 1888		LOUIS

Cem	Row	Name	Maiden Name	DOD	DOB	Parents	Spouse
125	L162	BERKOWITZ, DAVID		19 DEC 1956	1894		
119	G61	BERKOWITZ, ESSIE		30 OCT 1978	1896		
125	I118	BERKOWITZ, ESTHER	GREENSTEIN	27 JUN 1939	1864	SAMUEL & SARAH (KATZ)	MORRIS
119	G60	BERKOWITZ, HARRY		25 FEB 1978	1896		
125		BERKOWITZ, HS (FEMALE)		16 MAR 1917	1916	BENJAMIN & BESSIE (LEVINE)	
248	N76	BERKOWITZ, IDA		29 OCT 1924	1901		SIDNEY
248	L57	BERKOWITZ, ISADORE		11 NOV 1944	1887		
329	D 1	BERKOWITZ, JACOB		21 OCT 1986	20 APR 1889		
125	L 90	BERKOWITZ, JENNIE	WELINSKY	3 APR 1958	15 MAY 1873	MENDEL & DINAH MERYL (WINTZ)	SAMUEL
374	I49	BERKOWITZ, LENA L		1958	1886		LOUIS
125	Q194	BERKOWITZ, LOUIS		17 JAN 1962	SEP 1881	MORRIS & ESTHER (GREENSTEIN)	YETTA
372	B 4	BERKOWITZ, LOUIS		22 NOV 1973	12 OCT 1884		CLARA
374	I47	BERKOWITZ, LOUIS		1942	1880		LENA
125	E176	BERKOWITZ, MARCIA ANNE		17 MAY 1938	16 MAY 1938	ABRAHAM & ALICE (JEROME)	
125	R184	BERKOWITZ, MARY (MURKINEKOS	BERKOWITZ	26 FEB 1960	8 JAN 1899	MORRIS & ESTHER (GREENSTEIN)	JAMES
125	N110	BERKOWITZ, MAX		29 JUL 1928	1889	ISRAEL & LIBA (GOVZY)	IDA
125	H160	BERKOWITZ, MEYER "DICKIE"		9 MAY 1961	1895	MORRIS & ESTHER (GREENSTEIN)	
125	E138	BERKOWITZ, MORRIS		NDD			ALICE
125	L183	BERKOWITZ, MORRIS		7 AUG 1971	1909	DOV BER	
125	I119	BERKOWITZ, MORRIS JACOB		28 DEC 1934	15 SEP 1863	LEVI	ESTHER
101	A37	BERKOWITZ, SAM		23 JAN 1910	1865		
125	R164	BERKOWITZ, SAMUEL B		7 MAR 1944	10 FEB 1890	MORRIS & ESTHER (GREENSTEIN)	BESS
125	L 91	BERKOWITZ, SAMUEL DAVID		5 MAY 1924	8 JUL 1873	ABRAHAM & REBECCA	JENNIE WEL
372	I 4	BERKOWITZ, SARA		1958	1887		
125	ZA176	BERKOWITZ, SELMA RUTH		1990	15 AUG 1918	LOUIS & YETTA (GORFAIN)	
248	L56	BERKOWITZ, SIDNEY		1926	1922	ISADORE	IDA
102	A 7	BERKOWITZ, SOPHIE	COHEN	13 FEB 1931	1903		SAMUEL
125	Q193	BERKOWITZ, YETTA	GORFAIN	16 SEP 1963	10 JUL 1886	BENJAMIN & TZEREL (GREENSTEIN)	LOUIS
374	A32	BERLIN, IDA		1 AUG 1940	1878		
329	F21	BERLIN, MORRIS		17 FEB 1987	25 DEC 1897		
374	F14	BERLIN, SAMUEL		1932	1848		
125	EL34	BERMAN, (BABY)		20 OCT 1953	19 OCT 1953		
330	F37	BERMAN, AARON		5 OCT 1918	1883		
102	AE45	BERMAN, ANNA	SUDARSKY	23 AUG 1950	1885		
102	AG52	BERMAN, ANNA		25 MAY 1945	16 MAR 1891		
102	J14	BERMAN, ANNA		1904	1904		REUBEN
370	P28	BERMAN, ANNA		1960	1877		HYMAN
370	N14	BERMAN, ANNIE		1 MAR 1969	27 DEC 1889		PINCUS
330	B39	BERMAN, BELLA		27 JAN 1959	1880		
446	B13	BERMAN, BERTHA		1982	1912		EUGENE
101	M 7	BERMAN, BESSIE		9 APR 1942	1867		ISAAC
330	E32	BERMAN, CELIA		14 NOV 1957	1872		
105	G12	BERMAN, ELIOT		5 AUG 1941	16 DEC 1905		
102	J33	BERMAN, FRANCES	KASPROWICZ	1932	1894		NATHAN
102	AH55	BERMAN, FRANCES U		26 JAN 1992	25 JAN 1898		WILLIAM
102	J15	BERMAN, HAROLD J		1989	1928	REUBEN & ANNA	
330	AH 3	BERMAN, HELEN SARAH		1989	1908		HENRY
330	AH 4	BERMAN, HENRY MENDY		1989	1910		HELEN
370	P29	BERMAN, HYMAN		1928	1875		ANNA
101	M 6	BERMAN, ISAAC		11 OCT 1939	1867		BESSIE
125	O 83	BERMAN, ISAAC		16 FEB 1919	1890	HENRY & DORA	
330	F53	BERMAN, JACOB		18 MAR 1930	1878		
102	AG57	BERMAN, JEAN LIBBY		15 OCT 1948	19 JAN 1909		LOUIS
330	E30	BERMAN, KALMIN		9 APR 1936	1866		
330	G 9	BERMAN, KATIE		19 FEB 1953	1884		
330	G 7	BERMAN, LEAH		4 MAR 1951			
102	AG56	BERMAN, LOUIS		1 JUN 1987	22 MAR 1894		JEAN
330	AA12	BERMAN, LOUIS ABRAM		29 OCT 1980	1 SEP 1898		SAMUEL
121	E42	BERMAN, LYDA		12 MAY 1982	22 JAN 1908		
125	DA11	BERMAN, MARK		25 NOV 1953	1901	MAX & MINNIE	
125	J 25	BERMAN, MAX THEODORE		3 AUG 1918	1872		MINNIE
330	AA10	BERMAN, MILTON		23 AUG 1983	9 AUG 1921		
125	J 26	BERMAN, MINNIE		16 MAR 1950	1875		MAX
102	AJ224	BERMAN, MIRIAM Z		24 MAR 1986			
101	M 8	BERMAN, MORRIS		25 OCT 1967	1894	ISAAC & BESSIE	
330	AA 7	BERMAN, NATHAN		25 AUG 1979	21 SEP 1906		SARAH

Cem	Row	Name	Maiden Name	DOD	DOB	Parents	Spouse
102	J32	BERMAN, NATHAN H		1944	1884		
330	AB 8	BERMAN, NETTIE		1988	1904		FRANCES
370	N13	BERMAN, PINCUS		14 APR 1972	17 JUL 1889		ROBERT
102	J13	BERMAN, REUBEN		1905	1905		ANNIE
330	AB 9	BERMAN, ROBERT		1986	1902		ANNA
371	M36	BERMAN, ROSE		22 NOV 1953			NETTIE
377	S16	BERMAN, RUTH L		1970	1903		
330	AA11	BERMAN, SAMUEL H		5 JUL 1975	28 JAN 1890		
330	AA 9	BERMAN, SARAH		8 JAN 1974	13 DEC 1906		LOUIS
377	Q50	BERMAN, SHIMON M		9 JUN 1989	24 JAN 1904		NATHAN
127	N	BERMAN, STEVEN MICHAEL		11 JUL 1985	13 MAR 1939		
751	I29	BERMAN, SULLY I		11 JAN 1967	27 JAN 1902		
751	I28	BERMAN, SULLY I, JR		11 JUN 1953	6 JUN 1931	SULLY SR.	
750	A24	BERMAN, SUSAN	EPSTEIN	17 MAR 1980	22 APR 1936		
119	J65	BERMAN, SYLVIA	BACHNER	16 DEC 1991	26 JUN 1924		
102	CA13	BERMAN, SYLVIA E		31 DEC 1986	6 FEB 1904		
102	AH56	BERMAN, WILLIAM G		1 NOV 1964	1889		WILLIAM
102	CA12	BERMAN, WILLIAM L		31 JUL 1960	13 MAR 1899		FRANCES
330	E31	BERMAN, WOLFE		20 OCT 1936	1873		SYLVIA
374	E42	BERMANDE, EVA		10 SEP 1971	10 JUN 1906		
374	G10	BERMANDE, MAX		1979	1910		
374	G13	BERMANDE, SIMEON		1918	1879		
222	AC10	BERMANT, ANNA		10 FEB 1962	1883		JOSEPH
222	AA 2	BERMANT, JACOB					SARAH
222	AC 9	BERMANT, JOSEPH JACOB		19 AUG 1954	1875	JACOB	ANNA
222	AS 7	BERMANT, MANIA		3 JUL 1967	1894		SAMUEL
222	AS 8	BERMANT, SAMUEL J		24 MAY 1961	1893		MANIA
222	AA 3	BERMANT, SARAH					JACOB
222	AE18	BERMONT, MICHAEL J		25 DEC 1971	22 JUL 1905	JOSEPH JACOB & ANNA	
222	AE19	BERMONT, MORRIS		15 MAY 1924	1910	JOSEPH JACOB & ANNA	
222	AE 2	BERMONT, NATHAN		29 SEP 1976	1903	JOSEPH JACOB & ANNA	ROSE
222	AE 1	BERMONT, ROSE A		23 MAR 1957	1906		NATHAN
750	G27	BERNBACH, CELIA H		12 OCT 1972	28 MAR 1907		
446	C65	BERNHARD, CLARENCE H		16 JUL 1887	24 AUG 1886	HENRY & RACHEL	
446	A62	BERNHARD, HARRY S		2 DEC 1927	3 FEB 1872	HENRY & RACHEL	RENA
446	A60	BERNHARD, HENRY		13 JUN 1913	18 MAR 1846		RACHEL
446	A61	BERNHARD, RACHEL		9 SEP 1922	24 APR 1851		HENRY
446	A63	BERNHARD, RENA		7 FEB 1936	4 FEB 1874		HARRY
446	A64	BERNHARD, ROBERT		1963	1888	HENRY & RACHEL	
112	D 7	BERNHEIMER, JUSTIN		17 OCT 1979	13 MAY 1915		
377	T45	BERNS, MAX		27 JUL 1991	3 OCT 1906	SHALOM	
392	A57	BERNSTEIN, ABRAHAM T		23 JUN 1973	28 DEC 1899	LOUIS	EVA
102	CA37	BERNSTEIN, ABRAM Z		6 JAN 1972	12 JUL 1896		MARY
105	J54	BERNSTEIN, ANNA		15 JUN 1971	15 OCT 1889		JACOB
371	K16	BERNSTEIN, BENJAMIN		7 MAY 1987	25 DEC 1896		IDA
392	D47	BERNSTEIN, BENJAMIN		27 NOV 1957	1901	ARYEH LEV	
391	GE 1	BERNSTEIN, BERREL (CHILD)					
391	GI 7	BERNSTEIN, CHAIM (CHILD)					
433	I 9	BERNSTEIN, CHARLES		1 MAY 1975	9 MAR 1906	MEYER & SARAH	
371	AJ22	BERNSTEIN, DAVID L		8 MAY 1964			
125	M183	BERNSTEIN, EDITH	GELB	20 AUG 1968	23 DEC 1928		CHESTER
392	H12	BERNSTEIN, EVA		5 AUG 1967	1900	ZALMAN	ABRAHAM
101	J28	BERNSTEIN, FANNIE		29 NOV 1969	1884		NATHAN
113	B80	BERNSTEIN, HERBERT		15 MAY 1991	11 MAR 1911		
371	K17	BERNSTEIN, IDA HELENE		26 JUN 1963	16 JAN 1899		BENJAMIN
105	J55	BERNSTEIN, IRENE		28 SEP 1952	15 OCT 1906	JACOB & ANNA	
249	I 7	BERNSTEIN, ISADORE		29 SEP 1969	25 DEC 1895		
248	J 9	BERNSTEIN, ISRAEL		5 MAR 1937	1867		
105	J53	BERNSTEIN, JACOB		3 FEB 1963	15 JAN 1880		ANNA
125	Q174	BERNSTEIN, JACOB		29 NOV 1961	1897		
102	AB 2	BERNSTEIN, JEFFREY B		13 SEP 1968	1 MAY 1961		
392	G21	BERNSTEIN, LOUIS		23 SEP 1937	1874	ISAAC	
102	CA36	BERNSTEIN, MARY D		21 OCT 1979	15 JUN 1900		ABRAM
433	I11	BERNSTEIN, MEYER		12 JAN 1932	12 JAN 1932	ISAAC	SARAH
125	W183	BERNSTEIN, MILTON		4 MAY 1979	1919		
391	S44	BERNSTEIN, MOSES		3 DEC 1969	1883	DANIEL	ROSE

Cem	Row	Name	Maiden Name	DOD	DOB	Parents	Spouse
102	AB96	BERNSTEIN, MURIEL L		14 JUN 1989	17 OCT 1918		
101	B43	BERNSTEIN, NATHAN		9 JAN 1950	1894		FANNIE
391	GE 2	BERNSTEIN, NEIL (CHILD)					
102	AJ222	BERNSTEIN, RACHEL		7 MAY 1974	1904		
433	I12	BERNSTEIN, REUBEN		21 AUG 1990	1 OCT 1916	MEYER & SARAH	
330	G 1	BERNSTEIN, ROSE		24 SEP 1939			
391	S45	BERNSTEIN, ROSE	LAMPERT	4 MAR 1978	1888	MOSHE	MOSES
750	J29	BERNSTEIN, ROSE	OBERSTEIN	29 DEC 1978	18 OCT 1923		
494	B 6	BERNSTEIN, SAMUEL		1960	1901		
433	I10	BERNSTEIN, SARAH		14 JUL 1931	4 JUL 1931	ISRAEL	MEYER
248	K41	BERNSTEIN, SELINA		21 JUL 1982	24 NOV 1908		WILLIAM
377	Q 5	BERNSTEIN, SOL B		29 DEC 1974	30 OCT 1908		
113	J74	BERNSTEIN, STEVEN BARRY		17 JAN 1981	1 OCT 1946	HERBERT	
248	K42	BERNSTEIN, WILLIAM		8 NOV 1982	22 FEB 1902	ISRAEL	SELINA
125	ZB176	BERRETT, LEON G		21 MAY 1993	4 OCT 1912		BERTHA
102	E39	BERRETT, PAULINE		1966	1882		
125	I110	BERSON, ABRAHAM		4 AUG 1931	1855	SAMUEL	MARY
121	G31	BERSON, EFREM WALTER		21 MAR 1987	19 MAY 1927		
125	H145	BERSON, FANNYE REBECCA	BROOK	7 APR 1963	1891		GEORGE
125	H146	BERSON, GEORGE		19 OCT 1963	1882		FANNY
125	G144	BERSON, GLORIA		16 MAY 1994			
125	I111	BERSON, MARY	KRANY	25 AUG 1950	1852		ABRAHAM
125	J110	BERSON, NATHAN		6 JUL 1947	1888	ABRAHAM & CHAYA	SYLVIA
102	AA180	BERSON, SAUL L		1985	1916		
125	J111	BERSON, SYLVIA	GOLDBERG	8 DEC 1980	1889		NATHAN
377	Q53	BERSTEIN, SADIE		1993	1904		
433	G24	BERWICK, (INFANT)		3 SEP 1951			
433	E11	BERWICK, ROSALIND		14 DEC 1961	1 JAN 1914		
125	M100	BESSOFF, ALEX		30 NOV 1926	1881		ESTHER
125	M 99	BESSOFF, ESTHER		21 JUN 1956	1878		ALEX
377	O26	BESTERMAN, SIDNEY		30 NOV 1959	26 MAR 1913		
119	H27	BIALICK, BENJAMIN		20 JAN 1988	18 APR 1911		
119	H26	BIALICK, LILLIAN		19 FEB 1992	16 APR 1913		
371	I 8	BIALIK, RIVA		30 NOV 1948	1936		
447	D37	BIENSTOCK, HARRY		11 NOV 1929			
121	A 1	BIG, SADIE LILLIAN		30 MAY 1986	15 SEP 1898		
121	A 2	BIG, SAMUEL		28 FEB 1980	22 JUL 1898		
371	A15	BILOON, FANNIE R		5 SEP 1985	18 NOV 1895		
125		BIRENBAUM, (CHILD)		20 SEP 1915	20 SEP 1915	ISAAC & MALLE	
125		BIRENBAUM, (CHILD)		28 NOV 1915	28 NOV 1915	JOSEPH	
125	A 83	BIRENBAUM, ESTHER	SORTMAN	12 MAY 1969			ISRAEL
125	I115	BIRENBAUM, FANNIE R		13 MAY 1968	15 AUG 1887		REUBEN
377	A15	BIRENBAUM, HARRY		1993	1910		
125	A 82	BIRENBAUM, ISRAEL JACOB		19 JUL 1966	1878		ESTHER
377	B15	BIRENBAUM, JENNIE		1958	1885		JOSEPH
377	B16	BIRENBAUM, JOSEPH N		1937	1867		JENNIE
377	A16	BIRENBAUM, JOSEPH N		1970	1942	HARRY	
125	B185	BIRENBAUM, LILLY		22 AUG 1968	1906		
125	I114	BIRENBAUM, REUBEN LOUIS		9 MAY 1934	22 AUG 1878		FANNIE
222	AC 3	BIRMAN, LEON		27 JUL 1977	10 JUL 1889		TOMA
222	AC 2	BIRMAN, TOMA	DOBKIN	25 SEP 1967	1896	AARON & IDA	LEON
391	ZB62	BIRNBAUM, ANNE		3 DEC 1971	28 APR 1901	ZEV WOLF	ARNOLD
391	ZB61	BIRNBAUM, ARNOLD		26 APR 1967	25 MAR 1905	HIRSCH	ANNE
125	F 83	BIRNBAUM, BENJAMIN		27 MAY 1943	22 OCT 1906	MISHEL & LEAH	
125	G148	BIRNBAUM, BENJAMIN S		27 JAN 1984	1911		
751	I37	BIRNBAUM, BETTY				SIGMUND & LENA	
125	I152	BIRNBAUM, GEORGE		31 JUL 1946	17 DEC 1901	ABRAHAM	
125	B 79	BIRNBAUM, HAROLD		1988	1903		ROWENA
125	I 57	BIRNBAUM, HELEN		17 AUG 1915	1898		
125		BIRNBAUM, IDA		24 FEB 1922	17 JUL 1921	NATHAN	
125	N118	BIRNBAUM, ISAAC		18 SEP 1970	1887		MOLLIE
125	H109	BIRNBAUM, ISADORE		1 APR 1940	1884		
125	H112	BIRNBAUM, JACOB		10 OCT 1941	1886	DAVID & CHAYA	
751	I36	BIRNBAUM, LENA		30 SEP 1960			SIGMUND
125	B 83	BIRNBAUM, LEON		23 DEC 1968	5 MAY 1904		
125	H110	BIRNBAUM, LEONARD PAUL		7 DEC 1982	18 MAY 1919		

Cem	Row	Name	Maiden Name	DOD	DOB	Parents	Spouse
125		BIRNBAUM, LORRAINE		4 APR 1927	MAR 1927		
107	B21	BIRNBAUM, MILLIE	MATTS	23 APR 1991	9 JAN 1926		
125	N119	BIRNBAUM, MOLLIE	QUATINETZ	7 MAY 1932	1895		ISAAC
125	F 85	BIRNBAUM, MORRIS		27 FEB 1960	1883		PAULINE
125	I149	BIRNBAUM, NATHAN		13 SEP 1958	1890	SAMUEL	
125	F 84	BIRNBAUM, PAULINE		1959	1879		MORRIS
125	F148	BIRNBAUM, PHILIP H		1986	1906		
125		BIRNBAUM, REBECCA		13 DEC 1922	JUN 1854	SAMUEL & SARAH	
125		BIRNBAUM, RHODA		21 JUL 1925	MAR 1925		
125	H111	BIRNBAUM, ROSE L		12 DEC 1954	1898		
125	B 77	BIRNBAUM, ROWENA CLAIRE		4 AUG 1966	1908		HAROLD
751	I35	BIRNBAUM, SIGMUND		29 SEP 1963			LENA
391	GF 1	BIRNER, (CHILD)					
125	S182	BISHOFF, BLANCHE		1991	1901		JACK
125	S183	BISHOFF, JACK J		27 OCT 1957	1897		BLANCHE
433	G25	BISHOP, DIRK JOEL		19 FEB 1951	5 FEB 1948		
102	BF30	BISHOP, HARRY J		29 SEP 1987	30 JUN 1904		
248	M73	BITTAN, MINNIE		1 OCT 1941	1879		
446	C 8	BITTMAN, EVA		26 FEB 1948	19 JAN 1886		MORRIS
447	W14	BITTMAN, MARTHA		21 DEC 1963	5 MAY 1910		SAMUEL
446	B27	BITTMAN, MORRIS H		31 OCT 1918	15 MAY 1885		EVA
447	W13	BITTMAN, SAMUEL		28 JAN 1965	16 MAY 1903		MARTHA
121	H42	BLACK, BERNARD		25 DEC 1988	13 JUL 1918		
119	J61	BLACK, SEYMOUR		24 OCT 1985	4 OCT 1925		
103	C13	BLACKER, MOLLY		16 FEB 1983	7 FEB 1903		
103	C16	BLACKER, MORRIS		11 DEC 1989	7 JUL 1900		
125	S145	BLACKMAN, ELLIS		20 SEP 1938	1879	YITZCHOK & ESTHER	
125	L144	BLACKMAN, ESTHER C		19 MAY 1954	1906		
104	I13	BLACKMAN, FREDA	WEINBERG	11 OCT 1970	18 SEP 1911		
125	M178	BLACKMAN, SARAH ROSE		14 AUG 1969			
447	O20	BLAGODATNY, ELLA		30 APR 1947	1882		LEON
447	N23	BLAGODATNY, LEON		18 MAR 1936	12 DEC 1882		ELLA
377	K27	BLAIR, PETER	BELFOFF				
104	B35	BLAND, ANNA		18 SEP 1956			HYMAN
104	B36	BLAND, HYMAN		10 FEB 1969			ANNA
119	F69	BLANK, HERMAN		13 MAR 1982	13 MAY 1910		
119	F68	BLANK, IDA	ADOFF	12 MAR 1978	3 JUN 1913		
125	X153	BLANK, LILO	KNODT	1 JUN 1991	25 NOV 1919		
371	J 4	BLANK, MAJER		17 DEC 1972	20 APR 1911		
493	H25	BLANK, SAMUEL DR		2 OCT 1993	29 NOV 1914	ISRAEL	
391	R27	BLASKIN, ALEXANDER		2 NOV 1933	10 MAY 1883	MOSHE	
391	Z80	BLASKIN, BESSIE		25 SEP 1982	1 NOV 1892		
391	C 4	BLASKIN, DORA E		15 APR 1948	1886	ZELIG	
391	S26	BLASKIN, MORRIS		30 OCT 1915		ABRAHAM	
391	Q31	BLASKIN, RACHEL		14 MAR 1948	1865	SHLOMO	
447	H38	BLAU, JUDITH	ALBERT	7 JAN 1971	21 MAY 1942	DEWEY & SADIE	
374	E49	BLAUSTEIN, BELLA		1971	1889		ISADORE
374	E51	BLAUSTEIN, BESSIE		1978	1909		
374	E48	BLAUSTEIN, ISADORE		1962	1879		BELLA
374	E47	BLAUSTEIN, SAMUEL		1950	1910		
370	A61	BLAUZWERN, ELKE		FEB 1916			MEYER
370	A30	BLAUZWERN, MEYER		23 AUG 1904			ELKE
370	I 2	BLAZER, ANNIE		4 JUN 1924	1889		MAX
370	G29	BLAZER, MAX		24 JAN 1940			ANNIE
106	B20	BLECHERMAN, BENJAMIN		31 MAR 1987	13 FEB 1899		
106	B21	BLECHERMAN, SELMA		2 OCT 1975	6 JAN 1908		
391	B 3	BLECHNER, (BABY BOY)		28 MAR 1967	28 MAR 1967	STUART	
751	C12	BLEICH, BESSIE	BAZIL	1978	1902		JOSEPH
751	C13	BLEICH, JOSEPH S		1979	1897		BESSIE
391	ZF56	BLEIWEISS, DAVID		17 JUL 1990	18 APR 1902	MORDECHAI	JEAN
391	ZF57	BLEIWEISS, JEAN		16 JUL 1991	19 JUN 1912	HIRSCH	DAVID
119	E23	BLINDERMAN, EDNA		8 JAN 1975	7 APR 1905		
370	Q 8	BLINDERMAN, ELIAS		7 FEB 1922	1836		GOLDIE
374	C 5	BLINDERMAN, EVERETT K		9 JAN 1927	25 FEB 1917	WOLF	
374	D10	BLINDERMAN, FANNIE		14 MAY 1959	1882		
371	L21	BLINDERMAN, FRANK P		1 JUN 1968	13 MAY 1900		GUSSIE

Cem	Row	Name	Maiden Name	DOD	DOB	Parents	Spouse
370	Q 7	BLINDERMAN, GOLDIE		22 JAN 1916	1850		ELIAS
371	L20	BLINDERMAN, GUSSIE L		1 DEC 1973	6 OCT 1902		FRANK
370	K52	BLINDERMAN, IDA		8 DEC 1968	15 AUG 1890		
370	Q 2	BLINDERMAN, JENNIE		23 DEC 1956			SAMUEL
371	L18	BLINDERMAN, LOUIS		5 JUL 1985	16 FEB 1902		SHIRLEY
370	G27	BLINDERMAN, REUBEN		1946	1885		ROSE
370	G28	BLINDERMAN, ROSE		28 DEC 1919	1883		REUBEN
370	G26	BLINDERMAN, RUTHERFORD		12 JUN 1991	24 AUG 1908	REUBEN & ROSE	
370	Q 1	BLINDERMAN, SAMUEL L		13 SEP 1910			JENNIE
371	L19	BLINDERMAN, SHIRLEY M		22 DEC 1974	30 APR 1901		LOUIS
371	AG18	BLINDERMAN, SYDNEY P		21 NOV 1989	4 JUL 1911		
374	C 6	BLINDERMAN, WOLFE		11 MAR 1929	1880		
370	A23	BLISS, YEHUDA LEV		14 OCT 1934		AARON	
373	G 7	BLITZSTEIN, EFRAIM		27 FEB 1971			
372	I 9	BLOCH, JACOB		17 SEP 1971	1896		
106	A30	BLOCK, ALBION L		11 JAN 1984	24 MAR 1930		
102	I21	BLOCK, ANNA B		1 OCT 1959	1890		AUSHER
102	I20	BLOCK, AUSHER		8 DEC 1963	1887		ANNA
110	H26	BLOCK, BARRY RODNEY		25 MAY 1942	1933		
104	C27	BLOCK, ELIZABETH	LEVY	11 SEP 1978	15 JAN 1896		HARRY
102	AH85	BLOCK, FAYE B	WAXMAN	30 MAR 1962	23 JAN 1923	JOSEPH & HILDA	LOUIS
104	C26	BLOCK, HARRY G		3 AUG 1951	1895		ELIZABETH
102	AH84	BLOCK, LOUIS H DR		22 OCT 1977	5 APR 1921		FAYE
102	I22	BLOCK, MIRIAM SALLY		26 APR 1935	4 FEB 1925	AUSHER & ANNA	
125	J109	BLOMENBERG, HELEN	WINKLE	7 DEC 1939	1875		
446	D31	BLOMER,					
370	X15	BLONDER, FRIEDA		1961	1880		
370	Y 1	BLONDER, MORTON		1964	1921		
370	Z12	BLONDER, SAMUEL		1942	1873		
222	AT13	BLONSTEIN, LOTTIE		6 MAY 1990	1901		REUBEN
222	AT14	BLONSTEIN, REUBEN		3 JUN 1958	1899		LOTTIE
329	A 9	BLOOM, BERNARD		14 SEP 1961	1902		
330	C20	BLOOM, BERTHA DORA		12 SEP 1945	1867		JACOB
370	I12	BLOOM, CHANA SARA	FINE	11 OCT 1918	9 SEP 1878		SIMON
123		BLOOM, FRANK J		11 JUL 1952	1891		TINA
330	C19	BLOOM, JACOB		5 DEC 1943	1860		BERTHA
112	E29	BLOOM, JERALD		16 JAN 1992	25 JUN 1906		
370	D 3	BLOOM, JOHN		9 JUN 1935	1864	SHMUEL & HELEN (TEPPER)	SLAVA
101	K26	BLOOM, MAIMIE		11 OCT 1938	1874		
391	S40	BLOOM, MAMIE K		9 SEP 1955		JACOB	
370	P50	BLOOM, MAX		4 SEP 1970	25 APR 1896	YAKOV	MINNIE
370	P51	BLOOM, MINNIE	MOPSIK	28 FEB 1981	2 FEB 1903	HARRY & RACHEL LEAH	MAX
370	M 2	BLOOM, SIMON ISAAC		24 MAR 1950	20 SEP 1874	SHMUEL & HELEN (TEPPER)	CHANA
370	I10	BLOOM, SLAVA	BLOOM	18 JAN 1920	1865		JOHN
123		BLOOM, TINA	TUBIN	13 DEC 1956	1899		FRANK
750	J18	BLOOMBERG, LEAH	PLUTZIK	8 MAY 1979			MAXWELL
750	J19	BLOOMBERG, MAXWELL H		9 OCT 1968	24 FEB 1899		LEAH
116	BK11	BLOOMFIELD, DAVID I		11 JUL 1986	1 NOV 1900		
391	GC 4	BLOTSKY, MORRIS		25 OCT 1955	1883	AARON LEV	SARAH
391	GD 6	BLOTSKY, SARAH		3 AUG 1945	1880	YESHIYAHU	MORRIS
370	V24	BLUM, ABRAHAM		13 JUL 1920	1862	YEHUDA LEIBE	GITEL
102	Z86	BLUM, ANNA	DAVIS	15 JUN 1964	22 FEB 1886		MAX
370	O47	BLUM, DAVID		31 JAN 1957	1886	ABRAHAM & GITEL	MARY
374	D 6	BLUM, FANNIE FRUMI	BRENNER	31 OCT 1942			JOHN
119	I54	BLUM, FLORENCE E		21 APR 1988	14 JAN 1922		
374	D39	BLUM, GEORGE		18 FEB 1980	14 SEP 1899	JOHN & FANNIE	
370	V25	BLUM, GITEL	STEINBACH	18 FEB 1930	1857		ABRAHAM
115	E70	BLUM, HAROLD		15 MAR 1992			
374	D 8	BLUM, HARRY I		26 OCT 1973	12 JAN 1894	JOHN & FANNIE	
102	Z84	BLUM, HOWARD S PFC		15 MAR 1944	14 NOV 1911	MAX & ANNA (DAVIS)	
222	AJ18	BLUM, JACOB M		16 DEC 1931	1878		LENA
374	A 1	BLUM, JENNIE		6 SEP 1913	1891	JOHN & FANNIE	
374	D 7	BLUM, JOHN		17 AUG 1954			FANNIE
222	AJ17	BLUM, LENA		15 DEC 1967	1878		JACOB
102	BA 7	BLUM, LEONARD DAVIS		1988	1917		
125	E 84	BLUM, LOUIS		1990	1901		

Cem	Row	Name	Maiden Name	DOD	DOB	Parents	Spouse
370	V21	BLUM, LOUIS		8 DEC 1919	NOV 1887	ABE & GITEL	
370	O48	BLUM, MARY	SACK	14 JAN 1958	1894		DAVID
102	Z87	BLUM, MAX B		3 OCT 1961	2 APR 1884		ANNA
370	V22	BLUM, MICHAEL		18 FEB 1945	JUN 1884	ABE & GITEL	
447	U29	BLUM, SEYMOUR A		28 DEC 1977	3 MAY 1928		
370	A64	BLUM, YEHUDA LEIBE		25 OCT 1914	1830	ARON & LILLE	
447	J39	BLUMAN, ROSE		1987	1915		SAM
447	J40	BLUMAN, SAM		20 FEB 1972	1915		ROSE
391	C20	BLUMBERG, CHARLES ISAAC		17 MAY 1936		MATATHIAS	
116	BJ80	BLUMBERG, ROBERT L		20 AUG 1972	12 FEB 1905		
102	AB152	BLUME, JOSEPH		22 SEP 1990	27 APR 1900		MARIAN
102	AB151	BLUME, MARIAN	GLATT	26 FEB 1962	19 OCT 1909		JOSEPH
105	AA11	BLUMENTHAL, ALFRED		27 MAR 1978	14 APR 1934		
374	F33	BLUMENTHAL, ALICE I		1984	1915		HAROLD
101	F26	BLUMENTHAL, ANNA	GORDON	19 APR 1987	11 JAN 1898		ISADOR
102	Z79	BLUMENTHAL, ANNA	GREENBERG	22 JUL 1962	1888		MAX
392	J43	BLUMENTHAL, BENJAMIN W		21 AUG 1941	1879	ARYEH LEV	ETHEL
102	AC188	BLUMENTHAL, CHARLES A		15 AUG 1985	19 JUL 1918		FLORINE
125	U144	BLUMENTHAL, DAVID		14 FEB 1980	27 NOV 1917	SAMUEL & SARAH	
374	G38	BLUMENTHAL, DORA		1948	1898		NATHAN
102	Z78	BLUMENTHAL, ELLIOTT EDWARD		1925	1915	MAX & ANNA (GREENBERG)	
125	N145	BLUMENTHAL, ESTHER		21 OCT 1950	1889		SAMUEL
374	G32	BLUMENTHAL, ETHEL		24 DEC 1986	11 APR 1902		MOSES
392	J42	BLUMENTHAL, ETHEL L		1 APR 1971	1884	BARUCH	BENJAMIN
374	I52	BLUMENTHAL, EVELYN W		10 JAN 1979	29 FEB 1936		
111	2	BLUMENTHAL, FANNYE	WIEDER	30 JUN 1976	15 AUG 1899	MILTON & CARRIE (BIRCH)	JESSIE
102	AC189	BLUMENTHAL, FLORINE	SCHIFF	10 AUG 1971	25 DEC 1926		CHARLES
374	F32	BLUMENTHAL, HAROLD S		NDD	1924		ALICE
101	F27	BLUMENTHAL, ISADOR		4 NOV 1978	11 SEP 1895		ANNA
102	AA80	BLUMENTHAL, JACOB N		11 OCT 1952	2 JUL 1883	MEYER & SARAH (ARNOFSKY)	LEE
111	2	BLUMENTHAL, JESSIE S		15 NOV 1963	5 SEP 1893	SAMUEL & THERESA (BRUNEMAN)	FANNYE
111	2	BLUMENTHAL, JESSIE S		17 FEB 1934	8 JUN 1927	JESSIE & FANNYE (WIEDER)	
102	AA81	BLUMENTHAL, LEE B	BERKOWITZ	15 MAR 1976	26 FEB 1886		JACOB
102	Z80	BLUMENTHAL, MAX		2 DEC 1939	1885	MEYER & SARAH (ARNOFSKY)	ANNA
121	C32	BLUMENTHAL, MAY		23 AUG 1989	23 FEB 1914		
102	AJ52	BLUMENTHAL, MEYER		26 SEP 1944	1890		SARAH
374	G34	BLUMENTHAL, MEYER		1941	1872		REBECCA
374	G33	BLUMENTHAL, MOSES		1952	1906	MEYER & REBECCA	ETHEL
374	G37	BLUMENTHAL, NATHAN		12 DEC 1986	24 MAY 1894	MEYER & REBECCA	DORA
222	D 1	BLUMENTHAL, NETTIE	PEIZER	17 SEP 1992			
374	G35	BLUMENTHAL, REBECCA		1936	1873		MEYER
125	N144	BLUMENTHAL, SAMUEL		24 FEB 1969	1888		ESTHER
374	G36	BLUMENTHAL, SAMUEL J		1951	1895	MEYER & REBECCA	
102	AJ51	BLUMENTHAL, SARAH		7 APR 1963	1898		MEYER
374	F38	BLUMENTHAL, SHEILA		1968	1938		
102	A43	BLUMER, DAVID BURTON		26 JAN 1938	18 MAR 1932		
102	A49	BLUMER, MORRIS		6 DEC 1942	1894		
125	V184	BLUMSTEIN, BENJAMIN		9 SEP 1977	1922		
371	J12	BLUSTEIN, SAUL		13 AUG 1970	28 DEC 1907		
433	H 2	BOARDMAN, JEROME		30 JAN 1945	24 FEB 1939	ISAAC	
119	C 1	BOBICK, MORRIS (CANTOR)		24 FEB 1993	1929		
433	F20	BOCKSTEIN, DAVID		11 OCT 1957	13 MAR 1885		DOROTHY
433	F21	BOCKSTEIN, DOROTHY		18 FEB 1960	15 JUL 1887		DAVID
391	ZE56	BODENSTEIN, BENJAMIN		12 SEP 1967	27 APR 1891	NATAN	LILLIAN
391	ZE57	BODENSTEIN, LILLIAM P	PILPAS	12 JAN 1966	19 DEC 1893	JONAH	BENJAMIN
102	AK233	BODIAN, ABRAHAM		11 JUL 1985	2 DEC 1906		CELIA
102	AK234	BODIAN, CELIA M		16 APR 1976	26 SEP 1906		ABRAHAM
119	A47	BODY, BENJAMIN		26 AUG 1989	25 APR 1906		
125	O144	BOEHUR, ADELE	GOLDSTEIN	1 JUL 1970	13 OCT 1898		
113	B31	BOGATZ, ARNOLD		3 DEC 1985	4 DEC 1931		
391	GD 3	BOGUSLOFSKY, IDA		21 SEP 1971	1883	SHNAOR	JOSEPH
391	GD 4	BOGUSLOFSKY, JOSEPH		19 OCT 1955	1883	MORDECHAI	IDA
101	C30	BOIMEL, JACOB		4 NOV 1925	1855		SHEINDEL
101	J15	BOIMEL, SHEINDEL		8 MAR 1919	1859		JACOB
371	AI18	BOKOFF, DAVID		13 FEB 1967	1901		LENA
371	AM12	BOKOFF, ESTHER ANN		15 JUL 1966	1900		

Cem	Row	Name	Maiden Name	DOD	DOB	Parents	Spouse
370	J 8	BOKOFF, FANNIE		31 MAR 1932			
372	C15	BOKOFF, HARRY M		8 AUG 1991	18 JAN 1929		ZENA
371	AI17	BOKOFF, LENA		16 MAR 1980	1902		DAVID
371	AL13	BOKOFF, MORRIS		3 APR 1958	1890		
371	AL12	BOKOFF, PHILIP YALE LT		1944	1921	MORRIS	
101	D34	BOLOCHOFSKY, DAVID		10 MAY 1947	1885		LENA
101	D35	BOLOCHOFSKY, LENA	DRESSLER	16 JAN 1949	1888		DAVID
119	B37	BOLOCOFSKY, SAMUEL		8 JUN 1981	23 SEP 1907		
125	ZA179	BOLZ, CYRIL E		1990	1919		
119	E27	BONITO, MICHAEL A		18 AUG 1991	15 JUN 1969		
493	G15	BONOFF, LEO EDWARD		21 OCT 1983	24 JAN 1901		SALLIE
493	G16	BONOFF, SALLIE	GOLDBERG	27 SEP 1993	21 AUG 1899		LEO
105	C29	BOOTH, CHARLES		19 FEB 1990	6 DEC 1903		
105	C22	BOOTH, DOROTHY	LASSMAN	28 MAR 1965	1910		
102	M17	BORDEN, BARNEY		20 JUN 1956	1894		ROSE
222	AH 2	BORDEN, EVA		25 AUG 1950	1893		
102	AG82	BORDEN, IDA	PLOTKIN	13 APR 1965	1896		ISADORE
102	AG83	BORDEN, ISADORE		15 DEC 1968	15 MAR 1892	ABRAHAM & GNESSIE	IDA
392	B 8	BORDEN, LOUIS		14 FEB 1952	1899		ELKA
102	O32	BORDEN, MOLLIE	SIGAL	14 AUG 1971	24 AUG 1899		HAROLD
102	O34	BORDEN, MORRIS		30 JUN 1936	1860		MALKA
102	M18	BORDEN, ROSE	GOLD	9 DEC 1963	1898		BARNEY
391	P37	BORDON, ELKA		22 MAR 1915		MOSHE	LOUIS
102	O33	BORDON, HAROLD		15 JAN 1973	7 MAY 1897	MORRIS & MALKA	MOLLIE
102	O35	BORDON, MOLKA		25 SEP 1924	1864		MORRIS
104	J16	BORENSTEIN, SOL		17 OCT 1960	1918		
330	F54	BORETZ, JACOB		9 JUL 1955	1879		SARAH
330	AD 3	BORETZ, MYER		14 AUG 1970	15 JUL 1907	JACOB & SARAH	
330	F53	BORETZ, SARAH H		9 JUN 1952	1879		JACOB
102	Z207	BORIS, ABRAHAM		1983	1902		
101	K32	BORNSTEIN, FANNIE		21 SEP 1977	1898		JACOB
101	K33	BORNSTEIN, JACOB		13 OCT 1958	1890	HARRY & DORA (EDELSTEIN)	FANNIE
248	I25	BORODACH, ABRAHAM		27 DEC 1959	14 APR 1890		HELEN
248	I26	BORODACH, HELEN		26 MAR 1993	1896		ABRAHAM
248	I24	BORODACH, SAMUEL		17 MAR 1944	24 JUL 1892		
116	BJ120	BORTMAN, JOSEPH		10 FEB 1986	2 AUG 1910		
127	H	BOTNICK, ABRAHAM JOSEPH		6 APR 1982	3 OCT 1913		
374	C28	BOTNICK, FRIMA SARAH		8 NOV 1937			ISRAEL
374	C29	BOTNICK, ISRAEL		31 AUG 1942			FRIMA
330	F19	BOTNIK, ABRAHAM JOSEPH		3 JUL 1910	1854		
370	P 1	BOTWICK, MILDRED		15 FEB 1973	19 APR 1914		
102	Y200	BOVITZ, SAMUEL S		21 OCT 1986	27 MAY 1902		
106	D8	BOWER, MURRAY		10 DEC 1971	1922		
391	S29	BOYER, FANNY		8 DEC 1929	1861	ABRAHAM DAVID	MEYER
377	O 3	BOYER, MAX		1945	1888		
391	S28	BOYER, MEYER		1925	1865	MORDECHAI	FANNY
102	A72	BOYLAND, HATTIE	GREENWALD	22 AUG 1951	1875		
102	A25	BOYLAND, ISAAC		1936	1873		
125	J178	BOZARNICK, BEATRICE	ROSENTHAL	1 FEB 1980	1924		
125	I158	BOZARNICK, JOSEPH		17 JAN 1968	1893		ROSE
125	I159	BOZARNICK, ROSE		21 JUN 1962	1886		JOSEPH
116	AZ21	BRADMAN, SARAH		14 APR 1990	15 SEP 1902		
125	X186	BRADY, BARBARA	RUBINSTEIN	30 JUL 1982	29 APR 1950		
751	E33	BRAM, ABRAHAM H		1956	1904		
447	V37	BRAND, BERTHA		1968	1894		
125	O120	BRAND, RICHARD		9 OCT 1974	1916		
447	Z14	BRANDON, JOSEPH B		18 SEP 1972	1918		
110	D22	BRANKSY, ALEC		5 OCT 1974	1900		
101	D36	BRASS, FRANK		31 JAN 1947	1882		SARAH
101	D37	BRASS, SARAH		14 MAY 1978	1884		FRANK
113	O17	BRAUNBERG, ROSEL	WEIL	8 MAY 1986	6 SEP 1908		
751	A34	BRAUNSTEIN, ELLA		28 MAR 1923	10 MAR 1895		
330	B42	BRAUNSTEIN, FANNIE		28 JUL 1956	1862		
391	O51	BRAVERMAN, ELLA		17 JAN 1960	1866	CHAIM HILLEL	HERMAN
125	J 31	BRAVERMAN, FRANK					
391	O50	BRAVERMAN, HERMAN		24 JAN 1947	1871	SHLOMO	ELLA

Cem	Row	Name	Maiden Name	DOD	DOB	Parents	Spouse
447	A23	BRAVERMAN, HERMAN		25 NOV 1977	1898		
391	Q54	BRAVERMAN, IRVING		26 SEP 1960	1901	NEHEMYA	
447	G 9	BRAVERMAN, LOUIS S		24 MAR 1975	16 OCT 1933		ROSE
102	BG14	BRAVERMAN, MARINA A DR		1 APR 1991	5 MAR 1942		
391	Q53	BRAVERMAN, ROSE		5 APR 1993	1901	MENDEL	IRVING
106	D27	BRECHER, ISADORE		30 SEP 1976	16 JAN 1914		
119	K43	BREGMAN, ISRAEL		19 APR 1985	1922		
123		BREGMAN, MORRIS		27 MAY 1940	1894		
447	U13	BREITBART, BARBARA M	PECK	1961	1937		
447	U14	BREITBART, MITCHEL WALTER		1961	1929		BARBARA
494	C 4	BREITMAN, ISAAC HARRY		26 JAN 1987	14 APR 1886	ABRAHAM	MITCHELL
125	ZB174	BRENNER, FAYE		14 FEB 1993			
447	R13	BRENNER, JEANETTE		9 JUL 1962	1892		JOSEPH
447	R14	BRENNER, JOSEPH E		20 APR 1936	1886		JEANETTE
123		BRENNER, MILTON		22 DEC 1963	1916		
112	E11	BRENNER, MIRIAM		10 AUG 1986	4 JAN 1916		
110	B12	BRENNER, NATHAN		17 SEP 1931	1856		SARAH
110	B13	BRENNER, SARAH		19 JUL 1929	1861		NATHAN
222	A011	BRENNER, SYLVIA	FUHR	31 AUG 1968	1923		
125	I 64	BRENNERT, HANNAH		30 MAR 1924			
433	P 9	BRESLOW, BELLA		1992	1901		
433	E15	BRESLOW, CLARA		7 FEB 1962	12 APR 1905	SOFSEL	
433	S 1	BRESLOW, JAY		27 APR 1984	1929	MEYER	
102	H41	BRESNERKOFF, DOROTHY		19 DEC 1986	16 SEP 1905		JACOB
102	H42	BRESNERKOFF, JACOB		7 JUL 1965	10 MAY 1904		DOROTHY
374	G 1	BRESS, CHIA			6 APR 1916		
222	I12	BRESSLAU, FLORENCE	HALPERN	1967	1912		HERMAN
222	I11	BRESSLAU, HERMAN		18 MAR 1986	1911	MAX & ROSE	FLORENCE
222	J10	BRESSLAU, MARTIN		9 MAY 1989	1949		
222	I 9	BRESSLAU, MAX		22 MAY 1954	1876		ROSE
222	J11	BRESSLAU, ROBERT AARON		30 JAN 1987	1943		
222	I10	BRESSLAU, ROSE		19 AUG 1960	1887		MAX
222	J12	BRESSLAU, SOLOMON		20 NOV 1992			
248	G25	BRETTSCHNEIDER, ABRAHAM		18 AUG 1957	24 DEC 1921		
249	C14	BRETTSCHNEIDER, BERTHA		10 JUL 1989	27 JUL 1916		
248	G30	BRETTSCHNEIDER, ESTHER		2 OCT 1948	1855		NECHEMYA
248	F34	BRETTSCHNEIDER, HARRY		15 NOV 1973	1895	NECHEMYA & ESTHER	
248	F35	BRETTSCHNEIDER, HERMAN		8 JUN 1973	1895	NECHEMYA & ESTHER	
248	F25	BRETTSCHNEIDER, JACOB		13 MAY 1958	15 JUL 1906	NECHEMYA & ESTHER	
248	G32	BRETTSCHNEIDER, LENA		29 FEB 1984	13 OCT 1895		LOUIS
248	I78	BRETTSCHNEIDER, LOUIS		29 MAY 1935	1880		
248	G31	BRETTSCHNEIDER, LOUIS		26 JAN 1957	15 JUL 1890	NECHEMYA & ESTHER	LENA
248	G28	BRETTSCHNEIDER, MAX		30 JUL 1969	1888	NECHEMYA & ESTHER	REBECCA
248	F26	BRETTSCHNEIDER, PAULINE		16 AUG 1964	5 OCT 1883	NECHEMYA & ESTHER	
248	G29	BRETTSCHNEIDER, REBECCA		4 JUN 1950	1888		MAX
249	B12	BRETTSCHNEIDER, SYLVIA		NDD	28 APR 1915		
248	J65	BRETTSCHNIEDER, NECHEMYA		15 OCT 1917	1858		ESTHER
102	SR88	BREWER, ANNA	CRAMER	5 JUN 1941	1873		ISSAC
371	AM23	BREWER, EDITH		12 DEC 1967		ELIZABETH	
371	AM24	BREWER, ELIZABETH		1962	1878		
102	AE87	BREWER, MAE		18 DEC 1970	1904	ISAAC & ANNA (CRAMER)	
370	G31	BRICKMAN, ANNIE		11 AUG 1915			
392	J 9	BRICKMAN, BAILA PESHA		24 JAN 1916		TZVI HIRSH	
392	D38	BRICKMAN, HARRY		21 MAR 1956	8 MAY 1888		
391	ZA68	BRICKMAN, ISADORE		8 SEP 1973	1918	JACOB	
392	J38	BRICKMAN, ROSE S		10 SEP 1990	4 JUL 1900		
102	Z66	BRIGHTMAN, BENJAMIN		11 MAY 1987	24 NOV 1913	IDA	
101	E36	BRIGHTMAN, EDITH B		9 JAN 1965	1916		
102	Z67	BRIGHTMAN, IDA S		11 FEB 1964	1892		
372	G26	BRILL, RUTH		1977	1897		
125	J100	BRIN, ANNA		29 JAN 1966	1882		LOUIS
125	J 99	BRIN, LOUIS J		27 JUN 1971	1878		ANNA
125	M 85	BRIN, NETTIE		8 MAY 1921	FEB 1908	LOUIS & ANNA	
125	K136	BRIN, ROSE ZELDA		30 JAN 1933	13 JUN 1909		
102	T20	BROD, BENJAMIN H		7 DEC 1938	1891	MARCUS & GOLDA	
102	T21	BROD, GOLDA		24 NOV 1944	1868		MARCUS

Cem	Row	Name	Maiden Name	DOD	DOB	Parents	Spouse
102	T22	BROD, MARCUS		16 MAY 1939	1865		GOLDA
330	G16	BRODER, FANNIE		22 JAN 1959	1881		
330	AA15	BRODER, JACOB		31 JUL 1970	5 OCT 1909	LEON	
330	G15	BRODER, LEON		31 AUG 1957	1873		
330	AA16	BRODER, MORRIS HYMAN		20 SEP 1965	2 NOV 1907	LEON	
125	N162	BRODIE, HANNAH D		13 JUN 1951	1873		
391	Q69	BRODIE, HYMAN DON		23 AUG 1966	14 MAY 1904	AARON	AARON
391	Q68	BRODIE, IDA H		24 JAN 1976	8 AUG 1904		
391	Q66	BRODIE, ROBERT		27 NOV 1981	24 FEB 1913	AARON	
494	G 5	BRODINSKY, MARY	STEUTEVILLE	1991	1917		
391	G24	BRODSKY, BESSIE		2 JUN 1913	10 AUG 1898	LOUIS & ROSE	
126		BRODSKY, ELIAS		14 FEB 1891	24 FEB 1858		
112	B30	BRODSKY, HARRY		6 AUG 1988	10 AUG 1911		
392	G25	BRODSKY, LOUIS		16 DEC 1929	1861	ISRAEL	ROSE
392	G24	BRODSKY, ROSE		28 MAR 1937	1868	JACOB TZVI	LOUIS
102	F27	BRODY, ARCHY STEPHEN		1946	1904		KAY
101	M30	BRODY, BELLA		25 APR 1934	1883		JACOB
392	D20	BRODY, BENJAMIN		25 JUN 1957	1898	TZVI REUBEN	BESSIE
392	D19	BRODY, BESSIE S		29 MAR 1993	1900	JOSEPH	BENJAMIN
391	Q41	BRODY, ETTA		20 AUG 1941	1864	MICHAEL NOAH	
102	F26	BRODY, KAY	MAX	1990	1904		ARCHY
391	C19	BRODY, REUBEN		14 SEP 1936	1861	SIMON	
392	E 8	BRODY, ROSE D		15 JUL 1972	1901	BEN ZION	SAMUEL
392	E 7	BRODY, SAMUEL		7 JAN 1973	1898	TZVI REUBEN	ROSE
751	J11	BROKOPP, MAE	NIMAN	30 OCT 1938	16 DEC 1906		
751	N 2	BROKOPP, SARAH	NIMAN	1986	1902		
102	AE32	BROMBERG, MILTON A		1982	1880		RUBY
102	AE33	BROMBERG, RUBY	KOLODNEY	1954	1887		MILTON
104	M37	BRONERWEIN, BEN		22 NOV 1971	25 NOV 1905		
370	V 7	BRONERWINE, FANNIE		1977	1891		IRVING
370	V 8	BRONERWINE, IRVING M		1945	1890		FANNIE
391	P42	BRONITSKY, FANNIE I		3 JUN 1948	20 MAY 1896	MOSHE	WILLIAM
391	H35	BRONITSKY, GOLDIE		27 JAN 1925	1871	ZEV WOLF	SAMUEL
374	A 7	BRONITSKY, RICHARD PAUL		1953	1952		
391	P43	BRONITSKY, WILLIAM		13 FEB 1964	29 JAN 1894	ISRAEL	FANNIE
391	O28	BRONITZKY, ISRAEL		18 MAY 1909	1867	ELIYAHU	
222	AL23	BRONOWITZ, CARA	WOLFBEIN	1945	1895		ISAAC
222	AL22	BRONOWITZ, ISAAC		1935	1892		CARA
115	D55	BRONSON, HARRY E		5 FEB 1992			
125	L131	BRONSTEIN, MARILYN ALICE		26 SEP 1931	MAR 1925		
391	L26	BRONSTEIN, SAMUEL		9 JAN 1925	10 MAY 1870	ISRAEL	GOLDIE
391	GN 2	BRONSTEIN, YETTA		20 JUN 1934	14 MAR 1875	SHIMON	
392	E48	BROOK, EVELYN		13 DEC 1953	6 JAN 1908	JACOB	
127	A	BROOKS, ABRAHAM ABNER		5 DEC 1983	8 OCT 1913		
125	H165	BROOKS, GEORGE S		12 JUN 1947	1917	MEYER LEV	
106	C14	BROOKS, LOIS S		5 JUN 1982	28 DEC 1926		
125	I166	BROOKS, MAX		7 JAN 1961	1888		REBECCA
125	I165	BROOKS, REBECCA	RIVKIN	27 NOV 1984	1895		MAX
222	G 9	BROSOFSKY, JOSEPH		19 MAR 1977	19 APR 1926		
102	AB22	BROSS, THEODORE		1985	1905		
330	A24	BROUNSTEIN, ISADORE		29 APR 1961	1890		SARAH
329	A30	BROUNSTEIN, ROSE		18 JUL 1966	1889		
330	A26	BROUNSTEIN, SAMUEL		8 JUL 1975	15 APR 1921	ISADORE & SARAH	
330	A25	BROUNSTEIN, SARAH		18 SEP 1976	1895		ISIDORE
125		BROWN, (CHILD)		28 DEC 1916	28 DEC 1916	YOEL & PAULINE	
373	J 4	BROWN, BENJAMIN B		18 DEC 1972	14 NOV 1909		
112	E25	BROWN, BERNARD RABBI		19 MAR 1991	11 JUN 1913		
222	F 3	BROWN, BERTHA	EISENBERG	8 OCT 1969	1889		MORRIS
751	B19	BROWN, BESSIE	GOORIN	31 MAY 1955	1890		JOSEPH
102	O17	BROWN, CHARLES		30 JUL 1955	12 OCT 1899		
372	B 1	BROWN, EDWIN		1971	1889		IDA
125	M106	BROWN, HARRIS		13 DEC 1937	1856	YITZCHAK & CHANA	RACHEL
372	B 2	BROWN, IDA R		1973	1891		ERWIN
751	B20	BROWN, JOSEPH		23 OCT 1966	1885		BESSIE
119	D40	BROWN, MAX B		3 SEP 1973	21 NOV 1908		
222	F 4	BROWN, MORRIS		14 JUN 1956	1889		BERTHA

Cem	Row	Name	Maiden Name	DOD	DOB	Parents	Spouse
112	C35	BROWN, PETER B		13 AUG 1987	17 NOV 1894		
125	M107	BROWN, RACHEL L		1 MAR 1937	1858		
371	AQ 7	BROWN, RAE		17 AUG 1988	19 NOV 1904		HARRIS SAMUEL
371	AQ 6	BROWN, SAMUEL		11 FEB 1971	1 NOV 1898		RAE
447	T26	BROWNSTEIN, IDA		30 DEC 1954			
446	A47	BROWNSTEIN, ISRAEL DMD		1987	1901		
374	E 8	BRUCKNER, ABRAHAM		4 NOV 1953	15 AUG 1883		BELLA
374	E 9	BRUCKNER, BELLA R		13 JUL 1960	15 MAR 1883		ABRAHAM
374	E 3	BRUCKNER, BENJAMIN		1975	1909	ESTHER & MEYER	
374	F53	BRUCKNER, BESSIE		9 JUL 1963	15 JUN 1887		
374	E 4	BRUCKNER, ESTHER		18 DEC 1934	1862		MEYER
374	C41	BRUCKNER, GOLDIE		30 AUG 1967	10 JUL 1907		
371	AF15	BRUCKNER, HANNAH	CURLAND	19 OCT 1991			
374	E 6	BRUCKNER, HERMAN A		23 APR 1945	8 APR 1888		LENA
374	E 7	BRUCKNER, LENA		27 AUG 1979	24 DEC 1894		HERMAN
371	AF14	BRUCKNER, LEON S		13 OCT 1963	1896	MORRIS & HANNAH	
374	F52	BRUCKNER, LOUIS		18 JAN 1960	15 MAR 1886		
374	E 5	BRUCKNER, MEYER I		21 NOV 1928	1862		ESTHER
371	AF16	BRUCKNER, MORRIS		30 AUG 1978			
391	ZD65	BRUCKNER, SELMA		31 JUL 1980	22 JUL 1931	TZVI HIRSH	
446	C39	BRUMMEL, JOACHIM		30 MAR 1917	1 JUN 1882		JOSEPHINE
446	C38	BRUMMEL, JOSEPHINE		8 AUG 1908	23 MAY 1843		JOACHIM
446	D27	BRUMMEL, ROSIE		19 SEP 1900	23 MAR 1879	JOACHIN & JOSEPHINE	
119	J34	BRUNO, FAY	WAINGROW	1984	1911		
119	B65	BRUNSWICK, SIDNEY J		5 JUL 1991	7 NOV 1916		
370	O64	BRYER, JEANNIE	MOPSIK	1983	1897		
370	Q35	BRYNAN, ISADORE		1963	1885		ROSE
370	Q36	BRYNAN, ROSE		1963	1886		ISADORE
125	Z194	BUCH, MILTON		25 DEC 1988	30 MAR 1912		
125	Y193	BUCHALTER, JENNIE D		31 DEC 1984	15 AUG 1894		
125	J138	BUCHALTER, NATHAN		27 APR 1936	1862	ABRAHAM & ZELDA D	REBECCA
125	J137	BUCHALTER, REBECCA		23 MAR 1950	1868		NATHAN
330	G79	BUCHALTER, SAMUEL		29 MAY 1918			
248	L80	BUCHBINDER, ARTHUR KRISCHER		8 JUN 1981	25 OCT 1922		
377	X27	BUCHBINDER, RUBIN		16 MAY 1961	20 NOV 1904		
115	L51	BUCHMAN, CONSTANCE		16 OCT 1991			FREDERICK
119	H30	BUCHMAN, DELLA		6 NOV 1990	12 JUN 1909		
115	L50	BUCHMAN, FREDERICK DLS		3 JUL 1991	15 MAR 1923		CONSTANCE
119	H31	BUCHMAN, SOLOMON		5 APR 1984	10 JUN 1907		
370	J75	BUCHOVETSKY, CECELIA		13 MAR 1988	1907		MYER
370	J76	BUCHOVETSKY, MYER		7 FEB 1952	1897		CELIA
370	Z10	BUCK, ISAAC		1940	1866		MASHA
370	Z11	BUCK, MASHA		1943	1863		ISAAC
370	K50	BUCOVETSKY, CECILIA		13 MAR 1988	1907		MEYER
370	R 2	BUCOVETSKY, CELIA		18 FEB 1945		JACOB & RACHEL	
370	R 3	BUCOVETSKY, JACOB		1942	1868		RACHEL
370	K51	BUCOVETSKY, MYER		7 DEC 1952	1897		CELIA
370	R 1	BUCOVETSKY, RACHEL		1925	1868		JACOB
377	Y11	BUDD, EDITH	FABIAN	2 DEC 1973	11 DEC 1901	CHAIM	LOUIS
377	Y12	BUDD, LOUIS		14 FEB 1983	2 JAN 1895	SHALOM	EDITH
370	J32	BUDNICK, BESSIE MOLLIE		1937	1868		
370	B 8	BUDNICK, EPHRIAM A		4 JUN 1925	1862		SARAH
370	W10	BUDNICK, ESTHER		1962	1900		
370	V11	BUDNICK, HERMAN		12 JUL 1945	12 MAR 1893		
371	AH 8	BUDNICK, ISRAEL		26 JUN 1973	6 JAN 1900		
370	S31	BUDNICK, JOSEPH		27 MAR 1958			
370	I25	BUDNICK, SARAH		1 JUN 1927			EFFRIAM
370	S30	BUDNICK, SAUL		15 DEC 1965	7 SEP 1906		
102	AH181	BUECHLER, HANNAH		11 JUN 1989	26 SEP 1910		JOSEPH
102	AH182	BUECHLER, JOSEPH		9 APR 1984	10 APR 1904		HANNAH
119	I59	BUKSBAUM, HARRY		23 OCT 1987			
119	I60	BUKSBAUM, SYLVIA		30 DEC 1988	2 JUL 1908		
433	D30	BULA, BEA	URVATER	26 MAR 1989	19 OCT 1946	ABRAHAM	
447	V39	BURACK, BORIS		26 OCT 1968	10 APR 1929		
374	I35	BURCHMAN, HYMAN		1944	1885		LENA
374	A15	BURCHMAN, ISIDORE		7 JUL 1919	1910		

Cem	Row	Name	Maiden Name	DOD	DOB	Parents	Spouse
374	I34	BURCHMAN, LENA		1941	1879		HYMAN
108	C12	BURDAY, IDA		30 OCT 1974	1 APR 1908		
108	B15	BURKE, ALBERT S		8 AUG 1965	28 AUG 1907		
108	C17	BURLOCK, JOSEPH		7 FEB 1964	26 SEP 1911		
102	R30	BURNESS, IRVING LT		14 DEC 1944	1917	LEON & SYLVIA	
102	Z200	BURNESS, LEON B		21 SEP 1989	1886		SYLVIA
102	Z199	BURNESS, SYLVIA R		23 MAR 1984	1898		LEON
114	F20	BURNS, IRWIN M		24 SEP 1992			
391	P59	BURNS, JOSEPH LEWIS		9 OCT 1991	18 SEP 1913	MOSHE HALEVI	
114	F22	BURNS, LIONEL		24 MAY 1990	21 MAY 1902		
391	P36	BURNSTEIN, BERTHA		12 MAR 1918	1888	YEHUDA MOSHE	
391	X51	BURNSTEIN, PAULINE		5 JAN 1963	1885	ISAAC	SAMUEL
391	X50	BURNSTEIN, SAMUEL		11 SEP 1955	1880	JOSEPH	PAULINE
101	B17	BURRES, LOTTIE		18 OCT 1948	1868		NATHAN
101	B18	BURRES, NATHAN		11 JAN 1943	1867		LOTTIE
125	P196	BURROS, MOLLIE CATHERINE		24 SEP 1963	1901		MORRIS
125	P195	BURROS, MORRIS		1986	1896		MOLLIE
113	O62	BURSACK, BERNARD		17 APR 1970	10 DEC 1903		
330	C22	BURSTEIN, ABRAHAM I		20 JAN 1957	1869		REBECCA
125	N105	BURSTEIN, BLANCHE		8 OCT 1928	1877	DANIEL & KOBODY	
447	G40	BURSTEIN, EDWARD		16 AUG 1981	3 MAR 1895	HARRY & SARAH	FRIEDA
447	G39	BURSTEIN, FRIEDA		17 OCT 1974	18 AUG 1897		EDWARD
121	N 8	BURSTEIN, GUSSIE		14 SEP 1969	1897		
447	G38	BURSTEIN, HARRY		10 SEP 1928	1874		SARAH
121	N 7	BURSTEIN, JULIUS		27 SEP 1979	19 SEP 1915	GUSSIE	
328	A34	BURSTEIN, LOUIS		2 NOV 1973	5 OCT 1895		PAULA
328	A35	BURSTEIN, PAULA		4 OCT 1988	4 JUL 1904		LOUIS
330	C21	BURSTEIN, REBECCA		15 MAR 1948	1867		ABRAHAM
447	F37	BURSTEIN, SARAH		26 MAY 1935	1876		HARRY
121	N 6	BURSTEIN, SYLVIA		15 OCT 1972	13 AUG 1916		
125	E 24	BUSHELL, DORA		1991	1890		JOSEPH
125	M177	BUSHELL, ELIZABETH J		1970	1918		
125	F 21	BUSHELL, JOSEPH		24 MAY 1974	1881		DORA
377	R16	BUSKER, HELEN	WEINSTEIN	NDD	1901		MANFRED
377	R15	BUSKER, MANFRED		1962	1905		HELEN
125	N166	BUSKER, MAX		21 OCT 1951	1896		
248	G50	BUTLEMAN, ABRAHAM		11 JUL 1949	1882		ANNIE
248	G51	BUTLEMAN, ANNIE		10 NOV 1961	1883		ABRAHAM
377	Q26	BUTLEMAN, HAROLD J		18 SEP 1976	24 OCT 1925		
377	S14	BUTLEMAN, MARY		1983	1896		PHILIP
377	S13	BUTLEMAN, PHILIP G		1956	1886		MARY
116	AC17	BUTLER, HAROLD M		1985	1920		
125	L 26	BUTNICK, ANNA		8 SEP 1928	1890	MAX & RACHEL	
248	J22	BYCEL, BENJAMIN		4 SEP 1921	1890		TILLIE
248	I32	BYCEL, EVA		9 FEB 1922	1877	AARON & MOLLIE	
248	I31	BYCEL, MOLLIE		10 JAN 1933	1857		AARON
248	I29	BYCEL, TILLIE J		23 OCT 1947	1888		BENJAMIN
248	J24	BYCLE, AARON		3 APR 1914	1849		MOLLIE
125	S166	BYER, BELLA		21 AUG 1946	20 AUG 1862	MOSHE & ALTA PESHA	JOSEPH
125	R162	BYER, IRVING S		10 OCT 1942	3 DEC 1898	JOSEPH & BELLA	LENA
125	B118	BYER, JACOB		4 FEB 1970	1909	JOSEPH & BELLA	
125	O101	BYER, JOSEPH		18 MAR 1922	1855		BELLA
125	R163	BYER, LENA ANNA	BLUMENTHAL	13 JUN 1962	1899		IRVING
125	S165	BYER, LOUIS		15 OCT 1941	15 SEP 1892	JOSEPH & BELLA	LENA
125	Q171	BYER, PERCY		28 NOV 1963	1900	JOSEPH & BELLA	
102	AH189	BYRON, HARRY		29 DEC 1981	18 SEP 1907		
248	J25	BYSEL, SAMUEL M		23 SEP 1910	1873	AARON & MOLLIE	
370	F29	CADMONISH, SHRUGA					
370	F30	CADMONISH, YEHUDA					
391	L52	CAMASSAR, ANNA		22 DEC 1963	1881	ABRAHAM	
391	L53	CAMASSAR, HARRY		29 SEP 1950	1872	SHNAOR ZALMAN	
377	J 7	CAMASSAR, SELMA	SELLECK	13 MAR 1968	13 MAR 1918	JENNIE	
102	V18	CAMERON, GREGORY J		6 DEC 1984	24 JUN 1980		
377	V 9	CAMP, JEANETTE	GINSBERG	4 OCT 1975	1917	LEV	
116	BH62	CAMPBELL, EILEEN	YUSH	25 APR 1990	10 JUN 1952	LEONARD	
102	J24	CANTAROW, HELEN	KARP	1937	1878		JOSEPH

Cem	Row	Name	Maiden Name	DOD	DOB	Parents	Spouse
102	J23	CANTAROW, JOSEPH		1948	1873		
222	M 2	CANTOR, BESSIE		28 MAY 1974	1891		HELEN
125	K147	CANTOR, DAVID C		27 NOV 1964	14 SEP 1896		MAX
222	AL 3	CANTOR, LEIZER		31 MAR 1933	1865		MOLLY
222	K 6	CANTOR, MARY		9 SEP 1990	1896		SARAH
222	M 1	CANTOR, MAX		12 DEC 1983	1886		NATHAN
222	AM 1	CANTOR, MELVIN		25 AUG 1992			BESSIE
125	K146	CANTOR, MOLLY L	LIGHT	8 FEB 1985	28 JUL 1902		RITA
222	K 5	CANTOR, NATHAN		18 JAN 1960	1891		DAVID
222	AM 2	CANTOR, RITA B		31 AUG 1985	1929		MARY
377	Q43	CANTOR, ROSE		2 JUN 1983	30 MAR 1904		MELVIN
222	AL 4	CANTOR, SARAH		27 JAN 1932	1859		LEIZER
751	C33	CANZER, ARI		29 APR 1901	1871		
116	H 9	CAPLAN, DAVID		7 DEC 1990	21 AUG 1912		
102	E22	CAPLAN, EVA	TELECHANSKY	2 MAY 1986	20 JAN 1901		
249	N 5	CAPLAN, HYMAN		19 MAY 1987	23 NOV 1906		
116	AY12	CAPLAN, MOLLIE	ROCK	7 JUL 1973	1891		WILLIAM
125	J 28	CAPLAN, MORRIS L		4 FEB 1918	1852	YECHIEL & RIVA	SARAH
125	J 27	CAPLAN, SARAH F		1936	1853		MORRIS
116	AY11	CAPLAN, WILLIAM		22 MAR 1978	1886		MOLLIE
392	A13	CAPLOWE, LOUIS		12 JAN 1980	11 NOV 1925		
370	K 9	CARASHICK, ANNA		24 AUG 1948			
371	A 8	CARASHICK, JACOB B		18 JAN 1988	15 MAR 1912		
371	K10	CARASHICK, JACOB ZELIG		12 OCT 1962			
371	A 9	CARASHICK, ORRIN		2 APR 1990	18 APR 1908		
123		CARLSON, CARL		11 OCT 1963	1892		
371	M33	CAROLINE, CELIA		1977	1892		CELIA
371	M32	CAROLINE, EDWARD N		1952	1888		LOUIS
370	B46	CAROLINE, HYMAN		15 JUN 1931	1871	RISHE	
371	J33	CAROLINE, IDA		1964	1884		MORRIS
371	J32	CAROLINE, MORRIS		1967	1875		IDA
370	I28	CAROLINE, RISHE		21 NOV 1917	1849		
370	A57	CARPELMAN, SHAPIRA		6 AUG 1909	1843		
376	D11	CARPENOS, JANET		26 DEC 1981	28 FEB 1922		
127	S	CARR, SARAH ANNE		26 DEC 1981			
105	H25	CARROLL, AARON JOSEPH		30 APR 1967	1870		LEAH
105	H23	CARROLL, BENJAMIN		31 JUL 1956	1901	AARON & LEAH	
105	H24	CARROLL, LEAH		20 NOV 1941	1873		AARON
102	F42	CARSON, ETHEL	KRAUSS	13 JUL 1957	2 MAY 1906		
102	AB94	CARTEN, LOUIS S		13 MAY 1953	MAR 1888	ABRAHAM & YETTA	MINNIE
102	AB95	CARTEN, MINNIE B	RESNICK	5 FEB 1966	1894		LOUIS
102	T13	CARTIN, EDWARD L		31 MAY 1943	1925	MORRIS	
102	T14	CARTIN, MORRIS B		23 APR 1937	1893		
125	B 86	CASLOWITZ, AARON N		21 JUL 1985	26 SEP 1909	JOSEPH & ROSE	
125	G125	CASLOWITZ, JOSEPH		25 JUN 1933	1881		ROSE
125	G123	CASLOWITZ, ROSE		24 MAR 1970	1885		JOSEPH
101	J30	CASSEL, ELIZABETH		23 APR 1967	1887		MORRIS
101	J31	CASSEL, MORRIS		6 APR 1962	1892		ELIZABETH
118	C14	CASSIN, WALTER		24 NOV 1966			
447	X40	CASSYD, CASPER		8 JUL 1971	10 MAY 1907		JENNIE
447	X39	CASSYD, JENNIE		20 FEB 1990	2 JUN 1909		CASPER
105	F30	CAVAL, MYRA H	WYNN	2 JUL 1984	18 JAN 1953		
101	M20	CELINSON, CHANA		7 JUL 1910	1878		
114	H26	CHABACK, NATALIE	LITCHMAN	13 MAY 1991	7 FEB 1919		
371	AH24	CHADOW, ABRAHAM		11 SEP 1964	1903		
370	K23	CHAFITZ, ANNA		14 FEB 1945	1888		JOSEPH
370	L 5	CHAFITZ, JOSEPH		10 MAY 1944	1883		ANNA
102	AJ56	CHAIKIND, HARRY		1 SEP 1951	1896		SARAH
102	AJ55	CHAIKIND, SARAH M		1 DEC 1988	1898		HARRY
103	B20	CHAIN, SYDNEY		5 MAY 1989	14 NOV 1914		
374	D42	CHAIT, ISRAEL		1988	1905	LOUIS	ROSE
374	D44	CHAIT, LOUIS		1941	1870		
374	D43	CHAIT, ROSE		1985	1904		ISRAEL
248	A64	CHAITOW, HENRY		8 MAY 1992	14 AUG 1903		
372	B16	CHAMANSKY, ADOLPH BENNO		6 MAR 1937	1868		
372	B15	CHAMANSKY, DAVID		1893	1814		

Cem	Row	Name	Maiden Name	DOD	DOB	Parents	Spouse
372	B20	CHAMANSKY, HENRIETTA		1899	1840		
372	B19	CHAMANSKY, JOSEPH		1889	1827		JOSEPH
372	B18	CHAMANSKY, LOUIS J		12 NOV 1929	1866		HENRIETTA
372	B17	CHAMANSKY, PAULINE K	KUTNER	8 SEP 1938	1870	JOSEPH & HENRIETTA	PAULINE
222	AA 8	CHANIN, EMMA	KAMP	24 FEB 1927	2 AUG 1893		LOUIS
433	I 3	CHANNIE, BEATRICE ANN		1993	1914		
222	AP 7	CHANNIN, ANNA		30 JAN 1941	1867		NATHAN
222	AP 8	CHANNIN, ARTHUR N		25 DEC 1945	1892	NATHAN & ANNA	
121	E10	CHANNIN, HILDA	BERGER	25 APR 1969	24 MAR 1922		
222	AP 9	CHANNIN, IRVIN H		14 APR 1949	1903	NATHAN & ANNA	
222	AQ 1	CHANNIN, MYRON A		15 JAN 1983	23 SEP 1897		YETTA
222	AP 6	CHANNIN, NATHAN		8 APR 1933	1861		ANNA
222	AQ 2	CHANNIN, YETTA V		6 JUL 1988	5 JAN 1900		MYRON
330	F41	CHANSKY, DAVE		5 MAR 1922	1852		
113	M33	CHAPNICK, HYMAN		11 APR 1958	17 SEP 1875		LEONA
113	M34	CHAPNICK, LEONA		29 JUN 1971	14 OCT 1884		HYMAN
113	M35	CHAPNICK, MORTON		31 DEC 1976	29 NOV 1903	HYMAN & LEONA	
113	K59	CHARLAMB, JUNE R		7 AUG 1991	17 AUG 1926		
391	P40	CHARLOP, ANNA		5 DEC 1942	10 SEP 1872	JOSEPH	
377	Y38	CHARLOP, CARL M		11 SEP 1966	21 APR 1903	YEHUDA	
391	D29	CHARLOP, JULIUS		12 NOV 1949	1877	BARUCH	
391	H34	CHARLOP, SARAH		3 JAN 1925	1842	MOSHE DAVID	
377	Q54	CHARLOP, SOL		28 DEC 1991	7 MAR 1907		
328	B18	CHARMAC, LEA		13 JAN 1960	1898		
391	ZG57	CHARNEY, MINA		15 NOV 1993	5 SEP 1913	ISRAEL	
370	M 3	CHASANOFF, HILLEL		1947	1880	NACHMAN & JUDITH	SADIE
370	J17	CHASANOFF, JUDITH		1935	1852		MACHMAN
370	E 3	CHASANOFF, MACHMAN		1940	1852		JUDITH
370	H 6	CHASANOFF, SADIE	FRANK	29 FEB 1988	1 APR 1892		HILLEL
103	C1	CHASE, ABRAHAM		2 JUN 1970	1908		
391	E13	CHASE, ABRAHAM M		24 APR 1971	1900	AARON	GUSSIE
391	E14	CHASE, GUSSIE L		7 MAR 1992	1900	ISAAC	ABRAHAM
248	J45	CHASE, WILLIAM S DR			1 MAR 1908		
249	C 8	CHASEN, CELIA		16 DEC 1953	26 SEP 1888		
249	D 7	CHASEN, CELIA RAE		21 AUG 1987	4 SEP 1916		PHILIP
248	K67	CHASEN, EVELYN		14 JUL 1949	1914	PAUL & MINNIE	
371	N28	CHASEN, FANNIE E	SAFENOVITZ	30 OCT 1982	14 APR 1906		
248	J69	CHASEN, HARRY		6 AUG 1920	1875		
248	J68	CHASEN, HYMAN		31 DEC 1919	1880		
248	L69	CHASEN, HYMAN N		17 FEB 1955	1902		
248	K68	CHASEN, MINNIE		16 DEC 1962			PAUL
248	K69	CHASEN, PAUL		30 JUN 1941	2 JUL 1897		MINNIE
249	D 6	CHASEN, PHILIP		26 SEP 1992	17 APR 1914		CELIA
125	J 61	CHASINSKY, ANNIE		23 MAY 1910	1875		
125		CHASINSKY, RIVA		16 MAY 1917	1841	NISAN	
330	H19	CHASNOFF, NORMAN I		1945	1943		
125	J108	CHATINER, ABRAHAM		25 MAY 1943	10 FEB 1873	MOSHE & CHANA	MINNIE
125	P174	CHATINER, GUSSIE		15 JUL 1973	15 MAY 1895		HERMAN
125	P175	CHATINER, HERMAN		29 OCT 1962	12 MAY 1886		GUSSIE
125	J107	CHATINER, MINNIE		13 MAR 1955	1880		ABRAHAM
113	B65	CHATZKY, SAMUEL		15 NOV 1987	27 AUG 1912		
125	M174	CHAZEN, DAVID HARRY		5 JUN 1974	1901		
125	M173	CHAZEN, JOSEPH		4 FEB 1968	1903		
125	Q186	CHAZEN, MEYER L		20 MAR 1962	1892		
125	W194	CHAZEN, ROSE OFSTEIN	BYER	2 SEP 1981	1899		
446	D33	CHECK, AVRAM DANIEL		5 JAN 1988			
102	Z111	CHEIFFETZ, CECILE		1929	1902		ISADORE
102	Z110	CHEIFFETZ, ESTHER		1926	1868		
102	Z113	CHEIFFETZ, ETTA		1967	1892		SAMUEL
102	Z112	CHEIFFETZ, ISADORE B		1930	1903	ESTHER	CECILE
102	Z114	CHEIFFETZ, SAMUEL		25 APR 1979	26 JUL 1896	ESTHER	ETTA
113	D33	CHEIKIN, SYLVIA		4 FEB 1991	18 FEB 1946		MEYER
116	AU27	CHELL, RUTH	LONDON	28 FEB 1966	28 AUG 1920		
330	AC14	CHEPLOW, MORRIS		22 DEC 1962	1 MAY 1905		
391	R23	CHERKASKY, BENJAMIN		4 SEP 1923	1865	MENACHEM MENDEL	
391	R25	CHERKASKY, MAX		23 APR 1919	1842	ABRAHAM	

Cem	Row	Name	Maiden Name	DOD	DOB	Parents	Spouse
391	R25	CHERKASKY, MAX		23 APR 1919	1842	ABRAHAM	
391	S34	CHERKASKY, REBECCA		2 MAY 1920	1836	NACHMAN SIMON	
391	G 2	CHERKASKY, SAMUEL		30 AUG 1935	1873	MENACHEM MENDEL	
125	Q196	CHERNIAK, DAVID		26 APR 1962	1898		LENA
125	I 50	CHERNIAK, JACOB		1908	1869		LENA
125	L 23	CHERNIAK, LENA		19 MAR 1917	1858	SOLOMON	JACOB
125	Q195	CHERNIAK, LENA		26 OCT 1983	1899		DAVID
125	EL18	CHERNIAK, MRS GORDON H		26 JUN 1938	1872	JACOB & LEAH	GORDON
391	Q39	CHERNKASKY, ROSE		20 NOV 1934	26 DEC 1867	MORDECHAI	
125	L 27	CHERNOFF, BERTHA		8 OCT 1914	1894		
116	N 1	CHERNOFF, DONALD PHILSON		23 AUG 1981	13 SEP 1931		
125	N149	CHERNOFF, MENAS MISHA		14 JUN 1956	25 SEP 1871		SONIA
125	N148	CHERNOFF, SONIA		27 JAN 1951	14 APR 1875		MENAS
377	T20	CHERTOFF, SAMUEL		1980	1892	MOSHE	SARAH
377	T21	CHERTOFF, SARAH		1985	1892	ABRAHAM BER	SAMUEL
249	N14	CHERTOW, BORIS W		15 JUN 1970	18 FEB 1891		ELIZABETH
249	N15	CHERTOW, ELIZABETH K		3 FEB 1975	6 AUG 1896		BORIS
102	AD68	CHESKY, BENJAMIN F		26 SEP 1968	30 MAY 1894	HARRIS & RAIZEL (LERNER)	DORA
102	AD67	CHESKY, DORA	BLOCK	11 FEB 1953	1899		BENJAMIN
102	AD69	CHESKY, HAROLD L		1988	1918	BENJAMIN & DORA (BLOCK)	
102	AC62	CHESKY, HARRIS	OF LIPOVITZ	6 JAN 1941	1866		ROSE
102	AC65	CHESKY, JACKIE		1938	1929		
102	AC63	CHESKY, PAULINE		1918	1904		
102	AC63	CHESKY, ROSE	LERNER	1923	1869		HARRIS
102	AC61	CHESKY, WILLIAM		1949	1893	HARRIS & RAIZEL (LERNER)	
123		CHESLER, ABRAHAM		20 NOV 1952	1890		
377	G22	CHESLER, RONALD ALAN		17 AUG 1952	7 NOV 1944	ISRAEL	
123		CHESLER, SAM		16 MAY 1967	1896		
447	L15	CHESNER, FLORENCE	GOLDMAN	15 APR 1986	9 APR 1898		HARRY
447	P16	CHESNER, GOLDA		13 NOV 1959	1883		HARRY
447	P15	CHESNER, HARRY		28 OCT 1948	1879		GOLDA
125	Q147	CHESTER, MARY	COHEN	21 OCT 1981	1889		NATHAN
125	Q146	CHESTER, NATHAN		4 SEP 1944	1882		MARY
447	A10	CHESTLER, IRVING		27 JUN 1979	1907		SHIRLEY
447	A 9	CHESTLER, SHIRLEY		15 AUG 1987	1909		IRVING
447	S15	CHESTNER, MAX		3 DEC 1960	10 JUL 1893		
121	J46	CHIEL, MARTIN		18 MAR 1982	14 JUN 1927		
116	BL 7	CHINITZ, IDA		1 DEC 1959			
125	V180	CHINITZ, ISRAEL		10 NOV 1976	1897		
117	A10	CHINITZ, J RAYMOND		22 APR 1989	20 MAY 1922		
116	BL 5	CHINITZ, MILDRED		28 JAN 1991			
116	BL 6	CHINITZ, NATHAN		2 MAR 1982			
102	Z17	CHIPMAN, EVA		NDD	4 JAN 1906		MAX
102	Z16	CHIPMAN, MAX		28 APR 1977	10 OCT 1900		EVA
102	AJ178	CHORCHES, IDA	COHEN	8 AUG 1981	1898		ISRAEL
102	AJ177	CHORCHES, ISRAEL		23 JAN 1967	1894	JOSEPH & HILDA (MOSCOV)	IDA
102	Y172	CHORCHES, LOUIS		25 MAR 1975	15 MAY 1905		
121	G 5	CHORNEY, ANNA		24 FEB 1973			
125	X171	CHOTINER, FANNIE		6 MAR 1981	13 JUL 1911		
125	X170	CHOTINER, MOLLIE L		6 OCT 1983	22 JUL 1904		
125	P 60	CHOTINER, SAMUEL					
119	I43	CHOZICK, ANNA		26 JUL 1982	15 SEP 1910		
372	D18	CHURCH, CAROLINE		1958	1864		
249	C 5	CHUS, ESTHER		1974	1894		JACOB
248	F51	CHUS, IDA		15 OCT 1956	1864		SOLOMON
249	C 4	CHUS, JACOB		1952	1892		ESTHER
248	I74	CHUS, MEYER		6 JUL 1930			
248	F50	CHUS, SOLOMON		26 MAR 1949	1862		IDA
102	Z19	CION, ANNE	MILLER	29 APR 1982	12 NOV 1914	HARRY & JENNIE	IRVING
102	Z18	CION, IRVING		22 JUL 1977	8 NOV 1905		ANNE
102	G30	CION, SADIE	GOLDSTEIN	18 DEC 1964	1 MAR 1876		
446	A23	CITRON, BENJAMIN		2 MAR 1922			DEBORAH
447	R24	CITRON, BESSIE P		29 JAN 1992	1897		JACOB
446	A22	CITRON, DEBORAH		25 JUL 1936			BENJAMIN
447	T31	CITRON, HELEN	BRODOW	16 DEC 1981	1918		WILLIAM
447	R23	CITRON, JACOB N		1 NOV 1955	1898		BESSIE

Cem	Row	Name	Maiden Name	DOD	DOB	Parents	Spouse
447	T32	CITRON, WILLIAM MICHAEL		7 JUN 1976	29 AUG 1896		HELEN
105	G14	CLARE, BELLA		22 AUG 1972	1885		MEYER
102	Z175	CLARE, GERTRUDE	KAPLAN	29 JUL 1986	28 NOV 1912		
105	G13	CLARE, MEYER		15 MAY 1944	1884		BELLA
371	AG 5	CLARK, ANNA	RUBIN	16 OCT 1967	1895		RAYMOND
125	D132	CLARK, BERNARD FRANCIS		20 MAR 1981	1894		ELIZABETH
125	D131	CLARK, ELIZABETH	TITTLE	7 SEP 1957	1898		BERNARD
125	I 36	CLARK, ESTHER		4 APR 1955	1876		SAMUEL
125	I 38	CLARK, IDA		1 FEB 1916	1897	SAMUEL & FRUME	
116	A 3	CLARK, JANET S		27 APR 1982	24 SEP 1947		
370	X 4	CLARK, MINNIE B		1941	1871		SAMUEL
371	AG6	CLARK, RAYMOND LOUIS		23 NOV 1965	1890		ANNA
116	V 4	CLARK, RUTH		17 MAY 1977	28 DEC 1922		
125	I 37	CLARK, SAMUEL		22 AUG 1923	1873	DAVID BER & DEVORAH	ESTHER
370	X 3	CLARK, SAMUEL S		1938	1865		MINNIE
222	AJ 4	CLAVANSKY, ROSHA JUDITH		12 OCT 1918	1856		
446	A 4	CLEMENS, EDWARD		29 MAR 1924	1860		
447	O10	CLEMENS, MINNIE	BERNWALD	18 JUL 1933	1862		
113	J21	CLEMENTS, FREIDA	WOLFRUM	23 JAN 1988	22 DEC 1913		
110	D 5	CLIMAN, ANNA		13 FEB 1960	1881		
110	D30	CLIMAN, FRED		21 APR 1982	28 SEP 1900		MARY
102	W41	CLIMAN, HERMAN		20 APR 1973	19 MAY 1899	ISRAEL & LEAH	LEOLA
222	AU17	CLIMAN, HILDA INEZ		1992	1909		
102	W46	CLIMAN, ISRAEL		7 MAR 1927	1866		LEAH
102	W45	CLIMAN, LEAH		3 NOV 1936	1864		ISRAEL
102	W42	CLIMAN, LEOLA	SOLOMON	31 MAR 1973	26 NOV 1900		HERMAN
102	K49	CLIMAN, MARSHALL E		1984	1927	MAX & MINERVA	
110	D31	CLIMAN, MARY		13 FEB 1987	15 JUL 1902		FRED
102	K48	CLIMAN, MAX MD		1948	1892		MINERVA
102	K47	CLIMAN, MINERVA E		1957	1892		MAX
104	G32	CLYMER, ABRAHAM		30 JAN 1978	1896		REVA
104	G33	CLYMER, REVA M		21 DEC 1983	1897		ABRAHAM
114	H11	COAN, LINDA C		18 JUL 1984	30 MAY 1940		
108	C34	COBB, GRACE	CUTLER	26 JUL 1962	19 SEP 1894		
104	H40	COBLE, EDYTHE	ROME	21 JAN 1988			
222	N 1	COCHRAN, FREDERICK		1 NOV 1991	19 APR 1911		FREIDA
222	N 2	COCHRAN, FRIEDA		29 JUL 1985	5 MAY 1921		FREDERICK
222	AT16	COFFEY, JERROLD		1947	1943		
101	L22	COGAN, SARAH		10 APR 1916	1900		
116	AY14	COHAN, JACK		4 DEC 1976	1910		
111	12	COHAN, MILTON		1 AUG 1989	29 JUN 1916		
104	G 2	COHEN,		1992			
391	GH 3	COHEN, (BOY)		1921	1908	ISAAC	
391	GH 4	COHEN, (BOY)				ISAAC	
125		COHEN, (CHILD)		3 OCT 1922	3 OCT 1922	MORRIS & FANNIE	
125		COHEN, (CHILD)		6 AUG 1916	JUL 1916	MORRIS & MIRIAM	
125		COHEN, (CHILD)		28 JAN 1915	28 JAN 1915	MORRIS & MIRIAM	
125	O 85	COHEN, (CHILD)		3 MAR 1918	3 MAR 1918	MORRIS & MIRIAM	
391	GJ 3	COHEN, (GIRL)					
125	J155	COHEN, ABE		19 FEB 1971	15 MAR 1883		IDA
370	W 9	COHEN, ABE		1924	1906		
104	E26	COHEN, ABRAHAM		27 JUN 1980			ESTHER
125	L157	COHEN, ABRAHAM		12 DEC 1955			REBECCA
376	C 7	COHEN, ABRAHAM		27 OCT 1977	22 MAY 1913	MOSHE	
101	G10	COHEN, ABRAHAM LEO		15 OCT 1992			
248	M62	COHEN, ADELAIDE K		24 JUN 1982	21 DEC 1914		
447	B23	COHEN, ADELE N		1985	1907		NATHAN
125	D127	COHEN, ALAN BARRY		28 FEB 1954	1946		
125	F 6	COHEN, ALEX		23 JAN 1973	28 OCT 1896		JENNIE
249	D40	COHEN, ANITA T		2 DEC 1961	1896		TOM
125	N127	COHEN, ANNA	WAX	29 JAN 1972	30 MAY 1904		MICHAEL
125	N165	COHEN, ANNA		5 NOV 1956	1887		
104	M40	COHEN, ANNA B		10 MAY 1972			JULIUS
125	I154	COHEN, ANNA R		16 SEP 1946	25 JAN 1891	JOSEPH & LEAH	
222	J15	COHEN, ANNIE		18 NOV 1964	1888		JOSEPH
370	I63	COHEN, ANNIE		1945	1879		

Cem	Row	Name	Maiden Name	DOD	DOB	Parents	Spouse
377	Q32	COHEN, ARNOLD H		13 MAR 1979	28 OCT 1920		
370	F10	COHEN, AZRIEL AARON		4 SEP 1921			
116	L19	COHEN, BARBARA S		15 JAN 1992	14 FEB 1932		TOVA
125	O 98	COHEN, BARNET		6 JAN 1921	1884		
370	W 6	COHEN, BARNET		1929	1880		YETTA
125	A134	COHEN, BENJAMIN		5 FEB 1994			BETTY
125	F143	COHEN, BENJAMIN		25 JAN 1985	1898		YETTA
329	C46	COHEN, BENJAMIN		3 FEB 1957	1890		
751	M 7	COHEN, BENJAMIN	12 JAN 1961*	31 DEC 1961*	1887		
125	R172	COHEN, BENNY JOE		5 APR 1959	1892	MORRIS	BESSIE
102	AH69	COHEN, BERTHA	BASSEVITCH	21 APR 1976	10 FEB 1898	JULIUS	LEO
114	A16	COHEN, BERTHA		4 JUL 1989	2 SEP 1918		
102	O 4	COHEN, BESSIE		17 SEP 1965	1870		SIMON
125	L 99	COHEN, BESSIE	BOROWITZ	29 OCT 1928	1889	MENDEL	WILLIAM
125	R171	COHEN, BESSIE		25 MAY 1985	1895		BENNY
447	U22	COHEN, BESSIE		10 APR 1936	1877		
125	A133	COHEN, BETTY G			1911		BENJAMIN
446	B78	COHEN, BYRON		30 AUG 1882	1860	LOUISA (DEBARRE)	
119	B 7	COHEN, CELIA	SHREDOFF	1980	1898		
330	A20	COHEN, CELIA	DINNERSTEIN	2 DEC 1960	8 APR 1917		
371	AL14	COHEN, CELIA		8 JAN 1967	10 JAN 1891		ISAAC
376	B 2	COHEN, CELIA		6 OCT 1956			MORRIS
222	AF11	COHEN, CHAIM		30 MAY 1929	1858		
374	B 9	COHEN, CHARLES		6 SEP 1964			IDA
751	A33	COHEN, CHASA SHANAH		2 FEB 1899			
125	G117	COHEN, CLARA		7 DEC 1955			
125		COHEN, DAVE BARNET		5 NOV 1921	1885	CHAIM	
222	O 1	COHEN, DAVID		3 JUN 1987	18 JUL 1914		
370	Q58	COHEN, DAVID		1953	1883		
374	F43	COHEN, DAVID		1946	1893		
391	GF 3	COHEN, DAVID		7 SEP 1912			
101	E26	COHEN, DORA		8 APR 1985	1913		
370	J16	COHEN, DORA	GORDON	25 NOV 1934			HERMAN
118	E11	COHEN, DOROTHY		1 JAN 1983			
125	F 52	COHEN, DOROTHY	CHERNIACK	18 AUG 1977	1893		SAMUEL
370	O24	COHEN, DOROTHY HANNAH	AGE 11 MOS				
123		COHEN, DOROTHY S		27 FEB 1960	24 SEP 1924		
391	GJ 1	COHEN, EDITH		2 FEB 1931			
750	A30	COHEN, EDITH	BLOCK	8 FEB 1988	12 DEC 1917		SAMUEL
391	GJ 2	COHEN, EDWARD H		1 DEC 1929			
751	M22	COHEN, EDWARD M		7 SEP 1983	25 JUL 1900		
371	K 2	COHEN, ELEANOR		1992	1920		
371	A13	COHEN, ELI		1982	1920	HYMAN & ROSE	
119	K50	COHEN, ELSIE	BRENNER	25 JUN 1985	1921		
370	A60	COHEN, ELSIE		1956	1916		SAMUEL
105	L16	COHEN, ELY		25 JAN 1955	1879		GUSSIE
329	C23	COHEN, EMANUEL		22 FEB 1967	1908	MORRIS & ROSE	
104	E27	COHEN, ESTHER		13 AUG 1956			ABRAHAM
446	B76	COHEN, ESTHER		17 FEB 1882	1814		JOSEPH
370	O23	COHEN, ESTHER BESSIE	AGE 3				
102	AB65	COHEN, ESTHER G		27 JAN 1951			
105	D15	COHEN, ESTHER G		30 AUG 1969	1885		SIMON
125	K129	COHEN, ETHEL	BELMAN	20 OCT 1935	1875	HERTZEL & ANNA	
105	C48	COHEN, EVE T		3 OCT 1963	20 SEP 1909		
370	V 3	COHEN, FAIGA		4 NOV 1894		DAVID	
125	O188	COHEN, FANNIE	FEIGENBAUM	13 APR 1966	1893		
222	AS 3	COHEN, FANNIE		1 MAY 1979	1892		LOUIS
330	E 7	COHEN, FANNIE		6 FEB 1931			HARRIS
371	M10	COHEN, FRANCES ESTHER		1981	1889		SAMUEL
105	F35	COHEN, GEORGE E		5 FEB 1992			
121	F 1	COHEN, GEORGE S		12 JAN 1990	3 SEP 1904		
105	L17	COHEN, GUSSIE		3 SEP 1965	1895		ELY
330	C24	COHEN, GUSSIE F		10 FEB 1978	1 MAY 1899		MURRAY
330	B 4	COHEN, HARRIS		9 DEC 1937	1855		FANNIE
391	F26	COHEN, HARRIS		3 NOV 1897	1832	BENJAMIN	
125	M150	COHEN, HARRY		20 MAR 1952	1885		

Cem	Row	Name	Maiden Name	DOD	DOB	Parents	Spouse
222	J 4	COHEN, HARRY		23 MAY 1976	1911	JOSEPH & ANNIE	
494	C13	COHEN, HARRY R		1972	1896		
102	O 2	COHEN, HARRY S		26 AUG 1979		SIMON & BESSIE	
248	J42	COHEN, HATTIE		29 NOV 1963	1884		ROSE
102	AC48	COHEN, HATTIE E	MARKOWITZ	6 MAR 1984	3 SEP 1892		JACOB
101	K 7	COHEN, HERMAN		27 NOV 1962	1885		JACOB
125	V173	COHEN, HERMAN		16 SEP 1976	19 JUL 1918		SOPHIE
751	N 7	COHEN, HERMAN		15 JAN 1965	19 MAY 1914		
370	C15	COHEN, HERMAN B		1 JAN 1935			DORA
127	K	COHEN, HORTENSE		27 JUN 1991	14 SEP 1918		
101	A34	COHEN, HYMAN		30 JAN 1910	1878		
371	A 6	COHEN, HYMAN		1971	1896	ELIYAHU	ROSE
121	H14	COHEN, HYMAN I		8 APR 1975	22 MAR 1893		
125	V198	COHEN, HYMAN JOSEPH		10 JAN 1978	1888		
101	D31	COHEN, HYMAN M		16 NOV 1956	1891		
102	CA 6	COHEN, HYMAN M		20 MAR 1961	13 AUG 1893		JANE
125	ZA183	COHEN, IDA		17 NOV 1991	20 JUN 1901		MORRIS
249	K11	COHEN, IDA		17 DEC 1965	16 SEP 1879		MAX
374	B10	COHEN, IDA		23 JUN 1938			CHARLES
751	M24	COHEN, IDA		2 JUL 1948	1881		
125	J156	COHEN, IDA SARAH		8 MAY 1961	15 DEC 1886		ABE
222	I 5	COHEN, ISAAC		27 DEC 1959	1878	ABRAHAM	SOPHIE
371	AL15	COHEN, ISAAC		4 MAR 1970	10 APR 1882		CELIA
125	F 38	COHEN, ISAAC MARKUS		25 NOV 1938	20 JUN 1864		ROSA
370	I62	COHEN, ISIDORE		1946	1905	ANNIE	
105	I18	COHEN, JACK		19 MAY 1941	1908		
125	U175	COHEN, JACK		1990	1911		
125	R196	COHEN, JACOB		5 JAN 1961	1897		
222	AF12	COHEN, JACOB		10 MAR 1971	16 JAN 1882	CHAIM	TILLIE
248	J41	COHEN, JACOB		5 DEC 1962	1881		HATTIE
392	E45	COHEN, JACOB		25 MAR 1949	1875	ABRAHAM	
102	AC49	COHEN, JACOB L		27 JAN 1967	26 DEC 1888	AVRUM DAVID & ETTA (STERN)	HATTIE
102	CA 5	COHEN, JANE G		28 NOV 1969	21 NOV 1894		HYMAN
118	B10	COHEN, JEAN		30 DEC 1986			
102	AB66	COHEN, JEANETTE B		28 FEB 1974			
125	F 5	COHEN, JENNIE		9 MAY 1990	28 SEP 1897		ALEX
125	T148	COHEN, JENNIE		22 JUN 1939	1886	ZUSHE & EVA	
222	J16	COHEN, JOSEPH		2 FEB 1960	1884		ANNIE
392	G31	COHEN, JOSEPH		3 SEP 1926	1868	SHALOM	
446	B77	COHEN, JOSEPH		4 NOV 1889	1811		ESTHER
751	K31	COHEN, JOSEPH		28 DEC 1928	1863		
104	M39	COHEN, JULIUS		30 SEP 1985			ANNA
125	AA143	COHEN, JULIUS		1986	1908		
376	A 1	COHEN, LAWRENCE		5 AUG 1988	17 JAN 1919		
121	H15	COHEN, LENA	KOTKIN	17 JUL 1977	20 JAN 1902		
102	AH68	COHEN, LEO A		5 DEC 1988	2 MAR 1898		BERTHA
119	K51	COHEN, LEONARD A		30 SEP 1985	1923		
121	P 2	COHEN, LIBBY		11 MAR 1991	13 FEB 1913		
117	D 8	COHEN, LILLIAN		16 DEC 1990	27 MAR 1920		
391	T58	COHEN, LILLIAN		9 OCT 1983	1902	ZENDEL	
391	J44	COHEN, LILLIAN H		3 JAN 1962	1900	MOSHE	
125	N164	COHEN, LOUIS		9 JUL 1951	1891		
222	AS 4	COHEN, LOUIS		23 AUG 1960	1889		FANNY
392	B18	COHEN, LOUIS		1942	1875		
248	K62	COHEN, LOUIS JACOB		1 DEC 1958	27 AUG 1907	PHILIP & REBECCA	
446	B79	COHEN, LOUISA	DEBARRE	22 JAN 1893	1837	JOSEPH & ESTHER	
377	M30	COHEN, LUBA T		9 MAY 1985	15 SEP 1897	TZVI	
447	E17	COHEN, MARCUS		2 MAY 1944			
119	A61	COHEN, MARY	GLANZ	7 SEP 1991	15 NOV 1910		
125	F 39	COHEN, MATHEW		8 SEP 1972	1894	ISAAC & ROSA	
248	I61	COHEN, MAX		2 MAR 1922	1881		
249	K10	COHEN, MAX		1 DEC 1951	15 MAR 1881		IDA
329	B29	COHEN, MAX		5 MAR 1946	1886		MOLLY
751	M23	COHEN, MEYER J		6 MAR 1957	1913		
125	N128	COHEN, MICHAEL M		11 MAY 1992	1 OCT 1903		ANNA
222	J14	COHEN, MIRIAM		1 JUN 1992			SAUL

Cem	Row	Name	Maiden Name	DOD	DOB	Parents	Spouse
104	L30	COHEN, MIRIAM I		26 JAN 1986	8 JAN 1923		RABBI WILI
125	E 39	COHEN, MOLLIE	WEINERMAN	3 MAR 1989	25 OCT 1901		SAMUEL
329	B30	COHEN, MOLLY		31 MAR 1967	1886		MAX
121	T 1	COHEN, MORRIS		3 JUL 1988	9 DEC 1898		
125	K 40	COHEN, MORRIS		28 JUL 1913	1862		
125	X166	COHEN, MORRIS		5 NOV 1993			
329	C24	COHEN, MORRIS		12 FEB 1965	1877		ROSE
376	B 1	COHEN, MORRIS		29 JUN 1958			CELIA
391	F16	COHEN, MORRIS		20 JUL 1931	1868	SHRUGA	
751	K29	COHEN, MORRIS		10 NOV 1927	1873		
105	F13	COHEN, MORRIS J		14 SEP 1943	1873		REBECCA
110	A22	COHEN, MORRIS J		13 JAN 1958	1876		REBECCA
125	ZA182	COHEN, MORRIS S		11 JUN 1991	22 APR 1892		IDA
372	B 8	COHEN, MOSES		20 JUN 1890			
330	C23	COHEN, MURRAY		27 JAN 1948	8 MAY 1894		GUSSIE
112	A40	COHEN, MYRON A		17 OCT 1991	26 JUN 1928		
391	A1	COHEN, NANCY		20 SEP 1942	1939		
330	AH13	COHEN, NATHAN		3 MAY 1988	27 SEP 1907		SYLVIA
370	G30	COHEN, NATHAN		10 JUL 1940	28 JUN 1910		
447	B22	COHEN, NATHAN A		7 DEC 1957	1891		ADELE
125	T166	COHEN, NETTIE	LUZINSKY	6 AUG 1940	1882	HYMAN LOUIS & MARTHA	
751	E24	COHEN, PHILIP		11 JAN 1965	21 MAY 1896		
248	K61	COHEN, PHILIP R		28 MAY 1942	1869		PHILIP
125	N184	COHEN, RAE B		14 MAY 1983	1904		WILLIAM
371	AH22	COHEN, RALPH		3 JAN 1965			
377	M38	COHEN, RAY	HIRSCHFIELD	1963	1880		
105	F14	COHEN, REBECCA		6 JAN 1971	1887		MORRIS
110	A23	COHEN, REBECCA		22 DEC 1975	1879		MORRIS
125	L156	COHEN, REBECCA		13 SEP 1967	1886		ABRAHAM
751	M 8	COHEN, REBECCA	SCHNEDER	1958	1889		
248	K60	COHEN, REBECCA R		25 MAY 1968	1881		REBECCA
102	O 1	COHEN, REUBEN		5 OCT 1970		SIMON & BESSIE	
125	F144	COHEN, RICHARD L		25 JUN 1989	1942		
102	AJ211	COHEN, RITA	REINBLATT	11 AUG 1971	13 OCT 1932		
117	C 8	COHEN, ROBERT		20 APR 1984	22 FEB 1952	SIDNEY	
125	F 37	COHEN, ROSA		18 FEB 1947	1869	ABRAHAM	ISAAC
102	O 3	COHEN, ROSE	STAMBUL	11 OCT 1968			HARRY
125	L197	COHEN, ROSE	HABER	9 JUN 1975	1895		SAMUEL
329	C22	COHEN, ROSE		4 SEP 1971	1879		MORRIS
371	A 5	COHEN, ROSE		1979	1895	JACOB JOSEPH	HYMAN
104	I12	COHEN, SADIE		3 AUG 1973	1893		
115	B21	COHEN, SALLY		4 NOV 1991			
101	A 4	COHEN, SAMUEL					
125	L196	COHEN, SAMUEL		19 FEB 1972	1887		ROSE
125	Q156	COHEN, SAMUEL		2 JUL 1952	1878		TILLIE
125	F 53	COHEN, SAMUEL A		1988	1893		DOROTHY
750	A27	COHEN, SAMUEL D		19 AUG 1980	12 SEP 1911		EDITH
371	M11	COHEN, SAMUEL LOUIS		1981	1889		FRANCES
370	A20	COHEN, SAMUEL MORDECHAI		6 JUL 1906		SADOK DAVID	ELSIE
125	E 40	COHEN, SAMUEL R		22 DEC 1988	26 APR 1898		MOLLIE
392	H22	COHEN, SARAH		6 AUG 1938	1871	TOVYA	
222	J13	COHEN, SAUL DDS		15 FEB 1990	1911	JOSEPH & ANNIE	MIRIAM
117	C10	COHEN, SIDNEY		7 JAN 1990	22 NOV 1916		
125	G 43	COHEN, SIDNEY PETER		4 MAY 1994	11 MAR 1915	ELICK & ESTHER (KAGAN)	LUCILE
102	O 5	COHEN, SIMON		9 DEC 1925	1870		BESSIE
105	D14	COHEN, SIMON		13 NOV 1949	1879		ESTHER
113	N52	COHEN, SOL R		28 MAY 1990	14 JUL 1910		SYLVIA
101	K 6	COHEN, SOPHIE		17 OCT 1980	1885		HERMAN
222	I 4	COHEN, SOPHIE		5 OCT 1961	1880		ISAAC
391	K43	COHEN, SOPHIE		21 NOV 1948	1866	JOSEPH	
121	W 7	COHEN, STEVEN JON		17 OCT 1968	17 DEC 1967		
113	N51	COHEN, SYLVIA	WORTHMAN	31 MAR 1982	28 FEB 1914		SOL
125	E 52	COHEN, SYLVIA	KRECHEVSKY	05 FEB 1971	1924		
125	T144	COHEN, SYLVIA		24 APR 1938	5 NOV 1919	MORRIS & FANNY	
330	AH14	COHEN, SYLVIA		26 NOV 1974	30 JUL 1909		NATHAN
751	M22	COHEN, SYLVIA		23 DEC 1987	9 JUL 1901		

Cem	Row	Name	Maiden Name	DOD	DOB	Parents	Spouse
125	Q155	COHEN, TILLIE		8 OCT 1955	1 FEB 1881	ABRAHAM & SARAH RIVKAH	SAMUEL
222	AF13	COHEN, TILLIE		7 NOV 1956	4 OCT 1883		JACOB
249	D39	COHEN, TOM		9 JUL 1973	1890		ANITA
370	H 8	COHEN, TOVA		5 APR 1893		MOSHE	AZRIEL
751	M23	COHEN, ULE M		28 FEB 1986	15 NOV 1899		
125	L100	COHEN, WILLIAM		31 DEC 1955	1880		BESSIE
125	N185	COHEN, WILLIAM D		20 APR 1966	1903		RAE
125	F142	COHEN, YETTA	KRAMER	29 JUL 1978	1905		BENJAMIN
370	W 7	COHEN, YETTA		1952	1884		BARNET
391	GG 7	COHEN, ZEV WOLF		26 JAN 1905		ISAAC	
105	J 6	COHN, (BABY GIRL)		20 FEB 1948			
105	F15	COHN, ABARAHAM		9 DEC 1959	1888		IDA
105	M21	COHN, ABRAHAM		2 DEC 1972	1901	BARNEY & ANNA	
374	A47	COHN, ABRAHAM		8 JAN 1959	1880		NETTY
102	AD198	COHN, ALBERT		24 MAR 1966			
370	Y 7	COHN, ALIX		1 JAN 1987	6 JAN 1911		GERTRUDE
105	M23	COHN, ANNA		25 DEC 1935	1868		BARNEY
121	O20	COHN, ANNA		3 JAN 1976	1892		
102	AC 6	COHN, ANNA O		6 SEP 1981	1991		
102	AJ96	COHN, BAILE		23 APR 1941	1877		SAMUEL
370	Y10	COHN, BARNET		26 NOV 1953	4 MAY 1931		
105	F23	COHN, BARNEY		3 AUG 1986	24 JUL 1913		BESSIE
105	M22	COHN, BARNEY		16 MAR 1945	1869		ANNA
102	H49	COHN, BEN		15 FEB 1958	1895		MOLLIE
105	F24	COHN, BESSIE		29 AUG 1988	26 APR 1915		BARNEY
119	J52	COHN, CELIA		7 NOV 1990	1901		
102	AB186	COHN, DAVID		13 AUG 1985	22 SEP 1906		LAURA
102	A 5	COHN, DORA		4 JAN 1938	1854		
119	J51	COHN, ELIAS		17 SEP 1981	21 DEC 1904		
101	K14	COHN, ESTHER		10 AUG 1916	1841		
119	J50	COHN, FANNIE		3 JUN 1982	12 FEB 1908		
105	E13	COHN, FANNY		7 MAR 1966	1894		RUBIN
119	J26	COHN, GEORGE J		8 OCT 1984	9 JUN 1909		
370	Y 8	COHN, GERTRUDE J	SIZKIN	1948	1909		ALIX
370	Y 9	COHN, HARRY		1966	1904		
119	J53	COHN, HYMAN		22 JAN 1982	1907		
376	B 7	COHN, HYMAN		1918	1885		
105	F16	COHN, IDA		31 DEC 1959	1887		ABRAHAM
125	F 92	COHN, IDA MARTHA		21 MAR 1935	1882		MORRIS
105	N34	COHN, IRENE	GOLDSMITH	28 AUG 1981	23 FEB 1922		
102	P 1	COHN, JACOB		23 FEB 1982	17 NOV 1916		
121	O19	COHN, JACOB		19 OCT 1980	1886		
108	D 5	COHN, JOSEPH (CANTOR)		2 JUN 1975	10 APR 1921		
102	AB187	COHN, LAURA K		14 JAN 1982	4 SEP 1912		DAVID
102	AI196	COHN, LOUIS		1982	1902		
374	B50	COHN, LOUIS		6 JAN 1989	12 SEP 1916		
116	M13	COHN, LOUIS R		28 JUN 1987			
125	D128	COHN, MAX		26 MAY 1978			
105	G28	COHN, MEYER		6 AUG 1978	1883		MINNIE
105	G27	COHN, MINNIE		16 APR 1967	1887		MEYER
102	H48	COHN, MOLLIE	HAYMOND	8 NOV 1955	1895		BEN
105	B21	COHN, MORRIS		1959	1915		
125	F 91	COHN, MORRIS		27 JUL 1951	1882		IDA
374	A49	COHN, MORRIS		6 JAN 1989	15 DEC 1908	ABRAHAM & NETTY	
106	C3	COHN, MYRNA		23 SEP 1977	26 SEP 1941		
374	A48	COHN, NETTY		28 AUG 1959	1885		ABRAHAM
102	A85	COHN, ROSE		16 JAN 1945	1885		SAMUEL
105	E14	COHN, RUBIN		14 JUL 1945	1887		FANNY
105	C45	COHN, RUTH		17 AUG 1990	28 DEC 1930		
105	C44	COHN, SADIE		29 JUL 1968	1917		
102	A 4	COHN, SAMUEL		18 JAN 1931	1886	DORA	
102	A86	COHN, SAMUEL		25 JUN 1964	1880		ROSE
102	AJ97	COHN, SAMUEL		6 JAN 1944	1865		BAILE
125	L122	COHN, SAMUEL D		22 DEC 1930	1851		
105	E19	COHN, SAMUEL H		26 DEC 1956	1889		SOPHIE
105	E18	COHN, SOPHIE		4 OCT 1972	1889		SAMUEL

Cem	Row	Name	Maiden Name	DOD	DOB	Parents	Spouse
112	A32	COHN, VIRGINIA S		4 APR 1992			
447	X17	COHNS, LILLIAN		2 SEP 1980			RUBIN
447	X18	COHNS, RUBIN		24 SEP 1987			LILLIAN
370	U30	COIT, ANNA ROSE		1943	1885		SAMUEL
370	H26	COIT, IDA SARAH		1910	1879		SIMON
370	V31	COIT, LOUIS		1967	1903	SAMUEL & ANNA	LYNN
370	V30	COIT, LYNN	BRONROTT	1984	1908		LOUIS
370	U29	COIT, SAMUEL		1945	1869		ANNA
123		COLANGELO, JOSEPH		8 FEB 1972	1899		FANNY
116	BL70	COLE, MANUEL		10 JAN 1990	27 NOV 1907		
116	W 6	COLE, MILTON C MD	COLEDSKY	31 MAY 1981	1904	ABRAHAM & SARA (DAVIS)	
102	AH61	COLEDESKY, IDA	LEVY	22 NOV 1987	30 NOV 1903		LOUIS
102	AH62	COLEDESKY, LOUIS E		10 OCT 1961	30 MAY 1903		IDA
119	F20	COLEMAN, NANCY E		11 FEB 1976	5 MAR 1897		
101	G32	COLER, SIMON ELI		19 OCT 1990	4 JAN 1922		
330	H 4	COLISHMAN, HARRY		10 NOV 1915	1910		
123		COLMAN, MARTIN		19 AUG 1950	1918		
391	ZC51	COMASSAR, ARLINE	SCHOENBERG	NDD	1922		
392	F44	COMBS, BARBARA ELLEN	LUPKAY	22 JAN 1983	19 SEP 1952	GIDALYAH	
125	N 90	COMINICK, LOUIS		20 JUL 1924	1876		
391	ZB80	COMMASSAR, ARTHUR ABRAHAM		3 AUG 1983	1901	TZVI HIRCH	
222	AF21	COMPAINE, BENJAMIN M		26 JUL 1943	1890		LILLIAN
222	AF20	COMPAINE, LILLIAN L		22 FEB 1968	1895		BENJAMIN
222	AE22	COMPAINE, M WILLIAM		27 MAY 1919	26 JUN 1907	SAMUEL & OLGA	
222	AF22	COMPAINE, MARQUE PAUL		15 MAR 1917	20 JUN 1914	BENJAMIN & LILLIAN	
222	AE21	COMPAINE, OLGA H		24 MAY 1935	8 FEB 1874		SAMUEL
222	AE20	COMPAINE, S SAMUEL	OF KHARKOV RUSS	24 JAN 1958	28 AUG 1874	SOPHIE	OLGA
222	AE23	COMPAINE, SOPHIE		7 SEP 1923	1848		
125	V186	CONN, MIRIAM	LIVINGSTON	9 FEB 1977	18 APR 1896		NATHAN
125	V187	CONN, NATHAN		2 APR 1979	18 APR 1890		MIRIAM
113	A 5	CONOLLY, HELEN		24 MAY 1985	4 AUG 1913		
370	B27	CONTROVITCH, HYMAN B		9 MAY 1925	1862		
370	J 3	CONTROVITCH, MOLLIE		1930	1850		
119	E19	COOK, EDWARD		25 FEB 1980	21 JAN 1890		
119	E20	COOK, REBECCA		24 FEB 1975	15 JUN 1888		
127	R	COOLBAUGH, SARAH ALANA		27 APR 1992			
121	P 9	COOPER, ANN		29 AUG 1967	29 AUG 1911		
102	Q25	COOPER, BENJAMIN		1 MAY 1973	1911		
330	AD12	COOPER, BERNARD		13 JAN 1970	13 DEC 1913	WILLIAM & SADIE	
370	T32	COOPER, EDITH		1988	1918		HYMAN
125	M152	COOPER, ESTHER		7 MAY 1952	1888		
391	O59	COOPER, ESTHER	KOSS	15 JUN 1958	1931	SHRUGA FIVEL	
370	T29	COOPER, FANNIE		1947	1889		JOSEPH
370	T30	COOPER, H JOSEPH		1948	1882		FANNIE
370	O61	COOPER, HANNAH RUTH		1981	1904		JULIUS
113	C22	COOPER, HILLARY BETH		29 SEP 1988	2 OCT 1957		
370	T31	COOPER, HYMAN A		1966	1913		EDITH
370	O58	COOPER, JACOB		1951	1882		MARY
371	AA 5	COOPER, JACOB		4 JAN 1974	2 NOV 1899		
370	O60	COOPER, JULIUS		1982	1907		HANNAH
113	N54	COOPER, LORA E		11 SEP 1979	12 JUL 1909		
371	AB 2	COOPER, LOUIS		31 JAN 1983	1916		
370	O59	COOPER, MARY		1956	1881		JACOB
447	F23	COOPER, MIRIAM		2 DEC 1961	1873		
329	B 9	COOPER, MORRIS		4 MAR 1946	1866		
391	T53	COOPER, RACHEL CEILIA		22 MAR 1963	1883	BZALEL ISAAC	
391	Y56	COOPER, RUBEN		2 NOV 1958	1880	YECHIEL	
330	A 1	COOPER, SADIE	NORWITZ	22 FEB 1958	1896		WILLIAM
330	A 2	COOPER, WILLIAM		29 MAR 1963	1895		SADIE
370	G34	COOPERMAN, CELIA		2 SEP 1977			ISAAC
370	G35	COOPERMAN, ISAAC		30 DEC 1953			CELIA
105	O53	COOPERMAN, LOUIS		18 JUN 1971	1894		SARAH
105	O52	COOPERMAN, SARAH	COHN	26 MAY 1986	1895		LOUIS
370	G33	COOPERMAN, SARAH BEATRICE		JUL 1934	1917	ISAAC & CELIA	
116	BE 8	COOPERSMITH, EDNA		21 OCT 1992			
433	D14	COOPERSTOCK, ANNA		24 APR 1982	18 MAY 1895		

Cem	Row	Name	Maiden Name	DOD	DOB	Parents	Spouse
391	F 8	COPELAND, ABRAHAM DAVID		20 DEC 1935	1864	JACOB	
391	G23	COPELAND, ANNIE		15 MAY 1914	7 OCT 1898	ABRAHAM DAVID	
391	U65	COPELAND, JACOB S		19 DEC 1968	1909	ABRAHAM DAVID	
377	Q12	COPELAND, JENNIE		5 JAN 1990	18 JAN 1908		
377	O43	COPELAND, LOUIS		3 FEB 1947	6 NOV 1899		
391	R34	COPELAND, ROSA		3 JUL 1919	1865	ISAAC	
125	K140	COPELAND, SARAH		25 JAN 1932	26 FEB 1882		SIMON
125	K139	COPELAND, SIMON		1 AUG 1952	1869		SARAH
391	G17	COPELAND, VERA	GRANN	1931	1902		
222	AT 1	COR, ANNIE		8 SEP 1983	1893		JACOB
222	AT 2	COR, JACOB		20 JUN 1966	1886		ANNIE
222	AF18	COR, MINNIE		6 DEC 1985			SAMUEL
222	AF19	COR, SAMUEL		9 OCT 1977			MINNIE
125	3C38	CORBET, LILLIAN		26 JAN 1919	1893	MOSHE MORDECHAI	
119	J39	CORDOVA, JACK		6 FEB 1982	22 SEP 1924		
101	M26	CORENTSMITH, CILIE		27 APR 1913	1893		
114	G29	CORMIER, FREDA S		22 MAR 1990	12 OCT 1911		GEORGE
114	G28	CORMIER, GEORGE J		19 JUN 1986	2 AUG 1904		FREDA
750	B22	CORN, DORA		30 AUG 1963	1897		JOSEPH
750	B23	CORN, JOSEPH		19 SEP 1968	1893		DORA
101	L31	CORNTZVEET, ISAAC		31 AUG 1934	1840		
222	AC 8	CORR, IDA M		17 AUG 1953	1904	ISRAEL & RUTH	
222	AC 6	CORR, ISRAEL		24 NOV 1940	1863		RUTH
222	AD 4	CORR, LILLIAN S		20 OCT 1992			
222	AC 7	CORR, RUTH		14 OCT 1937	1863		ISRAEL
370	D 6	CRAMER, ABRAHAM		28 OCT 1935	1871		
371	O24	CRAMER, ANNA C		4 MAR 1983	19 FEB 1900		SAMPSON
371	AN 9	CRAMER, BETTY		27 JUN 1990	23 MAY 1908		ELLSWORTH
751	I26	CRAMER, DAVID		22 JUN 1981	21 JUL 1902		
371	AO 8	CRAMER, DIANA R					
371	AN10	CRAMER, ELLSWORTH		29 APR 1984	19 DEC 1906		BETTY
370	R 8	CRAMER, ESTHER		1942	1878		ISAAC
371	AP25	CRAMER, GERTRUDE		5 MAY 1968	14 DEC 1904		LOUIS
370	R 7	CRAMER, ISAAC		1934	1875		ESTHER
371	AP26	CRAMER, LOUIS M		26 NOV 1964	24 SEP 1901		GERTRUDE
222	F10	CRAMER, PAUL M		9 FEB 1956	1903		
371	U23	CRAMER, SAMPSON		29 JAN 1988	28 NOV 1897	TILLIE	ANNA
101	D 7	CRAMER, SAMUEL		18 APR 1969	1902		SOPHIE
101	D 8	CRAMER, SOPHIE		29 JUN 1968	1901		SAMUEL
371	O25	CRAMER, TILLIE		1955	1869		
370	F 6	CRAMER, WILLIAM		1923	1894	ISAAC & ESTHER	
391	R48	CRANE, LOUIS		28 MAR 1954	1879	DOV BER	
391	R47	CRANE, MINNIE	BAKER	1 MAY 1964	1883	KALMON	
101	J17	CREIFER, ELKA S		19 FEB 1922	1863		
116	O16	CREMER, HELENE	WINICK	6 JUN 1980	2 APR 1934		
125		CROLL, (CHILD)		6 AUG 1916	1916		
125	U142	CROLL, DAVID NATHAN		9 AUG 1985	23 OCT 1910		MINNIE
125	F 31	CROLL, ESTHER		9 OCT 1958	1884	DAVID	LOUIS
125		CROLL, JACOB		30 MAY 1918	1852		SLAVA
125	F 33	CROLL, JACOB L		24 NOV 1966	1921	LOUIS & ESTHER	
125	X180	CROLL, JOY LESLIE		9 MAY 1982	11 AUG 1961	JACOB LEV	
125		CROLL, LILLIAN R		19 JUN 1985	16 AUG 1922		
125	F 32	CROLL, LOUIS JOSEPH		18 FEB 1961	1881		ESTHER
125	O 75	CROLL, MARC TOBY		1 FEB 1955	1953		
125	U143	CROLL, MINNIE	ROTHSTEIN	5 OCT 1992	12 DEC 1909	MORRIS & NETTIE (GREENSTEIN)	DAVID
125	E 34	CROLL, ROSE		14 JUN 1983			
125	L 25	CROLL, SLAVA		MAR 1915			JACOB
377	Q15	CRON, BENJAMIN FREDERICK		9 AUG 1971	24 MAR 1924		
125	O195	CROWN, G EDWIN		10 JUN 1965	30 OCT 1907		
370	O66	CRUMB, ELI		1958	1901		
370	Q15	CRUMB, HARRY		14 OCT 1921	1890	ISAAC & REBECCA	MARY
370	Q17	CRUMB, ISAAC		3 APR 1924	1861		REBECCA
370	O51	CRUMB, JACOB		20 MAY 1954	1876	ISSAC & REBECCA	JENNIE
370	O50	CRUMB, JENNIE		6 AUG 1953	1878		JACOB
370	Q16	CRUMB, MARY BERTHA		24 MAY 1920	1892		HARRY
370	J73	CRUMB, MOLLIE		14 FEB 1879			

Cem	Row	Name	Maiden Name	DOD	DOB	Parents	Spouse
370	Q18	CRUMB, REBECCA		8 JAN 1938	1861		
370	O49	CRUMB, SELMA		17 OCT 1917			ISAAC
391	G18	CRUSKIN, SOPHIE R		26 DEC 1929	1910	CHAIM TZVI	
125	L 49	CUNARD, DANIEL		22 AUG 1909	21 MAY 1896		
125	L 48	CUNARD, JOSEPH		3 SEP 1922	1908	MYER & REBECCA	
371	D 2	CURHAN, JAMES		23 APR 1992	1 NOV 1909		
447	C 7	CURKIN, ABRAHAM		24 FEB 1939	1893	SARAH	BERTHA
447	AB34	CURKIN, ARTHUR		27 MAY 1990	3 OCT 1905		
447	C 6	CURKIN, BERTHA		11 SEP 1990	1895		ABRAHAM
447	T19	CURKIN, CELIA		27 JAN 1960	18 OCT 1899		HERMAN
447	F21	CURKIN, DAVID S		5 JUL 1978	1890		FREDA
446	A31	CURKIN, EVA		11 MAR 1918	1915		
447	F22	CURKIN, FREDA R	3 JAN 1942*	22 DEC 1942*	1895		DAVID
447	T18	CURKIN, HERMAN		4 SEP 1965	2 FEB 1895		CELIA
446	C17	CURKIN, IDA		2 DEC 1923	1898		
446	B26	CURKIN, PAULINE		1918	1897		
447	C 5	CURKIN, PHILIP		9 OCT 1974	5 JUL 1895	SARAH	
447	C 8	CURKIN, SARAH B		15 JUN 1938	1866		
370	P55	CURLAND, ABRAHAM		3 AUG 1954	21 AUG 1890		AUGUSTA
374	B16	CURLAND, BELLA		29 APR 1940			SAMUEL
374	B17	CURLAND, SAMUEL		23 MAR 1934			BELLA
370	S18	CURLINJICK, SADIE		1948	1898	SIMON & SARAH	
370	S15	CURLINJICK, SARAH		1941	1877		SIMON
370	S16	CURLINJICK, SIMON		1958	1879		SARAH
391	GL 4	CURRAN, SAMUEL		27 MAR 1943	28 JAN 1885	ELIEZER	SARAH
391	GK 6	CURRAN, SARAH		15 MAR 1958	5 OCT 1881	ZELIG	SAMUEL
377	K15	CURTIS, ELIZABETH M		1961	1896		
377	X19	CUSHNER, ABRAHAM		13 MAR 1963	2 FEB 1880	CHAIM	HELEN
377	X18	CUSHNER, HELEN C		8 MAY 1969	27 APR 1888	JOSEPH	ABRHAM
108	C 5	CUTLER, ABRAHAM		14 NOV 1942	1885		LOTTIE
108	C16	CUTLER, ANNE		26 APR 1989	19 AUG 1910		FRANK
108	C 7	CUTLER, BENJAMIN		29 MAR 1948	1891		REBECCA
330	D 5	CUTLER, DORA		20 APR 1945	10 JAN 1875		PINCHAS
330	G30	CUTLER, ELIZABETH	LEVIN	6 JUL 1918	1886		
108	C15	CUTLER, FRANK		20 AUG 1984	27 SEP 1910		ANNE
125	O 79	CUTLER, IDA		8 DEC 1918	1891	MORRIS & FREIDA	
108	C 6	CUTLER, LOTTIE K		27 NOV 1965	1887		ABRAHAM
108	C 9	CUTLER, MORRIS J		10 OCT 1985	9 DEC 1906		
330	D 4	CUTLER, PINCHAS		16 APR 1940	10 SEP 1871		DORA
108	C 8	CUTLER, REBECCA		27 MAR 1978	1887		BENJAMIN
125	M 82	CUTLER, ROCHE LEIKE		28 FEB 1919	1889		
108	C13	CUTLER, SAMUEL		12 MAR 1971	18 APR 1909	PINCUS & DORA (DAVIDSON)	TILLIE
108	C14	CUTLER, TILLIE		15 JUN 1975	1 SEP 1912		SAMUEL
447	P24	CYCAN, ALEX S		11 MAY 1950	1881		ROSE
447	P25	CYCAN, ROSE LEAH		19 MAR 1962	1883		ALEX
391	N38	DACTOR, CECELIA		10 MAY 1916	1890	JACOB	
116	BL76	DAMPSKY, MORRIS		30 SEP 1964	1897		
119	E15	DANEN, CHARLES		27 MAR 1975	1900		
119	E16	DANEN, FANNIE		22 JAN 1984	1903		
101	A22	DANIEL, SIMON		20 OCT 1916	1841		
447	W27	DANIELS, LAUREN JILL		1947	1946		
330	AH19	DANIELS, MARY J		1991	1910		
751	H26	DANKIN, CELIA		24 FEB 1970	12 MAY 1886		MORRIS
751	H27	DANKIN, MORRIS		29 AUG 1967	12 MAY 1881		CELIA
102	AH135	DANSEYAR, MORTON, L		1991	1923		
104	O35	DARACK, BETTY		12 SEP 1988	1912		CHARLES
104	O34	DARACK, CHARLES J		13 AUG 1989	1909		BETTY
104	J21	DARACK, NATHAN I		4 SEP 1966	1916		
447	Q38	DARDECK, CELIA		2 JAN 1965	1878		BARUCH
447	O21	DARDECK, JOSEPH		2 AMR 1946	1870		
447	O24	DARDECK, LOUIS		17 MAY 1977	1899	JOSEPH	ROSE
447	O25	DARDECK, ROSE		2 FEB 1983	1899		LOUIS
392	F25	DAREN, BARNY		29 JUL 1925	1916		
377	Y28	DAREN, GLADYS E		1 DEC 1988	26 SEP 1918	CHAIM	THEODORE
377	S 3	DAREN, JULIUS		1974	1888		MAMIE
377	S 4	DAREN, MAMIE		1968	1895		JULIUS

Cem	Row	Name	Maiden Name	DOD	DOB	Parents	Spouse
377	Y29	DAREN, THEODORE S		26 AUG 1983	29 OCT 1913	YEHUDA	
101	D32	DASHEFSKY, ESTHER		4 JUL 1948	1879		GLADYS
101	D33	DASHEFSKY, JACOB		3 APR 1950	1883		JACOB
331		DAVIDSOHN, THERESA		23 JUN 1894	15 SEP 1880		ESTHER
392	B48	DAVIDSON, ABRAHAM		14 FEB 1972	22 JUN 1898		
751	C 8	DAVIDSON, ALFRED		4 OCT 1975	22 JAN 1925		
377	V48	DAVIDSON, ALICE C		19 OCT 1981	27 FEB 1914	CHAIM ZELIG	
105	N36	DAVIDSON, ANNA		11 JUN 1986	15 APR 1892		
392	E37	DAVIDSON, DAVID		9 MAR 1938	1888	PHILIP	
116	A 9	DAVIDSON, EDWARD ROBERT		6 JUN 1987	24 FEB 1948		
125	I102	DAVIDSON, HARRY		31 OCT 1931	1880		
751	C 5	DAVIDSON, HARRY		5 MAY 1973	15 MAY 1882		SYLVIA
329	H25	DAVIDSON, IDA	GITLIN	21 DEC 1991	14 JAN 1892		ISADORE
101	I35	DAVIDSON, IRENE		23 JUN 1979	12 JUN 1914		
329	H26	DAVIDSON, ISADORE M		13 JAN 1965	17 NOV 1878		IDA
102	C 1	DAVIDSON, LILLIAN	COLLIER	7 DEC 1966	2 JUN 1908		
125	M149	DAVIDSON, LILLIAN		4 APR 1963	1898		MORRIS
751	B 4	DAVIDSON, M MORTON		1978	1920		
125	M148	DAVIDSON, MORRIS		1 MAR 1952	1874		LILLIAN
119	B81	DAVIDSON, MORRIS ISADORE		28 MAR 1990	20 AUG 1906		
392	E36	DAVIDSON, PHILIP ISAAC		6 OCT 1938	1868	ABRAHAM	
329	G27	DAVIDSON, ROSE B		21 NOV 1950	19 FEB 1889		WILLIAM
119	B80	DAVIDSON, SADIE	GEETER	25 SEP 1975	24 OCT 1907		
118	E1	DAVIDSON, SAUL J		3 JUN 1990			
372	E25	DAVIDSON, SELMA	PLAUT	1957	1878		
372	E24	DAVIDSON, SIDNEY		29 DEC 1980	20 MAR 1902		
125	I 61	DAVIDSON, SOLOMON		29 JUN 1901	16 AUG 1849	DAVID	
751	C 6	DAVIDSON, SYLVIA	BUDNICK	1 FEB 1960			HARRY
330	G66	DAVIDSON, TOBA		1 NOV 1943	1867		
329	G26	DAVIDSON, WILLIAM		19 JUL 1959	5 MAR 1883		ROSE
104	J13	DAVIS, ABRAHAM		4 APR 1962	1891		ROSE
433	C15	DAVIS, ANNA		17 JUL 1971	1890	JACOB KAFEL	DAVID
101	A 2	DAVIS, BAILA		1938	1853		BERNARD
101	A 3	DAVIS, BERNARD		24 DEC 1908	1840		BAILA
116	BL80	DAVIS, BERNARD JACOB		18 OCT 1962	25 OCT 1906		MOLLIE
116	BL81	DAVIS, BERTHA E		10 DEC 1987	7 MAY 1904		
102	AH73	DAVIS, BESS	ROMANSKY	3 JUL 1952	1902	BENJAMIN & HENRIETTA	
248	A51	DAVIS, CLARA		3 FEB 1965	1882		MAURICE
433	C14	DAVIS, DAVID		2 JUL 1969	11 FEB 1892	ZUSHA	ANNA
249	P 7	DAVIS, DORIS		1985	1926		
248	J 6	DAVIS, DOROTHY		16 MAR 1916	13 MAR 1916		
371	M 2	DAVIS, ESTHER		1976	1908		SIMEON
248	A60	DAVIS, HERMAN		11 JUL 1960	26 MAY 1907		
371	N 1	DAVIS, JACOB		1960	1911	LENA	
116	BL84	DAVIS, JOSEPH B		9 NOV 1963	10 MAR 1899		SOPHIE
125	A145	DAVIS, JOSEPH J		1 MAR 1980	1 APR 1894		
371	N 2	DAVIS, LENA		1960	1880		
116	BL77	DAVIS, LOUIS E		7 MAY 1981	15 AUG 1897		SID
248	A52	DAVIS, MAURICE		1951	1880		CLARA
101	B 1	DAVIS, MAX		24 MAR 1940	1882	BERNARD & BAILA	
116	BL79	DAVIS, MOLLIE	SALTIESKY	15 FEB 1975	27 OCT 1911		BERNARD
119	D 1	DAVIS, PAULINE D		31 DEC 1991	13 MAY 1929		
370	D15	DAVIS, PETER JOSEPH		2 FEB 1937	1867		
104	J12	DAVIS, ROSE	FISHMAN	7 DEC 1965	1893		ABRAHAM
116	BL78	DAVIS, SID	GREENBURG	20 JUN 1959	2 JUL 1897		LOUIS
371	M 1	DAVIS, SIMEON		1990	1903		ESTHER
116	BL83	DAVIS, SOPHIE	MESHKEN	10 JUL 1963	27 JUN 1906		JOSEPH
370	A41	DAVIS, WILLIAM		APR 1935			
102	AE83	DAVISON, BERNICE	SOFFER	27 SEP 1977	1918		
751	N17	DAVISON, ELLEN MARY		22 DEC 1987	12 MAR 1946		
125	K 97	DAVISON, IDA M		1 OCT 1919	1846		
102	AE86	DAVISON, JOSEPH		17 OCT 1962	1887	CHAIM MORDECAI & IDA	SARAH
102	AE85	DAVISON, SARA	BREWER	30 MAY 1961	1892		JOSEPH
371	AO22	DAVISSON, ELIZABETH ANN		1959	1955	ROBERT & IRENE	
391	ZG53	DE SIDAUY, ROSA	CORKIDI	28 FEB 1991	16 OCT 1907	DAVID	
377	T30	DEAN, ANNE		1971	1922	JOSEPH	HARRY

Cem	Row	Name	Maiden Name	DOD	DOB	Parents	Spouse
392	G20	DEAN, BENJAMIN		7 JAN 1938	1875	ISRAEL	
101	E14	DEAN, CEIL	DORFMAN				
377	T29	DEAN, HARRY		1989	1915	YODEL	ANNE
392	F 3	DEAN, JOSEPH		9 FEB 1969	1889	ISRAEL	RACHEL
377	ZA39	DEAN, LOUIS		10 JAN 1992	4 APR 1905	BEN ZION	
392	H47	DEAN, LOUIS		20 JUL 1983	6 APR 1904	DOV BEAR	
392	J 5	DEAN, MORRIS		1922	1912	BEN ZION	
392	F 4	DEAN, RACHEL		21 NOV 1963	1886	MEYER	JOSEPH
392	H14	DEAN, ROSE		31 JUL 1956	1878	SAMUEL	
119	E35	DEBOSAR, ELLIOTT		21 APR 1981	19 APR 1925		
433	I 4	DECK, SAMUEL		1933	1931	AARON	
104	I33	DEHAAS, DAVID		31 MAR 1982	9 OCT 1919		
104	G37	DEHAAS, LIESEL		19 OCT 1991			
330	AI15	DEITCH, ALEX		28 JUL 1982	13 APR 1916		GLADYS
330	AI16	DEITCH, GLADYS		NDD	1923		ALEX
330	AI 6	DEITCH, HARRY		1 SEP 1978	29 AUG 1911		
102	AF20	DEITCH, LILLIAN	WYNN	30 JAN 1985	1924	HARRY & CELIA	
391	C 3	DELATIZKY, ANNA		12 APR 1981	1890	YEHUDA	HYMAN
391	S53	DELATIZKY, BENJAMIN		30 APR 1955	1904	CHAIM	
391	C23	DELATIZKY, HYMAN		18 AUG 1938	1872	MORDECHAI	ANNA
371	A11	DELATIZKY, LEAH		11 JAN 1974	12 JAN 1904		
374	C12	DELINSKY, HARRIS		31 MAR 1932	1865		IDA
374	C11	DELINSKY, IDA		11 DEC 1948	1874		HARRIS
330	D 1	DEMBER, BARNET		1 NOV 1954	1864		CHIVA
123		DEMBER, BARNEY		10 AUG 1948	1894		
330	G 2	DEMBER, CHIVA		12 APR 1941	1860		BARNET
329	A 2	DEMBER, DORA		6 SEP 1963	26 APR 1895		JOSEPH
329	A 1	DEMBER, JOSEPH		16 OCT 1967	15 JUL 1895		DORA
370	O38	DEMBO, BELLA	HERMAN	8 DEC 1947	12 FEB 1890	JOSEPH & HELENA (SHEER)	HARRY
370	O37	DEMBO, HARRY		2 MAY 1950	1882	SHALOM SACHNA	BELLA
391	G45	DEMBROFF, MINNIE		28 APR 1950	1904	REUBEN	
391	ZG66	DEMBROFF, REUBEN		20 DEC 1985	25 JUN 1932		
371	K44	DEMBROW, AUGUSTA		7 DEC 1962	5 MAY 1914		JOSEPH
371	K41	DEMBROW, CYRIL		20 NOV 1971	2 MAY 1919		ROSE
371	K45	DEMBROW, ELEANOR R		7 SEP 1953	24 DEC 1900		
370	J12	DEMBROW, IDA RACHEL		23 SEP 1933			
371	K43	DEMBROW, JOSEPH A		30 MAY 1961			AUGUSTA
371	K42	DEMBROW, ROSE		24 JUN 1962			CYRIL
391	J32	DEMCHICK, BELLA		30 AUG 1932	25 NOV 1908	MICHAEL	
104	M32	DENMARK, FRIEDA		6 MAY 1978	7 FEB 1898		JACK
104	M31	DENMARK, JACK		14 APR 1968	15 FEB 1895		FREIDA
104	I18	DERER, KARL		13 JUN 1974	15 FEB 1897		
101	L 5	DERMER, BERL		29 MAY 1967	1883		
377	X 6	DETZ, ELLEN		10 OCT 1957	10 JAN 1945	ARYEH LEV	
377	Y 5	DETZ, EVELYN M		7 AUG 1989	23 APR 1921	MOSHE	
330	D22	DEUSCH, EZRA		10 JAN 1956	1887		REBECCA
330	D23	DEUSCH, REBECCA G		29 OCT 1971	1888		EZRA
116	BJ30	DEUTSCH, ALEXANDER S		28 OCT 1969	27 JUL 1893		MINNIE
374	E40	DEUTSCH, ESTHER R		11 FEB 1945	1885		LOUIS
370	Q27	DEUTSCH, JOSEPH		1936	1907	LOUIS & REBECCA	
433	B38	DEUTSCH, JOSEPHINE		18 JUL 1905	5 MAY 1887		
370	Q28	DEUTSCH, LOUIS		23 JUL 1927	1881		REBECCA
374	E39	DEUTSCH, LOUIS		30 JUN 1975	1875		ESTHER
116	BJ29	DEUTSCH, MINNIE T		28 NOV 1983	4 JUN 1894		ALEXANDER
370	Q29	DEUTSCH, REBECCA		29 SEP 1957	1884		LOUIS
370	Q30	DEUTSCH, REUBEN		13 OCT 1983	1912	LOUIS & REBECCA	
391	GE 3	DIAMOND, (CHILD)					
433	Q 1	DIAMOND, AARON		23 OCT 1980	12 JUN 1911	HEZIKIAH & FANNIE	SYLVIA
751	D 2	DIAMOND, ANNIE	SACHS	12 SEP 1953	1889		JOHN
102	H36	DIAMOND, DORA		1949	1871		ISRAEL
433	D18	DIAMOND, FANNIE		8 JUL 1968	5 DEC 1893	LABEL	HEZIKAH
392	J10	DIAMOND, FANNIE		27 AUG 1945	1872	ISAAC	
751	D14	DIAMOND, IRVING I		1974	1922	JOHN & ANNIE	
371	AE15	DIAMOND, ISADORE		23 NOV 1964	1886		SARAH
102	H35	DIAMOND, ISRAEL		1941	1871		DORA
751	D 1	DIAMOND, JOHN		5 DEC 1980	1894		ANNIE

Cem	Row	Name	Maiden Name	DOD	DOB	Parents	Spouse
102	D35	DIAMOND, MAURICE LIONEL		12 MAY 1973	17 FEB 1892		RUTH
370	G38	DIAMOND, MORRIS		15 FEB 1913			
102	D36	DIAMOND, RUTH	SHULINSKI	20 MAY 1949	27 AUG 1894		MAURICE
112	D12	DIAMOND, RUTH		2 JUL 1978	7 JAN 1912		
113	N71	DIAMOND, SAMUEL CHARLES		21 JUN 1967	21 AUG 1929		
371	AE16	DIAMOND, SARAH		17 APR 1963	1888		ISADORE
433	Q 2	DIAMOND, SYLVIA		1 MAR 1986	2 JUL 1914	DAVID	AARON
750	I26	DIBNER, SADIE		6 AUG 1977	10 MAR 1902		SAMUEL
750	I25	DIBNER, SAMUEL		25 NOV 1968			SADIE
101	C20	DICK, MAX		28 MAY 1958	16 DEC 1916		
114	E12	DICKMAN, ROBERT MARVIN		27 MAR 1990	17 SEP 1932		
119	J 1	DIMESKY, ELSIE A		23 JAN 1980	27 DEC 1919		
248	J19	DINER, ABE		30 JUL 1926			
125	R173	DINER, DAVID F		4 DEC 1960	1913		
125	L145	DINER, ELIZABETH LEE		23 JUN 1982			JUDD
125	S175	DINER, HENRIETTA		29 MAY 1957	1907		
125	L146	DINER, J JUDD		20 OCT 1954	1910		ELIZABETH
125	Q148	DINER, ROSE		2 OCT 1944	1888	YAKOV MOSHE & CHANA ALTA	
125	K 70	DINER, SAMUEL		25 SEP 1935	1880	JULIUS & MINAH	
115	A 2	DINERMAN, JANICE	KRUG	8 JAN 1991	11 NOV 1947		
330	A21	DINNERSTEIN, ABRAHAM J		20 SEP 1963	6 APR 1880		MARY
330	AC 8	DINNERSTEIN, BENJAMIN		1 MAR 1968	31 JAN 1912	ABRAHAM & MARY	
330	A22	DINNERSTEIN, MARY		4 MAY 1965	1 JUL 1880		ABRAHAM
371	L 4	DIRECTOR, IDA		1981	1905		JACK
371	L 3	DIRECTOR, JACK		1981	1896		IDA
104	A15	DISTEL, JOSEPH		13 JAN 1984	1 OCT 1911		
433	J19	DIVINS, ESTHER BARBARA		1944	1910		
374	A11	DIVITKIND, CHAIM		25 FEB 1914		JOSEPH	
371	A45	DIZENGOFF, CELIA		15 NOV 1986	27 MAY 1913		
102	L46	DOBIN, MYER		1957	1902		
222	AC 5	DOBKIN, AARON		6 MAY 1961	1868		IDA
125	I142	DOBKIN, CLARA LEAH		24 SEP 1944	1890	SHLOMO & FAGEL	LEON
222	C 3	DOBKIN, ESTHER		21 APR 1972	1884		MAX
222	AA14	DOBKIN, HARRY		23 JAN 1943	1889	JACOB & REBECCA	
222	C 5	DOBKIN, HYMAN		4 JUN 1943	1875		KATIE
222	AC 4	DOBKIN, IDA L		28 NOV 1943	1875		AARON
222	AA11	DOBKIN, JACOB		30 MAR 1924	1845		REBECCA
102	D 1	DOBKIN, JULIA		30 APR 1981	1900		SAMUEL
222	C 6	DOBKIN, KATIE		14 NOV 1941	1877		HYMAN
125	I143	DOBKIN, LEON		26 FEB 1950	1892		CHAYA
222	A10	DOBKIN, LEON		8 FEB 1987	5 JUL 1898		REBECCA
222	C 4	DOBKIN, MAX		16 MAR 1949	1881		ESTHER
222	A 9	DOBKIN, REBECCA		26 FEB 1979	14 MAY 1905		LEON
222	AA12	DOBKIN, REBECCA		26 FEB 1926	1849		JACOB
102	D 2	DOBKIN, SAMUEL D		25 DEC 1985	30 JUN 1912		JULIA
222	AA10	DOBKIN, SAMUEL S		11 JUL 1964	1891	JACOB & REBECCA	
493	B 1	DOBULER, PAUL ANDREW		1 SEP 1992	30 AUG 1989	SHLOMO	
125	R142	DOCHTERMAN, SAMUEL		17 MAY 1942	1877	MOSHE & MIRIAM	
751	G40	DODUCK, LENA		8 MAY 1937	1875		SAMUEL
751	F39	DODUCK, SAMUEL		17 MAR 1926	1874		LENA
102	AI180	DOLGORUCK, SADIE		11 JUL 1970	1892		SAMUEL
102	AI179	DOLGORUCK, SAMUEL		8 APR 1975	1894		SADIE
751	N30	DOLILNSKY, BENJAMIN L		1979	1900		
751	I19	DOLINSKY, BENJAMIN		1945	1865		FREIDA
248	I69	DOLINSKY, DAVID		6 JUL 1917	1852		
751	H15	DOLINSKY, DORA	FISCHER	1983	1898		MORRIS
751	I20	DOLINSKY, FREIDA S		1939	1875		BENJAMIN
751	H16	DOLINSKY, MORRIS H		25 SEP 1975	1896		DORA
102	M53	DONNER, JUDITH D		17 MAY 1988	30 MAR 1903		SAMUEL
102	M54	DONNER, SAMUEL MD		13 SEP 1962	30 APR 1896		JUDITH
119	E13	DORFMAN, BENJAMIN		22 APR 1975	14 APR 1894		
125	D104	DORFMAN, CLARA	SCHECTMAN	19 JUN 1977	28 MAY 1894		DAVID
125	D103	DORFMAN, DAVID		26 MAR 1985	21 JUL 1887		CLARA
125	C106	DORFMAN, GEORGE		1992	1919		
125	M172	DORFMAN, HELEN	HORN	1 FEB 1968	1915		MAXWELL
119	E14	DORFMAN, IDA		4 JAN 1986	7 SEP 1898		

Cem	Row	Name	Maiden Name	DOD	DOB	Parents	Spouse
249	I11	DORFMAN, JACOB		1987	1910		
750	I10	DORFMAN, JOSEPH		31 DEC 1990	27 DEC 1908		
125	M171	DORFMAN, MAXWELL		24 MAR 1968	1915		HELEN
249	I13	DORFMAN, ROBERTA		1987	1946		
123		DORMAN, BERTHA	WEISS	1967	1897		SAMUEL
125	L119	DORMAN, HARRY		20 SEP 1930	1868		
102	B19	DORMAN, HERMAN		13 SEP 1951	1879		IDA
102	B20	DORMAN, IDA	HALPERN	15 OCT 1972	1894		HERMAN
121	B37	DORMAN, MORRIS		11 FEB 1989	27 JUL 1918		
101	E15	DORMAN, MORRIS I		23 JUN 1969	5 OCT 1912		
123		DORMAN, SAMUEL		28 DEC 1958	1894		BERTHA
377	L27	DORSKY, JESSIE A		1985	1905	JACOB	LEON
377	L26	DORSKY, LEON B		1963	1892	HIRSCH	JESSIE
118	E 9	DOW, ESTHER		25 JUL 1980			
102	I40	DRAGAT, HARRIS		16 JAN 1952	15 JUN 1873		LENA
102	I41	DRAGAT, LENA IDA	STUCK	23 AUG 1941	1 JAN 1873		HARRIS
377	O14	DREIFUSS, FRED		1974	1897		GRETA
377	O15	DREIFUSS, GRETA		1963	1907		FRED
370	U14	DRELINGER, JOSEPH		18 MAY 1939			NAOMI
370	U13	DRELINGER, NAOMI		16 MAY 1947			JOSEPH
119	D20	DRESSLER, ALBERT		3 MAR 1978	1906		
102	AJ197	DRESSLER, ETTA	SOLOMON	8 JAN 1973	1889		
121	P11	DRESSLER, GERALD		2 OCT 1967	1936		
119	C21	DRESSLER, JACK		28 MAR 1983	24 MAR 1912		
377	L37	DREYFUS, BEATRICE	GOLDSMITH	30 MAR 1963	20 NOV 1880		NESTER
377	L36	DREYFUS, NESTER		24 MAY 1958	25 DEC 1872		BEATRICE
751	M30	DRUCKER, HENRY WILLIAN		7 JUN 1976	9 MAR 1908		
112	C18	DRUCKER, JACOB		20 NOV 1987	30 APR 1910		
446	B28	DRUCKER, MOLLIE		1918	1886		
112	E18	DRUCKMAN, CAROL ANN		15 OCT 1974	25 OCT 1939		
101	J10	DRUCKMAN, FANNIE		14 DEC 1944	1862		
101	M28	DRUCKMAN, SARAH		26 AUG 1912	1895		
447	P29	DUBIN, ABRAHAM		23 JUN 1949	1883		IDA
447	R 9	DUBIN, EMANUEL	5 JAN 1961*	24 DEC 1961*	1913		
447	P30	DUBIN, IDA		24 NOV 1950	1880		ABRAHAM
447	R10	DUBIN, SAMUEL SAUL		5 JAN 1961	10 MAR 1913		
446	C33	DUBINSKY, ANNIE		16 AUG 1912	1874		
116	O27	DUBINSKY, HARVEY		1980	1921		
102	AJ136	DUBINSKY, MINNIE	ELOVICH	24 NOV 1982	16 FEB 1898		MORRIS
102	AJ137	DUBINSKY, MORRIS M		8 DEC 1986	12 FEB 1900		MINNIE
102	CA19	DUBINSKY, PHILIP		11 APR 1977	1895		ROSALIE
102	CA18	DUBINSKY, ROSALIE M		5 APR 1960	1900		PHILIP
103	A37	DUBITZKY, GOLDIE		1992			JOSEPH
103	A36	DUBITZKY, JOSEPH ABRAHAM		2 JUN 1989	24 DEC 1900		GOLDIE
121	U17	DUBOSAR, ABRAHAM R		1971	1922		
105	L38	DUBOSAR, BERTHA	ROSETSKY	22 AUG 1961	1881		
125	O 92	DUBOSSAR, ABRAHAM		18 JUL 1920	1872	SAMUEL & CHANA RIVA	
125	M195	DUBOW, SAUL		20 MAY 1971	1915		
125	B 26	DUBOWY, ANNA	JACOBSON	21 AUG 1981	1897		
125	B 27	DUBOWY, ANNA		7 JAN 1956	20 MAR 1898		HYMAN
125	F 81	DUBOWY, BENJAMIN		11 JUL 1923	1864	LAZER & CHAYA	ROSE
125	B 28	DUBOWY, HYMAN NATHAN		2 OCT 1970	12 APR 1884		ANNA
125	E174	DUBOWY, ROSE	ELKINS	2 OCT 1941	1881	SHLOMO	
125	F 82	DUBOWY, ROSE		7 APR 1938	1868		BENJAMIN
125	B 24	DUBOWY, SADIE		10 OCT 1986	1 JAN 1897		SOLL
125	E 82	DUBOWY, SAMUEL D		27 FEB 1954	1893		
125	B 25	DUBOWY, SOLL		23 APR 1941	16 MAY 1886		SADIE
125	K 32	DUBOWY, SOLOMON		16 OCT 1924	1852		YETTA
125	K 33	DUBOWY, YETTA		16 JUL 1914	5 MAY 1856		SOLOMON
102	AI 5	DUBROW, BARRY MAKR		14 JUN 1943	23 MAY 1943		
104	A35	DUBROW, ESTELLE S		16 NOV 1980			MORRIS
125	Q185	DUBROW, EVA K		1 AUG 1961	1894		SAMUEL
102	BF14	DUBROW, GEORGE A		10 JAN 1990	30 JAN 1917		
102	M12	DUBROW, ISRAEL R		1990	1902		
104	A36	DUBROW, MORRIS		3 JUL 1965			ESTELLE
125	Q184	DUBROW, SAMUEL D		16 JUN 1985	1894		EVA

Cem	Row	Name	Maiden Name	DOD	DOB	Parents	Spouse
102	AA186	DUBROW, SAMUEL J		6 OCT 1966	1903		
374	G 9	DUEL, GITTEL		13 SEP 1918			
125	L 46	DUNN, (BABY)		27 JUN 1917	1917	EDWARD	
125	I194	DUNN, ALBERT DR		19 JAN 1970	1924	BESSIE	
125	J195	DUNN, ALBERT J		19 FEB 1985	1920		MINNIE
125	J148	DUNN, ANNA	COHEN	6 SEP 1980	1892		MEYER
125	X169	DUNN, BARBARA		1989	1933		
114	K23	DUNN, BEATRICE H		12 APR 1988	24 MAR 1925		BENJAMIN
102	AA 1	DUNN, BENJAMIN		15 FEB 1941	1898		
114	K24	DUNN, BENJAMIN		21 NOV 1980	6 AUG 1922		BEATRICE
125	I195	DUNN, BESSIE		1989	1899		
125	J154	DUNN, EDWARD		8 JAN 1960	1893		GERTRUDE
123		DUNN, ERNESTINE		1975	1924		JOSEPH
125	J153	DUNN, GERTRUDE	MUSSMAN	17 JAN 1961	1895		EDWARD
102	AJ67	DUNN, HARRY ABRAHAM		7 JUN 1969	24 DEC 1897		
110	B10	DUNN, HYMAN		1936	1874		
125	I117	DUNN, IDA		26 DEC 1934	1870		MICHAEL
102	AC40	DUNN, JACOB		15 JAN 1985	18 OCT 1903		
123		DUNN, JOSEPH R		18 FEB 1966	1924		ERNESTINE
125	J194	DUNN, LIBBIE		9 NOV 1993			ALBERT
125	L 47	DUNN, LIBBIE ELLA		13 JAN 1911			MICHAEL
102	AJ207	DUNN, MARION L		27 MAY 1971	16 JAN 1906	PETER	
102	CA21	DUNN, MAURICE J		29 OCT 1959	1896		MIRIAM
125	R148	DUNN, MAX B		30 MAR 1942	1893	MESHEL & LIBA	
125	I116	DUNN, MICHAEL YECHIEL		3 JUL 1934	1861	ABRAHAM	IDA
125	J152	DUNN, MORRIS L		6 APR 1960	1886		ROSE
125	J147	DUNN, MYER DAVID		6 OCT 1952	1885		ANNA
371	B 2	DUNN, NELLIE		18 JAN 1965			
125	X193	DUNN, PAULINE	ROSENZWEIG	8 JUN 1983	26 JUL 1918		
102	AJ68	DUNN, PEARL FLORENCE		14 NOV 1954	2 APR 1929	HARRY	
102	AJ206	DUNN, PETER		8 MAR 1975	5 MAY 1930		
110	B14	DUNN, REBECCA		27 JAN 1929	1850		
125	J151	DUNN, ROSE J	KALINSKY	19 DEC 1963	1886		MORRIS
119	D45	DUNN, SADIE		23 NOV 1992			
119	H58	DUNN, SAMUEL J		12 FEB 1988	1 APR 1903		
371	B 3	DUNN, STANLEY		8 JAN 1965		NELLIE	
248	J21	DURSHT, MAX		24 JUL 1911	1869		
125	Q175	DWARSKI, HARRY		10 APR 1961	1896		
125	M162	DWORIN, LOUIS		20 MAR 1954	15 JUL 1892		SADIE
125	M163	DWORIN, SADIE		4 OCT 1986	5 MAY 1889		LOUIS
125	H131	DWORSKI, DAISY	KOPLOWITZ	8 OCT 1970	1900		
125	B137	DWORSKY, DORIS	EISEMAN	16 FEB 1983	10 MAY 1931		
125	K 77	EASERMAN, FANNIE	GUTE	19 MAR 1919	1839	MOSES STRAL	
750	H32	EASTON, ELIZABETH		3 JUL 1986	30 MAR 1920		
125	IA32	ECHELSON, BESSIE	BUCHALTER	26 FEB 1985	1896		
102	A84	ECHELSON, JOSEPH R		22 NOV 1944	4 SEP 1944		
104	E34	ECHELSON, MRS					NATHAN
104	E35	ECHELSON, NATHAN		21 FEB 1967	23 SEP 1898		
493	G17	ECKER, ADAM		12 JAN 1990	8 DEC 1921		
222	AI 1	ECKER, MAURICE		12 MAR 1974	1898		
330	B38	ECOCHARD, KATHRYN	GAY LINDER	25 MAR 1990	22 FEB 1956		
102	Q27	EDDY, EDWARD G		9 AUG 1961	4 APR 1887		EVA
102	Q29	EDDY, EMANUEL H		1931	1911		
102	Q26	EDDY, EVA	MILLER	3 OCT 1956	8 AUG 1896		EDWARD
447	Y11	EDELBERG, ANN W		13 JUN 1967	19 MAY 1921		
447	Y17	EDELBERG, HARVEY		16 DEC 1978	6 APR 1937		
447	C14	EDELBERG, HESSIE		27 JUN 1934	1885		SIMON
447	C12	EDELBERG, SARAH	STROH	14 JUN 1964	1891		SIMON
447	C13	EDELBERG, SIMON		9 JUN 1978	12 FEB 1885		SARAH
125	E 30	EDELSON, (BABY)		3 MAY 1929	30 JUN 1929	MYER & LEAH	
125		EDELSON, (CHILD)		13 NOV 1926	1924		
125	I170	EDELSON, ABRAHAM		9 DEC 1975	1890		SADIE
125	B 66	EDELSON, ESTHER	SAVAL	29 APR 1988	10 MAR 1896		MAX
125	H 62	EDELSON, FANNIE		17 NOV 1932	1864		LOUIS
120	B 9	EDELSON, HARRY		21 DEC 1989	31 MAR 1917		
125	A 67	EDELSON, HOWARD		5 FEB 1957	1908		

Cem	Row	Name	Maiden Name	DOD	DOB	Parents	Spouse
125	G 63	EDELSON, LEAH		2 SEP 1942	MAY 1892		MYER
125	H 63	EDELSON, LOUIS		3 SEP 1945	1863	ELIMELCH & MATTA	FANNIE
125	B 65	EDELSON, MAX		21 FEB 1972	1894		ESTHER
125	H 64	EDELSON, MILDRED		4 FEB 1946	DEC 1918	MYER & LEAH	
125	G 61	EDELSON, MYER		3 NOV 1947	18 SEP 1887	LOUIS	LEAH
120	B10	EDELSON, RUTH	LEVINE	NDD	22 JUL 1918		
125	I173	EDELSON, SADIE	KRECHEVSKY	15 JAN 1984			ABRAHAM
391	M44	EDWARDS, MAX		27 FEB 1953	15 JUL 1875	JOSHUA EFFRAIM	
113	A36	EFRON, MINNIE	ROOT	12 JAN 1990	12 SEP 1904		
248	J 8	EFROS, ROBERT		22 AUG 1916	FEB 1915	M & C	
102	A32	EGGERT, RACHEL	CINCIMER	1937	1865		
371	M37	EHRENBERG, IDA		23 MAY 1952	JUN 1876		
447	AC37	EHRENBERG, MORRIS		12 FEB 1981	3 APR 1907		
370	C16	EHRENBERG, SAMUEL		11 APR 1935	1877		
103	A40	EHRLICH, ERIC SCOTT		17 SEP 1990	27 OCT 1959	STANLEY	
121	D37	EHRLICH, EUGENE L DR		18 APR 1980	6 JUN 1915		
377	S46	EHRLICH, FRANCES		12 JUL 1992	6 JAN 1915		LOUIS
107	F15	EHRLICH, IDA N		1 OCT 1985	14 FEB 1910		
377	S45	EHRLICH, LOUIS		2 NOV 1986	2 DEC 1913		FRANCES
125	V182	EHRLICK, JACK		28 JAN 1977	11 JAN 1902		
125	J 52	EICHELMAN, REBECCA		21 JAN 1905	1830		
391	GE 4	EINHORN, AARON ZEV (CHILD)					
330	AI21	EINHORN, ABRAHAM		6 APR 1978	1923		
391	M42	EINHORN, ANNIE		17 SEP 1946	1879	ELIYAHU	ISSAC
391	Y69	EINHORN, ARTHUR W		16 JAN 1972	6 JAN 1906	SHMARYAHU ISAAC	
329	B31	EINHORN, EVA		7 OCT 1945	1888		SAMUEL
391	M43	EINHORN, ISAAC		7 APR 1960	1876	SHMARYAHU ISAAC	ANNIE
330	Z1	EINHORN, LOUIS		28 JUL 1931			
329	B20	EINHORN, MOLLIE		12 OCT 1955	18 SEP 1906	SAMUEL & EVA	
391	ZF75	EINHORN, MORRIS		22 JUN 1988	27 MAR 1915	SHAMRYAHU ISAAC	
329	B32	EINHORN, SAMUEL		21 JUN 1953	1885		EVA
391	H32	EINSTEIN, FRIEDA		12 DEC 1928	1858	SAMUEL	
125	B139	EISEMAN, THEA		8 MAY 1988	31 DEC 1896		MEINHOLD
125	B138	EISEMANN, MEINHOLD		19 APR 1982	14 APR 1897		THEA
116	BE125	EISENBAUM, IRVING		1989	1923		
248	G43	EISENBERG, BENJAMIN		6 JAN 1963	22 FEB 1892	SAMUEL & MINNIE	FLORENCE
125	H 30	EISENBERG, BERTHA	KRANOWITZ	24 JUN 1978	1886		JULIUS
125	F 29	EISENBERG, ELLA S		5 JUN 1974	1907		
125	P172	EISENBERG, ETHEL		14 NOV 1963	1889		
248	G44	EISENBERG, FLORENCE		16 FEB 1962	26 MAR 1895		BENJAMIN
111	4	EISENBERG, HELENE A		1985	1896		
104	A10	EISENBERG, HILDA		27 DEC 1985	1 MAR 1916		
121	B42	EISENBERG, IRVING H		27 JAN 1992			
125	H 29	EISENBERG, JULIUS		13 NOV 1956	1875		BERTHA
248	G42	EISENBERG, MINNIE		6 AUG 1936	1863		SAMUEL
249	I 2	EISENBERG, MINNIE		4 JAN 1952	1894		
248	G41	EISENBERG, SAMUEL		1 JAN 1933	1861		MINNIE
121	J 8	EISENBERG, SARAH K		1980	1897		
249	C11	EISENBERG, SOLOMON		6 DEC 1978	30 JUN 1892		
222	AH 1	EISENSTADT, ADELE	WALL	18 MAY 1989	18 FEB 1922		
371	K34	EISENSTADT, JACK H		12 JAN 1977	8 SEP 1913		LIBBY
371	K33	EISENSTADT, LIBBY	HECHT	19 AUG 1973	23 MAR 1911		JACK
447	C34	EISENSTEIN, ETTA		13 OCT 1967	16 JUL 1898		JOSEPH
447	A34	EISENSTEIN, FANNIE E		6 FEB 1929	18 JUL 1870		MORRIS
370	Q32	EISENSTEIN, IDA		1941	1870		SAMUEL
447	B35	EISENSTEIN, JENNIE	ELLIS	8 DEC 1979	1895		MYER
392	D 7	EISENSTEIN, JOSEPH		14 JAN 1983	1 JAN 1891	SIMON & CHAYA SARAH	SARAH
447	C35	EISENSTEIN, JOSEPH		30 APR 1977	18 APR 1892	MORRIS & FANNIE	ETTA
447	O40	EISENSTEIN, MAVINA		11 FEB 1986	1911		
447	B34	EISENSTEIN, MEYER		27 SEP 1946	1890	MORRIS & FANNIE	JENNIE
447	A35	EISENSTEIN, MORRIS H		18 MAY 1931	16 DEC 1868		FANNIE
447	C32	EISENSTEIN, NORMAN N		14 DEC 1954	1903	MORRIS & FANNIE	
370	Q33	EISENSTEIN, SAMUEL		1957	1869		IDA
392	D 8	EISENSTEIN, SARAH REBECCA		22 MAR 1973	25 DEC 1896	DAVID	JOSEPH
447	S39	EISENSTEIN, SOLOMON		15 OCT 1967	1895	MORRIS & FANNIE	
125		EISENTEIN, ELIZABETH		25 JAN 1914			

Cem	Row	Name	Maiden Name	DOD	DOB	Parents	Spouse
392	J44	EISMAN, REBECCA		10 MAR 1943	1888	YECHEZKEL	SOLOMON
392	J45	EISMAN, SOLOMON		29 JUN 1953	1887	ABBA	REBECCA
391	O38	EISNER, BATHSHEVA				LEV HIRSH	ISAAC
370	I48	EISNER, TAUBE		7 JAN 1933	1856		
391	K35	EIZELOWITZ, FIVISH		25 OCT 1909		SHMARYAHU	
119	B 1	ELANSKY, (BABY GIRL)		20 MAR 1979			
121	I36	ELANSKY, JOSEPH DAVID		18 MAR 1986	8 MAY 1923		
121	I37	ELANSKY, ROSLYN		20 JAN 1989	15 SEP 1928		
373	H 4	ELBAUM, ALBERT		1976	1906		
375	F10	ELENOWITZ, HARRY		3 NOV 1979	1906	SIMCHA	MIRIAM
375	F 9	ELENOWITZ, MIRIAM MAYE		8 OCT 1969	1906	ZEV JOEL	HARRY
377	J 2	ELFENBEIN, EMANUEL		1965	1892	LOUIS & SARAH	SAMUEL
377	I 4	ELFENBEIN, HELEN	WEIL	21 APR 1991	17 MAR 1909		
377	J 5	ELFENBEIN, HERMAN		1960	1890	LOUIS & SARAH	LAURA
377	J 1	ELFENBEIN, IDA B		1980	1894		EMANUEL
377	J 6	ELFENBEIN, LAURA B		1970	1890		HERMAN
377	J 4	ELFENBEIN, LOUIS		1943	1867		SARAH
377	I 2	ELFENBEIN, MIRIAM L		1987	1909		
377	J 3	ELFENBEIN, SARAH MOLLY		1940	1867		LOUIS
330	D12	ELGART, ARTHUR		1950			BESSIE
330	E11	ELGART, BERNARD		28 NOV 1969	1880	MOSES & CELIA	
330	D13	ELGART, BESSIE		16 JAN 1944			ARTHUR
330	E13	ELGART, CELIA		10 NOV 1925	1847		MOSES
330	E14	ELGART, ELIZABETH		12 SEP 1979	1900		JACOB
330	E15	ELGART, JACOB		2 MAY 1985	1890	MOSES & CELIA	ELIZABETH
494	D20	ELGART, JOSEPH J		1968	1908		
330	F14	ELGART, LOUIS		19 FEB 1922	1883	MOSES & CELIA	
330	E12	ELGART, MOSES DAVID		27 FEB 1925	1847		CELIA
377	N34	ELGART, NATHAN		13 JUL 1948	15 MAY 1880		
125	B 33	ELIAS, SOPHIE	WEINBERG	1 FEB 1943	29 SEP 1897		
447	R15	ELIGATOR, EMIL		1954	1892		EMMA
447	R16	ELIGATOR, EMMA		1976	1897		EMIL
102	BE 8	ELINSKY, LOUIS		22 JAN 1991	10 MAY 1909		RUTH
102	BE 7	ELINSKY, RUTH M	WEINSTOCK	19 JUN 1991	22 MAY 1912		LOUIS
104	G 9	ELINSON, BER		4 SEP 1985	22 APR 1907		RIVA
104	G10	ELINSON, RIVA		4 AUG 1990	28 MAY 1913		BER
377	D21	ELION, FANNIE R		17 OCT 1985	5 MAY 1890	ABRAHAM	JOHN
377	D23	ELION, GEORGE O		23 JUN 1963	5 DEC 1890	ISAAC JACOB	
392	E26	ELION, HARRY B		25 JUL 1959	10 MAY 1910	LOUIS & PEARL	
377	D24	ELION, HARRY R		19 SEP 1974	1895	ISAAC JACOB	IDA
377	C26	ELION, HENRY		1956	1893		
377	D25	ELION, IDA E		1983	1902	ISRAEL	HARRY
391	C11	ELION, IMAN		21 MAY 1947	1867	JACOB	BERNARD
377	C25	ELION, JOHN		21 APR 1987	1894	CHAIM	ROSE
377	D22	ELION, JOHN EDWARD LT		3 FEB 1946	9 MAR 1912	GEORGE	FANNIE
392	E24	ELION, LOUIS (JUDAH LEV)		13 JUL 1954	1886	JACOB	PEARL
392	D12	ELION, MAX		8 FEB 1960	1912	LOUIS & PEARL	
392	E25	ELION, PEARL		9 OCT 1962	1886	MOSHE JUDAH	LOUIS
377	C24	ELION, ROSE R		16 MAR 1990	1915	SAMUEL	JOHN
377	O27	ELION, SAM		1963	1882		
392	J22	ELIONSKY, BASHEVA		2 OCT 1933	1853	AARON ISAAC	
391	E33	ELIONSKY, BERNARD					IMAN
391	I38	ELIONSKY, REBECCA		10 MAY 1933		MOSHE ELIYAHU	
391	J27	ELIOTT, MORRIS		2 OCT 1921	1890	ISAAC CHAIM	
433	B 6	ELKIN, BERTHA		13 AUG 1981	15 NOV 1890	ELEAZER	MICHAEL
391	ZA57	ELKIN, CELIA		29 MAY 1968	1901	REUBEN	NATHAN
433	B 5	ELKIN, MICHAEL		9 JUL 1976	7 APR 1892	SCHLOMO	BERTHA
391	ZA58	ELKIN, NATHAN		6 MAR 1963	1906	CHAIM	CELIA
102	BC 1	ELKINS, MARGIT S		30 OCT 1990	18 FEB 1933		
102	AJ158	ELLENBERG, ERNESTINE		23 MAY 1964	1884		
222	AC 1	ELLIN, BARUCH		28 FEB 1985	26 MAY 1901		
102	AG117	ELLIN, HARRY		24 FEB 1970	25 SEP 1896	CHAIM & TEMMA (LOVE)	DOROTHY
102	S10	ELLIN, HYMAN		21 NOV 1944			TEMAN
102	S 9	ELLIN, TEMA		21 OCT 1934	1859		HYMAN
391	X80	ELLION, HERMAN		30 MAY 1988	8 AUG 1910	SAMUEL	
119	F34	ELLIS, DAVID		1986	1899		

Cem	Row	Name	Maiden Name	DOD	DOB	Parents	Spouse
119	F35	ELLIS, ETHEL		1988	1899		
113	C26	ELLIS, FREIDA	GREENBERG	12 APR 1987	18 DEC 1903		
113	M49	ELLIS, JONATHAN GEORGE		10 APR 1966	19 APR 1951		SIDNEY
447	V25	ELLIS, MAX		1 FEB 1928			
377	V44	ELLIS, MOLLIE	SOKOL	17 FEB 1981	9 JUL 1950	LABEL	
432		ELLIS, ROSA		22 JUL 1898			
113	C27	ELLIS, SIDNEY		17 NOV 1991	13 SEP 1900	JACOB & ELLIS	FREIDA
102	AI167	ELLISH, GOLDIE	MURZIN	9 SEP 1991	29 JAN 1912		LEWIS
102	AI166	ELLISH, LEWIS		27 OCT 1991	13 SEP 1908		GOLDIE
102	L31	ELLOVICH, CHARLES		16 OCT 1946	16 AUG 1876		TOBA
102	O10	ELLOVICH, DORA	GROSS	13 AUG 1930	1878		
102	U43	ELLOVICH, ELIAS		9 OCT 1928	1 APR 1869		ELIZABETH
102	U42	ELLOVICH, ELIZABETH		16 SEP 1954	15 JUL 1870		ELIAS
102	U44	ELLOVICH, MORRIS		25 JAN 1930	17 MAY 1911	ELIAS & ELIZABETH	
102	U51	ELLOVICH, MYER		5 JAN 1990	6 FEB 1907	ELIAS & ELIZABETH	ROSE
102	U50	ELLOVICH, ROSE W		15 DEC 1976	9 JUL 1908		MYER
102	L30	ELLOVICH, TOBA		1 APR 1941	17 APR 1877		CHARLES
102	AI216	ELLOVITCH, ANNIE		16 NOV 1976	6 MAY 1886		
102	T 8	ELMAN, ALICE	GREENBERG	24 APR 1958	1891		BERNARD
102	T 9	ELMAN, BERNARD H		27 APR 1967	1888	LAZAR & KAYLA (PODEROWITZ)	ALICE
102	T 7	ELMAN, LAWRENCE LT		27 JUL 1944	15 MAY 1920	BERNARD & ALICE (GREENBERG)	
374	E50	ELMAN, LOUIS		1990	1905		
102	A30	ELMAN, MORRIS		2 AUG 1936	1887	LAZAR & KAYLA (PODEROWITZ)	
102	K42	ELOVICH, EMANUEL		20 JUL 1939	10 JUL 1896	LOUIS & FANNIE	
102	K43	ELOVICH, FANNIE		9 MAY 1942	1 APR 1866		LOUIS
102	J38	ELOVICH, HARRY C		15 NOV 1978	3 DEC 1890		REBECCA
102	K44	ELOVICH, LOUIS		25 FEB 1944	16 JUL 1866		FANNIE
102	J37	ELOVICH, REBECCA G		24 JUL 1967	17 JUN 1891		HARRY
123		ELSNER, BERTHA		NDD	18 NOV 1890		
119	J60	ELSTEIN, ILSE EDITH		9 JAN 1986	24 JUN 1910		
119	J59	ELSTEIN, ISAAC ABRAHAM		18 FEB 1985	7 APR 1894		
446	B36	EMANUEL, DAVID		1941	1869		LILLIAN
446	B37	EMANUEL, LILLIAN	BERNHARD	1943	1875	HENRY & RACHEL	DAVID
114	A17	EMANUEL, RUTH J		19 SEP 1989	15 MAY 1928		
105	C49	ENFELDT, ROSALIE DEE		24 AUG 1962	17 MAY 1958		
110	B 7	ENGEL, ANNIE		15 AUG 1947	1869		SOLOMON
750	E24	ENGEL, FREIDA G		16 AUG 1985	12 JUL 1916		
101	M19	ENGEL, MINNIE		21 MAY 1910	1893		
110	B 6	ENGEL, SOLOMON		12 JAN 1939	1855		ANNIE
377	O 1	ENNIS, DAVID		1944	1897		
125	R174	ENOCH, ELINOR	GREENBERG	23 MAY 1959	1887		
447	X32	ENOWITCH, ELLIOT HAROLD		1988	1908		
370	O45	EPSTEIN, ABRAHAM		2 FEB 1895			
125	N 85	EPSTEIN, ABRAHAM ISAAC		5 FEB 1924	1856	BENJAMIN	
102	AB103	EPSTEIN, ABRAM I		1932	1863		ELIZABETH
102	J 6	EPSTEIN, ADELE	ZIMMERMAN	12 MAY 1977	12 DEC 1922		JOSEPH
125	Y175	EPSTEIN, ALBERT		12 FEB 1984	25 APR 1899		
114	A 1	EPSTEIN, ANDREW L		7 JUL 1989	31 DEC 1964		
222	AL 9	EPSTEIN, ANNA		17 NOV 1920	1855		
102	AC90	EPSTEIN, ANNA CELIA		20 JUN 1935	1868		
102	CA17	EPSTEIN, CHARLES		8 MAR 1961	1885		PAULINE
222	AA 7	EPSTEIN, DAVID BENJAMIN		14 MAR 1965	1882	ANNA	
222	J 3	EPSTEIN, DAVID H		22 JUL 1935	30 OCT 1920	IRVING & SARAH	
371	AD21	EPSTEIN, DINA M		18 JAN 1964	1886		
102	AD96	EPSTEIN, DORA	SIEGEL	1941	1884		HERMAN
102	Q19	EPSTEIN, DORA SCHWARTZ	GABERMAN	28 FEB 1991	1 APR 1899		
102	AB102	EPSTEIN, ELIZABETH D		1932	1867		ARAM
249	C 9	EPSTEIN, ESTHER RACHEL		29 JUN 1958	15 AUG 1893		SAM
329	A 3	EPSTEIN, FANNIE		27 MAR 1959	1896		HYMAN
119	B 9	EPSTEIN, FLORENCE		26 JUN 1985	22 AUG 1901		
110	A17	EPSTEIN, FREIDEL C		9 MAY 1956	1869		MENDEL
392	E52	EPSTEIN, FRIEDA		30 JUL 1952	1869	CHAIM	
125	L190	EPSTEIN, GOLDIE	SACKROWITZ	9 APR 1981	1903		HERMAN
376	C 6	EPSTEIN, HELEN P		13 JUN 1974	25 NOV 1900	ABBA HIRSH	
102	AC156	EPSTEIN, HERBERT		1991	1922		
125	L191	EPSTEIN, HERMAN		14 OCT 1971	1902		GOLDIE

Cem	Row	Name	Maiden Name	DOD	DOB	Parents	Spouse
102	AD95	EPSTEIN, HERMAN ISRAEL		20 JUL 1960	1880		DORA
222	AR 1	EPSTEIN, HYMAN		11 NOV 1985	1909	LENA	
329	A 4	EPSTEIN, HYMAN		17 MAY 1972	1887		FANNIE
119	I52	EPSTEIN, IDA		31 MAR 1987	30 OCT 1907		
119	D30	EPSTEIN, IDA Z	SEARLEMAN	20 JAN 1980	16 DEC 1902		
119	I51	EPSTEIN, IRVING		3 JUN 1987	26 DEC 1906		
222	J 1	EPSTEIN, IRVING		3 FEB 1958	11 NOV 1888		SARAH
222	AL 8	EPSTEIN, ISAAC		19 AUG 1921	1892		
751	J38	EPSTEIN, ISIDORE		1951	1886		
121	D45	EPSTEIN, ISRAEL N		31 JAN 1988	26 NOV 1925		
102	A13	EPSTEIN, JENNIE P		9 DEC 1979	10 OCT 1886		MORRIS
102	AC91	EPSTEIN, JOSEPH		24 DEC 1944	1894		
750	A22	EPSTEIN, JULIAN ABRAHAM		25 SEP 1978	22 DEC 1922		
125	ZB159	EPSTEIN, JULIE MERLE		4 JUN 1991	9 MAY 1963		
125	J119	EPSTEIN, LENA	ABRAHAMSON	13 OCT 1964	1890		SAMUEL
222	AR 2	EPSTEIN, LENA		30 DEC 1944	1880		
125	L172	EPSTEIN, LILLIAN	GOLDSTEIN	5 SEP 1983	1887		LOUIS
123		EPSTEIN, LOUIS		10 DEC 1956	1903		
125	L173	EPSTEIN, LOUIS		8 JAN 1971	1891		LILLIAN
447	T23	EPSTEIN, LOUIS		7 JUN 1958	1900		
119	D29	EPSTEIN, MAX HERMAN		13 MAY 1985	1 JAN 1898		
102	AB100	EPSTEIN, MAX M		1974	1893		VERA
110	A16	EPSTEIN, MENDEL		17 OCT 1943	1864		FREIDEL
222	AL 6	EPSTEIN, MINNIE		17 SEP 1986	1886		MORRIS
222	AL 7	EPSTEIN, MORRIS		24 SEP 1927	1885	ANNA	MINNIE
370	O44	EPSTEIN, MORRIS		26 SEP 1961	1896		REBECCA
102	A12	EPSTEIN, MORRRIS L		10 MAY 1932	15 JUL 1888		JENNIE
102	CA16	EPSTEIN, PAULINE M		6 APR 1968	1886		CHARLES
370	O43	EPSTEIN, REBECCA		8 OCT 1948	1898		MORRIS
104	E30	EPSTEIN, ROSE		29 JAN 1981			
222	AR 3	EPSTEIN, RUEBEN		5 NOV 1990	1910	LENA	
249	C10	EPSTEIN, SAM		26 JUN 1979	15 DEC 1890		ESTHER
125	J120	EPSTEIN, SAMUEL		22 JUN 1937	1879		LENA
391	F19	EPSTEIN, SAMUEL		18 JAN 1930	1866	ARYEH LEV	
222	J 2	EPSTEIN, SARA		9 JUN 1966	14 AUG 1892		IRVING
125		EPSTEIN, SARAH R		10 OCT 1944	1855	FAGEL	
392	A48	EPSTEIN, SOL		4 FEB 1977	7 SEP 1902		
119	B10	EPSTEIN, SOLOMON		16 SEP 1982	14 MAR 1899		
102	AB101	EPSTEIN, VERA G		1968	1898		MAX
391	GC 7	ERSOFF, RITA	RAY	30 SEP 1947	1930	JACOB	
123		ERTMAN, BENJAMIN		25 JUL 1955	3 MAR 1925		
105	I41	ERTMAN, MORRIS		17 SEP 1987	18 DEC 1912		TILLIE
105	I40	ERTMAN, TILLIE	PORTNER	19 DEC 1980	10 JUL 1916		MORRIS
112	B 4	ESAKOV, IDA A		2 JUN 1991	16 OCT 1901		
391	O36	ESCOWITZ, BRYNA		11 JAN 1912	1842	JOSEPH KALMAN	
391	O29	ESCOWITZ, EPHRAIM		1908	1836	ISSAC JACOB	
391	F18	ESCOWITZ, ISAAC		13 AUG 1930	1868	YESHUA EFFRAIM	
391	N44	ESCOWITZ, MINNIE		7 APR 1965	18 APR 1910	SAMUEL & ROSE G	
391	I36	ESCOWITZ, NELLIE		30 DEC 1924	1882	JACOB	
391	H36	ESCOWITZ, ROSE G		23 DEC 1925	1873	SHLOMO	
391	M40	ESCOWITZ, SARAH REBECCA		12 DEC 1940	1865	SHABBATAI	
102	O15	ESSERMAN, DOROTHY		5 DEC 1943			HERMAN
102	O14	ESSERMAN, HERMAN		29 JUL 1958			DOROTHY
102	O11	ESSERMAN, JENNIE M		28 JUL 1970			
102	O16	ESSERMAN, SARAH		16 NOV 1926			
391	F24	ESSMAN, MAX		3 SEP 1927	1890		
370	G32	ETELMAN, ETIE		1933	1875		
125	Q166	ETELSON, ABRAHAM		2 AUG 1950	1879	SAMUEL	ANNA
125	Q165	ETELSON, ANNA D		2 DEC 1946	1877	MADAH & ATTA	ABRAHAM
125	J182	ETKIND, MINNIE		10 DEC 1987	10 JUL 1895		NATHAN
125	J183	ETKIND, NATHAN		2 NOV 1976	13 NOV 1885		MINNIE
391	J39	ETTINGER, BELLA	ESCOWITZ	1933	1866	JOSHUA EFFRAIM	
248	C21	EVANS, ARTHUR W		10 JUN 1989	17 APR 1917		ROSALIE
118	D14	EVANS, EVELYN	KAZDEN	19 NOV 1984			
248	C22	EVANS, ROSALIE B			21 AUG 1921		ARTHUR
101	J 1	EVERY, WILLIAM		15 MAR 1982	15 DEC 1902		ZELDA

Cem	Row	Name	Maiden Name	DOD	DOB	Parents	Spouse
101	J 2	EVERY, ZELDA L		24 MAR 1968	1906		
446	C12	EWNOWITCH, ANNA		22 APR 1929	1867		WILLIAM
446	B30	EWNOWITCH, BENJAMIN		11 SEP 1918	1863	ESTHER	BENJAMIN
446	C13	EWNOWITCH, ESTHER		10 NOV 1927	1844		ANNA
446	C48	EWNOWITCH, JULIA		2 JAN 1914	13 JAN 1899		
446	A44	EWNOWITCH, MINNIE		11 JUL 1919	18 SEP 1896	BENJAMIN	
446	B20	EWNOWITCH, SAUL		1916	1903	BENJAMIN & ANNA	
446	B 3	FABIAN, BERNARD M		1931	1876	MARCUS & LILLIAN	
446	B 9	FABIAN, FRED H		1938	1921	BERNARD & ROSE	ROSE
446	C16	FABIAN, LILLIAN		11 DEC 1924	1861		
446	A10	FABIAN, MARCUS		1930	1857		MARCUS
447	X38	FABIAN, MORRIS J		15 FEB 1969	1906		LILLIAN
447	Y10	FABIAN, ROBERT		5 NOV 1967	1912		
446	B 2	FABIAN, ROSE	TRAIER	1955	1881		BERNARD
391	Z59	FABRICANT, BERNARD W		29 JAN 1960	1901	ISAAC	MINNIE
377	S29	FABRICANT, DORIS S		12 OCT 1984	26 JAN 1918		MORRIS
391	D13	FABRICANT, FRED ISAAC		7 JAN 1940	1881	CALEB	LENA
391	ZB79	FABRICANT, GERTRUDE		8 JAN 1990	1903	ISAAC	
391	ZA55	FABRICANT, JEANNETTE	AGRONOVITCH	1961	1892		
391	Z55	FABRICANT, JESSIE PEARL		NDD	1921	FAGLACH	
391	G43	FABRICANT, LENA		21 JAN 1943	1882	JACOB	FRED
493	E22	FABRICANT, MAX WINTHROP		1981	1885		
377	S28	FABRICANT, MILTON W		15 APR 1970	12 DEC 1911		DORIS
391	Z58	FABRICANT, MINNIE	CAMMISSAR	23 MAY 1983	1904	HIRSHEL	BERNARD
110	E35	FACTOR, BESSIE	COHN	18 MAY 1986	20 JAN 1896		
110	A 8	FACTOR, HYMAN		28 FEB 1939	1889		
110	E34	FACTOR, MORRIS L		24 OCT 1990	10 APR 1918	BESSIE (COHN)	
110	C23	FACTOR, SARAH	BLOCK	14 FEB 1965	1 JAN 1893		
101	K17	FADEN, CLARA		4 MAR 1929	1846		NATHAN
101	J36	FADEN, MAMIE ROSE		7 NOV 1977			
101	C27	FADEN, NATHAN		10 AUG 1922	1841		CLARA
125	T162	FAIGEN, EDWARD		15 MAR 1940	24 JAN 1906	HARRIS & FANNIE	
125	1C31	FAIGEN, FANNIE		27 OCT 1919	1873	JACOB & HENNIE	HARRIS
125	T163	FAIGEN, HARRIS		9 JUL 1955	11 JAN 1871		FANNIE
125	S170	FAIGEN, IDA		30 JUL 1981	9 AUG 1904		MARION
125	S171	FAIGEN, MARION		2 JAN 1958	7 JUL 1909		IDA
125		FALK, (CHILD)		23 FEB 1919	1919	ELI & BESSIE	
125	P154	FALK, ANNA	CHINITZ	31 JUL 1963	1882		ELI
116	AY25	FALK, ARTHUR L		25 MAR 1968	4 JUN 1918		
125	P155	FALK, ELI		5 MAY 1948	1882	ABRAHAM	ANNA
391	O58	FALK, ESTHER	KOSS	6 FEB 1961	1912	SHRUGA FIVAL	
104	B39	FALK, EVA S		7 FEB 1990	15 DEC 1901		IRVING
330	AB13	FALK, FLORA F		10 JUN 1978	10 APR 1914		HYMAN
330	AA14	FALK, FRANK		15 APR 1969	16 APR 1889		REBECCA
116	AZ 5	FALK, GEORGE E		15 OCT 1987	12 APR 1910		MIRIAM
330	AB12	FALK, HYMAN J		4 AUG 1975	24 NOV 1913		FLORA
104	B38	FALK, IRVING H		13 SEP 1973	29 JUL 1900		EVA
116	AZ 4	FALK, MIRIAM	PESKIN	24 NOV 1972	18 JUL 1912		GEORGE
123		FALK, MORRIS S		1976	1887		DOROTHY
125	O186	FALK, PAULINE	HANDLER	28 NOV 1970	1889		SAMUEL
330	AA13	FALK, REBECCA		22 APR 1980	16 JUN 1889		FRANK
125	O187	FALK, SAMUEL		1 JAN 1965	1890		PAULINE
391	O35	FALK, TILLIE		22 JUL 1909	1856	MOSHE	
101	M34	FARBER, DOROTHY H		6 APR 1955	1911		
103	L1	FARBER, JACOB		30 DEC 1979	6 APR 1902		
121	L19	FARKAS, PAUL		5 FEB 1981	12 AUG 1920		
433	H13	FAST, EVA		26 APR 1947	1886	ARON	SAM
433	H14	FAST, SAM		28 MAY 1944	1885	PESACH	EVA
447	W30	FATELMAN, SADELLE		12 JUL 1895			
123		FAUST, JOSEPH J		21 JUL 1968	1919		CHARLES
377	T 8	FEDERMAN, ELIZABETH		1993	1897	BENJAMIN	MORRIS
377	T 7	FEDERMAN, MORRIS		1972	1894	AARON	ELIZABETH
391	ZB50	FEIBIS, HARRY M		9 NOV 1976	1890	MOSHE	SARAH
391	ZB51	FEIBIS, SARAH R		11 FEB 1980	1887	MORDECHAI ABRAHAM	HARRY
447	T30	FEIDEN, DAVID		1980	1903		KITTIE
330	E 8	FEIDEN, GOLDIE		22 MAY 1929			

Cem	Row	Name	Maiden Name	DOD	DOB	Parents	Spouse
447	T29	FEIDEN, KITTY		1976	1901		DAVID
330	B43	FEIDEN, SARAH	LEVINE	18 APR 1957	1872		
432		FEIERBERG, SAMUEL		9 DEC 1899			
248	L70	FEIGELSTOCK, ALBERT		3 SEP 1957	12 DEC 1896		BEATRICE
248	L71	FEIGELSTOCK, BEATRICE		4 DEC 1960	16 NOV 1899		ALBERT
125	B 49	FEIGENBAUM, ANNA	NAIR	18 SEP 1964	21 NOV 1900	CHAIM & JULIA (SILVERSTEIN)	HERMAN
125	B 43	FEIGENBAUM, BERTHA		16 MAR 1947	26 JAN 1898		JOSEPH
125	K 27	FEIGENBAUM, CILIA CHAVA		19 AUG 1917	1867	MOSHE CHAIM	ISAAC
125	A 45	FEIGENBAUM, DANIEL MORDECHA		14 MAR 1961	FEB 1957	FENMORE & GLADYS	
125	B 48	FEIGENBAUM, HERMAN		6 NOV 1964	15 APR 1899	ISAAC & CILIA	ANNA
125	K 28	FEIGENBAUM, ISAAC		9 SEP 1968	1869	JOSEPH	CILIA
125	B 42	FEIGENBAUM, JOSEPH L		29 MAR 1976	1894	ISAAC & CILIA	BERTHA
125	I 31	FEIGENBAUM, JULIA	SILVERSTEIN	7 JUL 1941	JUL 1871	MILTON & HANNAH (SILVERSTEIN)	CHAIM
125	B 46	FEIGENBAUM, MAX		13 MAR 1974	1898	ISAAC & CILIA	MINNIE
125	B 45	FEIGENBAUM, MINNIE	DUBOWY	1 SEP 1973	1900		MAX
102	F34	FEIGIN, ANNA		24 NOV 1951			
102	F36	FEIGIN, LEON A		20 JUL 1963			
102	F35	FEIGIN, LOUIS		29 JAN 1946			
102	AJ105	FEIN, AARON		1 MAY 1955	1890		
102	AJ225	FEIN, BENJAMIN		12 APR 1978	19 DEC 1902		
370	G36	FEIN, R MINNIE		1934	1900		
330	D 2	FEINBEN, AARON		21 JUN 1952	1860		
102	U 7	FEINBERG, ABRAHAM A		1979	1895		EMMA
102	F29	FEINBERG, ANNA		21 JUL 1964	1874		MAX
248	G61	FEINBERG, DAVID		16 FEB 1971	12 MAR 1897		LENA
102	U 4	FEINBERG, EMMA E		6 JAN 1944	1892		ABRAHAM
102	AI27	FEINBERG, ESTHER		5 OCT 1965	1887		
377	J37	FEINBERG, GERTRUDE S		1966	1897	NAOH LEV	RUDOLPH
125	N178	FEINBERG, IDA		29 FEB 1984	1893		JULIUS
102	T42	FEINBERG, IDA H	HERRUP	30 NOV 1967	1 JUL 1885		LOUIS
102	F31	FEINBERG, JACOB		18 NOV 1985	20 OCT 1900	MAX & ANNA	
125	N179	FEINBERG, JULIUS		5 FEB 1966	1898		IDA
248	G60	FEINBERG, LENA		28 SEP 1983	8 APR 1897		DAVID
102	T41	FEINBERG, LOUIS	OF AUSTRIA	17 APR 1953	26 AUG 1879	MOSES & RACHEL	IDA
102	F30	FEINBERG, MAX		8 NOV 1958	1864	MAX & ANNA	ANNA
102	U 6	FEINBERG, ROSE	GOLDMAN	3 NOV 1932	1875		ROSS
102	U 5	FEINBERG, ROSS H		20 APR 1933	1852		ROSE
377	J36	FEINBERG, RUDOLPH I		1969	1897	MORDECHAI	GERTRUDE
102	T40	FEINBERG, SELMA		16 MAR 1923	26 OCT 1908	IDA & LOUIS	
125	N101	FEINGOLD, BESSIE		16 MAY 1934	1872		DAVID
447	E13	FEINGOLD, CELIA		3 APR 1933	1868		
102	R40	FEINGOLD, DAVID		2 DEC 1943	7 MAR 1868	SAMUEL & MARY (ROTH)	JENNIE
125	N100	FEINGOLD, DAVID		29 MAR 1926	1859	DAVID & FAYA	BESSIE
102	R39	FEINGOLD, ETHEL SYLVIA		13 MAY 1940	16 FEB 1914	DAVID & JENNIE F	
125	N 92	FEINGOLD, HARRY		21 OCT 1924			
102	R38	FEINGOLD, JENNIE	KATZ	12 OCT 1954	7 JUN 1885		DAVID
433	F24	FEINGOLD, LOUIS		23 MAR 1960	23 JAN 1889		
125	K 53	FEINGOLD, MOLLIE		15 JUN 1910	1898		
102	B16	FEINMAN, BELLE		30 MAY 1975	13 JAN 1895		
101	K 9	FEINSTEIN, BERTHA		8 MAY 1935	1873		
101	I 2	FEINSTEIN, HARRY		26 APR 1990	12 SEP 1903	BERTHA	SARAH
116	BK135	FEINSTEIN, JACOB		15 OCT 1971	15 DEC 1891		SADIE
116	BK134	FEINSTEIN, SADIE		22 JAN 1981	27 MAY 1893		JACOB
101	K 8	FEINSTEIN, SARAH		NDD	1908		HARRY
371	M18	FEISTER, DAVID		1960	1900		
370	D12	FEISTER, FANNIE A		15 JUN 1965	20 MAY 1906	SOLOMON & SARAH	
370	D13	FEISTER, SARAH		24 JUL 1963	20 OCT 1876		SOLOMON
370	D14	FEISTER, SOLOMON J		14 NOV 1936	28 MAY 1874		SARAH
222	AL10	FEITELBERG, HANNA		16 JUL 1925			
222	AL13	FEITELBERG, LOUIS		26 AUG 1983	12 AUG 1897		MOLLY
222	AL12	FEITELBERG, MOLLY	GROSS	1 MAR 1976	25 SEP 1900	ZARA	LOUIS
222	AL11	FEITELBERG, ZARA		3 JUL 1966	1874		
750	I22	FEITELSON, LOUIS		31 JUL 1978	5 JUL 1882		
372	E 2	FELD, BERENICE		18 MAY 1954			SIMON
372	E 4	FELD, ROSE			1892		
372	E 3	FELD, SIMON E		25 JUN 1966			BERENICE

Cem	Row	Name	Maiden Name	DOD	DOB	Parents	Spouse
102	A28	FELDBERG, ANNA		28 MAY 1940	15 NOV 1866		LEVI
102	A27	FELDBERG, LEVI		2 SEP 1935	14 JAN 1862		ANNA
125	L 43	FELDBLUM, BENNIE		9 OCT 1902	1893		JENNIE
125	L 44	FELDBLUM, JENNIE		15 MAR 1908	1892		BENNIE
249	A15	FELDER, BESSIE		22 DEC 1970	22 APR 1900		
372	C 1	FELDMAN, ABRAHAM		12 JAN 1989	10 JAN 1910		LILLIAN
329	D42	FELDMAN, ANNA		17 DEC 1974	17 MAY 1896		HARRY
370	M32	FELDMAN, ANNA		20 DEC 1956			PHILIP
751	H25	FELDMAN, BELLA		1949	1881		ISAAC
105	F19	FELDMAN, BENJAMIN		24 NOV 1978	1890		ROSE
125	F 16	FELDMAN, BLANCHE		1990	1920		MORRIS
106	E18	FELDMAN, EDWARD		18 DEC 1989	22 MAY 1912		
125	H118	FELDMAN, EDWARD		13 JUL 1950	1885	SHLOMO	SALLIE
125	V153	FELDMAN, ELEANOR	KAPLAN	14 JUN 1978	28 APR 1921		
105	H19	FELDMAN, EVA		11 FEB 1957	1877		
123		FELDMAN, HARRY		7 OCT 1961	1893		SAMUEL
329	D43	FELDMAN, HARRY		18 APR 1981	22 FEB 1887		ANNA
447	AA38	FELDMAN, HOWARD M		6 MAY 1985	23 DEC 1937		
751	H24	FELDMAN, ISAAC		17 NOV 1946	1880		BELLA
101	K37	FELDMAN, ISSIE		2 FEB 1910	1908		
105	H16	FELDMAN, JACOB		16 FEB 1941	1866		
107	C15	FELDMAN, JOSEPH	FIELDS	30 APR 1978	21 MAY 1895		
447	A28	FELDMAN, JUDITH M		1983	1940		
125	P 56	FELDMAN, LESTER		23 NOV 1926	1 JUL 1924		
372	C 2	FELDMAN, LILLIAN		22 JUL 1969	17 JUL 1911		ABRAHAM
370	D11	FELDMAN, LIPA		4 DEC 1897		ELIYAHU	
106	E19	FELDMAN, LOUIS R		1971	1904		
125	F 17	FELDMAN, MORRIS		28 AUG 1975	1916		BLANCHE
370	M33	FELDMAN, PHILLIP		16 JUN 1950			ANNA
370	M31	FELDMAN, PHYLLIS		29 DEC 1956			
117	C 3	FELDMAN, RICHARD NOAH		11 FEB 1987	9 OCT 1926		
105	F20	FELDMAN, ROSE		10 JUL 1965	1890		BENJAMIN
391	S48	FELDMAN, ROSE		15 DEC 1944			
125	H117	FELDMAN, SALLIE JULIA		23 SEP 1943	28 AUG 1898	ALEXANDER LEV	EDWARD
105	F21	FELDMAN, SAMUEL		27 OCT 1936	1915	BENJAMIN & ROSE	
105	H18	FELDMAN, SOLON PVT		3 APR 1945	1917	JACOB & EVA (DOBIN)	MARSHA B
330	E27	FELDMAN, WILLIAM		8 FEB 1935	1884		YETTA
330	G56	FELDMAN, YETTA		1929	1888		WILLIAM
125	O 86	FELDSTEIN, ASHER YOUDEL		10 APR 1919	1879	ISAAC SHMUEL & RIVKA RACHEL	
330	F66	FELDSTEIN, JEAN ANITA		6 MAR 1954	4 MAR 1954		
123		FELIX, BENJAMIN		15 SEP 1958	1889		FLORENCE
377	L10	FELLMAN, ISRAEL ELY		1957	1884		
125		FELMAN, (CHILD)		15 SEP 1924	1924		
123		FELMAN, MORRIS		25 OCT 1951	1895		
101	M21	FELMAN, SARAH		25 MAR 1911	1827		
329	A18	FELNER, AARON		18 FEB 1975	15 MAR 1891		GUSSIE
329	A19	FELNER, GUSSIE I		6 OCT 1962	15 FEB 1890		AARON
329	A33	FELNER, IRVING M		14 JAN 1972	15 AUG 1911	AARON & GUSSIE	
329	A13	FELNER, JOSEPH		31 MAR 1962	8 JUL 1913	AARON & GUSSIE	
391	E17	FELSEN, DAVID MEYER		4 AUG 1971	8 JUL 1907	MOSHE	
370	V 9	FELTCORN, ABNER MOSES		4 FEB 1927			JUDITH
370	V10	FELTCORN, JUDITH		17 NOV 1922			ABNER
374	G31	FELTERMAN, ISRAEL IRVING		11 JUL 1983	26 MAR 1923		
374	F31	FELTERMAN, ROY IVAN		17 JUL 1958	11 SEP 1906		
120	G 5	FELTMAN, ALFRED		31 JUL 1992	15 JAN 1912		
392	B14	FELTMAN, ASHER		4 MAY 1917			
113	M57	FENDELL, LILLIAN GERTRUDE		24 MAR 1971	9 JUN 1899		MANNING
113	M56	FENDELL, MANNING		4 OCT 1966	23 MAR 1897		LILLIAN
102	BG25	FENOLD, SAMUEL HASKEL		20 APR 1991	13 MAR 1903		
249	F42	FENROW, MORRIS L		1967	1913		
102	AG136	FENSTER, HARRY H		24 JUL 1981	9 JAN 1922		TILLIE
102	AG135	FENSTER, TILLIE D		24 FEB 1970	1897		HARRY
117	E 2	FEOLA, JANICE K		24 AUG 1988	9 OCT 1919		
391	Y53	FERBER, CYLA		3 NOV 1958	1909	ELIEZER	
371	O26	FERBER, JOSEPH		6 DEC 1968	6 JAN 1910		
105	L51	FERDMAN, ALEXANDER		16 SEP 1989	1 JUL 1923		

Cem	Row	Name	Maiden Name	DOD	DOB	Parents	Spouse
105	M48	FERDMAN, GOLDA		4 JUN 1988	1895		ISAAC
105	M50	FERDMAN, HINDA RISA		1 FEB 1944	1874		SAMUEL
105	M49	FERDMAN, SAMUEL		14 SEP 1960	1895		HINDA
377	F 6	FERN, ESTHER		5 OCT 1961	24 MAR 1890		MAX
377	F 4	FERN, HERBERT M		8 JUL 1976	11 DEC 1907	MAX & ESTHER	
391	R36	FERN, LEAH		29 MAY 1934		MENACHEM MENDEL	
377	F 2	FERN, MAE	LAHN	12 OCT 1973	1 JAN 1901		SAMUEL
377	F 5	FERN, MAX		5 MAY 1965	28 JAN 1886		ESTHER
377	F 3	FERN, SAMUEL		17 SEP 1974	21 JAN 1893		MAE
391	D23	FERN, SAUL		2 MAY 1930		ELI	
377	E 4	FERN, SIDNEY		17 MAR 1970	25 NOV 1899		
377	E12	FETCHER, LEE F		13 JAN 1987	12 JUL 1922		
116	N23	FEUER, ANNA		4 MAY 1991	23 OCT 1918		BENJAMIN
116	N24	FEUER, BENJAMIN		28 MAR 1989	8 JAN 1913		ANNA
101	L 4	FIALKOFF, FRIDA		15 JUL 1983	1899		
101	L 3	FIALKOFF, KAISEL		16 MAR 1966	1904		
113	B60	FIALKOFF, RUBEN		7 SEP 1991	17 JUN 1922		
110	C10	FIALKY, ISRAEL		13 OCT 1962	18 MAR 1905		RACHEL
110	C11	FIALKY, RACHEL	KAPLAN	13 MAR 1960	15 SEP 1906		ISRAEL
102	P32	FICHMAN, ALFRED M		24 OCT 1945	1894		
125	M129	FICHMAN, DORA I		6 OCT 1968	1876		
102	E44	FICHMAN, EFFIE E		11 JAN 1984	10 JUL 1894		MORRIS
102	F52	FICHMAN, MERRILL S		30 JUN 1990	3 JUN 1914		
102	E45	FICHMAN, MORRIS M		1 SEP 1961	15 SEP 1888		EFFIE
102	P33	FICHMAN, MORTON D		20 MAR 1969	1922	ALFRED	ROSLYN
102	P34	FICHMAN, ROSLYN NITA		20 NOV 1982	4 MAR 1924		MORTON
372	F 3	FIEDLER, ANNE M		1967	1891	ISADORE & MARY	
372	F 1	FIEDLER, ISADORE		1943	1858		MARY
372	F 2	FIEDLER, MARY G		1944	1873		ISADORE
447	L31	FIELD, BENJAMIN		11 APR 1986	12 DEC 1906		PAULINE
447	I34	FIELD, CELIA		11 DEC 1946	1889		HARRY
447	L34	FIELD, DORA B		17 JAN 1978			LOUIS
446	B24	FIELD, ELLEN ICE		1918	1886		JACOB
447	G32	FIELD, ERNEST N		29 APR 1969	1918	MORRIS & HELEN	
447	Q 8	FIELD, FRANK EPHRIAM		9 AUG 1942	1876		ROSE
447	O33	FIELD, GERTRUDE		1987	1909		
447	I33	FIELD, HARRY		28 MAR 1951	1879		CELIA
447	G33	FIELD, HELEN		28 MAY 1979	1896		MORRIS
447	Q 6	FIELD, ISRAEL		1 MAR 1959	1907	FRANK & ROSE	
447	N33	FIELD, JACOB		7 JAN 1940	1874		
447	L35	FIELD, LOUIS		10 JUN 1964			DORA
447	G34	FIELD, MORRIS	3 JAN 1955*	24 DEC 1955*	1888		HELEN
447	L30	FIELD, PAULINE		NDD	6 JAN 1911		BENJAMIN
446	B25	FIELD, REBECCA		1918	1908	JACOB & ELLEN	
447	Q 7	FIELD, ROSE		18 AUG 1940	1877		FRANK
433	C16	FIELDING, RAYMOND O		11 SEP 1973	1909	ABRAHAM	
751	E38	FIELDMAN, EDWARD		13 MAY 1928	1899		
751	O 2	FIELDMAN, FRED		31 DEC 1961	1897		
751	I40	FIELDMAN, FREIDA		1 OCT 1941	1869		SAMUEL
751	J37	FIELDMAN, MORRIS		11 JUN 1950	1899		
751	I39	FIELDMAN, SAMUEL		7 FEB 1944	1864		FREIDA
113	M43	FIELDS, HAROLD PAUL DR		13 APR 1972	12 MAY 1925		SYBIL
113	M42	FIELDS, SYBIL	MANDEL	5 JUL 1990	27 FEB 1929		HAROLD
125	S149	FIEN, MARTIN		17 DEC 1940	16 OCT 1897		
102	E35	FIERBERG, ELSIE S		27 AUG 1957	1896		MORRIS
102	AJ57	FIERBERG, FANNIE	MATCHTON	20 NOV 1967	17 OCT 1891		MAURICE
102	AJ58	FIERBERG, MAURICE RAPHAEL	OF BUCHEREST	25 DEC 1945	18 MAY 1889	MENDEL & ROSE (ROTHMAN)	FANNIE
102	E36	FIERBERG, MORRIS A		9 DEC 1948	1894		ELSIE
125	J106	FIERSTEIN, EDWARD		9 AUG 1943	1888	JACOB & REBECCA	
125	M 27	FIERSTEIN, JOSEPH M		3 MAY 1916	28 JAN 1915	JULIUS & REBECCA	
125	J105	FIERSTEIN, LENA		19 MAR 1968	1889		EDWARD
125	G105	FIGHTLIN, ABRAHAM		1 SEP 1946	4 JUL 1901		IDA
125	G106	FIGHTLIN, IDA W		19 MAY 1971	1904		ABRAHAM
751	D17	FILANSKY, JACOB S		31 MAR 1951	20 JAN 1869		SARAH
751	D16	FILANSKY, SARAH M		3 JAN 1957	9 JAN 1878		JACOB
113	N47	FILLER, BETTY		14 FEB 1986	8 JAN 1911		CHARLES

Cem	Row	Name	Maiden Name	DOD	DOB	Parents	Spouse
113	N48	FILLER, CHARLES PHILLIP		14 APR 1970	1 FEB 1905		BETTY
104	N38	FINE, ADA K		15 OCT 1972	1883		MORRIS
110	A31	FINE, DORA		15 FEB 1927	1908		
106	F21	FINE, FRANCES		19 JUL 1976			SAMUEL
370	G46	FINE, JULIUS		1924	1909		
494	B 8	FINE, MAX		23 DEC 1961	15 JUN 1897		TILLIE
104	N37	FINE, MORRIS S		14 DEC 1959	1878		ADA
106	F22	FINE, SAMUEL		12 SEP 1990			FRANCES
494	B 9	FINE, TILLIE		31 MAR 1991	3 JUN 1898		MAX
105	L37	FINESILVER, ANNA		19 APR 1937	1855		
105	L36	FINESILVER, DAVID		28 NOV 1943	1889	ANNA	
105	L34	FINESILVER, PAULINE		5 SEP 1975	1886		WILLIAM
105	L35	FINESILVER, WILLIAM L		29 MAY 1970	1881	ANNA	PAULINE
116	BK 3	FINGER, CELIA		1 JAN 1981	18 NOV 1898		HARRY
116	BK 2	FINGER, HARRY		26 AUG 1961	4 AUG 1905		CELIA
102	AC177	FINK, ELI		25 MAY 1986	1902		MABEL
102	W10	FINK, HARRY		1926	1896	NATHAN & LEAH	ROSE
102	W14	FINK, LEAH		1946	1867		NATHAN
102	AC176	FINK, MABEL		27 MAY 1984	1908		ELI
125	A 13	FINK, MARY		4 MAR 1974	1916		
102	W15	FINK, NATHAN		1943	1868		LEAH
102	W11	FINK, ROSE		1947	1905		HARRY
119	D48	FINKEL, SAUL		1 FEB 1980	9 JUN 1926		
446	B19	FINKELBRAND, JACOB M		27 JAN 1916	16 SEP 1881		
125	M 29	FINKELSTEIN, ABRAHAM		21 JUL 1914	DEC 1905	HENRY & RENA	
125	M113	FINKELSTEIN, DAVID		14 JUL 1928	16 DEC 1884	HENRY & LENA	
125	H 8	FINKELSTEIN, HENRY		18 NOV 1939	1857	DAVID MOSHE & S MARY	LENA
249	L 1	FINKELSTEIN, JACOB		24 SEP 1960	1 JAN 1900		
101	L12	FINKELSTEIN, JENNIE		1 JUN 1913	1840		
125	O165	FINKELSTEIN, JENNIE HELEN		14 JAN 1988	6 AUG 1896		LOUIS
125	H 7	FINKELSTEIN, LENA		8 JAN 1953	1874		HENRY
125	O164	FINKELSTEIN, LOUIS PHILIP		18 APR 1950	20 JAN 1893	HENRY & LENA	JENNIE
447	Y33	FINKELSTEIN, SIDNEY		1987	1910		
125	J188	FINKELSTEIN, ZUNDIE		1986	1898		
119	C26	FINMAN, EDWARD		31 JUL 1992	20 JAN 1909		
125	B 75	FIRESTONE, ABRAHAM W		17 OCT 1985	1912		
125	B 74	FIRESTONE, ANNA GAIER		29 MAR 1958	1913		
125	B 76	FIRESTONE, EVELYN		23 APR 1971	1915		
113	N39	FIRESTONE, MORRIS L		18 APR 1976	19 AUG 1910		
101	C33	FISCHBERG, WILLIAM		3 MAR 1934	1859		
371	AI20	FISCHBURG, JACK		13 SEP 1974	23 DEC 1917	LOUIS	
371	AI19	FISCHBURG, LOUIS		10 SEP 1958	1 OCT 1890		
119	I34	FISCHER, MARTIN		11 NOV 1986	27 JAN 1919		
249	H41	FISCHER, MAX		13 MAR 1987	12 FEB 1905		
751	A37	FISCHER, SAMUEL		22 DEC 1922	1860		
125	O 87	FISHBEIN, JOSEPH		9 OCT 1918	1888	SOLOMON & ROSA (SHULMAN)	
329	E25	FISHBEIN, ROBERT EMANUEL		2 JUL 1991	1 AUG 1906		
101	L34	FISHBERG, ANNA		30 DEC 1939	1872		
121	AA22	FISHBERG, ESSA		20 FEB 1980	15 MAY 1895		
105	C46	FISHBERG, JACK		16 OCT 1964	1913		
103	A30	FISHBERG, SYLVIA	ZIEKY	13 SEP 1989	17 SEP 1915	MAX & ANNA	ABRAHAM
329	B45	FISHBONE, (BABY GIRL)					
374	F17	FISHBONE, ABRAHAM		1922	1865		
374	C50	FISHBONE, ABRAHAM		1982	1916		
391	C 9	FISHBONE, ANNE	SNITKIN	11 JUL 1945	1914	MORDECHAI	
374	D11	FISHBONE, ANNIE		15 JUL 1965	12 MAY 1881		ISADORE
374	C52	FISHBONE, BARNEY		9 JUL 1974	24 OCT 1912		
374	D20	FISHBONE, BERTHA	RESNICK	25 AUG 1964			
374	D16	FISHBONE, CELIA	ROSNER	1947	1887		HARRY
374	D19	FISHBONE, GILBERT		26 MAY 1930	1914		
374	B12	FISHBONE, HARRY		8 APR 1974			
374	D17	FISHBONE, HARRY		NDD	1880		CELIA
374	C16	FISHBONE, HENRIETTA	5 JAN 1982*	26 DEC 1982*	1901		ISADORE
374	D12	FISHBONE, ISADORE		13 DEC 1955	10 FEB 1890		ANNIE
374	C15	FISHBONE, ISIDORE		1983	1897		HENRIETTA
374	D15	FISHBONE, JACOB		17 OCT 1929	1910	ISADORE & ANNIE	

Cem	Row	Name	Maiden Name	DOD	DOB	Parents	Spouse
374	D18	FISHBONE, MAX		26 MAY 1934	1877		
101	B33	FISHER, ALEX		19 OCT 1918	1900		
102	T12	FISHER, ANNA G		5 OCT 1972	1 JAN 1879		
102	N38	FISHER, ANNIE		24 DEC 1968	1883	JENNIE	LOUIS
123		FISHER, BENJAMIN		16 MAR 1952	1894		
494	E 7	FISHER, EVA	10 JAN 1988*	28 DEC 1988*	1909	ISAAC	
371	M 3	FISHER, FANNIE	BOKOFF	5 JUL 1962	1901		
371	M38	FISHER, FRADIE R		1951	1884		
370	F 1	FISHER, HARRY		25 FEB 1947	1869		LENA
125	K182	FISHER, HYMAN		4 JUN 1973			
125	E 44	FISHER, IDA	LEADES	10 JUL 1958	1893	ISAAC & ANNA	
102	N39	FISHER, JENNIE		14 JUL 1956	1866		
370	J24	FISHER, LENA		21 JUL 1937	1879		HARRY
102	T11	FISHER, LOUIS J		30 APR 1940	17 MAR 1878		ANNA
373	C 1	FISHER, MAX		1952	1905		
222	D 6	FISHER, MOLLIE	MILLER	3 MAR 1989			WILLIAM
125	N124	FISHER, MORRIS		6 OCT 1970	1894		RAE
125	N123	FISHER, RAE		18 FEB 1974	1902		MORRIS
370	E 1	FISHER, SAMUEL		15 AUG 1949	15 MAR 1904	HARRY & LENA	
222	AT 9	FISHER, SARAH		4 APR 1980			
102	T10	FISHER, STANLEY D		21 JAN 1979	28 SEP 1909	LOUIS & ANNA	
222	D 5	FISHER, WILLIAM		5 FEB 1977	2 SEP 1901		MOLLIE
376	B19	FISHKIN, ANNIE		1960	1880		ISAAC
376	B21	FISHKIN, EVA		20 NOV 1941	5 FEB 1909	ISAAC & ANNIE	
376	B20	FISHKIN, ISAAC JACOB		7 FEB 1951	1876	CHAIM	ANNIE
376	B22	FISHKIN, LIBBY		7 NOV 1925	25 JUN 1839	MOSHE	
248	N67	FISHKIN, MAITA REESA		16 MAR 1933	1862		
376	D23	FISHKIN, PAUL		15 APR 1975	16 JAN 1914	SAMUEL & SARAH	
376	A25	FISHKIN, PAUL H		1985	1915		
376	D21	FISHKIN, SAMUEL		28 JUL 1950	1 MAR 1883	CHAIM	SARAH
391	E 1	FISHKIN, SAMUEL		13 MAY 1965	1903	ISAAC	
376	D22	FISHKIN, SARAH		2 MAR 1966	15 OCT 1892	JACOB	SAMUEL
123		FISHMAN, ABRAHAM		30 SEP 1945	1908		
110	E24	FISHMAN, ANNA		23 APR 1989	27 OCT 1903		LOUIS
102	X20	FISHMAN, HERMAN		20 MAY 1969	8 JUL 1899		MAYBELLE
104	A37	FISHMAN, JOSEPH H		15 JAN 1990	27 NOV 1904		
114	C26	FISHMAN, LORRAINE K		18 NOV 1988	29 APR 1928		
110	E25	FISHMAN, LOUIS		29 JUL 1990	5 JUL 1905		ANNA
102	AJ142	FISHMAN, MAX		20 FEB 1964	29 SEP 1884		MINNIE
102	X19	FISHMAN, MAYBELLE		3 SEP 1985	1 NOV 1904		HERMAN
102	AJ143	FISHMAN, MINNIE GERTRUDE		18 JAN 1959	6 JUN 1885		MAX
391	ZC75	FISHMAN, MORRIS		20 AUG 1982	17 MAR 1919	ABRAHAM	
110	H28	FISHMAN, MORRIS MARSHALL		11 APR 1927	4 DEC 1925		
102	AG61	FISHMAN, ROSE R	ROSENTHAL	27 NOV 1970	6 MAR 1901		WILLIAM
102	AG60	FISHMAN, WILLIAM M		24 DEC 1969	15 APR 1895	CHAIM & HINDA (STARR)	ROSE
102	AO173	FIXMAN, MIRIAM B		20 SEP 1969	8 JUN 1934		
102	AD119	FLADGER, LOUIS		24 JAN 1963	24 MAY 1893		LYMAN
102	AD118	FLADGER, LYMAN		1978	1895		LOUIS
248	H66	FLAUM, SOLOMON J		6 MAY 1961	12 JUL 1900		
119	D59	FLAXMAN, ANNE		1 OCT 1984	10 JUN 1905		
330	G74	FLAXMAN, HARRY		6 MAY 1952			
119	D60	FLAXMAN, SAMUEL		26 APR 1976	6 MAY 1903		
391	N37	FLAYER, SARAH		22 MAY 1907	1861	ABRAHAM	
377	I30	FLEDER, HILDA	SHERIFF	1960	1924	YEHUDA LEV	
751	E23	FLEISHER, BENJAMIN		13 FEB 1964	15 APR 1893		IDA
751	B 9	FLEISHER, HAROLD		1976	1930	BENJAMIN & IDA	
751	E22	FLEISHER, IDA		7 DEC 1987	4 MAY 1902		BENJAMIN
113	O72	FLEISHMAN, DOROTHY		29 APR 1975	26 FEB 1927		
110	B18	FLEISHMAN, JENNIE		23 JUL 1926	1869		NATHAN
113	O75	FLEISHMAN, MOLLY		5 JAN 1972	10 DEC 1894		
110	B17	FLEISHMAN, NATHAN		3 NOV 1924	1866		JENNIE
121	K11	FLEISHMAN, ROSE		1987	1890		
121	K12	FLEISHMAN, SAMUEL		1948	1890		
125	N121	FLETCHER, FRANCES		2 SEP 1972	12 APR 1902		
110	E 7	FLETCHER, IRVING A		20 JUN 1976	25 SEP 1911		
330	AF 2	FLOM, DAVID		11 AUG 1983	24 NOV 1924		

Cem	Row	Name	Maiden Name	DOD	DOB	Parents	Spouse
102	BB11	FLORENCE, KENNETH SPENCER M		18 JUN 1987	31 DEC 1961		
370	K19	FLORMAN, IDA		1945	1885		
371	AH 2	FLORMAN, ISADORE		21 APR 1975	1904		
371	AH 1	FLORMAN, SAMUEL		10 APR 1963	1880		
125	H 11	FOGELSON, ABBA YEHOSHUA		1 MAY 1921	1869	SAMUEL & MARY	SARAH
125	K152	FOGELSON, DAVID		14 AUG 1982	1 OCT 1897		RAE
125	G 11	FOGELSON, ESTHER		16 AUG 1985	15 SEP 1900		HERMAN
125	J167	FOGELSON, HANNAH		7 AUG 1980	1905		HARRY
125	J168	FOGELSON, HARRY		25 NOV 1960	1899		HANNAH
125	G 10	FOGELSON, HERMAN		2 FEB 1953	1896		ESTHER
125	H 12	FOGELSON, MARY		19 MAR 1978	1892		
125	H 9	FOGELSON, MARY ESTHER		1974	1914		
125	K153	FOGELSON, RAE M		15 MAR 1980	2 APR 1904		DAVID
125	O 64	FOGELSON, ROSIE		1908	1904		
125	G 12	FOGELSON, SADIE E		5 SEP 1985	25 SEP 1900		
125	H 10	FOGELSON, SARAH		26 APR 1933	1871		ABBA
102	AC192	FORMAN, MORRIS H		6 NOV 1985	20 AUG 1902		
102	AC194	FORMAN, SAMUEL		15 JAN 1990	28 SEP 1900		
328	A40	FORST, MAX		27 OCT 1979	1 FEB 1912		
222	AP24	FORSTOT, HARRY		1946	1879		JENNIE
222	AP23	FORSTOT, JENNIE		1956	1886		HARRY
113	N58	FOSTER, DAVID SHERMAN		1 SEP 1964	12 AUG 1944	LOUIS	
248	H76	FOSTER, DORA		1974	1890		MORRIS
111	I2	FOSTER, LENA		6 FEB 1985	12 DEC 1903		MAURICE
113	N59	FOSTER, LOUIS L		8 APR 1976	5 SEP 1906		
111	I2	FOSTER, MAURICE		24 MAR 1982	25 DEC 1894		LENA
115	D16	FOSTER, MICHAEL		1 NOV 1991	9 JUN 1906		
248	I76	FOSTER, MILTON		11 OCT 1934	1915	MORRIS & DORA	
248	H77	FOSTER, MORRIS		1966	1892		DORA
391	C21	FOSTOFSKY, ------					
391	C22	FOSTOFSKY, ------					
391	L25	FOUNTAIN, VERNON R		29 MAY 1937	14 MAY 1937		
370	A27	FOX, ABRAHAM		21 JAN 1910	1867		ZELDA
374	B51	FOX, ANNIE R		18 DEC 1955	18 SEP 1890		WILLIAM
125	V171	FOX, BEATRICE	BRENNER	9 SEP 1976	6 APR 1917		MITCHELL
101	I32	FOX, BENJAMIN		9 MAY 1984	4 NOV 1909		
248	I44	FOX, DINA		9 FEB 1978	6 JUL 1884		
125	V170	FOX, H MITCHELL		13 AUG 1985	5 OCT 1909		BEATRICE
248	I45	FOX, HARRY		22 JUN 1971		DINA	TOBY
125	M104	FOX, LAURA		2 MAY 1956	1876		M. H.
377	Q11	FOX, LILLIAN		24 AUG 1986	11 MAR 1915		MICHAEL
125	M103	FOX, M H		29 OCT 1927	1880		LAURA
377	Q10	FOX, MICHAEL		8 OCT 1974	21 MAR 1910		LILLIAN
371	M26	FOX, MORRIS		13 NOV 1933	14 OCT 1894		SADIE
102	AJ83	FOX, NATHAN		4 OCT 1944	1888		ROSE
102	A88	FOX, NICK		17 FEB 1952			
371	A27	FOX, REUBEN		NDD	22 FEB 1922		RUTH
102	AJ82	FOX, ROSE A		23 OCT 1971	1889		NATHAN
371	A28	FOX, RUTH D		3 MAR 1981	1 JUL 1926		REUBEN
371	M25	FOX, SADIE		16 FEB 1976	10 MAY 1897		MORRIS
119	A64	FOX, SUSAN	SHNEIDER	19 MAY 1988	25 NOV 1898		
248	I46	FOX, TOBY		16 DEC 1991	5 JUL 1905		HARRY
374	B52	FOX, WILLIAM N		24 NOV 1958	1 JAN 1887		ANNIE
370	U25	FOX, ZELDA		6 AUG 1940			ABRAHAM
102	H 7	FRADIN, JULIUS		6 OCT 1958	1884		LILLIAN
102	H 8	FRADIN, LILLIAN	KAVALIER	16 FEB 1973	1895	MAX & IDA	JULIUS
104	J 3	FRAIDOWITZ, REBECCA		18 MAY 1968	1896		
377	F 5	FRANK, ABRAHAM		15 DEC 1963	29 SEP 1889		SARAH
121	H32	FRANK, ANNE I		19 NOV 1987	1913		
103	D3	FRANK, DEBRA SUSAN		20 MAY 1981	20 OCT 1955		
104	A21	FRANK, GERTRUDE G		1988	1904		
447	F19	FRANK, HARRY S MD		1970	1900		PAULINE
370	L 2	FRANK, HYMAN		1945	1853		ROSE
391	E41	FRANK, MANDEL					
447	F18	FRANK, MAX		1944	1869		RAE
447	F20	FRANK, PAULINE T		1978	1917		HARRY

Cem	Row	Name	Maiden Name	DOD	DOB	Parents	Spouse
447	F17	FRANK, RAE STERN	ADLER	1942	1881		
370	K12	FRANK, ROSE		1948	1860		MAX
370	C20	FRANK, SAMUEL		26 AUG 1928	1901	HYMAN & ROSE	HYMAN
102	W19	FRANK, SAMUEL M		1980	1905		
377	D 4	FRANK, SARAH	BECKER	13 MAY 1961	25 DEC 1885		ABRAHAM
123		FRANK, SAUL		22 FEB 1960	1912		
249	C36	FRANKEL, CARLMAN		10 SEP 1983	6 JAN 1909		ESTHER
330	B25	FRANKEL, DAVID		30 AUG 1951	15 JUN 1884		ROSE
249	C35	FRANKEL, ESTHER		NDD	18 NOV 1910		CARLMAN
104	A27	FRANKEL, EUGENE G		8 MAR 1992	12 JAN 1911		LILLIAN
433	J13	FRANKEL, FREDA		NDD	20 NOV 1903		HERMAN
330	B19	FRANKEL, GERTRUDE		21 OCT 1948	17 MAR 1915	MAX & SADIE	
433	J12	FRANKEL, HERMAN M		26 AUG 1980	1 MAY 1898	MOSHE & ROSE	FREDA
249	D31	FRANKEL, HYMAN		27 JAN 1963	17 MAR 1916		
377	O11	FRANKEL, LILLIAN		16 OCT 1952	6 OCT 1865		
104	A28	FRANKEL, LILLIAN R		27 DEC 1984	6 SEP 1912		EUGENE
330	B18	FRANKEL, MAX		5 FEB 1958	1884		SADIE
121	S24	FRANKEL, REBECCA	GOLDMAN	24 NOV 1986	17 JUL 1891		
433	J10	FRANKEL, ROSE		15 DEC 1939	1854	ABRAHAM	ROSE
330	B26	FRANKEL, ROSE YETTA		MAY			DAVID
330	B17	FRANKEL, SADIE		26 MAR 1947	1887		MAX
119	A14	FRANKL, GERTRUDE		12 APR 1992	9 MAY 1915		
222	A 8	FRANKLIN, ALBERT MORRIS		1937	1875		ESTHER
370	Y11	FRANKLIN, C		21 JUN 1907			
248	L41	FRANKLIN, ELLEN	SWARTZ	1985	1942		
222	A 7	FRANKLIN, ESTHER		1943	1877		ALBERT
125	V151	FRANKLIN, GRACE		5 NOV 1986	14 JUL 1904		
222	B 3	FRANKLIN, HERMAN		30 JAN 1980	12 MAY 1915	MARCUS & ROSETTA	
222	AA23	FRANKLIN, IDA		23 MAY 1913	1848		LOUIS
222	AA24	FRANKLIN, LOUIS		24 FEB 1925	1851		IDA
222	B 5	FRANKLIN, MARCUS I		24 FEB 1980	15 OCT 1885		ROSETTA
222	A 4	FRANKLIN, MARCUS IRVING		1965	1897	ESTHER & ALBERT	
392	G13	FRANKLIN, MAX		10 JAN 1945	1873	YECHIEL MICHAEL	SONIA
222	B 6	FRANKLIN, NEUMAN G		3 NOV 1980	17 FEB 1922	MARCUS & ROSETTA	
222	B 4	FRANKLIN, ROSETTA		29 APR 1967	18 JUN 1891		MARCUS
751	N 4	FRANKLIN, SEYMOUR H		1969	1917		
392	H21	FRANKLIN, SONIA		28 APR 1941	1882	YESHIYAHU	MAX
102	AB166	FRAUENGLASS, JACOB JOSEPH		19 AUG 1979	22 NOV 1899		LILLIAN
102	AB167	FRAUENGLASS, LILLIAN	MARCUS	9 MAR 1968	3 APR 1907		JACOB
371	AN11	FREED, MIRIAM	GORDON	1992	1915		
102	AC120	FREED, MORRIS L		28 MAR 1968	1 JAN 1896	SAMUEL & RAISEL	ROSE
102	AC121	FREED, ROSE L	LEVIN	8 APR 1980	16 DEC 1900		MORRIS
392	F15	FREEDHAND, MEYER		21 SEP 1944	1879	MOSHE	
101	B24	FREEDMAN, ABRAHAM		28 APR 1926	1853		
125	N197	FREEDMAN, ALFRED		30 MAR 1972	1900		CHARLOTTE
125	J131	FREEDMAN, ANNA I	LEVINE	4 JUN 1936	1874	MEYER	BENJAMIN
121	J23	FREEDMAN, ANNABEL		1989	1902		
371	K26	FREEDMAN, ARTHUR		16 NOV 1963	17 MAY 1883		MARY
125	J130	FREEDMAN, BENJAMIN		30 MAY 1951	1876		ANNA
104	J35	FREEDMAN, BETTY	ROME	1965	1894		
113	C29	FREEDMAN, BEVERLY	BURSACK	23 SEP 1983	21 MAY 1932		
125	N198	FREEDMAN, CHARLOTTE		20 SEP 1967	1898		ALFRED
102	I48	FREEDMAN, DAVID		1 AUG 1959	1880		IDA
121	J22	FREEDMAN, EDWARD		1989	1898		
104	L52	FREEDMAN, ETHEL		19 JAN 1979	1885		
125	O117	FREEDMAN, GOLDIE		11 FEB 1974	1912		
248	I41	FREEDMAN, HARRY C		16 MAR 1955	1898		
750	E25	FREEDMAN, HENRIETTA		5 OCT 1983	27 DEC 1902		JACK
391	I35	FREEDMAN, HUDA		24 DEC 1924	1853	JOSEPH	MORRIS
102	AF60	FREEDMAN, HYMAN D		18 SEP 1949	15 JAN 1904	PHILIP & ANNA (YEDINSKY)	ROSE
102	I47	FREEDMAN, IDA		5 MAY 1952	1884		DAVID
750	F10	FREEDMAN, JACK		4 MAR 1973	22 JUN 1903		HENRIETTA
125	J 43	FREEDMAN, JACOB		3 JUN 1906	1878		
102	A 3	FREEDMAN, JEROME M		13 MAY 1932	27 MAY 1927		
123		FREEDMAN, JOSEPH D		1 NOV 1948	1892		
125		FREEDMAN, LENA					

Cem	Row	Name	Maiden Name	DOD	DOB	Parents	Spouse
371	K25	FREEDMAN, MARY		12 FEB 1970	2 MAY 1893		ARTHUR
391	C24	FREEDMAN, MORRIS		14 OCT 1939	1849	JACOB	HUDA
330	AA 6	FREEDMAN, RACHEL		16 JUN 1984	15 SEP 1902		
102	AF61	FREEDMAN, ROSE CHORCHES	SCHWARTZ	2 DEC 1991	4 APR 1904		HYMAN
377	U42	FREEDMAN, RUTH	DAVIES	21 JUN 1988	3 SEP 1924		
377	N30	FREEDMAN, SARAH		2 APR 1975	16 MAR 1887	MOSHE	
102	AK245	FREEMAN, BERNARD		20 DEC 1987	6 JUN 1922		
117	C13	FREEMAN, CHAYA		18 JAN 1985			
222	AU 9	FREEMAN, DAVID S		22 DEC 1965	1900		IRENE
102	AI153	FREEMAN, ESTHER	ROSENTHAL	24 JUN 1985	24 DEC 1905		JACOB
391	T56	FREEMAN, GEORGE A		27 APR 1969	1900	SHLOMO ZALMAN	SYLVIA
391	U58	FREEMAN, IDA		1 AUG 1952	1862	CHAIM MOSHE	SAMUEL
222	AU 8	FREEMAN, IRENE F		10 FEB 1985	1906		DAVID
377	Y23	FREEMAN, JACOB		14 JUN 1964	26 JUN 1892	SHLOMO ZALMAN	
391	R53	FREEMAN, JULIUS		26 SEP 1973	5 JUL 1894	SHLOMO ZELIG	
125	N188	FREEMAN, LYDIA R		2 MAY 1993	4 FEB 1910		MORTON
125	N189	FREEMAN, MORTON		17 NOV 1966	1904		LYDIA
391	U57	FREEMAN, SAMUEL		2 DEC 1953	1861	SAMUEL	IDA
391	T57	FREEMAN, SYLVIA H		22 JUN 1975	1915	BER	GEORGE
102	AJ110	FREHM, ANDREW MICHAEL		29 SEP 1973	30 MAR 1946		
391	M38	FREIBERG, ESTHER MOLLIE		27 SEP 1919		MOSHE	
112	C 4	FREIDEN, OSCAR		5 FEB 1982	15 SEP 1904		
371	A41	FREIDLAND, SARAH		26 DEC 1977	1888		
371	AB 9	FREIDMAN, ALAN W		1 MAY 1980	3 MAR 1921		
377	O41	FREIDMAN, BELLE	WEINSTEIN	1960	1903		
101	L16	FREIDMAN, DEBRA		29 MAY 1926	1842		
101	E22	FREIDMAN, FANNIE CLARA		22 JUN 1988	12 MAY 1909		MYER
377	Q22	FREIDMAN, LOUIS B		22 JUL 1967	16 APR 1899		
102	A42	FREIDMAN, MORRIS		24 AUG 1937	1892		
113	A11	FREIFELD, BESSIE		29 APR 1990	14 SEP 1903		
107	B14	FREILICH, FREIDA		22 FEB 1980	1920		
121	I51	FREIMAN, ETHEL E		18 JUL 1989	2 APR 1925		
116	J 5	FREIMAN, HAROLD		21 DEC 1987	10 JAN 1918		RIVA
116	J 6	FREIMAN, RIVA		26 FEB 1991	24 AUG 1917		HAROLD
123		FREUND, BELLE	STERN	1 MAY 1966	26 JUL 1875		
751	O34	FREUND, ERIC		2 FEB 1989	15 MAR 1905		
123		FREUND, SIMON		11 OCT 1971	1877		
119	K23	FREUND, THELMA J		14 APR 1986	21 AUG 1916		
114	A33	FRIED, BESSIE		13 JUL 1991	2 APR 1909		
370	K28	FRIEDBERG, BETSEY		4 AUG 1943	1857		HYMAN
370	P47	FRIEDBERG, HERMAN		NDD	1882	HYMAN & BETSEY	JEANNIE
370	L 8	FRIEDBERG, HYMAN		23 MAY 1941	1854		BETSY
370	P46	FRIEDBERG, JEANNIE		1953	1888		HERMAN
101	B31	FRIEDBERG, LOUIS		17 JAN 1919	1888		
370	R35	FRIEDBERG, MICHAEL		14 APR 1969	20 DEC 1897	HYMAN & BETSEY	TOBIE
370	R36	FRIEDBERG, TOBIE	SOLTZ	27 DEC 1970	22 SEP 1896		MICHAEL
104	I31	FRIEDEBERG, BERT		28 APR 1988	9 JAN 1910		
116	T17	FRIEDLAND, KENNETH ROGER		2 OCT 1977	1934		
370	L 3	FRIEDLAND, SAUL		26 DEC 1944	1890		
101	I 9	FRIEDLANDER, ADOLPH		31 AUG 1973	19 APR 1910		CLARA
101	I10	FRIEDLANDER, CLARA		30 JUN 1980	14 APR 1912		ADOLPH
391	P38	FRIEDLANDER, ROSE		27 MAY 1918		PESACH	
105	A12	FRIEDMAN, ABRAHAM I		23 JAN 1961	17 OCT 1902		
105	O41	FRIEDMAN, ANNA		8 JUN 1980	1899		BENJAMIN
105	G15	FRIEDMAN, ANNA W		10 JAN 1946	1892		
102	AA91	FRIEDMAN, ANNE	GARBER	25 DEC 1961	1894	MOSHE & RIVKE (KESSEL)	
370	H 4	FRIEDMAN, ANNIE		27 SEP 1893			
104	H36	FRIEDMAN, ARLENE		11 MAR 1988	19 JUN 1911		
447	V14	FRIEDMAN, ARTHUR		8 MAR 1963	27 JUL 1903		CORA
447	B17	FRIEDMAN, BELLA		12 FEB 1948	1901		HYMAN
105	O42	FRIEDMAN, BENJAMIN		3 OCT 1976	1891		ANNA
370	T43	FRIEDMAN, BENNIE P		2 DEC 1937	1892		
106	D7	FRIEDMAN, BERTHA S		14 MAR 1979	15 JAN 1903		
433	P 5	FRIEDMAN, BERTRAM J		20 OCT 1991	29 NOV 1911	ZALMAN ELIEZER	
222	AL 1	FRIEDMAN, BESSIE	KAUFMAN	13 JAN 1962	4 JUL 1898		
105	E20	FRIEDMAN, BESSIE		27 FEB 1987	1890		HARRY

Cem	Row	Name	Maiden Name	DOD	DOB	Parents	Spouse
116	AX15	FRIEDMAN, BLANCHE Z		13 APR 1981	23 DEC 1895		SAMUEL
374	C46	FRIEDMAN, CHARLES SAMUEL		19 JAN 1978	1911		
125	E117	FRIEDMAN, CLARENCE		17 DEC 1979	6 DEC 1901		
447	V13	FRIEDMAN, CORA R		24 JAN 1969	19 OCT 1904		ARTHUR
118	A4	FRIEDMAN, DAVID		14 JUN 1989			
371	L27	FRIEDMAN, DOROTHY V		1963	1910		LOUIS
102	S45	FRIEDMAN, ELEANOR	MINTZ	22 JUL 1991	1919		
222	AO 8	FRIEDMAN, ELI		4 FEB 1967	1911	MAX & SARAH	
330	C 9	FRIEDMAN, EVA		11 DEC 1932	1865		ISRAEL
447	H 7	FRIEDMAN, FRIEDA		1 NOV 1931	1877		KIWA
370	P49	FRIEDMAN, HARRIS		1937	1856		RACHEL
105	E21	FRIEDMAN, HARRY		6 NOV 1945	1888		BESSIE
391	U56	FRIEDMAN, HARRY		13 JAN 1968	1879	JUDAH LEV	KATE
222	AD 1	FRIEDMAN, HELEN A		17 NOV 1991	11 APR 1923		
391	ZA65	FRIEDMAN, HERMAN		9 JUL 1984	22 JUN 1912	MOSHE	
222	AT 7	FRIEDMAN, HERMAN		18 JUN 1967	1889		MARY
105	O37	FRIEDMAN, HUDEL		6 SEP 1958	1883		MORRIS
447	B16	FRIEDMAN, HYMAN		17 APR 1980	15 APR 1900		MINNIE, BE
118	B14	FRIEDMAN, IDA		19 OCT 1964			
222	AO 6	FRIEDMAN, IRVING		29 JUN 1948	19 FEB 1908	MAX & SARAH	
116	S17	FRIEDMAN, IRVING MD		11 JUN 1974	18 APR 1905		
330	F38	FRIEDMAN, ISRAEL		5 JUN 1919	1855		EVA
116	AY19	FRIEDMAN, ISRAEL EDWARD		1986	1907		
392	J36	FRIEDMAN, JACOB		1914	1880	ABRAHAM	
102	I42	FRIEDMAN, JOSEPH		2 OCT 1945	1895		
370	Q13	FRIEDMAN, JOSEPH		6 OCT 1971			RACHEL
116	W11	FRIEDMAN, JOSEPH Y		1976	1911		
391	U55	FRIEDMAN, KATE		2 FEB 1951	1877	ABRAHAM	HARRY
447	H 6	FRIEDMAN, KIWA		18 JAN 1954	1874		FREIDA
222	AL 2	FRIEDMAN, LIONELL OVID DR		23 JUN 1972	25 AUG 1931	BESSIE	
248	J20	FRIEDMAN, LOUIS		11 JAN 1916			
371	A44	FRIEDMAN, LOUIS		16 SEP 1985	26 JUN 1908		DOROTHY
377	O24	FRIEDMAN, LOUIS J		11 MAY 1952	10 SEP 1881		SARAH
372	K14	FRIEDMAN, LUDWIG		1943	1889		
222	AT 8	FRIEDMAN, MARY		16 JUN 1981	1899		HERMAN
104	C38	FRIEDMAN, MARY		21 OCT 1958	1916	SARAH	
222	AA 1	FRIEDMAN, MAURINE	RONNER	25 JAN 1980	16 SEP 1929		
222	AO 7	FRIEDMAN, MAX		11 NOV 1949	1884		SARAH
118	B13	FRIEDMAN, MAX		16 DEC 1975			RAE ANN
105	G54	FRIEDMAN, MAX		21 JAN 1992	16 AUG 1906		
392	I39	FRIEDMAN, MICHAEL		6 NOV 1953	1884	ABRAHAM	
447	B15	FRIEDMAN, MINNIE		12 JUN 1986	15 JUL 1902		HYMAN
371	O29	FRIEDMAN, MORRIS		20 NOV 1948	1882		
105	O36	FRIEDMAN, MORRIS		26 DEC 1960	1877		HUDEL
101	E23	FRIEDMAN, MYER I		20 MAR 1992	24 FEB 1906		FANNIE
370	Q12	FRIEDMAN, RACHEL		1 DEC 1960			JOSEPH
105	B19	FRIEDMAN, RACHEL		15 OCT 1950	1886		
370	P48	FRIEDMAN, RACHEL		1943	1857		HARRIS
118	B13	FRIEDMAN, RAE ANN		23 SEP 1954			MAX
391	ZA66	FRIEDMAN, SAM		27 AUG 1985	19 OCT 1912	RAFEAL ALTER	
116	AX16	FRIEDMAN, SAMUEL		4 OCT 1969	4 MAR 1892		BLANCHE
330	B36	FRIEDMAN, SAMUEL		11 FEB 1955	7 SEP 1892		SARAH
391	U60	FRIEDMAN, SAMUEL		27 APR 1989	1909	TVI ZUNDEL	
105	I15	FRIEDMAN, SAMUEL W		13 APR 1939	1881		
119	C48	FRIEDMAN, SANDRA N		2 NOV 1985	24 DEC 1929		
222	AO 5	FRIEDMAN, SARAH		3 JUN 1964	1886		MAX
330	B37	FRIEDMAN, SARAH	BERMAN	12 OCT 1977	27 OCT 1908		SAMUEL
104	C39	FRIEDMAN, SARAH		20 MAY 1951	1892		
377	O25	FRIEDMAN, SARAH		21 OCT 1983	23 DEC 1891		LOUIS
125		FRIEDMAN, SIDNEY		21 APR 1921	1921		
391	U59	FRIEDMAN, VICTOR		NDD	1908	ZVI ZUNDEL	
433	R 3	FRIEDMAN, WILLIAM BAER		8 MAY 1990	24 JAN 1931	JOSEPH	
391	Z76	FRIEDSTEIN, ISADORE		27 APR 1978	1901	ELIEZER	
494	A 5	FRIEND, RACHEL		25 NOV 1955		SAMUEL ZEV	
116	BK40	FRITZ, HYMAN MARK		12 OCT 1969	11 JUL 1950		
116	BV 6	FROMSON, BECKY	SALZBERG	8 DEC 1975	6 APR 1898		ISIDORE

Cem	Row	Name	Maiden Name	DOD	DOB	Parents	Spouse
116	BV 7	FROMSON, ISIDORE		6 JUN 1963	1 JUN 1893		BECKY
116	BV 5	FROMSON, MORRIS FRANK		1977	1916	ISADORE & BECKY	
116	I 9	FROOT, BERNARD		13 APR 1989	18 DEC 1919		
102	AH161	FRUCHTMAN, FANNIE	KOCH	3 APR 1980	5 JAN 1890		JACOB
102	AH162	FRUCHTMAN, JACOB		10 NOV 1972	8 FEB 1915		FANNIE
102	AJ130	FRUCHTMAN, LILLIAN		20 APR 1989	7 MAY 1917		
248	I43	FUCHS, ABRAHAM I		13 JUN 1947	1878		
391	U68	FUCHS, WILLIAM		25 NOV 1983	2 MAY 1902	ISADORE	
125	S184	FUCKS, ADOFINA		15 SEP 1960	1875		JACOB
125	S185	FUCKS, JACOB		17 DEC 1957	1906		ADOLPHINA
125	P142	FUCKS, MICHAEL		20 MAR 1947	25 MAY 1871	ISAAC	
222	AN16	FUHR, CELIA C	COOPERMAN	28 FEB 1968	1892		MAX
222	AN19	FUHR, HELEN C	COHEN	16 SEP 1968	2 OCT 1915	SAMUEL & BESSIE (DOLGIN)	SAMUEL
222	AN15	FUHR, MAX		1 NOV 1953	1886		CELIA
222	AO10	FUHR, MORRIS		30 AUG 1991	1919	MAX & CELIA	
222	AN18	FUHR, SAMUEL		4 MAY 1964	27 NOV 1915	MAX & CELIA	HELEN
222	AN17	FUHR, STEVEN J		4 NOV 1983	1947	SAMUEL & HELEN	
391	S41	FUNK, ANNIE	SHIRB	18 OCT 1957	1870	JUDAH LEV	
371	AI14	FURMAN, AARON		23 APR 1983	1897		MOLLIE
102	AJ 2	FURMAN, CHARLES WILLIAM		14 JUN 1964	1872		SADYE
370	J13	FURMAN, MIRIAM		10 FEB 1934	1900		
371	AI13	FURMAN, MOLLIE		26 JAN 1983	1900		AARON
102	AJ 1	FURMAN, SADYE		5 JUN 1941	1889		CHARLES
494	B 3	FURST, KATHIE		11 JUN 1960	10 JAN 1873	MOSHE	
102	G15	GABERMAN, BEN		4 MAY 1970	1900		
125	R170	GABERMAN, LOUIS		21 MAR 1959	1917		
102	Q18	GABERMAN, LOUIS Y		28 JUN 1939	7 OCT 1892		
104	H31	GAER, ABRAHAM A		23 JAN 1972	1904		ELIZABETH
104	H30	GAER, ELIZABETH		3 JAN 1973	1904		ABRAHAM
102	AI80	GAER, MEYER		17 JAN 1963	10 JAN 1910		
125	S140	GAER, ROSE		27 OCT 1937	1911	RUBIN & SARAH	
101	B32	GAIER, MAX		23 OCT 1918	1891		
102	V17	GALANTIERE, CECILE	LURIE	1930	1863		
102	M51	GALANTIERE, LEWIS		20 FEB 1977	1896		
750	G26	GALINN, SYD F		24 NOV 1989	9 OCT 1899		
391	O33	GALINSKY, BELLE		24 JAN 1908	1884	ZEV	
107	H12	GALINSKY, BERTHA		6 MAR 1986			
102	AJ132	GALINSKY, DAVID MD		27 MAR 1976	1911		
107	I27	GALINSKY, JOSEPH		26 NOV 1984	10 DEC 1908		
113	I58	GALLOW, LOUIS		20 JAN 1990	3 AUG 1913		MIRIAM
113	I59	GALLOW, MIRIAM RUTH		18 DEC 1980	2 MAR 1917		LOUIS
751	A 4	GALTON, DAVID S		23 DEC 1985	22 NOV 1901		
447	U35	GAMER, HARRY R		30 JAN 1978	1912		
377	O42	GANG, PHILIP		1954	1896		
102	J46	GANN, HARRY		14 MAY 1984	5 SEP 1897		MINERVA
102	J47	GANN, MINERVA SYBIL		12 JUL 1981	3 JUN 1902		HARRY
102	A58	GANS, ESTHER	WEXLER	26 JAN 1941	1878		LOUIS
125	K103	GANS, GEORGE L		21 MAY 1958	1893	LOUIS	RAE
125	L 94	GANS, LOUIS		7 AUG 1925	1865		MINNIE
125	L 95	GANS, MINNIE		10 AUG 1946	18 FEB 1868		LOUIS
125	K102	GANS, RACHEL	HURWITZ	7 AUG 1983	1898		GEORGE
125	J 57	GANS, SAMUEL		10 MAR 1904	1824		
248	I67	GANZ, MAX		21 FEB 1914			
104	N53	GARBER, ANNA		31 JUL 1963	1884		ELIAS
104	N52	GARBER, BARNET B		9 SEP 1959	1909	ELIAS & ANNA	
102	Z93	GARBER, BEATRICE	DOLGENAS	18 JUN 1983	1886		ISRAEL
107	B17	GARBER, BETTY S		20 MAY 1985	2 MAY 1904		JACOB
102	AA92	GARBER, DAVID		24 MAY 1970	10 JUL 1886	MOSES & RIVKE (KESSEL)	FLORENCE
104	N54	GARBER, ELIAS		15 SEP 1956	1878		ANNA
102	AA95	GARBER, ESTHER B	BETTIGOLD	12 JAN 1958	1891		HARRY
102	AA96	GARBER, HARRY		15 MAR 1955	1886	MOSES & RIVKE (KESSEL)	ESTHER
102	Z92	GARBER, ISRAEL	OF LUDMIR	19 JAN 1949	15 SEP 1876	MOSES & RIVKE (KESSEL)	BEATRICE
107	B18	GARBER, JACOB A		12 DEC 1985	1 AUG 1902		BETTY
101	A14	GARBER, MITLA RACHEL		3 OCT 1920	1887		SIMON
102	A22	GARBER, NATHAN		7 OCT 1934	1914		
101	A15	GARBER, SIMON SAMUEL		10 JAN 1920	1888		MITLA

Cem	Row	Name	Maiden Name	DOD	DOB	Parents	Spouse
329	B25	GARBICH, MAX		19 MAY 1948	1875		VICTORIA
329	B24	GARBICH, VICTORIA		31 OCT 1968	1884		MAX
751	N 7	GARBUS, FRANK		6 MAY 1967	26 MAY 1885		
751	N 6	GARBUS, GUSSIE		26 JAN 1967	3 DEC 1889		
751	K11	GARBUS, ISADORE		12 JAN 1992	23 DEC 1912		
329	D40	GARDNER, CHARLES		12 OCT 1991	21 AUG 1911		
125	K 25	GARFINKEL, FANNIE		25 JAN 1918	1883		
125	K 24	GARFINKEL, MENDEL		23 DEC 1923			
125	L168	GARFINKLE, MICHAEL		7 APR 1953	22 AUG 1879		
102	AA198	GARIN, JOANN	BERGER	9 MAY 1975	2 DEC 1937		
102	AA197	GARIN, LISA KIM		30 OCT 1987	10 OCT 1960	JOANN	
113	M72	GARMAN, DAVID SETH		26 FEB 1971	31 JUL 1952		
102	CA 1	GARR, EDYTHE		18 DEC 1988	13 DEC 1898		
751	N 1	GARRY, BENJAMIN		18 JAN 1988	27 OCT 1913		
751	N 2	GARRY, FAYE	KAPLAN	21 MAY 1987	12 MAR 1914		
125	A 63	GARTNER, HERMAN		22 MAY 1993	21 FEB 1901		
116	AC25	GARTNER, PAUL		1980	1917		
125	B 61	GARTNER, PAULINE	RUBENSTEIN	31 JUL 1989	25 NOV 1905		HERMAN
750	D25	GARTZMAN, HENRY		7 MAR 1978			SONDRA
750	D22	GARTZMAN, SONDRA		21 JAN 1963	1942		HENRY
107	I23	GASSNER, DAVID		6 MAR 1987	11 AUG 1907		
102	H12	GASSNER, FANNIE S		1 FEB 1966	15 SEP 1904		LEONARD
102	H11	GASSNER, LEONARD M		21 MAR 1945	17 JUN 1904		FANNIE
121	U 6	GASTER, BERTHOLD		24 MAR 1992	29 OCT 1926		
447	O32	GATZEN, MORRIS		19 MAR 1950	1889		ROSE
447	O31	GATZEN, ROSE	FIELD	29 JAN 1975	1890		MORRIS
751	K28	GAULL, NATHAN	4 JAN 1961*	25 DEC 1941*	1885		
101	M18	GAYER, MARION		10 APR 1910	1887		
125	O163	GEARTNER, FANNIE		18 JAN 1950	1878		
119	D65	GEETER, GLADYS	MILLER	16 JUL 1968	21 NOV 1914		
102	AI200	GEETER, REBECCA	MERANSKI	11 DEC 1990	1 NOV 1906		
105	D31	GEFFNER, ALBERT		18 OCT 1977	1913		
447	Z37	GEIGES, EDWIN JAY		1971	1934		
125	M181	GEISINGER, BERNARD		11 JUL 1968	15 APR 1895		MINNE
125	S141	GEISINGER, DOROTHY		12 DEC 1937	1912		
125	M180	GEISINGER, MINNIE		30 JAN 1980	1906		BERNARD
125		GEISINGER, RUTH		10 OCT 1918	4 OCT 1917	ISADORE	
392	C23	GEISMAN, LOUIS		2 MAR 1971	1893		NESHA
392	C22	GEISMAN, NESHA		10 JUL 1962	1893		LOUIS
102	AJ183	GEITHEIM, LILLIAN		30 JUL 1980	1896		MAX
102	AJ182	GEITHEIM, MAX		19 JAN 1975	1896		LILLIAN
329	C27	GELBERT, HERSCHEL		30 APR 1966	1880		
329	E 7	GELBERT, NATHAN		27 MAY 1992	21 APR 1901	HERSCHEL	ROSE
329	E 8	GELBERT, ROSE		13 AUG 1981	11 JUN 1900		NATHAN
370	J43	GELFAND, FANNIE		12 APR 1932			
370	J45	GELFAND, ISAAC		12 MAR 1983			SARAH
370	J46	GELFAND, SARAH		7 SEP 1888			ISAAC
102	AD200	GELLER, JACOB		16 JUN 1966	1880		
330	G46	GELLER, ROSE		7 APR 1920	1880		
101	J38	GELLERMAN, JACK		1 APR 1985	1903		YETTA
101	J37	GELLERMAN, YETTA		29 OCT 1977	1909		JACK
751	D 5	GELLERT, ANNA		11 JUN 1957	1887		
330	B 9	GELLERT, JENNIE		26 JUL 1947	1892		SAMUEL
330	B10	GELLERT, SAMUEL		1 AUG 1956	1882		JENNIE
116	BV14	GELLIN, CHARLES		14 JAN 1984	20 FEB 1918		
116	BV11	GELLIN, SAMUEL		25 DEC 1991	26 SEP 1920		
433	F25	GELLMAN, (BABY BOY)		31 MAR 1966			
101	I24	GELMAN, BEILA		24 FEB 1978	25 DEC 1901		ISRAEL
102	AD100	GELMAN, HARRY		11 DEC 1947	19 APR 1896	MOSES & REBECCA (LAMBERT)	
101	I25	GELMAN, ISRAEL		22 FEB 1979	6 MAY 1898		BEILA
102	AD104	GELMAN, JOSEPH		10 FEB 1953	19 DEC 1892	MOSES & REBECCA (LAMBERT)	SADIE
102	AD98	GELMAN, MORRIS D	OF GRODNO	4 OCT 1929	1865	AVRAM & BATIA	REBECCA
102	AD99	GELMAN, SAMUEL		12 JAN 1941	1881	MOSES & REBECCA (LAMBERT)	
391	O42	GELMAN, SARAH K		15 MAR 1976	26 AUG 1894	HERAM	
375	F 7	GELTZER, FRANCES		7 JUN 1993	12 MAR 1918	SAMUEL	IRVING
375	F 8	GELTZER, IRVING		20 AUG 1978	28 JUL 1918	ISRAEL	FRANCES

Cem	Row	Name	Maiden Name	DOD	DOB	Parents	Spouse
329	F19	GENDLER, ISRAEL		5 AUG 1987	7 JAN 1909		OLGA
329	F20	GENDLER, OLGA		20 FEB 1987	12 JUN 1912		ISRAEL
750	E10	GENSBERG, BERNARD		7 MAR 1984	16 AUG 1911		
392	D49	GENSBURG, EMANUEL		20 JAN 1979	30 SEP 1901	ASHER	
104	L50	GER, ABRAHAM		11 APR 1983	1912		BELLE
104	L49	GER, BELLE L		28 SEP 1985	1914		ABRAHAM
103	D28	GER, ISADORE		8 FEB 1991	17 NOV 1910		
102	AH10	GERBER, BERTHA	SPIELMAN	12 OCT 1991	7 APR 1899		
121	K10	GERBER, IDA	DOIGAN	2 DEC 1991	8 FEB 1910		
102	AI10	GERBER, JACOB OSIAS		1940	20 APR 1890		
104	E31	GERBER, MARY	EPSTEIN	27 MAY 1973	30 APR 1885		
123		GERBER, MILTON A		3 DEC 1944	1913		
102	BF12	GERBER, NORMAN M		27 FEB 1990	7 DEC 1934		
119	F32	GERE, IRWIN		12 JAN 1973	15 MAR 1919		
119	H39	GERE, MEYER		23 JAN 1977	18 SEP 1907		
119	I39	GERE, NATHANIEL		16 JUN 1985	1914		
119	I40	GERE, SARAH		4 DEC 1979	1915		
119	H47	GERE, WILLIAM H		21 AUG 1992	13 APR 1945		
121	J45	GERMAIN, ESTHER		29 APR 1978	14 JUL 1900		
751	H 8	GERMAN, JOSEPH		1 OCT 1990	22 AUG 1920		
391	V68	GEROFSKY, SAMUEL		13 APR 1987	7 JUL 1916	ABRAHAM	
104	J11	GERSHBERG, ELIZABETH		14 JUN 1959	1898		ISADORE
104	J10	GERSHBERG, ISADORE		5 JAN 1960	1897		ELIZABETH
116	H30	GERSHELIS, HENRY		10 MAR 1989	20 NOV 1915		
101	B40	GERSHENFELD, HARRY		24 FEB 1913	1891		
119	K25	GERSHENOWITZ, ABRAHAM		8 FEB 1985	14 APR 1907		
119	K26	GERSHENOWITZ, EDWARD L		13 AUG 1984	12 JUN 1940	ABRAHAM	
105	M32	GERSHMAN, BENJAMIN		29 FEB 1966			
105	M31	GERSHMAN, CHARLES		10 FEB 1980	25 FEB 1904		EVELYN
105	M30	GERSHMAN, EVELYN		2 APR 1990	12 DEC 1907		CHARLES
105	M27	GERSHMAN, HARRY		29 DEC 1986	1897		MINNIE
105	M29	GERSHMAN, JENNIE		6 NOV 1963	1892		MORRIS
105	M26	GERSHMAN, MINNIE		26 OCT 1988	1900		HARRY
105	M28	GERSHMAN, MORRIS		21 MAY 1955	1884		JENNIE
392	H28	GERSHMAN, ROSE M	WATCHINSKY	8 MAR 1937	2 OCT 1900	AARON TZVI	
392	D22	GERSHOWITZ, BERTHA		26 JUL 1971	1883	BAER	SOLOMON
392	D21	GERSHOWITZ, SOLOMON		29 JAN 1959	1881	PINCHUS	BERTHA
392	A15	GERSHOWITZ, SYDNEY		7 MAY 1989	11 NOV 1915	SOLOMON & BERTHA	
370	S 9	GERSHUNI, IDA		1941	1867		PHILIP
370	A22	GERSHUNI, PHILIP		6 FEB 1907	1867		IDA
116	AV16	GERSTEIN, BESSIE		13 SEP 1970	1886		HYMAN
101	B 2	GERSTEIN, GUSSIE		27 NOV 1923	1848		
116	AV17	GERSTEIN, HYMAN		28 MAR 1964	1885		BESSIE
102	AA19	GERSTEN, CELIA	KAUFMAN	9 MAY 1957	1887		SAMUEL
330	H51	GERSTEN, DEBORAH		20 APR 1950	1870	MORRIS D & MINNIE (COHEN)	SELIG
329	D47	GERSTEN, ETTIE	LEVSON	1975	1905		JOSEPH
102	AA15	GERSTEN, HAROLD		23 NOV 1988	14 JUL 1927	SAMUEL & CELIA (KAUFMAN)	
330	H 5	GERSTEN, HYMAN		26 SEP 1914	1905	SELIG & DEBORAH	
329	D46	GERSTEN, JOSEPH		1972	1907		ETTIE
102	AC19	GERSTEN, RAYMOND		13 APR 1944	1916	SAMUEL & CELIA (KAUFMAN)	
102	AA18	GERSTEN, SAMUEL		18 MAY 1953	24 MAY 1882	ISAAC & FREDA	CELIA
330	H41	GERSTEN, SELIG		23 MAR 1943	1871		DEBORAH
330	A 8	GERTNER, GERTRUDE		18 NOV 1958	1901		SOLOMON
330	A 9	GERTNER, SOLOMON		2 MAR 1973	1896		GERTRUDE
329	B18	GETZOFF, IDA		22 FEB 1963	19 AUG 1893		LOUIS
329	B19	GETZOFF, LOUIS		31 DEC 1957	12 MAY 1892		IDA
447	S 8	GEWIRTZ, GLEN ALLAN		25 AUG 1970	11 APR 1958		
102	D37	GIBER, ALEX		6 APR 1946	14 SEP 1887		FANNIE
102	D38	GIBER, FANNIE		6 JAN 1955	28 JUL 1888		ALEX
102	AJ41	GIBER, PEARL	ROSOFF	3 OCT 1958	13 JAN 1914		
248	G54	GIBSON, ANNA M		1977	1884		
371	K 3	GILBERT, BARRY		1974	1910		IDA
371	K 4	GILBERT, IDA		1982	1900		BARRY
121	H18	GILBERT, LAWRENCE B		25 APR 1975	1936		
447	E24	GILFIX, IRMA	SCHWARTZ	21 SEP 1965	1898		JOSEPH
447	E25	GILFIX, JOSEPH W		1 AUG 1976	1901		IRMA

Cem	Row	Name	Maiden Name	DOD	DOB	Parents	Spouse
750	F27	GILLER, GUSSIE	LEBON	29 AUG 1971	16 APR 1897		MAX
750	F25	GILLER, MAX		27 JUL 1969	25 APR 1897		GUSSIE
119	C46	GILLMAN, IRVING L		6 AUG 1985	2 MAR 1922		
377	F34	GILMAN, CLARA	STERN	3 NOV 1980	18 DEC 1882	AMENDEL	NATHAN
330	E34	GILMAN, DAVID		10 APR 1937	1889	MOSES & REBECCA	
377	E38	GILMAN, EDNA	GRUBNER	1978	1914	MOSHE & HINDA	LAWRENCE
377	F30	GILMAN, GEORGE		20 MAR 1988	15 DEC 1904	NATHAN & CLARA	RUTH
329	B 1	GILMAN, HARRY		22 JUN 1968	25 MAY 1881		SARAH
329	D 4	GILMAN, HELEN		16 NOV 1969	20 JUN 1914		
115	A40	GILMAN, HERBERT		12 JUL 1990	25 DEC 1924		
391	F 4	GILMAN, JACOB			1940	1888	HARRY	
370	A34	GILMAN, JACOB M		8 JUL 1906	1883		
377	E37	GILMAN, LAWRENCE M		1991	1909		EDNA
125	G131	GILMAN, MANYA		10 AUG 1937	1865	ABRAHAM & MALKA	MICHAEL
377	E33	GILMAN, MARTIN JOHN		21 FEB 1979	18 NOV 1907	NISAN	
125	G130	GILMAN, MICHAEL		27 SEP 1952	1866		MANYA
125	G129	GILMAN, MOLLIE		26 MAR 1948	1900	MICHAEL & MINNIE	
330	F16	GILMAN, MOSES		18 MAY 1919			REBECCA
125	F131	GILMAN, MOYER		1989	1890		
377	F33	GILMAN, NATHAN		2 APR 1978	22 FEB 1879	MOSHE	CLARA
377	F35	GILMAN, PATRICIA A		1 MAR 1983	21 AUG 1914	NATHAN & CLARA	
330	G58	GILMAN, REBECCA		28 MAR 1930	1856		MOSES
377	F31	GILMAN, RUTH FERN		3 MAR 1986	15 AUG 1909		GEORGE
329	B 2	GILMAN, SARAH		29 JUN 1969	14 JUN 1886		HARRY
222	AJ19	GILMAN, USHER		24 JUL 1923	1865		
102	Z99	GILSTON, LEAH		24 MAR 1967	1892		MORRIS
102	AA99	GILSTON, LINA	GROSS	15 MAY 1990	10 FEB 1921		
102	Z100	GILSTON, MORRIS		14 NOV 1974	1882		LEAH
115	A 4	GINEWSKY, BELLE	YOUNG	17 OCT 1990	23 JAN 1918		
102	R20	GINEWSKY, FRANCES K		11 AUG 1980	3 APR 1883		JULIUS
102	R19	GINEWSKY, JULIUS H		10 JAN 1940	21 AUG 1880		FRANCES
102	R23	GINEWSKY, SYLVIA	LEAF	18 MAR 1973	5 NOV 1917		THEODORE G
433	C20	GINNIS, BEATRICE		1 JAN 1984	22 DEC 1915	JACOB	SAMUEL
433	C19	GINNIS, SAMUEL		21 NOV 1973	24 JUN 1905	AARON	BEATRICE
125	S150	GINSBERG, ANNA		22 AUG 1940	1883		
110	E 8	GINSBERG, BENJAMIN		4 DEC 1976			IDA
125	H157	GINSBERG, DAVID		3 JUL 1970	1910		
125	Q144	GINSBERG, EDWARD		25 JUN 1944	1882	ISAAC & HANNAH CHAYA	SARAH
125	O112	GINSBERG, ELIZABETH		3 DEC 1984	1904		PHILIP
116	BX79	GINSBERG, GOLDIE		5 APR 1993			GOLDIE
377	W 9	GINSBERG, GUSSIE	BRODY	20 SEP 1980	1892	REUBEN	LOUIS
125	L132	GINSBERG, HINDA		22 OCT 1931	15 MAY 1867		
116	T25	GINSBERG, HYMAN		10 APR 1978	10 JUL 1909		ROSE
125	K141	GINSBERG, HYMAN		8 DEC 1931	1869		
110	E 9	GINSBERG, IDA	KOSTIN	23 NOV 1990		JACOB & GITTEL LEAH (DION)	BENJAMIN
101	M36	GINSBERG, ISAAC H		5 NOV 1931			
125	D 13	GINSBERG, JACOB		14 APR 1955	1874		MAY
391	Y50	GINSBERG, JOSEPH		22 FEB 1958	1910	SHALOM	
101	C40	GINSBERG, JOSEPH		28 JUL 1929	1893		
750	A20	GINSBERG, JUDITH B		29 NOV 1989	15 DEC 1937		
101	L24	GINSBERG, LENA		21 MAR 1918	1888		
377	W10	GINSBERG, LOUIS		30 NOV 1961	1886	JOSEPH	GUSSIE
125	D 15	GINSBERG, MARCELLI		18 OCT 1968	1901	JACOB & MAY	
116	S 5	GINSBERG, MAURICE		18 JUN 1975	18 DEC 1914		
125	D 14	GINSBERG, MAY		19 SEP 1952	1876		JACOB
377	V10	GINSBERG, NORMAN M		8 JUN 1965	1921	YEHUDA LEV	
125	O113	GINSBERG, PHILIP		17 NOV 1973	1903		ELIZABETH
102	AC 1	GINSBERG, RACHEL		18 JUL 1946	1884		SAMUEL
116	T26	GINSBERG, ROSE		5 JUL 1987	5 APR 1912		HYMAN
102	AC 2	GINSBERG, SAMUEL		21 MAY 1936	1880		RACHEL
101	B44	GINSBERG, SAMUEL		23 APR 1946	1885		
125	Q145	GINSBERG, SARAH W		19 AUG 1944	SEP 1889	YOSEF LEV & HAMI PITEL	EDWARD
116	BX80	GINSBERG, SIMON LEONARD		13 MAR 1976	19 SEP 1898		SIMON
125	N161	GINSBERG, SOLOMON		27 APR 1951	DEC 1864		
125	e1-30	GINSBERG, SUSAN L		10 OCT 1950	30 SEP 1950		
119	B 8	GINSBURG, BEATRICE	FLITT	20 MAY 1981	4 DEC 1914		

Cem	Row	Name	Maiden Name	DOD	DOB	Parents	Spouse
125	L104	GINSBURG, EVA		1930	1864		
125	O175	GINSBURG, FANNIE		16 FEB 1964	1884		MICHAEL
125	P184	GINSBURG, FRANK		20 FEB 1963	1890		REBECCA
125	O166	GINSBURG, LOUIS		2 JUL 1950	1860		YETTA
125	O174	GINSBURG, MICHAEL		8 OCT 1981			FANNIE
392	F11	GINSBURG, MURRY J		1975	1909	NACHEM	
102	CA 4	GINSBURG, NATHAN A		18 APR 1961	1906		
125	P183	GINSBURG, REBECCA		27 MAR 1983			FRANK
102	C33	GINSBURG, SOPHIE D		3 MAR 1974	4 JAN 1893		
102	C31	GINSBURG, SOPHIE F		2 FEB 1983	27 NOV 1899		
446	C41	GINSBURG, WILLIAM		1908	1863		
377	C14	GIPSTEIN, LOUIS		7 OCT 1972	2 MAR 1908	SAMUEL & REBECCA	
377	D14	GIPSTEIN, MORRIS S		19 MAR 1963	4 FEB 1901	SAMUEL & REBECCA	
377	D15	GIPSTEIN, REBECCA	FALK	2 SEP 1977	1 MAY 1881		SAMUEL
377	D16	GIPSTEIN, SAMUEL		29 JUN 1967	15 AUG 1877		REBECCA
222	AR 6	GIRSHICK, HYMAN		11 MAY 1960			ROSE
222	AR 7	GIRSHICK, ROSE		31 MAR 1954			HYMAN
330	E19	GITLEN, ABRAHAM D		22 FEB 1931	1859		
222	AU 5	GITLEN, GERTRUDE		25 AUG 1969	1900		
116	BX73	GITLEN, HERBERT		8 MAY 1993			YETTA
330	G59	GITLEN, HILDA		29 MAR 1932			ISIDORE
330	E20	GITLEN, ISIDORE		3 FEB 1947			HILDA
222	I13	GITLEN, MORRIS		18 AUG 1943	1858		YETTA
116	BX72	GITLEN, YETTA	SMITH	2 OCT 1980	5 MAY 1896		HERBERT
222	I14	GITLEN, YETTA		11 FEB 1951	1854		MORRIS
377	O35	GITLIN, (BABY BOY)		22 OCT 1939	17 OCT 1939		
102	AA193	GITLIN, BERNARD E		27 FEB 1986	29 JUL 1907		
330	E45	GITLIN, CELIA		5 JAN 1940	1856		
392	J48	GITLIN, DORA E		17 MAY 1963	1884	GEDALIAH	HYMAN
392	J47	GITLIN, HYMAN I		6 JAN 1947	1883	JOSEPH	DORA
119	B15	GITLIN, MARY		2 JAN 1991	18 DEC 1907		
329	C48	GITLIN, MAX L		29 JUL 1967	2 FEB 1894	SAMUEL & SARAH	
329	B10	GITLIN, SAMUEL		4 MAY 1953	1873		SARAH
329	B11	GITLIN, SARAH		31 JAN 1960	1869		SAMUEL
330	D41	GITLIN, SOPHIE		12 AUG 1958	1902		
329	B44	GITLIN, SUSANA B		9 FEB 1954	16 OCT 1953		
125	N 82	GITLITZ, BASHE		6 JAN 1923	1862	MICHAEL & LIBBY	
125	AB118	GITLITZ, BELLA		30 MAR 1982	1902		ERWIN
125	AA115	GITLITZ, CELIA		1990	1900		
125	AB123	GITLITZ, ERWIN		25 NOV 1979			BELLA
125	AA117	GITLITZ, GOLDIE		9 APR 1981	1890		HARRY
125	AA116	GITLITZ, HARRY		24 AUG 1977	1891		GOLDIE
125	AB117	GITLITZ, LOUIS		16 OCT 1978	1888		MILLIE
125	AB116	GITLITZ, MILLIE	HOROWITZ	29 JUL 1982	1904		LOUIS
125	J169	GITLOVITZ, DOROTHY		NDD			
125	O160	GITLOVITZ, HYMAN		19 JAN 1963	15 JUL 1886		IDA
125	O159	GITLOWITZ, IDA		31 JUL 1949	30 SEP 1886		HYMAN
125	D 64	GITTLEMAN, EDITH		4 FEB 1994			
125	C 55	GITTLEMAN, IRVING		3 JUL 1959	1915		
125	D 61	GITTLEMAN, MAX		30 NOV 1965	1882		SADIE
125	D 62	GITTLEMAN, SADIE		6 JAN 1959	1885	HARRY	MAX
102	P10	GLADSTEIN, ROSE	POSNER	1975	1883		WILLIAM
102	P11	GLADSTEIN, WILLIAM		1977	1882		ROSE
105	D20	GLADSTONE, ARTHUR		1 NOV 1947	1889		SOPHIE
102	A24	GLADSTONE, BETTY	ROSENBERG	8 APR 1935	6 JUN 1903		
119	K46	GLADSTONE, MOE		29 APR 1984	17 NOV 1905		
119	K45	GLADSTONE, MOLLYE		16 NOV 1989	23 MAR 1913		
105	D19	GLADSTONE, SOPHIE		29 MAY 1983	1 JUN 1898		ARTHUR
127	P	GLAEBERMAN, BARBARA		5 DEC 1989	22 MAY 1940		
113	N24	GLAIBER, MAX K		22 NOV 1962	20 FEB 1909		SALLY
113	N25	GLAIBER, SALLY	HALPERN	9 MAY 1977			MAX
102	AE67	GLANZ, BESSIE	RUFFKESS	2 JAN 1970	17 DEC 1883		JOSEPH
102	AE69	GLANZ, ESTHER		21 APR 1950	7 APR 1909		
102	AE66	GLANZ, JOSEPH		18 MAR 1968	18 DEC 1883		BESSIE
102	AF65	GLANZ, SADIE		28 MAY 1981	24 DEC 1906		
102	BB 6	GLASER, RUTH		20 FEB 1986	3 JUN 1896		

Cem	Row	Name	Maiden Name	DOD	DOB	Parents	Spouse
248	K64	GLASKIN, MOLLIE		12 OCT 1960	1878		
248	D42	GLASS, BLIMA		1 FEB 1940	1866		RAPHAEL
330	A23	GLASS, DAVID		30 JAN 1961	1 APR 1908	MAX & LENA	
249	C41	GLASS, GUSSIE		17 JUL 1951	10 MAR 1884		LOUIS
330	A33	GLASS, LENA		20 APR 1969	1884		MAX
249	C40	GLASS, LOUIS G		1955	1889		GUSSIE
330	A32	GLASS, MAX		27 NOV 1963	1880		LENA
248	D41	GLASS, RAPHAEL		17 OCT 1935	1863		BLIMA
330	G32	GLASS, REBECCA	LEVIN	1 AUG 1911	1879		
330	H 6	GLASS, ZOLMAN		26 AUG 1909	9 JAN 1902	MAX & LENA	
391	Y52	GLASSBERG, BENJAMIN		17 FEB 1967	1901	ISAAC MEYER	
391	M41	GLASSBERG, EMMA		12 JUL 1941	1863	YEHUDA LEV	ISAAC
391	D19	GLASSBERG, ISAAC M		17 MAY 1935	1853	AARON ZEV	EMMA
377	L31	GLASSENBERG, CHARLES		1945	1892		
105	J60	GLASSMAN, ABRAHAM		26 AUG 1987	25 MAR 1890		GOLDIE
111	4	GLASSMAN, AMY		5 JAN 1981	16 AUG 1955		
105	J56	GLASSMAN, ANNA	BRASS	11 JUN 1983	15 MAY 1904		MAX
105	J44	GLASSMAN, ANNA S		1 MAR 1968	15 MAY 1898		HARRY
105	H51	GLASSMAN, BARNEY JEROME		11 FEB 1974			FANNY
377	N28	GLASSMAN, BERNARD		8 OCT 1965	22 DEC 1893	ZENDEL	EVELYN
105	H42	GLASSMAN, DAVID		8 JUN 1963	1908		
102	J41	GLASSMAN, ESTHER P		16 NOV 1973	27 MAR 1896		GEORGE
377	N29	GLASSMAN, EVELYN		25 DEC 1964	15 SEP 1892	CHAIM ELIYAHU	BERNARD
105	H52	GLASSMAN, FANNIE	HAVERBACK	27 FEB 1970			BARNEY
105	J50	GLASSMAN, FANNIE K		22 JUL 1983	15 APR 1898		JACOB
102	J40	GLASSMAN, GEORGE M		NDD	22 FEB 1891		ESTHER
105	J61	GLASSMAN, GOLDIE S		8 MAY 1978	27 JUN 1897		ABRAHAM
105	J43	GLASSMAN, HARRY I		9 MAR 1950	21 MAR 1888		ANNA
119	F30	GLASSMAN, IDA		9 OCT 1973	1882		
105	J14	GLASSMAN, IDA S		17 DEC 1941	1864		
105	J 5	GLASSMAN, INFANT					
105	J49	GLASSMAN, JACOB		25 MAR 1981	7 FEB 1891		FANNIE
119	I31	GLASSMAN, LENA R		13 DEC 1986	27 APR 1907		
111	4	GLASSMAN, LEON		NDD	29 AUG 1920		
102	F45	GLASSMAN, LOUIS H		1 FEB 1978	17 AUG 1912		
105	J57	GLASSMAN, MAX		25 JUN 1990	15 AUG 1902		ANNA
105	I44	GLASSMAN, MOLLY		7 SEP 1989	1897		
111	4	GLASSMAN, NANCY	MEMSER	NDD	25 DEC 1925		
105	H43	GLASSMAN, SAM		16 AUG 1961	1884		
105	I43	GLASSMAN, SOPHIE		16 MAR 1965	1889		
391	M54	GLATER, BERTHA		3 SEP 1993	31 MAY 1903	ISSAC	
391	M55	GLATER, FRIEDA		4 MAR 1990	20 OCT 1912	ISAAC	
101	A25	GLATER, HYMAN		6 MAY 1914	1880		
391	B 8	GLATER, IRENE		1955		PAULINE & JOSEPH	
391	L50	GLATER, ISADORE		21 JAN 1948	1880	SHALOM	
391	E 5	GLATER, JOSEPH		31 MAY 1971	1890	SOLOMON	PAULINE
391	D21	GLATER, LOUIS		15 FEB 1932	1863	SHALOM	SARAH
391	ZC68	GLATER, MARION		29 MAY 1980	1902	ELIYAHU	SAMUEL
391	E 4	GLATER, PAULINE	GOLD	5 DEC 1964	1890	YEHUDA LEV	JOSEPH
391	L51	GLATER, ROSE		12 MAY 1970	1883	ISAAC	
391	ZC69	GLATER, SAMUEL		25 JAN 1976	1897	SHLOMO	MARION
391	L42	GLATER, SARAH R		6 JAN 1936	1865	ISAAC JACOB	LOUIS
330	E17	GLAUBINGER, ELIYAHU		24 MAR 1926	1879		
331		GLAUBINGER, JOSEPH		3 JAN 1913			
110	E36	GLAUBMAN, BERNARD LEON		21 DEC 1979	1915		
110	F 5	GLAUBMAN, HENRY MITCHELL MD		29 MAR 1987	1904		
110	B32	GLAUBMAN, ISADORE CHARLES		3 OCT 1959	1881		
110	B29	GLAUBMAN, ROSE	BELDER	18 DEC 1947			
110	F 6	GLAUBMAN, WILLIAM MD		13 MAR 1987	1910		
447	Q27	GLAZER, ISRAEL HARRY		27 NOV 1964	1887		SARAH
374	A 4	GLAZER, LILLIAN		26 DEC 1963			
105	E29	GLAZER, MARCIA	FELDMAN	30 AUG 1990	27 OCT 1913		
374	G17	GLAZER, MOSHE YOSEPH		29 JUN 1913			
447	Q26	GLAZER, SARAH GITTEL		25 JAN 1955	1885		ISRAEL
119	E 4	GLAZIER, ANNA		16 JUN 1989	16 SEP 1905		
119	E 3	GLAZIER, BENJAMIN		4 JAN 1977	19 DEC 1904		

Cem	Row	Name	Maiden Name	DOD	DOB	Parents	Spouse
102	AH207	GLAZIER, DAVID		30 JUN 1972	12 AUG 1906		
116	V14	GLAZIER, DOROTHY		27 APR 1984	21 DEC 1909		RUTH
116	V13	GLAZIER, JULIUS		19 MAY 1979	12 SEP 1908		JULIUS
102	AH208	GLAZIER, RUTH		1 MAY 1991	8 FEB 1912		DOROTHY
112	E 2	GLECKMAN, LILLIAN H		1992	1907		DAVID
112	E 3	GLECKMAN, LOUIS D		1990	1900		LOUIS
112	E19	GLECKMAN, WADE HARRISON		27 JAN 1972	29 JAN 1968		LILLIAN
123		GLICK, EDWARD		27 SEP 1948	1892		
371	N32	GLICK, ISAAC		11 MAY 1952	1892		
447	V21	GLICK, MARY		27 FEB 1928	1864		
447	B21	GLICKMAN, HARRY		1985	1905		
447	B20	GLICKMAN, LILLIAN		1987	1905		LILLIAN
374	G 6	GLICKSMAN, ANNIE		5 AUG 1918	1891		HARRY
106	D39	GLICKSTEIN, ESTHER		20 JUL 1988	28 OCT 1898		SAMUEL
106	D38	GLICKSTEIN, SAMUEL		15 MAY 1972	1 JUN 1892		ESTHER
371	E 2	GLOBERMAN, MORRIS H		3 AUG 1987	19 JAN 1924		
106	B8	GLOBMAN, BENJAMIN		25 APR 1991	10 SEP 1916		
119	J21	GLOOSKIN, SHIRLEY M		28 FEB 1985	22 DEC 1931		
102	AI 9	GLOTZER, DAVID		19 AUG 1953	1878		FANNIE
102	AI 8	GLOTZER, FANNIE		28 OCT 1959	1881		DAVID
102	AJ212	GLOTZER, JOSEPH		3 DEC 1971	1900		RUTH
102	A55	GLOTZER, ROSE		25 FEB 1941	1874		SAMUEL
102	AJ213	GLOTZER, RUTH L		24 APR 1983	29 AUG 1911		JOSEPH
102	A54	GLOTZER, SAMUEL J		10 JUL 1940	1874		ROSE
248	J63	GLUSKIN, ABRAHAM		12 MAR 1933	1874		
248	N71	GLUSKIN, FANNIE		22 SEP 1920	1901		
102	A77	GODING, JENNIE	TOBIAS	13 APR 1948	1873		
102	A76	GODING, SAUL		20 JUN 1943	1870		
110	E 1	GOFFIN, DOROTHY	MAISLEN	7 MAR 1978	29 JUL 1907		
391	GG 4	GOLAS, MEYER					
125	O142	GOLD, ALEX ZELECK		13 JUN 1982	1912		SHIRLEY
101	I22	GOLD, ANNA		18 DEC 1982	25 APR 1911		BERNARD
101	I23	GOLD, BERNARD		15 JAN 1978	28 SEP 1911		ANNA
116	O14	GOLD, EDITH S		31 MAY 1990	3 APR 1906		WILLIAM
374	D 1	GOLD, ESTHER		26 JAN 1928			
102	AJ141	GOLD, EVA	BEIZER	26 AUG 1972	1892		JULIUS
222	AS 1	GOLD, GEORGE		24 MAR 1986	21 JUL 1910		SOPHIE
112	C19	GOLD, GOLDIE T		30 JAN 1985	29 MAR 1915		
125	E151	GOLD, HARRY LOUIS		16 OCT 1936	1858	PERETZ JOSEPH & YEHUDIS	
105	N37	GOLD, HERMAN		19 DEC 1986	2 SEP 1910		
101	B45	GOLD, HYMAN		4 APR 1952	1867		
222	AN 3	GOLD, ISIDORE		4 JAN 1967	5 SEP 1878		REBECCA
101	J29	GOLD, JENNIE	FADEN	20 JAN 1957	27 SEP 1896		
123		GOLD, JOSEPH		23 DEC 1945	1895		
102	AJ140	GOLD, JULIUS		26 NOV 1958	1889		EVA
125	T190	GOLD, MOLLY	LEVINE	11 FEB 1989	6 JUN 1913		
222	AN 4	GOLD, REBECCA	KAUFMAN	27 APR 1939	1882		ISIDORE
102	AC32	GOLD, ROSE	LIPMAN	1 MAR 1985			
101	J 8	GOLD, RUTH GLADYS		8 DEC 1966	1902		
102	Y177	GOLD, SAMUEL		26 MAY 1984			
125	I 44	GOLD, SARAH		21 FEB 1915	1861		
391	H38	GOLD, SARAH G		3 JAN 1928	1859	YEHUDA LEV	
116	U11	GOLD, SEYMOUR		22 NOV 1984	17 JUN 1923		
125	O143	GOLD, SHIRLEY RUTH FEINBERG	RABINOW	10 DEC 1972	26 MAR 1926		ALEX
106	E13	GOLD, SIDNEY		27 SEP 1981	19 AUG 1914		
222	AS 2	GOLD, SOPHIE		16 OCT 1989	24 MAR 1911		GEORGE
116	O13	GOLD, WILLIAM		1982	1906		EDITH
330	AF31	GOLDAPEL, HELENA		17 AUG 1983	1903		
248	J 5	GOLDBERG, ABRAHAM					
248	N75	GOLDBERG, ABRAHAM		6 FEB 1914	6 FEB 1914		
123		GOLDBERG, ABRAHAM		11 JUN 1948	1909		
370	J53	GOLDBERG, ABRAHAM		1989	1906	JACOB & ANNIE	
329	F11	GOLDBERG, ABRAHAM		31 DEC 1990	11 MAR 1913	ISAAC	YETTA
125	F123	GOLDBERG, ABRAHAM		5 DEC 1979		CHARLES	
371	AO26	GOLDBERG, ABRAHAM A DDS		24 OCT 1976	1913		ANNE
102	AD31	GOLDBERG, ABRAHAM M		9 DEC 1970	1899		

Cem	Row	Name	Maiden Name	DOD	DOB	Parents	Spouse
102	AJ63	GOLDBERG, ADA P		19 JAN 1957	1890		
102	AD33	GOLDBERG, ADELLE S		29 FEB 1988	20 OCT 1897		HARRY
370	J54	GOLDBERG, ALEX		1983	1908	JACOB & ANNIE	BARNEY
112	E 7	GOLDBERG, ALLEN JEROME		21 MAR 1987	8 JUN 1933		
371	AN20	GOLDBERG, ANNA	HECHT	14 MAR 1990	17 JUN 1904		
102	U 1	GOLDBERG, ANNA	TULIN	18 NOV 1930	10 JAN 1881		ISADORE
125	S164	GOLDBERG, ANNA		2 NOV 1951	1876		BENJAMIN
370	K15	GOLDBERG, ANNA		25 JUN 1947			
371	AO20	GOLDBERG, ANNA BESS		16 NOV 1959	1873		HYMAN
371	AO25	GOLDBERG, ANNE		1 JUL 1986	1914		ABRAHAM
102	A 6	GOLDBERG, ANNIE	TUCHMAN	4 JAN 1931			
370	J56	GOLDBERG, ANNIE		1964	1879		JACOB
121	I23	GOLDBERG, ARTHUR S		22 MAR 1987	1933		
102	AJ62	GOLDBERG, BARNEY		28 OCT 1957	1882	DAVID & RACHEL (ANTICOILSKI)	NANCY
102	AD34	GOLDBERG, BARNEY U		3 JAN 1967	22 JUN 1895		ADELLE
125	Z183	GOLDBERG, BECKY		9 OCT 1987	1895		HARRY
101	L17	GOLDBERG, BELLA		2 FEB 1914			
222	AU 2	GOLDBERG, BEN		12 JUL 1967	1887		CLARA
125	K115	GOLDBERG, BENJAMIN		1 MAR 1941	1882		BLANCHE
125	S163	GOLDBERG, BENJAMIN		11 OCT 1941	1880	SHLOMO	ANNA
102	AJ150	GOLDBERG, BERNARD MAISHE		19 NOV 1981	27 JUL 1913		
330	G13	GOLDBERG, BERTHA		8 JUL 1983	1895		
101	K34	GOLDBERG, BERTHA	OKRANT	17 OCT 1963	1897		BERTHA
119	B48	GOLDBERG, BERTHA		31 MAY 1992	8 FEB 1922		
104	G24	GOLDBERG, BESSIE		22 JUN 1987	10 JUL 1900		
370	P24	GOLDBERG, BEVERLY		1989	1915		
125	K116	GOLDBERG, BLANCHE	WELENCHIK	16 MAR 1934	1882	HYMAN & REBECCA	BENJAMIN
330	H43	GOLDBERG, CARL		26 JUN 1940	1899		
751	C16	GOLDBERG, CELIA	BAZIL	NDD			ISIDORE
370	B49	GOLDBERG, CHARLES		10 JUN 1936	15 JUN 1883		ESTHER
125	L102	GOLDBERG, CHARLES		11 JUN 1929	1853		ELIZABETH
330	G14	GOLDBERG, CHARLES		30 APR 1954	1890		CHARLES
125	Y194	GOLDBERG, CLARA		1986	1904		JACK
222	AU 1	GOLDBERG, CLARA R		7 OCT 1984	1900		BEN
330	G38	GOLDBERG, CLARA SARA		8 JAN 1910	7 MAY 1897		
102	U41	GOLDBERG, DANIEL	WAINGROW	27 APR 1989	23 SEP 1951		
329	B16	GOLDBERG, DANIEL ZADEL		10 APR 1973	1885		ROSE
104	M43	GOLDBERG, DAVID		14 AUG 1979	15 OCT 1910		FREDA
102	AB57	GOLDBERG, DAVID		1924	1863		RACHEL
371	N12	GOLDBERG, DAVID		1957	1893		FANNIE
750	C22	GOLDBERG, DAVID E		9 JUL 1963	21 FEB 1944	ISRAEL & KITTY	
102	U 3	GOLDBERG, DAVID L		14 NOV 1957	7 OCT 1904	ISADORE & ANNA	
125	Q173	GOLDBERG, DAVID MAX		31 MAR 1961	1909		
102	I52	GOLDBERG, EDITH	CARTIN	1985	1903		HARRY
125	K 35	GOLDBERG, ELIZABETH	BLIHES	17 APR 1914	1872	YITZCAK	CHARLES
121	N13	GOLDBERG, ESTHER		15 MAR 1965	1900		
370	B50	GOLDBERG, ESTHER		22 NOV 1967	9 FEB 1888		CHARLES
371	AO15	GOLDBERG, ESTHER D		9 NOV 1973	1909		LOUIS
371	AK17	GOLDBERG, ETHEL		31 MAR 1988	1892		ISADORE
447	R 7	GOLDBERG, ETHEL L		1981	1894		HARRIS
103	C2	GOLDBERG, EVA WOOD	CHASE	27 SEP 1980	1912		
391	H42	GOLDBERG, FANNIE		14 JUL 1943	1871	GEDALIAH LEV	
371	N13	GOLDBERG, FANNIE		1965	1900		DAVID
104	M44	GOLDBERG, FREDA	ROSENBERG	25 MAR 1962	17 SEP 1913		DAVID
107	F19	GOLDBERG, GARSON		2 DEC 1986	27 NOV 1911		
101	A 1	GOLDBERG, GITEL	PERLSTEIN	24 MAR 1940	1882		
447	R 8	GOLDBERG, HARRIS		1973	1896		ETHEL
370	B15	GOLDBERG, HARRY		11 OCT 1918	1893		IDA
102	AH210	GOLDBERG, HARRY		17 APR 1975	19 DEC 1908		
102	I51	GOLDBERG, HARRY		21 JUN 1992			EDITH
102	AJ64	GOLDBERG, HARRY		27 JUN 1941	1874		ADA
125	T153	GOLDBERG, HARRY		29 NOV 1939	1885	AARON JACOB & ANNA	
125	I161	GOLDBERG, HELEN		14 FEB 1949	1897	ASHER	HERMAN
116	U 3	GOLDBERG, HENRY JEROME		1986	1908		
102	T 6	GOLDBERG, HENRY R		1927	1902		
125	H122	GOLDBERG, HERMAN		3 OCT 1968			HELEN

Cem	Row	Name	Maiden Name	DOD	DOB	Parents	Spouse
125	L148	GOLDBERG, HYMAN		11 JAN 1955	1894		MARY
371	A019	GOLDBERG, HYMAN R		7 DEC 1962	1872		ANNA
104	J34	GOLDBERG, IDA		11 APR 1955	1897		
125	J123	GOLDBERG, IDA	PEDRO	17 AUG 1976	1898		WILLIAM
370	H27	GOLDBERG, IDA R		13 SEP 1955	28 JUL 1899		HARRY
102	T 2	GOLDBERG, IRVING A		1955	1901		
330	F 5	GOLDBERG, ISAAC		2 JUL 1939	1854		
116	S21	GOLDBERG, ISAAC		4 JAN 1978	18 FEB 1894		MOLLY
371	AK18	GOLDBERG, ISADORE		3 NOV 1969	1894		ETHEL
391	C13	GOLDBERG, ISADORE		31 MAR 1946	7 NOV 1898		
102	U 2	GOLDBERG, ISIDORE E		18 MAR 1938	25 DEC 1872		ANNA
751	C17	GOLDBERG, ISIDORE S		1986	1904		CELIA
371	A 2	GOLDBERG, ISRAEL		10 MAR 1976	1900		SUSAN
750	C23	GOLDBERG, ISRAEL		17 DEC 1991	10 MAR 1901		KITTY
125	Y195	GOLDBERG, JACK		17 FEB 1985	1894		CLARA
113	K49	GOLDBERG, JACK D		31 AUG 1985	1 DEC 1924		
102	A51	GOLDBERG, JACOB		19 DEC 1939	1891		
370	J55	GOLDBERG, JACOB		1960	1877		ANNIE
391	V59	GOLDBERG, JAMES F		1 JAN 1978	17 JUN 1896	MOSHE	
116	AC 8	GOLDBERG, JETTA		27 JUL 1986	26 MAR 1937		
330	AF12	GOLDBERG, JOSEPH		20 AUG 1969	14 FEB 1885		YETTA
371	N14	GOLDBERG, JULIUS		5 SEP 1984	12 MAY 1918	DAVID & FANNIE	
104	O43	GOLDBERG, JULIUS		28 FEB 1951	1880		TILLIE
102	T 5	GOLDBERG, JULIUS B		1982	1905		
102	T 4	GOLDBERG, KATE G		1982	1883		MICHAEL
330	E 3	GOLDBERG, KATIE		4 DEC 1945	1872		
125	I 35	GOLDBERG, KATIE DOROTHY	BERGER	2 OCT 1918	15 OCT 1888	BERL & LILLIE (GLIKAS)	
750	C24	GOLDBERG, KITTY		29 AUG 1992	27 FEB 1909		ISRAEL
371	A017	GOLDBERG, LEA	GOODMAN	22 OCT 1974	1914		SAUL
446	C 1	GOLDBERG, LILLIAN		27 DEC 1930	1902		
329	D15	GOLDBERG, LILLIAN JUNE		28 JUN 1976	19 JUN 1902		WILLIAM
391	GA 7	GOLDBERG, LOUIS		3 AUG 1939	1897	MEYER	
433	G 5	GOLDBERG, LOUIS		7 JUL 1939	1874	AKIVA	
121	A 9	GOLDBERG, LOUIS		1969	1883		
371	A016	GOLDBERG, LOUIS M		15 FEB 1975	1905	HYMAN & ANNA	ESTHER
125	F124	GOLDBERG, LOUIS S		4 MAR 1945	1883	BAISEL & BRIENA	
377	B 9	GOLDBERG, LOUISE	LIPTON	17 MAR 1982	26 SEP 1927		
330	H52	GOLDBERG, LUBA		21 MAY 1954	1886		
125	L147	GOLDBERG, MARY		28 AUG 1964	1899		HYMAN
447	AE38	GOLDBERG, MAX		14 SEP 1986	16 MAR 1911		
104	H49	GOLDBERG, MAX SAMUEL	AGE 75				MINNIE
102	T 3	GOLDBERG, MICHAEL G		1947	1872		KATE
104	H48	GOLDBERG, MINNIE	ROME	27 DEC 1973	1902	LIPMAN & NELLIE (KATZ)	MAX
370	H16	GOLDBERG, MIRIAM		29 APR 1959			PHILIP
116	S22	GOLDBERG, MOLLIE		1 JUN 1977	18 FEB 1894		ISAAC
433	F11	GOLDBERG, MORRIS		5 JUL 1954	1898	JACOB	
370	J38	GOLDBERG, MORRIS		6 FEB 1946			REBECCA
121	H19	GOLDBERG, MORRIS		14 APR 1971	1896		
102	AJ61	GOLDBERG, NANCY	DUBOFSKY	1984	1886		BARNEY
102	P28	GOLDBERG, PAULINE	SEGAL	1928	1866		MICHAEL
370	F21	GOLDBERG, PHILIP		13 OCT 1945	15 SEP 1871		
102	AB58	GOLDBERG, RACHEL		1943	1861		DAVID
125	I151	GOLDBERG, REBECCA		17 NOV 1965	1887	SAMUEL	SOLOMON
121	H20	GOLDBERG, REBECCA		20 AUG 1985	1900		
370	J37	GOLDBERG, REBECCA		22 DEC 1958			MORRIS
125	L140	GOLDBERG, REBECCA	SILVERMAN	29 FEB 1968	1886		
102	AJ13	GOLDBERG, REUBEN		28 FEB 1946	1870		
112	E30	GOLDBERG, ROBERT LOUIS		21 MAR 1992	7 AUG 1961		
329	B 3	GOLDBERG, ROSALYN	KATZ	26 DEC 1965	15 JAN 1919		
125	O115	GOLDBERG, ROSE		1 JAN 1974	1904		
329	B17	GOLDBERG, ROSE	LUCHNICK	18 MAR 1978	1896		DANIEL
248	N74	GOLDBERG, ROSE		22 JAN 1922	22 DEC 1914		
102	AD36	GOLDBERG, ROSE		24 OCT 1949	1898		
125	L103	GOLDBERG, ROSE		29 FEB 1936	1864		CHARLES
392	B40	GOLDBERG, ROSE R		1930	1864		
370	C 9	GOLDBERG, SAMUEL		7 DEC 1930	1872		

Cem	Row	Name	Maiden Name	DOD	DOB	Parents	Spouse
330	H48	GOLDBERG, SAMUEL		8 OCT 1948	1857		
107	C18	GOLDBERG, SAMUEL		1976	1914		
375	G15	GOLDBERG, SARAH	BELGRADE	14 JUL 1966	9 APR 1912	SIMCHA	
370	H19	GOLDBERG, SARAH		15 JUL 1902			
371	AO18	GOLDBERG, SAUL H		17 AUG 1963	1897	HYMAN & ANNA	LEAH
125	I150	GOLDBERG, SOLOMON		22 SEP 1954	1885	MOSHE	REBECCA
116	AU17	GOLDBERG, SOLON P		20 SEP 1978	8 AUG 1915		
371	B 1	GOLDBERG, SUSAN		1965	1891		ISRAEL
104	O42	GOLDBERG, TILLIE		23 NOV 1969	1880		JULIUS
392	B10	GOLDBERG, WILLIAM		6 DEC 1950	1908		
125	J124	GOLDBERG, WILLIAM		20 JAN 1937	1894	DAVID M & EVA R	IDA
329	D16	GOLDBERG, WILLIAM JAY		18 DEC 1990	19 SEP 1900		LILLIAN
330	AF11	GOLDBERG, YETTA		14 JUN 1970	26 DEC 1892		JOSEPH
329	F12	GOLDBERG, YETTA	HELRICH	NDD	2 MAR 1926		ABRAHAM
376	B 4	GOLDBLATT, AARON		6 NOV 1946	15 JUL 1888		BESSIE
376	D 8	GOLDBLATT, ABRAHAM H		5 MAY 1922	1920	AARON	
125	J 49	GOLDBLATT, ANNA		8 AUG 1898	SEP 1853		
102	N41	GOLDBLATT, ARNOLD J		23 DEC 1924	12 OCT 1918	CELIA	
376	D10	GOLDBLATT, AUGUSTA		20 AUG 1985	31 MAY 1914	AARON	
370	G17	GOLDBLATT, BARNETT L		30 OCT 1957	17 MAR 1876		MOLLIE
376	B 3	GOLDBLATT, BESSIE R		17 SEP 1973	28 JAN 1888		AARON
102	N40	GOLDBLATT, CELIA		18 SEP 1965	1897		
376	B 5	GOLDBLATT, DAVID		17 JUN 1953	24 JUL 1881		SARAH
371	AJ11	GOLDBLATT, JACOB		9 FEB 1964	29 AUG 1906		
377	W58	GOLDBLATT, JEFFREY NATHAN		30 JAN 1992	5 OCT 1960	SHAYA BEREL	
370	E 4	GOLDBLATT, JOSEPH		30 MAY 1949	1895		
370	G18	GOLDBLATT, LOUIS		31 MAY 1975	18 AUG 1904	BARNET & MOLLIE	
372	A 6	GOLDBLATT, MAURICE DR		1984	1908		
370	G16	GOLDBLATT, MOLLIE		3 APR 1946	10 JAN 1882		BARNETT
370	B 4	GOLDBLATT, PHILIP		1 JUL 1921	1847		SARAH
376	C 5	GOLDBLATT, PHILIP		28 MAR 1974	1 MAR 1924	AARON	
376	B 6	GOLDBLATT, SARAH	BENDETT	11 JUN 1944	1886		DAVID
370	H11	GOLDBLATT, SARAH L		2 JAN 1942	1847		PHILIP
370	J22	GOLDBLATT, SHEVA ROSE		6 APR 1936	1864		
102	N42	GOLDBLATT, STEVEN B		7 DEC 1969	4 AUG 1928	CELIA	
125	G 62	GOLDCHEN, LOUIS I		12 DEC 1931	1852		SOPHIE
125	E 79	GOLDCHEN, SOPHIE		13 DEC 1931	5 SEP 1858		LOUIS
105	A20	GOLDEN, EDNA		2 JUL 1966	1902		
117	D 9	GOLDEN, HELEN		5 MAR 1991	20 OCT 1909		
374	E11	GOLDEN, JEANNE KAY	SOLOFF	18 SEP 1959	29 APR 1939		
119	J43	GOLDEN, JULIUS		12 JUL 1983	24 JUN 1919		
103	B21	GOLDEN, JULIUS		19 OCT 1988	8 AUG 1913	BARNETT & ESTHER (SHUSTEMAN)	
101	I13	GOLDEN, LEONA		30 JUN 1974	12 APR 1935		
103	B11	GOLDEN, SAMUEL		3 JAN 1987	11 AUG 1911	BARNETT & ESTHER (SHUSTEMAN)	
102	AB172	GOLDENBERG, IDA		13 JUL 1972	19 FEB 1905		JACOB
102	AB173	GOLDENBERG, JACOB MD		8 JUN 1988	10 FEB 1901		IDA
102	AF34	GOLDENBERG, SAUL E		9 JUN 1952	1896		
127	M	GOLDENBERG, STACI LEA		12 APR 1988	5 APR 1988		
104	E34	GOLDENBLOOM, HELEN S		30 SEP 1989	24 MAR 1923		
102	AD26	GOLDENTHAL, ANNIE		10 MAR 1965	1876		
125	A 24	GOLDENTHAL, HELEN		18 MAR 1993			
102	CB57	GOLDENTHAL, JACK		28 JUL 1981	26 MAR 1915		
374	G20	GOLDER, DAVID		5 OCT 1920	14 SEP 1877		
370	I20	GOLDFADEN, ETAL		10 NOV 1926			MOSES
371	AP 8	GOLDFADEN, ETHEL S		1974	1892		HERMAN
371	AP 7	GOLDFADEN, HERMAN S		1962	1887		ETHEL
370	L21	GOLDFADEN, MOSES		16 JUL 1948	1862		ETAL
102	AE14	GOLDFARB, BENJAMIN		30 JUL 1983	6 SEP 1916		
370	I 5	GOLDFARB, DORA		8 OCT 1923	1848		
101	J27	GOLDFARB, DORIS		5 AUG 1956	1907		
115	F16	GOLDFARB, ELLEN		6 APR 1992			
248	H68	GOLDFARB, FANNIE		9 JUN 1978	1 MAY 1899		KURT
110	C27	GOLDFARB, FAY	FACTOR	27 JUL 1972	5 FEB 1916		
248	H67	GOLDFARB, KURT		29 JUL 1967	6 JUN 1905		FANNIE
123		GOLDFARB, LENA C		1973	1893		SAUL
222	AU11	GOLDFARB, LOUIS		28 APR 1991	7 JUN 1910	SARAH	

Cem	Row	Name	Maiden Name	DOD	DOB	Parents	Spouse
116	BU46	GOLDFARB, MEYER		24 FEB 1976	15 MAR 1883		
119	E33	GOLDFARB, MITZI		19 MAR 1993			SARAH
116	AZ11	GOLDFARB, ROBERT		31 OCT 1970	1915		
116	BU45	GOLDFARB, SARAH	GOLDPIN	14 NOV 1975	6 MAR 1887		
222	AU10	GOLDFARB, SARAH	COHEN	19 FEB 1963	1884		MEYER
123		GOLDFARB, SAUL M		12 JUN 1959	1883		
392	J23	GOLDFRIED, ROSE		10 SEP 1932	1884	JOSEPH	LENA
392	C19	GOLDFRIED, SAMUEL		16 AUG 1949	1876		SAMUEL
493	F22	GOLDHAMMER, JOAN R		14 AUG 1990	29 AUG 1930		ROSE
248	I64	GOLDIN, DANIEL		28 SEP 1933	1907		
371	K29	GOLDKNOFF, ISRAEL		7 FEB 1963	26 JUN 1889		
114	F25	GOLDMAN, ADELLE F		14 OCT 1988	6 FEB 1926		
377	Q49	GOLDMAN, ADRIAN H		17 SEP 1983	7 MAY 1919	JOSEPH	
102	Z89	GOLDMAN, ALEC		12 JAN 1964	9 AUG 1903		
391	G12	GOLDMAN, AMY		11 OCT 1918	26 AUG 1884	ZELIG	
751	D18	GOLDMAN, ANNA	DODUCK	23 AUG 1956	28 DEC 1897		EDWARD
330	H46	GOLDMAN, BENJAMIN		8 JUL 1941	1875		
106	E25	GOLDMAN, BESSIE S		17 OCT 1989	9 APR 1911		
328	A30	GOLDMAN, BRONIA		13 NOV 1991	5 DEC 1915		ISAAC
102	AJ80	GOLDMAN, CELIA		22 MAY 1962	30 SEP 1881		
751	D19	GOLDMAN, EDWARD H		31 JUL 1951	2 NOV 1895		ANNA
106	A37	GOLDMAN, ELI M		10 DEC 1988	12 APR 1910		
104	F33	GOLDMAN, ESTHER	KING	17 APR 1990	25 NOV 1912		HARRY
104	F32	GOLDMAN, HARRY		26 SEP 1982	25 DEC 1910		ESTHER
447	L16	GOLDMAN, HARRY ARTHUR		25 JUL 1943	1886		FLORENCE
328	A29	GOLDMAN, ISAAC		10 JUL 1968	21 NOV 1900		BRONIA
125	M120	GOLDMAN, JENNIE	GREENSTEIN	27 MAR 1929	1888	BEN & ROSIE (AHTEVSKY)	
751	D15	GOLDMAN, JOSEPH N		6 AUG 1954	1890		
222	AJ21	GOLDMAN, LOUIS		2 JUL 1985	9 APR 1907		
102	AJ81	GOLDMAN, LOUIS D		7 APR 1952	7 MAR 1901	CELIA	
248	K77	GOLDMAN, MORRIS		12 JAN 1980	6 APR 1941		
121	F28	GOLDMAN, PHILIP		10 OCT 1992			
102	AJ76	GOLDMAN, ROBERT		25 JAN 1990	18 AUG 1911	CELIA	
370	C24	GOLDMAN, SHINDEL				ABRAHAM	
116	BL68	GOLDMINTZ, ETTA		2 OCT 1971			
447	S 7	GOLDREICH, MAX		28 JUL 1951	1886		
447	S 5	GOLDREICH, SAMUEL		4 NOV 1983	20 MAY 1916	MAX	
447	S 6	GOLDREICH, SIDNEY		18 SEP 1980	1918	MAX	
110	C12	GOLDSCHMIDT, BESSIE		15 APR 1960	1890		
110	A26	GOLDSCHMIDT, DAVID		16 AUG 1955	1906		SAM
110	D15	GOLDSCHMIDT, DORA		28 SEP 1987	1920		SIMON
110	A28	GOLDSCHMIDT, HYMAN		1 MAY 1948	1865		
112	C 6	GOLDSCHMIDT, JOHN E		22 APR 1982	6 JUN 1922		
110	C24	GOLDSCHMIDT, MINNA B		23 JAN 1968	1909		
125	H163	GOLDSCHMIDT, MYER MD		29 MAY 1953	1911		
110	B24	GOLDSCHMIDT, REBECCA		22 JUL 1932	1870		
110	C13	GOLDSCHMIDT, SAM		26 JUL 1960	1890		BESSIE
110	D16	GOLDSCHMIDT, SIMON		17 JUL 1971	1908		DORA
125	L 20	GOLDSMITH, ANNA		2 APR 1940	10 SEP 1895	JONAH	
125	J 56	GOLDSMITH, CHANA		8 JAN 1904	14 MAR 1871		
125	B112	GOLDSMITH, HENRY B		17 FEB 1971	1903		
125	M118	GOLDSMITH, IDA		18 JUL 1937	1862	ABRAHAM & ANNA	
125	L 92	GOLDSMITH, JONAH		9 SEP 1952	12 MAR 1869		
125	Q177	GOLDSMITH, MYER		7 JUN 1961	1899		RACHEL
125	Q176	GOLDSMITH, RACHEL		20 SEP 1993			MYER
391	F29	GOLDSTEIN, AARON		14 SEP 1928	1864	ISAAC	
446	A21	GOLDSTEIN, ABRAHAM		6 APR 1921	1864		
371	O16	GOLDSTEIN, ABRAHAM		7 JAN 1963	8 AUG 1904		KATE
391	J30	GOLDSTEIN, ABRAHAM		16 APR 1921	1865	MORDECHAI	
125	G159	GOLDSTEIN, ABRAHAM		19 NOV 1975	10 JUN 1899		
125	R141	GOLDSTEIN, ABRAHAM I		14 MAY 1942	1872		
249	C32	GOLDSTEIN, ADOLPH		21 AUG 1961	1 SEP 1877		FANNY
125	R176	GOLDSTEIN, ALFRED		19 DEC 1985	23 JAN 1891		ELIZABETH
330	AG23	GOLDSTEIN, ALFRED D		3 DEC 1992			
330	AG22	GOLDSTEIN, ANNA		3 JUN 1990			
392	J27	GOLDSTEIN, ANNA		14 APR 1925	1895	MEYER	

Cem	Row	Name	Maiden Name	DOD	DOB	Parents	Spouse
391	C 7	GOLDSTEIN, ANNA		1919	1899	ABRAHAM	
392	C30	GOLDSTEIN, ANNA		20 JUN 1956	1870		
447	C18	GOLDSTEIN, ANNIE		29 JUN 1944	1874		ISRAEL
447	C16	GOLDSTEIN, ARTHUR		13 DEC 1974	29 OCT 1916	EDWARD & CELIA	
370	C11	GOLDSTEIN, BARNET		13 AUG 1931			JENNIE
447	F35	GOLDSTEIN, BARRY MARTIN		1993	1944	BERNARD	
392	D18	GOLDSTEIN, BELLA		4 NOV 1957	1894	SAMUEL JOSEPH	MAX
102	Z22	GOLDSTEIN, BENJAMIN		10 JUL 1966	10 OCT 1898		
330	D26	GOLDSTEIN, BENJAMIN		12 JAN 1956	1885		FANNIE
248	C45	GOLDSTEIN, BERNARD		18 APR 1977	17 MAY 1906		ROSE
447	F33	GOLDSTEIN, BERNARD S		2 JUN 1989	1921		
249	Q 6	GOLDSTEIN, BETH		17 AUG 1988	3 JUN 1958	HERBERT & CAROL (DAVIS)	
370	I44	GOLDSTEIN, BETSEY ROSE		12 DEC 1945			SAMUEL
105	F29	GOLDSTEIN, CECILIA		1 JUN 1992			ROBERT
447	C19	GOLDSTEIN, CELIA B		19 JUL 1991	1898	ANNIE	EDWARD
125	Z198	GOLDSTEIN, CHARLES		15 NOV 1990	22 JUL 1923		
370	T47	GOLDSTEIN, CORRINNE		22 MAR 1963			
330	F51	GOLDSTEIN, DAVID		22 JUL 1929	1861		
119	H22	GOLDSTEIN, DORIS A		3 APR 1991	23 JUL 1905		
371	J19	GOLDSTEIN, EDITH		1964	1931		
447	C20	GOLDSTEIN, EDWARD A		29 APR 1968	1896		CELIA
125	R175	GOLDSTEIN, ELIZABETH	GRUENBAUM	8 MAR 1982	1 JUL 1898		ALFRED
447	N 7	GOLDSTEIN, ESTHER	LUNTZ	8 SEP 1931	28 JUN 1895	SAUL & ANNIE	
391	Q35	GOLDSTEIN, ESTHER		22 FEB 1916		ISAAC	
125	K106	GOLDSTEIN, ESTHER S		18 MAR 1939	1868	YEKOIEL & LEAH	ISRAEL
377	T12	GOLDSTEIN, ETHEL		1988	1907	LEV	HARRY
373	K 4	GOLDSTEIN, EVELYN		27 JUN 1991	20 MAY 1914		MAX
330	D27	GOLDSTEIN, FANNIE		7 MAR 1970	1886		BENJAMIN
370	K20	GOLDSTEIN, FANNIE	BENDETT	27 SEP 1945	1880		JACOB
249	C33	GOLDSTEIN, FANNY		6 JUN 1956	1886		ADOLPH
433	H 9	GOLDSTEIN, FLORENCE		18 MAR 1943	17 APR 1902	ABRAHAM	
391	W54	GOLDSTEIN, FRANK		28 FEB 1958	1896	ZEV DOV	MOLLIE
447	T37	GOLDSTEIN, FRIEDA		14 DEC 1970	1903		JACOB
370	I45	GOLDSTEIN, GEORGE JOSEPH ·		14 SEP 1963	19 MAR 1907	SAMUEL & BETSEY	SARAH
101	I31	GOLDSTEIN, GOLDIE		12 MAY 1986	2 OCT 1912		
330	AG20	GOLDSTEIN, GRACE		15 NOV 1982	23 JAN 1905		GUSTAVE
330	AG19	GOLDSTEIN, GUSTAV		7 JUN 1974	30 MAY 1909		GRACE
433	G 3	GOLDSTEIN, HARRY		9 AUG 1946	31 JAN 1882	HESKEL	
377	T11 ·	GOLDSTEIN, HARRY		1981	1910	ISRAEL	ETHEL
119	J54	GOLDSTEIN, HARRY		29 AUG 1991	27 FEB 1909		
248	N79	GOLDSTEIN, HELEN	BASHEIN	15 NOV 1938	10 MAR 1881		
101	H31	GOLDSTEIN, HYMAN DDS		24 JUL 1991	15 OCT 1905		
125	R145	GOLDSTEIN, I C		8 JUL 1942	1872		
330	A31	GOLDSTEIN, IDA		26 JUN 1961	15 MAR 1886		IKE
330	A30	GOLDSTEIN, IKE		18 SEP 1977	26 DEC 1880		IDA
119	J55	GOLDSTEIN, IRMA	NORKIN	17 JAN 1984	20 SEP 1909		
125	P147	GOLDSTEIN, ISAAC		14 SEP 1947	5 JUN 1891	ISRAEL MOSHE & SIRYA	
102	C28	GOLDSTEIN, ISRAEL		9 MAY 1948	15 SEP 1898		
392	C31	GOLDSTEIN, ISRAEL		10 MAR 1950	1878		ANNA
125	K107	GOLDSTEIN, ISRAEL I		30 JAN 1939	1865	MORRIS AARON & SARAH SOPHIE	ESTHER
447	T36	GOLDSTEIN, JACOB		2 APR 1969	1905		FRIEDA
447	S21	GOLDSTEIN, JACOB		8 AUG 1958	1890		SARAH
370	L 7	GOLDSTEIN, JACOB		1943	1870		FANNIE
371	AE18	GOLDSTEIN, JENNIE		4 FEB 1968	1885		PHILIP
370	J 6	GOLDSTEIN, JENNIE		30 JUL 1931			BARNET
101	I27	GOLDSTEIN, JENNIE A		14 JUN 1978	20 JAN 1885		WILLIAM
101	I30	GOLDSTEIN, JESSIE PHILIP		23 NOV 1978	12 JUL 1949		
125	L198	GOLDSTEIN, JULIA	PRUZANSKY	28 MAY 1972	1900		
371	O15	GOLDSTEIN, KATE M		13 JUL 1975	28 NOV 1904		ABRAHAM
116	BK71	GOLDSTEIN, LAWRENCE M		15 JUL 1966	17 APR 1952		
102	AD47	GOLDSTEIN, LEAH	LEVEN	9 NOV 1949	31 OCT 1894		WILLIAM
751	B33	GOLDSTEIN, LEBA		1 MAY 1912	1837		
370	J31	GOLDSTEIN, LENA		1939	1879		
391	P41	GOLDSTEIN, LENA		26 FEB 1947	1868	SOLOMON BEREL	
375	E50	GOLDSTEIN, LENA		27 DEC 1907	1902		
433	D23	GOLDSTEIN, LEO MERRIS		25 AUG 1982	28 JUL 1911	HESHEL	

Cem	Row	Name	Maiden Name	DOD	DOB	Parents	Spouse
222	AT11	GOLDSTEIN, LIBBY ESTHER		9 JUL 1975	8 JAN 1902		
433	G20	GOLDSTEIN, LORETTA		16 MAY 1953	31 MAY 1886	ISAAC	
121	AA 1	GOLDSTEIN, LYDIA		6 FEB 1992	30 SEP 1915		
374	D 2	GOLDSTEIN, MARTIN ERWIN		1 AUG 1916	2 MAR 1915		
125	S197	GOLDSTEIN, MAURICE A		21 NOV 1958	1902	ISRAEL & ESTHER SASHA	SADIE
391	N26	GOLDSTEIN, MAX		3 NOV 1911	1840	JUDAH LEV	
373	K 3	GOLDSTEIN, MAX		14 SEP 1985	15 MAR 1914		EVELYN
370	L12	GOLDSTEIN, MAX		1929	1878		
392	D17	GOLDSTEIN, MAX		29 MAY 1966	1894	ISRAEL	BELLA
102	AD46	GOLDSTEIN, MAX R MD		10 OCT 1974	16 FEB 1917	WILLIAM & LEAH	
248	K52	GOLDSTEIN, MILDRED FRANCES		22 NOV 1988	11 DEC 1920		
391	W53	GOLDSTEIN, MOLLIE	GREENBLATT	8 JUL 1992	1895	BARUCH	FRANK
119	F29	GOLDSTEIN, MOLLY		1992	1892		
330	AG21	GOLDSTEIN, MORRIS		15 JUL 1977			
447	C17	GOLDSTEIN, MURIEL I		22 JUN 1944	1926	EDWARD & CELIA	
377	P 5	GOLDSTEIN, MYRIAM RACHEL		19 SEP 1962	27 MAR 1960		
447	S37	GOLDSTEIN, NATHAN		17 MAR 1878	24 NOV 1914		
248	K50	GOLDSTEIN, NETTIE		20 MAR 1993			
371	AE17	GOLDSTEIN, PHILIP		20 MAR 1963	1890		JENNIE
370	I56	GOLDSTEIN, ROBERT		3 JUN 1936	1892		
105	F28	GOLDSTEIN, ROBERT		27 SEP 1983	23 NOV 1906		CECILIA
248	C44	GOLDSTEIN, ROSE	BERGER	2 DEC 1981	8 NOV 1897		BERNARD
102	AA 4	GOLDSTEIN, ROSE		7 MAY 1947	1897		
433	I22	GOLDSTEIN, ROSE		16 FEB 1935	1855	ZUSEL	SAMUEL
391	I32	GOLDSTEIN, ROSE		23 MAR 1922	20 DEC 1897	ABRAHAM	
119	H23	GOLDSTEIN, S EDWARD		21 JAN 1990	9 DEC 1907		
125	S198	GOLDSTEIN, SADIE	FRIEDMAN	20 AUG 1979	1903		MAURICE
370	I43	GOLDSTEIN, SAMUEL		6 FEB 1953			BETSEY
249	C39	GOLDSTEIN, SAMUEL		17 JUN 1954	1 SEP 1874		
433	I23	GOLDSTEIN, SAMUEL		28 APR 1943	1855	SHLOMO ABBA	ROSE
370	T46	GOLDSTEIN, SARAH		6 AUG 1960			GEORGE
125	L130	GOLDSTEIN, SARAH	TROTSKY	16 AUG 1931	1864	NATHAN & BEATRICE (CHONE)	
447	S20	GOLDSTEIN, SARAH		17 MAR 1976	1887		JACOB
447	D15	GOLDSTEIN, SHIRLEY M	SHLIEN	20 FEB 1978	15 MAR 1907		
392	J28	GOLDSTEIN, SOPHIE		1 MAR 1925	1918	MORDECHAI	
371	N 9	GOLDSTEIN, SOPHIE		21 JUN 1966			
330	G51	GOLDSTEIN, TILLIE		21 DEC 1926	1857		
101	K16	GOLDSTEIN, TILLIE		24 NOV 1910	1825		
125	S176	GOLDSTEIN, WALTER		20 MAY 1959	31 MAR 1928		
330	A29	GOLDSTEIN, WILLIAM		25 JUN 1961	22 AUG 1909	IKE & IDA	
102	AD48	GOLDSTEIN, WILLIAM G		29 MAR 1965	22 FEB 1894		LEAH
101	I26	GOLDSTEIN, WILLIAM J		10 MAR 1978	25 DEC 1876		JENNIE
119	H53	GOLDWASSER, ELSIE		1 FEB 1988	29 JAN 1926		
370	P59	GOLDWATER, ADOLPH		1988	1901	MEYER & SADIE	
370	P57	GOLDWATER, MEYER		1943	1868		SADIE
370	P58	GOLDWATER, SADIE		1965	1879		MEYER
447	D 6	GOLENSKY, DAVID		3 JAN 1956*	23 DEC 1956*		1904
391	GN 3	GOLSMITH, SARAH		11 OCT 1928	1876	ABRAHAM ISAAC	
113	I22	GOLTZ, CHARLOTTE	RUBINOW	7 FEB 1991	13 MAY 1913	WILLIAM & MARY (BRODSKY)	
371	AE13	GOLUB, ANNA		3 AUG 1968	1885		SANDER
371	AE14	GOLUB, SANDER		23 OCT 1932	1882		ANNA
751	M19	GOLUBOFF, HELEN R		18 SEP 1967	19 FEB 1912		
751	M18	GOLUBOFF, SAMUEL		2 SEP 1973	10 APR 1906		
377	U15	GOLUMBIC, HARRIET S		7 JAN 1986	24 JUL 1907	HIRSCH	SAM
377	U14	GOLUMBIC, SAM W		14 MAR 1974	10 SEP 1899	ISAAC	HARRIET
102	A81	GOODFLEISH, ELIZABETH	LUTWACK	17 MAR 1944	1881		
123		GOODMAN, ABRAHAM		10 SEP 1969	1887		
102	G41	GOODMAN, ABRAHAM H		21 SEP 1962	1890		SADIE
102	E46	GOODMAN, ANDY NOAH		19 OCT 1974	14 FEB 1955		
102	CB18	GOODMAN, AUGUSTA R		13 AUG 1978	6 DEC 1896		
370	B31	GOODMAN, BENJAMIN		24 JAN 1970	15 APR 1880		SADIE
102	K57	GOODMAN, CARL		1962	1927	SAMUEL	
391	Z67	GOODMAN, CELIA KATE		12 NOV 1975	25 OCT 1894	SAMUEL JOSEPH	
127	U	GOODMAN, CELIA PEPPER		29 SEP 1989	31 OCT 1918		SIDNEY
377	Y20	GOODMAN, EVA S		24 JUL 1966	16 APR 1902	DAVID	
102	C 4	GOODMAN, EVELYN	DAVIDSON	12 SEP 1963	1899		

Cem	Row	Name	Maiden Name	DOD	DOB	Parents	Spouse
447	J 3	GOODMAN, FRANKLYN SHERWIN		16 FEB 1992	10 APR 1915		
376	D17	GOODMAN, HARRY		8 AUG 1968	1920	DAVID	
102	G42	GOODMAN, HENRY		25 JAN 1954	1911	ABRAHAM & SADIE	
102	AJ50	GOODMAN, HENRY H		1943	1887		
391	S46	GOODMAN, ISADORE		31 MAR 1943	1880	ISRAEL	REBECCA
751	E36	GOODMAN, ISRAEL		1 MAY 1924	1864		REBECCA
370	A52	GOODMAN, JENNIE A	PINCUS	1922	1886		MOSHE
374	B 3	GOODMAN, LIBBY		18 JUL 1985	2 JAN 1912		
447	J 2	GOODMAN, LISA RUTH		9 APR 1977	29 MAY 1952	FRANKLIN	
102	E12	GOODMAN, LOUIS		27 JAN 1965	24 MAR 1899		
102	AJ89	GOODMAN, MARY REICHLIN	SCHWARTZ	20 DEC 1972	15 MAR 1900		
370	D20	GOODMAN, MOSHE		22 FEB 1896			JENNIE
391	S47	GOODMAN, REBECCA		7 APR 1944	1884	NOAH MORDECHAI	ISADORE
102	AJ49	GOODMAN, REBECCA G K		1978	1895		HENRY
374	A 9	GOODMAN, ROSE		18 DEC 1935	1887		WILLIAM
102	G40	GOODMAN, SADIE		18 OCT 1984	1891		ABRAHAM
370	B32	GOODMAN, SADIE J		7 MAY 1973	26 OCT 1899		BENJAMIN
391	X58	GOODMAN, SAMUEL		16 JAN 1957	16 FEB 1888	ISRAEL	
102	K59	GOODMAN, SAMUEL		1960	1894		
371	D 3	GOODMAN, SAMUEL		28 MAR 1989	15 SEP 1902		
102	A62	GOODMAN, SARA		28 FEB 1941	1888		
248	M70	GOODMAN, SARAH		24 JUN 1942	1872		
116	V11	GOODMAN, SAUL		1978	1920		
127	U	GOODMAN, SIDNEY ARTHUR		22 SEP 1976	9 JUN 1913		CELIA
125	L153	GOODMAN, SOLOMON		19 JUN 1955	1884		
125	B 17	GOODMAN, SYLVIA	JAFFEE	14 MAY 1958	1880		
374	A 8	GOODMAN, WILLIAM		21 MAR 1939	1890		ROSE
113	N43	GOODSTINE, ALICE		4 JUL 1972	6 FEB 1909	ISRAEL & LENA	MAX
113	A35	GOODSTINE, HERMAN		1 FEB 1990	30 JUN 1910		
113	N45	GOODSTINE, ISRAEL		6 AUG 1958	15 OCT 1885		LENA
113	N44	GOODSTINE, LENA		18 MAR 1974	28 DEC 1893		ISRAEL
113	N42	GOODSTINE, MAX		29 NOV 1982	2 JUN 1913		ALICE
125	K178	GOODWIN, LEONARD		7 MAY 1973			
125	E123	GOOGEL, (TWIN BABIES)		6 APR 1940	JAN 1939	SAMUEL	
125	C 8	GOOGEL, CORINNE	GOLDBERG	28 FEB 1975	5 MAY 1911		SAMUEL
125	D 19	GOOGEL, FREDA		20 DEC 1946	1879	JOSEPH	NATHAN
125	D 18	GOOGEL, NATHAN		12 FEB 1941	1875	YITZHOK & SIFERAH	FREDA
125	C 7	GOOGEL, SAMUEL S		16 SEP 1988	16 DEC 1903		CORRINE
373	B 2	GOOR, HARRY		3 FEB 1956			MAMIE
373	H 7	GOOR, HYMAN		1979	1911		
373	B 1	GOOR, MAMIE		2 AUG 1951			HARRY
330	E29	GOOTERMAN, HARRY		25 FEB 1936	1862		
101	K35	GORALNEK, ETHEL		4 MAR 1960	1896		
119	C38	GORALNICK, ISADORE		7 FEB 1980	26 OCT 1918		
125		GORBACH, A		15 FEB 1926	1926	ABRAHAM	
125	I 65	GORBACH, MYER		10 DEC 1909	1855		SARAH
125	I 66	GORBACH, SARAH		1 AUG 1933	1861		MYER
125	N150	GORBACK, JOSEPH M		6 FEB 1951	1890		
125	C 6	GORBAN, CHARLES		26 MAY 1963	15 MAR 1901		
101	F28	GORBARD, HARVEY "HON"		1986	1938		
104	L51	GORBARD, SARAH		8 AUG 1992	1900		
391	J26	GORCHOW, HARRY B		16 OCT 1918	1 OCT 1893	DAVID	
105	P15	GORDES, ELIZABETH		15 JAN 1990	2 SEP 1905		
105	P17	GORDES, ESTHER		6 AUG 1970	1885		JACOB
125	S193	GORDES, GEORGE SIDNEY		11 SEP 1958	11 OCT 1912	JACOB & ESTHER	
105	P16	GORDES, JACOB		12 MAR 1944	1883		ESTHER
125		GORDON, (CHILD)		8 SEP 1925	7 SEP 1925		
370	C 6	GORDON, AARON		8 JAN 1929	1871		
391	E23	GORDON, ABRAHAM		6 MAY 1963	1875	ISRAEL	REBECCA
125	G 74	GORDON, ABRAHAM		22 NOV 1948	6 MAY 1877		
391	GI 4	GORDON, ABRAHAM ISAAC	4 MOS	22 DEC 1915		SAMUEL	
222	AP 2	GORDON, ALBERT		1963	1889		ROSABELLE
102	A48	GORDON, ALBERT		26 NOV 1938	1918		
376	D14	GORDON, ALBERT L		19 DEC 1985	29 DEC 1919		MURIAL
371	AN12	GORDON, ALEC		NDD	1911		
391	M51	GORDON, ANNA		19 DEC 1965	1879	ELIYAHU	BARNETT

Cem	Row	Name	Maiden Name	DOD	DOB	Parents	Spouse
125	I 67	GORDON, ANNA		1908	1901		
125	G 75	GORDON, ANNA	CHERNIAK	1938	1873		
371	AO 6	GORDON, ANNA		22 MAR 1964	1886		CHARLES
374	C14	GORDON, ANNA		29 SEP 1935	1870		MORRIS
125	I 51	GORDON, ANNA	FISH	3 FEB 1960	1876		GEORGE
102	AJ157	GORDON, ANNE	CHOZICK	19 DEC 1964	25 MAY 1908		JACK
370	F34	GORDON, ANNIE					
125	E 96	GORDON, B		9 JAN 1933			
391	M50	GORDON, BARNET		17 NOV 1953	1874	CHIAM	ANNA
125	G 50	GORDON, BENJAMIN		11 FEB 1970	28 JAN 1900		DOROTHY
377	P 6	GORDON, BENJAMIN		15 MAR 1953	17 JUL 1952		
104	I19	GORDON, BENJAMIN		1973	1905		HAZEL
391	S69	GORDON, BENJAMIN		21 FEB 1986		ABRAHAM	MYRTLE
125	G115	GORDON, BENJAMIN		6 MAR 1942	1903	NATHAN	SELMA
125	N107	GORDON, BERNARD		9 JUL 1933	7 JAN 1868		HENRIETTA
222	AP 4	GORDON, BESSIE		1957	1876		HERMAN
371	AO 7	GORDON, CHARLES M		15 SEP 1963	1884		ANNA
249	J 4	GORDON, CLARA		1951	1890		SAMUEL
125	H 50	GORDON, DAVID		12 OCT 1930	1870	SAMUEL	LENA
125	P163	GORDON, DAVID		26 AUG 1948	1885	SAMUEL	
447	T 1	GORDON, DAVID K		25 FEB 1958	14 MAY 1895		DOROTHY
370	N 8	GORDON, DAVID NATHAN		1965	1882		MINNIE
370	L31	GORDON, DEBORAH		12 FEB 1938	3 FEB 1938		
110	H25	GORDON, DIANE MERLE		10 OCT 1958	10 OCT 1958		
370	M 6	GORDON, DINA		18 AUG 1920	18 NOV 1917		
125	H116	GORDON, DORA		17 DEC 1968	1899	NATHAN & ETHEL	
447	T 2	GORDON, DOROTHY H		16 DEC 1966	2 AUG 1898		DAVID
125	G 51	GORDON, DOROTHY V		9 JUL 1979	1898		BENJAMIN
222	AP 3	GORDON, ELLIS		1943	1905	HERMAN & BESSIE	
102	U21	GORDON, ERNEST M		1980	1911	HARRY & RAE	
125	H115	GORDON, ETHEL		3 FEB 1957	1877		NATHAN
371	N30	GORDON, FLORENCE		1988	1895		SOLOMON
104	J15	GORDON, FREDERICK		21 AUG 1965	1909		RUTH
125	H 46	GORDON, GEORGE		10 JAN 1955	1872		ANNA
751	O 9	GORDON, GERTRUDE		9 JAN 1981	18 MAR 1888		
392	G23	GORDON, GERTRUDE	SOKARL	13 MAY 1943	5 MAY 1903	MOSHE AARON	
370	O13	GORDON, GERTRUDE		1962	1895		LEO
391	ZF79	GORDON, GERTRUDE S		21 DEC 1986		MENACHEM MENDEL	
391	M52	GORDON, HARRY		3 APR 1972	1903	BARNET & ANNA	MILDRED
125	B109	GORDON, HARRY		16 SEP 1963	1900		RUTH
125	L142	GORDON, HARRY		19 DEC 1954	1873		
102	U19	GORDON, HARRY		25 AUG 1943	1888		RAE
104	I20	GORDON, HAZEL		1981	1905		BENJAMIN
125	N106	GORDON, HENRIETTA	MENDELSON	15 FEB 1928	1874		BERNARD
125	A124	GORDON, HENRY		1963	1897		
370	Q47	GORDON, HERMAN		11 APR 1927			
447	L10	GORDON, HERMAN R		11 MAR 1929	1897	YALE & JENNIE	
222	AP 5	GORDON, HERMAN, M		1941	1874		BESSIE
125	M 88	GORDON, HIRSH		29 JAN 1923	1853	MYER SHERMAN & MARIA LEAH	
105	H36	GORDON, HYMAN		9 APR 1985	1903		
371	M 4	GORDON, IDA	SEGAL	17 MAR 1960			
370	J15	GORDON, IDA F		23 NOV 1941			
102	AJ156	GORDON, JACK		10 JUL 1991	28 MAR 1907		ANN
493	A15	GORDON, JACK I		1978	1901	JACOB	
370	A 1	GORDON, JACOB		22 SEP 1918	1869		
125	E185	GORDON, JANE		2 NOV 1938	13 FEB 1880		
447	L13	GORDON, JENNIE		27 JUN 1945	1874		YALE
391	S36	GORDON, JENNIE D	KAPLAN	6 MAR 1927	18 FEB 1903	WOLF	
370	A 7	GORDON, JOSEPH		7 OCT 1899			
125	T156	GORDON, JOSEPH		16 JAN 1940	15 APR 1878		
370	N 9	GORDON, JOSEPH		1991	1909		RUTH
125	O128	GORDON, JOSEPH		28 APR 1975	12 FEB 1901		ROSE
102	AB37	GORDON, JOSEPH G		1962	1888		LILLIAN
329	D 5	GORDON, JULIA		9 DEC 1972	15 MAY 1898		MAX
125	H 51	GORDON, LENA		14 OCT 1945	1877		LENA
370	O12	GORDON, LEO		1968	1885		GERTRUDE

Cem	Row	Name	Maiden Name	DOD	DOB	Parents	Spouse
102	AA230	GORDON, LEYB		5 JUN 1992	2 MAY 1912		
125	N172	GORDON, LILLIAN	WEINER	4 DEC 1982	1901		LOUIS
102	AB38	GORDON, LILLIAN R		1980	1888		JOSEPH
125	N173	GORDON, LOUIS		13 NOV 1965	1897		LILLIAN
125	O 96	GORDON, LOUIS		25 FEB 1921	1873	AARON & MARINA	
371	J36	GORDON, LOUIS A		23 FEB 1979	11 APR 1901		
330	F39	GORDON, MAIER		7 APR 1921	1851		
125	I 69	GORDON, MARY L	HORWITZ	13 AUG 1906	1832		MEYER
370	I17	GORDON, MARY LEAH		6 JUN 1916			
125	A123	GORDON, MAURICE		10 MAR 1980	1896		
329	D 6	GORDON, MAX		13 SEP 1977	5 MAY 1900		JULIA
125	I 68	GORDON, MEYER S		24 JUN 1904	1833		MARY
391	M53	GORDON, MILDRED		8 JUN 1986	1905	BENJAMIN	HARRY
370	N 7	GORDON, MINNIE		1974	1884		DAVID
125	D 55	GORDON, MONROE S		25 JAN 1984	1905		
374	C13	GORDON, MORRIS		5 OCT 1944	1866		ANNA
447	L11	GORDON, MORRIS		21 DEC 1965	31 DEC 1900	YALE & JENNIE	
376	D15	GORDON, MURIEL					ALBERT
391	S68	GORDON, MYRTLE	TANNER	29 MAR 1977		JUDAH LEV	BENJAMIN
125	H114	GORDON, NATHAN		15 JAN 1949	1866		ETHEL
374	E43	GORDON, RACHEL		3 JUL 1947			
102	U20	GORDON, RAE		8 DEC 1974	1889		HARRY
391	E24	GORDON, REBECCA		24 OCT 1949	1880		ABRAHAM
125	Y181	GORDON, RIA		8 MAR 1984	14 JAN 1907		
371	A16	GORDON, ROBERT M		1 NOV 1986	6 AUG 1955		
371	AN 7	GORDON, RONALD		20 JAN 1990	1922		ZOE
222	AP 1	GORDON, ROSABELLE	SCHIFF	2 MAY 1967			ALBERT
125	O127	GORDON, ROSE	COHEN	26 FEB 1981	21 MAR 1891		JOSEPH
370	U15	GORDON, ROSE I		22 JAN 1960	15 JUL 1876		
104	J14	GORDON, RUTH		1992			FREDERICK
125	E 56	GORDON, RUTH		23 OCT 1989	2 NOV 1904		
125	B110	GORDON, RUTH	PLOONSKY	9 MAY 1981	1906		HARRY
370	N10	GORDON, RUTH A		1989	1911		JOSEPH
113	C35	GORDON, SAMUEL		2 APR 1991	27 MAR 1913		
249	J 5	GORDON, SAMUEL		1955	1888		CLARA
125	V196	GORDON, SAMUEL		9 FEB 1979	12 JUL 1900		SARAH
125	V195	GORDON, SARA L	KATZ	4 OCT 1977	2 SEP 1903		SAMUEL
447	W38	GORDON, SARAH	APTER	1 JAN 1969	1904		
125	E112	GORDON, SARAH		29 APR 1934	1858		
125	Q151	GORDON, SARAH		4 MAR 1945	16 MAY 1883	RIVKA	
370	D22	GORDON, SAUL S		23 JAN 1917			
370	D19	GORDON, SAXTON		1915			
391	GI 5	GORDON, SELMA		7 SEP 1924	3 JUL 1924	SAMUEL	
125	G116	GORDON, SELMA		3 MAR 1973	1905		BENJAMIN
101	B38	GORDON, SOLOMON		30 SEP 1920	1850		
371	N29	GORDON, SOLOMON Z		1954	1889		FLORENCE
447	L14	GORDON, YALE		29 MAY 1939	1871		JENNIE
101	M37	GORDON, ZEV		16 SEP 1923			
371	AN 8	GORDON, ZOE M		NDD	1925		RONALD
125	E132	GORFAIN, (STILLBORN)		15 FEB 1951	15 FEB 1951	ALEX & MARY (MENKOWITZ)	
125	K179	GORFAIN, AARON		20 FEB 1975	30 APR 1907	NATHAN & ADELE (WOLSHINSKY)	MARTHA
125	A 41	GORFAIN, ABRAHAM		26 NOV 1968	5 MAY 1905	NATHAN & ADELE (WOLSHINSKY)	ROSE
125	A 39	GORFAIN, ADELE BUNNE	WOLOSHINSKY	16 JUL 1914	1878		NATHAN
125	P156	GORFAIN, ANNA		19 JAN 1960	1897	BZALELL	ISADORE
125	Q143	GORFAIN, BESSIE	RUBENSTEIN	4 MAY 1978	1881		
125	O 68	GORFAIN, CHARLES NATHAN		19 FEB 1922	1918	EDWARD & EDITH (BERNSTEIN)	
125	Q142	GORFAIN, DAVID		7 MAR 1944	27 DEC 1883	DOV HIRSH & TZEREL(GREENSTEIN)	BESSIE
125	R186	GORFAIN, EDITH	BERNSTEIN	26 JUN 1960	1888	PESACH	EDWARD
125	R185	GORFAIN, EDWARD DAVID		20 JUL 1962	24 APR 1883	DOV HIRSH & TZEREL(GREENSTEIN)	EDITH
125	M 95	GORFAIN, HARRY BENJAMIN		4 MAY 1926	1856	ABRAHAM & LEAH	TSERELLE
125	P157	GORFAIN, ISADORE		8 JUN 1948	26 FEB 1896		ANNA
125	B 41	GORFAIN, JOSEPH		3 APR 1972	1903	NATHAN & LILLIAN (LEVY)	LILLIAN
125	B 39	GORFAIN, LILLIAN	LEVY	18 APR 1964	1905	SHLOMO	JOSEPH
125	K180	GORFAIN, MARTHA	BERKMAN	15 MAY 1973	21 SEP 1908	JOSEPH	AARON
125	B 40	GORFAIN, NATHAN		3 JUL 1945	1877	DOV HIRSH & TZEREL(GREENSTEIN)	ADELE
125	A 40	GORFAIN, ROSE	WIENER	16 SEP 1982	18 SEP 1909	YAKOV	ABRAHAM

Cem	Row	Name	Maiden Name	DOD	DOB	Parents	Spouse
125	E 11	GORFAIN, THELMA PELTA		14 JUL 1928	1922	EDWARD (ISADORE) & RACHEL	
372	B21	GORIN, MARTHA		31 JUL 1977	6 AUG 1910		SAMUEL
372	B22	GORIN, SAMUEL L		21 JUN 1979	16 MAR 1907		MARTHA
125	V192	GORMAN, MAXIM		8 DEC 1978	1909		ROSE
125	V193	GORMAN, ROSE	GOLDBERG	22 SEP 1977	1911		MAXIM
751	F37	GORODSKY, MINNIE ZVENE		23 OCT 1924	1851		
103	G9	GOROFF, NORMAN NATHAN		26 OCT 1989	13 JUN 1925		
330	AG18	GOROSHNIK, PHILIP		1978	1904		
102	I12	GORSKY, BEULAH EDNA		15 MAR 1974	29 MAR 1912		SAMUEL
102	I13	GORSKY, KENNETH		6 JUL 1944	2 JAN 1939	SAMUEL & BEULAH	
102	I11	GORSKY, SAMUEL		17 NOV 1984	23 JAN 1910		BEULAH
375	A10	GOSSETT, MINNIE GERTRUDE		18 DEC 1976	25 APR 1903	MENDEL	
330	C17	GOTFRIED, ANNA		22 FEB 1936			
371	J 7	GOTKIN, MAX		6 OCT 1968	15 MAY 1916		
102	BH16	GOTSULYAR, GENYA		14 JUL 1992	14 FEB 1916		
392	E43	GOTTESDIENER, ISADORE		31 JAN 1947	1893	NATTA	
392	D43	GOTTESDIENER, LENA B		21 JAN 1967	1900	KIDDISH	
371	L 2	GOTTESFELD, BERTHA		1969	1900		PHILIP
371	L 1	GOTTESFELD, PHILIP		1984	1896		BERTHA
121	C 5	GOTTESMAN, RUTH	KOWALSKY	21 MAY 1967	17 APR 1926		
330	H34	GOTTFREID, SAUL		7 JAN 1949			
433	F 7	GOTTFRIED, ANNA		23 APR 1954		DAVID HAIKEL	ISADORE
433	F 6	GOTTFRIED, ISADORE		16 AUG 1953		SHAYA LEV	ANNA
433	I25	GOTTFRIED, LOUIS		23 JUL 1948	1857	ARYEH	REBECCA
116	AZ25	GOTTFRIED, MURRAY J		27 JAN 1970	9 SEP 1922		
433	I24	GOTTFRIED, REBECCA LENA		15 JUN 1939	1864	JACOB	LOUIS
372	E33	GOTTHELF, BERTHA	FRIEDBERGER	11 FEB 1922	4 APR 1847		MOSES
372	E32	GOTTHELF, MOSES		24 MAY 1886	29 SEP 1832		BERTHA
392	C 4	GOTTLIEB, ALBERT				JACOB & HANNAH	ANNA
330	AH 6	GOTTLIEB, ANNA		22 AUG 1990	15 MAR 1892		DAVID
392	C 5	GOTTLIEB, ANNA	ROTH	25 JUN 1990	1915		ALBERT
330	AH 5	GOTTLIEB, DAVID		11 APR 1976	15 MAY 1891		ANNA
392	C 8	GOTTLIEB, HANNAH LEA		17 FEB 1947	1878		JACOB
330	AF 9	GOTTLIEB, IDA L		24 AUG 1971	11 DEC 1899		SAMUEL
392	C 7	GOTTLIEB, JACOB		6 AUG 1960	1880		HANNAH
392	C 2	GOTTLIEB, JUDITH	LOEB			JACOB & HANNAH	
106	A9	GOTTLIEB, MARY	ROSNER	19 DEC 1987	5 FEB 1912		SIDNEY
392	C 6	GOTTLIEB, ROSE				JACOB & HANNAH	
104	A 7	GOTTLIEB, ROSE	KLEIN	26 JAN 1989	1898		
330	AF10	GOTTLIEB, SAMUEL D		15 NOV 1977	7 MAY 1891		IDA
106	A10	GOTTLIEB, SIDNEY S		17 NOV 1970	26 NOV 1907		MARY
113	I66	GOTTLIEB, SYLVIA		29 SEP 1986	21 OCT 1925		
392	C 3	GOTTLIEB, WILLIAM				JACOB & HANNAH	
102	G23	GOULD, ANNIE		6 DEC 1953	1876		LOUIS
125	R192	GOULD, BELLE	DAVIDSON	1 NOV 1964	25 DEC 1889		HENRY
125	R191	GOULD, HENRY		25 SEP 1960	14 MAR 1887		BELLE
102	G22	GOULD, LOUIS		4 MAY 1966	1872		ANNIE
446	XXX	GOUREVITCH, ANNA		1981	1897		
125	J145	GOURSON, LOUIS		13 OCT 1952	1874		REBECCA
125	J146	GOURSON, REBECCA	SCHWARTZ	7 JUN 1963	1881		LOUIS
125	Z197	GOURSON, SELIG		16 JAN 1989	19 MAY 1911	LOUIS & REBECCA	
374	A50	GRABELEFSKY, ESTHER	ZUBOW	5 JUL 1983	1888		
371	F 1	GRABLE, FLORENCE		3 OCT 1981	1912		
370	C17	GRABLEFSKY, JACOB DAVID		23 MAY 1963			JENNIE
370	K 7	GRABLEFSKY, JENNIE SARAH		12 JUN 1949			JACOB
125	L115	GRABOIS, FRANK		6 MAY 1930	APR 1862		PAULINE
125	N112	GRABOIS, PAULINE		17 NOV 1945	1871	HYMAN HORACE & GITTLE SHANA	FRANK
750	I18	GRABOW, MORRIS		6 JAN 1964	1893		
116	W18	GRABOW, PAUL DAVID		2 MAR 1978	15 FEB 1952		
116	AW27	GRABOWSKY, REBECCA		19 JAN 1971	1893		
116	T15	GRACEMAN, EDWARD M		14 JUN 1986	11 JUL 1909		MARY
116	T16	GRACEMAN, MARY R		8 MAR 1976	10 DEC 1884		EDWARD
101	K27	GRACIERSTEIN, FANNIE		14 SEP 1941	1886		
101	L 6	GRACIERSTEIN, SAMUEL		28 JUN 1967	1880		
372	G12	GRAFF, ADELHEIDE		12 APR 1912		CASPER & ROSE	
372	G11	GRAFF, CASPER		1952	1867		ROSE

Cem	Row	Name	Maiden Name	DOD	DOB	Parents	Spouse
371	AN 2	GRAFF, ELLA	SOLOVEITZIK	5 APR 1965	25 DEC 1907		MORTON
372	H 6	GRAFF, FANNIE	BERGER	1962	1898		NATHAN
102	BE 5	GRAFF, GERTRUDE LILLIAN		3 FEB 1989	18 NOV 1910		JULIUS
102	BE 6	GRAFF, JULIUS Y		22 NOV 1990	11 NOV 1910		GERTRUDE
372	H 8	GRAFF, MILTON		1979	1898		
371	AN 1	GRAFF, MORTON LEO		25 DEC 1962	26 DEC 1905		ELLA
372	H 7	GRAFF, NATHAN		1967	1893		FANNIE
372	G10	GRAFF, ROSE	WERNER	1963	1875		CASPER
392	C43	GRAND, HARRY JOHN		5 FEB 1989	1911		LILLIAN
392	C44	GRAND, LILLIAN	WEINSTEIN	22 JUN 1978	1912		HARRY
377	H 3	GRANN, ANITA		1944	1882		ESSAK
377	H 2	GRANN, ESAAK		1949	1878		ANITA
377	O22	GRANN, JACK		1945	1893		
102	AJ45	GRANSTEIN, CARRIE	GROSS	28 MAR 1982	25 AUG 1893		CHARLES
102	AJ46	GRANSTEIN, CHARLES I MD		11 APR 1947	10 MAY 1887		CARRIE
115	AA 6	GRANSTEIN, EDITH A		9 JAN 1987	1 AUG 1917		HERBERT
115	AA 7	GRANSTEIN, HERBERT L			25 JAN 1916		EDITH
447	S27	GRANT, GARY RICHARD		14 SEP 1970	26 OCT 1936		
330	AA 2	GRANT, HELEN		12 JUN 1982	24 JUN 1897		SAMUEL
102	AJ73	GRANT, IDA	HALPER	26 DEC 1943	17 APR 1898		LEON
102	AJ74	GRANT, LEON WILLIAM		30 JAN 1964	15 SEP 1895		IDA
330	AA 1	GRANT, SAMUEL		15 MAR 1984	21 JUN 1893		HELEN
377	Z39	GRATENSTEIN, HERMAN L		1978	1902	MESHALOM	
125	N139	GRAVITCH, ABRAHAM		24 FEB 1973	1907		SYDELLE
125	N138	GRAVITCH, SYDELLE		1990	1907		ABRAHAM
102	CA 8	GREEN, BENJAMIN		26 SEP 1961	1910		
392	F19	GREEN, BERTA		30 OCT 1945	1871	SAMUEL JUDAH	SIMON
125	N157	GREEN, FANNY LEAH		20 APR 1951	1901		MAX
102	AJ228	GREEN, IRVING		1984	1917		
371	I 1	GREEN, JONAH ULIC		1973	1909		JUDITH
371	I 3	GREEN, JUDITH E	WEISMAN	1955	1912		JONAH
377	R37	GREEN, LOUIS		18 NOV 1992	8 MAY 1908		
125	N158	GREEN, MAX		4 MAR 1978	25 DEC 1903		FANNY
114	L14	GREEN, MELANIE HOPE		17 SEP 1982			
392	F20	GREEN, SIMON DAVID		8 NOV 1931	14 MAY 1877		BERTA
102	AH214	GREENBAUM, JACK S		21 AUG 1984	27 SEP 1909		
102	AJ215	GREENBAUM, SAMUEL		30 OCT 1989	21 DEC 1907		
433	F17	GREENBERG, AARON		8 AUG 1957	1878	JACOB	DAVID
493	E10	GREENBERG, AARON M MD		4 JAN 1983	16 FEB 1906		ADELINE
121	B 1	GREENBERG, ABRAHAM		3 APR 1980	25 APR 1891		
105	M37	GREENBERG, ABRAHAM J		13 MAY 1939	1877		FREIDA
493	E11	GREENBERG, ADELINE K		NDD			AARON
102	N50	GREENBERG, ALBERT A		1957	1894		
103	B4	GREENBERG, ALTA		14 NOV 1931	1883		MORRIS
102	AC 8	GREENBERG, ANNA		1937	1879		
328	A28	GREENBERG, ANNIE		5 JAN 1966	1888		MAX
102	AD59	GREENBERG, BERNARD		12 MAR 1974	25 SEP 1903		MOLLIE
104	G23	GREENBERG, BERTHA	WEXELSTEIN	11 AUG 1985	5 MAY 1910		
102	AD75	GREENBERG, BLUMA		29 MAR 1934	1871		HARRY
105	J 4	GREENBERG, BRANDON	LEIGH	22 MAR 1979	25 JUN 1978		
331		GREENBERG, BYELA		10 DEC 1896	1859		MORRIS
330	F32	GREENBERG, C. D.		17 OCT 1913	15 MAR 1862		GITTEL
121	B 2	GREENBERG, CELIA		30 JAN 1989	8 NOV 1898		
121	A24	GREENBERG, CHANA	HUREWITZ	13 MAY 1987	28 FEB 1897		
105	M44	GREENBERG, CHARLES		22 JAN 1943	1890		NELLIE
222	AI 7	GREENBERG, EDWARD A		1970	1898		
102	S17	GREENBERG, ELIZABETH W		31 MAY 1981			MAURICE
125	I128	GREENBERG, ESTHER		28 NOV 1946	1872	SADIE	JACOB
116	BJ71	GREENBERG, FRANCES M		5 MAY 1987	26 APR 1898		MAURICE
105	M38	GREENBERG, FREIDA		21 MOV 1949	1879		ABRAHAM
111	12	GREENBERG, GEORGE M		1968	1910		
330	G33	GREENBERG, GITTEL		15 SEP 1910	1866		C.D
102	AI 3	GREENBERG, HAROLD		1942	1905		
377	X35	GREENBERG, HARRIET	KREMS	6 FEB 1991	27 MAY 1921	HIRSCH TZVI	
102	AD76	GREENBERG, HARRY		1946	1866		BLUMA
105	L41	GREENBERG, HARRY S		1965	1890	ZELDA	NORA

Cem	Row	Name	Maiden Name	DOD	DOB	Parents	Spouse
103	B6	GREENBERG, HOWARD BURTON		3 JAN 1990	4 SEP 1933		
374	C 7	GREENBERG, ISAAC		27 DEC 1927	1858		LENA
329	C28	GREENBERG, JACK B		9 OCT 1958	17 JUL 1913		
125	I129	GREENBERG, JACOB		24 JAN 1948	1863	ASHER	ESTHER
329	B27	GREENBERG, JOE		21 MAR 1948	1881		LENA
102	Q 7	GREENBERG, JULIA		8 JUN 1931	1887		
102	S14	GREENBERG, KUNE		1942	1869		RACHEL
329	B26	GREENBERG, LENA		5 JAN 1959	1891		JOE
374	C 8	GREENBERG, LENA		9 JUN 1942	1858		ISAAC
125	B 89	GREENBERG, LILLIAN ELLE	MAXEN	16 FEB 1980	22 DEC 1912		
102	AD74	GREENBERG, LOUIS		12 JAN 1940	1891		MARY
118	E6	GREENBERG, LOUIS E		9 JAN 1961			
102	AD79	GREENBERG, MARY		13 MAR 1988	1888		LOUIS
116	BJ70	GREENBERG, MAURICE		18 JAN 1980	8 NOV 1900		FRANCES
102	S16	GREENBERG, MAURICE		22 FEB 1965			ELIZABETH
328	A27	GREENBERG, MAX		2 MAR 1971	1893		ANNIE
102	AD60	GREENBERG, MOLLIE		30 AUG 1987	16 APR 1903		BERNARD
103	B3	GREENBERG, MORRIS		5 JUN 1955	1875		ALTA
330	F43	GREENBERG, NATHAN		10 NOV 1922	1854		
105	M45	GREENBERG, NELLIE		2 APR 1986	1895		CHARLES
105	L42	GREENBERG, NORA		1982	1894		HARRY
125	I 46	GREENBERG, PEARL		9 JAN 1913	1868		
102	S15	GREENBERG, RACHEL		1951	1871		KUNE
102	N53	GREENBERG, RALEIGH		18 DEC 1983	11 JUL 1913	ALBERT	
433	F18	GREENBERG, ROSE		28 MAY 1973	1883	ABRAHAM	ROSE
102	AI 4	GREENBERG, SALLY		1949	1898		
102	F29	GREENBERG, SAMUEL		18 MAY 1951	1901		SARAH
125	H 1	GREENBERG, SAMUEL		6 SEP 1954	1871		SAMUEL
105	L40	GREENBERG, SARAH		14 SEP 1952	1877		
125	T142	GREENBERG, SARAH		17 SEP 1937	1868	GEDALYA & IDA	
125	H 2	GREENBERG, SARAH		18 FEB 1957	1882		SARAH
102	F28	GREENBERG, SARAH		18 MAR 1951	1903		SAMUEL
105	N45	GREENBERG, SIDNEY		28 OCT 1980	14 MAY 1916		
248	K25	GREENBERG, SOPHIE	TAFFEL	17 MAR 1991	1896		
105	M35	GREENBERG, SUSAN	STONE	19 DEC 1990	1898		VICTOR
102	AD 2	GREENBERG, SYLVIA		1933	1897	ANNA	
105	M36	GREENBERG, VICTOR		2 MAR 1954	1899		SUSAN
105	L39	GREENBERG, ZELDA		12 MAY 1941	1856		
372	G15	GREENBERGER, GEORGE		1942	1864		MARY
372	G16	GREENBERGER, MARY		1945	1864		GEORGE
391	W50	GREENBLATT, BARNETT		23 MAR 1967	1868	ISAAC	MARY
391	W55	GREENBLATT, DOROTHY		11 MAR 1967	1900	NATAN NATTA	MARTIN
125	J184	GREENBLATT, HAROLD J		30 DEC 1982	1911		
125	M194	GREENBLATT, HERMAN		26 DEC 1969	1916		
391	W52	GREENBLATT, JENNIE		16 MAR 1952		BARUCH	
125	Q182	GREENBLATT, JENNIE		20 AUG 1966	1889		NATHAN
391	W57	GREENBLATT, LOUIS		18 JAN 1973	1903	BARUCH	
391	W56	GREENBLATT, MARTIN		12 MAR 1983	1897	BARUCH	DOROTHY
391	W51	GREENBLATT, MARY		3 NOV 1957	1871	JACOB	BARNETT
106	C11	GREENBLATT, MAYE	KRUH	23 JAN 1980	29 DEC 1917		
125	Q183	GREENBLATT, NATHAN		26 JUL 1961	1889		JENNIE
102	AE60	GREENBLATT, ROSE	SHERRY	1 DEC 1980	1903		
372	G 2	GREENBURG, CHARLIE		1909	1884	NELLIE	SOPHIE
372	G 3	GREENBURG, NELLIE		1923	1845		
372	G 1	GREENBURG, SOPHIA		1892	1885		CHARLIE
117	F30	GREENE, SOL		29 NOV 1992	1 JUL 1913		
372	C11	GREENE, STEPHEN		9 APR 1966	16 DEC 1965		
102	R24	GREENE, THEODORE		5 MAR 1945	29 JUN 1918		SYLVIA
391	X77	GREENES, FRANCES		NDD	1903	ZALMAN	JESSE
391	X76	GREENES, JESSE		1992	1901	YESHIYAHU & PAULINE	FRANCES
391	X75	GREENES, PAULINE		1975	1874	BENJAMIN	
374	H56	GREENFIELD, ETHEL		1977	1912		
377	X46	GREENGRASS, BEATRICE		20 DEC 1991	12 DEC 1909	MORDECHAI	
377	Y46	GREENGRASS, MILTON		19 OCT 1993	18 FEB 1909	MOSHE	
119	A15	GREENHALGH, LAURA	BEIZER	1990	1910		
371	AH10	GREENLEAF, CHARLES		5 APR 1988	10 AUG 1897		IDA

Cem	Row	Name	Maiden Name	DOD	DOB	Parents	Spouse
371	AH 9	GREENLEAF, IDA		3 MAY 1992	16 OCT 1905		
392	F45	GREENSPAN, FRIEDA		20 FEB 1983	18 SEP 1916	MOSHE YOSEF	CHARLES
104	M47	GREENSPAN, SOLOMON		1 DEC 1976	1910		
102	G47	GREENSPON, ANNA M		6 APR 1968	4 AUG 1897		CHARLES
116	V17	GREENSPON, BENJAMIN		31 AUG 1975	6 NOV 1919		
102	G46	GREENSPON, BESSIE S		29 MAY 1987	5 OCT 1898		
102	G48	GREENSPON, CHARLES		3 MAY 1986	10 JUL 1894		ANNA
121	F10	GREENSPON, EVA		6 SEP 1989	1886		
121	G11	GREENSPON, FLORENCE		24 DEC 1991	9 AUG 1923		
102	AJ15	GREENSPON, JANET S		4 APR 1953	1914		JOSEPH
102	AJ16	GREENSPON, JOSEPH M		7 JAN 1991	1908		JANET
121	F11	GREENSPON, LOUIS		24 MAR 1976	1883		
119	H 2	GREENSPON, PAULINE	GROSS	11 SEP 1990	4 MAY 1895		
119	H 1	GREENSPON, SAMUEL		16 MAR 1984	5 MAY 1889		
116	BE14	GREENSPOON, LOUIS		3 MAY 1962	4 OCT 1896		NETTIE
116	BE13	GREENSPOON, NETTIE		12 APR 1990	30 DEC 1903		LOUIS
125	K110	GREENSTEIN, ANNA	GREENSTEIN	13 NOV 1934	1862	BEN & ROSIE (AHETOVSKY)	SAMUEL
125	I 34	GREENSTEIN, BEILA DORA	GOLDBERG	7 APR 1928	1859	LOUIS & YETTA	HARRY
125	I 63	GREENSTEIN, BENJAMIN		24 MAY 1917	1845	SAMUEL & SARAH (KATZ)	ROSIE
125	N195	GREENSTEIN, CHARLES JACOB M		30 JUN 1967	28 DEC 1886	SAMUEL & ANNA (GREENSTEIN)	DOROTHY
222	AR13	GREENSTEIN, CLARA		8 DEC 1957	1898		
125	N196	GREENSTEIN, DOROTHY	ZIERING	2 FEB 1978	3 FEB 1895		CHARLES
125	H 44	GREENSTEIN, EDWARD ALBERT		3 MAR 1932	8 MAR 1893	HARRY & BEILA (GOLDBERG)	SARAH
371	AO 2	GREENSTEIN, GERTRUDE	SOLOVEITZIK			SARAH	JOSIAH
125	I 33	GREENSTEIN, HARRY		28 JAN 1923	1860	SAMUEL & SARAH (KATZ)	BEILE
125		GREENSTEIN, JACOB BENJAMIN		17 JAN 1923	OCT 1921	EDWARD & SARAH (WELINSKY)	
371	AO 1	GREENSTEIN, JOSIAH		2 NOV 1975	28 NOV 1897	SAMUEL & ANNA	GERTRUDE
125	K 29	GREENSTEIN, LOUIS		12 AUG 1916	12 JUN 1895	HARRY & BEILA (GOLDBERG)	
125	I 62	GREENSTEIN, ROSIE	AHETOVSKY	6 SEP 1902	1842	MORRIS	BENJAMIN
125	K109	GREENSTEIN, SAMUEL		7 SEP 1949	1858	DOV BEAR & ANNA (EPSTEIN)	ANNA
125	H 43	GREENSTEIN, SARAH	WELINSKY	2 SEP 1963	1892	FRANK & LENA (SILVERSTEIN)	EDWARD
447	Y38	GREENWALD, GERTRUDE		5 AUG 1972	1924		
101	A17	GREIFER, JOSHUA		18 FEB 1924	1861		
102	P27	GREIFF, BELLE R		8 DEC 1989	7 DEC 1905		PHILIP
102	P26	GREIFF, PHILIP DAVID		20 FEB 1988	4 OCT 1906		BELLE
116	BU26	GREISS, BENJAMIN		26 JAN 1963	4 JAN 1892		ESTHER
116	BU25	GREISS, ESTHER S		30 SEP 1979	12 AUG 1899		BENJAMIN
329	E16	GRIM, JANICE Y		1991	1918		
102	CB31	GRINER, JENNIE U		12 NOV 1988	23 FEB 1902		SHERMAN
102	CB32	GRINER, SHERMAN		31 OCT 1981	15 JAN 1901		JENNIE
328	A 1	GRINFELD, JACK		24 MAY 1989	13 APR 1920		
391	G 1	GRODINSKY, MAX		20 DEC 1941	1871	ZEV	
102	AJ180	GRODY, EVELYN	LEMKIN	12 DEC 1975	18 MAR 1907		
102	J44	GRODY, GEORGE E		6 JUN 1952	1895		
102	AC114	GRODY, ISRAEL		13 MAY 1982	1896		REBECCA
102	AC115	GRODY, M LEONARD		22 AUG 1983	10 OCT 1933	ISRAEL & REBECCA	
102	AC113	GRODY, REBECCA		5 DEC 1968	1899		ISRAEL
113	N50	GROEGER, JOSEPH		22 DEC 1955	15 SEP 1903		MINNA
113	N49	GROEGER, MINNA	KELLER	4 OCT 1974	1 DEC 1906		JOSEPH
330	G37	GROLLMAN, ROSA		1909	1840		
371	E 5	GROSDOV, ADELE		8 OCT 1993	16 MAR 1919		WILLIAM
370	L 1	GROSDOV, BEN		23 MAY 1948			SADIE
370	K24	GROSDOV, SADIE		14 JAN 1945			BEN
371	E 4	GROSDOV, WILLIAM		16 SEP 1985	3 OCT 1904		ADELE
102	L49	GROSS, ALBERT E		29 JAN 1963	1894		
105	G34	GROSS, ANNA		16 AUG 1985	1890		HARRY
102	O 7	GROSS, BENJAMIN		6 MAY 1958	1891		ETHEL
102	A69	GROSS, ESTHER		17 JAN 1942	13 SEP 1886		
102	O 8	GROSS, ETHEL D	BLUMENTHAL	20 JUL 1967	1899		BENJAMIN
125	M 93	GROSS, FEIGA RACHEL		2 JUN 1925	1869	ISAAC MARK	JACOB
102	BD15	GROSS, GEORGE A		11 JUL 1988	10 JUL 1942		
125	J 36	GROSS, GOLDIE		21 MAR 1909	1833		
105	G35	GROSS, HARRY		7 DEC 1973	1891		ANNA
125		GROSS, HENRIETTA		15 OCT 1925	1855		
102	AJ44	GROSS, HERMAN		6 APR 1955	1864		MOLLY
125	F 4	GROSS, JACOB		25 MAY 1949	1874	AARON DAVID & RACHEL	

Cem	Row	Name	Maiden Name	DOD	DOB	Parents	Spouse
125	M 94	GROSS, JACOB M		25 MAY 1949	1868		
105	D25	GROSS, JACOB W		9 MAR 1961	15 DEC 1891		FEIGA
222	AQ 3	GROSS, JAMES		1975	1889		LENA
125	H140	GROSS, JOSEPH		13 JUN 1994			SELMA
125	D 23	GROSS, JULIUS YALE		1967	1900		
105	H17	GROSS, LENA		27 NOV 1954			SOPHIE
105	D26	GROSS, LENA E		15 APR 1893	15 APR 1893		
102	R37	GROSS, LEWIS I		29 FEB 1976	1893		JACOB
125	G 18	GROSS, LILLIAN	KENNEDY	10 MAY 1966	1892		SOPHIA
377	Q39	GROSS, MARTIN		5 AUG 1982	15 DEC 1895		
102	A70	GROSS, MATILDA TINA		14 DEC 1982	7 JUL 1896		
222	F 1	GROSS, MINNA B		30 AUG 1968	1946	SYLVIA	
102	AA84	GROSS, MIRIAM	LEIMSIEDER	1929	1867		ZELIG
102	AJ43	GROSS, MOLLIE		20 MAY 1943	1864		HERMAN
104	O32	GROSS, NORMAN D DR		26 MAY 1988	23 DEC 1921		
102	O 6	GROSS, PAUL ZACHARY		17 FEB 1961	1929	BENJAMIN & ETHEL	
102	O 9	GROSS, RACHEL		5 MAR 1951	1867		
222	AQ 4	GROSS, SELMA R	ROSENTHAL	1983	1889	EMIL & BERTHA (FORST)	JAMES
105	G37	GROSS, SHIRLEY TIBBY		10 JAN 1985	4 OCT 1920	HARRY & ANNA	
102	R36	GROSS, SOPHIA	HOROWITZ	3 JUN 1981	1893		LEWIS
101	K29	GROSS, SOPHIA		6 SEP 1951	1897		
125	D 24	GROSS, SOPHIE		1987	1907		JULIUS
102	AC205	GROSS, SOPHIE G		18 AUG 1977	10 NOV 1898		
222	F 2	GROSS, SYLVIA	BROWN	8 JAN 1990	1912		
102	AA85	GROSS, ZELIG		1930	1860		MIRIAM
101	H10	GROSSBERG, MEIRA SUSAN		1 MAY 1990	13 APR 1953		
391	S50	GROSSFELD, HARRY		17 MAR 1954	1891	JONAH	
125		GROSSMAN, (CHILD)		27 MAR 1917	1917	NATHAN & REIKEL	
328	A26	GROSSMAN, ANNA RUTH		3 OCT 1965	18 JUN 1910		
249	C20	GROSSMAN, BERNARD		27 NOV 1982	17 SEP 1916		
119	K49	GROSSMAN, CHAIM		20 JAN 1984	4 APR 1930	ISAAC	
107	G16	GROSSMAN, I MILDRED	ZAMEL	19 APR 1974			
119	K47	GROSSMAN, ISAAC		6 AUG 1981	7 OCT 1903		
105	I17	GROSSMAN, ISRAEL M		22 AUG 1940	1859		
249	D30	GROSSMAN, JACOB		21 NOV 1964	13 OCT 1903		
105	L14	GROSSMAN, MARY		1983	1882		
751	I 2	GROSSMAN, PAUL		NDD	9 JAN 1939		SUE
125	B 32	GROSSMAN, RACHEL	JARTMAN	15 NOV 1973			NATHAN
751	I 1	GROSSMAN, SUE		12 AUG 1988	6 AUG 1939		PAUL
125	A 31	GROSSMAN, YALE JULIUS		30 JUL 1967	1915	NATHAN & RACHEL (JARTMAN)	
104	I10	GROSZMANN, ILONA		29 OCT 1969	10 JUN 1896		
446	C31	GROVER, BESSIE		8 AUG 1911	1853		MAX
446	C34	GROVER, MAX		26 MAR 1913	14 SEP 1863		BESSIE
447	C22	GROWER, ANNIE JOSEPHINE		20 FEB 1982	1886		LOUIS
447	G31	GROWER, ISRAEL L DDS		5 NOV 1988	1910	LOUIS & ANNIE	
391	ZA59	GROWER, JACK		27 DEC 1960		MORDECHAI	
447	I12	GROWER, JULIUS H MD		1 MAR 1967	2 FEB 1898		
447	G18	GROWER, LEA		14 OCT 1979	10 SEP 1901		
447	C21	GROWER, LOUIS		31 OCT 1947	1882		ANNIE
447	C23	GROWER, MYER D		1964	1911	LOUIS & ANNIE	
102	U14	GRUBER, ISRAEL		22 AUG 1970	1887	WILLIAM & ROSE	SADIE
102	A63	GRUBER, JACOB		1941	1891		
121	F 8	GRUBER, JACOB J		11 JUL 1969	1892		
433	H23	GRUBER, LENA		27 JUN 1937	1848	ZALMAN	LOUIS
433	H24	GRUBER, LOUIS		15 JUL 1938	1858		LENA
102	U13	GRUBER, ROSE		20 MAR 1937	1866		WILLIAM
102	U15	GRUBER, SADIE H		14 APR 1974	1890		ISRAEL
102	U12	GRUBER, WILLIAM		OCT 1930	1862		ROSE
377	L35	GRUBNER, HELEN W		1964	1883		MAURICE
377	L33	GRUBNER, MAURICE		1959	1883		HELEN
377	K33	GRUBNER, MERIAM FRANCES		30 MAR 1910	10 APR 1908		
377	L34	GRUBNER, WALTER R		1942	1911	MAURICE & HELEN	
119	C18	GRUENBERG, ROBERT S		12 JUL 1987	18 JAN 1914		
391	R46	GRUSKIN, ADELAIDE IRENE	KNASIN	23 MAY 1949	10 MAR 1920	NATHAN & ESTHER (ABESS)	MURRAY
391	ZA51	GRUSKIN, ANNA	ROSOFSKY	16 SEP 1973	1 DEC 1884	ABRAHAM MORDECHAI	SAMUEL
391	E28	GRUSKIN, BESSIE	SIMON	6 APR 1945	1866	YEHUDA	HARRY

Cem	Row	Name	Maiden Name	DOD	DOB	Parents	Spouse
391	ZH66	GRUSKIN, ESTELLE	GERSTEIN	15 FEB 1995	30 JAN 1909	HYMAN & BESSIE (LABBINGER)	SAMUEL
391	E29	GRUSKIN, HARRY		15 MAR 1957	1871	ABRAHAM & BEILA (RUBENSTEIN)	BESSIE
391	U69	GRUSKIN, ISSER		31 OCT 1975	4 OCT 1898	HARRY & BESSIE (SIMON)	MILDRED
391		GRUSKIN, MILDRED	WLADAVER	8 OCT 1992	12 JUL 1902	MAX & LILY (SCHWARTZ)	ISSER
391	ZB55	GRUSKIN, MURRAY		8 OCT 1994	10 APR 1911	SAMUEL & ANNA (ROSOFSKY)	SARAH
391	ZA50	GRUSKIN, SAMUEL		11 JUL 1961	1 APR 1881	ABRAHAM & BEILA (RUBENSTEIN)	ANNA
391	ZB54	GRUSKIN, SOLLY		28 MAR 1995	14 JUN 1906	SAMUEL & ANNA (ROSOFSKY)	ADELAIDE
391		GRUSKIN, SOPHIE		22 FEB 1929	25 DEC 1910	HARRY & BESSIE (SIMON)	
112	D21	GUENZBURGER, EMMY R		30 NOV 1980	30 APR 1885		
125	K 51	GUNER, YETTIE		19 JUL 1898	1897		
116	A 7	GUNNER, TILLIE		9 JUN 1984	15 SEP 1898		
447	W 9	GUNTER, FAYE		8 JAN 1965	30 AUG 1912		WILLIAM
447	W10	GUNTER, WILLIAM DDS		25 NOV 1986	24 AUG 1905		FAYE
750	F13	GUNTHER, LOUIS A		6 AUG 1991	2 AUG 1913		
392	D 6	GUREWITZ, ROBERT		16 OCT 1985	5 OCT 1908	DAVID	
330	AC 4	GURIAN, HARRY		7 DEC 1970	18 MAY 1907		
751	F36	GURIN, ROSE		14 MAR 1926	1886		
446	B16	GURLAND, EDNA		17 DEC 1917	10 MAR 1915		
447	M38	GURLAND, HAROLD G		1976	1909		
372	C13	GUSS, HELEN	RABINOVITCH	NDD			LOUIS
372	C12	GUSS, LOUIS MD		25 SEP 1992	17 SEP 1914		HELEN
116	W 8	GUTCHEON, ALVIN		17 JAN 1974	21 MAR 1921		
116	N 5	GUTCHEON, IRVING		27 OCT 1990	27 FEB 1918		SHIRLEY
116	N 6	GUTCHEON, SHIRLEY	COHEN	7 NOV 1985	6 NOV 1922		IRVING
105	J18	GUTER, BETTY	KLEIMAN	NDD			LEON
105	J19	GUTER, LEON		28 OCT 1985	23 JUL 1911		BETTY
330	E48	GUTERMAN, ANNIE		25 FEB 1941	1874		
116	BK55	GUTHART, ABRAHAM		18 SEP 1976	15 DEC 1903		
121	G44	GUTKIN, ANNETTE		9 FEB 1989	1 MAR 1909		
125		GUTMAN, (BABY)		13 OCT 1928	9 OCT 1928	I & EMMA (GARST)	
125	I183	GUTMAN, BERNICE P		8 JAN 1983	1909		LEONARD
125	Q198	GUTMAN, BERTHA		19 JUL 1962	1902		
330	AH32	GUTMAN, JAMES JAY		12 MAR 1991	15 FEB 1952		
374	A39	GUTMAN, LEON		6 NOV 1974	1902		
125	I184	GUTMAN, LEONARD J		5 FEB 1971	1903		BERNICE
125	Q197	GUTMAN, MARY	SOKOL	21 MAR 1976	1896		
125		GUTMAN, SAM		8 MAR 1926	JUL 1925	SAMUEL	
329	A14	GUTTERMAN, HYMAN		31 DEC 1978	29 JUN 1901		PAULINE
329	A22	GUTTERMAN, JULIUS		9 SEP 1964	18 MAY 1903		SARA
329	A15	GUTTERMAN, PAULINE		14 FEB 1982	21 OCT 1912		HYMAN
329	A23	GUTTERMAN, SARA		23 NOV 1972	24 NOV 1912		JULIUS
447	AD40	GUY, MAYNARD N		24 MAY 1984	1931		
125	L 98	GWOSDOWF, ANNA		7 MAY 1932	1869		ANNA
125	S142	GWOSDOWF, ESTHER	POLSKY	4 JAN 1938	1866	YITZCHAK PERETZ	
125	L150	GWOSDOWF, MARY	MEREMINSKY	5 APR 1955	1868		
125	L 96	GWOSDOWF, MENDEL		13 MAY 1927	1901	SAMUEL & ANNA	
125	J160	GWOSDOWF, PAULINE ROSE		13 OCT 1991	28 OCT 1896		SAMUEL
125	K159	GWOSDOWF, REBECCA		2 DEC 1980	15 SEP 1900		WILLIAM
125	J159	GWOSDOWF, SAMUEL FELIX		3 SEP 1955	1894		PAULINE
125	L 97	GWOSDOWF, SAMUEL J		4 AUG 1960	1866		SAMUEL
125	K157	GWOSDOWF, WILLIAM MERREL		6 AUG 1968	2 OCT 1932		REBECCA
125	K160	GWOSDOWF, WILLIAM N		6 JAN 1960	17 NOV 1902		REBECCA
125	R183	HABER, FANNIE		16 FEB 1961	1880		
107	A17	HABER, IRENE B		11 DEC 1983	29 SEP 1904		
101	D20	HABER, ISADORE I		23 MAY 1959	1915		SHIRLEY
101	E18	HABER, ROSE		11 APR 1978	1891		SAMUEL
125	R159	HABER, ROSE		15 AUG 1944	1858	ASHER & LEAH	
101	E19	HABER, SAMUEL H		11 MAR 1977	1891		ROSE
125	O139	HABER, SAMUEL M		21 FEB 1976	1897		SIDELLE
101	D15	HABER, SHIRLEY H		25 DEC 1982	1927		ISADORE
125	O138	HABER, SIDELLE		14 MAR 1973	1899		SAMUEL
125	ZC169	HABER, SYLVIA		7 JUL 1993			
108	B13	HACK, ARTHUR		16 JUL 1976	1901		ETTA
108	B14	HACK, ETTA		26 JAN 1963	1908		ARTHUR
102	A79	HACKENBURG, BESSIE SILBERMA	GRUBER	16 DEC 1976	25 SEP 1896		
118	B11	HACKMAN, JENNIE E		16 APR 1965			

Cem	Row	Name	Maiden Name	DOD	DOB	Parents	Spouse
447	X 2	HAFTEL, EDITH		25 JUL 1984	1907		
447	X 3	HAFTEL, MORRIS		23 MAR 1981	1904		MORRIS
751	I13	HAGAN, JENNIE		27 FEB 1954	1863		EDITH
751	I14	HAGAN, MICHAEL		8 JUL 1943	1861		MICHAEL
446	A76	HAHN, ALBERT		24 FEB 1881	DEC 1880	LOUIS & ALICE	JENNIE
391	Q51	HAHN, ETHEL	LEADER	20 NOV 1961		ELIEZER	
391	Q55	HAHN, WILLIAM		8 JUN 1985		ELIEZER	WILLIAM
371	AM14	HAIMAN, ALBERT		6 APR 1983	16 JUL 1899		ETHEL
371	AM13	HAIMAN, YETTA		23 JUL 1972	10 SEP 1911		YETTA
103	E49	HAKIAN, EFRIAM		21 OCT 1985	28 MAY 1928		ALBERT
751	E19	HALBERSTAM, BERTHA M		1 MAY 1965		HARRY & SARAH	
751	E18	HALBERSTAM, BETTY		28 APR 1974		HARRY & SARAH	
751	D11	HALBERSTAM, CHARLES A		10 JUN 1950	9 FEB 1897		
751	D13	HALBERSTAM, EUGENE		1977	1900		
751	H20	HALBERSTAM, HARRY		1945	1867		SARAH
751	H19	HALBERSTAM, SARAH E		1949	1872		HARRY
121	F13	HALL, JEAN	KENT	14 AUG 1985	31 JAN 1904	CELIA	
370	A33	HALPERIN, ABRAHAM		1908	1877		
222	AB 2	HALPERIN, ROSE		11 NOV 1953	1879		
125	E 37	HALPERIN, SAMUEL ALBERT		18 DEC 1966			
447	Y16	HALPERN, ABRAHAM D		11 OCT 1983			ANN
447	Y15	HALPERN, ANN E		NDD			ABRAHAM
447	Z17	HALPERN, ANNE S		28 AUG 1982	1915		BENJAMIN
447	Z18	HALPERN, BENJAMIN		22 NOV 1991	1907		ANNE
117	E 1	HALPERN, DELORES ROSE		25 SEP 1987	5 SEP 1930		
125	P151	HALPERN, GUSSIE		15 MAR 1948	1 MAY 1877	SOLOMON & BELLA	
447	R 6	HALPERN, HARRY		19 SEP 1981	9 JAN 1912		
125	N 81	HALPERN, HARRY ALBERT		8 NOV 1922	1878	SOLOMON & BELLA	
330	F58	HALPERN, JULIUS		26 JUL 1931	1881		
391	GB 1	HALPERN, JULIUS V		24 NOV 1970	19 NOV 1896	ABRAHAM	PEARL
249	D32	HALPERN, MORRIS C		2 FEB 1981	6 SEP 1901		
391	GB 2	HALPERN, PEARL G		30 AUG 1965	14 FEB 1903	JACOB	JULIUS
391	F23	HALPERN, PHILIP		27 SEP 1927	9 FEB 1903	ABRAHAM	
222	L 3	HAMMER, FRANCES	CANTOR	31 OCT 1980	1894		LOUIS
371	AA21	HAMMER, GRACE	GANS	5 SEP 1984			ISADORE
371	AA20	HAMMER, ISADORE		23 JUL 1978			GRACE
222	L 4	HAMMER, LOUIS RABBI		20 MAR 1959	1892		FRANCES
370	V23	HAMMER, MAROLE		9 MAR 1920			
112	A42	HAMMERSCHLAG, MAX		21 SEP 1991	23 NOV 1909		
370	H25	HANDBERGE, OVA		1910	1858		
370	S25	HANDELMAN, DAVID		1 FEB 1945			GUTE
370	S24	HANDELMAN, GUTE CHASO		31 AUG 1911			DAVID
370	G48	HANDELMAN, MORRIS		30 JAN 1927	1901	SARAH	
370	A49	HANDELMAN, SARAH		17 APR 1921	1882		
373	I 1	HANDLEMAN, JACOB		13 JAN 1963	3 FEB 1914		
376	C21	HANDLEMAN, KATHERINE		14 MAY 1990	15 MAY 1924		
101	J19	HANDLER, FENY		10 OCT 1927	1851		
113	L24	HANDLER, IRVING		24 APR 1984	15 JUN 1909		
127	B	HANDLER, MARK STEVEN MD		8 JUN 1984	29 JUN 1945		
447	AB21	HANDLER, ZELDAMAE		1993	1927		
125	I125	HANIN, MARY	GERLOWIN	28 MAR 1939	1871		SAUL
125	I131	HANIN, NELLIE		1993		CHAIM & MINNIE	
125	I130	HANIN, SARAH		24 JUN 1983	1907		
125	I124	HANIN, SAUL L		8 JAN 1937	1877	DAVE N & BASHE R	MARY
370	P33	HANKIN, BAILE		30 JAN 1943			ISRAEL
371	J39	HANKIN, BESSIE	GOLUBCHICK	3 JUL 1978	5 JUL 1905		ORRIN
371	L35	HANKIN, HARRY		16 MAY 1953	1886	AARON & LENA	JENNIE
370	T 9	HANKIN, HERMAN I		10 FEB 1991	24 FEB 1914		ISABEL
370	L26	HANKIN, ISABEL		1940	1929		HERMAN
370	P32	HANKIN, ISRAEL		18 JAN 1928			BAILE
371	J41	HANKIN, JENNIE		22 DEC 1973	1891	ORBIN & BESSIE	HARRY
330	AG 7	HANKIN, LAWRENCE S		1 JUL 1980	23 FEB 1927		
370	B 3	HANKIN, LOUIS		20 MAY 1920			SARAH
376	A 5	HANKIN, MAX		13 JAN 1961	23 SEP 1888		ROSE
371	J40	HANKIN, ORRIN		8 OCT 1972	23 SEP 1914		BESSIE
370	J20	HANKIN, RAYE		1935	1893		

Cem	Row	Name	Maiden Name	DOD	DOB	Parents	Spouse
376	A 4	HANKIN, ROSE		29 JUL 1974	12 MAY 1888		MAX
370	I 6	HANKIN, SARAH		27 AUG 1922	1852		LOUIS
370	L28	HANKIN, SHANDEL		25 OCT 1919	19 JUN 1918		
371	L30	HANKIN, WILLIAM		1959	1894		
447	V23	HANTMAN, CELIA		28 MAR 1938	1861		
371	G 2	HANTMAN, FRANCES		11 JAN 1983	9 JAN 1906		
102	AJ170	HARRIS, A SHERRY		1965	1895		BEATRICE
102	A31	HARRIS, ADELINE	CINCIMER	1936	1883		
102	AJ171	HARRIS, BEATRICE		1986	1896		A SHERRY
433	C 9	HARRIS, BERTHA		13 JAN 1992	28 DEC 1906	HERSHEL	SOL
102	V14	HARRIS, CHARLES		12 APR 1929	1877		MAY
102	AC67	HARRIS, CLARA	GIBBS	12 AUG 1935	1862		HERMAN
751	N 6	HARRIS, DAVID H		1962	1890		
104	H21	HARRIS, DORA		11 FEB 1971			
102	AE111	HARRIS, ELIZABETH	ROSENBLATT	23 OCT 1971	13 JAN 1906		WILLIAM
377	B34	HARRIS, FRANK		12 MAY 1986	6 MAR 1896	NATHAN	
391	Y57	HARRIS, FREDERIC G		11 FEB 1973	26 JUL 1922	AARON ISAAC	
102	A75	HARRIS, GERTRUDE		31 JAN 1943	1873		
377	A32	HARRIS, GERTRUDE J		22 APR 1984	24 OCT 1906	HIRSHEL	LOUIS
101	A36	HARRIS, HARRY		8 APR 1919	1859		
377	B32	HARRIS, HATTIE		27 JUL 1939	14 DEC 1876	ISAAC	
377	A30	HARRIS, HATTIE R		20 APR 1988	7 MAR 1908	YECHIEL	HENRY
377	A31	HARRIS, HENRY		27 APR 1979	23 FEB 1901	CHAIM	HATTIE
102	AC68	HARRIS, HERMAN		26 SEP 1936	1860		CLARA
102	V16	HARRIS, JACOB A		1 MAY 1933			SARAH
102	AJ27	HARRIS, LEON		11 JUN 1944	1897	PHILIP & SARAH	MARY
377	A33	HARRIS, LOUIS		28 MAY 1985	6 JUL 1897	NATHAN	GERTRUDE
102	L32	HARRIS, LOUIS GABRIEL		4 NOV 1934	11 NOV 1877		SARAH
102	AJ28	HARRIS, MARY	KAYSER	22 DEC 1990	8 NOV 1903		LEON
102	V13	HARRIS, MAY G		3 JAN 1942	1882		CHARLES
377	B31	HARRIS, NATHAN		15 AUG 1939	15 JUN 1873	ISAAC	
102	AJ26	HARRIS, PHILIP		27 MAR 1944	1867		SARAH
751	N 5	HARRIS, ROSE	DANZIGER	1972	1891		
391	D15	HARRIS, SAMSON		8 JUL 1938		JACOB TZVI	
377	B30	HARRIS, SAMUEL		4 MAY 1988	1 FEB 1899	NATHAN	
102	L33	HARRIS, SARAH	TULIN	6 SEP 1962	7 JUL 1877		LOUIS
102	AJ25	HARRIS, SARAH		15 AUG 1964	1872		PHILIP
374	F18	HARRIS, SARAH	RACZKOWSKA	1922	1858		
102	V15	HARRIS, SARAH	BLAND	26 APR 1956			JACOB
433	C 8	HARRIS, SOL		4 JAN 1969	2 JAN 1904	ISAAC	BERTHA
112	D31	HARRIS, VICTOR		1979	1911		
377	B33	HARRIS, WILLIAM		7 APR 1953	18 OCT 1894	NATHAN	
102	AE112	HARRIS, WILLIAM		30 JAN 1988	24 JUL 1899		ELIZABETH
447	Q37	HARRISON, BARUCH DARDECK		5 JUL 1966	1883		CELIA
102	K 8	HARRISON, FLORENCE		17 FEB 1987	11 MAY 1902		
113	N36	HARRISON, PHILIP		25 JUL 1989	6 OCT 1916		
391	F 5	HARSHOWITZ, ISAAC		6 NOV 1939	1878	YEHUDA	
125		HART, EVA		20 JUN 1915	1871	LEISER & CHAYA	
125	Z170	HART, SHIRLEY	ALPERT	1 MAY 1986			
102	O28	HARTENBERG, BESSIE		1944	1879		JOSEPH
102	O27	HARTENBERG, JOSEPH		1934	1878		BESSIE
102	O29	HARTENBERG, SAMUEL L		1925	1901	JOSEPH & BESSIE	
374	D 4	HARTLING, (BABY)		1940			
374	J41	HARTLING, KATIE ANN		1981	1906		
370	K10	HARTMAN, EVA	ARBER	29 JUN 1948	1883		SAMUEL
330	AF 8	HARTMAN, PAULINE		17 AUG 1984	11 NOV 1898		SAMUEL
377	Q16	HARTMAN, RUDOLPH		28 OCT 1970	17 DEC 1912		
330	AF 7	HARTMAN, SAMUEL		8 SEP 1964	11 OCT 1898		PAULINE
370	K11	HARTMAN, SAMUEL		18 SEP 1956	1883		EVA
125	D 26	HARTSTEIN, ARNOLD		6 MAR 1963	1921		
102	J48	HARVEY, KENNETH		1979	1918		
125	S174	HARVEY, MINNA	ORENSTEIN	20 AUG 1959	1880		
105	C10	HARVEY, ROSE	NERMEROFF	2 MAY 1965			
102	U34	HASENFRATZ, RUTH	WALKER	25 JAN 1978	15 AUG 1919		
123		HASKIN, HARRIS		1989	1921		
119	L30	HATTEM, CHARLES		18 APR 1989	21 MAR 1922		

Cem	Row	Name	Maiden Name	DOD	DOB	Parents	Spouse
107	J27	HAUPTMAN, WILLIAM DOV		27 FEB 1988	10 JUN 1948		
447	X13	HAUSER, DOROTHY		22 JUN 1964	8 DEC 1891		PAUL
447	X14	HAUSER, PAUL		6 JUN 1968	28 JAN 1891		DOROTHY
102	AA75	HAUSS, DONALD MD		1 JAN 1991	20 NOV 1924		
377	N26	HAUSS, MORRIS		9 OCT 1966	7 APR 1893	CHAIM	REBECCA
377	N27	HAUSS, REBECCA R		31 JAN 1985	24 MAR 1896	NOACH	MORRIS
102	W26	HAYMOND, IDA		22 SEP 1945	1870		MORRIS
102	W25	HAYMOND, MORRIS		6 AUG 1953	1868		IDA
107	H20	HEALY, BRETTA	HENOWITZ	31 JUL 1972	1925	LOUIS & GUSSIE	
371	AI24	HECHT, ESTHER LEAH		20 NOV 1958	1880	FRANK & ESTHER	
373	I20	HECHT, ISRAEL		11 APR 1952	1905		
125	L133	HECHT, JACOB		23 OCT 1931	1860		
370	Q46	HECHT, SAMUEL ZEV		10 SEP 1934		ISRAEL	
391	W68	HECHTER, ABRAHAM I		21 FEB 1973	1910		
391	Y59	HECHTER, JODY LEWIS		23 JUL 1966	1949	ABRAHAM ISAAC	
447	AB10	HECKER, FANNIE F		23 OCT 1975	1 JUL 1885		
371	AI22	HECKT, ESTHER K		28 AUG 1964	1915		FRANK
371	AI23	HECKT, FRANK L		30 DEC 1989	1912		ESTHER
391	Z79	HECTER, RUTH G		4 NOV 1983	24 JUN 1908		
125	A 35	HEFFLER, LENA	KATZ	5 MAR 1986	12 MAR 1896		
125	B 36	HEFFLER, MEYER		11 NOV 1966	1884		REGINA
125	B 37	HEFFLER, REGINA	DUBOWY	7 MAR 1944	23 NOV 1889	SHLOMO & ATAH	MEYER
102	AA89	HEILPERN, GEORGE S		28 AUG 1992			
102	AA86	HEILPERN, JOSEPH S		21 JUL 1947	6 JUL 1876		SARAH
102	AA87	HEILPERN, SARAH G		3 JUN 1967	12 FEB 1888		JOSEPH
374	A37	HEILWEIL, ANITA	ORENSTEIN	15 JUL 1974	28 MAR 1932		JUDAH
374	G40	HEILWEIL, ISSAC W		20 APR 1956			
374	A36	HEILWEIL, JUDAH		12 OCT 1936			ANITA
374	A35	HEILWEIL, PHILIP		11 NOV 1934			
125	G 52	HEIMAN, AARON		20 JUL 1971	17 APR 1902		EVA
125	R199	HEIMAN, DAVID		1 MAR 1961	1901		
125	G 53	HEIMAN, EVA	KOPLOWITZ	13 FEB 1985	26 AUG 1902		AARON
372	A 2	HEIMAN, HELEN		26 JUL 1985	16 JUL 1892		
372	A 3	HEIMAN, MILDRED F		4 SEP 1964	12 NOV 1913		
116	BJ114	HEIMOV, ETHEL		22 OCT 1992	3 JUL 1906		MAX
116	BJ113	HEIMOV, HERBERT L		22 NOV 1975	1934	MAX & ETHEL	
116	BJ115	HEIMOV, MAX		4 DEC 1982	22 DEC 1907		ETHEL
102	AD186	HEIMOVITCH, BESSIE	UNGER	8 JUN 1964	1887		EDWARD
102	AD187	HEIMOVITCH, EDWARD		21 APR 1970	1883	SAMUEL & SARAH	BESSIE
102	S25	HEIMOVITCH, HANNAH S		3 MAY 1977	7 JUL 1888		WILLIAM
330	C25	HEIMOVITCH, HERMAN		20 JUN 1951	1887		
102	S24	HEIMOVITCH, SARAH		27 JAN 1926	1858		SAMUEL
102	S26	HEIMOVITCH, WILLIAM		31 MAY 1948	15 AUG 1879	SARAH	HANNAH
249	B 9	HELFGOTT, JACK		10 DEC 1959	1 MAY 1901		
105	C47	HELLBERG, EUGENE J		1964	1957		
392	C28	HELLER, ABRAHAM		1974	1890		DEINE
222	F14	HELLER, ALBERT		1982	1893		
391	P53	HELLER, ALEX		22 AUG 1945	1873	ABRAHAM	
392	J 6	HELLER, ARNOLD		13 SEP 1930		ABRAHAM	
329	F24	HELLER, BESSIE		15 OCT 1982	1917		
392	C29	HELLER, DEINE		1949	1892		ABRAHAM
249	B 2	HELLER, HARRY		26 SEP 1941	1909	ISIDORE & SARAH	
329	B37	HELLER, ISADORE		20 DEC 1942	1888		ROSE
249	B 4	HELLER, ISADORE JACOB		31 JUL 1969	1879		SARAH
249	B 1	HELLER, NORBERT HARRY		4 MAY 1957	26 DEC 1947		
329	A12	HELLER, ROSE		27 OCT 1961	1892		ISADORE
110	B27	HELLER, SADIE		14 NOV 1954	1891		
249	B 3	HELLER, SARAH LEAH	SCHEINMAN	14 FEB 1954	1881		ISADORE
391	L41	HELLER, SONIA		17 APR 1934	1866	ISAAC JACOB	
392	F36	HELLER, TILLIE		15 AUG 1949	1919	ABRAHAM PHALIK	
104	N40	HELLERMAN, MORRIS		20 AUG 1983	1899		
102	W 9	HELPER, CASPER		28 OCT 1956	1897		MOLLY
102	W 8	HELPER, MOLLIE	SIGAL	4 APR 1975	1897		CASPER
391	ZB66	HENDEL, BERNARD T		23 AUG 1979	22 JUL 1904	SHLOMO JACOB	
377	J21	HENDEL, DANIEL		1958	1913	PHILIP JACOB & REBECCA	
377	J34	HENDEL, ELIZABETH		9 OCT 1962	25 JAN 1892	ZALMAN	JULIUS

Cem	Row	Name	Maiden Name	DOD	DOB	Parents	Spouse
377	J26	HENDEL, HELEN		13 OCT 1964	1878	YEHUDA	RICHARD
377	H35	HENDEL, HILBERT		30 OCT 1986	22 AUG 1901	SOLOMON	
377	R11	HENDEL, IRVING G		1971	1897		LENA
377	I24	HENDEL, ISADORE MD		1975	1895	FIVEL ZELIG	
377	J33	HENDEL, JULIUS		8 NOV 1960	10 JUL 1884	SANDER	ELIZABETH
377	P 2	HENDEL, LAUREN ELIZABETH		28 AUG 1986	18 JAN 1986		
377	S17	HENDEL, LAWRENCE S		1959	1930		
377	R12	HENDEL, LENA G		1993	1900		IRVING
377	Z12	HENDEL, LILLIAN B		15 MAY 1991	23 MAR 1909	SAMUEL	
377	R13	HENDEL, MAURICE L		1972	1899		RUTH
377	J22	HENDEL, PHILIP JACOB	(FIVAL ZELIG)	1934	1872		REBECCA
377	J23	HENDEL, REBECCA S		1972	1873		PHILIP
377	J25	HENDEL, RICHARD		29 JUN 1938	1878	SANDER	HELEN
377	I34	HENDEL, ROWENA P		15 MAY 1978	6 APR 1926	ZEV	
377	R14	HENDEL, RUTH T		1976	1902		MAURICE
222	D 8	HENDERSON, ENID	PEARL	5 SEP 1989	22 MAR 1943	SAMUEL & GOLDIE	
370	J36	HENENSON, ETTA		19 NOV 1941	1875		JACOB
371	J26	HENENSON, HERMAN		24 AUG 1967	12 SEP 1907		
370	L 4	HENENSON, JACOB		14 AUG 1944	1869		ETTA
102	E30	HENKEN, MAX		16 JAN 1967	1883		PAULINE
447	R32	HENKEN, MINNIE		6 FEB 1975			SAMUEL
102	E29	HENKEN, PAULINE		30 AUG 1966	1895		MAX
447	R33	HENKEN, SAMUEL L		6 OCT 1960			MINNIE
107	H18	HENOWITZ, GUSSIE R		1980	1900		LOUIS
107	H14	HENOWITZ, JOSEPH GEORGE		14 OCT 1988	19 APR 1919		
107	H19	HENOWITZ, LOUIS		1 NOV 1975	12 MAR 1895		GUSSIE
370	M54	HENSCHEL, ANNA T		1944	1883		RUDOLPH
370	M55	HENSCHEL, RUDOLPH		1943	1880		ANNA
370	M57	HENSCHEL, STANLEY J		21 JAN 1959	17 SEP 1905	RUDOLPH & ANNA	
102	AB34	HERBERT, BAILA		1949	1871		NATHAN
102	AB33	HERBERT, HARRY S		6 OCT 1974	26 FEB 1900	NATHAN & BAILA	
113	A 9	HERBERT, JOSEPH		27 APR 1987	3 MAY 1926		
102	AB35	HERBERT, NATHAN		1947	1866		BAILA
330	AI 9	HERBST, JOSEPH		14 MAR 1983	26 NOV 1893		ROSE
330	AI 8	HERBST, ROSE		17 MAY 1979	15 APR 1899		JOSEPH
102	AG88	HERCHMAN, GEORGE J		29 NOV 1960	1904	SAMUEL & PAULA	
102	AG86	HERCHMAN, PAULA		27 AUG 1942	1877		SAMUEL
102	AG85	HERCHMAN, ROSE DR		29 JAN 1953	1893		ABRAHAM
102	AG87	HERCHMAN, SAMUEL		3 MAR 1936	1874		PAULA
116	AY20	HERLICK, ELEANOR A		13 APR 1971	25 APR 1925		
116	A 4	HERLICK, MILDRED		6 JUL 1983	17 SEP 1891		
102	B 1	HERMAN, ADA		30 NOV 1967	6 JAN 1890		LOUIS
374	E 1	HERMAN, ANNA		16 SEP 1927	1875		
374	F 2	HERMAN, BLUMA		14 1918	1853		
125	Y185	HERMAN, ELLIOT		13 JUL 1984	13 AUG 1907		
370	I55	HERMAN, FRED		1 MAR 1953	1889		
370	G37	HERMAN, HENRY		1911	1854		
331		HERMAN, JACOB		31 OCT 1917	1859		
330	D34	HERMAN, JERRY		20 JUL 1961	1893		
116	BF138	HERMAN, JOSEPH L		3 APR 1991	6 JUL 1924		
102	B 2	HERMAN, LOUIS		23 FEB 1965	29 JUN 1885		ADA
329	C37	HERMAN, MILTON B		27 FEB 1981	17 DEC 1909		
125	M124	HERMAN, MINNIE		24 JUN 1936	1871	DAVID & ETHEL	
370	I34	HERMAN, MOLLIE		23 JUL 1931			
102	BH33	HERMAN, MURRAY		29 JUL 1991	28 JUL 1905		
370	I65	HERMAN, OSCAR		27 FEB 1947			
125	S191	HERMANN, HARRY M		21 APR 1958	1898		TILLIE
125	S190	HERMANN, TILLIE	LEWIS	31 JUL 1961	1894		HARRY
102	T38	HERRUP, ELI		1927	1849		GUSSIE
102	T37	HERRUP, GUSSIE	POSANER	1922	1853		ELI
102	U 8	HERRUP, MORRIS		28 FEB 1952	17 MAR 1893		
102	U18	HERRUP, RHEA	NOLL	12 JUL 1951	20 MAY 1899	HARRIS & IDA	
102	T39	HERRUP, SOLOMON R		1939	1880	ELI & GUSSIE (POSANER)	
116	AU 5	HERSH, HAROLD S		20 MAR 1968	1916		LOTTIE
116	AU 4	HERSH, LOTTIE		13 SEP 1958	10 NOV 1918		HAROLD
101	A 5	HERSHMAN, GEDALIAH		5 DEC 1916	1839		

Cem	Row	Name	Maiden Name	DOD	DOB	Parents	Spouse
447	Q17	HERSHMAN, M MANNIE		16 OCT 1952	23 DEC 1914		
375	E46	HERSHMAN, MORRIS		27 JAN 1910	1895		
391	Y60	HERSHOWITZ, LENA		6 FEB 1981	1882	ABRAHAM	
125	C 25	HERSHOWITZ, SIDNEY J		4 DEC 1960	1905		JARTMAN
125	C 24	HERSHOWITZ, STEVEN WILLIAM		24 OCT 1957	1944	SIDNEY	
370	B14	HERTZ, ABRAHAM		21 FEB 1919			
370	L23	HERTZ, FRANK		4 FEB 1945			ROSE
391	E40	HERTZ, JEROME		7 JAN 1927	9 APR 1926		
391	Z51	HERTZ, MAX		15 FEB 1965	8 JUL 1898	EFFRAIM	ROSE
370	A15	HERTZ, ORRIN		1974	1893		
371	A21	HERTZ, PHILIP		1988	1900		
370	I19	HERTZ, ROSA		28 FEB 1923			
370	L22	HERTZ, ROSE D		3 OCT 1951			FRANK
391	Z50	HERTZ, ROSE E		22 FEB 1905	22 FEB 1905	ISAAC	MAX
370	B24	HERTZ, SAMUEL G		21 JUL 1924			
447	AA37	HERTZBERG, FAYE L		29 OCT 1975	1905		HERMAN
447	AA36	HERTZBERG, HERMAN L		19 JUL 1972	1900		FAYE
395	A 2	HESS, LENA		1944	1872		SIMON
395	A 3	HESS, SANFORD		1918	1894	SIMON & LENA	
395	A 1	HESS, SIMON		1926	1858		LENA
370	J 2	HEYMAN, BLUMA		18 OCT 1918		YECHIEL ASHER	
102	AI72	HEYMAN, FANNY	SCHOENBERG	15 SEP 1948	1868		
102	AI73	HEYMAN, JACK		1985	1905	FANNIE (SHOENBERG)	
102	AI74	HEYMAN, JOSEPH MD		25 MAY 1965	1896	FANNIE (SHOENBERG)	
125	N 84	HEYMAN, SAMUEL		19 OCT 1923	1893	SHLOMO	
330	F60	HEYMOWITZ, LOUIS		25 MAR 1943	1859		ROSE
330	F59	HEYMOWITZ, ROSE		27 JUL 1931	1857		LOUIS
391	P33	HEZKOWITZ, FANNIE		2 NOV 1916	1873	MOSHE YEHUDA	
391	S37	HIDOV, IDA	LAMPERT	31 JAN 1920	1890	MOSHE	
751	D36	HIGHSMITH, RACHEL ALANA		5 MAR 1985			
248	M71	HILLER, RACHEL		4 JAN 1942	1870		
392	J 3	HILLSBERG, (BABY GIRL)		21 JUN 1958			
392	B 2	HILLSBERG, BETHANY PERRI		21 MAR 1983	19 MAY 1977		
392	A21	HILLSBERG, CAROLINE	MILLER	16 NOV 1991	16 MAY 1926		
392	B 3	HILLSBERG, MAX		1992	1892		SARAH
392	B 1	HILLSBERG, RISA SUSAN		21 MAR 1983	2 MAR 1970		
370	I13	HILLSBERG, ROSE		11 OCT 1918			
392	B 4	HILLSBERG, SARAH		1970	1897		MAX
125	K118	HIMBERG, HARRY		13 FEB 1934	1882		LENA
125	K117	HIMBERG, LENA		23 FEB 1971	1886		HARRY
116	W17	HIMELSTEIN, DOROTHY J		6 SEP 1981	15 AUG 1896		
371	AD 6	HIMELSTEIN, MYRTLE		1993			
102	H43	HIMMELBLAU, BESSIE L		12 DEC 1987	10 DEC 1894		
102	A41	HIMMELBLAU, HARRY OSHER		16 JUL 1938	1895		
125	I172	HIMMELFARB, ALEX		30 OCT 1989	17 SEP 1899		ESTHER
125	I171	HIMMELFARB, ESTHER	SPIVAK	18 NOV 1989	5 NOV 1906		ALEX
330	D37	HIMMELSTEIN, DORA		3 JUN 1972	10 APR 1885		LOUIS
103	D8	HIMMELSTEIN, FANNIE		1985	1908		
330	C 4	HIMMELSTEIN, FRANK		20 JUL 1930			LIBBY
330	C 5	HIMMELSTEIN, LIBBY		30 SEP 1937			FRANK
330	D38	HIMMELSTEIN, LOUIS		13 MAR 1962	1 APR 1882		DORA
330	F46	HIMMELSTEIN, MAX A		3 NOV 1926	1885		
330	C 6	HIMMELSTEIN, RACHEL MAY				FRANK & LIBBY	
103	D9	HIMMELSTEIN, ROSE		1986	1910		
103	D7	HIMMELSTEIN, SIDNEY		1982	1914		
330	D36	HIMMELSTEIN, ZELDA		13 SEP 1967	22 JUL 1909	LOUIS & DORA	
391	F37	HIRSCH, ANNIE		28 JUL 1937	1869	ISAAC	ISAAC
372	E 6	HIRSCH, CARRIE		1963	1879		
392	C40	HIRSCH, CHARLES		7 SEP 1973	1893		ROSE
372	D 3	HIRSCH, CHARLOTTE	SOLOMON	1912	1848		HEYMAN
113	O74	HIRSCH, ELSA H		29 MAY 1981	9 MAR 1904		
372	D 2	HIRSCH, HEYMAN J		1925	1839		CHARLOTTE
391	F38	HIRSCH, ISAAC		29 JUL 1938	1860	ISAAC LEV	ANNIE
102	AI218	HIRSCH, JOSEPH L		28 MAY 1975	11 NOV 1908		
372	E 5	HIRSCH, MADELINE		1966	1882		
372	D 4	HIRSCH, MARION		1892	1876	HEYMAN & CHARLOTTE	

Cem	Row	Name	Maiden Name	DOD	DOB	Parents	Spouse
102	AI219	HIRSCH, MARY		30 NOV 1992			
370	B19	HIRSCH, MEYER R		27 JUL 1915	1827		
395	C12	HIRSCH, NATHAN		16 DEC 1979	15 OCT 1877	HEDER CHAIM	SARAH
392	C41	HIRSCH, ROSE		2 MAY 1960	1896		
370	I11	HIRSCH, SARAH G		13 SEP 1919	1831		CHARLES MEYER
102	AI220	HIRSCH, WILLIAM		7 JAN 1992		JOSEPH	
751	E20	HIRSCHBERG, LILLIAN	HALBERSTAM	1978	1907	HARRY & SARAH	THEODORE
751	E21	HIRSCHBERG, THEODORE J		1961	1891		LILLIAN
330	H 1	HIRSCHFELD, HARRY		20 MAY 1908	21 AUG 1906		
377	V50	HIRSCHMAN, GUSSIE	HIRSCHMAN	28 APR 1984	22 NOV 1906	SAMUEL	
102	AB159	HIRSH, ARTHUR M		1978	1907		
102	D11	HIRSHBERG, MANUEL		18 FEB 1985	14 AUG 1903		
391	ZD54	HIRTH, AMALIA		5 SEP 1986	1894	SHLOMO	MOSES
391	ZD53	HIRTH, MOSES		25 MAY 1965	1887	MEYER HIRSH	AMALIA
125	H137	HITTELMAN, EDWARD		5 JAN 1944	30 MAY 1919	SAMUEL & DWASHE	
125	H138	HITTLEMAN, DORA		NDD	1890		
125	H136	HITTLEMAN, SAMUEL		16 APR 1971	1888		
125	1C67	HOBERMAN, ANNA		8 APR 1920	1893		
125	K131	HOBERMAN, ANNA		24 JAN 1933	1863		ISADORE
125	O 84	HOBERMAN, BESSIE		15 MAR 1919	1889	RUBIN	
371	H 5	HOBERMAN, HINDA		8 MAY 1986	4 MAR 1904		OSHER
125	K132	HOBERMAN, ISIDORE		20 SEP 1941	1856	MORDECHAI	ANNA
447	N38	HOBERMAN, JACOB		20 JAN 1948	1894		
102	AA171	HOBERMAN, MAXWELL G		11 MAY 1981	16 AUG 1911		
371	H 4	HOBERMAN, OSHER		13 JUL 1974	30 APR 1900		HINDA
447	N37	HOBERMAN, RUTH		29 NOV 1928	17 JUL 1926	JACOB	
248	H41	HOCHBERG, ISAAC		13 APR 1936	12 DEC 1862		LENA
248	H47	HOCHBERG, JOSEPH		24 JAN 1979	1897		LILLIAN
248	H42	HOCHBERG, LENA		20 FEB 1948	5 MAY 1878		ISAAC
248	H44	HOCHBERG, LILLIAN		30 JAN 1992	15 JUN 1907		JOSEPH
377	P 1	HOCHMAN, (BABY GIRL)		27 MAR 1963		LOUIS & RUTH	
391	ZE58	HOCHMAN, ESTHER L		29 NOV 1965	1892	BENJAMIN	NATHAN
391	W59	HOCHMAN, FANNIE		11 DEC 1972	10 APR 1894	ISAAC MEYER	JACOB
391	W60	HOCHMAN, JACOB		22 JAN 1969	18 JAN 1891	ABRAHAM	FANNIE
391	ZF53	HOCHMAN, MOLLIE I		31 DEC 1989		SIMON	
391	ZE59	HOCHMAN, NATHAN		16 JUL 1970	1887	ABRAHAM	ESTHER
248	I20	HOCHMAN, SEYMOUR		26 SEP 1975	1924		
119	E31	HOCHMAN, WILLIAM		11 AUG 1991	3 AUG 1917		
391	M34	HOFF, HERMAN B		3 MAY 1960	1889	NACHMAN ELIEZER	
391	P26	HOFF, JOSEPH WILLIAM		17 OCT 1923	1897	NACHMAN ELIEZER	
121	J 1	HOFFENBERG, HERSCHEL B		13 SEP 1991	26 AUG 1917		
432		HOFFMAN,		16 AUG 1897			
121	I 9	HOFFMAN, AARON		8 OCT 1968	1 JUL 1901		
102	X 2	HOFFMAN, ABRAHAM		20 JUL 1933	1880		IDA
125	M199	HOFFMAN, ALBERT		23 AUG 1968	1895		CELIA
102	D 6	HOFFMAN, BARNEY		18 NOV 1985	1900		FLORENCE
125	M198	HOFFMAN, CELIA F		9 SEP 1988	1898		ALBERT
121	K 2	HOFFMAN, DORIS R		24 DEC 1981	6 APR 1907		
121	K 1	HOFFMAN, EDWARD J		25 FEB 1965	7 JAN 1901		
102	AA66	HOFFMAN, EVA	SCHULTZ	10 SEP 1959			
102	D 5	HOFFMAN, FLORENCE		6 JUN 1992	1902		BARNEY
121	I10	HOFFMAN, FREDA	VIZER	24 AUG 1986	26 FEB 1912		
447	L39	HOFFMAN, HYMAN		1989	1906		
102	X 1	HOFFMAN, IDA		20 JUN 1954	1882		ABRAHAM
123		HOFFMAN, IRVING J		14 MAR 1967			
102	AI169	HOFFMAN, ISAAC H		23 OCT 1983	10 APR 1904		
102	C 7	HOFFMAN, ISRAEL		22 AUG 1956	1896		ROSE
102	G 2	HOFFMAN, JACOB		6 NOV 1964	15 OCT 1871		MAMIE
102	A37	HOFFMAN, JOSEPH H		23 FEB 1937	16 AUG 1890		
125	Q157	HOFFMAN, KARL		27 OCT 1945	1888	MOSHE	REGINA
125	C140	HOFFMAN, LEON NOAH		21 JUL 1981	20 NOV 1920		
102	G 1	HOFFMAN, MAMIE	ROME	5 FEB 1970	17 JUL 1876		JACOB
121	K 3	HOFFMAN, PHYLIS H		2 MAR 1991	4 NOV 1934	EDWARD & DORIS	
102	R32	HOFFMAN, RAYMOND		10 APR 1957			SADIE
125	Q158	HOFFMAN, REGINA	WEISS	20 MAY 1971	1895		KARL
102	A44	HOFFMAN, RHODA	LUTWACK	11 FEB 1938	1898		

Cem	Row	Name	Maiden Name	DOD	DOB	Parents	Spouse
102	C 6	HOFFMAN, ROSE	RHEA	25 JAN 1992	1902		ISRAEL
102	R31	HOFFMAN, SADIE	PRANT	30 DEC 1959	1901		RAYMOND
102	X 3	HOFFMAN, SAMUEL K		1 OCT 1987	20 DEC 1903	ABRAHAM & IDA	
101	J22	HOFFMAN, SARAH		7 DEC 1931	1847		
391	N30	HOFFS, NATHAN L		23 JAN 1905	1852	ABRAHAM	
102	AC 3	HOFFSON, PHILIP		1972	1889		TILLIE
102	AC 4	HOFFSON, TILLIE R		1936	1888		PHILIP
102	H40	HOFSTATTER, ALLEN	OF NYC	22 MAR 1970	2 DEC 1894	TENA	GERTRUDE
102	H39	HOFSTATTER, GERTRUDE	ARONSON	12 SEP 1947	2 OCT 1900		ALLEN
391	N33	HOLANDESKY, FANNIE		10 NOV 1900		EFFRAIM	
125	N146	HOLBACK, ABRAHAM		22 DEC 1950	1890		
105	A24	HOLDTMAN, LOUIS		1 SEP 1982	24 MAY 1905		
248	D15	HOLIN, JACOB		3 MAY 1961	5 JUL 1897		
391	GC 1	HOLLANDER, HARRY		3 JUN 1967	6 JUL 1884	PHALIK	JENNIE
116	U14	HOLLANDER, JANET	GREEN	19 APR 1973	5 JUN 1901		PERRY
391	GC 2	HOLLANDER, JENNIE		21 AUG 1965	25 AUG 1882	ISAAC	HARRY
750	I27	HOLLANDER, MARIA		10 FEB 1988	14 MAR 1893		
116	U13	HOLLANDER, PERRY		29 MAY 1979	13 SEP 1904		JANET
391	S55	HOLLANDERSKY, ANNA	STROM	9 DEC 1983	30 JAN 1890	MOSES & GUTE LIEBE (SHAPIRO)	MEYER
391	S32	HOLLANDERSKY, CELIA		10 AUG 1921	1850	MOSHE	
391	M27	HOLLANDERSKY, CHARLES		24 AUG 1921	1848	PERETZ	
391	F17	HOLLANDERSKY, FALK		14 OCT 1930	16 MAR 1834	PERETZ	
391	M28	HOLLANDERSKY, FRANK P		22 SEP 1913	1895	ABBA JACOB	
391	D10	HOLLANDERSKY, JACOB		19 SEP 1942	1867	CALEB & FALK	
391	S54	HOLLANDERSKY, MEYER H		9 SEP 1967	1893	JACOB	ANNA
391	C10	HOLLANDERSKY, PERRY		24 DEC 1946	1888	JACOB	
391	G38	HOLLANDERSKY, SARAH		5 FEB 1931	12 MAR 1842	MOSHE	
391	V58	HOLLANDERSKY, WARREN D		13 AUG 1970	1919	MEYER	
123		HOLLM, CHARLES		16 JAN 1948	1893		
123		HOLLM, DOROTHY	HYMAN	2 JUN 1952	18 SEP 1900		
102	Z103	HOLSTEIN, EDWIN J		8 JAN 1925	27 SEP 1879		KITTIE
102	Z106	HOLSTEIN, HELEN J		23 MAR 1990	25 NOV 1922		IVAN
102	Z105	HOLSTEIN, IVAN M		20 JUL 1968	25 JUN 1907	EDWIN & KITTIE	HELEN
102	Z104	HOLSTEIN, KITTIE H		3 OCT 1971	15 MAY 1877		EDWIN
102	AJ120	HOLSTEIN, NATHANIEL L		18 NOV 1956	1904		
105	J11	HOLTMAN, ANNA		13 JUN 1968	1885		JOSEPH
105	I10	HOLTMAN, EVA	YOULOVSKY	27 SEP 1960	1898	ETTA LEAH	
105	L12	HOLTMAN, HYMAN		9 FEB 1964	4 JUL 1909		
105	J10	HOLTMAN, JOSEPH		3 NOV 1956	1884		ANNA
105	L6	HOLTMAN, PAULINE		12 MAY 1991	4 JUL 1914		
391	F28	HOLTZ, HYMAN		3 JUL 1903	1838		
375	C15	HOLTZ, JACK		1993	1917		
447	Y39	HOLZBERG, BETTY		6 FEB 1986	1919		JULES
447	Y40	HOLZBERG, JULES D		22 FEB 1978	1915		BETTY
371	H 6	HOLZSCHLAG, HERMAN		18 DEC 1978	1 MAY 1913		
222	M11	HOMELSON, BERT		25 JUL 1981	14 MAR 1891		NEOMI
222	F 5	HOMELSON, FRANCES	ROSENBERG	8 DEC 1950	1908		JOSEPH
222	F 6	HOMELSON, JOSEPH		29 MAR 1955	7 APR 1909		FRANCES
222	M10	HOMELSON, NEOMA		30 DEC 1983	25 DEC 1893		BERT
125	I135	HONEYMAN, ANNA ROSE		15 FEB 1954	1865		ISRAEL
125	M147	HONEYMAN, DOROTHY C		30 DEC 1983	1895		EDWARD
125	M146	HONEYMAN, EDWARD		23 FEB 1952	1892		DOROTHY
125		HONEYMAN, EVA		9 FEB 1921	05 DEC 1920	HARRY & MOLLY	
125	L177	HONEYMAN, HILDA	CHAZEN	18 JUN 1971	1914		
125	I134	HONEYMAN, ISRAEL		26 AUG 1940	1860	YEHUDA	ANNA
125	ZA175	HONEYMAN, STANTON		11 MAR 1990	22 AUG 1921		
102	AD172	HONIGBERG, LEON		25 FEB 1963	24 NOV 1897		OLGA
102	AD173	HONIGBERG, OLGA W		1 APR 1991	14 NOV 1902		LEON
371	AA18	HOPFER, HELEN L		29 JAN 1953			
372	K12	HOPFER, HERMAN		1959	1887		
392	C38	HOREN, GERTRUDE		28 MAY 1945	13 MAY 1896		
371	O30	HORENBLAS, HENRY		1948	1891		
125	O 97	HORENSTEIN, ABRAHAM		18 FEB 1921	1900	BENJAMIN & ESTHER	
125	J127	HORENSTEIN, BARNET		14 OCT 1936	1872	BARUCH & BRAYNA	
391	G28	HORENSTEIN, HIMAN		21 DEC 1906		PESACH	
125	M114	HORN, BERTHA	GISSER	2 JUL 1957	18 AUG 1894		

Cem	Row	Name	Maiden Name	DOD	DOB	Parents	Spouse
248	E53	HORN, FRANCES	ANTOKOL	25 MAY 1991	11 SEP 1920		
248	E52	HORN, JOSEPH		15 OCT 1957	4 MAY 1893		MARY
248	E51	HORN, MARY		6 AUG 1961	5 JUL 1894		JOSEPH
125	M112	HORN, MORDECHAI		27 DEC 1935	9 SEP 1884	SAMUEL & BREINA	
102	N49	HOROWITZ, ABRAHAM I		28 SEP 1948	1880		REBECCA
102	R33	HOROWITZ, ANN R		24 SEP 1966	1871	MAURICE & ROSETTA	
391	GB 5	HOROWITZ, BENJAMIN		5 DEC 1958	1891	JACOB	
102	AI29	HOROWITZ, BENJAMIN		13 MAY 1976	20 MAY 1916		BESSIE
102	AI28	HOROWITZ, BESSIE		11 AUG 1955	1890		BENJAMIN
371	A31	HOROWITZ, BYRON		30 AUG 1989	24 FEB 1921		
494	A11	HOROWITZ, GEORGE		25 JAN 1993	4 JAN 1926	SHMARYAHU	
116	I28	HOROWITZ, HARRY		27 AUG 1990	25 AUG 1913		
329	D26	HOROWITZ, HENRY		30 JUL 1970	1879		ROSE
370	G42	HOROWITZ, ISAAC		13 MAR 1936			
125	H 24	HOROWITZ, ISADORE		23 OCT 1969	1881		JENNIE
102	AD160	HOROWITZ, JACOB		1975	1894		
329	B42	HOROWITZ, JACOB		24 OCT 1955	1868		LENA
125	G 22	HOROWITZ, JENNIE	BURRIS	15 FEB 1976	16 APR 1883		ISADORE
104	O41	HOROWITZ, LAWRENCE		7 SEP 1950	1899		
102	AC167	HOROWITZ, LEE DANIEL		1963	1901		MOLLIE
329	B41	HOROWITZ, LENA		24 NOV 1941	1869		JACOB
377	N32	HOROWITZ, LENA F		9 MAY 1981	6 MAR 1891	MOSHE	MORRIS
102	R34	HOROWITZ, MAURICE J		22 AUG 1942	1894		ROSETTA
433	F 9	HOROWITZ, MINNIE		3 JUN 1954		JACOB	SAM
102	AC168	HOROWITZ, MOLLIE	LIBMAN	1985	1902		LEE
391	ZA56	HOROWITZ, MOLLIE		26 NOV 1966	1896	CHAIM	
377	N31	HOROWITZ, MORRIS DDS		29 NOV 1981	1 JAN 1894	MENDEL	LENA
101	B 9	HOROWITZ, MYER		23 JUL 1939	1875		SARAH
329	C43	HOROWITZ, OSCAR		9 NOV 1914		SAMUEL	
377	M29	HOROWITZ, PHYLISS, G		10 JUN 1983	1 MAR 1919	BENJAMIN	
116	AU14	HOROWITZ, REBECCA		5 FEB 1975			SAMUEL
102	N48	HOROWITZ, REBECCA I		10 OCT 1965	1879		ABRAHAM
329	D25	HOROWITZ, ROSE		4 OCT 1966	1884		HENRY
102	R35	HOROWITZ, ROSETTA		11 FEB 1982	1895		MAURICE
371	AF24	HOROWITZ, SAM		5 NOV 1951	1871		
433	F 8	HOROWITZ, SAM		16 MAY 1979		LEV	MINNIE
750	A25	HOROWITZ, SAMUEL		2 NOV 1983			
329	C42	HOROWITZ, SAMUEL		3 JUN 1978	6 JUL 1887		
116	AU15 .	HOROWITZ, SAMUEL		6 DEC 1946			REBECCA
101	B10	HOROWITZ, SARAH		17 NOV 1958	1875		MYER
116	U26	HORTON, DOROTHY S		4 AUG 1986	19 FEB 1914		SAMUEL
116	U25	HORTON, SAMUEL R		20 MAY 1979	16 NOV 1901		DOROTHY
125	N175	HORWITZ, ANN C		1990	1903		EDWARD
125	D 42	HORWITZ, BENJAMIN		20 MAY 1922	1889	KALMAN & CHAYA	IDA
330	E24	HORWITZ, BESSIE		15 APR 1963	1879		ISAAC
125	N174	HORWITZ, EDWARD NATHANIEL		3 JAN 1966	1898		ANN
125	B 70	HORWITZ, EMMA	GOURSON	8 FEB 1964	1867		
121	Q10	HORWITZ, ESTHER	SHAPIRO	30 MAR 1969	1 APR 1899		
125	I 48 ·	HORWITZ, EVA		6 NOV 1912	1876		MOSES
123		HORWITZ, FLORENCE L		1981	1897		
125	A 71	HORWITZ, HARRY		14 OCT 1964	1928	ROSE & MARTIN	
125	H 54	HORWITZ, HARRY		21 FEB 1923	11 AUG 1873	ABRAHAM & EVA (KOVAROFF)	
125	H 70	HORWITZ, HYMAN		21 APR 1938	1860	DOV BEAR & SARAH	SOPHIE
125	D 41	HORWITZ, IDA WILSON	GREENSTEIN	20 JUL 1946	1890	HARRY & BEILA (GOLDBERG)	BEN
330	E23	HORWITZ, ISAAC		31 MAR 1934	1872		BESSIE
372	H12	HORWITZ, JACOB		1992	1891		ROSE
248	C33	HORWITZ, JENNIE	ISRAEL	5 MAY 1968	1890		STANLEY
125	S199	HORWITZ, LEWIS ALEXANDER		15 FEB 1960	1886		
125	R194	HORWITZ, LOUIS		28 NOV 1960	17 AUG 1893		MOLLIE
125	G 68	HORWITZ, MARTIN		17 JUL 1972	1897	SARAH	NANCY
125	B 69	HORWITZ, MARTIN H		17 NOV 1968	1895	EMMA	ROSE
125	R193	HORWITZ, MOLLIE	TUBOWITZ	20 FEB 1970	10 JUL 1895		LOUIS
125	W181	HORWITZ, MOREY		16 MAR 1979	1901		
125	I 47	HORWITZ, MOSES L		13 FEB 1926	1853		EVA
125	G 69	HORWITZ, NANCY	WANSKER	20 MAY 1979	25 MAY 1905		MARTIN
125	M 87	HORWITZ, NATHAN		20 DEC 1921	1876		

Cem	Row	Name	Maiden Name	DOD	DOB	Parents	Spouse
121	Q 9	HORWITZ, PHILIP E		5 APR 1988	12 OCT 1896		
125	B 68	HORWITZ, ROSE	SABLOTSKY	4 APR 1968	1900		
372	H11	HORWITZ, ROSE		NDD	1903		MARTIN
123		HORWITZ, SAMUEL M		29 JAN 1968	1892		JACOB
125	G 67	HORWITZ, SARAH		21 MAR 1922	1847		
125	N199	HORWITZ, SIDNEY		28 DEC 1967	1923		
125	H 68	HORWITZ, SIMON		11 MAR 1919	1890	HYMAN & SOPHIE	
125	H 69	HORWITZ, SOPHIE	CROLL	4 OCT 1928	1858		HYMAN
125		HORWITZ, SYDNEY		28 DEC 1916	SEP 1916	HARRY & EMMA	
102	AE105	HOWARD, GEORGE J		3 MAR 1955	5 SEP 1906		LOIS
102	AE104	HOWARD, LOIS	BURR	17 JAN 1990	4 APR 1913		GEORGE
102	AE103	HOWARD, STEVEN		10 MAR 1946	28 JAN 1946	GEORGE & LOIS (BURR)	
125	O177	HOWELL, RUBEN		26 FEB 1964			
101	H 1	HUFNAGEL, FLORA		26 MAY 1981	25 DEC 1892		
101	D 6	HUFNAGEL, IRENE		31 DEC 1971	29 MAY 1922		
222	AP18	HUNTER, LESLIE (MALE)		1 MAR 1971	1909		
330	Z10	HURWIT, (BABY BOY)		13 JUN 1978			
102	AI56	HURWIT, BENJAMIN		27 JUL 1976	17 FEB 1897		HELEN
330	AC 6	HURWIT, ESTHER		27 AUG 1992			
102	AI55	HURWIT, HELEN		19 APR 1952	21 AUG 1904		BENJAMIN
102	AI57	HURWIT, JAMES S		4 OCT 1982	3 AUG 1898		MARY
102	AI58	HURWIT, MARY	GITLIN	8 SEP 1962	28 JAN 1901		JAMES
102	AI214	HURWITCH, EDWARD A		27 APR 1984	1901		EVELYN
102	AI215	HURWITCH, EVELYN S		21 MAY 1974	1906		EDWARD
447	T24	HURWITZ, ABRAHAM M		12 SEP 1955	1908		
101	C22	HURWITZ, BARNET H		5 JUN 1943	1894		
101	B27	HURWITZ, BASHE		8 MAY 1924			CEMACH
101	B28	HURWITZ, CEMACH		21 AUG 1922			BASHE
330	AD40	HURWITZ, CORRINE		24 APR 1986	3 JUL 1926		
119	B60	HURWITZ, DAVID S		10 JUL 1992	3 SEP 1903		
102	G38	HURWITZ, HERMAN MAX MD		16 JAN 1946	10 APR 1890		SOPHIE
121	T13	HURWITZ, ISADOR		6 DEC 1959			
330	AH25	HURWITZ, MARY		18 MAY 1983			MEYER
101	B25	HURWITZ, MENDEL		22 OCT 1948	1873		SARAH
330	AH26	HURWITZ, MEYER N		14 JUL 1972	5 MAR 1906		MARY
102	AD85	HURWITZ, MORRIS H		4 APR 1989	30 JUL 1909		
102	V27	HURWITZ, ROSE		29 DEC 1974	1892		SAMUEL
102	V26	HURWITZ, SAMUEL		5 JUN 1945	1888		ROSE
101	B26	HURWITZ, SARAH		21 FEB 1927	1870		MENDEL
102	G37	HURWITZ, SOPHIE	LUKASHOK	4 AUG 1960	13 APR 1893		HERMAN
330	H 2	HUTCHINSON, RUTH ANN		1978			
119	A59	HUTNER, ALBERT DAVID		25 NOV 1983	23 NOV 1909		
372	G24	HUTZLER, CHARLES M		1954	1867		ROSE
372	G25	HUTZLER, IRMA		1966	1895	CHARLES & ROSE	
372	G23	HUTZLER, ROSA	GOTTHELF	1945	1869		CHARLES
370	I26	HYATT, BESSIE		1926	1871		MOSES
392	C25	HYATT, LOUIS		6 JAN 1956	1906		
370	B34	HYATT, MOSES		1925	1872		BESSIE
374	G18	HYMAN, AARON		18 JUN 1912			
370	M61	HYMAN, ABRAHAM		9 MAR 1950	3 JAN 1881		MOLLIE
102	T16	HYMAN, ALBERT		23 OCT 1952	1902	LENA	
374	A41	HYMAN, ASA DAVID		19 SEP 1941	1901		
102	AD122	HYMAN, GEORGE M		28 APR 1985	25 DEC 1902		STELLA
374	F19	HYMAN, GUTEL		1938	1866		
102	AC179	HYMAN, HARRY		23 JAN 1986	27 JUL 1903		PAULINE
102	AD171	HYMAN, HYMAN		1962	1911		
374	G19	HYMAN, ISRAEL		1918	1860		
102	T15	HYMAN, LENA	HEROLD	6 SEP 1941	1876		
103	D1	HYMAN, MAURICE L		10 JAN 1973	1897		
370	M60	HYMAN, MOLLIE		1963	1895		ABRAHAM
374	G56	HYMAN, NATHAN D					
102	AC178	HYMAN, PAULINE	FINK	30 SEP 1953	19 AUG 1953		HARRY
102	AD120	HYMAN, RACHEL		1960	1892		
374	G55	HYMAN, REUBEN A		24 APR 1985	17 JUN 1904		
102	AD123	HYMAN, STELLA	KATZ	1975	1897		GEORGE
374	G50	HYMAN, WILLIAM					

Cem	Row	Name	Maiden Name	DOD	DOB	Parents	Spouse
374	F51	HYMAN, WILLIAM		NDD			
102	C37	HYNE, ROBERT		9 OCT 1979	4 MAY 1935		
121	T15	IDELKOPE, SYLVIA		11 OCT 1966	1922		
751	I 8	IGDALSKY, MORRIS		31 DEC 1988	8 DEC 1918		
125	I 55	IKOWITZ, HASHE		6 NOV 1905			
125	R153	IKOWITZ, MORRIS		25 APR 1943	10 JAN 1884	ISRAEL & CHASHA	REBECCA
125	R154	IKOWITZ, REBECCA		30 JAN 1967	1890		MORRIS
376	J50	IMBER, REGINA		10 DEC 1966	1918		
391	ZC58	IRSAY, GISELLE G		4 AUG 1967	13 JUN 1903	JUDAH	HERMAN
391	ZC59	IRSAY, HERMAN J		28 MAY 1965	10 MAY 1903	CHAIM ELIEZER	GISELLE
123		IRVING, MARSHALL		1982	1906		
377	B26	IRWIN, CHARLES MD (CAPT)		17 NOV 1951	12 NOV 1920	MORRIS & ESTHER	
377	B25	IRWIN, ESTHER P		27 JUN 1980	13 DEC 1899	BESALEL	MORRIS
377	R 4	IRWIN, GUSSIE		1979	1909		LOUIS
377	N14	IRWIN, HAROLD H MD		1981	1907		
377	R 3	IRWIN, LOUIS		1979	1898		GUSSIE
377	B24	IRWIN, MORRIS J		18 OCT 1984	2 OCT 1895	SHMARYAHU	ESTHER
751	N13	ISAACSON, BEATRIX	GORDON	1970	1909		
103	A5	ISAACSON, GUSSIE	ALBERT	22 AUG 1976	23 MAR 1873		HYMAN
103	A6	ISAACSON, HYMAN		16 AUG 1928	23 MAR 1873		GUSSIE
751	N14	ISAACSON, JOSEPH S		NDD			
751	K23	ISAACSON, LENA		15 MAY 1931			
116	S 8	ISENBERG, ESTHER R		20 MAY 1980	9 JAN 1895		ROBERT
121	B34	ISENBERG, MICHAEL ADAM		22 JUN 1985	2 JAN 1971		
116	S 7	ISENBERG, ROBERT		1979	1896		ESTHER
248	C31	ISRAEL, CARL		22 JUL 1976	1 SEP 1894	HYMAN & LENA	CELIA
248	C30	ISRAEL, CELIA S		6 SEP 1975	8 DEC 1897		CARL
248	C35	ISRAEL, HYMAN		5 JAN 1940	1862		LENA
102	V28	ISRAEL, IRENE F		31 JUL 1945	SEP 1944		
330	AF13	ISRAEL, IRWIN DR		1971	1927		
248	C34	ISRAEL, LENA	EHRLICH	14 AUG 1936	1863		HYMAN
103	B24	ISRAEL, LIONEL K		16 NOV 1986	10 SEP 1921		PEARL
103	B23	ISRAEL, PEARL L		9 NOV 1986	2 SEP 1922		LIONEL
370	O 7	ISRAELITE, ABRAHAM		17 DEC 1950			
373	F 9	ISRAELITE, ANNA		25 OCT 1992	14 JUL 1912		LEON
371	AE23	ISRAELITE, BORYS		29 DEC 1980	7 OCT 1902		CYLIA
371	AE24	ISRAELITE, CYLIA	SCHYMANSKI	5 FEB 1960	28 DEC 1912		BORYS
370	Y14	ISRAELITE, DOLOVER					
370	O 4	ISRAELITE, DORA		30 NOV 1973	11 JUL 1890		WILLIAM
373	F 8	ISRAELITE, LEON		30 MAY 1981	21 FEB 1912		ANNA
370	O 5	ISRAELITE, WILLIAM		29 MAR 1975	15 MAY 1892		DORA
248	F60	ISSELBACHER, HERMAN		8 APR 1978	19 OCT 1894		
248	F61	ISSELBACHER, LINA		18 JAN 1988	20 SEP 1902		LINA
370	A17	ITCHKAWICH, ECHIAL		29 SEP 1937	4 NOV 1874	BEZALEL ELIAHU	
447	V 5	ITKIN, BEATRICE		29 MAY 1967	1896		JOSEPH
102	AB147	ITKIN, FANNIE WILSON	WEINSTEIN	11 OCT 1981	1893		
447	V 8	ITKIN, JACK DAVID		31 AUG 1963	1916		
447	V 4	ITKIN, JASON BRETT		8 JUN 1989	20 MAY 1970		
447	V 6	ITKIN, JOSEPH		25 JUN 1971	1889		BEATRICE
391	D18	ITZKOWITZ, SAMUEL		24 DEC 1935	1861	YEHUDA LEV	
371	O 4	JABLON, BLIMA		25 DEC 1990	5 MAY 1901		
370	A40	JABLONSKY, MOSES ISAAC		18 OCT 1905			
125	W182	JACKAWAY, BETTY	HOROWITZ	28 DEC 1982	1893		
101	D38	JACKOWITZ, HYMAN		14 DEC 1948	1868		
125	Q141	JACKSON, BERTHA		26 JUL 1972			MORRIS
102	AJ116	JACKSON, CELIA		14 OCT 1988	1900		JOSEPH
125	L149	JACKSON, FRED L		1 MAR 1955	1895		
102	AJ115	JACKSON, JOSEPH		10 MAY 1956	1901		CELIA
125	Q140	JACKSON, MORRIS		17 DEC 1943	1888	ANCHIS	BERTHA
102	BF18	JACKSON, RAPHAEL		1988	1928		
330	D35	JACKTER, BENJAMIN		6 FEB 1963	1912		
330	AD11	JACKTER, JACK		23 NOV 1984	28 MAY 1914		
119	A 3	JACOB, FANNY	PARTNOY	21 JUL 1989	24 MAY 1910		
329	A31	JACOB, FRANCES E		28 SEP 1975	6 MAR 1906		
329	A20	JACOB, HELENA		26 JUN 1963	15 JAN 1915		HERBERT
329	A21	JACOB, HERBERT I		24 MAR 1990	21 FEB 1904		HELENA

Cem	Row	Name	Maiden Name	DOD	DOB	Parents	Spouse
447	A11	JACOBI, MARY	CHESTLER	11 JUL 1939	1906		
329	E18	JACOBOWITZ, MORRIS		1980	1901		IRVING
102	AA164	JACOBS, ALBERT SELIG		16 FEB 1982	17 MAR 1903		
125		JACOBS, ANDREW		19 MAR 1957	14 FEB 1957		EDYTHE
373	J25	JACOBS, CHARLES		27 FEB 1980	18 JAN 1917	WILLIAM & ETTA	ISABELLE
101	D10	JACOBS, DAVID M		22 DEC 1967	2 JUN 1951		
102	AA165	JACOBS, EDYTHE	YESSNER	5 DEC 1981	27 JUN 1905		ALBERT
377	V20	JACOBS, ERWIN		1980	1913	ISRAEL	VICTORIA
373	J20	JACOBS, ETTA IDA		13 JUN 1977	28 NOV 1895		WILLIAM
121	J48	JACOBS, FANNIE		1 NOV 1988	10 AUG 1904		
102	V24	JACOBS, HARRY		13 NOV 1986	28 MAY 1900		
102	AB210	JACOBS, HENRY		1986	1906		SADIE
373	J26	JACOBS, ISABELLE		17 MAR 1993	22 JAN 1920		CHARLES
377	W20	JACOBS, ISRAEL M		1964	1887	MORDECHAI	MOLLIE
373	J23	JACOBS, JACK		1941	1938	WILLIAM & ETTA	
370	X 9	JACOBS, JOHN		14 AUG 1992	17 JUL 1907		VIOLA
373	J24	JACOBS, JUDITH ANN		2 JAN 1962	28 JAN 1945	WILLIAM & ETTA	
377	W19	JACOBS, MOLLIE R		1959	1887	SAMUEL	ISRAEL
102	V22	JACOBS, RACHEL	BAGGISH	4 JAN 1936	1874		
374	G 3	JACOBS, RACHEL		1914	1873	MICHAEL	
102	V23	JACOBS, RAE	MARKUS	23 JUN 1942	19 JUN 1898		
102	E 1	JACOBS, ROBERT A		1945	1938		
102	V25	JACOBS, SADIE A		9 AUG 1992	14 APR 1904		HARRY
125	Q187	JACOBS, SAMUEL		6 OCT 1961	1883		
377	V19	JACOBS, VICTORIA		1967	1918		ERWIN
370	X10	JACOBS, VIOLA		27 APR 1993	22 AUG 1906		JOHN
373	J21	JACOBS, WILLIAM R		2 APR 1966	3 SEP 1893		ETTA
750	H31	JACOBSON, AARON		7 AUG 1983	14 DEC 1897		MOLLIE
121	N18	JACOBSON, ABRAHAM		17 APR 1988	8 FEB 1917		
370	T41	JACOBSON, ABRAHAM		1929	1873		MATTIE
373	I 5	JACOBSON, ANNE E		1976	1910		ELI
370	B38	JACOBSON, ANNIE		1905			
370	I40	JACOBSON, BARNET		31 MAY 1938			
370	H21	JACOBSON, BASSIE		31 JUL 1905	1874		ROSE
370	T45	JACOBSON, CHARLES		29 MAR 1969	23 APR 1892		MINNIE
371	A19	JACOBSON, DOROTHY		30 JUL 1986	17 FEB 1907		NATHAN
373	I 4	JACOBSON, ELI		1984	1903		ANNE
104	O46	JACOBSON, ESTHER		10 OCT 1976	15 JUL 1895		SAMUEL
751	N32	JACOBSON, FAY L		19 JUL 1988			
494	A 4	JACOBSON, ISADORE		1967	1891		
371	AO21	JACOBSON, LILLIAN R		1978	1918		
751	M 9	JACOBSON, LOUIS		10 FEB 1967			
370	F17	JACOBSON, LOUIS		1918	1900		
370	T42	JACOBSON, MATTIE	SEARS	1960	1881		ABRAHAM
370	T44	JACOBSON, MINNIE M		20 OCT 1945	29 MAR 1897		CHARLES
106	D5	JACOBSON, MIRIAM	STEIN	26 NOV 1974	11 OCT 1927		
750	H30	JACOBSON, MOLLIE		5 MAY 1970	10 MAR 1908		AARON
371	L22	JACOBSON, NATHAN PAUL		21 JUN 1988	6 APR 1909		DOROTHY
447	A12	JACOBSON, PHYLLIS	CHESTLER	9 OCT 1983	1932	IRVING	
370	I39	JACOBSON, ROSE LEAH		27 OCT 1963			BARNETT
104	O47	JACOBSON, SAMUEL		22 SEP 1987	14 FEB 1897		ESTHER
116	W25	JACOBY, ERIC STEPHEN		15 AUG 1979	13 JUL 1975		
751	I11	JAFFE, AARON		29 JAN 1947	1879		JENNIE
330	G18	JAFFE, ABRAHAM		20 MAR 1947	10 SEP 1887		
125	B 14	JAFFE, ANNA		12 SEP 1944	26 DEC 1892	TOBI & RACHEL BATYA	ZALMAN
125	B 10	JAFFE, ANNA	BELL	30 OCT 1975	20 MAY 1887		YALE
102	AH 3	JAFFE, ELIZABETH		23 JUN 1941	1850		
370	P13	JAFFE, ELLA SUSSMAN	CRANDEL		1907	MENACHEM	
433	P 4	JAFFE, FRIEDA		NDD			PAUL
125	B 18	JAFFE, GUTTE		19 DEC 1938	1865	NATHAN & IDA SARAH	JACOB ELI
102	D39	JAFFE, HARRY		28 JAN 1977	8 SEP 1900		MATTIE
125	C 15	JAFFE, HERBERT		29 SEP 1968	1916		SYLVIA
125	A 13	JAFFE, ISAAC		27 JUL 1970	1888		
125	B 19	JAFFE, JACOB ELI		3 DEC 1946	1868	MORRIS & SOPHIA	GUTTI
751	I12	JAFFE, JENNIE	SAPERSTEIN	2 DEC 1951	1880		AARON
125	B 20	JAFFE, JULIUS		27 NOV 1949	1899	YAKOV ELI & GUTTI	

Cem	Row	Name	Maiden Name	DOD	DOB	Parents	Spouse
371	L12	JAFFE, MARY		1961	1880		NATHAN
125	A 20	JAFFE, MARY S		25 JAN 1985			SIMON
102	D40	JAFFE, MATTIE	BOWMAN	24 JUN 1949	27 AUG 1907		HARRY
371	L14	JAFFE, MILTON		1 JUL 1978	3 MAR 1908	NATHAN & MARY	
125	B 9	JAFFE, MORRIS J		1985	1919	YALE & ANNA	
371	L13	JAFFE, NATHAN		1958	1871		MARY
125	A 18	JAFFE, NATHAN B		22 MAR 1959	1893	JACOB & GUTTI	
433	P 3	JAFFE, PAUL		1986	1899	YEHUDA JOSEPH	FREIDA
330	G17	JAFFE, ROSE		11 MAR 1963	21 SEP 1891		
392	F10	JAFFE, SAMUEL		2 APR 1951	1881	BARUCH	
125	A 19	JAFFE, SIMON M		3 AUG 1984	1898		MARY
391	F34	JAFFE, SOLOMON		4 NOV 1911	20 OCT 1876	ABARAHAM	
392	H17	JAFFE, SOPHIE		19 JUL 1949	1891	YECHEZKEL	
125	C 16	JAFFE, SYLVIA		6 NOV 1986	5 APR 1919		HERBERT
125	B 11	JAFFE, YALE		13 FEB 1966	1886		ANNA
125	B 12	JAFFE, ZALMAN MICHAEL		3 JAN 1968	1889		ANNA
116	M 2	JAFFEE, BARNET		25 DEC 1981	1892		IDA
331		JAFFEE, DIANA		8 JAN 1919	21 SEP 1917		
116	M 1	JAFFEE, IDA	MOPSIK	8 APR 1982	1895		BARNET
102	Q34	JAFFER, ANNA G		26 JUN 1940	1 AUG 1871		
102	Q35	JAFFER, DOROTHY		9 DEC 1937	4 JUN 1890		LOUIS
102	Q31	JAFFER, HERMAN		22 SEP 1949	17 APR 1905		IDA
102	Q30	JAFFER, IDA		11 FEB 1965	28 JUL 1893		HERMAN
102	Q32	JAFFER, LOUIS		3 NOV 1932	2 MAY 1892		DOROTHY
104	H12	JAINCHILL, CLARA		15 JAN 1985	1888		
123		JAINCHILL, EDWARD S		6 OCT 1954	1898		
105	F26	JAINCHILL, RUBEN		13 JUL 1984	1911		
377	W11	JAIVIN, LILLIAN K		15 APR 1974	5 JAN 1895	SHRUGA JOSEPH	PHILIP
377	W12	JAIVIN, PHILIP		7 APR 1963	25 JUN 1891	ELIEZER	LILLIAN
127	O	JAMPEL, HELEN		1990	1898		
116	W 7	JANES, ANITA		17 MAR 1972	2 JUL 1913		
125		JANOFSKY, LEONARD		4 AUG 1925	MAR 1925		
104	J20	JANOWSKY, IRVING		24 MAY 1964	8 MAR 1917		
102	Z177	JANOWSKY, ISADORE I	JASON	16 NOV 1974	30 DEC 1910		
125	B 31	JARTMAN, ANNA ROSE	WEINBERG	27 AUG 1939	1861	MATIS & YENTA	NATHAN
125	D 37	JARTMAN, BESSIE	BLOCK	30 DEC 1976	1895		ISRAEL
125	B 30	JARTMAN, FANNY		3 FEB 1971	1891	NATHAN & ANNA ROSE (WEINBERG)	
125	D 36	JARTMAN, ISRAEL W		1 SEP 1941	8 MAY 1893	NATHAN & ANNA ROSE (WEINBERG)	BESSIE
125	E 50	JARTMAN, LOUIS		17 SEP 1969	1896	NATHAN & ANNA ROSE (WEINBERG)	RUTH
125	K 74	JARTMAN, NATHAN		6 FEB 1920	1863	ISRAEL & MARY	ANNA ROSE
125	D 35	JARTMAN, NATHAN M		11 AUG 1958	1920	ISRAEL & BESSIE (BLOCK)	
125	E 51	JARTMAN, RUTH		1 MAR 1984	6 NOV 1900		LOUIS
125	A 30	JARTMAN, SARAH		12 NOV 1976	1901	NATHAN & ANNA ROSE (WEINBERG)	
125	F 97	JASOLOWITZ, ROSE		19 SEP 1951	1876		ALBERT
116	BH50	JAVIT, ORLY		2 JAN 1992	24 SEP 1955		
121	R19	JAYS, ANNE	REICH	8 AUG 1976	14 APR 1904		
121	H43	JAYS, BETTY	SACK	18 FEB 1992	16 NOV 1916		
121	R18	JAYS, CLARENCE K		13 JAN 1985	25 MAR 1906		
374	H33	JENNES, ANNA		1976	1890		
370	R 9	JENNES, ANNIE		1917	1841		
373	I23	JENNES, BELLE	BERCOWITZ	1952	1915		
374	H35	JENNES, EDITH		1954	1904		SAMUEL
374	F42	JENNES, ELI		23 MAR 1965	28 JUL 1909		
374	H37	JENNES, ELIZABETH		1941	1883		MOSES
374	H47	JENNES, ERNEST H		24 MAR 1970	8 SEP 1925		
370	Y 5	JENNES, FRANCES		15 JAN 1906	15 JAN 1906	JK & FANNIE	
374	H32	JENNES, HENRY		12 DEC 1959	1897		LEAH
374	H31	JENNES, LEAH		9 JUL 1981	19 MAR 1897		HENRY
374	H38	JENNES, MOSES		1940	1883		ELIZABETH
374	H34	JENNES, SAMUEL		1959	1896		EDITH
102	H32	JESS, ALBERT		3 JUL 1968	16 SEP 1882		IRENE
102	H34	JESS, BEATRICE Y		30 JUL 1934	31 MAY 1906	ALBERT & IRENE	
102	H33	JESS, IRENE C		3 JUL 1967	21 MAR 1884		ALBERT
377	B37	JOHL, HELOISE	MAIBRUNN	10 JAN 1957	19 AUG 1903		WILLIAM
377	B36	JOHL, WILLIAM W		24 OCT 1954	4 JUL 1903		HELOISE
106	B14	JOHNSON, CARYN	ROSOFF	15 FEB 1981	19 AUG 1949		

Cem	Row	Name	Maiden Name	DOD	DOB	Parents	Spouse
114	L12	JOHNSON, MARY	FRIED	28 SEP 1981	3 NOV 1910		
391	L37	JORDAN, BARNEY		25 JAN 1970	1893	ELCHANA	
102	M 6	JOSELFOF, HERBERT M		1929	1927		
125	F 96	JOSELOWITZ, ALBERT		1 OCT 1948	1876	JACOB	ROSE
125	F 98	JOSELOWITZ, JESSIE		29 NOV 1985	7 JUN 1901	ALBERT & ROSE	
102	AJ10	JOSEPH, ANNA	ADLER	15 NOV 1955	1886		MORRIS
102	A11	JOSEPH, BERTHA	ALLEN	1931	1896		
222	AH 7	JOSEPH, DORA		21 JUL 1977	1904		SAMUEL
113	O59	JOSEPH, ELSIE		8 JUN 1991	18 MAR 1918		KURT
222	AH10	JOSEPH, EZECHIEL DAVID		23 MAY 1917	1853		ROSE
102	AC81	JOSEPH, HENRY		22 FEB 1952	1881		SARAH
102	AC83	JOSEPH, IRVING		13 JUN 1951	1904	HENRY & SARAH	
113	O58	JOSEPH, KURT		16 DEC 1981	1 SEP 1912		ELSIE
248	F62	JOSEPH, LEO		26 JUN 1978	18 OCT 1900		HERMAN
102	AJ 9	JOSEPH, MORRIS		22 MAY 1947	1878		ANNA
222	AH 9	JOSEPH, ROSE RACHEL		1 AUG 1926	1854		EZECHIEL
222	AH 8	JOSEPH, SAMUEL		10 JUN 1964	1890	EZEKIEL & ROSE	DORA
102	AC80	JOSEPH, SARAH	RUBINSON	21 JAN 1973	1884		HENRY
391	Q28	JOSEPHSON, NATHAN		26 OCT 1911	1829	ISAAC	
118	B15	JOSOLOWITZ, PHILIP		26 NOV 1973			REBECCA
118	B15	JOSOLOWITZ, REBECCA		7 NOV 1991			PHILIP
391	N36	JOSPEHSON, HANNA		6 MAR 1903	1838	ELIYAHU	
125	M143	JOTKOWITZ, ESTHER RUTH	SKLARIWICZ	12 OCT 1980	1888		JACOB
125	M142	JOTKOWITZ, JACOB MORRIS		15 DEC 1951	1887		ESTHER
330	AC12	JUDENFRIEND, MIRIAM		29 JUN 1963	24 JUL 1920		
121	B21	JUSTER, MILTON R		3 SEP 1992			
494	H 2	KABAT, LUKE		1966	1939		SYRTILLER
447	G 5	KABATZNICK, ABNER		25 AUG 1984	1914	LOUIS & ANNIE	BETTY
447	G12	KABATZNICK, ANNIE		8 NOV 1963	15 MAR 1872		LOUIS
446	A30	KABATZNICK, BERTHA		15 JAN 1917	14 SEP 1910		SAUL
447	G 8	KABATZNICK, BETTY		21 MAY 1984	2 JAN 1902		ABNER
433	P 7	KABATZNICK, HERBERT		1993	1919	YAKOV	
447	G 7	KABATZNICK, JACOB		10 JUL 1931	27 JAN 1885	LOUIS & ANNIE	MINNIE
447	G13	KABATZNICK, LOUIS		21 AUG 1929	1868		ANNIE
447	G 6	KABATZNICK, MINNIE S		17 AUG 1968	20 APR 1887		JACOB
447	G10	KABATZNICK, MURRAY D		24 MAY 1956	25 NOV 1898		
447	G11	KABATZNICK, SAMUEL		4 DEC 1933	28 MAR 1903	LOUIS & ANNIE	
446	A35	KABATZNICK, SAUL		1924	1917	LOUIS & ANNIE	BERTHA
447	AA14	KABEL, DORA	STEINMULLER	9 OCT 1974	15 JUL 1894		
447	AA12	KABEL, JOYCE	LEFF	26 DEC 1980	20 DEC 1921		
329	B12	KABOT, AL		22 MAY 1957	1914		
112	B28	KADDEN, FRIEDA W		21 AUG 1988	24 JUN 1916		
102	AD108	KADIS, ANNE		10 NOV 1973			
102	AD107	KADIS, BESSIE		10 SEP 1978			
103	D20	KAGAN, CELIA		31 AUG 1986	1894		MORRIS
116	L 9	KAGAN, EVA B		16 MAR 1985	15 FEB 1919		
103	D19	KAGAN, MORRIS		10 OCT 1970	1896		CELIA
102	R11	KAHAN, ANNA	RAPAPORT	14 JUL 1925			ABRAHAM
222	AU 3	KAHAN, ESTHER		4 JAN 1968	30 MAY 1890		JACOB
222	AU 4	KAHAN, JACOB		7 DEC 1968	12 FEB 1884		ESTHER
114	E 1	KAHAN, MORRIS D		4 JUN 1991	24 MAY 1928		
113	C21	KAHANER, THELMA	EARNEST	5 SEP 1983	19 NOV 1912		
370	A53	KAHEVSKY, DEOBORAH		1922	1885		
101	L32	KAHN, ANNA R		1 MAR 1931	1903		
102	AB154	KAHN, BERNARD R		27 SEP 1978	2 OCT 1910		NORA
101	B39	KAHN, DAVEN		8 JUN 1913	1892		
102	BF10	KAHN, HARRIS DR		13 JUL 1990	3 JUL 1925		
750	I15	KAHN, HENRY		8 JUN 1980			MARCIA
113	A15	KAHN, IDA	BASS	6 DEC 1987	11 JUN 1899		
222	AR 9	KAHN, JOSEPH		21 FEB 1955	1876		ROSE
119	I 5	KAHN, LESTER H		16 MAY 1986	22 DEC 1925		
125	ZA173	KAHN, LOTHER		1990	1922		
101	L26	KAHN, LOTTA		12 SEP 1918	10 AUG 1859		
105	C25	KAHN, LOUIS		7 DEC 1984			SALLY
750	I16	KAHN, MARCIA		27 APR 1990			HENRY
102	AB153	KAHN, NORA		27 OCT 1962	23 AUG 1914		BERNARD

Cem	Row	Name	Maiden Name	DOD	DOB	Parents	Spouse
222	AR 8	KAHN, ROSE C		28 APR 1965	1876		JOSEPH
101	L 9	KAHN, SALLY		13 JUL 1972	1899		
105	C26	KAHN, SALLY	LASSMAN	23 DEC 1967			LOUIS
101	K15	KAISE, SARAH		14 SEP 1912	1842		
249	P11	KAISER, JUDITH SUSAN		3 JAN 1992	9 MAR 1943		
125	U140	KAITZ, MILTON ARTHUR		4 AUG 1976	1908		
115	B 5	KALAFA, YETTA		30 MAY 1991	14 MAY 1903		
116	BU79	KALIN, JOSEPH		7 JAN 1968	1891		TILLIE
116	BU77	KALIN, SUMNER ROBERT		30 MAR 1965	12 JUN 1929	JOSEPH & TILLIE	
116	BU78	KALIN, TILLIE		21 APR 1983			JOSEPH
391	K37	KALINSKY, ELYAHU			1906	MOSHE YEHUDA	
391	K36	KALINSKY, ISAAC		22 JUL 1900		MOSHE YEHUDA	
105	B18	KALINSKY, LOUIS		3 AUG 1950	1882		
109	E 2	KALLER, MARLENE		26 DEC 1985	1945		
125	Z187	KALLER, MARY E		6 NOV 1987	11 MAR 1911		
125	E 79	KALLERMAN, PEARL		5 MAY 1971	1895		
330	Z11	KALMAN, AARON		28 DEC 1921	6 DEC 1921		
113	K71	KALMAN, MYRON ISAAC		1 FEB 1977	11 APR 1929		
329	D45	KALMANOVITZ, GLADYS		15 MAR 1967			
329	B39	KALMANOVITZ, JACOB ISAAC		13 FEB 1941	1879		REBECCA
329	B40	KALMANOVITZ, REBECCA		6 JUN 1941	1880		JACOB
329	B38	KALMANOVITZ, SHIMON RABBI		8 FEB 1940			
125	I147	KALMANOWITZ, ESTHER D		7 NOB 1952	1883		HERMAN
125	I146	KALMANOWITZ, HERMAN K		1 JUL 1946	15 MAR 1884	DOV BEAR	ESTHER
125	H159	KALMANOWITZ, MORRIS		14 DEC 1961	1910		
391	F21	KALMANOWITZ, PHILIP		23 APR 1929	1881	ELI	
371	AG19	KALNITSKY, CHARLES		28 FEB 1982	1894		ETHEL
371	AG20	KALNITSKY, ETHEL SHAINA		1 SEP 1968	1896		CHARLES
119	K37	KAMEN, CLARA		26 OCT 1985	1 MAY 1909		
119	K36	KAMEN, MORRIS		21 SEP 1990	10 FEB 1900		
125		KAMENICK, ISRAEL		25 APR 1924	1871	ABRAHAM & SARAH	
114	B23	KAMINER, DORIS		29 DEC 1991	6 NOV 1908		
104	G25	KAMINS, ANNE		7 SEP 1971			
119	D54	KAMINS, BERNARD R		23 SEP 1992			
447	M36	KAMINS, MORRIS		9 AUG 1988	1905		ROSE
116	W 9	KAMINS, MORRIS		1987	1914		
116	AW16	KAMINS, MURRAY M		14 SEP 1958	1900		
102	N 9	KAMINS, ROBERT M		22 MAR 1988	12 MAY 1893		ROSE
102	N 8	KAMINS, ROSE	WETSTONE	23 SEP 1985	4 MAR 1895		ROBERT
447	M37	KAMINS, ROSE G		19 DEC 1977	1904		MORRIS
330	H13	KAMINSKY, ABRAHAM					
373	C 7	KAMINSKY, DAVID R		12 NOV 1983	21 MAR 1929	SARAH	
370	L20	KAMINSKY, EDITH BELLE	ANTOKOL	1980	1894	ISRAEL	
125	V190	KAMINSKY, FRANCES	WISNEFSKY	18 AUG 1977	1898		
114	G13	KAMINSKY, HARRY I		19 DEC 1987	17 JUL 1942	MAX	
370	P30	KAMINSKY, ISRAEL		1929	1858		
114	G12	KAMINSKY, MAX A		8 JUN 1990	28 FEB 1912		
391	H37	KAMINSKY, RACHEL I		16 MAR 1926	1841	DAVID	
125	H164	KAMINSKY, SAMUEL		5 FEB 1948	24 MAY 1896	YEHUDA	
373	C 6	KAMINSKY, SARAH R		13 JAN 1982	12 OCT 1905		
125	O144	KAMMERMAN, ELYSE	GOURSON	10 OCT 1992	1904		SYLVAN
125	O143	KAMMERMAN, SYLVAN DAVID		4 DEC 1948	MAY 1903		ELYSE
222	AF15	KAMP, HARRY M		19 OCT 1955	1869		OLGA
222	AF16	KAMP, OLGA		15 FEB 1942	1869		HARRY
119	J63	KANE, SAMUEL PAUL		1984	1942		
249	J 9	KANTER, ABRAHAM		6 OCT 1974	1892		ROSE
222	E 4	KANTER, BENJAMIN		6 DEC 1972	1 OCT 1880		CELIA
222	E 5	KANTER, CELIA	MOSES	12 JUN 1981	27 NOV 1889	DAVID & REBECCA (MENDELSON)	BENJAMIN
101	A19	KANTER, CHAIM L		15 MAY 1919	1867		
222	E 6	KANTER, ESTELLE H		21 DEC 1987	22 MAR 1923	BENJAMIN & CELIA	
222	AJ12	KANTER, ESTHER		10 SEP 1922	1882		
222	AK 4	KANTER, ESTHER DINA		1 MAY 1937	3 NOV 1936		
101	K19	KANTER, EVA K		10 MAY 1924	1875		
222	AB 1	KANTER, HARRY		27 FEB 1911	13 OCT 1910	BENJAMIN & CELIA	
104	G 7	KANTER, NATHAN		2 SEP 1983	28 NOV 1900		
249	J 8	KANTER, ROSE M		5 AUG 1964	1897		ABRAHAM

Cem	Row	Name	Maiden Name	DOD	DOB	Parents	Spouse
330	AD 6	KANTOR, BESSIE		30 APR 1967	1899		
104	A 1	KANTOR, CARL		29 APR 1981	1903		EMMA
104	A 2	KANTOR, EMMA		22 NOV 1973	1903		CARL
102	AK243	KANTOR, NATHAN S		27 DEC 1982	25 DEC 1915		
102	W 4	KANTROWITZ, GUSSIE		2 NOV 1981	13 JUN 1893		SAMUEL
125	K199	KANTROWITZ, MINNIE		17 JAN 1986	1904		SOL
248	J14	KANTROWITZ, ROSE		14 FEB 1917	1880		
102	W 5	KANTROWITZ, SAMUEL		15 SEP 1972	10 MAY 1888	MORRIS & IDA	GUSSIE
125	K198	KANTROWITZ, SOL		13 MAY 1974	1898		MINNIE
125		KAPLAN, (BABY)		11 JAN 1923	9 JAN 1923	ALBERT & LENA	
125		KAPLAN, (BABY)		31 MAY 1938	30 MAY 1938	SADIE (MILSTEIN)	
125		KAPLAN, (CHILD)		3 DEC 1920	3 DEC 1920	AA	
125		KAPLAN, (CHILD)		12 OCT 1925	11 OCT 1925		
105	N41	KAPLAN, ABRAHAM		6 MAY 1989	25 SEP 1899		
391	GN 5	KAPLAN, ABRAHAM		18 MAR 1936		NATAN NATTA	YETTA
374	F57	KAPLAN, ABRAHAM MILTON		9 OCT 1975	1 JUN 1913		
125	I138	KAPLAN, ALBERT A		17 FEB 1942	1891	YITZCHAK & LEAH	LENA
116	BY44	KAPLAN, ALBERT L		29 DEC 1980	12 FEB 1914		OLIVE
248	E44	KAPLAN, ANNA		14 AUG 1972	1879		LEWIS
391	U51	KAPLAN, ANNA LENA		4 DEC 1945	1869	SHIMON	ISAAC
121	Q15	KAPLAN, BECKIE	KAMINS	14 MAY 1978	1892		
377	H24	KAPLAN, BENJAMIN		12 AUG 1976	3 NOV 1892	NATHAN	BERTHA
377	J27	KAPLAN, BENJAMIN		13 AUG 1989	1891	JOEL	
121	Q16	KAPLAN, BENJAMIN MORRIS		9 JUL 1969	1889		
377	H25	KAPLAN, BERTHA	WILK	25 MAR 1980	7 DEC 1896	JOSEPH	BENJAMIN
121	Q19	KAPLAN, BESSIE	TULMAN	1 AUG 1988	15 OCT 1901		
101	F34	KAPLAN, BESSIE		20 JUN 1992	1903		
110	A 5	KAPLAN, BETTY		10 JUL 1954	1901		SAMUEL
751	M15	KAPLAN, CARL		26 DEC 1955	31 JAN 1920		
110	A18	KAPLAN, CHAYE		19 JUL 1950	1858		
102	AH 2	KAPLAN, DAVID		3 JUL 1960	15 APR 1871		ELLA
102	G18	KAPLAN, DAVID		21 DEC 1961	1875		
391	GI 6	KAPLAN, DAVID SAMUEL		1906	1901		
121	O11	KAPLAN, DAWN	SOLOMKIN	7 JUN 1970	9 AUG 1923		
105	L48	KAPLAN, DORA		25 JUL 1948	1870		HARRY
751	K 9	KAPLAN, EDWARD		1990	1920		
125	B 23	KAPLAN, ELIHU		12 DEC 1940	12 SEP 1926	WILLIAM	
102	AH 1	KAPLAN, ELLA		8 MAR 1940	15 MAY 1879		DAVID
248	E23	KAPLAN, ESTHER		7 MAY 1970	25 SEP 1885		SAMUEL
110	A34	KAPLAN, ESTHER		14 AUG 1978			
105	N40	KAPLAN, ESTHER M		8 JUN 1980	2 DEC 1913		
102	AD130	KAPLAN, ETHEL	MARCUS	18 JAN 1990	6 DEC 1894		SAMUEL
125	M 84	KAPLAN, ETHEL EMMA		31 OCT 1919	1877	AARON	
751	O28	KAPLAN, EVA		1988	1895		HARRY
102	G39	KAPLAN, EVA	LEVIN	26 JUN 1947	21 AUG 1905		GEORGE G
392	E47	KAPLAN, EVELYN		16 JUL 1953	1917	JOSHUA	
110	C 2	KAPLAN, FANNIE		25 AUG 1922			FRANK
110	C 1	KAPLAN, FRANK		29 APR 1941			FANNIE
751	K10	KAPLAN, FRIEDA		NDD			
370	A 6	KAPLAN, HARRIS		11 OCT 1930	1868	JACOB & LENA	
110	D 7	KAPLAN, HARRY		11 APR 1964	1879		PAULINE
751	O29	KAPLAN, HARRY		1978	1888		EVA
105	L47	KAPLAN, HARRY		26 MAR 1950	1867		DORA
392	B11	KAPLAN, HARRY		27 DEC 1979	3 NOV 1900		
116	BY42	KAPLAN, HARRY H		28 OCT 1962	1886		SADYE
105	N42	KAPLAN, HENRY DAVID		3 DEC 1970	1902		
391	GM 6	KAPLAN, HERBERT H		28 JUN 1935	10 MAY 1919	JUDAH LEV	
105	N44	KAPLAN, HERMAN		5 FEB 1944	1897		JENNIE
391	C39	KAPLAN, HORACE S		25 JAN 1925	22 JAN 1925	BENJAMIN & LENA	
391	ZC66	KAPLAN, HOWARD ALFRED		11 NOV 1994	17 SEP 1938	HERSHEL	
110	D10	KAPLAN, IDA	LEVY	28 JUL 1962	1906		
330	AG 6	KAPLAN, IRWIN I		14 FEB 1985	27 MAY 1909		
391	U52	KAPLAN, ISAAC		13 JUN 1950	1874	TZVI	ANNA
392	D24	KAPLAN, ISADORE		6 DEC 1968	1885	TZVI HIRSH	REBECCA
102	AG 6	KAPLAN, ISADORE		20 MAY 1939	1872		RACHEL
370	G50	KAPLAN, JACOB					LENA

Cem	Row	Name	Maiden Name	DOD	DOB	Parents	Spouse
102	AJ179	KAPLAN, JACOB		4 APR 1967	1884		
105	L46	KAPLAN, JACOB		15 JAN 1955	1878		REVA
125	B 21	KAPLAN, JACOB R		28 JUN 1960	1869		ROSE
105	N43	KAPLAN, JENNIE		13 FEB 1966	1899		HERMAN
392	B33	KAPLAN, JOHN R		5 JUL 1945			SARAH
248	C50	KAPLAN, JOSEPH		16 JAN 1980	16 JUN 1914		
248	E26	KAPLAN, JOSEPH		29 AUG 1957	1880		SOPHIE
248	J72	KAPLAN, JULIUS		16 AUG 1917			
370	H13	KAPLAN, LENA		4 AUG 1890	1835		JACOB
371	E 1	KAPLAN, LENA		6 MAY 1988	22 DEC 1902		
392	E40	KAPLAN, LENA		27 JUL 1957	1892	ISAAC MEYER	SAMUEL
377	J28	KAPLAN, LENA C		20 DEC 1947	1893		
371	J 1	KAPLAN, LEON		4 NOV 1988	23 JUL 1918		
391	GM 3	KAPLAN, LEON		5 MAR 1942	1897		
125	H148	KAPLAN, LEON S		27 NOV 1977	1902		MURIEL
248	E45	KAPLAN, LEWIS		24 JAN 1946	1873		ANNA
377	L 7	KAPLAN, LOUIS		1982	1898		
110	A 9	KAPLAN, LOUIS		20 JAN 1930	1872		
121	Q20	KAPLAN, LOUIS "KID"		26 OCT 1970	15 OCT 1901		
447	AA35	KAPLAN, MARUICE		17 JAN 1982	26 MAY 1914		
391	ZB69	KAPLAN, MARY	MALLEN	10 DEC 1977	1901	ELCHANON	
391	GM 4	KAPLAN, MAX		28 AUG 1940	1871	TZVI	
125	T160	KAPLAN, MAX		28 FEB 1940	1870	ISRAEL	ROSE
391	GC 3	KAPLAN, MAY		20 JUL 1958	1896	NACHMAN	
391	C38	KAPLAN, MENDEL		3 JUL 1924	14 JUN 1924	BENJAMIN & LENA	
125	H147	KAPLAN, MINNIE	GLASS	27 JUL 1970	1902		LEON
102	G21	KAPLAN, MOLLIE		13 AUG 1951	1886		
392	H49	KAPLAN, MORRIS		10 JUN 1993	22 FEB 1912	ISAAC	
110	D24	KAPLAN, MORRIS		18 JUL 1973	1898		
391	GK 4	KAPLAN, MORRIS		19 MAY 1948	1881	ABRAHAM ISAAC	
125	W174	KAPLAN, MORRIS		20 DEC 1977	10 AUG 1911		
119	F26	KAPLAN, MORRIS		22 OCT 1973	4 JUL 1902		
248	F41	KAPLAN, MORRIS H		26 MAR 1938	1874		
116	BY43	KAPLAN, OLIVE S		25 MAY 1987	25 FEB 1914		ALBERT
110	D 6	KAPLAN, PAULINE		4 NOV 1961	1882		HARRY
391	S35	KAPLAN, PAULINE		31 DEC 1919	1903	JOSEPH	
110	A 3	KAPLAN, RACHEL		6 SEP 1974	1906		
102	AG 5	KAPLAN, RACHEL		26 MAR 1949	1876		ISADORE
391	GG 1	KAPLAN, RAE	PINCUS	1 JUL 1962	19 SEP 1890	ABRAHAM	
105	N39	KAPLAN, RAYMOND B		19 AUG 1977	21 DEC 1942		
102	C11	KAPLAN, REBECCA	NITKIN	22 NOV 1984			
392	D23	KAPLAN, REBECCA		28 OCT 1969	1894	SAMUEL	ISADORE
105	L45	KAPLAN, REVA	ROSETSKY	1 JUL 1959	1879		JACOB
105	L43	KAPLAN, ROBERTA N		15 JUL 1972	15 SEP 1908		
125	T161	KAPLAN, ROSE		3 FEB 1955	1880		MAX
105	H20	KAPLAN, ROSE	FELDMAN	11 JUN 1954	1908		
111	4	KAPLAN, ROSE		15 JUL 1975	20 SEP 1900		
125	B 22	KAPLAN, ROSE		21 JUL 1942	11 JUN 1874		JACOB
119	B 6	KAPLAN, RUTH		10 OCT 1991	24 SEP 1928		
116	BY41	KAPLAN, SADYE	LEVY	13 JUN 1968	1893		HARRY
119	I 6	KAPLAN, SAMUEL		8 JUN 1987	22 JUL 1909		
392	E39	KAPLAN, SAMUEL		21 AUG 1947	1890		LENA
248	E24	KAPLAN, SAMUEL		29 JAN 1958	15 SEP 1883		ESTHER
110	A 4	KAPLAN, SAMUEL		30 OCT 1960	1898		BETTY
102	AD129	KAPLAN, SAMUEL L		26 APR 1971	25 SEP 1892		ETHEL
125	E139	KAPLAN, SARAH	MILSTEIN	9 JAN 1936	1858	MOSHE & MIRIAM	
248	F44	KAPLAN, SARAH		13 APR 1959	1884		
392	B32	KAPLAN, SARAH		15 NOV 1932			JOHN
110	D 3	KAPLAN, SARAH GITAL		10 FEB 1952	1887		
392	H23	KAPLAN, SARAH L		9 JUN 1938	1912	ZALMAN	
113	C25	KAPLAN, SEYMOUR		7 NOV 1983	1 JUL 1924		
110	D 4	KAPLAN, SILVIA		4 APR 1957	1865		
110	A21	KAPLAN, SIMON		15 MAY 1955	1900		
110	E 3	KAPLAN, SOLOMON		31 MAR 1975	5 DEC 1902		
105	M43	KAPLAN, SONIA K		30 MAR 1983			
119	F25	KAPLAN, SONYA		19 JUN 1990	10 APR 1905		

Cem	Row	Name	Maiden Name	DOD	DOB	Parents	Spouse
248	E25	KAPLAN, SOPHIE		26 FEB 1976	1888		JOSEPH
110	E 2	KAPLAN, SUSAN D		6 JAN 1987	13 MAY 1941	SOLOMON	
391	GK 3	KAPLAN, WILLIAM		17 NOV 1955	1877	ABRAHAM	
125	A 21	KAPLAN, WILLIAM I		3 SEP 1983	1900		
116	BY45	KAPLAN, WILLIAM S		21 JAN 1970			
391	GN 4	KAPLAN, YETTA C		29 JAN 1936	1873	ISAAC	ABRAHAM
751	A36	KAPLOWITZ, ESTHER		14 AUG 1925	1873		
751	N31	KAPLOWITZ, MORRIS		25 JAN 1976	14 MAY 1910		
101	K11	KAPROVE, GOLDY		13 APR 1924	1854		
119	B 2	KAPROVE, SAMUEL		30 SEP 1979	15 AUG 1892		
119	B 3	KAPROVE, SOPHIE		7 JUN 1988	15 AUG 1897		
330	AH17	KARAL, JERRY		1974	1939		
391	GG 6	KARAN, RIFKA		1909			
102	A65	KARASEK, TONI	LEOPOLD	24 OCT 1988	1907		
104	E29	KARGMAN, BELLA		1984	1891		MAX
119	F 2	KARGMAN, CHARLES KENNETH		3 JUN 1974	30 JAN 1914		
119	F 1	KARGMAN, CHARLOTTE		12 MAY 1992			
111	12	KARGMAN, HAROLD		2 OCT 1986	19 SEP 1912		
104	E28	KARGMAN, MAX		1973	1892		BELLA
116	K 8	KARL, ROSE L		1 NOV 1986	12 FEB 1907		
102	BF16	KARLIN, BENYAMIN		1992	1902		NEDEZHDA
113	L72	KARLIN, DANIEL		8 FEB 1983	14 MAY 1900		FANNIE
113	L71	KARLIN, FANNIE		1 FEB 1990	28 SEP 1903		DANIEL
102	BF15	KARLIN, NADEZHDA		1989	1905		BENYAMIN
102	AJ181	KARLINER, ERNST		25 APR 1967	29 OCT 1887		
102	AJ17	KARLINER, HILDE	EPSTEIN	23 MAY 1943	15 APR 1915		
374	C17	KARNATER, HELEN ROSE	RUBIN	13 NOV 1975	25 DEC 1898		
104	B29	KARNO, G KATHERINE		1 MAR 1978	1895		PHILIP
104	B28	KARNO, PHILIP		21 DEC 1951	1895		G KATHERII
102	I50	KAROTKIN, ALBERT		11 JUL 1956	1902		CHARLOTTE
102	I49	KAROTKIN, CHARLOTTE		12 FEB 1980	1901		ALBERT
102	AD106	KAROTKIN, ROBERT H DR		19 FEB 1975	1909		
125	S162	KARP, DORA	HONEYMAN	5 SEP 1941	1897	ISRAEL	
123		KARP, GEORGE		8 MAR 1949	1921		
123		KARP, HYMAN A		24 SEP 1944	12 DEC 1917		
102	K31	KARP, JENNIE		1933	1875		
392	D41	KARP, PHILIP		27 MAR 1956	1877	MOSHE	
102	K30	KARP, ROSE		1932	1880		
377	S24	KARPEL, SAUL		JUL 1970	MAR 1910		
110	C20	KARPMAN, ANNA		14 NOV 1968	1883		TEVIE
110	B 2	KARPMAN, BASSIE		5 SEP 1927	1851		BARUCH
110	B 1	KARPMAN, BORUCH		9 JUL 1933	1851		BASSIE
119	C 4	KARPMAN, IDA L		29 APR 1988	17 JUN 1917		
110	C21	KARPMAN, TEVIE		27 DEC 1964	1868		ANNIE
330	AB 7	KASHKIN, IDA		14 JUL 1969	10 APR 1891		PHILIP
330	AB 6	KASHKIN, PHILIP		31 AUG 1968	20 MAY 1888		IDA
111	4	KASHMANN, HOWARD J		12 FEB 1992	22 OCT 1900		
121	J21	KASIN, JOSEPH		1975	1905		
121	J20	KASIN, SYDE M		1980	1908		
102	BH34	KASLER, ELLEN		22 JUL 1991	4 NOV 1923		
447	W 3	KASLER, JENNIE W		1982	1898		
370	P34	KASLOFSKY, BESSEY		1926	1866		LOUIS
370	G47	KASLOFSKY, LOUIS		27 MAR 1926	1864		BESSEY
102	L39	KASOV, CECELIA	SHAPIRO	17 FEB 1969	1887		PHILIP
102	L38	KASOV, PHILIP		4 SEP 1939	1887		CECELIA
249	F40	KASSMAN, ANNIE S		7 MAR 1971	15 MAR 1902		MAX
249	G31	KASSMAN, ANNNETTE M		23 FEB 1985	25 DEC 1929		
330	AG15	KASSMAN, BENJAMIN		1 JAN 1985	15 MAR 1892		SADIE
249	G38	KASSMAN, ELIZABETH SARAH		14 MAR 1983	10 JUN 1982		
249	F39	KASSMAN, MAX		6 JAN 1985	24 DEC 1896		ANNIE
330	AG30	KASSMAN, MORRIS		29 MAR 1991	13 APR 1923	BENJAMIN & SADIE	
248	K66	KASSMAN, RAPHAEL AARON		12 APR 1946	25 JUL 1921		
330	AG14	KASSMAN, SADIE		6 MAY 1971	3 SEP 1894		BENJAMIN
112	A38	KATTEN, BETTY		11 NOV 1991	3 JUL 1900		
112	D29	KATTEN, JULIUS		27 JUN 1978	10 MAY 1901		MARGOT
112	D30	KATTEN, MARGOT	MANNES	21 MAR 1989	19 JAN 1894		JULIUS

Cem	Row	Name	Maiden Name	DOD	DOB	Parents	Spouse
391	B 2	KATZ, (BABY BOY)		10 OCT 1963			
371	K39	KATZ, AARON S		29 APR 1953	1899		BERTHA
102	AG109	KATZ, ABRAHAM		3 FEB 1984	2 JAN 1892		IDA
392	H33	KATZ, ABRAHAM		20 NOV 1964	1885	ISRAEL	
116	U27	KATZ, ABRAHAM		21 MAY 1990	26 JUN 1924		
391	F27	KATZ, ABRAHAM D		22 JUN 1934	15 SEP 1890	ISAAC	
102	F41	KATZ, ABRAHAM I		12 DEC 1948	3 JUN 1890		MARY
105	G 9	KATZ, ANNA	SOSIN	18 SEP 1990	3 JAN 1898		HERMAN
391	T50	KATZ, ANNA		23 OCT 1941	1866	SHIMON	
102	G31	KATZ, ARCHIE H		12 OCT 1972	8 OCT 1900		GLADYS
103	E5	KATZ, BELLA	NEIKRE	21 FEB 1990	17 APR 1917		
121	V10	KATZ, BENJAMIN		9 AUG 1983	10 JAN 1895		
102	Q11	KATZ, BENJAMIN		18 JUN 1934	1870		ROSE
125	L141	KATZ, BENJAMIN		30 MAY 1953	31 JAN 1890		
113	O57	KATZ, BERNARD L		24 NOV 1979	27 NOV 1922		
371	K40	KATZ, BERTHA		19 NOV 1991	1900		AARON
102	W20	KATZ, BERTHA	ADAMS	1926	1873		
125	O131	KATZ, BESSIE		13 JUL 1990	1904		MICHAEL
113	J44	KATZ, BLUMA	RUBIN	4 FEB 1984	24 OCT 1906		SAMUEL
125	E113	KATZ, DAVID S		3 MAR 1985	13 AUG 1912		
102	CB36	KATZ, DEBORAH F		31 JUL 1981	17 JAN 1959		
119	C42	KATZ, EDWARD		29 MAR 1980	20 OCT 1901		
105	G11	KATZ, ELINOR	BLUMENTHAL	30 SEP 1987	23 MAR 1926		
102	AB74	KATZ, ELIZABAETH		19 DEC 1982	1893		NATHAN
102	AG54	KATZ, EMMA	GLAZER	3 SEP 1973	13 JUL 1925		
119	F64	KATZ, ESTHER		15 JUL 1976			
391	R33	KATZ, ETTA		9 JUN 1919		ABRAHAM	
370	Z 2	KATZ, GITEL ESTHER		4 SEP 1942			
102	G32	KATZ, GLADYS	CION	12 AUG 1952	2 FEB 1900		ARCHIE
751	C 9	KATZ, HARRY		1967	1905		
377	S22	KATZ, HARRY M		1970	1916		
102	AC20	KATZ, HENRY		3 OCT 1981	13 MAR 1895		
105	G 8	KATZ, HERMAN		1976	1897		ANNA
102	F18	KATZ, HILDA	LEVY	3 APR 1970	15 SEP 1899		HYMAN
391	G31	KATZ, HYMAN		16 MAR 1928	1891	ISAAC	
102	F19	KATZ, HYMAN CY		12 MAY 1947	7 NOV 1897		HILDA
102	C30	KATZ, IDA	SELTZER	1950	1880		WILLIAM
104	C30	KATZ, IDA		1962	1899		MAX
102	AG110	KATZ, IDA		24 MAR 1986	2 SEP 1894		ABRAHAM
119	H24	KATZ, IRVING		16 DEC 1989	1917		
391	T51	KATZ, ISAAC		16 JAN 1941	1867	SHIMON	
125	T155	KATZ, ISAAC		19 FEB 1946	1872		JENNIE
119	B54	KATZ, JACK		29 JAN 1992	2 JAN 1920		
391	ZF77	KATZ, JACOB		5 SEP 1985	21 NOV 1915	ELIEZER	
125	K144	KATZ, JACOB LOUIS		4 DEC 1931	MAR 1893		
751	N17	KATZ, JAKE		5 AUG 1966	21 OCT 1894		
111	4	KATZ, JANE E		22 JUL 1970	2 SEP 1948		
125	T154	KATZ, JENNIE		6 JAN 1940	1877		ISAAC
125	O 56	KATZ, JEROME					
125	E120	KATZ, JEROME		2 NOV 1934	1930	MICHAEL	
121	N14	KATZ, JOSEPH A		15 NOV 1989	15 JUN 1902		
114	C13	KATZ, JOSEPH H		15 JAN 1981	9 SEP 1957		
102	Q13	KATZ, JOSEPH J		30 MAR 1955	1894		LUCY
102	AC87	KATZ, LENA A		30 APR 1943	1885		LOUIS
125	G132	KATZ, LEON EDWARD		29 DEC 1962	1892		
105	H29	KATZ, LIBBY ESTHER		6 FEB 1944	1874		
391	ZB59	KATZ, LILLIAN	HIRSCH	5 AUG 1965	27 SEP 1915	ABRAHAM	
102	AC88	KATZ, LOUIS H		18 FEB 1959	1881		LENA
102	AB164	KATZ, LOUIS Y		3 OCT 1989	4 AUG 1899		
102	Q12	KATZ, LUCY	PAUSMENTIER	12 SEP 1971	1893		JOSEPH
119	H33	KATZ, MARION C		20 MAR 1984	15 JUL 1915		
102	F40	KATZ, MARY E		31 OCT 1963			ABRAHAM
222	AL21	KATZ, MAX		30 SEP 1921	1878		
104	C31	KATZ, MAX Z		1959	1887		IDA
125	O132	KATZ, MICHAEL S		13 DEC 1975	1899		BESSIE
391	GM 2	KATZ, MORRIS		7 JAN 1949	1880	NATNEL	

Cem	Row	Name	Maiden Name	DOD	DOB	Parents	Spouse
125	G133	KATZ, MYRON		18 MAY 1945	1925		
102	AE30	KATZ, NATHAN		4 MAR 1970	15 MAR 1898	YEHUDA YITZCHAK	
102	AB73	KATZ, NATHAN		13 JAN 1961	1893		
102	N32	KATZ, RAY		14 OCT 1923	1868		ELIZABETH
391	L47	KATZ, REBECCA T		22 MAR 1989	23 OCT 1894	MEYER	SAMUEL
330	C 3	KATZ, ROSE		13 AUG 1961			
391	U50	KATZ, ROSE		19 JUL 1944	1925	JACOB	SAMUEL
102	Q10	KATZ, ROSE	GREENBERG	29 JAN 1934	1874		
111	4	KATZ, ROSLYN N		1975	1918		BENJAMIN
102	G13	KATZ, SADIE	GABERMAN	4 DEC 1982	15 SEP 1905		
125	G 1	KATZ, SAMUEL		11 JUL 1964	1908		
391	P28	KATZ, SAMUEL		14 JAN 1917	1839	DAVID	
330	C 2	KATZ, SAMUEL		15 MAY 1949			
119	F65	KATZ, SAMUEL		18 MAY 1986			ROSE
391	T52	KATZ, SAMUEL		20 JUN 1944	1901	ISAAC	
102	N31	KATZ, SAMUEL		20 NOV 1947	1874		RAY
392	H41	KATZ, SAMUEL (SHIBTAL ELIEZ		27 JUN 1987	29 JUL 1893	ISAAC	
113	J45	KATZ, SAMUEL S		6 JUN 1979	25 JUL 1899		BLUMA
121	K 8	KATZ, SARAH L		11 MAR 1975			
111	4	KATZ, SIDNEY	OF SPRINGFIELD	13 OCT 1965	2 AUG 1910	ABRAHAM & MAY	
125	G134	KATZ, SOPHIE		1985	1902		
125	O 69	KATZ, SYLVIA		10 OCT 1921	JUL 25 1920	PHILIP	
102	C29	KATZ, WILLIAM		1946	1876		IDA
123		KATZEL, HARRY		12 SEP 1949	1893		
125	J114	KATZEN, EDWARD		28 JAN 1933	1877		MINNIE
119	F18	KATZEN, JOSEPH		7 MAR 1986	1900		
125	J115	KATZEN, MINNIE		14 FEB 1953	1880		EDWARD
119	F17	KATZEN, SARAH		4 MAR 1974	1904		
125	D 98	KATZENSTEIN, SALLYE S		1993	1899		WILLIAM
125	D 97	KATZENSTEIN, WILLIAM		19 JAN 1948	28 DEC 1896		SALLYE
751	N 9	KATZIN, JUDITH		24 OCT 1973			
751	B 7	KATZIN, LORI DENNISE		28 APR 1976	13 APR 1956		
751	N 8	KATZIN, NATHAN		14 SEP 1975			
121	M18	KATZMAN, LENA		21 MAR 1986	1900		
751	M25	KATZMAN, PETER		26 AUG 1968	9 SEP 1897		
121	M19	KATZMAN, RAYMOND		18 APR 1976	1895		
112	D 5	KAUFHERR, MINNA		7 MAY 1979	2 JUN 1889		
391	GG 3	KAUFMAN, (BOY)					
391	GH 1	KAUFMAN, ABRAHAM				ZADOK	
222	AF 8	KAUFMAN, ABRAM		1 NOV 1943	1879		THELMA
125	M132	KAUFMAN, ADOLPH S		1 MAY 1970	19 MAR 1880		HILDE
125	M123	KAUFMAN, ANNA SARAH		26 APR 1929	1887	SHLOMON & SARALE	
110	B 3	KAUFMAN, BELLA		1 MAY 1932	1902		
102	AI185	KAUFMAN, BENJAMIN		21 APR 1970	1886		IDA
222	AA17	KAUFMAN, BESSIE		1 OCT 1975	22 FEB 1903	MOSES & MALKA	
377	D38	KAUFMAN, CHARLES MD		8 AUG 1959	18 JUN 1895		IDA
104	H28	KAUFMAN, EDWARD		12 MAR 1971	8 JUL 1912		SARAH
116	BL73	KAUFMAN, ETHEL S		11 JUL 1991	28 NOV 1908		MURRAY
222	AF 9	KAUFMAN, EVA R		27 MAR 1939	1861		SOLOMON
102	AF77	KAUFMAN, EZRA JEROME		13 OCT 1987	19 OCT 1901		
125	G 20	KAUFMAN, FANNIE	LIPMAN	19 OCT 1950	1890		
104	G18	KAUFMAN, FAY	DUBOW	20 APR 1972			
105	L24	KAUFMAN, FREDA M		10 JUN 1982	1902		
222	AJ 6	KAUFMAN, GERTRUDE		25 OCT 1921	1919		ISRAEL
102	N 1	KAUFMAN, GLADYS S		9 JAN 1977	14 OCT 1928		
371	AJ15	KAUFMAN, HARRY J		3 NOV 1969	1901		SAUNDER
222	AG 6	KAUFMAN, HELEN	CHALPHIN	18 JAN 1981	30 OCT 1908		JACOB
329	C50	KAUFMAN, HERMAN		29 JUN 1962			ROSE
125	M131	KAUFMAN, HILDE F		16 JAN 1986	4 FEB 1894		ADOLPHE
330	E43	KAUFMAN, IDA	STOCK	5 FEB 1939	1905		
102	AI186	KAUFMAN, IDA		16 MAY 1971	1888		BENJAMIN
105	L27	KAUFMAN, IDA		19 FEB 1963	1902		NATHAN
377	D37	KAUFMAN, IDA	SLOSSBERG	20 DEC 1978	14 JUL 1901		CHARLES
102	N 3	KAUFMAN, IRVING L		9 MAR 1950	26 MAR 1893		
105	L25	KAUFMAN, ISRAEL		28 DEC 1970	1897		FREDA
447	A15	KAUFMAN, ISRAEL		29 MAY 1958	1890		MARY

Cem	Row	Name	Maiden Name	DOD	DOB	Parents	Spouse
222	AG 5	KAUFMAN, JACOB		26 JUL 1973	15 OCT 1898		HELEN
222	AJ 7	KAUFMAN, JONAS		29 NOV 1920	1859		
102	AF85	KAUFMAN, JONAS A		6 DEC 1963	27 JUN 1911	MORRIS & MINNIE	
101	A32	KAUFMAN, LOUIS		26 JUN 1910	1856		
102	F 1	KAUFMAN, LOUIS E		2 SEP 1974	31 DEC 1903		
222	AA16	KAUFMAN, MALKA		24 DEC 1918	1882		MOSES
447	A17	KAUFMAN, MARY	ADLER	12 OCT 1962	1889		ISRAEL
447	K36	KAUFMAN, MARY		1970	1915		
329	D44	KAUFMAN, MEYER		3 MAY 1986	28 OCT 1895		
102	AF86	KAUFMAN, MINNIE	RICKMAN	19 MAY 1958	13 MAR 1881		MORRIS
751	K18	KAUFMAN, MORRIS		26 MAY 1936	1867		
102	AF87	KAUFMAN, MORRIS GABRIEL		4 DEC 1966	17 MAR 1884		MINNIE
222	AA15	KAUFMAN, MOSES		20 OCT 1926	1877		MALKA
116	BL74	KAUFMAN, MURRAY		15 MAY 1988	24 NOV 1908		ETHEL
105	L26	KAUFMAN, NATHAN		13 DEC 1970	1894		IDA
222	AJ 5	KAUFMAN, PAUL		12 APR 1928	18 OCT 1913		
102	N 4	KAUFMAN, RICHARD F		13 JAN 1929	27 JUL 1927	IRVING	
329	C51	KAUFMAN, ROSE		11 APR 1962			HERMAN
104	H29	KAUFMAN, SARA		22 APR 1979	8 NOV 1916		EDWARD
102	F 2	KAUFMAN, SARAH	HURWITZ	19 JUL 1966	3 JUN 1966		
391	P34	KAUFMAN, SARAH		31 MAR 1917	1873	SIMON	
102	N 2	KAUFMAN, SAUNDER JOSEPH		1984	1925	IRVING	GLADYS
222	AF10	KAUFMAN, SOLOMON S		3 JAN 1938	1859		EVA
222	AF 7	KAUFMAN, THELMA		11 APR 1969	1890		ABRAM
107	G20	KAUFMANN, ERICH		4 FEB 1973	4 JUL 1901		
102	H 1	KAVALIER, ESTHER H		7 JUL 1944	1905		
102	H 4	KAVALIER, IDA		27 JAN 1937	1869		MAX
102	H 6	KAVALIER, MAURICE A		24 JUN 1959	1901	MAX & IDA	
102	H 3	KAVALIER, MAX		23 NOV 1940	1870		IDA
102	H 5	KAVALIER, SAMUEL		29 OCT 1952	1903	MAX & IDA	
102	H 2	KAVALIER, SANDRA LOIS		6 JUL 1944	1938	ESTHER	
102	T18	KAWARE, BERTHA B	BROD	DEC 1962	NOV 1902	MARCUS & GOLDA	JAY
102	T19	KAWARE, JAY		23 DEC 1970	14 JAN 1896		BERTHA
102	T17	KAWARE, STANLEY MARSHALL		19 MAY 1977	6 JUL 1923	JAY & BERTHA (BROD)	
370	Q59	KAY, ADOLPH		2 JUL 1953	26 DEC 1899		REBECCA
102	AG119	KAY, ARNOLD J		1990	1921		FAE
102	AG118	KAY, FAE	ELLIN	24 JUL 1981	9 JAN 1922		ARNOLD
447	K11	KAY, POLLY	LONDON	30 JUN 1953	1900	BENJAMIN & MARCIA	
370	Q61	KAY, REBECCA		27 DEC 1989	13 DEC 1901		ADOLPH
125	M197	KAYE, ANNETTE B		16 FEB 1970			
101	I11	KAYE, BARNEY		4 NOV 1985	24 MAR 1907		
125	H 55	KAYE, EDWARD N		22 SEP 1956	1911		
370	U 7	KAYE, FRANCES	ALOFSIN	13 NOV 1990	30 OCT 1918		
113	B33	KAYE, PAUL MANUEL		21 MAY 1984	19 MAY 1907		
121	AA31	KAYE, ROSE		20 AUG 1984	10 DEC 1890		
125	L143	KAYE, SOPHIE		9 SEP 1953	1908		
125	K169	KAYSER, JAMES G		9 JAN 1962	6 AUG 1901		
106	D10	KEARNEY, FAYE		17 DEC 1981	9 APR 1931		
102	T53	KEEFE, ELSIE	JONAS	7 JAN 1981	6 MAR 1892		
125		KEINOVITZ, (BABY)		11 SEP 1917	1917	ISRAEL & ANNA	
116	BU84	KEIZERSTEIN, ELSIE		19 JAN 1973	15 JAN 1900		MYRON
116	BU85	KEIZERSTEIN, MYRON		7 APR 1989	7 JAN 1899		ELSIE
113	O49	KELLER, ANNIE		11 JUN 1962	15 FEB 1887		
102	I17	KELLIN, MIKE		26 AUG 1983	26 APR 1922	SAMUEL & SOPHIE	
102	I16	KELLIN, SAMUEL		3 FEB 1977	23 NOV 1903		SOPHIE
102	I14	KELLIN, SHIRLEY		6 JUL 1944	14 AUG 1927	SAMUEL & SOPHIE	
102	I15	KELLIN, SOPHIE		3 NOV 1988	29 JUN 1902		SAMUEL
102	K40	KELMAN, ANNA	CARTIN	4 JUL 1968	1918		JACOB
102	K41	KELMAN, BERNICE		13 JUL 1938	4 DEC 1919		JACOB
248	G45	KELMAN, HARRY		17 SEP 1943	1909	MORRIS & IDA	
248	G47	KELMAN, IDA	EISENBERG	11 AUG 1976	1888	SAMUEL & MINNIE	MORRIS
102	K39	KELMAN, JACOB		20 NOV 1943	1891		ANNA
248	G46	KELMAN, MORRIS		29 NOV 1963	1883		IDA
248	L58	KELMAN, ROSE		17 JUN 1981	1 FEB 1894		
102	D25	KEMLER, BENJAMIN S		2 MAY 1966	1893		ROSE
102	T28	KEMLER, ESTHER	WEDEEN	19 JAN 1923	1892		LOUIS

Cem	Row	Name	Maiden Name	DOD	DOB	Parents	Spouse
102	T27	KEMLER, LOUIS E		3 NOV 1932	1883		ESTHER
102	D24	KEMLER, ROSE MINTZ		7 MAR 1971	1898		BENJAMIN
433	I21	KEMMALMAN, BEN ZION		2 APR 1923	1863	CHAIKEL	
127	K	KEMPINSKI, MIRIAM		6 FEB 1990	5 MAY 1927		
372	G 9	KEMPNER, ANNIE	RAPHAEL	1927	1848		JACOB
372	G 8	KEMPNER, JACOB		3 OCT 1912	1849		ANNIE
372	G 7	KEMPNER, LOUIS		1941	1880	JACOB & ANNA	
370	K40	KENDALL, AIDA	KESSLER	1968	1901		
125	N143	KENDZUR, LOUIS		14 AUG 1950	1883		
123		KENDZUR, MAX S		15 JUN 1944	1917		
125	Q161	KENDZUR, SEYMOUR		31 MAR 1946	24 JUN 1921	LOUIS & SARAH	
125	R151	KENDZUR, SONIA		25 FEB 1943	5 FEB 1888	SHIMON & CHANA	
109	C 7	KENIG, AARON	OF AUSTRIA	10 APR 1949	1865	JULIUS & MOLLY	REBECCA
119	C62	KENIG, ALBERT		25 SEP 1987	27 MAR 1925		
374	B26	KENIG, DORA		11 JUL 1993	1897		ISRAEL
374	B29	KENIG, ISAAC		1 OCT 1943	1871		LENA
374	B27	KENIG, ISRAEL		23 FEB 1953	1897		DORA
374	B28	KENIG, LENA		23 JUL 1938	1876		ISAAC
109	E 8	KENIG, MINNIE		6 JUL 1988	1903	AARON & REBECCA (SHIMELMAN)	
109	E 7	KENIG, PEARL		19 SEP 1990	22 JUN 1907	AARON & REBECCA (SHIMELMAN)	
109	C 6	KENIG, REBECCA	SHIMELMAN	12 OCT 1958	1877		AARON
447	S24	KENIGSBERG, MORRIS		21 APR 1957	1890		
446	B70	KENNAY, MARION	STRAUSS	17 DEC 1928	6 JAN 1864		
125		KENNEDY, (MISCARRIAGE)		10 DEC 1920	10 DEC 1920	MAX & BELLA	
125	K 98	KENNEDY, BELLA		3 FEB 1921	1893	SAMUEL & ROSE	
125	P148	KENNEDY, BEN		24 JAN 1948	1893	ZVI HIRSH	
113	H27	KENNEDY, BESSIE L	ESSMAN	26 MAY 1976	27 MAY 1893		
125	I 60	KENNEDY, DAVID F		26 MAY 1905	27 APR 1828		
125	H 4	KENNEDY, DORA K		11 JAN 1957	1870		SAMUEL
125	I 58	KENNEDY, ETTA		27 FEB 1899	15 JAN 1827	MEYER	
125	I106	KENNEDY, HARRY		28 JUN 1942	1858	DAVID	REBECCA
125	M161	KENNEDY, MAX		6 OCT 1952	1887		
125	G 4	KENNEDY, MAXWELL S		1988	1901		SADIE
125	K 69	KENNEDY, MYER		1 JUL 1935	1898	TZVI HIRSH & RIVKAH	
125	I105	KENNEDY, REBECCA		1929	1863		HARRY
125	G 6	KENNEDY, SADIE		13 SEP 1973	1907		MAXWELL
125	H 5	KENNEDY, SAMUEL		10 MAY 1939	1867	DAVID	DORA
125	K192	KENNEDY, SAMUEL		31 MAR 1974	1894		SYLVIA
125	H 18	KENNEDY, SARAH D		25 MAR 1939	1869		SIMON
125	H 17	KENNEDY, SIMON		9 DEC 1942	1870	DAVID	SARAH
125	K193	KENNEDY, SYLVIA		1992	1904		SAMUEL
126		KENRICH, HENRIETTA		27 SEP 1924	25 SEP 1841		ISAAC
126		KENRICH, ISAAC		9 MAY 1916	4 MAY 1849		HENRIETTA
121	F15	KENT, ALAN MARTIN		12 AUG 1978	5 JAN 1916	CELIA	
125	J197	KENT, BARRY JAY		3 JUN 1984	1934		HYLA
121	F14	KENT, CELIA		5 JUL 1975	22 FEB 1882		
125	J198	KENT, HYLA		25 JAN 1993	1935		BARRY
121	M13	KENT, JEFFREY		1969	1945		
116	S20	KEPPNER, HELEN	LEVINE	16 JUN 1976	14 OCT 1910		
116	S27	KEPPNER, JACK		13 SEP 1988	31 MAR 1933		
330	AC11	KERACHSKY, MARSHA		4 JAN 1967	1878		
249	D10	KERACHSKY, MIRIAM C		27 FEB 1982	21 MAR 1917		MORRIS
249	D 9	KERACHSKY, MORRIS		18 MAY 1986	25 DEC 1912		MIRIAM
328	A 4	KERACHSKY, NATHAN L		17 JAN 1988	7 JAN 1907		
119	A60	KERN, MORRIS		31 OCT 1981	1898		
370	F22	KERSMAN, ZALMAN		JUL 1925		AARON	
222	AJ 3	KESSER, FRANCES	SILVERHERZ	1935	1903	MORRIS & REBECCA	
101	A23	KESSLER, BORACH		29 DEC 1915	1831		
377	G 5	KESSLER, GERTRUDE		1958	1875		
377	O23	KESSLER, HERMAN		1950	1874		
370	K38	KESSLER, JACOB		11 MAY 1939	1864		SHIMA
330	C16	KESSLER, MINNIE		11 JAN 1944	1860		MORRIS
391	L30	KESSLER, MORDECHAI		27 APR 1922	1844	CHAIM	
330	C15	KESSLER, MORRIS		12 JUL 1934	1863		MINNIE
370	Q53	KESSLER, SAMUEL		2 MAY 1938			
370	K39	KESSLER, SHIMA		16 JUL 1933	1863		JACOB

Cem	Row	Name	Maiden Name	DOD	DOB	Parents	Spouse
121	A 5	KESTIN, JOSEPH		4 JUL 1974	2 NOV 1888		
110	D28	KEYSER, ANNA		16 JUL 1989	1903		HARRY
110	D29	KEYSER, HARRY		25 OCT 1974	1900		ANNA
110	B15	KEYSER, MORRIS		4 DEC 1926	1863		VELFEL
104	H35	KEYSER, MRS					SAMUEL
104	H34	KEYSER, SAMUEL H		18 FEB 1986	22 FEB 1922		
110	B16	KEYSER, VELFL		21 OCT 1952	1870		MORRIS
377	ZA52	KIERSTEIN, HYMAN		24 JAN 1993	18 AUG 1913	SITZEL & RACHEL	
377	Z43	KIERSTEIN, KEVIN ROBERT		6 SEP 1991	24 JAN 1973	CHANINA & RAZZA	
391	Z75	KIL, BORIS		22 JUN 1976	14 JUL 1914	GERSHON	
391	A 2	KIL, JOSHUA SMITH		4 MAR 1976	31 JAN 1975	ABRAHAM	
112	E 1	KINER, HARRY		25 JAN 1991	15 OCT 1912		
391	I33	KING, ADA JENNIE	LEVITZ	15 DEC 1926	1854	YEHUDA LEV	
377	T31	KING, GEORGE W		12 DEC 1980	1894	CHAIM	LILLIAN
391	Q26	KING, JACOB		28 OCT 1923	1830	ZELIG	
377	T32	KING, LILLIAN M		27 MAR 1991	1899	ISAAC	GEORGE
118	D18	KING, LOUIS		2 JUL 1956			
391	X59	KING, MOSES		11 DEC 1956		JACOB	
391	W58	KING, ROSE		29 MAR 1955		JACOB	
102	AJ173	KINNARD, NEAL P		18 DEC 1966	1920		
328	A 8	KIOTIC, ETHEL I		6 MAY 1982	4 DEC 1924		
328	A33	KIOTIC, SAMUEL		14 APR 1972	1886		
110	A33	KIPPERMAN, SADIE		18 NOV 1989	21 JAN 1904		SIMON
110	A32	KIPPERMAN, SIMON		7 AUG 1976	6 OCT 1898		SADIE
371	L32	KIRSCH, AARON		4 AUG 1953	14 JAN 1865		LENA
371	L31	KIRSCH, HELEN C		24 MAR 1984	9 DEC 1910		
371	J25	KIRSCH, HUGO		24 FEB 1982	29 APR 1906		
371	L33	KIRSCH, LENA ADA		5 JUN 1952	16 JUL 1875		AARON
371	L34	KIRSCH, NATHAN		6 NOV 1963	12 MAY 1901	AARON & LENA	
391	ZD52	KIRSCHENBAUM, ABRAHAM L		7 NOV 1982	28 DEC 1895	PINCUS ISAAC	
330	G39	KIRSHENBAUM, RACHEL		5 JUN 1911	1843		
330	H35	KIRSHNER, BARNET		11 DEC 1947	1870		ROSE
330	E49	KIRSHNER, ROSE		27 JAN 1941	1883		BARNET
125	R143	KIRSHNIT, FANNIE		27 MAY 1942	1898		SAMUEL
125	F121	KIRSHNIT, LOUIS		2 FEB 1945	1 DEC 1878	ZVI HIRSH & DWASHE	MINNIE
125	F120	KIRSHNIT, MINNIE		21 JAN 1963	1885		LOUIS
102	G16	KIRSHNIT, ROSE	GABERMAN	8 JUL 1981	7 NOV 1901		
125	R144	KIRSHNIT, SAMUEL		22 AUG 1972	1898		FANNIE
125	K 44	KIRSHNITZ, DORA		1912	1861		
125	O 95	KIRSHNITZ, HARRY		19 FEB 1921	1859	DAVID & ESTHER	
370	P 2	KIRSTEIN, ABRAHAM		1994	1913		LOUIS
372	K 5	KIRSTEIN, ELSIE	ROSENTHAL	1969	1913	JOSEPH & CHARLOTTE	
370	R40	KIRSTEIN, LOUIS		19 OCT 1966	1 APR 1915		ABRAHAM
371	AD22	KIRSTEIN, MIRIAM		2 FEB 1966	1900		
370	Q 3	KIRSTEN, ETHEL	WOLFE	26 FEB 1956			PHILIP
370	Q 4	KIRSTEN, PHILIP		1967	1894		ETHEL
370	Q 5	KIRSTIN, ANNA		6 MAR 1949			HYMAN
370	Q 6	KIRSTIN, HYMAN		1943	1911		ANNA
371	M31	KIVELEWITZ, AARON		9 MAY 1966			
370	K18	KIVELEWITZ, ETHEL L		12 MAY 1946	1887		
446	A33	KLAPPER, JULIUS		20 MAR 1919		LOUIS & SALLIE	
446	B29	KLAPPER, LOUIS		1918	1878		SALLIE
446	A34	KLAPPER, MEYER		20 MAR 1919		LOUIS & SALLIE	
446	C 3	KLAPPER, SALLIE		7 SEP 1955	1884		LOUIS
446	C 4	KLAPPER, SAMUEL		20 JUL 1988	1904	LOUIS & SALLIE	
433	G23	KLAR, KENNETH		1953			YETTA
433	H22	KLAR, YETTA		22 JUL 1957	1889	NACHEM	KENNETH
125	P188	KLASZ, ELIZABETH SYLVIA	GORFAIN	2 APR 1963	10 JUN 1893	BENJAMIN & TZEREL (GREENSTEIN)	JACOB
125	P187	KLASZ, JACOB HARRY		9 JAN 1971	5 MAR 1891		ELIZABETH
121	G33	KLAU, JOSEPH EDWARD		10 MAY 1988	25 JUL 1902		
101	C35	KLAZ, HARRY		6 OCT 1937	1869		
105	J22	KLEIMAN, FALEK		26 MAR 1943	1884		SOPHIE
447	Z32	KLEIMAN, MAX RABBI		8 JUL 1979	11 OCT 1915		
105	J17	KLEIMAN, REBECCA		19 APR 1984	1898		
105	J15	KLEIMAN, SAMUEL		10 APR 1942	1887		
105	J23	KLEIMAN, SOPHIE		27 JUL 1957	1887		FALEK

Cem	Row	Name	Maiden Name	DOD	DOB	Parents	Spouse
102	A21	KLEIN, ABRAHAM		10 FEB 1934	1886		
116	BI32	KLEIN, ALAN		13 JUL 1985	11 JAN 1934		
391	P35	KLEIN, BESSIE		19 JAN 1915			
370	B18	KLEIN, FERENCZ RABBI		3 MAY 1958		DANIEL	
102	J45	KLEIN, MORRIS		30 JUL 1965	1911		
751	H11	KLEIN, NATHAN RABBI		3 MAR 1946	3 JAN 1908		
392	J35	KLEIN, SAM		1914	1891		
377	U33	KLEIN, ZOLTAN		1980	1889	JUDAH	
433	F 1	KLEINBERG, GUSSIE		10 MAY 1969	1913	YERUCHEM	SAMUEL
433	F 2	KLEINBERG, SAMUEL		28 FEB 1953	15 JAN 1895	ABRAHAM	GUSSIE
751	C21	KLEINER, ABRAHAM		13 DEC 1954	16 MAR 1891	YONAH	
751	J33	KLEINER, KLARA R		1949	1872		
116	BX31	KLEINMAN, HARRY H		29 NOV 1981	1895		RUTH
116	BX30	KLEINMAN, RUTH	NESTOR	12 JAN 1982	18 SEP 1908		HARRY
105	J25	KLEMAN, FANNY		1 MAY 1971	15 MAY 1917	LOUIS & GERTRUDE	JACOB
105	J24	KLEMAN, JACOB		22 NOV 1955	1890		FANNY
105	I25	KLEMAN, ROSE		29 DEC 1978	1886		
113	O54	KLEMENS, IDA		28 DEC 1979	30 JAN 1914		
116	BG 3	KLEPAK, JOSEPH B		23 MAR 1988	19 JAN 1899		
102	AJ20	KLEPER, FANNY	SHERRY	15 APR 1969	3 MAR 1912		HYMAN
102	AJ19	KLEPER, HYMAN		28 OCT 1954	1888		FANNY
101	J40	KLETSKY, LENA		16 MAY 1978	1884		
113	O61	KLIBANOFF, ABRAHAM		8 JUN 1975	1893		
102	AB174	KLINE, HARRY		20 AUG 1973	16 OCT 1926		
101	K31	KLINE, JAMES		20 SEP 1958	25 JUL 1903		
114	L13	KLINE, JESSE ALEXANDER		11 OCT 1983	1906		
371	AB22	KLINE, REAH		24 MAY 1961			
371	AQ 9	KLINGON, FRANCES S		1991	1897		LOUIS
371	AQ 8	KLINGON, LOUIS E MD		1961	1887		FRANCES
222	I 8	KLOTHE, LOUIS		1 MAR 1959	1906		
248	L66	KLUG, HENRY		22 MAY 1963	30 OCT 1894		
249	J10	KNIEBERG, HARRY		8 JAN 1964	1887		
328	B19	KOENIG, BEATRICE		18 OCT 1957	1894		
249	A16	KOENIGSBERG, HARRY		17 OCT 1983	4 APR 1900		
371	AA15	KOFKOFF, NATHAN		24 JAN 1974	1884		
370	I36	KOFKOFF, REBECCA		29 OCT 1931	1881		
106	B12	KOFKSY, ABRAHAM		15 JUL 1990	9 SEP 1909		
103	D16	KOFMAN, HANA			8 JAN 1901		
102	AA169	KOGEN, ELEANOR	GEIGER		13 JAN 1906		LAWRENCE
102	AA168	KOGEN, LAWRENCE			7 NOV 1915		ELEANOR
111	4	KOGUT, RUTH B		NDD	20 APR 1918		
101	I21	KOHN, EDWARD L		22 FEB 1977	22 SEP 1941		
391	ZC52	KOHN, FREDA	HENDEL	18 MAR 1964	18 MAY 1907	SAMUEL LEV	
102	CB41	KOLBIN, ABARAHAM J		16 JUN 1980	13 JAN 1900		HANNAH
102	CB42	KOLBIN, HANNAH		26 JAN 1986	15 MAR 1903		ABRAHAM
125	K119	KOLBRIN, SAMUEL		14 NOV 1971	1877		
125	D101	KOLODNEY, ABRAHAM J		19 FEB 1983	11 SEP 1903		
125	F 60	KOLODNEY, ABRAHAM JACOB		29 MAY 1927	1851		ROSE
125	F 62	KOLODNEY, ANNA		22 APR 1959	1887	ABRAHAM & ROSE	
102	R41	KOLODNEY, BESSIE		24 JAN 1990	1 JAN 1894		RALPH
125	J 64	KOLODNEY, CHAYA SARAH		12 MAR 1918			
125	D 67	KOLODNEY, DAISY P		1985	1896		NEIL
125	D102	KOLODNEY, DORA	FRISHMAN	13 MAR 1963	21 JAN 1887		JOSEPH
125	F101	KOLODNEY, ESTHER	WELINSKY	23 MAY 1984	1 JUL 1902	FRANK & LENA (SILVERSTEIN)	SAMUEL
125	C100	KOLODNEY, EVA	SWILLING	1 JUL 1962	27 DEC 1907		
125	E 66	KOLODNEY, ISAAC		4 OCT 1956	1890		MARY
125	K 34	KOLODNEY, JOSEPH		17 MAY 1914	1862	ARYEH LEV	DORA
125	E 68	KOLODNEY, MARY		8 FEB 1970	1890		ISAAC
125	F 99	KOLODNEY, MARY IDA	MILLER	27 SEP 1947	1899		
125	D 66	KOLODNEY, NEAL		27 NOV 1976	1900		DAISY
102	R42	KOLODNEY, RALPH		21 NOV 1979	16 AUG 1888		BESSIE
125	E101	KOLODNEY, RALPH J		31 DEC 1978	27 AUG 1901		SYLVIA
125	F 61	KOLODNEY, ROSE GITEL		12 APR 1950	1861	JOSEPH & DORA	ABRAHAM
125	F100	KOLODNEY, SAMUEL		9 OCT 1953	7 MAR 1897	JOSEPH & DORA	ESTHER
125		KOLODNEY, SARAH		13 MAR 1918	1855	ABRAHAM	
125	E100	KOLODNEY, SYLVIA		6 JAN 1955	24 NOV 1905		RALPH

Cem	Row	Name	Maiden Name	DOD	DOB	Parents	Spouse
114	L28	KOLP, LAURENCE		18 MAR 1980	15 JUL 1934		
377	O32	KOMISKY, FRANCES		6 SEP 1948	5 JAN 1898		
125	A105	KOMISS, EUNICE Z		7 OCT 1987	3 NOV 1903		
125	A 36	KOMISS, LAURA		3 JAN 1933	27 DEC 1871		
125	B 90	KOMISS, LEO O		30 MAR 1973	29 JUL 1905		
102	A20	KONE, ANNA I	ROSENBERG	26 OCT 1933	5 MAR 1891		SAMUEL C
125	G 16	KONE, JENNETTE	KENNEDY	26 MAR 1984	1894		SAMUEL
116	M 3	KONE, JOSEPH M		15 NOV 1982	25 JAN 1926		
125	G 17	KONE, SAMUEL C		2 FEB 1951	1882		JENNETTE
371	J11	KONOPNY, ABRAHAM		1973	1915		ELISE
371	J10	KONOPNY, ELISE		1963	1919		ABRAHAM
391	GJ 4	KONOVITZ, RIVKA		AUG 1912	1907		
121	F40	KONTNER, EDITH		24 MAR 1986	23 MAY 1918		
116	K 3	KOPEJKA, FEIGA S		23 JAN 1988	19 APR 1903		
222	AC11	KOPLIN, STELLA		21 DEC 1922	1839		
125		KOPLOWITZ, (BABY)		6 JUN 1917	1917	EDWARD & STELLA	
125	E131	KOPLOWITZ, ANNA	HODES	12 FEB 1964	1882		
125	S155	KOPLOWITZ, ANNA		15 OCT 1965	1881		GEORGE
125	E130	KOPLOWITZ, BESSIE		3 SEP 1954	1901		
119	F27	KOPLOWITZ, DOLORES R		31 DEC 1989	24 DEC 1929		
125	S154	KOPLOWITZ, GEORGE		17 DEC 1942	1879	HYMAN & CHAYA SARAH	ANNA
125	S158	KOPLOWITZ, GEORGE		27 MAY 1941	1865	HYMAN YAKOV	
125	E132	KOPLOWITZ, HAROLD I		10 SEP 1990			
125	E134	KOPLOWITZ, HARRY		26 JUN 1964	1879		SOPHIE
125	O192	KOPLOWITZ, HENRIETTA		28 AUG 1982	1896		MORRIS
125	L129	KOPLOWITZ, HYMAN S		27 AUG 1931	1845		
125	M 90	KOPLOWITZ, IDA DINA		3 APR 1923	25 AUG 1883	HUSH & DOWASHE	
125	N 95	KOPLOWITZ, IDA SARAH		24 MAY 1925	1846	ABRAHAM DAVID	
125		KOPLOWITZ, INFANT		1 JUL 1931	1931	HENRY	
125	H130	KOPLOWITZ, ISAAC S		29 APR 1943	1873	HYMAN SHIMON & CHAYA SARAH	SARAH
125	I 30	KOPLOWITZ, LENA		14 MAY 1944	10 APR 1867		
125		KOPLOWITZ, M		13 AUG 1923	1923	HENRIETTA	
125	ZA171	KOPLOWITZ, MARIA		27 DEC 1989	25 DEC 1921		
125	J134	KOPLOWITZ, MAX		8 APR 1936	1881	HYMAN & ROSE F	ROSE
125	O193	KOPLOWITZ, MORRIS		24 APR 1965	1894		HENRIETTA
125	M157	KOPLOWITZ, MORRIS L		21 MAY 1952	1880		
125	K142	KOPLOWITZ, NATHAN		15 DEC 1931	1869		
125	Z171	KOPLOWITZ, ROSE		13 JUL 1988	19 OCT 1909		
125	J139	KOPLOWITZ, ROSE		25 JAN 1935	1880	SAMUEL & MICHELE	MAX
125	H 53	KOPLOWITZ, ROSE		28 OCT 1950	1880		SIMON
125	K122	KOPLOWITZ, SADYE		1 NOV 1933	1904	HARRY	
125	H129	KOPLOWITZ, SARAH		28 DEC 1959	1873		ISAAC
125	H 52	KOPLOWITZ, SIMON COPELAND		8 AUG 1930	1870		ROSE
125	E133	KOPLOWITZ, SOPHIE	HODES	18 NOV 1963	1876		HARRY
113	B50	KOPMAN, JOSEPH		17 NOV 1987	22 MAR 1913		
330	AA31	KOPP, EVA S		29 MAY 1993			
125	K188	KOPP, JOAN		14 AUG 1986	5 NOV 1907		SAMUEL
125	K187	KOPP, SAMUEL		7 JAN 1974	2 MAY 1904		JOAN
125		KOPPEL, (BABY GIRL)		4 JUL 1962	03 JUL 1962	MORTON	
125	I196	KOPPEL, A MORRIS		7 FEB 1974	1901		
125	Z172	KOPPEL, BURTON L		26 MAY 1986	1 AUG 1942		
125	L192	KOPPEL, DAVID		4 JUN 1974	1902		SUSAN
125	M130	KOPPEL, IDA ROSE		27 DEC 1968	1870		
125	K133	KOPPEL, NATHAN		28 OCT 1932	1870		
125	L193	KOPPEL, SUSAN	LEVY	27 OCT 1971	1902		DAVID
102	S27	KOPPELL, FLORENCE	HEIMOVITCH	31 OCT 1977	29 APR 1918	WILLIAM & HANNAH	ERNEST
125	P199	KOPPELMAN, JENNIE	SALKOWITZ	10 DEC 1963	1882		
125	N160	KOPPELMAN, JOSEPH		24 APR 1951	1878		
102	AA72	KOPPLEMAN, (BABY)		9 FEB 1928			
102	AA77	KOPPLEMAN, ABRAHAM		26 AUG 1977	20 DEC 1889		RACHEL
102	Z75	KOPPLEMAN, ADELINE	GREENSTEIN	20 JAN 1968	1885		HERMAN
102	Z74	KOPPLEMAN, HERMAN P	OF ODESSA	11 AUG 1957	1 MAY 1880	HENRY & JESSIE (MINTZ)	ADELINE
102	Z72	KOPPLEMAN, JOSEPH H		7 APR 1939	1903		
102	AA76	KOPPLEMAN, RACHEL S		6 JUL 1987	10 JAN 1895		ABRAHAM
102	S28	KOPPPELL, ERNEST B		8 MAR 1983	28 DEC 1906		FLORENCE
392	J30	KORCHINKSY, REBECCA		21 SEP 1924	1871	JACOB JOSEPH	

Cem	Row	Name	Maiden Name	DOD	DOB	Parents	Spouse
392	C34	KORCHINSKY, MILDRED		30 NOV 1966	1873		SAMUEL
392	C33	KORCHINSKY, SAMUEL		3 AUG 1948	1863		MILDRED
103	E39	KORDUNER, BELLA		5 NOV 1987	2 NOV 1907		ISAK
103	C43	KORDUNER, FREDA		1988	1900		WOLF
103	E38	KORDUNER, ISAK		7 JUN 1987	5 MAY 1907		BELLA
103	C38	KORDUNER, TOBY		19 MAY 1984	15 APR 1925	WOLF & FREIDA	
103	C42	KORDUNER, WOLF		1990	1895		FREIDA
102	Z134	KORET, ARTHUR S (CANTOR)		8 JAN 1990	20 FEB 1916		
119	C50	KORMAN, ALBERT E		2 OCT 1987	6 OCT 1917		
329	A 8	KORMAN, GEORGE		25 AUG 1961	1886		
370	J18	KORMAN, JENNIE	LAHN	1935	1892		
329	D29	KORMAN, JULIUS		18 NOV 1967	1908		
329	A37	KORMAN, MAX		22 MAY 1974	18 MAR 1922		
751	K32	KORNICH, SAUL E		16 OCT 1947	17 JUL 1923		
330	F44	KOROTSKY, SAMUEL		6 MAY 1923		MOSHE YITCHY	
121	A 8	KORZENNIK, MEYER		16 FEB 1970	1902		
392	C46	KOSAKOW, BARNEY		1966	1891		SARAH
392	C47	KOSAKOW, LEONARD		1967	1922	BARNEY & SARAH	
391	D17	KOSAKOW, LOUIS		3 APR 1936	1874	ELIEZER	
392	C45	KOSAKOW, SARAH K		1974	1898		BARNEY
370	B 1	KOSLOFSKY, JOSEPH		23 MAR 1924			
391	R29	KOSOWSKY, GETEL		1918	1873	MOSHE	
391	C26	KOSOWSKY, HAROLD		22 OCT 1957	1870	SHMARYAHU	
391	ZB76	KOSS, BENJMAIN ALPERT		19 DEC 1983	7 FEB 1907	HILLEL	EDITH
391	ZB75	KOSS, EDITH	BENDETT	4 APR 1980	9 FEB 1909	VELVEL	BENJAMIN
391	X56	KOSS, HARRY		16 JAN 1957	1880	BENJAMIN ZEV	JENNIE
391	X55	KOSS, JENNIE		4 APR 1980	1887	MORDECHAI	HARRY
391	ZB77	KOSS, MAURICE		28 JUN 1989	4 NOV 1911		
391	O55	KOSS, PAULINE Z		18 NOV 1958	1889	NACHMAN	PHILIP
391	O54	KOSS, PHILIP		1 JUL 1950	1886	BENJAMIN ZEV	PAULINE
102	S 8	KOSSOFF, ELLA	ELLIN	1966	1891		SAMUEL
102	S 7	KOSSOFF, SAMUEL		1924	1885		ELLA
101	C 5	KOSTIN, BENJAMIN		23 NOV 1917	1877		FANNIE
110	D 9	KOSTIN, BERTHA	KAPLAN	3 FEB 1990	22 FEB 1900		MORRIS
330	AH 1	KOSTIN, DORIS	BENDER	2 FEB 1984	14 AUG 1927		MIRON
101	D 4	KOSTIN, FANNIE	KAPLAN	7 OCT 1960	1883		BENJAMIN
330	AH 2	KOSTIN, MIRON STANLEY		12 JUN 1989	5 JAN 1925		DORIS
110	D 8	KOSTIN, MORRIS		21 FEB 1962	27 APR 1894		BERTHA
110	B21	KOSTIN, PAUL		5 JUL 1945	4 MAY 1910	RACHEL	
110	B22	KOSTIN, RACHEL		25 OCT 1958	1883		
110	E 5	KOSTIN, SADIE		9 FEB 1976	3 DEC 1909		
102	AA223	KOSTIN, SAMUEL J		1 NOV 1987	31 JAN 1913		
114	F28	KOSTIN, TILLIE		28 MAY 1990	8 NOV 1917		
110	A 2	KOSTINSKY, GITEL LEAH	DION	1935	1873		JACOB
110	A 1	KOSTINSKY, JACOB		1933	1866		GITEL
101	C 4	KOSTINSKY, LOUIS		2 FEB 1933	1847		MINNIE
101	C 3	KOSTINSKY, MINNIE		8 MAY 1926	1839		LOUIS
110	A10	KOSTINSKY, PETER		13 MAY 1939	1882	JACOB & GITTEL LEAH (DION)	
222	AF14	KOSTOLEFSKY, SAMUEL		30 JUL 1952	1898		
125	K 39	KOTCH, RAPHAEL		27 JUN 1913	31 MAR 1874		
102	Z185	KOTCHEN, ALFRED		25 JUL 1980	5 MAY 1908		
125	J144	KOTKIN, ABRAHAM		6 MAR 1994			
125	I112	KOTKIN, EDITH		3 OCT 1939	1879		MORRIS
121	I11	KOTKIN, FRANK		26 APR 1979	17 JUN 1906		
121	I12	KOTKIN, MAX		9 MAR 1981	25 DEC 1897		
125	I113	KOTKIN, MORRIS		19 APR 1934	1876		EDITH
121	G41	KOTON, DAVID ISAAC		20 OCT 1988	17 AUG 1959		
114	K16	KOVALIK, LEO A JR		12 OCT 1990	4 NOV 1924		
101	C42	KOVNOVITZ, SAUL		26 OCT 1935			
125	A 81	KOWALESKI, NANCY	BIRNBAUM	26 JUL 1964	1942		
391	ZC56	KOZEK, EVA RUTH		1986	1899	ELCHANON	WILLIAM
391	ZE77	KOZEK, PAUL MARVIN		2 OCT 1985	1936		
391	ZC55	KOZEK, WILLIAM		1965	1901	HAGAD	EVA
375	E35	KOZLIN, DORA		13 MAY 1967	1897	MORDECHAI	LOUIS
391	E32	KOZLIN, IDA		10 SEP 1919			
375	E34	KOZLIN, LOUIS	9 JAN 1974*	29 DEC 1974*	1898	NACHEM	DORA

Cem	Row	Name	Maiden Name	DOD	DOB	Parents	Spouse
391	D 5	KOZLIN, NATHAN		19 JAN 1948	1868	JACOB	SARAH
391	C 5	KOZLIN, SARAH		10 AUG 1949	1870	FLORA & JACK	NATHAN
125	N134	KRAFT, BESSIE	LEVITZ	16 SEP 1972	17 NOV 1895		MEYER
125	A106	KRAFT, LILLIAN	KOMISS	24 DEC 1990	28 MAY 1900		
125	N135	KRAFT, MEYER		3 JUN 1982	25 JUN 1900		BESSIE
102	AJ191	KRAM, GLICKA	TAYLOR	13 MAR 1969	19 AUG 1914	YAKOV	
101	B34	KRAMER, DAVID M		9 SEP 1917			
249	D33	KRAMER, HARRY		5 FEB 1965	15 JAN 1885		ROSE
102	AC209	KRAMER, JACOB		17 NOV 1982	3 APR 1898		SADIE
125	N 99	KRAMER, MALKE	KUNITZ	23 MAR 1926	1882	LEIB	
249	D34	KRAMER, ROSE		12 SEP 1962	1 FEB 1889		HARRY
102	AC210	KRAMER, SADIE C		17 JAN 1991	22 JAN 1902		JACOB
370	F18	KRAMER, SAMUEL		28 JUL 1915		ZALMAN	
370	C18	KRANC, JOEL		20 JUN 1969	1891		
106	D30	KRANDLER, SOPHIE		5 FEB 1991	15 FEB 1899		
125	G 30	KRANOWITZ, AARON		26 DEC 1916	1863	LEIBEL & BERTHA	SOPHIE
125		KRANOWITZ, BERNARD		19 MAR 1971	1902		
102	M41	KRANOWITZ, BERNARD G		19 MAR 1971	1 MAY 1901		
125	F 50	KRANOWITZ, HELEN	RAPHAEL	5 JUL 1984	4 JUN 1898		WILLIAM
125	T158	KRANOWITZ, JANE ROSE		14 AUG 1966	5 FEB 1901	SUZANNE	LOUIS
125	G 28	KRANOWITZ, LENA E		29 NOV 1954	1888		
125	T159	KRANOWITZ, LOUIS H		7 OCT 1960	7 OCT 1892		JANE
125	G 29	KRANOWITZ, SOPHIE		17 JUN 1930	1865		AARON
125	T157	KRANOWITZ, SUZANNE		23 JAN 1940	9 MAY 1932	LOUIS	
125	F 49	KRANOWITZ, WILLIAM		2 MAY 1965	31 JAN 1896		HELEN
331		KRANZLER, ABRAHAM		6 DEC 1912	1862		
376	D50	KRAPKO, ALBERT		1921	1920	DAVID	
391	P32	KRAPP, SARAH REBECCA		9 MAR 1921	1884	NACHMAN ELIEZER	
248	J67	KRASNICK, ISIE		17 MAR 1919	1904		
116	T 3	KRASNOFF, MAURICE		5 JUN 1987	21 JUN 1904		
105	P24	KRASNOW, BORIS		10 OCT 1944	1876		MINNIE
105	P23	KRASNOW, MINNIE		28 JUL 1944	1886		BORIS
370	U31	KRASOFSKY, MARY		1930	1875		
751	K 1	KRASSNER, SCOTT DAVID		30 AUG 1985	4 JUL 1956		
112	C10	KRAUS, HEINRICH (HARRY)		5 MAR 1983	23 JUL 1932		
371	N 3	KRAUSHAR, ISAAC		1976	1895		
102	AB59	KRAUSKOFF, HANNAH G		1978	1897		JOSEPH
102	AB60	KRAUSKOFF, JOSEPH		2 AUG 1970	1895		HANNAH
119	B 5	KRAVET, SAMUEL B		1979	1910		
446	C28	KRAVETSKY, ELI		1910	1872		
125	N190	KRAVETZ, ABRAHAM		12 DEC 1966	19 NOV 1902	MAX & EDITH	
125	O145	KRAVETZ, EDITH	GORFAIN	29 DEC 1948	DEC 1880	HARRY & TZERELLE (GREENSTEIN)	MAX
113	B35	KRAVITZ, ALLAN WILLIAM		7 AUG 1984	11 MAR 1926		
113	M73	KRAVITZ, MARK		4 AUG 1979	31 AUG 1920	SAMUEL & ROSE	
113	M76	KRAVITZ, ROSE		28 FEB 1979	19 OCT 1897		SAMUEL
113	M75	KRAVITZ, SAMUEL		23 SEP 1972	25 MAR 1891		ROSE
118	D10	KRAVITZ, SEYMOUR		9 NOV 1983			
125	1C65	KRECHEVSKY, (CHILD)		13 FEB 1920	10 JAN 1920	YEDEL & TAMERA	
102	L47	KRECHEVSKY, ANNA		8 JUL 1969	18 SEP 1896		MORRIS
125	I120	KRECHEVSKY, JOSEPH		11 MAR 1937	1867	YEHUDA	SARAH
102	L48	KRECHEVSKY, MORRIS		13 NOV 1957	5 NOV 1894		ANNA
125	H155	KRECHEVSKY, ROBERT		27 MAY 1968	1900		RUTH
125	H156	KRECHEVSKY, RUTH	MARK	10 JAN 1992	1908		ROBERT
125	I121	KRECHEVSKY, SARAH	RABINOWITZ	10 JUN 1936	1873	SAMUEL	JOSEPH
116	BI71	KREFETZ, WALTER		21 SEP 1986	6 SEP 1917		
101	H 9	KREGER, BENJAMIN		15 DEC 1991	15 JUL 1908		
370	B40	KREIGER, BENJAMIN		2 MAR 1953	1890	MOSES & REBECCA	ROSE
370	B41	KREIGER, ROSE E		18 AUG 1961	1892		BENJAMIN
374	F 3	KREMEN, ESTHER		10 FEB 1913			
125	N 96	KREPSHAN, KOPEL		4 AUG 1925	1868	BERIL & LEA	
125	L101	KREPSHAN, MINNIE		11 NOV 1935	1893	MORDECHAI & RACHEL LEAH	
125	O155	KREPSHONE, HARRY		7 APR 1949	1891	BOPEL	
249	C37	KRESEWITZ, EVA	GREENSTEIN	21 SEP 1955	1883		JACOB
249	C38	KRESEWITZ, JACOB		17 OCT 1961	1879		EVA
447	R17	KRESS, CHARLES		2 DEC 1954	18 APR 1919		
371	AN25	KRIEGER, ABRAHAM		18 MAY 1953	1897		LEE

Cem	Row	Name	Maiden Name	DOD	DOB	Parents	Spouse
371	K15	KRIEGER, BERNARD		5 APR 1964	1897		
371	K14	KRIEGER, BESS R		13 SEP 1969	1899		BESS
371	AN15	KRIEGER, GEORGE J		30 AUG 1981	1901		BERNARD
222	H 4	KRIEGER, LEAH M DR		14 MAY 1985	6 NOV 1916		
371	AN24	KRIEGER, LEE L		8 MAY 1983	1901		
371	AN16	KRIEGER, LOUIS		23 AUG 1968	16 JUL 1899		ABRAHAM
370	F20	KRIEGER, MOSES		12 FEB 1945	1863		
370	J30	KRIEGER, REBECCA		8 AUG 1939	1867		REBECCA
447	W40	KRIGER, EVA		1973	1888		MOSES
125	O102	KRIM, MORRIS		1 OCT 1922	1857		
751	A25	KRINICK, EDITH		7 MAR 1977	21 DEC 1917		
377	Y62	KRINSKY, CHARLES M		9 JUL 1992	17 NOV 1908	MOSHE MEYER	
377	R31	KRINSKY, DOROTHY Z		13 MAR 1985	21 AUG 1913		WILLIAM
104	M46	KRINSKY, JACOB		1960	1891		LEA
104	M45	KRINSKY, LEA		1975	1906		JACOB
377	R30	KRINSKY, WILLIAM V		21 APR 1969	1 AUG 1899		DOROTHY
447	F11	KRITSICK, MINNIE		10 OCT 1929	1882		
102	D41	KRIVITZ, SADIE R		27 DEC 1950	30 OCT 1898		
249	I12	KRIVITZ, SHIRLEY		NDD	1913		
101	C 8	KRIWITSKY, TILLIE		19 NOV 1989			
101	C 9	KRIWITZKY, ARON		23 JAN 1980	1882		
101	C10	KRIWITZKY, CLARA		27 FEB 1970			CLARA
101	B 5	KRIWITZKY, SAMUEL		31 OCT 1921			ARON
101	B 6	KRIWITZKY, SARAH		17 SEP 1956			
372	H15	KROLL, BERTHA	HUTZLER	26 SEP 1970	24 SEP 1893		NATHAN
372	H14	KROLL, NATHAN		1 JUN 1933	1 JAN 1895		BERTHA
370	A13	KROM, ABIE		19 APR 1895			SHEVA
370	H17	KROM, SHEVA		25 NOV 1901		JACOB	ABIE
750	A 1	KRONES, ROSE		18 SEP 1989	25 FEB 1928		
121	I46	KRONICK, IDA		21 JAN 1990	2 SEP 1908		
113	L38	KRONICK, ROSE	TULIN	25 SEP 1977			WILLIAM
113	L39	KRONICK, WILLIAM		1 NOV 1966	30 JUN 1897		ROSE
372	E16	KRONIG, BETTY		1940	1858		SAMUEL
372	E17	KRONIG, LEO		1923	1886	SAMUEL & BETTY	
372	E15	KRONIG, SAMUEL		1921	1859	SAUL	BETTY
372	E14	KRONIG, SAUL		1886	1809		
119	D51	KROOPNECK, MAX		8 JUN 1977	10 MAY 1914		
116	G22	KROOPNICK, LORRAINE	ARIKER	1 AUG 1991	30 DEC 1935		
125	N 97	KROUSE, YETTA		14 OCT 1925	1887		
248	H48	KRUG, ABRAHAM		3 MAY 1957	5 APR 1882		MOLLIE
248	I48	KRUG, BERNARD		27 MAR 1991	13 JUL 1917	ABRAHAM & MOLLIE	
248	I49	KRUG, HYMAN		3 JUN 1986	6 AUG 1915	ABRAHAM & MOLLIE	
248	I50	KRUG, IRWIN I		24 APR 1967	9 SEP 1909	ABRAHAM & MOLLIE	
248	H49	KRUG, MOLLIE		19 APR 1965	1884		ABRAHAM
248	I53	KRUG, RAE	WILENSKY	15 AUG 1976	6 SEP 1907	ISRAEL & REBECCA	WILLIAM
248	I52	KRUG, WILLIAM M		25 MAY 1980	19 OCT 1906	ABRAHAM & MOLLIE	RAE
447	U36	KRUGER, ABRAHAM		22 APR 1968	12 JAN 1912		
108	A27	KRUH, HEIDI T		24 MAR 1949	4 MAY 1943		
106	C5	KRUH, HOPE		1985	1963		
392	F31	KRUMBEIN, GUSSIE S		31 AUG 1986	24 SEP 1896	LAZAR BARUCH	
102	AD182	KRUMHOLZ, MATHEW		31 AUG 1965	13 FEB 1913		
331		KRUPNICK, PAULINE L		2 MAY 1921	1914		
331		KRUPNICK, WILLIE		27 FEB 1917	1879		
123		KRUPNIKOFF, ABRAHAM B		25 MAY 1962	1913		
102	AJ198	KRUTT, SOLOMON		22 OCT 1970	29 AUG 1910		
377	S26	KUBLANOV, BORIS		1981	1894		
248	L62	KUDROSHOFF, ELIZABETH		12 JUN 1967			
222	AG 2	KUMMER, F RUTH		22 JUL 1981	3 MAY 1926		
105	M47	KUNIK, ANN	SELTZER	28 JUN 1990	5 JAN 1915		ANN
105	M46	KUNIK, ISAAC J		3 SEP 1981	10 NOV 1912		
105	L50	KUNIK, JOSEPH		5 MAR 1967	1889		SARAH
105	L49	KUNIK, SARAH		1 SEP 1959	1892		JOSEPH
112	D33	KUNSTADT, SOLOMON		1 MAR 1979	27 AUG 1894		
750	E16	KUPERMAN, ABRAHAM S		26 SEP 1977	25 SEP 1897		DOROTHY
750	E13	KUPERMAN, DOROTHY		3 MAR 1983	29 DEC 1900		ABRAHAM
105	L23	KUPERSMITH, GERTRUDE		7 OCT 1961	1901		MAX

Cem	Row	Name	Maiden Name	DOD	DOB	Parents	Spouse
105	L22	KUPERSMITH, MAX		12 FEB 1981	1889		GERTRUDE
371	AJ20	KUPERSTEIN, ZACHERY (CANTOR		16 JUN 1973	1920		
377	X17	KUPFER, ALBERT		1978	1905		FLORA
377	X16	KUPFER, FLORA	REICH	17 SEP 1962	1907	ABRAHAM HIRSH	ALBERT
102	AJ85	KUPPERSTEIN, H WILLIAM MD		18 APR 1944	14 FEB 1894		
102	A64	KUPPERSTEIN, JANET	GRUBER	1961	1919		
377	Q18	KUPTZIN, AARON		1970	1894		
377	U32	KUPTZIN, ESTHER M		1985	1887	ABRAHAM	
377	U31	KUPTZIN, FLORENCE		1980	1917	AARON	
104	I49	KURLAND, HEIDE-JO		24 JUN 1979	30 JAN 1962		
113	O29	KURLAND, REBA F		1 AUG 1974	23 JUL 1901		REUBEN
113	O30	KURLAND, REUBEN B		19 FEB 1962	16 JAN 1897		REBA
102	AD111	KURLAND, SIMON		14 DEC 1945			
249	L 2	KURLANDER, ESTHER		6 MAR 1938	1870		
391	I41	KURLANSIK, BESSIE		26 AUG 1943		ISRAEL	
391	Q36	KURLANSIK, ESTHER BAYLA		29 MAR 1916		ISAAC	
391	ZE80	KURLANSIK, ETHEL		13 JUL 1985		NATHAN	
391	L46	KURLANSIK, EVA		9 JAN 1962		NATHAN	
391	F 7	KURLANSIK, NATHAN		26 MAR 1938		JACOB	
102	AA158	KURNITSKY, SARAH	DUBROW	21 SEP 1985	26 SEP 1907		
111	4	KURTZ, ETHEL		NDD		JULIUS & MARIAM	
116	K12	KURTZ, JENNIE R		4 JUN 1967	5 MAY 1905		MAX
111	4	KURTZ, JULIUS		1963	1885		MARIAM
111	4	KURTZ, MARRIAM		5 JUL 1992	1893		JULIUS
116	K11	KURTZ, MAX M		8 APR 1989	15 SEP 1901		JENNIE
330	D28	KURTZ, ROSE		14 DEC 1958	1899		SAMUEL
330	D29	KURTZ, SAMUEL		5 JAN 1970	1897		ROSE
329	E23	KUSHELEFSKY, HERMINA		8 MAY 1987	1893		SAM
329	A29	KUSHELEFSKY, SAM		3 JUN 1966	1896		HERMINA
125	G128	KUSHLAN, BESSIE		12 MAR 1946	1876	ABRAHAM	DAVID
125	G126	KUSHLAN, CHARLES		1 OCT 1965	1900		
125	G127	KUSHLAN, DAVID		14 JAN 1933	1870		BESSIE
330	G69	KUSHLAN, EMMA	GLAZER	11 NOV 1946			
377	D 7	KUSHMAN, ETTA		1940	1868		
222	AU16	KUSHNER, ANNA	SELENGUT	11 OCT 1979	27 SEP 1894		
392	J50	KUSHNER, HARRY		22 JAN 1971	9 AUG 1887	CHAIM	
392	J51	KUSHNER, LOTTIE		25 SEP 1977	8 APR 1890	PESACH	
121	U 9	KUSHNER, MAX		29 DEC 1967	3 JUN 1918		
377	Z26	KUSHNER, MOLLY	BECKMAN	14 JAN 1972		JONAH	
121	F 4	KUSHNET, GEORGE GILBERT		29 FEB 1988	10 DEC 1913		
222	AH18	KUSLANSKY, CELIA L		9 NOV 1955	1906		WILLIAM
222	AH17	KUSLANSKY, IDA K		9 JAN 1935	1872		
222	AH19	KUSLANSKY, WILLIAM		16 OCT 1972	1898	IDA	CELIA
377	O36	KUTCHER, MEYER		1961	1910		
102	AD21	KUTNER, ABE W		21 JAN 1992	7 MAY 1901		
447	E34	KUTNER, ESTHER		7 DEC 1939	1869		JULIUS
447	A36	KUTNER, IDA		3 APR 1968	1877		MAX
447	E32	KUTNER, ISRAEL J		8 APR 1927	1898		MINNIE
447	E35	KUTNER, JULIUS		7 JUN 1932	1870		ESTHER
447	A37	KUTNER, MAX		8 MAY 1942	1877		IDA
447	E33	KUTNER, MINNIE		15 MAR 1938	1896		ISRAEL
125	G165	KUZNEOW, SAM		28 FEB 1981	6 JUN 1913		
125	Q159	KUZNETZOW, MENDEL		18 DEC 1945	1879	MORDECHAI & DWOSHE	SARAH
125	Q160	KUZNETZOW, SARAH		22 DEC 1949	1891		MENDEL
125	P160	KUZNOW, SOLOMON		24 JUL 1948	1916	MENACHEM MENDEL	
121	O15	LABB, ADA M		17 FEB 1989	22 MAR 1900		
121	D 6	LABB, ANN L		15 OCT 1969	12 DEC 1903		
121	O16	LABB, CHARLES		23 MAR 1990	4 JUN 1900		
121	D 7	LABB, FRANK		28 JUL 1988	4 OCT 1898		
377	S 9	LABEL, BENJAMIN		12 MAY 1967	20 FEB 1911		
116	BU37	LABELL, ABRAHAM D		29 NOV 1978	1912	REBECCA	EDNA
116	BU38	LABELL, EDNA		10 JAN 1991	1910		ABRAHAM
116	BU39	LABELL, REBECCA		16 MAY 1962	1881		
395	A 6	LABENSKY, ELIAS		6 MAY 1933	22 JUL 1846		
395	C10	LABENSKY, LEONARD		7 MAR 1886	7 JUN 1885	ELIAS & PAULINE	
395	A 7	LABENSKY, PAULINE		9 FEB 1941	3 SEP 1855		

Cem	Row	Name	Maiden Name	DOD	DOB	Parents	Spouse
391	GH 2	LABENSKY, WACHNA (GIRL)		1910	1907	LEV	
750	F20	LABOVITZ, CHARLES LEE		9 FEB 1965	2 AUG 1905		IDA
750	F15	LABOVITZ, IDA E		10 APR 1966	12 MAY 1898		CHARLES
370	I64	LACKENBACH, ELSIE		1937	1908		
104	F24	LACKER, RUTH G			5 OCT 1920		
116	BJ11	LACKMAN, JOHN J		17 JUL 1982	25 DEC 1890		MARCIA
116	BJ10	LACKMAN, MARCIA		25 DEC 1987	12 MAY 1891		JOHN
116	BJ12	LACKMAN, STUART ALAN		22 JAN 1970	27 JAN 1950		
370	O10	LAHN, ABRAHAM		30 JUL 1967	25 DEC 1893		JEAN
370	K 2	LAHN, AKIVA H		17 FEB 1955	1862		ANNA
370	K 5	LAHN, ANNA	GOTTLIEB	1949	1866		AKIVA
370	X 7	LAHN, BENJAMIN A		28 OCT 1970	1889		
391	G16	LAHN, DORA	LUBOW	1932	1901	DOV BER	
371	M 8	LAHN, DORA VERA	SOLOMON	1957	1887		JOSEPH
374	G21	LAHN, ESTHER		1940	1903		
371	L10	LAHN, HARRY		2 DEC 1988	11 JUN 1896		
374	G22	LAHN, ISRAEL		1941	1940	ESTHER	
370	O 9	LAHN, JEAN S		26 NOV 1965	23 JUN 1893		ABRAHAM
371	M 7	LAHN, JOSEPH M		1988	1886		DORA VERA
371	M 6	LAHN, LEO S		1983	1914	JOSEPH & DORA VERA	
371	M 9	LAHN, LOUIS MD		1958	1895		
370	Q26	LAHN, MAX		24 FEB 1942			ROSE
371	M 5	LAHN, NATHAN		1961	1890		
370	Q25	LAHN, ROSE		16 SEP 1935			MAX
751	L36	LAMBERT, GENE ALAN		1959	1958		
370	Q50	LAMM, DAVID		29 MAR 1954	4 JAN 1897		FRANCES
370	Q51	LAMM, FRANCES		29 OCT 1987	1 AUG 1905		DAVID
391	S30	LAMPERT, ESTHER		17 SEP 1931	1861	TZVI	
447	T 3	LAMPERT, FRANCES		13 JUN 1979	22 DEC 1904		
391	C14	LAMPERT, LOUIS		14 JUN 1945	1877	JOSEPH	
391	V56	LAMPERT, LOUIS		18 DEC 1957	1888	MOSHE	
391	O41	LAMPERT, MARY		1 OCT 1941	1871	CHAIM TZVI	
391	D24	LAMPERT, MORRIS		20 DEC 1928	1864	JOSEPH	
372	C 7	LAND, HARRY M		1965	1880		MATIE
377	N33	LAND, MARY	ELGART	23 MAY 1965	18 AUG 1882	MOSHE	
372	C 8	LAND, MATIE F		1949	1883		HARRY
447	Y 3	LANDAU, BEATRICE M					MITCHEL
106	B1	LANDAU, FRANCIS A		1982	1914		
447	Y 4	LANDAU, MITCHEL		1970	1904		BEATRICE
125	D133	LANDER, SARAH	GROSS	24 FEB 1990	20 AUG 1901		
104	I 3	LANDERMAN, PAUL D		27 JUL 1964	1917		
125		LANDERS, ANNA LOUISE		23 MAY 1921	1921	LOUIS & CLARA	
391	Y58	LANDLER, ZOLTAN		1 OCT 1958	1898	DAVID	
102	AJ94	LANDSBERG, ALBERT		22 JAN 1955	1898		REBECCA
106	F14	LANDSBERG, ANDREA BETH		19 JUN 1986	29 JUL 1965		
102	AJ95	LANDSBERG, REBECCA W		2 MAR 1986	1899		ALBERT
125	O109	LANDWALD, EMMA		12 NOV 1973	1900		
121	I41	LANES, JACOB J		8 JUL 1992	1 JUL 1900		
121	I40	LANES, MARY		23 MAY 1990	17 SEP 1903		
447	M12	LANGER, BENJAMIN		10 JUN 1985	1 JUN 1893	SAMUEL & BESSIE	ESTHER
447	MAA	LANGER, ESTHER		22 MAY 1984	25 DEC 1897		BENJAMIN
102	BB 1	LANGER, MOLLIE E		22 MAY 1986	4 MAR 1901		
447	M13	LANGER, ROSE		5 JUL 1932	1900	SAMUEL & BESSIE	
391	K38	LANN, FANNIE		10 AUG 1933		NAFTALI TZVI	
391	ZC60	LANN, FRANK		25 NOV 1966	4 JAN 1897	ISAAC	
391	O26	LANN, ISAAC		20 OCT 1915	1867	JUDAH	
102	K16	LANSING, BENJAMIN		1 OCT 1974	24 AUG 1884		ROSE
102	K15	LANSING, ROSE B		13 MAY 1949	26 AUG 1890		BENJAMIN
391	GD 2	LAPIN, BENJAMIN		15 JAN 1962	1886	MENACHEM MENDEL	
391	GD 1	LAPIN, JENNIE		29 MAR 1976	1889	JOSEPH	
377	R 5	LAPIN, MILTON		16 NOV 1992	16 DEC 1914		
101	H34	LAPP, EDA		26 APR 1983	7 JUL 1913		MICHAEL
101	H11	LAPP, IDA		1982	1902		
101	H35	LAPP, MICHAEL		13 AUG 1989	24 APR 1908		EDA
119	F36	LAPPEN, BENJAMIN		8 MAY 1987	1901		
102	AJ245	LAPPIN, SYLVIA F		5 JUN 1984	27 AUG 1920		

Cem	Row	Name	Maiden Name	DOD	DOB	Parents	Spouse
330	C14	LAPPING, ABRAHAM ISAAC		25 NOV 1943			HANNAH
330	A36	LAPPING, HANNAH		15 JAN 1906			ABRAHAM
123		LAPUK, ABRAHAM		23 OCT 1942	1896		
102	P30	LASCHEVER, RACHEL		25 MAY 1944	1876		
125	F 71	LASH, JACK E		10 JUL 1943	29 JAN 1892		
125	E 78	LASH, LILLIAN		7 NOV 1966	30 NOV 1899		
104	I 7	LASHIN, DAVID		15 FEB 1965	1907		
330	F25	LASKA, DAVID		7 NOV 1907	1875		
374	A40	LASKOWITZ, GOLDIE		21 AUG 1952	1881		
374	F13	LASKOWITZ, HARRY		1926	1872		
370	A55	LASKY, BESSIE		1941	1873		HW
370	B48	LASKY, H W		26 MAR 1934			BESSIE
105	C21	LASSMAN, ANNA		22 SEP 1955	1878		
105	H40	LASSMAN, BARNEY		11 MAY 1947			MOLLIE
105	G50	LASSMAN, HARRY B		21 JAN 1992		PHILIP & LILLIAN	
105	H47	LASSMAN, ISRAEL		16 OCT 1989	1909		
105	C27	LASSMAN, JENNIE		19 NOV 1985			
105	G52	LASSMAN, LILLIAN		10 OCT 1970	1905		PHILIP
105	H49	LASSMAN, MOLLIE		1 OCT 1954			BARNEY
105	G53	LASSMAN, PHILIP		23 JAN 1984	1904		LILLIAN
101	M14	LASSMAN, SVIYA		31 JAN 1933			
103	E1	LASSOFF, ISADORE		2 FEB 1985	15 SEP 1907		
105	I14	LASSOW, HARRY I		12 DEC 1937	19 JAN 1905		
119	D33	LASSOW, MARY		8 OCT 1984	7 JUL 1900		
119	D34	LASSOW, SAMUEL		16 NOV 1984	14 SEP 1897		
107	E16	LATER, ANNE	LEVIN	1 MAY 1991	1 JAN 1911		CHARLES
107	E17	LATER, CHARLES WILLIAM		26 FEB 1976	26 JUN 1893		ANNE
370	O36	LATER, DORA		1982			
391	B 1	LATHEM, MICHAEL		23 OCT 1967	30 OCT 1966		
248	L45	LAUTER, REGINA			1920		SIGISMUND
248	L46	LAUTER, SIGISMUND		1972	1906		REGINA
102	A23	LAVENBERG, MARVIN JAY		29 JAN 1935	MAR 1930		
121	AA35	LAVENBERG, MILTON		21 SEP 1989	27 JAN 1902		
121	AA34	LAVENBERG, SARAH	FLAXMAN	25 DEC 1987	22 JUL 1901		
114	D23	LAVENBURG, JOHN ARLEN		30 MAR 1989	10 OCT 1963		
102	T51	LAVIETES, DAVID P		3 NOV 1952	5 OCT 1887		ELIZA
102	T52	LAVIETES, ELIZA	JONAS	16 DEC 1959	30 SEP 1887		DAVID
370	B11	LAVINE, ABRAHAM		15 JUN 1923			ETTY
123		LAVINE, BENJAMIN		28 JUL 1938	1889		MATILDA
370	I 4	LAVINE, ETTY		5 FEB 1924			ABRAHAM
446	C32	LAVINE, JENNIE		28 AUG 1911	1866		
123		LAVINE, MATILDA	RICHMAN	31 MAR 1958	1890		BENJAMIN
222	F 8	LAVITT, CELIA		10 DEC 1968	1876		PAUL
222	AG 1	LAVITT, EUDICE	HYATT	1 MAR 1988	12 MAY 1916		
222	AF 6	LAVITT, FANNIE	ROSENBERG	26 DEC 1969	13 JAN 1894		JOSEPH
222	AF 5	LAVITT, JOSEPH		11 MAY 1950	1 MAY 1895	MAX & REBECCA	FANNIE
222	AF 3	LAVITT, MAX		1936	1868		REBECCA
222	F 7	LAVITT, PAUL		11 JUN 1952	1875		CELIA
222	AF 4	LAVITT, REBECCA	SAUNDERS	27 FEB 1951	20 MAY 1873		MAX
222	AI 2	LAVITT, SADIE	GREENSTEIN	14 JAN 1973	1900		
222	AF 2	LAVITT, SAMUEL		19 JAN 1965	1893	MAX & REBECCA	
222	F 9	LAVITT, SAMUEL MARK CAPT		25 FEB 1991	1915	PAUL & CELIA	
376	D 9	LAWALL, ARNOLD J		29 FEB 1980	14 OCT 1911	JUDAH	
377	G 6	LAWRENCE, JOSEPH		1935	1899		
121	H24	LAZAROWITZ, ANNA		18 OCT 1988	2 JUL 1905		
391	V52	LAZAROWITZ, GUSSIE		18 FEB 1960	1893	ABRAHAM MORDECHAI	JOSEPH
391	V51	LAZAROWITZ, JOSEPH		21 OCT 1987	1896	LEV	GUSSIE
392	D50	LAZAROWITZ, NETTIE		31 DEC 1989	1899	LABEL	
377	T36	LAZARUS, ALEX		1994	1917		
101	H32	LAZARUS, ELIZABETH LOUISE		31 MAR 1983	15 MAY 1910		MAURICE
101	H33	LAZARUS, MAURICE ARTHUR		20 SEP 1984	8 MAY 1910		ELIZABETH
750	I20	LAZARUS, SIMON		31 JUL 1984	10 JUL 1913		
371	L37	LAZEROFF, ABRAHAM		14 MAR 1954	15 APR 1885		SARAH
371	A32	LAZEROFF, HAROLD		21 DEC 1986	3 NOV 1911	ABRAHAM & SARAH	
371	L36	LAZEROFF, SARAH L		1979	1893		ABRAHAM
371	A26	LAZEROFF, SIDNEY		7 JUN 1989	3 AUG 1915	ABRAHAM & SARAH	

Cem	Row	Name	Maiden Name	DOD	DOB	Parents	Spouse
392	D39	LAZEROW, ELIZABETH		31 DEC 1966	1897	SAMUEL	JACOB
392	D40	LAZEROW, JACOB		14 JUL 1957	1894	ISRAEL	ELIZABETH
119	K28	LAZEROW, RUBIN		29 MAY 1989	7 OCT 1887		
330	D42	LAZINSK, ABRAHAM		13 SEP 1956	1865		CELIA
330	E47	LAZINSK, CELIA		6 DEC 1940	1868		ABRAHAM
330	AH28	LAZINSK, JACK		3 MAY 1976	9 OCT 1904	ABRAHAM & CELIA	LILLIAN
330	AH27	LAZINSK, LILLIAN S		2 JUL 1972	23 OCT 1906		JACK
121	F36	LAZOWSKI, JOSEPH		7 OCT 1990			
121	F37	LAZOWSKI, ROSE	ALTER	10 FEB 1986			
391	Q49	LEADER, JOSEPH		16 OCT 1952	1887	JACOB	SARAH
391	Q50	LEADER, SARAH R		26 MAR 1988	1894	ELIEZER	JOSEPH
102	Z98	LEADER, SYLVIA	GILSTON	3 AUG 1988	7 APR 1912	MORRIS & LEAH	
391	Q52	LEADER, WILLIAM M		20 JUN 1980	16 SEP 1952	JACOB ELIEZER	
125		LEADES, (BABY)		5 JUL 1917	1917	LOUIS & REBECCA	
125	F 44	LEADES, ANNA		3 MAY 1949	20 APR 1868	ELEAZER	ISAAC
125	F 43	LEADES, CELIA		29 SEP 1946	1895	ISAAC & ANNA	
125	E 46	LEADES, HARRY		23 AUG 1977	1898		ISAAC
125	F 45	LEADES, ISAAC		7 JUL 1925	1856		ANNA
125	E 45	LEADES, SAUL		4 JUN 1974	1901		
371	AA 1	LEAK, ROSE		1973	1884		
391	E12	LEAR, JOSEPH F		18 APR 1976	13 JUL 1891	SAMUEL	MOLLIE
391	E11	LEAR, MOLLIE		18 JUL 1976	31 JUL 1897	MENACHEM MENDEL	JOSEPH
751	D20	LEAVITT, MAE	MINTZ	2 FEB 1958	1879		SAMUEL
222	AC17	LEAVITT, PAULINE	LEVINE	1973	1886	BENJAMIN & VERA	
751	D21	LEAVITT, SAMUEL M		15 JUL 1955	1877		MAE
102	D42	LEAVY, ANN	KRIVITZ	1 MAR 1970	13 JUN 1895		
102	F17	LEAVY, SAMUEL		7 OCT 1957	28 MAY 1890		
121	I47	LEBED, ALEX BRIAN		1 AUG 1989	3 MAR 1904		
222	AJ14	LEBESHEVSKY, ESTHER		8 JAN 1947	1872		NATHAN
222	AM 3	LEBESHEVSKY, LOUISE		4 OCT 1923	17 JUN 1921		
222	AJ13	LEBESHEVSKY, NATHAN		27 SEP 1922	1866		ESTHER
222	AM 4	LEBESHEVSKY, NATHANIEL		21 MAR 1928	21 MAY 1924		
102	O18	LEBON, FRIEDA	MISSAL	11 SEP 1982	19 FEB 1906	ABE & GOLDA	SAMUEL
102	O20	LEBON, RACHEL H		7 SEP 1950	15 JAN 1874		
102	O19	LEBON, SAMUEL		24 JUL 1977	12 JUN 1904	RACHEL	FRIEDA
371	K37	LEBOVITZ, BENJAMIN		1 JUN 1982	7 APR 1887		CELIA
374	G 7	LEBOVITZ, BROCHA		1927	1872		
371	K38	LEBOVITZ, CELIA		14 NOV 1959	18 AUG 1889		BENJAMIN
119	C58	LEBOWITZ, ETTA	DUNN	7 MAY 1989	29 APR 1901		
119	C59	LEBOWITZ, HARRY		14 NOV 1991	30 MAY 1901		
121	B25	LEBOWITZ, LOUIS		29 DEC 1985	14 NOV 1895		
125	O 93	LECHOWITZ, YIDEL MENACHEM		2 AUG 1920	1870	AARON & FEIGE MALKE	
249	G42	LEDERER, ELLA		HOLOCAUST		MORITZ	
249	G42	LEDERER, FREDERIKA		HOLOCAUST		MORITZ	
249	G42	LEDERER, GUSTAV		HOLOCAUST		MORITZ	
249	G42	LEDERER, HILDA		HOLOCAUST		MORITZ	
249	G42	LEDERER, HUGO		9 OCT 1982	15 NOV 1902		
249	G42	LEDERER, IRENE		HOLOCAUST		MORITZ	
249	G42	LEDERER, OSKAR		HOLOCAUST		MORITZ	
249	G42	LEDERER, SOPHIE	DEUTSCH	HOLOCAUST		IGNATZ	
447	X37	LEFF, REUBEN		25 JAN 1970	1892		VERA
447	X36	LEFF, VERA	11 JAN 1969*	30 DEC 1969*	1898		REUBEN
121	L 4	LEFKOWITZ, GERTRUDE		22 JAN 1986	1898		
330	F64	LEFKOWITZ, LOUIS		15 DEC 1937	1886		
121	L 5	LEFKOWITZ, SAMUEL		12 FEB 1975	1894		
330	G73	LEGOMSKY, MICHAEL		18 AUG 1976	1903	SAMUEL	
330	G78	LEGOMSKY, ROSE		25 APR 1965			SAMUEL
330	G77	LEGOMSKY, SAMUEL		17 AUG 1941	1878		ROSE
330	G76	LEGOMSKY, SAMUEL		19 NOV 1970			
372	G27	LEHMAN, WALTER		14 SEP 1977	10 NOV 1892		LEAH
102	W48	LEHRER, BARNEY		11 MAR 1963	15 DEC 1888		
125	M111	LEHRER, BENJAMIN		11 MAY 1928	1891	ABRAHAM & REBECCA	
125	D 63	LEHRER, C RUDY		4 NOV 1974	29 FEB 1904		LEAH
102	AC95	LEHRER, ISADORE ALBERT		1977	1915		LEAH
102	AC94	LEHRER, LEAH	RUTT	28 JUN 1989	2 NOV 1918		ISADORE
102	W47	LEHRER, LENA		13 MAR 1981	15 DEC 1888		BARNEY

Cem	Row	Name	Maiden Name	DOD	DOB	Parents	Spouse
125	O108	LEHRER, LENA B		7 NOV 1973	21 MAR 1891		
125	E 63	LEHRER, MARC BARNET		25 AUG 1976	28 DEC 1972		
125	F 57	LEHRER, MARY		2 MAY 1940	1875		SAMUEL
102	W50	LEHRER, MORRIS J		26 APR 1990	26 JAN 1913	BARNEY & LEAH	
125	D 64	LEHRER, NELLIE	FLEISHER	28 SEP 1984	17 DEC 1904		
125	E 65	LEHRER, P BENJAMIN		4 JUN 1962	1900		
125	F 55	LEHRER, PEARL L		1988	1915		
101	M25	LEHRER, RACHEL R		20 APR 1913	1884		KELMAN
125	F 56	LEHRER, SAMUEL		10 AUG 1931	1874	MORRIS	MARY
102	W49	LEHRER, SAUL		26 FEB 1958	26 MAR 1920	BARNEY & LEAH	
371	A46	LEHRER, SOLOMON B		30 SEP 1988	15 MAR 1909		
392	D29	LEHRMAN, SALLEY E		22 AUG 1990	20 NOV 1907	LEV	
447	AE40	LEIB, ESTELLE H		28 AUG 1986	2 SEP 1917		
102	AI191	LEIB, LEO W		27 SEP 1988	22 JUL 1896		
433	T 1	LEIBER, LIBBY		6 JUL 1984	28 APR 1911		HELMAN
116	AV21	LEIBERT, MARJORIE	SPEARO	27 JAN 1966	19 SEP 1921	MORRIS	
116	AV25	LEIBERT, MORRIS ELIAS		26 MAR 1978	5 DEC 1889		
370	R19	LEIBOVITZ, ABRAHAM		28 FEB 1945	10 JUL 1873		SARAH
371	AB11	LEIBOVITZ, EDWARD L		21 FEB 1993	21 JUN 1902		EVELYN
371	AB10	LEIBOVITZ, EVELYN R		30 JUN 1975	15 SEP 1903		EDWARD
370	R21	LEIBOVITZ, GERTRUDE		8 SEP 1983	19 AUG 1914	ABRAHAM & SARAH	
371	AB 8	LEIBOVITZ, MIRIAM B		17 SEP 1993	7 OCT 1900		PHILIP
371	AB 7	LEIBOVITZ, PHILLIP R		13 MAY 1959	6 NOV 1896		MIRIAM
370	R20	LEIBOVITZ, SARAH		18 JUN 1946	15 DEC 1874		ABRAHAM
249	J 7	LEIBOWITZ, ABRAHAM		20 AUG 1963	1877		
370	I15	LEIBOWITZ, HINDA		6 APR 1917		ABRAHAM & SARAH	
110	F 4	LEIBOWITZ, ROBERT A		1988	1916		
371	AA10	LEIBSON, EUNICE		4 FEB 1978	2 MAR 1925		
102	C32	LEICHNER, ETHEL B		19 MAY 1948	1898		
126	O 63	LEIKIN, BERNARD		13 SEP 1894	1853		
125	R152	LEIKIN, ELIZABETH	NAIR	26 FEB 1943	15 AUG 1891	LOUIS & REBECCA	
108	C28	LEIKIN, LEONARD B		1964	1915		
125	M 30	LEIKIN, MIRIAM		7 MAY 1914	5 JAN 1913		
125	K135	LEIKIN, WILLIAM		27 AUG 1932	21 APR 1881		
102	X23	LEIKIND, ABRAHAM		1950	1874		MIRIAM
102	X24	LEIKIND, MIRIAM GITTEL		1949	1876		ABRAHAM
102	X22	LEIKIND, SIDNEY B		24 MAR 1985	20 OCT 1905	ABRAHAM & MIRIAM	
102	X21	LEIKIND, SIMON BURR		22 MAR 1987	7 MAY 1902	ABRAHAM & MIRIAM	
447	AF36	LEINWAND, BARBARA	LUBOW	11 FEB 1987	19 MAR 1951		
447	Q12	LEIPZIGER, MARCUS		7 SEP 1968	1909		
751	H 2	LEIT, SOL		23 OCT 1992	2 OCT 1927		
102	P 3	LEITERMAN, ANNE	SCHREYEK	20 JUN 1943	15 MAR 1878		MORRIS
102	P 4	LEITERMAN, MORRIS		9 NOV 1953	22 OCT 1867		ANNE
447	Z 7	LEITZES, ANNA M		1980	1908		HARROLD
447	Z11	LEITZES, ARLINE	10 JAN 1974*	30 DEC 1974*	1905		
447	B12	LEITZES, DAVID		19 JUL 1949			ESTHER
447	B13	LEITZES, ESTHER		18 JUN 1935			DAVID
447	Z 8	LEITZES, HAROLD		NDD	1907		ANNA
330	AF33	LEJFER, BERL		9 APR 1985	2 FEB 1911		
330	AF36	LEJFER, DAVID		21 MAR 1985	15 FEB 1906		
330	AF37	LEJFER, JACOB		9 OCT 1986	1920		
102	T34	LEMKIN, ANN	NEWMAN	12 APR 1984	25 DEC 1913		HENRY
102	T31	LEMKIN, HENRY		2 SEP 1992			ANN
102	T33	LEMKIN, ISADORE		1959	1882		ROSE
102	T32	LEMKIN, ROSE	MARCUS	1976	1884		ISADORE
493	G19	LEMKIN, SANDRA R		23 FEB 1991	23 JAN 1939		
377	I11	LENCHEK, PHILIP		10 JAN 1961	17 AUG 1899		SALLY
377	I12	LENCHEK, SALLY		26 JAN 1985	5 APR 1904		PHILIP
391	R66	LENOROWITZ, BERTHA		5 AUG 1981		JACOB	
391	R65	LENOROWITZ, MORRIS E		29 MAR 1986		CHAIM TZVI	
391	C42	LENOROWITZ, ROSELLE		19 FEB 1932	21 APR 1930		
113	B28	LEON, MILTON		17 JAN 1992	28 MAR 1919		
102	A66	LEOPOLD, BERTHA		26 JUL 1944	1878		
116	BI95	LEOPOLD, FAY L		12 JUL 1991	17 JUL 1921		
121	S 1	LEPKOFKER, EMIL		30 APR 1991	6 SEP 1900		
121	S 2	LEPKOFKER, LENA		24 AUG 1988	19 FEB 1903		

Cem	Row	Name	Maiden Name	DOD	DOB	Parents	Spouse
447	P11	LERNER, ANNA S		12 DEC 1967	22 JUN 1896		ANNA
447	P12	LERNER, DAVID T		22 APR 1968	26 AUG 1891		DAVID
447	P 9	LERNER, FANNIE LILLIAN		2 AUG 1971	3 JUN 1906		LOUIS
105	B20	LERNER, HARRY		4 MAR 1952	1883		
447	P10	LERNER, LOUIS		4 NOV 1982	10 JUL 1900		FANNIE
102	A39	LERNER, MAXWELL E		1950	1898		
447	P13	LERNER, MOLLIE G		26 JUN 1952	1871		NATHAN
102	CB53	LERNER, MYRNA B		21 MAR 1979	24 NOV 1934		
447	P14	LERNER, NATHAN		28 JUL 1935	1870		MOLLIE
123		LEROY, BETTY		1954	1911		
125	P180	LESHIN, ESTHER	GANS	8 FEB 1963	1885		
392	C39	LESSER, ELLA		18 OCT 1977	11 AUG 1908		
125	K 65	LESSER, HERMAN					ROSE
447	B14	LESSER, ISRAEL H		5 JUN 1939	24 DEC 1855		
446	C20	LESSER, MIRIL		17 MAY 1922	1857		
125	K 64	LESSER, ROSE		10 JUN 1917	1889	MORRIS & BEILE	HERMAN
750	H23	LESSER, WILLIAM MORRIS		28 JUN 1985	23 AUG 1931		
113	M32	LESSNER, ESTHER	MARGULIES	2 APR 1990	14 SEP 1913		
102	AJ90	LESSOW, NATHAN		26 NOV 1971	1886		SADIE
102	AJ91	LESSOW, SADIE	RAPHAEL	16 MAY 1969	1888		NATHAN
123		LESTER, NETTIE	TUBIN	1969	1895		PAUL
123		LESTER, PAUL		29 DEC 1956	1887		NETTIE
375	E38	LETNIKOWITZ, LENA		24 APR 1905	1837	AARON	
101	K24	LEV, ANNIE R		22 FEB 1936	1864		
102	AD40	LEVEN, SAMUEL		29 JUN 1948	2 FEB 1889		
329	A25	LEVENE, IRVING H		10 FEB 1965	1902		
392	D45	LEVENE, REBECCA		8 NOV 1951		JACOB	
391	ZD75	LEVENE, SELMA R		2 AUG 1983	1918	ZEV WOLF	
125		LEVENSON, ABRAHAM DAVID		14 MAY 1925	1923	YEHUDA LEIB & FRIEDA	
113	O39	LEVETT, FREDA	GOODINSKY	13 JUL 1984	16 SEP 1906		MEYER
113	O38	LEVETT, MEYER		11 MAY 1991	15 AUG 1901		FREDA
113	O40	LEVETT, STANLEY		25 NOV 1983	19 SEP 1928	MEYER & FREDA	
121	A33	LEVI, JULIUS		8 SEP 1992			
330	F 3	LEVILOFF, BARNET		7 SEP 1953	1873		MOLLIE
330	G 8	LEVILOFF, MOLLIE		9 MAR 1951	1876		BARNET
372	C 4	LEVIN, ABRAHAM		14 MAY 1989	11 OCT 1898		JEANNETTE
125	I163	LEVIN, ABRAHAM		1987	1910		JESSIE
102	P12	LEVIN, ADOLPH		17 NOV 1969	18 FEB 1890		RENEE
372	B 7	LEVIN, ALFRED		28 NOV 1984	25 NOV 1908		FANNIE
370	G 4	LEVIN, ANNA	SLOSSBERG	1965	1879		MICHAEL
125	J126	LEVIN, ANNA TZERIL		18 NOV 1936	1871		ARYEH
102	H44	LEVIN, ANNIE		14 APR 1962	1865		HARRY
125	J125	LEVIN, ARYEH LEV		27 APR 1943	1870		ANNA
447	F13	LEVIN, BEATRICE		21 SEP 1985	15 MAR 1895		MAX
391	N54	LEVIN, BELLE	RIFKIND	5 FEB 1964	29 MAR 1905	MOSHE	
102	AJ 6	LEVIN, BERNARD D		7 DEC 1943	1884		LENA
330	E 4	LEVIN, BESSIE ETTA	SCHULTZ	24 MAR 1940	1857		SAMUEL
119	A32	LEVIN, CELIA		30 DEC 1985	12 DEC 1907		
125	B140	LEVIN, CHARLES		24 FEB 1989	12 MAY 1905		
372	C 6	LEVIN, CHARLES ALEC		1958	1894		
102	AC171	LEVIN, DAVID		19 NOV 1981	2 OCT 1892		
125	N108	LEVIN, DEBRA DORA		5 MAY 1928	1853		SOLOMON
125	D135	LEVIN, EDWARD		4 OCT 1991	28 DEC 1906		
104	H10	LEVIN, ELIAS ABRAHAM		23 JUN 1977	24 MAR 1887		
125	D 57	LEVIN, ESTELLE		23 OCT 1991	29 OCT 1900		
330	G29	LEVIN, ESTHER		21 FEB 1924	1838		JOSEPH
125	L118	LEVIN, ESTHER MALKA	LAKOWSKY	17 SEP 1930	1875	DAVID	
372	B 6	LEVIN, FANNIE		13 JUL 1986	26 OCT 1908		ALFRED
370	K22	LEVIN, FIA RIVKA		12 AUG 1945			SAMUEL
119	J33	LEVIN, GERTRUDE		6 APR 1984	11 MAR 1916		
102	P14	LEVIN, GITEL		5 AUG 1938	1866		TOBIAS
446	A27	LEVIN, H H DR		6 OCT 1913	1883		
102	H45	LEVIN, HARRY		30 APR 1950	1867		ANNIE
370	D 4	LEVIN, HARRY J		1 JUL 1935			LIBBY
751	D39	LEVIN, HEIMIE		2 JUL 1913			
391	F13	LEVIN, HENRY		10 JAN 1932	1865	ARYEH LEV	

Cem	Row	Name	Maiden Name	DOD	DOB	Parents	Spouse
377	U45	LEVIN, HERMAN EDWARD		10 JUN 1989	22 FEB 1908	MENDEL	
125	I164	LEVIN, ISRAEL		28 DEC 1955	1881		
119	J32	LEVIN, JACK		4 AUG 1988	19 MAY 1915		
102	Z120	LEVIN, JACOB		11 DEC 1981	15 FEB 1894		
391	K27	LEVIN, JACOB		27 SEP 1918	1894		MARY
372	C 3	LEVIN, JEANETTE W		9 DEC 1992	7 SEP 1901		ABRAHAM
125	I162	LEVIN, JESSIE		15 NOV 1993			ABRAHAM
372	C 5	LEVIN, JOHN EDWARD		12 JUL 1961	3 MAY 1956		
330	F 9	LEVIN, JOSEPH		10 NOV 1929	1840		
125		LEVIN, JOSEPH		22 APR 1919	OCT 1893	SAMUEL & ROSE	ESTHER
104	A12	LEVIN, JULIAN		25 JUL 1974	1915		
125	O191	LEVIN, JULIUS		6 FEB 1965	1879		
102	AJ 5	LEVIN, LENA		5 JUN 1941	1889		BERNARD
104	I11	LEVIN, LIBBIAN	FISHER	4 AUG 1970	16 APR 1898		
370	J 9	LEVIN, LIBBY		1932	1848		HARRY
102	Z174	LEVIN, LILLIAN GERTRUDE		9 MAR 1977	7 SEP 1908		LOUIS
125	K125	LEVIN, LILLIE	LEVINE	11 APR 1933	15 AUG 1886	SHIMON	
102	Z173	LEVIN, LOUIS I		21 JAN 1989	10 JUN 1904		LILLIAN
391	S43	LEVIN, MARY		26 SEP 1961	1 OCT 1872	JACOB	
102	Z121	LEVIN, MARY	CRAMER	27 FEB 1990	18 NOV 1897		JACOB
102	AH159	LEVIN, MAURICE		31 DEC 1968	1897		
447	F14	LEVIN, MAX		11 JUL 1940	24 JUL 1897	REBECCA	BEATRICE
370	G 5	LEVIN, MICHAEL		1960	1871		ANNA
105	L32	LEVIN, MOLLIE K		2 SEP 1991	10 JAN 1925		
125		LEVIN, NATHAN		10 FEB 1918	JUN 1915	AARON & ESTIE	
113	B63	LEVIN, NEJEMIA		6 MAR 1992	24 JUN 1902		NEJOMA
113	B62	LEVIN, NEJOMA	KAPLAN	3 MAY 1988	10 JAN 1904		NEJEMIA
447	F12	LEVIN, REBECCA		27 SEP 1929	1854		
102	P13	LEVIN, RENEE		16 MAR 1959	21 JUN 1890		ADOLPH
125	C134	LEVIN, ROSE		1 OCT 1990	1900		SAMUEL
125		LEVIN, SAM		19 MAR 1918	1916	MORRIS & SADIE	
125	C133	LEVIN, SAMUEL		23 DEC 1959	1894		ROSE
119	A33	LEVIN, SAMUEL		27 MAY 1981	10 AUG 1907		
370	K 3	LEVIN, SAMUEL		28 MAY 1973	1888		FIA
330	F 8	LEVIN, SAMUEL JACOB		21 NOV 1931	1855		BESSIE
125	I101	LEVIN, SAMUEL L		2 APR 1928	1863		SARAH
370	V20	LEVIN, SARAH	BLUM	18 FEB 1926	14 OCT 1888	ABE & GITEL (STEINBACH)	HARRY
125	I100	LEVIN, SARAH	WEXLER	19 MAR 1941	1878	HYMAN	SAMUEL
125	N109	LEVIN, SOLOMON SHALOM		25 JUL 1928	1855		DEBORAH
102	P15	LEVIN, TOBIAS		22 AUG 1925	1867		GITEL
433	B30	LEVINE, (BABY BOY)		18 JAN 1960		DAVID	
222	AA18	LEVINE, A JACOB S		16 AUG 1916	28 DEC 1873	SAMUEL & GITTEL	
330	E35	LEVINE, AARON		3 AUG 1937			
125	B107	LEVINE, ABE H		22 SEP 1983	18 JAN 1901		
125	I157	LEVINE, ABRAHAM		9 JUL 1948	1882		ANNE
330	H40	LEVINE, ABRAHAM		13 APR 1943	1858		
330	F62	LEVINE, ABRAHAM		24 MAR 1934			
370	C12	LEVINE, ABRAHAM D		12 JAN 1933	1858		
370	M50	LEVINE, ABRAHAM L		1 OCT 1983	13 APR 1892		BESSIE
392	J49	LEVINE, ADA		14 JAN 1952	1898		
107	H17	LEVINE, ADAM DANIEL		28 JUN 1985	10 MAY 1985		
116	N22	LEVINE, ALBERT L		3 JUL 1987	12 NOV 1918		
374	F22	LEVINE, ALEX		20 JAN 1987	5 FEB 1911		
391	R35	LEVINE, ALTA DEVORAH	KALINSKY	4 DEC 1933	1887	DOV BER	
494	A 3	LEVINE, ANN	SAMUELS	3 OCT 1966	27 JUL 1904		
392	E18	LEVINE, ANNA		23 DEC 1967	1884	ISRAEL	JACOB
104	G30	LEVINE, ANNA REBECCA	MONASTERSKY	29 DEC 1969	1896		MAX
104	K49	LEVINE, ANNA V		21 APR 1992			GABRIEL
125	I156	LEVINE, ANNE		28 JAN 1960	1887		ABRAHAM
102	W 6	LEVINE, ARTHUR		7 NOV 1964	1901		RUTH
104	J22	LEVINE, BARBARA	DAVIS	1967	1923		
104	K48	LEVINE, BARRY Z		6 NOV 1983	24 APR 1939	GABRIAL & ANNA	
110	C 7	LEVINE, BASHE NECHAME	PINSKY				
102	L50	LEVINE, BELLA	WEDEEN	13 JUL 1976	15 JUN 1906		
447	W12	LEVINE, BENJAMIN		4 NOV 1964	1900		
125	F 12	LEVINE, BENJAMIN		24 DEC 1961	1898		

Cem	Row	Name	Maiden Name	DOD	DOB	Parents	Spouse
222	AC15	LEVINE, BENJAMIN S DR		12 OCT 1970			
116	BL139	LEVINE, BERNICE W		29 NOV 1986	1910		VERA
370	M51	LEVINE, BESSIE S		11 JUN 1968	1 APR 1900		MORTON
447	Y34	LEVINE, CELIA		8 MAR 1985	9 JAN 1896		ABRAHAM
125	D 45	LEVINE, CHARLES		6 FEB 1979	1908		LOUIS
330	E37	LEVINE, CHARLES		22 JUN 1941			
222	AB 6	LEVINE, CHARLES H		24 AUG 1938	1882		
330	AA 8	LEVINE, DAVE		6 MAR 1963	20 JAN 1923		ESTHER
433	B35	LEVINE, DAVID		6 NOV 1948	1912		
330	F18	LEVINE, DAVID		10 APR 1912	1832		
222	AB 3	LEVINE, DAVID S		27 NOV 1958	1894		RUTH
102	AG 1	LEVINE, DORA	BASHNER	1942	1891		JOSEPH
125	U146	LEVINE, DORIS	SOCKUT	2 OCT 1982	31 JUL 1923		
222	AC14	LEVINE, DOROTHY	GOLDBERG	26 SEP 1951	1882		SINCLAIR
125	W179	LEVINE, E HERMAN		10 JUL 1978	1901		LENA
371	J 2	LEVINE, ELLA W		10 JUL 1987	14 OCT 1910		SAUL
330	AA17	LEVINE, ESTHER	SCHREIBER	9 FEB 1963			
222	AB 5	LEVINE, ESTHER		21 APR 1969	1887		CHARLES
330	AD 1	LEVINE, ESTHER K		1975	1894		ISADORE
125	L151	LEVINE, ETHEL S	KESSLER	13 JUN 1978	1888		HARRY
330	G19	LEVINE, ETTA		5 JAN 1959	1882		
119	C66	LEVINE, EVELYN	SHNEIDER	16 OCT 1991	30 DEC 1907		
433	D35	LEVINE, EVELYN		27 MAY 1992	26 JUL 1900	BARUCH	MORRIS
125	B106	LEVINE, FANNIE		13 JAN 1963	1878		
116	BL136	LEVINE, FANNIE		24 MAR 1981	15 NOV 1891		HARRY
371	O 3	LEVINE, FANNIE S		4 MAR 1980	1 FEB 1894		NICHOLAS
125	E 15	LEVINE, FLORENCE	SPIVAK	15 MAR 1972	1919		LESTER
391	R31	LEVINE, FLORENCE MAE	CLARK	11 OCT 1918	15 MAR 1894	SAMUEL & MINNIE	SAMUEL
125	L169	LEVINE, FRIEDA	BALLI	16 OCT 1955	1858		
330	AG 4	LEVINE, GERTRUDE		16 JUN 1992	29 APR 1902		SAM
222	AA21	LEVINE, GITTEL		31 MAY 1928			SAMUEL
330	E50	LEVINE, HANNAH		9 MAY 1941	1862		
125	E152	LEVINE, HANNAH ZIREL		17 NOV 1936	1876	MORRIS & YACHNE	
330	B11	LEVINE, HAROLD		9 NOV 1943	4 MAY 1917	HYMAN	
125	L152	LEVINE, HARRY		6 MAY 1955	1885		ETHEL
330	G20	LEVINE, HARRY		13 DEC 1958	1883		
125	D121	LEVINE, HARRY		17 JUN 1977	1895		SARAH
447	Z 1	LEVINE, HARRY		19 DEC 1986	1909		
116	BL137	LEVINE, HARRY		22 APR 1970	1885		FANNIE
330	F48	LEVINE, HARRY S		14 JAN 1929	1888		
447	F 5	LEVINE, HATTIE		5 FEB 1938	1894		JOSEPH
370	M49	LEVINE, HENRY S		9 JUL 1977	18 OCT 1900		
125	D 29	LEVINE, HOWARD		16 NOV 1981	1916		
121	E30	LEVINE, HOWARD		24 JUL 1978	6 MAY 1921		
102	L25	LEVINE, HYMAN		19 JUN 1955	14 APR 1902		
330	B12	LEVINE, HYMAN		25 OCT 1956	21 DEC 1881		IDA
330	G68	LEVINE, IDA		2 APR 1946	1881		
330	B13	LEVINE, IDA		14 APR 1968	25 AUG 1891		HYMAN
125	Q199	LEVINE, IRVING R		11 AUG 1963	1911		
222	AA20	LEVINE, ISAAK S		11 APR 1926	1877	SAMUEL & GITTEL	
125	F 11	LEVINE, ISADORE		14 APR 1974	1891		LOTTIE
330	AD 2	LEVINE, ISADORE		1974	1892		ESTHER
329	C35	LEVINE, JACOB		8 AUG 1974	1887		SYLVIA
330	G21	LEVINE, JACOB		9 MAR 1945	1862		
392	E19	LEVINE, JACOB		29 MAR 1948	1879	MOSHE	ANNA
370	B 6	LEVINE, JACOB M		23 APR 1925	1834		
370	A56	LEVINE, JENNIE		29 JUN 1908			
371	N 7	LEVINE, JOSEPH		16 DEC 1954	1884		LENA
447	F 4	LEVINE, JOSEPH		18 APR 1962	1895		HATTIE
102	AG 2	LEVINE, JOSEPH J		1940	1887		DORA
330	AA19	LEVINE, LARRY H		22 MAY 1974	27 FEB 1945		
102	AK244	LEVINE, LAURA L		3 JAN 1985	1912		
370	K 4	LEVINE, LEAH		28 SEP 1950			
371	N 8	LEVINE, LENA		20 OCT 1960	1890		JOSEPH
125	W180	LEVINE, LENA C		4 JUL 1988	1898		HERMAN
330	B20	LEVINE, LEONARD		22 JUN 1981	4 MAY 1920		

Cem	Row	Name	Maiden Name	DOD	DOB	Parents	Spouse
222	AB 7	LEVINE, LEONARD W		2 JAN 1949	1913	CHARLES & ESTHER	
125	E 16	LEVINE, LESTER		11 APR 1972	1918	SAMUEL	FLORENCE
248	E42	LEVINE, LIBBY		26 FEB 1951	8 JAN 1881		MAX
101	D14	LEVINE, LILLIAN		3 FEB 1969	1914		
370	F 8	LEVINE, LINDA SUSAN		18 MAR 1959	12 DEC 1958		
125	F 10	LEVINE, LOTTIE		13 FEB 1958	1893		ISADORE
330	AC 7	LEVINE, LOUIS		5 FEB 1984	14 OCT 1909		
446	C 7	LEVINE, LOUIS		17 JUN 1948	1873		SADIE
447	Y35	LEVINE, LOUIS		18 JAN 1978	9 JAN 1897		CELIA
125	J125	LEVINE, LOUIS		26 APR 1943	31 JAN 1876		
377	Y18	LEVINE, LOUIS		29 APR 1964	12 MAY 1904		
330	D32	LEVINE, MAMMIE		10 NOV 1977	17 APR 1890		
330	AC 5	LEVINE, MARCIA		8 APR 1979	16 MAY 1925		
102	AG71	LEVINE, MARION L		8 DEC 1974	29 OCT 1912		
119	C67	LEVINE, MAURICE		17 NOV 1985	15 DEC 1905		
104	G31	LEVINE, MAX		19 MAR 1972	1892		ANNA
125	N192	LEVINE, MAX		2 JAN 1967	1888		SOPHIE
248	E41	LEVINE, MAX RABBI		30 MAY 1934	2 DEC 1880		LIBBY
102	AJ 3	LEVINE, MELVIN H		24 JAN 1944	16 SEP 1913		
125	L194	LEVINE, MICHAEL		27 JAN 1972	1900		RAY
377	T 1	LEVINE, MORRIS		6 APR 1973	6 MAY 1915	JACOB	
433	D36	LEVINE, MORRIS		10 FEB 1959	1884	DAVID	EVELYN
391	C25	LEVINE, MORRIS		10 MAY 1943	1868	JOSEPH ZEV	
116	BL138	LEVINE, MORTON J		24 JUL 1982	1912	HARRY & FANNIE	BERNICE
447	F 1	LEVINE, NATHAN		30 JAN 1932	1887		
371	O 2	LEVINE, NICHOLAS		30 MAR 1968	15 MAR 1885		FANNIE
222	AA19	LEVINE, NOAH S		13 JUL 1913	31 DEC 1889	SAMUEL & GITTEL	
391	GG 2	LEVINE, PHILIP		30 JAN 1955	1910	ISAAC	
248	I65	LEVINE, PHILIP H		18 APR 1927	1907		
125	P171	LEVINE, PHYLIS	BYER	22 OCT 1968	5 JAN 1924		
391	J40	LEVINE, RACHEL		29 MAY 1936		JUDAH ELIEZER	
125	L195	LEVINE, RAY		1 MAY 1972			MICHAEL
125		LEVINE, REBECCA		8 SEP 1926	7 SEP 1926	HERMAN & LEAH	
119	F38	LEVINE, ROSE		29 JAN 1990	12 AUG 1906		
125	O 99	LEVINE, ROSIE SARAH	HESSE	4 JAN 1922	1857		
102	W 7	LEVINE, RUTH	SIGAL	19 APR 1972	1902		ARTHUR
249	C21	LEVINE, RUTH		24 DEC 1982	19 FEB 1923		
222	AB 4	LEVINE, RUTH W		28 DEC 1990	1899		DAVID
446	C35	LEVINE, SADIE		5 OCT 1913	3 DEC 1897		LOUIS
330	G47	LEVINE, SADIE		1923			
330	AG 3	LEVINE, SAM		2 JUN 1980	20 JAN 1898		GERTRUDE
125	E 17	LEVINE, SAMUEL		11 APR 1962	1887		
222	AA22	LEVINE, SAMUEL		13 OCT 1928			GITTEL
121	L14	LEVINE, SAMUEL		27 JAN 1973	1927		
125	Q164	LEVINE, SAMUEL		9 OCT 1960	1901		
330	G28	LEVINE, SARA RIVA		17 APR 1924			
125	D120	LEVINE, SARAH	BYER	15 FEB 1962	1896		HARRY
125	T151	LEVINE, SARAH		15 OCT 1939	1890	ISAAC & BAYLE	
329	C17	LEVINE, SARAH		16 FEB 1969	15 SEP 1883		
371	J 3	LEVINE, SAUL H		22 APR 1985	28 MAR 1893		ELLA
102	AC86	LEVINE, SELMA	KATZ	19 FEB 1981	1911		
222	AC13	LEVINE, SINCLAIR S MD		14 NOV 1955	1883		DOROTHY
125	Q163	LEVINE, SOLOMON H		23 NOV 1946	1873	ISRAEL & LEAH	
125	N191	LEVINE, SOPHIE		14 AUG 1974	1884		MAX
125	ZA160	LEVINE, SYLVIA		18 FEB 1993	27 OCT 1927		
329	C34	LEVINE, SYLVIA		26 SEP 1967	1887		JACOB
329	C 7	LEVINE, TYLLY		2 JAN 1971	31 OCT 1896		
222	AC16	LEVINE, VERA	JOSEPH	4 SEP 1969			BENJAMIN
116	N11	LEVINSON, ABRAHAM		3 JUL 1990	28 JUN 1905		SARAH
391	E21	LEVINSON, ABRHAM J		17 OCT 1948	1871	PESACH	PAULINE
125	S179	LEVINSON, ANNA	GORFAIN	20 JUL 1957	18 OCT 1896	DOV ZVI & TSEREL(GREENSTEIN)	REUBEN
392	A59	LEVINSON, BERTHA	ADAMSKY	30 DEC 1973	26 MAY 1894		ELI
392	I30	LEVINSON, BESSIE		16 APR 1946	15 DEC 1857		
392	J32	LEVINSON, DAVID		16 DEC 1918	5 MAY 1858	ISRAEL LEV	
377	V 1	LEVINSON, EDWARD C		25 FEB 1975	25 JUN 1897	ABRAHAM JACOB	
392	A58	LEVINSON, ELI WHITNEY		29 JUL 1971	16 NOV 1893		BERTHA

Cem	Row	Name	Maiden Name	DOD	DOB	Parents	Spouse
377	X59	LEVINSON, GRACE ANNE		12 APR 1987	18 JAN 1987		
102	A 2	LEVINSON, HERBERT		17 MAY 1933	1929		
127	F	LEVINSON, HERBERT I		19 MAR 1989	4 APR 1920		
116	AX 2	LEVINSON, IDA	AKABAS	18 JUN 1976	6 JAN 1892		LOUIS
222	J17	LEVINSON, ISRAEL		8 AUG 1986	10 MAY 1905	SAMUEL & ROSEMARY	
101	B41	LEVINSON, JACOB		15 JUL 1912	1882		
116	AX 3	LEVINSON, LOUIS P		9 JUN 1972	17 FEB 1881		IDA
391	E22	LEVINSON, PAULINE		24 JAN 1969	1876	MENACHEM MENDEL	ABRAHAM
105	D18	LEVINSON, PETER B		8 MAR 1956	21 MAY 1949		
377	F12	LEVINSON, ROBERT I		6 MAR 1973	12 OCT 1903		
222	I 7	LEVINSON, ROSMARY	HOLLANDER	17 DEC 1954	1879		SAMUEL
125	S178	LEVINSON, RUBEN		2 NOV 1989	18 JUL 1896		ANNA
222	I 6	LEVINSON, SAMUEL		5 JUL 1946	1874		ROSMARY
116	N12	LEVINSON, SARAH C		24 JAN 1989	22 AUG 1905		ABRAHAM
104	K34	LEVINSON, TYBEL		4 MAR 1966	1911		
102	B 6	LEVISON, ALICE G		22 JUL 1967	19 JUL 1901		SAMUEL
102	B 5	LEVISON, SAMUEL		24 JAN 1978	1 JUN 1901		ALICE
104	H18	LEVIT, HARRY		1982	1882		SARAH
104	H19	LEVIT, SARAH LEAH		1990	1885		HARRY
330	C29	LEVITA, ANNA CLAIRE		28 JUL 1968	15 MAR 1951	MORRIS & HELEN	
330	F63	LEVITA, HARRY		30 SEP 1934	1892	JACOB	
330	AI 3	LEVITA, HELEN		NDD	16 APR 1911		MORRIS
330	C 1	LEVITA, JACOB		22 APR 1956	1863		
330	AI 4	LEVITA, MORRIS		30 NOV 1980	15 SEP 1898	JACOB	HELEN
116	B26	LEVITAN, DAVID		20 FEB 1990	7 AUG 1919		EVA
116	B27	LEVITAN, EVA F		2 FEB 1991	19 APR 1920		DAVID
116	B25	LEVITAN, HERMAN		31 MAY 1980	28 JUN 1908		
370	B13	LEVITT, ABRAHAM G		8 DEC 1919			
370	I33	LEVITT, ANNA		6 JAN 1929	1879		
119	J48	LEVITT, CELIA		25 JUN 1981	20 MAR 1916		
105	C13	LEVITT, DAVID		21 NOV 1947	1896		
371	AQ21	LEVITT, EDNA		15 MAY 1976	1 JAN 1903		HERMAN
371	AQ20	LEVITT, HERMAN		20 SEP 1970	14 OCT 1902		EDNA
370	I16	LEVITT, IDA		24 MAY 1940			
125	R190	LEVITZ, JULIUS		15 AUG 1960	16 SEP 1912		
125	O189	LEVITZ, ROSE	HOFFMAN	29 JAN 1965	30 JAN 1888		
119	J24	LEVITZ, SALLEY	KRUGER	29 OCT 1984	22 APR 1911		
433	D12	LEVOWITZ, FLO		6 JUL 1964	4 DEC 1907		IRVING
433	D11	LEVOWITZ, IRVING		10 JUL 1988	21 JUL 1905		FLO
447	D 3	LEVSON, MORRIS		9 OCT 1970	1910	PHILIP & SELINA	THELMA
447	D 8	LEVSON, PHILIP		6 MAR 1951	1870		SELINA
447	D 7	LEVSON, SELINA		15 OCT 1946	1877		PHILIP
447	D 2	LEVSON, THELMA	RADNOR	2 JUN 1981	1903		MORRIS
330	A35	LEVY, ADA		26 DEC 1982	1902		ISIDORE
125	O126	LEVY, ALFRED		28 APR 1975	1910		
330	AE 1	LEVY, BERTHA		28 JUL 1980	1898		CHARLES
330	AF 1	LEVY, CHARLES		13 SEP 1967	1893		BERTHA
374	B36	LEVY, DAVID		26 OCT 1940	25 DEC 1893	MAYER JOEL & SARAH (GARBER)	DINA
374	B37	LEVY, DINA	ROSENWASSER	4 FEB 1951	1895	YITCHAK & FREIDA	DAVID
447	N39	LEVY, DORA	HOBERMAN	10 OCT 1986	1897		
125	G164	LEVY, EMIL		5 JUN 1979	1912		
125	O124	LEVY, ESTHER	ROTH	14 APR 1975	1908	JOSEPH & JENNIE (WINN)	SAMUEL
102	O13	LEVY, ESTHER	ESSERMAN	20 JUL 1968		HERMAN & DOROTHY	WILLIAM
116	R18	LEVY, ETHEL	TULIN	1 SEP 1972	12 APR 1915		SAMUEL
447	H35	LEVY, GEORGE		19 DEC 1989	11 AUG 1910		GERTUDE
447	H34	LEVY, GERTRUDE		NDD	20 DEC 1909		GEORGE
105	E15	LEVY, HARRY		15 JAN 1948	1885		PULINE
125	R140	LEVY, HENRIETTA		15 FEB 1942	14 AUG 1873		
119	H48	LEVY, HERMAN VICTOR		4 JUN 1992			
102	K 4	LEVY, IDA	LOVE	1 DEC 1948	1889		MEYER
371	A 1	LEVY, IRVING		6 JAN 1977	16 AUG 1901		
330	A34	LEVY, ISIDORE		22 DEC 1964	1889		ADA
102	A36	LEVY, JACOB		24 JAN 1937	1893		
370	K16	LEVY, JENNIE		25 MAR 1947			
447	I35	LEVY, JOAN	RHODES	11 DEC 1979	18 MAR 1941	GEORGE & GERTRUDE	
119	B82	LEVY, LEONARD		21 MAR 1973	3 JUL 1918		

Cem	Row	Name	Maiden Name	DOD	DOB	Parents	Spouse
391	S52	LEVY, LOUIS		26 JUN 1954	1895	CHINACH	SARAH
102	AH211	LEVY, MARSHA	LEWIS	14 MAY 1976	18 JUL 1942		
371	N34	LEVY, MAX		1950	1887		PAULA
102	K 3	LEVY, MEYER		23 SEP 1935	1886		IDA
125	I 43	LEVY, MORRIS		22 NOV 1915	1882		
391	Y76	LEVY, NATHAN H		1978	1905		SALLY
371	N33	LEVY, PAULA		1967	1893		MAX
105	E16	LEVY, PAULINE		13 NOV 1952	1888		HARRY
102	CA22	LEVY, ROSE	MAGRILL	7 JUN 1962	20 NOV 1898		SAMUEL
391	Y75	LEVY, SALLY S		1976	1904		NATHAN
125	O123	LEVY, SAMUEL		16 SEP 1982	1907		ESTHER
116	R17	LEVY, SAMUEL		30 APR 1987	1 OCT 1913		ETHEL
102	CA23	LEVY, SAMUEL H		25 SEP 1959	9 JUN 1894		ROSE
391	S51	LEVY, SARAH		31 MAY 1964	1899	MENACHEM MENDEL	LOUIS
119	B83	LEVY, SYLVIA	GEETER	4 JUN 1992	28 OCT 1920		
102	O12	LEVY, WILLIAM		25 DEC 1960			ESTHER
102	AH60	LEVY, WILLIAM M		5 DEC 1971	1 AUG 1906		
102	AJ214	LEVY, WILLIAM MYRON		26 AUG 1973	10 DEC 1900		
330	AG33	LEW, ISRAEL		22 APR 1987	6 FEB 1922		
330	AG34	LEW, JOHANAN		5 NOV 1988	13 OCT 1953	ISRAEL	
377	O38	LEWI, MARY	TRAUTMAN	1972	1897		MORITZ
377	O37	LEWI, MORITZ		1943	1891		MARY
330	D 3	LEWIN, ISHOK NACHUM		4 JUN 1952			
116	BU 6	LEWIS, ALBERT		9 JUN 1967	1897		MINNIE
102	V 8	LEWIS, MARY	SCHWOLSKY	8 NOV 1983	19 OCT 1896	LOUIS & RACHEL	
102	G36	LEWIS, MAX S		12 MAR 1970	1895		
116	BU 5	LEWIS, MINNIE S		10 FEB 1988	10 JUL 1897		ALBERT
102	AC172	LEWIS, ROBERT REUBEN		30 DEC 1966	17 AUG 1908		
330	AG 8	LEWIT, ABRAHAM		1973	1918		
125	H 13	LEWITT, ALFRED		16 MAY 1928	1898	MICHAEL & BETTY	
125	G 14	LEWITT, BELLA		9 FEB 1988	2 AUG 1904		
125	H 15	LEWITT, BETTIE		20 OCT 1934	1877		MICHAEL
125	G 15	LEWITT, MERWIN		4 MAY 1919	25 OCT 1918	MICHAEL & BETTY	
125	H 14	LEWITT, MICHAEL C		9 DEC 1934	1868		BETSY
125	G 13	LEWITT, NELLIE		11 AUG 1987	15 APR 1903	MICHAEL & BETTY	
125	J141	LEWITT, SOPHIE	APPELL	3 JUN 1978	1888		
125	M137	LEWTAN, HERMAN		11 MAR 1969	1891		
391	J35	LEWYANT, EDYTHE		9 SEP 1992	1914	BEN ZION	FRANK
391	J34	LEWYANT, FRANK		28 FEB 1976	1910	MICHAEL	EDYTHE
391	H44	LEWYANT, GUSSIE		9 APR 1948	1876	NAFTALI	
391	C16	LEWYANT, MAX		19 DEC 1941	1868	CHAIM SAMUEL	
391	H26	LEWYANT, MITCHEL		2 APR 1927	1874	CHAIM SHMUEL	
391	J33	LEWYANT, REBECCA	DEAN	20 FEB 1955	1887	ISRAEL	
391	F 1	LEYBOVITCH, BESSIE		7 JUN 1969	1880	MORDECHI	
391	S27	LEYBOVITCH, GEORGE		1925	1879		
375	A12	LEYBOVITCH, LOUIS		1977	1905		
222	F13	LIBBY, BESSIE		16 APR 1955			JACOB
751	J29	LIBBY, DAVID		18 JAN 1986	22 JAN 1905		
222	AL17	LIBBY, HARRY		1986	1893		
222	F12	LIBBY, JACOB		23 FEB 1957			BESSIE
222	N 6	LIBBY, ROSAMOND G		25 APR 1985	3 MAY 1904		
103	D23	LIBHABER, AARON			20 JUN 1921		MIRIAM
103	D24	LIBHABER, MIRIAM			22 JUN 1922		AARON
101	A27	LIBIN, HARRIS		1 APR 1913	1848		
249	G33	LIBITZKI, JOSEPH		3 MAY 1984	19 APR 1911		
116	AW22	LIBMAN, ANN B		2 JAN 1988	26 APR 1919		
102	CA51	LIBMAN, BERNARD		1 FEB 1959	8 NOV 1907		
371	AQ13	LIBO, ANNETTE		17 JAN 1973	1895		ASHER
371	AQ14	LIBO, ASHER		9 JUL 1978	1897		ANNETTE
371	M23	LIBO, BETTY A		16 JUN 1979	15 APR 1900		LOUIS
370	J19	LIBO, KUNA		25 OCT 1935			UDA
371	M24	LIBO, LOUIS		14 APR 1971	1 JAN 1898		BETTY
370	C 7	LIBO, UDA ARON		18 NOV 1929			KUNA
371	A23	LIBOU, ANNA W		17 OCT 1989	7 APR 1896		
125	L155	LICHT, JOSEPH		1 DEC 1955	5 SEP 1886		LILLIAN
125	L154	LICHT, LILLIAN	GINSBURG	28 APR 1977	23 JUN 1890		JOSEPH

Cem	Row	Name	Maiden Name	DOD	DOB	Parents	Spouse
102	I38	LICHTENSTEIN, BERNARD		24 APR 1938	15 SEP 1876		
102	I39	LICHTENSTEIN, PEARL B		19 FEB 1958	25 JUN 1885		PEARL
112	D 9	LICHTENSTEIN, THEODOR		21 OCT 1978	13 NOV 1902		BERNARD
121	B 3	LICHTER, ROSE		12 DEC 1992			
370	M53	LICHTMAN, GUS		30 JAN 1975			
370	M56	LICHTMAN, JOE		3 JUN 1958			JOE
330	G 4	LICKER, FANNIE		2 NOV 1946			GUS
330	F 4	LICKER, ISRAEL		10 JUL 1947			ISRAEL
119	E17	LICTENBAUM, JACOB		25 MAR 1975	5 SEP 1952		FANNIE
377	O12	LIEBENAV, KURT		1964	1889		
377	O13	LIEBENAV, LOLA HELENE		1987	1898		LOLA
110	B23	LIEBER, FANNIE		14 SEP 1943	1891		KURT
433	T 2	LIEBER, HELMAN		4 AUG 1987	4 NOV 1904		
110	B34	LIEBER, JOSEPH		23 MAR 1975	1886		LIBBY
371	N11	LIEBER, LENA CHIA		17 FEB 1956	1880		
371	N10	LIEBER, RUBIN		20 AUG 1955	1876		RUBIN
107	H1	LIEBERMAN, ANNA H		11 APR 1981	8 FEB 1891		LENA
391	C 8	LIEBERMAN, CARRIE		1909	1888		
117	H 1	LIEBERMAN, DAVID JOSHUA		30 NOV 1990	11 JUL 1990		
392	B36	LIEBERMAN, DEBRA		12 JUN 1935			
391	N40	LIEBERMAN, DORA D		6 JUL 1943	1866	AARON	JULIUS
447	AA39	LIEBERMAN, ELAINE RUTH		18 FEB 1980	24 DEC 1920		
370	K41	LIEBERMAN, FAGE		2 JUN 1958	15 NOV 1913		
391	ZA61	LIEBERMAN, FANNIE W		31 OCT 1972	1897	JUDAH	MORRIS
447	X11	LIEBERMAN, FAY S		10 MAY 1986			MORRIS
391	B 7	LIEBERMAN, HERMAN		23 AUG 1907			
330	B40	LIEBERMAN, HIRSCH		6 DEC 1955	1907		
249	L13	LIEBERMAN, ISABELLE	YOFFE	19 JUL 1990	14 SEP 1918		
447	B 8	LIEBERMAN, JACOB I		7 NOV 1940	1884		SARAH
391	N41	LIEBERMAN, JULIUS		22 FEB 1945	1867	ARYEH LEV	DORA
104	A33	LIEBERMAN, LOUIS		18 AUG 1959	1887		ROSE
121	Q 6	LIEBERMAN, LOUIS A		24 NOV 1980	15 JUN 1926		
391	ZA60	LIEBERMAN, MORRIS		1 APR 1977	1902	JUDAH	FANNIE
447	X12	LIEBERMAN, MORRIS		24 JAN 1967	1893		FAY
104	A34	LIEBERMAN, ROSE		25 MAY 1964	1889		LOUIS
447	B 7	LIEBERMAN, SARAH		31 MAY 1975	1893		JACOB
493	B25	LIEBLER, ERIC KENNETH		18 APR 1986	3 JUL 1945	TZVI	
104	J 8	LIEBLICK, WILLIAM		4 MAR 1957	1905		
328	A12	LIEBMAN, BARNEY		4 MAR 1957	1901		
328	A14	LIEBMAN, BELLA		11 FEB 1967	15 APR 1897		BENJAMIN
328	A13	LIEBMAN, BENJAMIN		22 FEB 1983	15 DEC 1891		BELLA
222	AA 5	LIEBMAN, CHAIM		22 FEB 1910	1847		MALKA
222	H 7	LIEBMAN, HARRY		1983	1892		
222	C 9	LIEBMAN, LOUIS		8 APR 1937	1880		REBECCA
222	AA 6	LIEBMAN, MALKA		20 NOV 1931	1853		CHAIM
222	AA 4	LIEBMAN, PAUL		30 AUG 1928	8 DEC 1889	CHAIM & MALKA	
222	C10	LIEBMAN, REBECCA		15 JUL 1949	1892		LOUIS
101	M15	LIEBOVITZ, DOBBISH		2 DEC 1912	1832		
104	M35	LIEBOWITZ, EDIS	SLUSKY	24 MAR 1973	3 JUN 1926		
391	GE 5	LIEBOWITZ, GETZEL (CHILD)		9 SEP 1911			
249	K 9	LIEBOWITZ, HYMAN		2 OCT 1947	14 JUN 1908		
107	E6	LIEBOWITZ, JACK		15 JUL 1989	24 NOV 1907		
123		LIEBOWITZ, MOLLIE		7 OCT 1983	14 APR 1894		
249	K 8	LIEBOWITZ, MOLLIE	LAZAROWITZ	26 MAR 1953	1885		ABRAHAM
116	K 9	LIEBOWITZ, SEYMOUR A MD		14 JUN 1987	5 SEP 1936		
370	J44	LIFSCHITZ, DORA		6 APR 1936		YITCHAK YAKOV	
102	AF49	LIFSET, ESTHER S		29 DEC 1991	19 MAY 1897		
125	H128	LIFSHITZ, ANNIE	RABINOW	20 JUN 1961	1886		NATHAN
110	A19	LIFSHITZ, CHAYA ESTHER		22 APR 1951	1870		MENDEL
751	K13	LIFSHITZ, GUSSIE		13 DEC 1935	1865		
125	Q192	LIFSHITZ, IDA		7 DEC 1961	1874		SAMUEL
110	A20	LIFSHITZ, MENDEL	OF MALTZ, RUSSI	6 JUN 1951	1868	ELEAZER & FEIGE ADEL	CHAYA
101	C31	LIFSHITZ, MEYER		16 DEC 1929	1859		
371	A40	LIFSHITZ, MOSHIA		11 SEP 1953	1877		MYER
371	A39	LIFSHITZ, MYER		23 MAR 1951	1874		MOSHIA
125	H127	LIFSHITZ, NATHAN		26 APR 1942	1882	MOSHE & HAMDA	ANNIE

LIST OF BURIALS IN CONNECTICUT

Cem	Row	Name	Maiden Name	DOD	DOB	Parents	Spouse
101	J20	LIFSHITZ, ROSE		17 NOV 1930	1861		
125	Q191	LIFSHITZ, SAMUEL		12 APR 1962	1879		IDA
125	O181	LIFSHITZ, WILLIAM		24 SEP 1964	1890		
102	L45	LIFTIG, MAURICE D		26 SEP 1972	1888		SARAH
102	L44	LIFTIG, SARA DOROTHY		27 AUG 1952	12 MAY 1892		MAURICE
125	J121	LIGHT, BERNARD		20 MAY 1956	1869		MINNIE
125	J122	LIGHT, MINNIE		28 FEB 1937	1870		BERNARD
376	D31	LILLIE, IRVING		1 DEC 1974		FIVEL	
751	B10	LINDER, IDA		27 FEB 1976	25 DEC 1895		MAX
377	H31	LINDER, MARY	JAFFE	30 AUG 1984	1892	JACOB ELI	MORRIS
751	B11	LINDER, MAX		6 MAR 1976	16 JUL 1891		IDA
377	H30	LINDER, MORRIS L		3 OCT 1957	1886	TZVI	MARY
119	B35	LINET, FREDA	SACK	12 APR 1989	8 FEB 1914		
377	Y16	LINZ, BERTOLD		1979	1895	MEYER	
377	Y15	LINZ, RECHA		27 OCT 1988	1902	MEYER	
371	AH20	LIPCHANSKY, EVA	SOLOMON	22 DEC 1966			
391	C15	LIPCHANSKY, ISRAEL		18 JUN 1944	18 MAY 1876	NOAH	
108	A.7	LIPKIN, JEROME I		27 JAN 1977	17 OCT 1925		
107	A22	LIPKIND, MAX		21 SEP 1987	21 DEC 1908		TANYA
107	A21	LIPKIND, TANYA P		19 NOV 1984	30 JUN 1911		MAX
125		LIPMAN, (BABY)		MAY 1958	MAY 1958		
125	G 21	LIPMAN, AARON		30 DEC 1918	1883	SIMON & PESHE	
125	F118	LIPMAN, ABRAHAM D		3 MAR 1948	15 NOV 1883	YAKOV	ANNIE
125	F117	LIPMAN, ANNIE		8 DEC 1979	1884		ABRAHAM
249	I10	LIPMAN, ARTHUR		29 MAR 1970	29 NOV 1920		
374	F 5	LIPMAN, BESSIE	BRUCKNER	26 FEB 1923	1901		
102	AC33	LIPMAN, CELIA		24 AUG 1968			SAMUEL
102	R29	LIPMAN, DAVID A		31 AUG 1976	1 JAN 1894		ESTHER
125	P173	LIPMAN, EDWARD B		22 OCT 1962	1903		
447	V22	LIPMAN, ELLA		7 MAY 1928	1842		
102	R28	LIPMAN, ESTHER S		17 MAR 1972	20 MAR 1898		DAVID
125	D117	LIPMAN, EVELYN		2 MAR 1990	6 MAR 1910		ISRAEL
125	J117	LIPMAN, GRACE		11 SEP 1938	1871	SAMUEL & RASHE	
125	W193	LIPMAN, HAROLD E		23 FEB 1980	25 AUG 1906		
125	G 19	LIPMAN, HILLYAR		7 SEP 1933	1871		
125	D118	LIPMAN, ISRAEL M		5 JUN 1992	18 MAY 1905		EVELYN
125	H152	LIPMAN, JACK		1991	1915		
222	AU 6	LIPMAN, LEONARD AARON		16 MAY 1975	2 SEP 1951	RALPH	
116	BK 5	LIPMAN, LOUIS		23 FEB 1988	10 SEP 1917		
125	F115	LIPMAN, LOUIS		25 MAY 1941	1872	YAKOV	MASHA
125	F114	LIPMAN, MASHA M		9 JAN 1976	1871		LOUIS
102	AC35	LIPMAN, MORRIS		12 JAN 1976	13 JAN 1910		
125	F119	LIPMAN, NATHAN		1985	1911	ABRAHAM & ANNIE	
125	H 21	LIPMAN, PEARL BESSIE		31 MAR 1941	1863		SIMON
222	AU 7	LIPMAN, RALPH		5 JAN 1981	9 OCT 1912		
102	AC34	LIPMAN, SAMUEL		21 APR 1957			CELIA
125	H 20	LIPMAN, SIMON		21 APR 1941	1861	YAKOV	PEARL
125	E122	LIPMAN, STEPHEN		14 NOV 1939	18 SEP 1939	ISADORE	
102	AI64	LIPNER, HARRY		1 JUL 1972	1923		
374	A30	LIPOVITCH, ABRAHAM		25 OCT 1932	1870		
102	AD180	LIPPMAN, BERNARD B		4 MAY 1990	22 DEC 1905		
102	AG40	LIPPMAN, BERNARD E		28 JUL 1992			
102	AG45	LIPPMAN, JACOB H		1 NOV 1967	1893		
114	I16	LIPPMAN, MARILYN R		24 SEP 1981	21 DEC 1929		
126		LIPPMAN, WILLIE		18 MAY 1893	1866		
392	J40	LIPPS, RACHEL		8 DEC 1935		ABRAHAM LIPA	
392	I38	LIPPS, WILLIAM M		14 AUG 1951	1876	ZEV WOLF	
222	N 4	LIPSCHITZ, BEATRICE		17 AUG 1974	2 NOV 1897		LOUIS
222	N 5	LIPSCHITZ, LOUIS		2 MAR 1982	1 JAN 1892		BEATRICE
125	1C68	LIPSHITZ, MIRIAM		20 MAR 1920	1847		
118	E13	LIPSON, GERTRUDE		9 AUG 1974			HARRY
118	E13	LIPSON, HARRY G		20 JAN 1983			GERTRUDE
125	S143	LIPSON, SAMUEL H		6 JUL 1938	15 MAR 1877	JACOB & RAIZA	SARAH
125	S144	LIPSON, SARAH		18 JAN 1967	10 APR 1884		SAMUEL
125	H108	LIPSTEIN, PAULINE F	BIRNBAUM	21 JUL 1959	9 APR 1892		
391	E35	LIPTON, (DAUGHTER)		29 MAR 1916	14 MAR 1916	IRVING & SARAH	

Cem	Row	Name	Maiden Name	DOD	DOB	Parents	Spouse
115	C65	LIPTON, HAROLD MD		1988	1907		
222	N 3	LIPTON, HERMAN		8 SEP 1976	19 OCT 1923		
377	B 8	LIPTON, IRVING H		14 MAY 1976	1 MAY 1888		SARAH
377	B 7	LIPTON, SARAH	BARATZ	18 AUG 1963	2 APR 1891		IRVING
751	D34	LISKIN, BELLA		19 APR 1918	1861		DAVID
751	D33	LISKIN, DAVID		1938	1857		BELLA
751	K38	LISKIN, ESTHER		7 FEB 1953	17 AUG 1898		
751	L40	LISKIN, MYER		1973	1882		
751	G37	LISKIN, YETTA		4 SEP 1944	1894	DAVID & BELLA	
102	AH177	LISS, ETHEL	KAUFMAN	10 SEP 1969			
102	AA21	LISS, ETHEL MARIE	GERSTEN	20 NOV 1980	1919	SAMUEL & CELIA	
494	H 6	LISSITZ, EVA		1972	1888		
104	C23	LITCHMAN, MATHILDA C		11 AUG 1972	31 AUG 1889		RALPH
104	C24	LITCHMAN, RALPH P		26 JUN 1957	19 SEP 1888		MATHILDA
377	T14	LITINSKY, DORA		1987	1896	RIVKA	MORRIS
377	T13	LITINSKY, MORRIS		1961	1891	ABRAHAM	DORA
371	AG 1	LITMAN, IDA	KAPLAN	28 OCT 1962	1878		
125	L187	LITSKY, HERMAN		26 AUG 1971	1911		IDA
125	L186	LITSKY, IDA V		24 JUN 1989	22 FEB 1901		HERMAN
391		LITTMAN, SIDNEY		6 FEB 1995	22 MAR 1906		STELLE
391	ZB52	LITTMAN, STELLE	GRUSKIN	11 MAY 1993	2 JAN 1904	SAMUEL & ANNA (ROSOFSKY)	SIDNEY
222	C 2	LITWIN, EMMA	DOBKIN	28 JUL 1974	1895		MORRIS
222	C 1	LITWIN, MORRIS		30 JUN 1944	1893		EMMA
330	AA20	LIVERANT, BENJAMIN		8 AUG 1985	25 AUG 1918	NATHAN & ESTHER	SYLVIA
330	AA22	LIVERANT, ESTHER		24 SEP 1973	18 JUL 1890		NATHAN
330	AA21	LIVERANT, NATHAN		11 APR 1973	10 APR 1890		ESTHER
330	Z14	LIVERANT, SAMUEL		22 MAR 1918	8 NOV 1913	NATHAN & ESTHER	
330	AA23	LIVERANT, SYLVIA		24 OCT 1982	29 JUL 1924	NATHAN & ESTHER	BENJAMIN
370	P56	LIVINGSTON, AUGUSTA CURLAND	WOLF	11 APR 1985	1 JUL 1893	PHILIP & ANNA (DUKE)	ABRAHAM
447	AC38	LIVITSKY, FAITH ANN		2 SEP 1992	30 JAN 1937	GEORGE & EDITH (HERMAN)	EDWARD
370	O46	LOCHENBACK, GUSTAVE		1963	1869		
392	J26	LOEW, ZLOTA		25 DEC 1924		ISAAC	
249	L 4	LOFMAN, SEENA SARA		28 OCT 1991	29 SEP 1924		
377	T10	LONDON, ALTE		9 SEP 1970	2 JAN 1908	SIMON ISAAC	
447	K12	LONDON, BENJAMIN		7 MAY 1928	1864		MARCIA
330	F11	LONDON, BENJAMIN		11 AUG 1924	1879		
330	C 7	LONDON, CHAYA SARAH	MARTISMA	JUN 1931	FEB 1869		ISAR
446	C22	LONDON, HINDE		2 NOV 1920	1837		
330	C 8	LONDON, ISAR CHAIM		JAN 1947	MAR 1866		CHAYA SARA
447	K14	LONDON, JEAN		24 OCT 1927	1904	BENJAMIN & MARCIA	
125	M138	LONDON, JEROME		16 MAY 1970	23 NOV 1933		
330	B24	LONDON, JOSEPH		10 APR 1962	1893	ISAR & CHAYA	LENA
330	B23	LONDON, LENA		27 FEB 1969	1895		JOSEPH
330	H38	LONDON, LEON MORTIMER		6 JAN 1946	4 JAN 1917	JOSEPH & LENA	
447	K13	LONDON, MARCIA		8 APR 1961	1870		BENJAMIN
446	C42	LONDON, MICHAEL		23 OCT 1906	10 AUG 1893	HINDE	
117	C11	LONDON, SPITZER		3 SEP 1983			
105	J39	LORBER, ABRAHAM R		10 DEC 1962	18 AUG 1890		MANYA
105	J40	LORBER, MANYA	HOFFMAN	18 MAY 1982	12 JUN 1898		ABRAHAM
374	H50	LORINSKY, CANDI		13 SEP 1991	2 SEP 1956		
374	H41	LORINSKY, CLARA		10 APR 1957	1889		LOUIS
125	V191	LORINSKY, JACK		21 SEP 1977	1915		
374	H48	LORINSKY, KOPELAND H		25 MAY 1971	15 OCT 1930		
374	H40	LORINSKY, LOUIS		24 MAR 1941	1878		CLARA
391	ZC76	LORINSKY, MIRIAM		NDD			MYER
391	ZC77	LORINSKY, MYER		11 SEP 1993	26 OCT 1912	LABEL	MIRIAM
374	H44	LORINSKY, SAMUEL B		15 FEB 1967	1908		
371	L 6	LOSHIN, GERTRUDE		23 AUG 1967	15 DEC 1900		SAMUEL
371	L 5	LOSHIN, SAMUEL W		21 FEB 1964	12 JUL 1896		GERTRUDE
116	O 9	LOTSTEIN, RAYMOND S		16 JUN 1980	5 FEB 1929		
106	C19	LOVESKY, LOUIS		11 APR 1980	30 AUG 1904		
391	F42	LOVITCH, JENNIE		26 SEP 1949	1876	AARON YEHUDA	JULIUS
391	F43	LOVITCH, JULIUS		17 FEB 1958	1868	ELCHANON	JENNIE
112	E14	LOVITZ, ALBERT		6 AUG 1980	11 APR 1922		BEATRICE
112	E12	LOVITZ, BEATRICE		10 AUG 1986	4 JAN 1916		ALBERT
112	E21	LOWELL, JEAN		18 NOV 1968	14 JUL 1900		LEO

Cem	Row	Name	Maiden Name	DOD	DOB	Parents	Spouse
112	E22	LOWELL, LEO		6 AUG 1975	5 FEB 1891		JEAN
112	D14	LOWENSTEIN, ALBERT		6 APR 1978	1902		MARGRET
112	D13	LOWENSTEIN, MARGARET		29 MAR 1986	1905		ALBERT
125	Q149	LOWENSTEIN, ROSE		25 OCT 1944	23 NOV 1868	MOSHE	
125		LOWEY, MORRIS		24 NOV 1915	1881	DAVID & DEBORAH	
391	F14	LOWITCH, HARRY		16 AUG 1931	22 FEB 1899	AHRON YEHUDA	
101	L10	LOWY, ALEXANDER		14 JUL 1991	7 AUG 1898		MARY
101	M12	LOWY, FRIEDA		NDD	19 AUG 1906		GUSTAV
101	M11	LOWY, GUSTAV		NDD	7 AUG 1898		FRIEDA
101	L11	LOWY, MARY		NDD	15 MAY 1906		ALEXANDER
391	P67	LUBCHANSKY, ABRHAM A		3 JUN 1984	9 OCT 1910	NOAH	
391	Q48	LUBCHANSKY, BESSIE	GORVENUS	9 FEB 1977	1890	ISAAC	DAVID
391	Q47	LUBCHANSKY, DAVID L		12 NOV 1944	1888	AARON	BESSIE
391	F33	LUBCHANSKY, ESTHER		26 FEB 1952	1888	CHAIM	MORRIS
391	Q33	LUBCHANSKY, IDA		3 DEC 1912	1854	JOSEPH	
391	R50	LUBCHANSKY, IDA		11 MAY 1958	1885		LOUIS
391	G42	LUBCHANSKY, IDA		15 FEB 1942	1870	ISAAC	
391	R49	LUBCHANSKY, IRVING		5 APR 1954	14 OCT 1911	YEHUDA LEV	
391	D30	LUBCHANSKY, JACOB		11 JUN 1956	1872	AARON	
391	P65	LUBCHANSKY, JACOB H DR		18 OCT 1982	29 MAR 1906	NOAH	
391	A 5	LUBCHANSKY, KIM LAUREN		24 OCT 1968	15 AUG 1968		
370	J27	LUBCHANSKY, LEAH		1940	1864		MICHAEL
391	O65	LUBCHANSKY, LILLIAN D		5 FEB 1985	26 OCT 1903	NACHMAN NETTA	
391	F30	LUBCHANSKY, LOUIS		20 SEP 1928	1887	MOSHE	
391	D16	LUBCHANSKY, LOUIS		27 JUN 1938	1880	ISAAC	
391	Q30	LUBCHANSKY, MAX		1911	1851	ZEV	
330	F24	LUBCHANSKY, MEYER		1 FEB 1907	1865		
370	C 8	LUBCHANSKY, MICHAEL		31 JAN 1930			LEAH
377	D10	LUBCHANSKY, MILDRED F		31 DEC 1980	22 OCT 1891		MORRIS
391	F31	LUBCHANSKY, MORRIS		11 FEB 1964	1878	AARON	ESTHER
377	D11	LUBCHANSKY, MORRIS		17 JUN 1968	7 APR 1890		MILDRED
391	E30	LUBCHANSKY, NATHAN		25 AUG 1937	12 JAN 1884	AARON	SARAH
391	G 3	LUBCHANSKY, REUBEN		12 JAN 1935	1870	ISAAC	
391	D22	LUBCHANSKY, REUBEN		31 AUG 1930	1873	AARON	
370	V 1	LUBCHANSKY, ROSE		18 JAN 1977		MICHAEL & LEAH	
391	O67	LUBCHANSKY, ROSE K	MARKOWITZ	17 JUN 1988	10 JUN 1913	SAMUEL & REBECCA	SAMUEL
330	F30	LUBCHANSKY, SAMUEL		1 SEP 1911	1890		
391	V57	LUBCHANSKY, SAMUEL		5 APR 1955			ROSE
391	D25	LUBCHANSKY, SAMUEL		23 SEP 1933	1844	ELIYAHU	
391	E31	LUBCHANSKY, SARAH	GROVIS	2 SEP 1950	25 AUG 1886	ISAAC	NATHAN
391	R37	LUBCHANSKY, SARAH		4 NOV 1934		ISACHAR DOV	
391	W65	LUBCHANSKY, STUART IRA		30 DEC 1970	1953	AARON	
391	P66	LUBCHANSKY, WILLIAM R		1 AUG 1966	7 DEC 1907	NOAH	
249	K 7	LUBETSKY, MAX		24 JUN 1947	1884		
391	Y54	LUBIN, DORIS	BODENSTEIN	19 JUL 1966	1917	ZION	HARRY
330	G 6	LUBIN, ETHEL		6 JAN 1955	1874		
391	Y55	LUBIN, HARRY		4 NOV 1961	1914	JACOB	DORIS
330	E22	LUBIN, JOSEPH		15 JAN 1934	1859		
101	M10	LUBIN, SARAH		17 JUL 1964	1866		
391	W77	LUBIN, SHIRLEY		19 FEB 1980	30 APR 1912	JACOB	
377	S19	LUBITZ, ROBERT S		6 JUL 1959	13 JUL 1915		
104	F25	LUBKA, BERNARD		1 JUN 1992			
104	E31	LUBKA, MOSES FELIX		5 OCT 1982	30 APR 1917		
102	C20	LUBLIN, JOAN R		10 AUG 1981	13 JAN 1941		JOAN
102	C19	LUBLIN, KAREN		10 AUG 1981	25 JUL 1971	JOAN	
391	S42	LUBOVITZ, BESSIE		1 JUL 1961	1874	MENACHEM MENDEL	
391	R24	LUBOVITZ, NATHAN		20 JUN 1919	1864	REUBEN	
391	ZA52	LUBOW, ANNIE		14 APR 1963	1880	DOV BER	BANNETT
391	ZA53	LUBOW, BANETT		21 JUL 1961	1877	MORDECHAI	ANNIE
377	D 8	LUBOW, BELLA	KUSHMAN	11 MAR 1972	15 MAR 1887	ETTA	NATHAN
391	Q29	LUBOW, DAVID		17 OCT 1970	1886	MORDECHI	
377	O18	LUBOW, EUGENE HENRY		11 SEP 1952	4 SEP 1943		
377	C10	LUBOW, MILTON L		1985	1920		
377	D 9	LUBOW, NATHAN E		20 JUL 1947	15 APR 1885		BELLA
370	S12	LUCAS, JEFFREY LEE		24 JUL 1973	7 DEC 1953		
392	C 1	LUCAS, MACK LOEB		26 AUG 1988	6 JUN 1903	YEHUDA	

Cem	Row	Name	Maiden Name	DOD	DOB	Parents	Spouse
371	AI 8	LUCHANSKY, AARON		25 JAN 1955	1878		
391	S39	LUCHANSKY, BESSIE		17 MAR 1924	1851	JACOB	ETHEL
371	AI 7	LUCHANSKY, ETHEL		29 AUG 1962	1882		SAMUEL
329	B13	LUCHNICK, CELIA		16 JUN 1962	1879		AARON
330	F 6	LUCHNICK, HARRY		3 DEC 1938	1856		
105	B12	LUCKMAN, JULIUS		2 MAY 1947	1886		
105	B13	LUCKMAN, MINNIE		12 DEC 1965	1892		MINNIE
101	C41	LUDVIG, AZKIEL		21 FEB 1919	1896		JULIUS
447	N 9	LUNTZ, A SAUL		10 JUN 1931	18 APR 1859		
447	N 8	LUNTZ, ANNIE		15 APR 1943	10 OCT 1867		SAUL
447	N 5	LUNTZ, BENJAMIN DDS		1 DEC 1982	14 FEB 1891	SAUL & ANNIE	JENNIE
447	N11	LUNTZ, BERTHA		16 AUG 1977	3 OCT 1888	SAUL & ANNIE	FLORENCE
432		LUNTZ, CHARLES	OF E HAMPTON	27 MAY 1900			
447	N 6	LUNTZ, FLORENCE		16 MAR 1947	4 AUG 1894		BENJAMIN
447	N 3	LUNTZ, FRANK		30 NOV 1959	28 AUG 1900	SAUL & ANNIE	SARA
447	N12	LUNTZ, IDA		16 NOV 1973	31 DEC 1902	SAUL & ANNIE	
447	N14	LUNTZ, LENORA		23 JUN 1967	7 JUL 1896	SAUL & ANNIE	
447	N 4	LUNTZ, SARA K		28 FEB 1963	13 JAN 1903		FRANK
125		LURIE, (CHILD)		18 JAN 1917	1917	SAM & MARY	
102	V19	LURIE, AARON		1946	1872		PAULINE
102	V21	LURIE, ANDREA LEE		22 DEC 1973	17 NOV 1951		
371	A20	LURIE, EVA H		1993	1907		
102	BC11	LURIE, HOWARD L		1991	1917		
127	C	LURIE, MANDEL		11 JUN 1974	11 JUL 1902		ROSE
125	F126	LURIE, MARY	CAPLAN	15 NOV 1970	1900		SAMUEL
370	A 8	LURIE, MOSES RABBI		10 OCT 1918			
102	V20	LURIE, PAULINE	ZUCKER	1929	1875		AARON
125	F127	LURIE, SAMUEL A		21 MAY 1951	1 APR 1894		MARY
125	N176	LURYEA, DAVID		23 JUN 1966	1906	JOSEPH & MILLIE	
125	S146	LURYEA, JOSEPH		15 DEC 1938	1882	ZALMAN & DORA	
125	O140	LURYEA, MOLLIE		28 OCT 1948	17 FEB 1881	SHIMON DAVID	
119	C40	LUTIN, ESTHER N		15 JUL 1983	14 APR 1906		
119	C39	LUTIN, FELIX J		22 JUL 1977	8 SEP 1900		
102	U11	LUTWACK, AUGUSTA		22 JAN 1967	1886		MORRIS
125	L 26	LUTWACK, GUSSIE		23 JAN 1915			GUSSIE
102	U 9	LUTWACK, HAROLD S		17 AUG 1966	1909	MORRIS & AUGUSTA	
125	L 46	LUTWACK, ISAAC		1 MAR 1910	1830		ISAAC
102	U10	LUTWACK, MORRIS S		13 OCT 1943	1882		AUGUSTA
101	A31	LUTZMER, JAKE		22 MAR 1911	1876		
391	E27	LYNN, ESTHER E		10 MAR 1948		ABRAHAM JACOB	SAMUEL
391	D26	LYNN, SAMUEL Z		17 NOV 1957	1862	YEHUDA	ESTHER
372	H 5	MAAS, HENRY	ROLF	1968	1910		IRMA
372	H 4	MAAS, IRMA	GRAFF				HENRY
372	E 7	MACHOL, DAVID		1929	1854		MINNIE
372	D 5	MACHOL, ISADORE		1936	1865		
372	E 8	MACHOL, MINNIE		20 MAY 1911			DAVID
372	E 9	MACHOL, SALOMON		24 SEP 1890			
370	S17	MACHT, JANETTE C		1964	1907		JEROME
370	S19	MACHT, JEROME		1952	1908		JEANETTE
118	D21	MACK, ANN L		12 MAY 1972	2 DEC 1907		
102	G49	MACKENZIE, SOPHIE	YANOWETZ	3 MAR 1983			
102	J52	MACKLER, HAROLD		1992	1908		NELLIE
102	J51	MACKLER, NELLIE		NDD			HAROLD
102	AF104	MACKLER, ROSE		3 OCT 1990	2 OCT 1907		
116	R19	MACKTA, SAMUEL J		18 SEP 1972	18 JUN 1901		
114	G19	MADOR, SOPHIE	BROWN	10 MAR 1982	20 APR 1895		
125	H 74	MAG, NATHAN E		12 MAY 1937	1869	ELI	REBECCA
115	B40	MAG, RAYMOND		26 FEB 1992	19 DEC 1912		
125	D 86	MAG, RAYMOND SIDNEY		1993	1943		
125	H 75	MAG, REBECCA		24 OCT 1944	1872	RAFAEL & ESTHER ALTA	NATHAN
125	G 76	MAG, ROBERT ELIOT		20 MAR 1931	14 APR 1929	SAMUEL & REBECCA	
125	G 75	MAG, SAMUEL ELIOT		5 JUN 1972			REBECCA
433	K 7	MAGER, ANNA		29 MAR 1946	1911	CHAIM HALEVI	MORRIS
433	H 1	MAGER, CLARA		4 OCT 1973	12 JUL 1904	VELVEL	
433	K 8	MAGER, MORRIS		13 JUN 1953	1891	SHLOMO ZALMAN	ANNA
116	AX10	MAGUN, BENJAMIN C MD		24 SEP 1992			FRANCES

Cem	Row	Name	Maiden Name	DOD	DOB	Parents	Spouse
116	AX 9	MAGUN, FRANCES	LEVIV	1 JUN 1972	22 OCT 1914		BENJAMIN
116	AX25	MAGUN, HARRY L		2 OCT 1967	5 JUN 1911		
750	F24	MAHLER, PHILIP		25 MAR 1962	19 MAR 1908		
119	D 5	MAIDMAN, ROSLYN		1986	1922		
391	ZC67	MAIN, ROSE	EINHORN	10 APR 1978	22 OCT 1910	SHMARYAHU ISAAC	
330	D16	MAIOFES, BARNET		10 MAY 1943	1880		LENA
330	D17	MAIOFES, LENA		25 DEC 1960	1889		BARNET
114	E13	MAISEL, BERTHA E		7 DEC 1991	4 JUN 1909		SELIG
114	E14	MAISEL, J SELIG		23 NOV 1987	17 NOV 1898		BERTHA
125	I181	MAISEL, JAMES		24 JUN 1969			
125	I140	MAISEL, MICHAEL		19 JUN 1944	16 MAR 1885	ABRAHAM & GITTEL PRADA	PEARL
125	I141	MAISEL, PEARL	SICKLICK	21 NOV 1959	1899		MICHAEL
102	H21	MAISLEN, ARNOLD MD DDS		18 JUN 1954	1925	SAMUEL & IDA	
125	G 74	MAISLEN, ELIZABETH	AISENBERG	11 JUN 1937	1892	ABRAHAM	SAMUEL
102	H19	MAISLEN, IDA	EPSTEIN	24 DEC 1988	19 OCT 1901		SAMUEL
102	H20	MAISLEN, SAMUEL MD		1981	1891		IDA
371	A12	MAJOR, KENNETH		21 APR 1977	14 JUL 1955		
751	O24	MALKIN, HERMAN		3 DEC 1982	18 JUL 1912		
751	O25	MALKIN, PHILIP		13 JUL 1980	28 NOV 1907		
125	K 43	MALL, ABRAHAM		13 MAR 1914			
391	G34	MALLEN, TOBEY R		16 OCT 1931	1868	ISRAEL JACOB	
116	D 5	MALLEY, SHERMAN L		25 FEB 1991	25 MAY 1933		
377	Y31	MALLOVE, HARVEY N		29 JUN 1989	30 JUN 1927	MOSHE	
392	F40	MALLOVE, LIBBY		12 AUG 1931	18 NOV 1923	MOSHE	
377	Y33	MALLOVE, MORRIS		17 MAR 1973	19 AUG 1894	ABRHAM	
125	P 63	MALOMED, JACOB		5 DEC 1925	JUL 1921	ALEX	
391	GM 1	MALOVE, FANNIE		14 OCT 1956	1892	MOSHE	
329	F 7	MANAKER, DAVID		20 AUG 1988	8 AUG 1905		
111	12	MANAKER, MAURICE		26 JUL 1979	21 DEC 1903		
446	C 9	MANASEWICH, LOUIS		27 NOV 1939	1882		LOUISA
446	C10	MANASEWICH, LOUISE M		12 NOV 1932	1878		LOUIS
102	BB 2	MANCALL, ROSAMOND	SCHWARTZ	2 FEB 1986	11 DEC 1926		DANIEL
447	W15	MANCARELLA, LENA		13 MAR 1953			
391	W75	MANCHESTER, DORA		21 DEC 1978	27 DEC 1898	BEREL	
392	F 6	MANCHESTER, SAMUEL ELI		6 JAN 1970	1878	JOSEPH ISAAC	
102	AF136	MANCOLL, EDITH	MALLAMED	28 DEC 1978	4 NOV 1903		MORRIS
102	AF135	MANCOLL, MORRIS MAX MD		22 MAR 1983	1 APR 1903		EDITH
370	J26	MANDEL, DORA		12 NOV 1937	1890		
377	D36	MANDEL, GLORIA	KAUFMAN	1962	1923	CHARLES & IDA	
370	A35	MANDEL, ISRAEL		7 SEP 1982	11 JUN 1891		
370	A45	MANDEL, JACK		2 APR 1956	8 APR 1895		
113	M41	MANDEL, LOUIS		4 JUN 1989	17 DEC 1903		
391	ZC50	MANDEL, MISCHA		1963	1916	ISRAEL CHAIM	
370	L32	MANDEL, TOBE		9 JAN 1915			
370	B47	MANDEL, WOLF		12 JAN 1933	20 SEP 1885		
104	O49	MANDELL, ANN L		7 MAR 1973			MEYER
447	H36	MANDELL, ANNA T		15 JAN 1985	1898		MILTON
370	T13	MANDELL, ANNIE		20 FEB 1973			PHILIP
370	T12	MANDELL, BENJAMIN		4 FEB 1977			GOLDIE
101	B15	MANDELL, BENJAMIN		26 AUG 1950	1864		LENA
101	H29	MANDELL, BENJAMIN		26 OCT 1985	20 MAR 1892		
248	A22	MANDELL, CELIA		11 NOV 1975	1879		MAX
102	BB 4	MANDELL, DANIEL I		8 APR 1988	15 APR 1901		ROSAMOND
370	T18	MANDELL, FANNIE		25 MAR 1930			SAMUEL
370	T11	MANDELL, GOLDIE		18 MAY 1992			BENJAMIN
248	B20	MANDELL, H LOUIS		25 JAN 1969	1904	MAX & CELIA	
371	AJ24	MANDELL, HARRY		22 FEB 1964	1894		
370	R11	MANDELL, IDA	SWATZBURG	27 AUG 1922	4 MAY 1899		
248	A23	MANDELL, JACOB		11 SEP 1978	1906	MAX & CELIA	
101	B16	MANDELL, LENA		12 MAY 1946	1874		BENJAMIN
248	A21	MANDELL, MAX		8 MAR 1962	1881		CELIA
104	O48	MANDELL, MEYER R		1 APR 1977			ANN
447	H37	MANDELL, MILTON S		12 NOV 1970	1894		ANNA
370	T14	MANDELL, PHILIP		7 MAY 1960			ANNIE
370	T15	MANDELL, ROSE		27 FEB 1950			SIMON
370	T17	MANDELL, SAMUEL		7 OCT 1944			FANNIE

Cem	Row	Name	Maiden Name	DOD	DOB	Parents	Spouse
370	O42	MANDELL, SIDNEY		29 NOV 1927	8 AUG 1927		
370	T16	MANDELL, SIMON		25 MAR 1956			ROSE
104	O39	MANDELL, WILLIAM		14 JUN 1983	30 JUN 1910		
447	W 8	MANDELOWITZ, ALEX		8 DEC 1966	3 JAN 1907		
447	E14	MANEVITZ, ANNIE		28 OCT 1929	1890		JOSHUA
446	B23	MANEVITZ, IDA M		1918	1876		
446	A32	MANEVITZ, JOSEPH		6 FEB 1919	1915	IDA	
447	E11	MANEVITZ, JOSHUA		17 MAR 1937	1889		ANNIE
126		MANEWITCH, JONEH		8 SEP 1893	31 AUG 1891		
391	GK 5	MANHEIMER, HARRY		7 JUL 1940	2 SEP 1891	SAMUEL ISAAC	
116	O18	MANISCHEWITZ, PAULA		29 APR 1982	5 DEC 1915		
750	H24	MANN, HARRY		3 FEB 1962	1913		
125	Q154	MANN, MILDRED	PIZER	4 MAY 1945	1907	ABRAHAM & LEAH	
125	V150	MANN, WILLIAM H		8 SEP 1982	1922		
370	Z13	MANOVIL, BERNHARD		21 NOV 1946	28 MAY 1892		DORTHEA
370	Z14	MANOVIL, DORTHEA	LEISERSOHN	21 DEC 1954	28 FEB 1898		BERNHARD
377	O33	MANOVIL, LUCIE		1963	1894		
391	I37	MANOWITZ, ETHEL		7 FEB 1960	1875	ISRAEL SAMUEL	MORRIS
391	D14	MANOWITZ, MORRIS		1939	1863	YEHUDA ANSHEL	ETHEL
112	E28	MANTEL, FRED MD		2 JAN 1992	6 JUN 1939		
370	S33	MAPSIK, HARRY		9 DEC 1960	15 JUL 1879		RACHEL
370	S32	MAPSIK, RACHEL LEAH		6 FEB 1955	25 JUN 1884		HARRY
101	M29	MARCOLIN, SARAH ELISE		29 OCT 1917	1890		AARON
102	AJ11	MARCUS, BARNEY		19 DEC 1943	30 SEP 1865		MOLLY
102	AA 2	MARCUS, BELLA	PYSER	5 NOV 1945	1861		HARRIS
104	E29	MARCUS, EMANUEL		9 AUG 1975	27 JAN 1909		
392	J39	MARCUS, EVA A		3 JAN 1931	1848	JOSEPH	
392	H13	MARCUS, FANNIE		1958	1875	SAMUEL	
102	AA 3	MARCUS, HARRIS		30 MAR 1933	1854		BELLA
374	F 9	MARCUS, HARRY		18 JAN 1929	6 JAN 1890		
392	D33	MARCUS, HENRY		11 JUN 1952	1866	DAVID BAER	
121	G 1	MARCUS, IRA G		1 MAY 1987	1 JUL 1917		
222	AM 5	MARCUS, JACOB		19 AUG 1961	11 JUL 1883		ROSE
121	H26	MARCUS, LARRY NEAL		7 SEP 1986	14 JUL 1955		
123		MARCUS, MAX		7 MAR 1943	1909		
102	AJ12	MARCUS, MOLLY		29 JUN 1947	21 SEP 1866		BARNEY
222	AM 7	MARCUS, NATHAN DDS		12 DEC 1992	7 OCT 1926	JACOB & ROSE	
222	AM 6	MARCUS, ROSE C		17 DEC 1970	1 SEP 1895		JACOB
392	F17	MARDER, ISRAEL		1 NOV 1938	1892		
121	A 6	MAREK, RAFAEL		10 AUG 1971	20 MAY 1914		
391	N43	MARGOLIS, FANNIE		5 JUN 1945		SANDER	LOUIS
392	A 2	MARGOLIS, FANNIE		29 OCT 1990	12 JAN 1900		
371	N31	MARGOLIS, ISIDOR		11 OCT 1953	1896		
102	V12	MARGOLIS, LOUIS		18 MAR 1987	18 APR 1903		
391	N42	MARGOLIS, LOUIS		20 FEB 1974	17 MAR 1889	ISAAC	FANNIE
391	G39	MARGOLIS, RACHEL		24 JUL 1930	1857	ABRAHAM MEYER	
391	L33	MARGOLIS, RACHEL T		15 NOV 1963	1899	DAVID MOSHE	
391	Q38	MARGOLIS, ROSE		7 OCT 1918	1893		
102	A80	MARGOLIS, SILVIA B		29 FEB 1944	1905		LOUIS
751	B22	MARGULIES, DIANA GAIL		1961	1952	RALPH	
751	C22	MARGULIES, JEAN		1954	1902		MAX
751	C23	MARGULIES, MAX V		1959	1900		JEAN
751	B21	MARGULIES, S RALPH		1967	1924		
125	K 96	MARHOLIN, BENJAMIN		14 JUL 1930	1858		SYLVIA
102	AA33	MARHOLIN, DAVID		30 AUG 1979	30 OCT 1908		
102	AA34	MARHOLIN, DAVID II		22 NOV 1978	7 APR 1949	DAVID	
125	M 96	MARHOLIN, ELI		26 MAY 1926	1868	ABRHAM ISAAC & MASHE	
125	K148	MARHOLIN, JENNIE		17 JAN 1973	1888		SAMUEL
125	N168	MARHOLIN, JOSEPH YALE		2 JAN 1952	1899		
125	S147	MARHOLIN, MAX		25 DEC 1938	1868	AARON ISAAC & MASHE	RACHEL
125		MARHOLIN, N		2 MAY 1917	1866	YOEL & LANE	
125	S148	MARHOLIN, RACHEL		9 APR 1950	1873		MAX
125	K149	MARHOLIN, SAMUEL		02 FEB 1956	1888		JENNIE
125	K 47	MARHOLIN, SARAH		18 SEP 1912	1862		MORRIS
125	J 62	MARHOLIN, SARAH D		9 AUG 1909	9 DEC 1881		
125	K 78	MARHOLIN, SYLVIA	BASS	20 MAR 1919	1857	DAVID	BENJAMIN

Cem	Row	Name	Maiden Name	DOD	DOB	Parents	Spouse
751	L38	MARINE, WENDY KAY		5 JAN 1956	7 MAY 1955		
113	B24	MARK, DAVID		5 SEP 1983	2 OCT 1907		
433	G19	MARK, RACHEL		13 AUG 1952	1915	HILLEL	
107	A11	MARK, WILLIAM		1990	1913		
330	AH12	MARKIEWICZ, ABRAM		4 DEC 1976	15 MAY 1910		
370	I35	MARKOFF, ANNA		9 SEP 1930			
370	T40	MARKOFF, BESSIE	FOX	1957	1902		
370	V19	MARKOFF, CLARA		1976	1901		KOPELAND
370	F13	MARKOFF, HARRY E		1939	1884		ROSE
330	D30	MARKOFF, HARRY NATHAN		4 FEB 1959	24 APR 1885		MARCIA
370	H 3	MARKOFF, JENNIE		7 JUL 1890			
370	J33	MARKOFF, JULIA		11 OCT 1939	1871		MORRIS
370	V18	MARKOFF, KOPELAND		1951	1896		CLARA
370	V 6	MARKOFF, LAZAR		15 DEC 1926			ROSE
371	A43	MARKOFF, LENA		22 JUN 1988	13 MAY 1896		
370	E10	MARKOFF, LOUIS		5 SEP 1949			
330	D31	MARKOFF, MARCIA		15 FEB 1976	16 JUN 1889		NATHAN
370	C19	MARKOFF, MORRIS		29 NOV 1936	1876		JULIA
370	F 3	MARKOFF, ROSE		16 MAR 1971	2 FEB 1893		HARRY
370	F11	MARKOFF, RUBIN		5 MAY 1920	10 NOV 1902		SARAH
370	V 2	MARKOFF, SARAH		14 FEB 1955			LAZAR
370	H 7	MARKOFF, SARAH		1965	1901		RUBIN
370	K29	MARKOFF, TOBY ANNA		20 JUN 1943			
370	R 5	MARKOW, ELLA		1917	1844		LOUIS
372	K16	MARKOW, ETHEL		1955	1893		LOUIS
370	R 4	MARKOW, ISRAEL		30 SEP 1934		LOUIS & ELLA	
370	B10	MARKOW, JACOB		9 APR 1923			MINNIE
370	R 6	MARKOW, LOUIS		1904	1841		ELLA
372	K15	MARKOW, LOUIS		1942	1894		ETHEL
370	I 9	MARKOW, MINNIE		3 JUL 1920			JACOB
446	B11	MARKOWITZ, ANNA		5 FEB 1923			
447	W29	MARKOWITZ, PAULA M		30 JAN 1941	2 JUL 1940		
447	R36	MARKOWITZ, PHILIP		21 AUG 1960	1 JUL 1901		
432		MARKOWITZ, SAMUEL		5 NOV 1900			
102	AI160	MARKS, ANN	BARON	30 JUN 1988	1926		MATTATHIAS
330	A10	MARKS, ISADORE		19 SEP 1959	22 JUL 1919		SHIRLEY
102	AI159	MARKS, MATTHIAS W		19 JUL 1969	1905		ANN
116	G11	MARKS, MELVYN B		23 MAY 1989	18 AUG 1942		
330	AD13	MARKS, SAMUEL		8 DEC 1970	21 JUN 1903	ISRAEL & SHIRLEY	
248	L65	MARKS, SARAH	FRAGER	1963	1913		
330	A 7	MARKS, SHIRLEY P	GERTNER	2 APR 1984	7 NOV 1922	SOLOMON & GERTRUDE	ISIDORE
113	K36	MARLOW, LENA		1 MAY 1972	27 FEB 1885		NATHAN
113	K35	MARLOW, NATHAN		18 MAR 1975	18 MAY 1878		LENA
113	K33	MARLOW, WILMA	DUBIN	25 OCT 1973	23 APR 1917		
127	E	MARMER, BENJAMIN		22 JUN 1989	1913		
102	G24	MARMER, ROSE	WAXMAN	29 JAN 1970			
102	A19	MARMOR, BORIS		5 JUN 1939	1863		IDA
102	A18	MARMOR, IDA		22 OCT 1933	1866		BORIS
125	D119	MARON, JEFFREY BRUCE		5 AUG 1991	30 APR 1963		
125	C121	MARON, WENDY	LIPMAN	4 JUL 1961	1959		
330	G62	MARRUS, BREINA		24 APR 1936			
125	C110	MARSHALL, MORRIS		11 APR 1974	1912		SYLVIA
125	D108	MARSHALL, ROSE	MIRSKY	29 DEC 1971	1881		WILLIAM
248	D10	MARSHALL, SAMUEL		5 AUG 1991	25 DEC 1902		
125	C111	MARSHALL, SYLVIA	AROTSKY	4 NOV 1979	1915		MORRIS
125	D109	MARSHALL, WILLIAM		8 JAN 1947	27 APR 1874	YITGAL MOSHE	ROSE
125	R147	MARTIN, ANNA		9 MAR 1964	1886		JOSEPH
125	O 66	MARTIN, ISADORE		12 JUN 1925	29 DEC 1920	JACOB & MARTHA	
125	R146	MARTIN, JOSEPH		16 SEP 1942	1882	WILLIS	ANNA
112	B15	MARX, HENRY		23 JUL 1990	22 JUN 1928		
222	AJ24	MASKEL, CORA	FRANKLIN	19 DEC 1954	1881		SIMON
222	AR14	MASKEL, HERMAN		26 AUG 1987	3 SEP 1915	SIMON & CORA (FRANKLIN)	
222	AI12	MASKEL, MOSES NATHAN		18 JUN 1968	2 MAY 1912	SIMON & CORA (FRANKLIN)	IDA
222	AJ22	MASKEL, NAHOM, I		4 NOV 1923	1856		
222	AJ23	MASKEL, SIMON M		27 JUL 1950	1876	NAHOM	CORA
751	M 4	MASKOVSKY, BENJAMIN		NDD			

Cem	Row	Name	Maiden Name	DOD	DOB	Parents	Spouse
751	M 3	MASKOVSKY, EMMA		NDD			
751	J13	MASKOVSKY, JENNIE		1945	1902		
371	AH 4	MASOFSKY, LEONARD J		19 DEC 1989	1899		
104	N50	MASS, CLARA	ROSEN	30 DEC 1983	13 SEP 1908		SAMUEL
104	N47	MASS, SAMUEL		1 FEB 1987	15 NOV 1902		CLARA
432		MASSER,		12 SEP 1899			
370	A39	MASSOVER, LOUIS JACOB		24 MAR 1892	1852		
447	A33	MASTER, (BABY)		30 JAN 1934			
374	D31	MASTERS, FANNIE		29 SEP 1938			ISRAEL
328	A 5	MASTERS, GUSTAVE		8 OCT 1985	16 MAR 1892		
374	D32	MASTERS, ISRAEL I		1943	1865		FANNIE
330	H53	MASTERS, ROSE		30 JUN 1954	1895		
113	O41	MATHEWS, ESTHER	SMOLOWITZ	22 MAY 1984	18 MAR 1899		
371	A42	MATIKAN, JEAN		30 APR 1991	10 JAN 1912		
101	K23	MATTELSON, SADIE		12 JAN 1933	1908		
101	C25	MATTELSON, SAMUEL		5 FEB 1932	1878		
446	A69	MATTES, BESSIE A		1915	1891	JACOB & MAGGIE	
446	B75	MATTES, ISRAEL		31 AUG 1973	23 DEC 1896	JACOB & MAGGIE	
446	A71	MATTES, JACOB		11 NOV 1941	1865		MAGGIE
446	C74	MATTES, L		1888	1888	JACOB & MAGGIE	
446	B73	MATTES, LILLIAN		1889	1886	JACOB & MAGGIE	
446	A70	MATTES, MAGGIE S		1956	1865		JACOB
101	F30	MATTLESON, REUBEN		10 OCT 1986	13 JUL 1913		
101	C19	MATUSOV, PETER		21 AUG 1951	1877		ROSE
101	C18	MATUSOV, ROSE		11 APR 1954	1881		PETER
102	Z34	MAX, MOLLIE	WEBER	26 DEC 1964	15 JUL 1892		ZELAK
102	Z33	MAX, ZELAK A		26 MAR 1963	26 SEP 1890		MOLLE
125	M108	MAXEN, GUSSIE	BROWN	10 MAR 1928	1890	H & SHAINA	
125	D 92	MAXEN, HARRY		14 FEB 1963	1888		
125	W187	MAXEN, LOUIS		10 AUG 1979	1892		VIVIAN
125	C 95	MAXEN, MYRON I		1990	1928		
125	C 94	MAXEN, NATHAN		5 FEB 1947	3 MAY 1918	HARRY & GUSSIE	
125	W188	MAXEN, VIVIAN	ROSENFIELD	22 FEB 1982	1901		LOUIS
374	F34	MAY, DENISE	BLUMENTHAL	19 JUL 1992	15 FEB 1950	HAROLD & ALICE	
392	A52	MAY, HELEN K		1 JUL 1978	14 FEB 1902		SAMUEL
392	A53	MAY, SAMUEL S		30 JUN 1974	2 OCT 1902		HELEN
377	P 3	MAY, SARAH		19 MAY 1975			
328	A23	MAYER, ALFRED		31 DEC 1964	24 MAR 1890		
125	J 35	MAYER, MOSES		17 JUN 1908	1853		
114	C37	MAYER, RUBIN		14 MAR 1989	23 DEC 1904		
447	E37	MAYER, STEPHEN F		27 MAY 1970	25 JUN 1945		
248	K11	MAYERSON, JACOB		1958	1896		RAE
248	K10	MAYERSON, RAE E		1986	1899		JACOB
371	AL23	MAYERSON, SAMUEL J		28 JAN 1952	1905		
433	K 5	MAZER, MAYER		19 JAN 1942	1876	MENACHEM MENDEL	PAULINE
433	K 6	MAZER, PAULINE		4 JAN 1939	1872	MORDECHAI	MAYER
102	AB88	MAZIE, PAULINE		22 NOV 1958	1880		
392	H24	MAZUR, BERTHA		12 SEP 1936	17 JUN 1887	DAVID AARON	SAMUEL
392	D46	MAZUR, MORRIS		3 APR 1957	1883	ISAAC	
392	G14	MAZUR, SAMUEL H		23 MAY 1943	1909	MOSHE EZRA	BERTHA
751	I16	MCMAHON, SARAH	TILLES	3 OCT 1980	10 AUG 1897		
106	D31	MCMILLIN, JANET		31 DEC 1976	4 APR 1926		
116	N13	MEADE, JAY A		1986	1927		
110	A29	MEDNICK, JOSEPH		25 JAN 1948	1882		
222	AU12	MEIERFELD, VERA LUCILLE		17 APR 1991	1916		
330	D40	MEISLER, PHILIP		10 FEB 1960	1867		
329	C 8	MEISLER, REBECCA		28 FEB 1964	15 MAR 1880		
222	M 5	MEISNER, EVA Z		30 JUN 1960	1869		
222	M 3	MEISNER, SYLVIA		15 AUG 1974	12 NOV 1904		
751	O35	MEISTRICH, JEANNE	WAXLER	1980	1914		
377	O34	MELAMED, MARY	SUISMAN	1952	1915		
112	B10	MELCHER, SIDNEY		21 AUG 1990	29 JUN 1905		
121	A23	MELL, LILLIAN		13 JUN 1992			
102	AJ29	MELLAMED, ANN R		5 NOV 1952	9 APR 1901		
123		MELLAMED, HENRY L		27 DEC 1958	1888		
125	B 6	MELLINS, BERT		20 OCT 1980	1892		ELFREIDA

Cem	Row	Name	Maiden Name	DOD	DOB	Parents	Spouse
125	B 7	MELLINS, DONALD		15 SEP 1944	1926	BERT & ELFREDA	
125	B 8	MELLINS, ELFREIDA	GINSBERG	10 FEB 1983			BERT
125	ZB169	MELLION, JACOB MD		23 FEB 1991	25 DEC 1897		
105	I52	MELLMAN, JUDITH L		17 JUN 1963	16 MAR 1947		
222	K 7	MELNICK, ABRAHAM		25 OCT 1962	1863		
102	AC41	MELROSE, SAYNE	DUNN	29 AUG 1984	29 DEC 1938		
330	AF 3	MELTZ, ABRAHAM		4 NOV 1972	1889		SOPHIE
117	I 5	MELTZ, ROBERT		23 FEB 1993			
330	AF 4	MELTZ, SOPHIE		10 APR 1981	1896		ABRAHAM
104	J46	MELTZER, ALLAN DAVID		22 NOV 1950	4 OCT 1950		
125	E125	MELTZER, FLORENCE FELICE		23 SEP 1943	JUN 1943		
125	J 55	MELTZER, HERBERT P		9 JAN 1903			IDA
104	H47	MELTZER, IDA	ROME	11 NOV 1986	5 FEB 1900		JOSEPH
125	I 59	MELTZER, IDA ROSE		7 JUL 1899			HERBERT
104	H46	MELTZER, JOSEPH D		21 NOV 1961	1900		IDA
104	O28	MEN, ANNA		12 JUL 1992	13 AUG 1918		
113	J75	MENCHELL, BERNARD		24 APR 1989	14 MAR 1916		
447	B32	MENDELOWITZ, SOLOMON		22 JUL 1978	1909		
102	AE108	MENDELSOHN, HARRY		15 DEC 1947	9 AUG 1880		HELEN
102	AE107	MENDELSOHN, HELEN		12 AUG 1980	31 JUL 1888		HARRY
117	F 1	MENDES, JOSEPH H JR		13 MAR 1993			
125	D 60	MENUS, ADA	AXELROD	1988	1900		
125	F111	MENUS, AUGUSTA	LEWIN	23 MAR 1941	7 JUL 1888	SAMUEL	SAMUEL
125	E114	MENUS, MOLLIE G		29 AUG 1967	31 OCT 1899		
125	F112	MENUS, SAMUEL W		15 JUL 1985	23 MAR 1885		AUGUSTA
102	N17	MERIDY, EMMA L		1951	1891	MORRIS	
102	AJ161	MERIDY, LOUIS		6 FEB 1975	25 OCT 1894		SARAH
102	N15	MERIDY, MORRIS		1937	1865		
102	N16	MERIDY, MURRAY		1932	1924		
102	AJ164	MERIDY, SARAH		12 MAR 1966	19 JUN 1902		LOUIS
391	S38	MERIMS, JENNIE		17 NOV 1920	1874	JACOB	
391	D11	MERIMS, MAX		6 NOV 1940	1873	PHELEK	
112	B 1	MERIN, GOLDY	KAUFMAN	29 JUL 1991	29 NOV 1911		
330	AD30	MERLIS, AL		22 SEP 1987	23 MAR 1896		
116	BL101	MERLIS, DOROTHY	FREEDMAN	4 JUN 1961	28 NOV 1894		LEWIS
116	BL100	MERLIS, LEWIS H		1978	1894		DOROTHY
392	H20	MERRAN, REBECCA		19 DEC 1941	1882	YESHIYAHU	
392	D42	MERRIMS, REBECCA		5 JUL 1956	1880	JUDAH	
125	J 30	MESHKEN, BASIA	FOX	18 SEP 1915	1858	ZALMAN & LEAH	
125	I 28	MESHKEN, EDWARD		22 SEP 1940	1872		
125	J 29	MESHKEN, ELIZABETH		2 OCT 1916	9 MAR 1877		
328	A19	MESSINGER, BESSIE		3 JUN 1958	1892		WILLIAM
116	B23	MESSINGER, CLARA	MARCUS	6 JUN 1980	1 JUL 1892		
328	A37	MESSINGER, SARA	BROOK	29 MAR 1976	1 JUN 1920		
328	A18	MESSINGER, WILLIAM		4 MAY 1968	1890		BESSIE
102	AI199	METANSKI, ESTHER T		22 OCT 1981	19 NOV 1894		
102	AD110	METTER, ETHYLE	KADISKY	21 SEP 1988	1 NOV 1908		
113	O31	METTER, LILLIAN R		4 MAR 1979	1 DEC 1899		MORRIS
113	O32	METTER, MORRIS		25 OCT 1959	10 JAN 1891		LILLIAN
371	J20	METZENDORF, ABRAHAM M		1966	1892		ESTHER
371	J21	METZENDORF, ESTHER		1982	1887		ABRAHAM
391	Y65	MEYER, ABRAHAM ISAAC		10 JUL 1971	25 DEC 1892	SAUL	
391	GB 4	MEYER, ABRAHAM JACOB		14 JAN 1960	1870	JUDAH	
372	K18	MEYER, ANITA S		1957	1894		ISAAC
370	H23	MEYER, ANNIE		21 SEP 1903			ISSAC
391	O32	MEYER, BESSIE		1 JUN 1946	1863	MEYER	SAUL
391	U76	MEYER, HANNAH		15 APR 1983	1905	JUDAH	ISADORE
391	C40	MEYER, HORTENSE R		7 JAN 1926	FEB 1925		
370	C10	MEYER, ISAAC		10 JUN 1931	1854		ANNIE
372	K19	MEYER, ISAAC		1937	1890		ANITA
447	AB37	MEYER, ISAAC		1973	1888		ROSE
391	U75	MEYER, ISIDORE S RABBI		8 SEP 1992	1903	MORDECHAI	HANNAH
372	C14	MEYER, JOHN		1974	1923		
371	O 9	MEYER, MAURICE W		15 JUN 1956	26 NOV 1899		
391	K50	MEYER, MAX		28 APR 1960	1880	YEHUDA	RACHEL
377	I 6	MEYER, MAYME E		1976	1894		

Cem	Row	Name	Maiden Name	DOD	DOB	Parents	Spouse
391	R32	MEYER, RACHEL LEAH		11 APR 1919	1835	JUDAH LEV	
391	K51	MEYER, RACHEL PEARL		12 DEC 1955	1881	YAKOV YEHUDA	
447	AB36	MEYER, ROSE		1975	1890		MAX
374	E10	MEYER, RUTH	BRUCKNER	18 SEP 1954			ISAAC
391	N31	MEYER, SAUL		1918	1863		
372	K10	MEYEROWITZ, KATE		1956	1881		BESSIE
372	K17	MEYERS, KARL		2 APR 1977	23 JUL 1909		BENNO
222	AL14	MEYERS, KATIE		27 JUL 1931	1866		
447	P36	MEYERS, ROSE	BATTALIN	4 SEP 1942	2 SEP 1896	HENRY & RACHEL	
329	D41	MICEGENDLER, JENNIE		22 APR 1966	25 APR 1885		
391	L32	MICHAEL, HANNAH		13 MAR 1893	19 FEB 1893	JOSEPH & ROSA	
107	C23	MICHAELS, RONALD A		26 DEC 1973	28 MAR 1935		
107	G17	MICHELS, BELLA	SHUMSKY	1988	1908		EDWARD
107	G18	MICHELS, EDWARD		1989	1906		BELLA
119	H60	MICHELSON, CAROLINE J		29 JAN 1990	7 NOV 1909		
102	AJ 4	MICHELSON, CHARLES		1946	1903		
102	AJ188	MICHELSON, HYMAN		13 APR 1977		NAFTALI	
102	H52	MICHELSON, ISAAC		29 JAN 1957	1909		ROSALYN
102	AJ189	MICHELSON, JANE		11 JUL 1969		NAFTALI	
102	AJ187	MICHELSON, LOUIS		21 FEB 1976		NAFTALI	
121	D41	MICHELSON, MARLENE ANN		31 AUG 1981	30 MAR 1935		
102	CB15	MICHELSON, MARTIN S		1982	1926		
102	AJ186	MICHELSON, MAYER		9 DEC 1968		NAFTALI	
110	E17	MICHELSON, PEARL K		24 APR 1987	27 FEB 1912		
102	AJ190	MICHELSON, RENA		4 SEP 1973		NAFTALI	
102	H53	MICHELSON, ROSLYN	KATZ	16 APR 1983	18 DEC 1913		ISAAC
121	D39	MICHELSON, SIDNEY A		8 APR 1980	3 DEC 1930		
125	K108	MICHLIN, HYMAN		11 AUG 1938	1892	MENDEL & PRODA	
125	N177	MICHLIN, IDA		31 JAN 1966	1899		
123		MIKKELSON, PETER		6 JUL 1942	1904		
372	G18	MIKOLASI, ROSA		20 OCT 1936	25 NOV 1855		SANDOR
372	G17	MIKOLASI, SANDOR		20 OCT 1916	12 FEB 1855		ROSA
123		MILAVSKY, FAY	MARCUS	13 JUN 1957	1913		
125	F129	MILAVSKY, GERTRUDE		14 OCT 1968	1912		
123		MILAVSKY, JACK		11 FEB 1974	4 JUL 1908		
125	K 71	MILCOWITZ, LENA		12 FEB 1932	1882		
125	M119	MILCOWITZ, MAX		5 OCT 1961	1879		
123		MILEFSKY, SAMUEL		1983	1894		
248	G53	MILEVITZ, ALBERT		2 NOV 1966			MIRIAM
248	G52	MILEVITZ, MIRIAM		23 MAY 1963			ALBERT
125	F110	MILKOWITZ, ANNA		4 MAR 1948	1867	SHMUEL MOSHE	ISAAC
125	M145	MILKOWITZ, CLARA		8 MAR 1955	1887		
125	F109	MILKOWITZ, ISAAC		23 JAN 1965	1870		ANNA
125	E111	MILKOWITZ, NORMA		31 OCT 1937	22 OCT 1831	HARRY & SYLVIA	
125	E109	MILKOWITZ, SYLVIA	WEISSMAN	22 OCT 1980	6 NOV 1903		
330	B22	MILLER, AARON EARL RABBI		22 FEB 1965	1910	ISAAC & ANNA	SONIA
370	G45	MILLER, ABRAHAM		1922	1887		
102	AI155	MILLER, ABRAHAM H		14 JUN 1969	25 DEC 1893		REBECCA
121	A10	MILLER, ALEX		20 MAY 1968	15 MAR 1900		
330	B16	MILLER, ANNA		2 OCT 1944	1872		ISAAC
116	BU56	MILLER, ANNA	DAVIS	8 DEC 1964	20 AUG 1893		JOSEPH
101	K22	MILLER, ANNA		13 FEB 1930	1858		
101	H 2	MILLER, BARBARA T		16 FEB 1981	5 OCT 1937		
222	L12	MILLER, BARNET		22 MAR 1963	19 MAY 1892		
447	O15	MILLER, BELLA		22 AUG 1948	1877		
116	BL21	MILLER, BENJAMIN		1 JAN 1959	1888		ESTHER
751	N16	MILLER, BENJAMIN		1972	1898		
125	A 22	MILLER, BERNARD		25 JUL 1939			
102	M48	MILLER, BERTHA		9 APR 1975	1883		DAVID
125	F 75	MILLER, BETTY	KALLMAN	31 JUL 1969	1883		
125	F 69	MILLER, CELIA Z		18 AUG 1972	1882		NATHAN
102	C36	MILLER, CHARLES H		4 FEB 1982	4 NOV 1896		
447	U18	MILLER, DANIEL		1949	1879		
102	M49	MILLER, DAVID		23 MAY 1964	1882		BERTHA
751	N15	MILLER, DOROTHY		1980	1902		
222	AJ 9	MILLER, ELEAZAR		29 AUG 1924	1856		NEHAMAH

Cem	Row	Name	Maiden Name	DOD	DOB	Parents	Spouse
102	AF111	MILLER, ERIC J		28 DEC 1988	14 DEC 1958		
392	H30	MILLER, ESTHER		19 DEC 1928	1870		SAMUEL
373	A 1	MILLER, ESTHER		1947	1883		ISRAEL
116	BL20	MILLER, ESTHER	WEINBERG	27 APR 1969	1891		BENJAMIN
125	X179	MILLER, ETHEL	LURYEA	10 DEC 1984	1905		MURRAY
125	K 36	MILLER, ETTA		30 MAR 1914	24 SEP 1898		
329	A16	MILLER, FRANCES		2 MAY 1962	1903		HYMAN
370	U32	MILLER, GOLDIE		1932	1915		
447	Y37	MILLER, HARRY		21 JAN 1970	1902		IRENE
101	C34	MILLER, HARRY		29 NOV 1934	1861		
125	K 67	MILLER, HARRY ALBERT		9 OCT 1918	1892	ISRAEL	
102	Z20	MILLER, HARRY B		7 JAN 1946	10 JUL 1888		JENNIE
102	AA181	MILLER, HARVEY JOEL		18 JUN 1965	1935		
103	C21	MILLER, HENRY R		1982	1901		SALLY
329	A17	MILLER, HYMAN		3 NOV 1976	1894		FRANCES
105	M16	MILLER, HYMAN RUBIN		23 DEC 1951	1888		ROSE
125	K121	MILLER, IDA SARAH		23 AUG 1950	1872		JULIUS
447	Y36	MILLER, IRENE		16 MAY 1971	1909		HARRY
330	C13	MILLER, ISAAC		1939	1871		ANNA
391	GL 2	MILLER, ISADORE		20 APR 1947	11 MAR 1886	SOLOMON	
373	A 2	MILLER, ISRAEL		19 OCT 1927			ESTHER
447	T 7	MILLER, JACK		17 AUG 1960	14 JUL 1901		
102	Z21	MILLER, JENNIE G		17 JUL 1968	3 DEC 1893		HARRY
222	L13	MILLER, JEREMY		12 JUL 1991	5 JUL 1991		
121	A11	MILLER, JESSIE		20 NOV 1979	29 AUG 1908		
391	X52	MILLER, JOSEPH		3 OCT 1966	12 OCT 1930	ISAAC	
373	I21	MILLER, JOSEPH		1949	1900		
222	D 4	MILLER, JOSEPH		24 FEB 1958	1878		RACHEL
123		MILLER, JOSEPH C		1 SEP 1953	1898		
116	BU57	MILLER, JOSEPH S		18 MAY 1963	2 AUG 1891		ANNA
125	K120	MILLER, JULIUS		3 JAN 1934	1866		IDA
127	R	MILLER, JULIUS		19 NOV 1987	15 SEP 1892		
392	J17	MILLER, KAY		8 JUL 1947	20 APR 1898	JOSEPH	
391	GM 5	MILLER, MAMIE		8 MAR 1940	19 SEP 1889	ISRAEL LEV	
110	E10	MILLER, MARSHA	KOSTIN	20 MAY 1990		JACOB & GITTEL LEAH (DION)	MORRIS
125	J 41	MILLER, MARY		16 SEP 1914	1868	ABNER	SIMON
102	AC196	MILLER, MAX		30 SEP 1983	24 DEC 1904		SOPHIE
127	C	MILLER, MILDRED		27 JUL 1989	17 OCT 1910		
447	O16	MILLER, MIRIAM	LENDER	12 SEP 1975	15 JUL 1896		
110	E11	MILLER, MORRIS		21 JUN 1979			MARSHA
125	X178	MILLER, MURRAY H		29 JAN 1982	1899		ETHEL
125	D 77	MILLER, NATHAN D		14 JAN 1990	8 APR 1931		
125	F 70	MILLER, NATHAN M		1918	1878		CELIA
222	AJ 8	MILLER, NEHAMAH		31 MAY 1921	1855		ELEAZER
329	A36	MILLER, PAULINE		15 FEB 1974	1897		
222	D 3	MILLER, RACHEL	RADZIVILOW	30 APR 1962	1884		JOSEPH
371	AE11	MILLER, RALPH		9 MAR 1976	18 DEC 1912		
371	AJ25	MILLER, RAPHAEL		29 DEC 1962	2 JAN 1883		
102	AO156	MILLER, REBECCA	DUBIN	5 JAN 1973	3 APR 1893		ABRAHAM
370	I68	MILLER, REBECCA		19 SEP 1949			
116	BU55	MILLER, ROBERT D		23 APR 1989	7 NOV 1920	JOSEPH & ANNA	SIMI
106	E35	MILLER, RONALD		12 APR 1985	30 DEC 1941		
105	M17	MILLER, ROSE	SHLIEN	30 JUL 1991	1898		HYMAN
103	C20	MILLER, SALLY L		1984	1904		HENRY
392	H29	MILLER, SAMUEL		16 OCT 1936	1871	ABRAHAM	ESTHER
370	C 5	MILLER, SAMUEL		1927	1878		SOPHIE
116	S15	MILLER, SAMUEL HENRY		26 OCT 1973	22 MAR 1896		
370	D 2	MILLER, SAMUEL JACOB		21 MAY 1934	1890		
125	L123	MILLER, SARAH		20 JAN 1931	15 DEC 1871	KALMAN LOUIS	
125	D 75	MILLER, SIDNEY S		1985	1903		
125	J 42	MILLER, SIMON		12 JUN 1906	1857	ABRAHAM	MARY
125		MILLER, SIMON		3 MAY 1918	1873	ISRAEL	SARAH
330	B21	MILLER, SONIA		28 APR 1981	28 MAR 1903		EARL
102	AC197	MILLER, SOPHIE		16 AUG 1991	22 MAY 1907		MAX
370	I21	MILLER, SOPHIE		1926	1876		SAMUEL
377	Q21	MILLER, THERESA	GOODMAN	18 JAN 1991	28 APR 1894		

Cem	Row	Name	Maiden Name	DOD	DOB	Parents	Spouse
249	H40	MILLER, VERA		9 SEP 1987	22 FEB 1908		
125	F157	MILLER, WILLIAM C		22 APR 1981	1893		
391	M33	MILLIAN, MARKUS EDEL		10 FEB 1893	1853		
121	D31	MILLROD, MAX P		30 APR 1981	16 SEP 1896		
121	D30	MILLROD, MINNA	HYATT	25 DEC 1978	6 FEB 1900		
119	C22	MILLSTEIN, MAX D		7 OCT 1987	28 AUG 1904		
119	C23	MILLSTEIN, RUTH I		3 MAY 1982	11 OCT 1907		
119	D22	MILLSTEIN, YETTA S		29 JUL 1977	1913		
125	T165	MILSTEIN, MORRIS		26 JUN 1940	1870		
125	M140	MILSTEIN, ROSE		4 DEC 1951	1874		SAMUEL
125	L148	MILSTEIN, SADYE E		6 APR 1957	1904		
125	M141	MILSTEIN, SAMUEL		15 MAR 1956	1874		ROSE
330	A41	MILTON, RUTH		23 NOV 1968	23 NOV 1929		
330	D24	MINCH, CARA		4 AUG 1957	1910		
374	A33	MINDEL, CELIA		15 AUG 1967	2 SEP 1889		SHAIL
374	E33	MINDEL, IDA PEARL		1951	1915		
374	A34	MINDEL, SHAIL		7 MAY 1935	7 MAY 1882		CELIA
102	G19	MINDELL, JACOB		16 SEP 1959	4 MAR 1906		
370	G 7	MINDELL, MAX		30 NOV 1956	1880		TOBE
370	G 6	MINDELL, TOBE RIFKA		15 MAY 1956	1881		MAX
121	D35	MINDES, ABRAHAM		13 MAR 1983	18 DEC 1903		
121	D34	MINDES, RUTH		16 MAR 1982	28 FEB 1907		
105	H13	MINSK, ESTHER		28 NOV 1971	1899		KELLMAN
330	E 5	MINSK, GUSSIE		6 JUN 1939	1887		HARRIS
330	D21	MINSK, HARRIS B		17 JUL 1952			GUSSIE
105	H12	MINSK, KELLMAN		16 JAN 1968	1898		ESTHER
330	E42	MINTZ, ANNA M		14 MAR 1930	1856		LOUIS
102	D33	MINTZ, BENJAMIN A		6 MAR 1963	1879		TILLIE
102	S42	MINTZ, BERNARD L		21 JUN 1990	1910	JAMES & BESSIE	DORIS
102	S44	MINTZ, BESSIE		9 SEP 1968	1888		JAMES
330	E 9	MINTZ, CHAYA RISHA		5 APR 1927	1862		
373	C 4	MINTZ, DORA		30 SEP 1970	1887		LOUIS
102	S41	MINTZ, DORIS		15 MAY 1983	1906		BERNARD
102	D32	MINTZ, ERNEST ELI SGT		23 JUL 1944	19 FEB 1909	BENJAMIN & TILLIE MARY	
374	G 8	MINTZ, ESTHER J		1928	1865		
374	F12	MINTZ, HARRY		1927	1864		
330	F17	MINTZ, HYMAN		1 DEC 1918	1857		
330	G57	MINTZ, IDA		25 OCT 1929			
330	F61	MINTZ, ISADORE		18 APR 1934			
102	S43	MINTZ, JAMES		19 NOV 1962	1879		BESSIE
373	C 5	MINTZ, LOUIS		19 JUN 1974	1886		DORA
330	E41	MINTZ, LOUIS		24 OCT 1929	1855		ANNA
330	G35	MINTZ, MARY		25 MAY 1936	1882		
370	K45	MINTZ, MAXINE M		1944	1918	MORRIS	
370	E 8	MINTZ, MORRIS		31 MAY 1949	1886		
330	AG10	MINTZ, SAMUEL		24 NOV 1979	6 MAY 1905		
102	AJ107	MINTZ, SAMUEL F		20 APR 1962	1886		
376	B11	MINTZ, SIMA	RUTCHIK	29 JUN 1971	1902		
102	D34	MINTZ, TILLE H		22 NOV 1970	1890		BENJAMIN
446	C29	MIRIN, BITAH		31 DEC 1900		ISRAEL	
493	H35	MIRKIN, ESTHER		26 MAR 1991	27 MAY 1914	JUDAH	
447	W36	MIRSKY, ROSE		4 DEC 1968	1911		
116	AU 7	MISCHEL, ANNIE	BERMAN	18 FEB 1960	1891		MORRIS
116	AU 6	MISCHEL, MORRIS		26 JUL 1930	1890		ANNIE
101	E28	MISKIN, ABRAHAM		5 SEP 1978	1890		
101	L30	MISKIN, CELIA		21 JUL 1930	1862		
101	I 5	MISKIN, CHARLOTTE				SAMUEL & ROSE	
101	C36	MISKIN, ISAAC		6 DEC 1938	1855		
101	I 4	MISKIN, ROSE		13 JUN 1979	1897		SAMUEL
101	I 3	MISKIN, SAMUEL		19 APR 1972	1884		ROSE
102	O25	MISSAL, ABE		6 DEC 1943	8 APR 1882		GOLDA
102	AC170	MISSAL, CECELIA	PIERSON	15 MAY 1990	5 NOV 1909		
102	AJ114	MISSAL, CELIA L		30 JAN 1968	25 DEC 1894	MAYER & RACHEL (GOLDBERG)	
102	AI 1	MISSAL, FANNIE D		1963	1878		ISAAC
102	O26	MISSAL, GOLDA	BERKOVITCH	25 JUN 1928	21 JUN 1883		ABE
102	O23	MISSAL, HAROLD PAT		28 JAN 1977	21 JUL 1904	ABE & GOLDA	LILLIAN

Cem	Row	Name	Maiden Name	DOD	DOB	Parents	Spouse
102	AI 2	MISSAL, ISAAC S		1941	1875		FANNIE
102	O22	MISSAL, LILLIAN	CION	4 JAN 1966	1 MAY 1903		HAROLD
116	BJ 9	MISSAL, SARAH	LIFTIG	18 JUL 1976	4 OCT 1885		
102	A 8	MISSAL, SIDNEY		1 MAR 1945	1889		
248	H50	MISSAN, HANNAH H		11 JAN 1960	1 JAN 1901		
102	AJ243	MISSAN, MAX		3 JAN 1992	5 APR 1906		
102	P 5	MISSAN, MICHAEL		12 JUN 1960	6 APR 1904		MOLLIE
102	P 6	MISSAN, MOLLIE	SCHWARTZ	13 JAN 1972	30 APR 1909	NATHAN & REBECCA	MICHAEL
375	E40	MISSING STONE (HALE INSCRIP		30 SEP 1895			
391	ZA75	MITCHELL, BESSIE A		23 DEC 1979	1 NOV 1894	SHMERRYL	
107	D11	MITCHELL, BETTY		1980	1897		
102	AF81	MITNICK, DAVID		3 MAR 1963	27 NOV 1877		ROSE
102	AG81	MITNICK, JENNIE D		8 MAY 1970	1892		MAX
102	AE80	MITNICK, LOUIS		2 DEC 1985	20 JUL 1887		
102	AG80	MITNICK, MAX		30 MAR 1959	1886		JENNIE
102	AF82	MITNICK, MORTON M		30 MAR 1976	16 OCT 1906	DAVID & ROSE	
102	AF79	MITNICK, RALPH R		10 SEP 1953	29 AUG 1908	DAVID & ROSE	
102	BE13	MITNICK, REGINA H		25 JUL 1991	27 MAY 1912		
102	AF80	MITNICK, ROSE		10 MAY 1950	31 JAN 1885		DAVID
447	G15	MITTELMAN, DAVID		15 DEC 1951			MINNIE
370	A38	MITTELMAN, ELIYAHU		31 AUG 1892			
446	D32	MITTELMAN, IDA		9 AUG 1903	8 OCT 1902		
447	G16	MITTELMAN, MINNIE		5 FEB 1943			DAVID
102	F25	MITTELMAN, REUBEN		15 NOV 1937	19 JUL 1896		
446	XXX	MITTLEMAN, BENJAMIN D		1976	1893		SADIE
446	XXX	MITTLEMAN, CAROL P		1965	1927	BENJAMIN & SADIE	
446	A49	MITTLEMAN, CORRINE		1977	1890		LOUIS
446	A25	MITTLEMAN, ISRAEL		2 NOV 1920	1867		LENA
446	C24	MITTLEMAN, JUDAH		4 MAR 1921			
446	A24	MITTLEMAN, LENA B		1957	1869		ISRAEL
446	A50	MITTLEMAN, LOUIS		1988	1890		CORRINE
446	A53	MITTLEMAN, REUBEN		1962	1895		RUTH
446	A54	MITTLEMAN, RUTH C		1977	1899		REUBEN
446	XXX	MITTLEMAN, SADIE		1985	1897		BENJAMIN
329	A32	MITZEN, ANNA		20 NOV 1969	1894		
119	K54	MOGEL, BEN		31 AUG 1975	1897		
119	K55	MOGEL, IDA		28 SEP 1990			
392	E17	MOGELEFSKY, SADIE	LEVINE	18 FEB 1987	20 MAY 1904	JACOB & ANNA	
392	F18	MOGOLESKY, MORRIS		21 APR 1932	1860	ARYEH DOV	
125	G120	MOHILL, BERNARD		7 OCT 1957	1896		
125	H120	MOHILL, DORA	TOBIAS	30 AUG 1970	1888		LOUIS
125	H121	MOHILL, LOUIS		26 APR 1951	1888		DORA
125	I108	MOHILL, MARTHA		7 MAY 1930	1857	MORRIS	REUBEN
125	I109	MOHILL, REUBEN		13 SEP 1932	1858		MARTHA
376	D30	MOHIN, MAX		17 JUN 1961		ABRAHAM	
377	W24	MOHLMAN, WILLIAM		1 MAR 1991	12 FEB 1919	KALMAN	
112	D38	MOIDEL, ABRAHAM M		8 APR 1981	4 AUG 1904		ANNA
112	D39	MOIDEL, ANNA		30 MAR 1984	18 OCT 1905		ABRAHAM
102	AC180	MOIGER, WILLIAM		1 JUL 1968	1917		
102	W57	MOLANS, EDWARD H		7 FEB 1949	1881		REBECCA
102	L43	MOLANS, PAULINE HOFFMAN	SHAFER	7 OCT 1977	28 MAR 1896		ALEXANDER
102	W58	MOLANS, REBECCA		26 MAY 1943	1884		EDWARD
116	BJ 4	MOLIN, HARRY D		2 MAY 1990	3 DEC 1906		LILLIAN
116	BJ 3	MOLIN, LILLIAN		19 JAN 1969	25 APR 1907		HARRY
391	GL 1	MOLLOVE, MORRIS		2 MAR 1949	1892	MICHAEL NOAH	
392	F39	MOLTZ, CLARA		25 MAR 1981	25 MAR 1883	AARON DAVID	
391	GK 1	MOLTZ, HARRY		26 MAR 1959	1892	SAMUEL	
104	G28	MONASTERSKY, DAVID H		1 MAY 1967	1899		
374	K31	MONDSCHEIN, ARON		17 FEB 1985	2 JAN 1922		
102	H54	MONDSHEIN, HAROLD M		13 FEB 1984			
371	AH 3	MOONEY, HYMAN E		19 ADR 1963	1880		LILLIAN
371	AI 2	MOONEY, LILLIAN F		11 JUN 1975	1889		HYMAN
125	O142	MOORE, LOUIS		14 MAY 1967	1885		
125	D 58	MOORE, SUSAN ERICA		15 MAY 1969			
125	O141	MOORE, YETTA		20 NOV 1948	18 SEP 1885		LOUIS
370	O63	MOPSIK, ALLEN		NDD			

Cem	Row	Name	Maiden Name	DOD	DOB	Parents	Spouse
370	M70	MOPSIK, JEROME DR		1959	1918		
125	P143	MORANS, ETTA		30 MAY 1947	1869	MOSHE CHAIM	
125	H100	MORANS, ETTA		5 FEB 1936	13 NOV 1872		HENRY
125	H101	MORANS, HENRY		17 MAR 1932	24 JUN 1872		ETTA
125	G100	MORANS, HERBERT E		9 NOV 1976	23 OCT 1904		
125		MORANS, L		2 FEB 1935	1899	HENRY & ETTA (GORE)	
102	BD 4	MOREL, CHARLES		2 MAY 1988	15 SEP 1896		FARROKH
102	BD 3	MOREL, FARROKH	PARI	4 OCT 1990	9 OCT 1916		CHARLES
751	E15	MORGANSTEIN, CAROL LYNN		7 APR 1962	22 AUG 1955	JOANNE	
751	E16	MORGANSTEIN, JOANNE H		1 NOV 1958	13 MAR 1929		
751	E17	MORGANSTEIN, RICHARD S		31 AUG 1953	18 APR 1953	JOANNE	
329	C 5	MORGENSTEIN, BELLA		27 MAY 1987	20 JUL 1902		
116	S24	MORI, RACHEL	BEHAR	24 DEC 1980	13 DEC 1930		
125	M151	MORRIS, ALFRED		18 OCT 1984			
373	A 3	MORRIS, CLARA YOSELEVSKY	MILLER	25 MAY 1990	26 NOV 1908		DAVID
373	A 4	MORRIS, DAVID		18 OCT 1989	3 SEP 1909		CLARA
377	S 8	MORRIS, MARION	KRAMER	7 FEB 1968	18 JUL 1900		NATHAN
377	S 7	MORRIS, NATHAN		6 DEC 1948	1 JAN 1886		MARION
330	AI11	MORSE, MICHAEL DAVID		24 SEP 1976	31 MAR 1952		
329	D30	MORSON, LESLIE		17 DEC 1968	2 MAR 1909		
104	N41	MOSCOV, NATHAN		4 JAN 1968	26 OCT 1900		
374	A20	MOSCOWITZ, LACY		1 AUG 1922	1909		
102	AH91	MOSCOWITZ, LEAH		13 AUG 1954			
222	H 1	MOSES, ADRIENNE G		26 NOV 1986	27 MAR 1927	HERMAN & LILLIAN	
127	C	MOSES, BARNEY B		10 MAY 1974	10 MAY 1901		GRETA
222	AN 5	MOSES, DAVID		28 APR 1931	1860		REBECCA
222	H 6	MOSES, ELI MORRIS		23 SEP 1956	14 OCT 1887	DAVID & REBECCA (MENDELSON)	IDA
127	C	MOSES, GRETA	WESTERFIELD	19 OCT 1991	25 OCT 1923	LILLY LEHMAN	BARNEY
222	H 2	MOSES, HERMAN A		15 DEC 1981	4 APR 1892	DAVID & REBECCA (MENDELSON)	HERMAN
222	H 5	MOSES, IDA ROSE	LUBLIN	19 SEP 1989	23 SEP 1888		ELI
222	G 3	MOSES, IRENE B		8 MAY 1985	27 MAR 1902		SAMUEL
222	G 5	MOSES, KATHRYN	SHAREFF	4 APR 1966	30 MAY 1900		MAXWELL
222	H 3	MOSES, LILLIAN		15 DEC 1981	4 APR 1892		LILLIAN
222	AO 4	MOSES, MAE S		25 OCT 1982	22 JAN 1913		NATHAN
222	G 4	MOSES, MAXWELL		30 AUG 1978	4 MAR 1896	DAVID & REBECCA (MENDELSON)	KATHRYN
222	G 1	MOSES, MAY R		1982	1933	SAMUEL & IRENE	
222	AO 3	MOSES, NATHAN		23 AUG 1985	15 JAN 1905	DAVID & REBECCA (MENDELSON)	MAE
222	AN 6	MOSES, REBECCA	MENDELSON	14 DEC 1941	1860		DAVID
222	G 2	MOSES, SAMUEL H		30 NOV 1989	7 JAN 1897	DAVID & REBECCA (MENDELSON)	IRENE
222	AN 7	MOSES, SARAH		18 JUN 1989	1903	DAVID & REBECCA (MENDELSON)	
102	AJ40	MOSESSON, HATTIE		12 JAN 1957	1887		SOLOMON
102	AJ39	MOSESSON, SOLOMON		30 NOV 1951	1888		HATTIE
110	D14	MOSHINSKY, ESTHER	SONN	30 JUN 1969	1888		
371	AG23	MOSKOWITZ, ALBERT		26 JUL 1982	25 DEC 1898		FANNIE
370	V29	MOSKOWITZ, ANNE R		1992	1899		MAX
371	AG24	MOSKOWITZ, FANNIE		23 OCT 1970	25 MAY 1898		ALBERT
248	B48	MOSKOWITZ, IRA		23 MAR 1944	20 MAR 1944		
370	I59	MOSKOWITZ, ISAAC		1943	1863		SARAH
331		MOSKOWITZ, JOE		27 JUN 1913			
371	AD11	MOSKOWITZ, JULIUS		1 MAR 1976	1910		LUBA
328	A31	MOSKOWITZ, LILLIAN		7 JUN 1970	25 JUL 1900		
370	V28	MOSKOWITZ, MAX E		1960	1900		ANNE
222	B 1	MOSKOWITZ, REBECCA SUGARMAN	SPITELNIK	25 JUL 1974	18 JUL 1893		MORRIS
248	B47	MOSKOWITZ, ROBIN C		8 APR 1973	5 APR 1973		
370	I58	MOSKOWITZ, SARAH		9 JUN 1933	1875		ISAAC
114	F16	MOSKOWITZ, STANLEY		30 OCT 1988	14 MAR 1930		
113	N23	MOSLER, FLORENCE BLANCHE		2 SEP 1983			SIDNEY
113	N22	MOSLER, SIDNEY		28 MAY 1954			FLORENCE
113	J52	MOSLER, STUART C		29 APR 1978	31 OCT 1935		
125	O179	MOSS, ALFRED		28 AUG 1964	1902		HILDA
447	Z 2	MOSS, ANN R		1993	1913		
119	A16	MOSS, EVELYN S		18 JAN 1988	12 OCT 1909		
125	O178	MOSS, HILDA	OSTFELD	24 MAR 1983	1912		ALFRED
751	K14	MOSS, JOSEPH		3 APR 1934	1866		MILLIE
447	Z 4	MOSS, LEWIS STEVEN		17 SEP 1981	8 NOV 1939		
751	K15	MOSS, MILLIE		10 AUG 1945	1862		JOSEPH

Cem	Row	Name	Maiden Name	DOD	DOB	Parents	Spouse
119	A17	MOSS, NEWTON		17 NOV 1980	11 AUG 1909		
751	J16	MOSS, PINKUS		31 AUG 1983	20 JAN 1888		
391	ZF51	MOSS, SAMUEL W		17 NOV 1987	9 NOV 1907	ABRAHAM	
102	AH80	MOTT, JOSEPH P		16 DEC 1987	19 MAY 1907		
370	L24	MOYEL, BEN ZION		4 FEB 1945	1881		KALIE
370	A11	MOYEL, BENJAMIN TZVI		14 OCT 1950			MIRIAM
370	L25	MOYEL, KALIE TOBIE		6 MAR 1969	1883		BEN ZION
370	D 8	MOYEL, MAX		22 JUN 1959	1901		
370	A12	MOYEL, MIRIAM LEAH		28 JUL 1964			BENJAMIN
377	Z36	MOYEL, ROBERT B		3 FEB 1979	22 DEC 1929	MORDECHAI JONAH	
101	C28	MUGERMAN, ISADORE		30 JUN 1922	1864		
330	E25	MULLER, IGNATZ		26 MAY 1934	1858		JENNIE
330	E26	MULLER, JENNIE		NDD	NBD		IGNATZ
330	F52	MULLINDORF, DAVID		10 AUG 1929	1858		FANNIE
330	G67	MULLINDORF, FANNIE		25 NOV 1943	1867		DAVID
330	C10	MULSTEIN, GUSSIE		26 SEP 1934	1854		
115	E40	MUNCH, RUTH	BAMBERGER	17 MAR 1991	23 JAN 1908		
112	C42	MUNIC, ABE		25 AUG 1987	5 MAY 1915		
370	I23	MUNTER, SARA HINDA		24 SEP 1926			
370	Z15	MUSKIN, JOSEPH		3 SEP 1950	20 MAY 1903		
125	E24	MUSMAN, MOINIS		14 MAR 1929	AUG 1928	LEWIS	
125	M168	MUSSMAN, LENA		25 JAN 1953	1899		LOUIS
125	M167	MUSSMAN, LOUIS		10 OCT 1968	1893		LENA
107	H26	MYER, HERMAN H		1979	1905		WILMA
107	H25	MYER, WILMA		2 SEP 1990	30 NOV 1906		HERMAN
222	AN12	MYEROWITZ, CALMAN		4 SEP 1987	7 MAY 1907	JOSEPH & FEIGA	
222	AN13	MYEROWITZ, FEIGA RIVKA		27 MAY 1969	1871		JOSEPH
222	AN14	MYEROWITZ, JOSEPH		16 MAY 1957	1876		FEIGA
125	V194	MYEROWITZ, REBECCA	GOLDBERG	13 APR 1979	18 DEC 1904		
494	XXX	MYERS, EDGAR		1981	1893		SENA
372	D 6	MYERS, SADIE	MACHOL	1962	1890	ISADORE	
494	XXX	MYERS, SENA K		1981	1891		EDGAR
125	I 52	MYERSON, CHASHA		16 DEC 1945	1872	HIRSH & CHANA	RALPH
125	R178	MYERSON, JOSEPH L		22 JUL 1959	21 JAN 1906		SARAH
125	L110	MYERSON, MYER		23 AUG 1929	20 NOV 1902	RALPH & SARAH	
114	F 1	MYERSON, MYRON		21 NOV 1991	14 JUL 1939		
105	D28	MYERSON, NATHAN, M		28 OCT 1964	1898		THELMA
125	I 53	MYERSON, RALPH		2 MAR 1908	APR 1868		CHASHA
125	R177	MYERSON, SARAH	RODENSKY	28 DEC 1977	18 MAY 1909		JOSEPH
105	D27	MYERSON, THELMA	TONKEN	7 APR 1972	1908		NATHAN
330	G48	NADEL, SARAH		21 JUN 1923	1885		
374	G 2	NADLER, (BABY GIRL)			1915	BAREF	
101	C 7	NADLER, FANNIE		15 JAN 1960	1882		WILLIAM
119	A12	NADLER, JACOB		19 APR 1992			
493	A 6	NADLER, MICHAEL ARON		15 JUL 1982	13 JUL 1982		
101	C 6	NADLER, WILLIAM		18 APR 1952	1883		FANNIE
391	U54	NAGDYMAN, BERTHA G		24 JUN 1982	1889	MOSHE	LOUIS
391	U53	NAGDYMAN, LOUIS		5 JUN 1949	1891	JOSHUA	BERTHA
102	AJ236	NAHUM, DORA	MITNICK	6 OCT 1980	25 APR 1904		MILTON
102	AJ235	NAHUM, MILTON		18 NOV 1980	19 MAY 1901	SAMUEL & TILLIE (KOSCHER)	DORA
125	W198	NAIER, IDA	HERMAN	28 NOV 1980	1906		JACK
125	A 51	NAIER, JACK		12 JAN 1957	9 APR 1898	CHAIM & JULIA (SILVERSTEIN)	IDA
125		NAIR, (BABY BOY)		1 APR 1961	1 APR 1961		
125	E125	NAIR, (BABY GIRL)		7 FEB 1954	6 JAN 1954		
125	E134	NAIR, (STILLBORN)		18 SEP 1952	1952		
125		NAIR, DAVID ALON		23 NOV 1962	25 OCT 1962	MONROE & RUBY (FIELDING)	
125	F106	NAIR, DAVID L		7 APR 1950	1897		DORA
125	F105	NAIR, DORA	ROKAU	23 NOV 1950	1897		DAVID
102	AJ53	NAIR, ESTHER	CRAVZOW	7 DEC 1942	1 JUL 1900		LOUIS
125	F103	NAIR, FRANK		30 MAY 1966	1876		SOPHIE
125	I133	NAIR, LOUIS		16 JUN 1941	1867		REBECCA
125	A 52	NAIR, LOUIS J		4 MAY 1979	25 NOV 1895	CHAIM & JULIA (SILVERSTEIN)	EVELYN
102	AJ54	NAIR, LOUIS L MD		22 JUN 1982	7 AUG 1898		ESTHER
125	I132	NAIR, REBECCA		17 JAN 1940	1875		LOUIS
125	F102	NAIR, SOPHIE	ADLER	8 MAR 1953	1883		FRANK
125	G 36	NAPHTOLIN, ABRAHAM		26 NOV 1955	1876		

Cem	Row	Name	Maiden Name	DOD	DOB	Parents	Spouse
249	C15	NASH, ISIDOR DR		6 SEP 1974	10 MAY 1895		
102	A15	NASHNER, DORA M		4 JAN 1982	1889		LOUIS
102	AD197	NASHNER, FLORENCE		20 FEB 1971			MAX
102	A14	NASHNER, LOUIS S		12 NOV 1932	1888		DORA
102	AD196	NASHNER, MAX		11 NOV 1985		SIDNEY & ANNA (ROSENTHAL)	FLORENCE
102	AJ106	NASHNER, SYDNEY		15 AUG 1955	1912	SAMUEL & YETTA (GILLS)	
102	CB23	NASSAU, FLORA D		9 FEB 1990	9 FEB 1906		ISAAC
102	CB26	NASSAU, ISAAC		24 MAR 1981	29 JUN 1899		FLORA
115	F50	NASSAU, MARLENE E		30 OCT 1991	25 APR 1936		
391	G46	NASSER, BECKY BAHIA		20 APR 1962	1892	SHLOMO	
391	ZE51	NASSER, BESSIE		25 APR 1979	1901	JOSEPH	NATHAN
391	ZG50	NASSER, MAURICE		5 NOV 1990	8 OCT 1919	NATAN NATTA	
391	ZE50	NASSER, NATHAN		7 SEP 1964	1895	SHLOMO	BESSIE
391	ZE52	NASSER, PAULINE		23 NOV 1965	1890	SHLOMO	SAM
391	G41	NASSER, RACHEL NIZHA		6 FEB 1938			
391	ZE53	NASSER, SAM		28 DEC 1977		NATHAN NATTA	PAULINE
447	AA 7	NASTIR, MARLA KAREN		1 MAR 1975	5 OCT 1957		
107	A14	NATAF, PAULINE		9 DEC 1987	14 JUL 1901		PERLINE
107	A15	NATAF, PERLINE		1 AUG 1987	1 JAN 1914		PAULINE
123		NATHAN, LEO ELIAS		2 FEB 1952	1914		
114	O18	NATTER, ARTHUR		27 MAY 1983	29 MAY 1929		
494	XXX	NATTER, NOAH		1980	1915		
121	T12	NAVIASKY, JULIA	GALINSKY	8 APR 1962	4 OCT 1920		
371	AM19	NAVICK, JACOB		25 AUG 1988	1909	LOUIS & REBECCA	
371	AM20	NAVICK, LOUIS		3 OCT 1971	1884		REBECCA
371	AM21	NAVICK, REBECCA IDA		24 NOV 1964	1885		LOUIS
121	P 8	NEEDELMAN, SIDNEY		1957	1920		
447	R28	NEEDLE, MAX B		8 MAR 1955	1892		SADIE
447	R29	NEEDLE, SADIE		15 OCT 1980	1895		MAX
751	K30	NEEDLES, ISAAC S		3 OCT 1929	1845		
751	D24	NEEDLES, JACOB J		1961	1883		
751	B36	NEEDLES, YETTA		8 FEB 1919	1852		
116	AW 4	NEIDITCH, DIANE	STICKLOR	20 JUN 1990	17 MAR 1928		SEYMOUR
102	AB80	NEIDITCH, DOROTHY	SIEGEL	5 DEC 1970	1896		ISRAEL
102	AB79	NEIDITCH, GOLDIE	GLOTZER	10 AUG 1953	1862		
102	AB81	NEIDITCH, ISRAEL S		30 APR 1968	1893	GOLDIE	DOROTHY
102	AB78	NEIDITCH, MELVIN		1933	1921	ISRAEL & DOROTHY	
116	AW 3	NEIDITCH, SEYMOUR "TIM"		19 MAR 1986	25 SEP 1924		DIANE
102	AG36	NEIDITZ, DAVID H		28 DEC 1981	18 NOV 1930	MOSES & RACHEL	
102	AG34	NEIDITZ, MOSES J		1 AUG 1985	2 JUN 1899		RACHEL
102	AG35	NEIDITZ, RACHEL P		15 MAY 1983	12 JUL 1903		MOSES
102	AG32	NEIDITZ, RAYMOND J		15 JAN 1982	16 DEC 1895		
102	L52	NEIDITZ, SAMUEL J		3 FEB 1990	7 FEB 1897		TILLIE
102	L51	NEIDITZ, TILLIE		23 DEC 1990	16 MAR 1903		SAMUEL
330	AC 9	NEIDLE, ABRAHAM I DR		28 AUG 1989	28 MAY 1908		SALLIE
330	B15	NEIDLE, MARY		12 MAR 1962	1876		MORRIS
330	AD 9	NEIDLE, MAX		19 JUN 1987	11 OCT 1910		RITA
330	H33	NEIDLE, MAX		28 OCT 1948			
330	B14	NEIDLE, MORRIS		8 FEB 1944	1875		MARY
330	AD10	NEIDLE, RITA		20 NOV 1989	15 NOV 1909		MAX
330	AC10	NEIDLE, SALLIE C		10 AUG 1986	28 FEB 1907		ABRAHAM
103	A11	NEIKRIE, BERNARD		11 OCT 1981	27 FEB 1902		SYLVIA
102	BF33	NEIKRIE, M JOSEPH		4 JUL 1987	23 JUN 1928		
103	A12	NEIKRIE, SYLVIA		12 MAR 1985	25 MAR 1902		BERNARD
370	S22	NEIMAN, ABRAHAM		14 MAR 1946			FANNY
370	I 3	NEIMAN, ESTHER		31 MAR 1924			
370	S23	NEIMAN, FANNY ROSE		11 OCT 1953			ABRAHAM
493	C20	NEIMAN, HAROLD		26 NOV 1979	24 OCT 1919	TOV	
125	M 33	NEISTAT, ANNIE C		27 SEP 1901			
125	L 38	NEISTAT, ANNIE G		6 MAY 1903	27 SEP 1891		
392	I46	NEISTAT, BENJAMIN S		1964	1879	ABRAHAM	SARAH
105	C50	NEISTAT, BERNICE	POST	16 AUG 1958	4 JUN 1910		
125	N125	NEISTAT, FRANCES		5 JAN 1972	1902		RALPH
125		NEISTAT, JULIUS		7 FEB 1916	1914	MORRIS	
125	J 40	NEISTAT, LIZZIE		16 SEP 1906	3 MAR 1879		
125	R158	NEISTAT, MORRIS		19 MAR 1943	1871		

Cem	Row	Name	Maiden Name	DOD	DOB	Parents	Spouse
125	N126	NEISTAT, RALPH		30 DEC 1991			FRANCES
392	I45	NEISTAT, SARAH		1959	1887	LEV	BENJAMIN
330	A14	NELEBER, ANNA		24 OCT 1968	3 MAR 1899		BENJAMIN
330	A16	NELEBER, AUGUSTA L		31 JAN 1969	12 JUN 1893		HARRY
330	A13	NELEBER, BENJAMIN NATHANIEL		25 MAR 1960	29 MAR 1892		ANNA
330	A15	NELEBER, HARRY		10 AUG 1979	28 FEB 1889		AUGUSTA
330	A18	NELEBER, LOUIS		18 JAN 1982	28 JUN 1895		
330	F23	NELEBER, REBECCA		22 DEC 1945	1863		SIMON
330	F22	NELEBER, SIMON		10 MAY 1905	1862		REBECCA
751	M20	NELKEN, BELLA S		22 AUG 1960			
751	M21	NELKEN, JULIUS		6 JUN 1968			
330	F40	NELKIN, FRANK		16 SEP 1921	1849		
330	E38	NELKIN, FREDA		9 JUL 1930	1858		
370	D 7	NELKIN, JACOB		15 FEB 1936			KALA
370	K 8	NELKIN, KALA		20 OCT 1948			JACOB
371	O18	NELKIN, LOUIS		26 JAN 1971	22 MAR 1886		MARY
371	O17	NELKIN, MARY		2 MAR 1982	8 MAY 1884		LOUIS
330	F33	NELKIN, MAX		13 APR 1915	1881		
370	O52	NELKIN, SAMUEL DAVID		26 APR 1990	22 MAR 1908	JACOB & KALA	
371	O19	NELKIN, SAUL A		17 DEC 1972	4 NOV 1918	LOUIS & MARY	
105	D11	NEMEROFF, CHARLES		20 SEP 1946	1889		
105	A14	NEMEROFF, JACOB		25 NOV 1970	1891		SARAH
105	A15	NEMEROFF, SARAH		27 SEP 1980	1897		JACOB
125		NEMIROW, LILLIAN		15 MAR 1919	1896		
222	AI11	NEMSER, CHARLES		24 MAR 1978	1 NOV 1900		
125		NERENBERG, (BABY GIRL)		10 SEP 1954	9 SEP 1954		
125	E138	NERENBERG, (BABY GIRL)		30 AUG 1955	29 AUG 1955		
116	BX34	NESTOR, GERTRUDE	STAYMAN	25 NOV 1957	16 MAR 1892		LOUIS
116	BX37	NESTOR, JOSEPH		24 SEP 1983	16 NOV 1916	LOUIS & GERTRUDE	
116	BX35	NESTOR, LOUIS		16 JAN 1969	15 MAR 1893		GERTRUDE
125	E119	NETUPSKY, HERMAN		21 SEP 1934	15 FEB 1930	HARRY	
104	H20	NEUFIELD, RACHEL		11 JUN 1977	1928		
112	D42	NEUHAUS, ROSE		31 DEC 1983	12 JUL 1892		
446	XXX	NEUMAN, ANNE	KURITZKES	1954	1904		SIGMUND
377	R44	NEUMAN, LEON		7 OCT 1989	11 OCT 1909		
446	XXX	NEUMAN, SIGMUND		1962	1904		ANNE
377	R45	NEUMAN, WIFE OF LEON					LEON
102	A16	NEVILLE, JAMES A		1932	1912		
447	I27	NEWBERG, ANNETTE	GOLD	13 SEP 1950	19 JAN 1915		MENDEL
447	I23	NEWBERG, EVA	LESSER	18 AUG 1971	17 APR 1885		MAX
447	U 6	NEWBERG, FERNE				ELIMELECH	
447	U 4	NEWBERG, HERTZEL		9 JUN 1989	1918	ELIMELECH	
447	I24	NEWBERG, IVON C		24 SEP 1975	1907	MAX & EVA	
447	U 5	NEWBERG, MAURICE S				ELIMELECH	
447	I22	NEWBERG, MAX		20 NOV 1941	4 MAR 1882		EVA
447	I26	NEWBERG, MENDEL		13 FEB 1976	1909	MAX & EVA	ANNETTE
222	AF 1	NEWBURGER, HANNA	LAVITT	17 NOV 1989	25 DEC 1914		
447	B24	NEWFIELD, JOSEPH		1962	1870		
125	2C52	NEWMAN, (CHILD)		7 APR 1919	1919		
102	AA 5	NEWMAN, ABRAHAM		10 JUL 1934	1898		
371	K27	NEWMAN, BENJAMIN		1972	1890		KATE
751	A22	NEWMAN, EDNA A		1990	1917		
125	C131	NEWMAN, HARRY		19 MAR 1983	1888		JENNIE
125	C132	NEWMAN, JENNIE DOROTHY		8 NOV 1991	1898		HARRY
371	K28	NEWMAN, KATE	GOLD	1963	1894		BENJAMIN
125	O 89	NEWMAN, MALKA		12 MAY 1919	MAR 1881	BARUCH & PEARL	
391	ZA77	NEWMAN, WILLIAM		6 JAN 1982	20 JAN 1903	SHIMON	
127	I	NICHOLAS, AARON CHARLES		1 JAN 1978	8 FEB 1977		
103	C5	NIDRIGER, JACK J		9 DEC 1989	1 OCT 1914		EDITH
328	B14	NIDZON, JACK		4 OCT 1985	1904		
371	J17	NIEDERMAN, EDWARD		6 DEC 1972	6 DEC 1891		
371	J16	NIEDERMAN, MIRIAM RUTH		4 MAR 1982	12 OCT 1912	EDWARD	
751	A 3	NIMAN, A B		196-			
751	J12	NIMAN, ANNA YETTA		20 OCT 1941	1871		
751	M 1	NIMAN, LENA	GORDON	1965	1900		
751	N 1	NIMAN, SAMUEL		1 NOV 1959			

Cem	Row	Name	Maiden Name	DOD	DOB	Parents	Spouse
121	W 8	NIRENSTEIN, (BABY BOY)		5 JUN 1970	4 JUN 1970		
105	J26	NIRENSTEIN, BEATRICE N		30 JAN 1949	1900		SAMUEL
116	N 8	NIRENSTEIN, J BERNARD		16 FEB 1992	27 DEC 1919		RITA
103	C8	NIRENSTEIN, PHILIP		24 JAN 1982	1913		
116	N 7	NIRENSTEIN, RITA	COHEN	13 SEP 1985	3 DEC 1921		J BERNARD
105	J27	NIRENSTEIN, SAMUEL L		10 JAN 1988	1893		BEATRICE
108	A15	NISOFF, CHARLES		12 FEB 1982	8 JAN 1930		MYRNA
108	A16	NISOFF, MYRNA	BURKE	5 SEP 1979	17 SEP 1934		CHARLES
125	E16	NISSANSON, FANNIE		19 SEP 1928	MAY 1928	WOOLF & BARCHA	
391	Q37	NISSENBERG, HELENE		20 APR 1916	1844		HERMAN
391	L29	NISSENSON, HERMAN		15 MAR 1900	22 NOV 1851		
751	H18	NITKIN, ABRAHAM		1940	1880		BERTHA
751	H17	NITKIN, BERTHA	DANZIGER	1954	1880		ABRAHAM
102	C10	NITKIN, GERTRUDE CATHERINE		11 AUG 1969			
751	I18	NITKIN, MILTON		1963	1905		
117	E10	NIXON, TRACEY		28 JAN 1991	16 MAR 1979		
392	J12	NODELMAN, ISAAC		22 SEP 1992	1909	MOSHE	
123		NOLL, CECILE	DIWINSKY	7 JAN 1965	1900		NATHAN
125	M188	NOLL, FANNIE	ZUCKER	22 JUL 1969			SAMUEL
102	U16	NOLL, HARRIS		25 FEB 1941	1872		IDA
102	U17	NOLL, IDA	EPSTEIN	27 MAR 1959	1871		HARRIS
102	AC154	NOLL, JACOB		17 OCT 1984	16 JAN 1902		
123		NOLL, NATHAN		8 OCT 1951	1896		CECILE
125	M189	NOLL, SAMUEL I		23 FEB 1980	1906		FANNY
370	I67	NORDEN, HANS E		8 OCT 1948	25 NOV 1884		
372	K13	NORDHEIMER, CLAIRE	HERTZ	29 APR 1978	23 JUN 1877		
377	Q46	NORMAN, FRANCIS	SHARAF	23 JUL 1985	24 OCT 1912		
370	B20	NORWICH, N	GOLDBERG	20 FEB 1915			
330	B 5	NORWITZ, JOSEPH		26 DEC 1935	1863		REBECCA
330	B 6	NORWITZ, REBECCA		25 OCT 1942	1867		JOSEPH
102	J56	NORWITZ, ROSE P		15 SEP 1977	29 JAN 1891		REUBEN
102	J57	NORWITZ, RUBIN		30 SEP 1964	12 AUG 1886		ROSE
116	AW 8	NORWITZ, SIDNEY S		20 OCT 1965	10 JUL 1921		
330	AI18	NOVA, IRVING		5 OCT 1991	15 JAN 1902		
105	E12	NOVACK, SAMUEL		14 JUL 1944	1893		
125	O180	NOVECK, CHARLES		22 DEC 1964	1908		
106	C13	NOVECK, NATHAN		24 NOV 1984	25 APR 1892		
125	C136	NOVICK, BELLA		21 AUG 1969	1 JAN 1885		
102	AG48	NOVICK, FRANK		14 DEC 1990	3 JUN 1900	SARAH	BELLA
102	AG45	NOVICK, HARRY		19 JAN 1957	3 SEP 1902	SARAH	
125	C135	NOVICK, ISADORE		18 SEP 1964	1 MAY 1879		ISADORE
125	C137	NOVICK, JOSEPH		20 NOV 1986	10 JAN 1907	ISADORE & BELLA	
116	U19	NOVICK, JOSEPH H		23 APR 1977	15 AUG 1908		
376	B 8	NOVICK, MEYER L		22 JUL 1928	1899		
102	AG49	NOVICK, SARAH	KRASNITSKY	28 JAN 1939	22 DEC 1879		
102	AG50	NOVICK, STUART I		25 APR 1948	18 JAN 1927		
113	I75	NOVIN, MURRAY H		7 MAR 1990	28 JUN 1902		
391	M36	NOVITCH, ASHER	WEINGER	8 JUL 1971	25 JUN 1894	MOSHE MORDECHAI	SADIE
391	L39	NOVITCH, DINAH B		9 NOV 1953	1873	AARON YESHAYHU	MORRIS
391	L38	NOVITCH, MORRIS M		6 JAN 1954	1873	JOEL	DINAH
391	M35	NOVITCH, SADIE AZIA		12 MAY 1986	10 JUL 1907	ABRAHAM	ASHER
127	A	NOVOGRAD, HENRY		13 JUN 1985	21 NOV 1920		
370	Q 9	NOWICK, DAVID		2 MAY 1946	1878		KATE
370	Q10	NOWICK, KATE		19 MAR 1971	1885		DAVID
370	Q11	NOWICK, SIDNEY		1976	1919	DAVID & KATE	
102	A59	NOZETTE, ANNA	ROSENFELD	6 NOV 1940	16 JAN 1888		
101	J13	NUESSLE, AUGUSTA		10 FEB 1919	1891		
112	D28	NUSSBAUM, BERTHA	STERN	23 JAN 1978	24 MAR 1910		
125	O158	NUSSBAUM, FRANZISKA	COHEN	13 JUN 1949	25 JAN 1885	JOSEPH	
222	J 8	NUSSDORF, JACOB		1972	1880		YETTA
222	J 9	NUSSDORF, YETTA		1964	1884		JACOB
222	M 7	OBER, DOROTHY	HOMELSON	24 APR 1991	6 OCT 1910		
222	M 6	OBER, MICHAEL DAVID		19 JUN 1968	4 AUG 1944	DOROTHY	
750	J28	OBERSTEIN, RALPH		7 MAY 1964	4 JUN 1899		SONIA
750	J27	OBERSTEIN, SONIA		11 JAN 1968	28 OCT 1899		RALPH
391	K34	OCKOONEFF, ANNETTE J		1907	1806	SOL & FRANCES	

Cem	Row	Name	Maiden Name	DOD	DOB	Parents	Spouse
391	F12	OCKOONEFF, SOLOMON		27 MAY 1932	11 NOV 1871	NAPHTALI	
101	A 9	OFENGAND, PEARL		14 OCT 1940	1856		
102	W51	OFSHE, ANNA H		1929	1857		
248	J66	OGGINS, SIMON M		25 DEC 1914	1858		
376	B15	OGULNICK, JOHN		2 JAN 1962			SIFCAH
376	B17	OGULNICK, SIFCALAH		17 APR 1943			JOHN
101	L 2	OGUSHEWITZ, ANNA BELLA		11 JAN 1984	1902		
249	K 5	OGUSHEWITZ, BENJAMIN		5 APR 1952	1868		JULIA
101	L 1	OGUSHEWITZ, HARRY		9 MAR 1966	1900		
249	M 6	OGUSHEWITZ, JACK		1981	1898		
249	A 6	OGUSHEWITZ, JOSEPH T		10 DEC 1988	30 JUL 1908		
249	K 4	OGUSHEWITZ, JULIA	PLOWSKY	8 APR 1949	1870		BEMJAMIN
101	K39	OHLBAUM, MICHAEL D		7 APR 1961	1958		
101	D 5	OKEN, SIMON G		19 APR 1991	8 AUG 1910		
446	C72	OKOROFSKY, GERALD SANFORD		1921	1921		
101	I38	OKRANT, (BABY)		12 FEB 1991			
391	Z61	OKRANT, ETHEL		7 DEC 1982	1910	BEREL	REUBEN
102	Y199	OKRANT, GERALD		15 OCT 1992			
391	J42	OKRANT, IDA		23 JUN 1942	1876	ELCHANA	MORRIS
391	J43	OKRANT, MORRIS		30 JAN 1955	1873	JACOB	IDA
391	Z60	OKRANT, REUBEN		26 JUN 1967	1903	MOSHE	ETHEL
370	A28	OK___ED, JOSEPH MARK					
376	B24	OLSTEIN, IDA S		11 FEB 1941	1876	MOSHE	JOSEPH
376	B25	OLSTEIN, JOSEPH		21 FEB 1941	1873	SAMUEL	IDA
125	G 64	OPALINSKY, ESTHER	APPELL	6 FEB 1967	1897		LOUIS
125	G 65	OPALINSKY, LOUIS HENRY		17 NOV 1969	1896		ESTHER
377	K26	OPOTOWKSY, BETTY		28 AUG 1952	20 JUN 1882	NATHAN	
377	T23	OPOTOWSKY, REA		13 NOV 1987	5 JUN 1910	GIDALYA	RUBIN
377	T22	OPOTOWSKY, RUBIN		12 JUN 1973	19 AUG 1907	SAMUEL	REA
112	D34	OPPENHEIMER, ARTHUR		30 NOV 1980	4 MAR 1897		GERTA
112	D35	OPPENHEIMER, GERTA	WOLF	14 FEB 1986	27 JUN 1903		ARTHUR
112	C43	OPPENHEIMER, JEANNE S		2 MAR 1991	11 APR 1929		MARTIN
372	B 5	OPPENHEIMER, KURT MD		1976	1897		
105	D 9	OPPENHEIMER, MANNIS		24 JUL 1981	3 AUG 1903		
112	C44	OPPENHEIMER, MARTIN G		27 MAR 1988	28 OCT 1927		JEANNE
373	J 7	OPPENHIEMER, HEDWIG		5 JUN 1978	2 JAN 1888		
125	B140	ORBACH, EDITH JULIANE		3 SEP 1972	12 MAY 1898		EGMONT
125	B141	ORBACH, EGMONT JULIUS		22 MAY 1990	19 JAN 1900		EDITH
328	A16	ORBUCH, NANCY		2 AUG 1974	1952		
391	G25	ORDANSKY, BIRDIE		23 JAN 1912	1892	ELCHANA	
330	D19	ORELOWITZ, FRIEDA		9 FEB 1949			MENDEL
330	H45	ORELOWITZ, JOSEPH AARON		17 JAN 1941	1905		
330	D18	ORELOWITZ, MENDEL		17 MAY 1946			FRIEDA
374	B35	ORENSTEIN, ABRAHAM		24 APR 1980	10 JUL 1903		RUTH
371	J 6	ORENSTEIN, BEN		24 JUL 1973	14 MAY 1904		FANNY
373	G 1	ORENSTEIN, DOROTHY		16 NOV 1960	5 MAR 1900		
330	E44	ORENSTEIN, ESTHER PEARL		8 FEB 1939	1877		
374	A44	ORENSTEIN, FANNIE		5 NOV 1959	1894		PHILIP
371	J 5	ORENSTEIN, FANNY		15 APR 1993	15 AUG 1902		BEN
329	B28	ORENSTEIN, HARRY		9 MAY 1946	1867		
123		ORENSTEIN, JOHN J		13 JAN 1963	1898		
102	AD193	ORENSTEIN, LOUIS		8 DEC 1964	2 OCT 1896		
121	C31	ORENSTEIN, MILTON J		16 DEC 1989	1916		
374	A43	ORENSTEIN, PHILIP		4 JAN 1956	15 APR 1895		FANNIE
374	B34	ORENSTEIN, RUTH		6 DEC 1991	10 JUN 1904		ABRAHAM
373	G 2	ORENSTEIN, SAMUEL B		5 JUL 1968	15 APR 1900		
374	D 3	ORINSKY, SHIRLEY					
110	B25	ORTIN, LIEY BACUA	ROMINE	18 APR 1934			
102	CA31	OSBER, ALLEN B		11 AUG 1959	1909		PEARL
102	K50	OSBER, BETTY	MILLER	23 OCT 1952	4 JUL 1904		BURTON
102	CA30	OSBER, PEARL S		3 DEC 1988	1911		ALLEN
102	K51	OSBER, S BURTON		30 NOV 1964	16 JUL 1899		BETTY
222	AE12	OSCAR, BERNHARD J		29 OCT 1943	1866		
113	M39	OSHINSKY, WILLIAM		10 DEC 1977	5 OCT 1924		
125	C 12	OSSEN, BETTY	GOOGEL	13 AUG 1980	1911		JAY
751	N11	OSSEN, HARRY		29 JUN 1980	10 APR 1905		

Cem	Row	Name	Maiden Name	DOD	DOB	Parents	Spouse
125	C 13	OSSEN, JAY		1992	1909		BETTY
110	D13	OSTER, IDA		10 OCT 1988	16 NOV 1920		
110	D12	OSTER, MICHAEL		16 AUG 1970	1897		MINNIE
110	D11	OSTER, MINNIE		1 MAR 1969	1896		MICHAEL
103	A50	OSTER, SAUL		1989	1900		
392	C35	OSTRAUF, LEON H		28 JUN 1916	22 MAY 1885		ANNIE
248	B43	OSTROFSKY, ABRAHAM I		7 FEB 1959	1893	MICHAEL & FANNIE	
248	B42	OSTROFSKY, FANNY		14 DEC 1940	1868		MICHAEL
248	B41	OSTROFSKY, MICHAEL		7 JAN 1940	1865		FANNY
114	M16	OSTROV, FRIDA		8 AUG 1992	7 DEC 1912		
447	S11	OSTROVITZ, MORTON		1936	1932	SAUL & ROSE	
392	J34	OSTROW, MOSHE		29 MAR 1915		ISSAC	
392	F43	OSTROW, SAMUEL CHAIM		5 FEB 1920	1918	MOSHE	
493	F25	OTTENHEIMER, ELSIE	MOOS	28 OCT 1992	23 NOV 1894		
114	L31	OVRUTSKAYA, RAISA		8 JAN 1977	19 JAN 1903		
377	T28	OWAROFF, EVE V		27 DEC 1971	6 JUL 1914	ABRHAM ISRAEL	
125	L 51	OXENDLER, HELEN		16 JAN 1912			JOSEPH
125	L 52	OXENDLER, JOSEPH		1922	1848		HELEN
125	N115	OZAROFF, ALICE	NEDELMAN	1992	1901		BENJAMIN
125	N116	OZAROFF, BENJAMIN		5 JUN 1970	1891		ALICE
391	GB 6	PACKER, BERNARD		3 DEC 1966	1888	MORDECHAI	LILLIAN
113	L43	PACKER, DORIS	MEHR	2 FEB 1984	19 MAR 1902		MORRIS
391	GB 7	PACKER, LILLIAN		16 AUG 1955	1898	ISAAC	BERNARD
113	L42	PACKER, MORRIS		21 APR 1956	25 DEC 1896		DORIS
105	H22	PADOWITZ, BARBARA RUTH		NDD	1916		LOUIS
105	H21	PADOWITZ, LOUIS		1978	1903		BARBARA
105	J20	PADOWITZ, OSNE		23 APR 1954	1880		SAMSON
105	J21	PADOWITZ, SAMSON		2 JAN 1940	1877		OSNE
101	J 5	PAHUSKIN, FLORA	TISLER	22 JUL 1984	1892		MORRIS
494	B16	PALAIS, FRANCES	SILVERMAN	28 NOV 1991	21 JAN 1918		
751	H12	PALETSKY, JOSEPH		1959	1883		
447	S17	PALEY, REBECCA		13 JAN 1967	1894		SOL
447	M10	PALEY, SIDNEY		31 JUL 1992	21 DEC 1916		
447	S16	PALEY, SOL		7 APR 1960	1893		REBECCA
392	B17	PALLITZ, DAVID		18 NOV 1940	1893		
248	J62	PALLOCK, FANNIE		9 MAR 1955	1876		
248	I62	PALLOCK, NATHAN		9 FEB 1931	1873		
447	O 9	PALMER, AARON J		1971	1904		
447	M22	PALMER, ABRAHAM H		13 NOV 1954	1885		HELEN
112	C20	PALMER, ANNE H		23 FEB 1987	18 JAN 1911		
447	O 3	PALMER, BERTHA		15 DEC 1992	1908	MORRIS & SARAH	
447	O11	PALMER, BETHIA C		1971	1883		ISADORE
446	A26	PALMER, CHARLES		8 MAY 1912	15 MAR 1888		MURIEL
447	L21	PALMER, DAVID		3 JUN 1966			DORA
447	L22	PALMER, DORA		25 NOV 1943			DAVID
447	M23	PALMER, HELEN		9 JUN 1973	1899		ABRAHAM
447	O 7	PALMER, IDA LEAH		30 JUL 1933	1850		
447	O12	PALMER, ISADORE		4 AUG 1931	1878		BETHIA
447	P 6	PALMER, MARVIN "BUD"		1974	1927		
447	O 5	PALMER, MORRIS		7 AUG 1939	1881	IDA	SARAH
446	B17	PALMER, S MURIEL		7 APR 1914	11 NOV 1913		CHARLES
447	P 7	PALMER, SADIE J		3 NOV 1939			SAMUEL
447	P 8	PALMER, SAMUEL H		2 MAR 1939			SADIE
447	O 4	PALMER, SARAH W		5 JUN 1971	1884		MORRIS
446	D29	PALMER, SOFEA				CHARLES & MURIEL	
125	E133	PALMUCCI, LEAH	EDEN	17 JAN 1952	APR 1950		
102	AE25	PALTEN, HARRY		26 MAY 1950	15 OCT 1875	MORRIS & TYBA	SYLVIA
102	AE27	PALTEN, RICHARD D		4 AUG 1983	7 JUN 1958	PAUL M	
102	AE26	PALTEN, SYLVIA	KOTICK	29 NOV 1973	17 DEC 1883		HARRY
494	C 3	PAPISH, SOPHIA		26 JAN 1987	14 APR 1886		
110	D25	PAPPAS, MARK WARREN		17 JUN 1974	1 DEC 1953		
391	Z69	PARKER, AARON M		29 JUN 1973	8 MAY 1902	REUBEN	
377	R 8	PARKER, BENJAMIN		1973	1909		
116	BK96	PARKER, HARRY		26 OCT 1989	28 JUL 1909		
377	R 7	PARKER, LOUIS		1966	1903		
377	Q37	PARKER, MILTON M		29 APR 1980	10 MAR 1895		

Cem	Row	Name	Maiden Name	DOD	DOB	Parents	Spouse
377	O40	PARKER, PAULINE		1956	1875		REUBEN
377	O39	PARKER, REUBEN		1945	1871		PAULINE
371	K 5	PARKIN, IDA FLORENCE		22 SEP 1967	30 MAY 1890		
111	11	PARSONS, SAM ALLEN		17 JUN 1972	24 MAY 1903		
372	I16	PASNIK, ALEXANDER		1940	1880		BETTIE
372	I17	PASNIK, BETTIE H		1952	1877		ALEXANDER
113	N73	PASS, MAURICE A		9 NOV 1988	4 JUL 1916		
102	AJ128	PASSETT, DORA A		1959	1906		MAX
102	AJ129	PASSETT, MAX		1965	1897		DORA
370	P27	PASTER, ANNIE		1918	1895		ISAAC
376	D 7	PASTER, EVELYN		1929	1916	MOSHE ELI	
370	G44	PASTER, ISAAC		1917	1900		ANNIE
370	L18	PASTER, JOSEPH P		17 JAN 1944	1923	ISAAC & ANNIE	
371	J13	PASTER, LOUIS		21 JUN 1976	1888		ROSE
371	J14	PASTER, ROSE		21 AUG 1970	1885		LOUIS
370	K17	PASTER, SARAH RIVA		2 FEB 1947	1864		SOLOMON
370	F23	PASTER, SOLOMON A		22 FEB 1952	1865		SARAH
123		PASTERNAK, AARON B		3 APR 1951	1894		
116	E26	PASTOR, EDITH A		15 JAN 1990	4 APR 1907		
115	A60	PATRON, MARVIN MEYER		28 MAR 1990	14 MAY 1915		
112	E10	PATTEN, RICHARD		17 APR 1982	22 FEB 1916		
447	O23	PAUL, ABRAHAM		7 SEP 1945	15 MAY 1883		BESSIE
447	O22	PAUL, BESSIE DOROTHY		27 NOV 1950	1 AUG 1885		ABRAHAM
447	N28	PAUL, HYMAN N		8 NOV 1981	1910	ABRAHAM & BESSIE	
102	Z171	PAULL, HILDA		19 JUL 1991	2 FEB 1907		JACK
102	Z170	PAULL, JACK		21 JUL 1980	7 OCT 1897		HILDA
102	Z172	PAULL, RICHARD L		5 FEB 1975	16 MAR 1929	JACK & HILDA	
433	S 3	PEAR, ALBERT L		13 MAY 1991	24 MAR 1912		
446	A19	PEAR, MORRIS		18 JUN 1923	1877		
433	P 1	PEAR, SAMUEL		30 MAR 1980	15 MAY 1907	MORDECHAI MOSHE	
248	K75	PEARL, ANNA		16 OCT 1952	1882		MORRIS
222	C 7	PEARL, BENJAMIN		19 OCT 1955	1874		DORA
222	C 8	PEARL, DORA	MILLER	16 AUG 1963	1874		BENJAMIN
222	F11	PEARL, ETHEL		6 MAY 1984	26 NOV 1906	BENJAMIN & DORA	
116	AV 2	PEARL, EUNICE TOBY		9 AUG 1958	5 FEB 1921		
125	M 98	PEARL, FRANK		21 NOV 1926	1889	SHIMON	IDA
222	D 9	PEARL, GOLDIE		25 SEP 1991	13 DEC 1917		SAMUEL
125	M 97	PEARL, IDA		27 OCT 1973			FRANK
116	T11	PEARL, JOSEPH		8 AUG 1972	16 OCT 1910		
391	P27	PEARL, MAX		5 FEB 1919	1879	SHABATAI FIVAL	
248	K74	PEARL, MORRIS		5 DEC 1946	1880		ANNA
105	I28	PEARL, SALLY	SIGAL	15 JAN 1979	1936		
222	D 7	PEARL, SAMUEL WILLIAM		4 MAY 1986	23 JUL 1910	BENJAMIN & DORA	GOLDIE
116	AZ20	PEARSON, ETHEL		1 DEC 1981	26 JUL 1901		ROBERT
370	W19	PEARSON, HARRY		1924	1910	MORRIS & IDA	
370	W18	PEARSON, IDA		1965	1881		MORRIS
370	W17	PEARSON, MORRIS		1947	1875		IDA
370	W16	PEARSON, NATHAN		21 MAY 1933		MORRIS & IDA	
116	AZ19	PEARSON, ROBERT		21 JAN 1989	10 NOV 1907		ETHEL
248	C41	PECK, AARON		13 FEB 1933	1 JUN 1831		
447	U11	PECK, ANNE		1990	1908		EDWARD
248	C43	PECK, CLARA F		4 SEP 1950	1882	AARON	JOSEPH
447	U12	PECK, EDWARD		1986	1906		ANNE
331		PECK, FANNIE		31 MAR 1894			
433	C22	PECK, HYMAN		26 NOV 1975	5 DEC 1910	ISRAEL	
121	T 9	PECK, IRA STUART		10 OCT 1972	9 MAY 1948		
102	M47	PECK, ISAAC		1946	1894		MINNIE
248	C42	PECK, JOSEPH		4 APR 1952	1878		CLARA
377	Q30	PECK, LEWIS		1977	1916		
433	C26	PECK, LILLIAN		24 APR 1992	12 MAR 1923	PHILIP	
102	M46	PECK, MINNIE		1988	1898		ISSAC
104	O54	PECK, MURIEL		10 APR 1973	28 JAN 1911		
377	S20	PECK, NATHAN		1962	1878		PAULINE
377	S21	PECK, PAULINE		1960	1880		NATHAN
113	O20	PECK, WILLIAM		19 MAY 1981	3 OCT 1909		
433	C11	PECKEROFF, ABRAHAM		24 JUN 1969	12 AUG 1887	ISRAEL	

Cem	Row	Name	Maiden Name	DOD	DOB	Parents	Spouse
433	G18	PECKEROFF, ESTHER		2 MAR 1962	1884	PESACH	ISADORE
433	G17	PECKEROFF, ISADORE		1 MAR 1952	1884	CHAIM GABRIAL	ESTHER
433	C24	PECKEROFF, PHILIP		26 NOV 1980	24 MAY 1909	ISRAEL	
371	J18	PEIKES, IRVING		1983	1909		
101	A24	PEIZER, ISRAEL		23 SEP 1914	1856		
101	K28	PEIZER, LEAH	SHKOLNIK	12 OCT 1945	1858		LEAH
222	D 2	PEIZER, SAUL L		15 JAN 1952	1897		
328	A21	PELKISON, JACOB		6 JUN 1963	15 JAN 1888		ROSE
328	A22	PELKISON, ROSE		9 JUN 1967	10 MAY 1888		JACOB
116	AW28	PELZEL, MAX		28 OCT 1963	3 AUG 1887		
125	O156	PERETZ, JOSEPH		13 MAY 1949	1889	LITA & MALCAH	REBECCA
125	O157	PERETZ, REBECCA		27 SEP 1955	1882		JOSEPH
330	AF34	PEREW, EVELYN	LEVINE	30 SEP 1984	14 FEB 1918		
116	BI108	PERL, BELLE		8 JUN 1987	25 DEC 1910		GUSTAVE
102	R 1	PERL, EUNICE		26 AUG 1971	31 DEC 1916		HARRY
116	BI109	PERL, GUSTAV G		18 JAN 1976	21 FEB 1909		BELLE
102	R 2	PERL, HARRY		13 DEC 1985	21 MAR 1905	SAMUEL & IDA	EUNICE
125		PERL, IKUCIAL		7 MAR 1922	14 FEB 1922	FRANK	
116	BI107	PERL, JEFFREY W		16 NOV 1981	14 FEB 1947	GUSTAVE & BELLE	
447	AC35	PERLIN, LOUIS		9 SEP 1991	5 MAY 1928		
372	K11	PERLIS, ROSA		1956	1876		
377	S 2	PERLMAN, CELIA K		1981	1902		
102	AI133	PERLMAN, CHARLES		16 DEC 1989	6 NOV 1905		IDA
102	AI134	PERLMAN, IDA		16 APR 1991	29 MAR 1909		CHARLES
116	R13	PERLMAN, MAX H		30 DEC 1971	3 MAR 1910		
125	O103	PERLMAN, SARAH MARY		4 AUG 1926	1886		WILLIAM
125	O 78	PERLMAN, WILLIAM		30 OCT 1918	1881		SARAH
125	N111	PERLMUTER, ANNA H		18 MAR 1929	1893	ERWIN	
102	W52	PERLMUTTER, BELLE		18 OCT 1963	1890		LOUIS
249	H43	PERLMUTTER, JACK		25 FEB 1987	6 SEP 1914		
102	W56	PERLMUTTER, JACOB		1 NOV 1943	1863		TOBE
102	W54	PERLMUTTER, LOUIS I		26 OCT 1948	1889	JACOB & TOBE	BELLE
102	E 4	PERLMUTTER, MATILDA		27 APR 1974	1912		WILLIAM
102	W53	PERLMUTTER, SIDNEY A		14 MAY 1942	1914	LOUIS & BELLE	
102	W55	PERLMUTTER, TOBE		25 AUG 1950	1868		JACOB
102	E 3	PERLMUTTER, WILLIAM		8 NOV 1974	14 JUL 1913		MATILDA
121	T 8	PERLSTEIN, ABRAHAM		15 AUG 1981	19 APR 1909		
102	W23	PERLSTEIN, ALEXANDER Z		1971	1894		SARAH
101	B 3	PERLSTEIN, BELLA	BEREZOVITZ	4 JUL 1939	1857		
121	W10	PERLSTEIN, JENNY ELIZABETH		18 NOV 1981	17 NOV 1981		
102	W24	PERLSTEIN, NORMAN H		1982	1919	ALEXANDER & SARAH	
102	W22	PERLSTEIN, SARAH	GLAZER	1987	1893		ALEXANDER
121	T 7	PERLSTEIN, SARAH		27 DEC 1990	16 MAR 1911		
102	F38	PERLYSKY, BARNEY B		6 FEB 1971	1894		MOLLIE
102	F37	PERLYSKY, GERALD H LT		17 DEC 1944	10 APR 1921	BARNEY & MOLLIE	
102	R 3	PERLYSKY, IDA		30 JUN 1958	16 APR 1871		SAMUEL
101	B35	PERLYSKY, MAX		8 JUN 1917	1859		
102	F39	PERLYSKY, MOLLIE	TORETSKY	20 DEC 1991	21 JAN 1896		BARNEY
102	R 4	PERLYSKY, SAMUEL		15 APR 1947	21 MAR 1864		IDA
377	W55	PERRY, CLAIRE M		8 AUG 1991	11 JUN 1932	MORDECHAI	
377	J13	PERRY, FRANCES L		19 NOV 1989	3 JAN 1897		WILLIAM
377	J11	PERRY, MATHEW L		13 OCT 1944	7 JAN 1925	WILLIAM & FRANCES	
377	J12	PERRY, WILLIAM B		21 FEB 1965	5 NOV 1895		FRANCES
110	B36	PERSKY, DAVID		30 MAR 1977	1920		
370	P52	PERSOFF, AUGUSTA		26 MAR 1974	25 AUG 1902		LEWIS
370	Q48	PERSOFF, LEWIS DR		19 APR 1953	6 DEC 1896		AUGUSTA
391	C30	PESKOFF, ETTA	SOLTZ	12 JUN 1957	1886	CALEB	MEYER
391	C31	PESKOFF, MEYER JOEL		18 FEB 1950	1887	JACOB	ETTA
102	AJ69	PESSIN, CELIA G		6 JUN 1975	1890		DAVID
102	AJ70	PESSIN, DAVID L		12 APR 1944	1890		CELIA
123		PESSIN, HAROLD L		19 JAN 1945	1920		
102	AH195	PESSIN, ISRAEL GEORGE		12 JUL 1975	14 MAR 1894		GUSSIE
374	F45	PETERS, FAE	STRACKMAN	1975	1907		
376	B13	PETERS, JOHN STANLEY		30 JUL 1987	28 JUN 1943		
374	F21	PETERS, NAT		1966	1902		
114	I23	PETRUSHANSKY, MORRIS		12 AUG 1987	25 DEC 1908		

Cem	Row	Name	Maiden Name	DOD	DOB	Parents	Spouse
370	I60	PEVNER, MAX		1946	1880		SARAH
370	I61	PEVNER, SARAH		1972	1885		MAX
447	O36	PFEFFER, CIMA E		24 OCT 1983	1901		NATHAN
447	O39	PFEFFER, LEAH		7 APR 1936			MICHAEL
106	C31	PFEFFER, LEE R		5 APR 1991	18 JUN 1917		
447	O38	PFEFFER, MICHAEL		1 DEC 1935			LEAH
447	I31	PFEFFER, MORRIS		1978	1908		SARAH
447	O37	PFEFFER, NATHAN		7 APR 1986	1901		CIMA
447	I32	PFEFFER, SARAH F		NDD	1906		MORRIS
125		PHILIPS, (CHILD)		15 JAN 1926	JAN 1926	ABRAHAM	
102	I54	PHILIPS, MURRAY		29 JUL 1959	25 AUG 1884		SARAH
104	D27	PHILIPS, SARA		28 JAN 1975	1 JAN 1892		SIMON
102	I53	PHILIPS, SARAH	BERMAN	1 APR 1958	6 APR 1889		MURRAY
104	D26	PHILIPS, SIMON		8 JAN 1956	4 DEC 1890		SARAH
446	C69	PHILLIPS, A D		30 NOV 1939	28 NOV 1851		HENRIETTA
391	K31	PHILLIPS, ANNIE		5 OCT 1926	27 MAY 1850	YEHUDA LEV	
370	J 7	PHILLIPS, BESSIE		1931	1873		
446	B69	PHILLIPS, CLARA	STRAUSS	8 MAR 1950	8 JUL 1875		
446	C67	PHILLIPS, ERNEST				A D & HENRIETTA	
391	ZD58	PHILLIPS, EVA	RITCH	3 JAN 1993	1900	MICHAEL	MAX
392	A23	PHILLIPS, HARRY		22 NOV 1990	25 JUL 1912		HENRIETTA
392	A24	PHILLIPS, HENRIETTA		2 MAR 1990	12 FEB 1914		HARRY
446	C68	PHILLIPS, HENRIETTA	STRAUSS	6 NOV 1904	6 APR 1857		ABRAHAM D
371	A22	PHILLIPS, JOSEPH		1978	1900		
446	C66	PHILLIPS, MAX				A D & HENRIETTA	
391	ZD59	PHILLIPS, MAX CARL		11 FEB 1971	1898	ISAAC MOSHE	EVA
391	K30	PHILLIPS, MORRIS		14 APR 1916	31 DEC 1831	EFFRAIM	
391	O27	PHILLIPS, MORRIS		17 OCT 1909	1844	ELIEZER	
113	B55	PIATOK, MURRAY		18 NOV 1988	1 JUL 1926		
112	D 1	PICK, HENRY		5 JUL 1980	14 JAN 1904		
101	J12	PICKMAN, EVA BERTHA		9 MAR 1933	1898		
377	U 9	PIEL, IRVING W		10 APR 1991	8 MAY 1904	ZEV DOV	
125	D124	PIERSON, DIANA	BERKOWITZ	24 MAY 1963	10 DEC 1899	SAMUEL & JENNIE (WELINSKY)	ARTHUR
102	AE35	PIERSON, HENRY		1951	1911		
102	AC169	PIERSON, WILLIAM L		12 AUG 1963	29 APR 1902		
751	E27	PINCUS, ESTHER		11 DEC 1951	13 JAN 1882		JOSEPH
751	C18	PINCUS, INA	GRANT	17 DEC 1954	11 JAN 1946	JACK & JANET (GRANT)	
751	C20	PINCUS, JACK J		21 NOV 1990	12 MAY 1906		JANET
751	C19	PINCUS, JANET	GRANT	4 JUL 1978	24 MAY 1917		JACK
751	E26	PINCUS, JOSEPH		27 DEC 1947			ESTHER
392	B41	PINE, ABRAHAM		5 APR 1911	1875		
377	Z57	PINE, HYMAN R		3 AUG 1992	20 MAY 1906	ABRAHAM	
392	B 9	PINE, LOUIS		6 APR 1982	15 APR 1902		
101	D40	PINKES, ANNA		29 DEC 1982	1889		DAVID
101	D39	PINKES, DAVID		4 MAY 1956	1896		ANNA
110	C26	PINKES, HERMAN		27 AUG 1977	1897		TOBE
102	BF 1	PINKES, SAM MD		26 NOV 1987	11 NOV 1924		
110	C25	PINKES, TOBE		2 JUL 1971	1901		HERMAN
125	L113	PINKUS, AARON		29 DEC 1929			IDA
125	L114	PINKUS, IDA	GELLER	4 JUL 1962	1880		AARON
125	O190	PINKUS, SAMUEL		7 OCT 1965	1900		
447	A 7	PINSKER, ESTHER M		20 OCT 1968			JOSEPH
447	A 8	PINSKER, JOSEPH J		8 JAN 1937			ESTHER
447	A 1	PINSKER, SAMUEL D		17 FEB 1950	27 NOV 1900		
110	B11	PINSKY, BENJAMIN		11 NOV 1934	1847		
751	J36	PINSKY, DAVID L		25 NOV 1949	1872		
751	K36	PINSKY, GEORGE		1 FEB 1956	1916		
751	K35	PINSKY, HYMAN		1956	1879		
116	N10	PINSKY, JULES		22 JUN 1985	13 OCT 1913		
751	F35	PINSKY, LIBBY		1978	1892		
110	H29	PINSKY, MILTON		9 DEC 1926	1900		
751	K16	PINSKY, NATHAN		20 AUG 1948	1886		
116	V21	PISETSKY, MARVIN S		15 MAY 1978	12 DEC 1933		
113	A 7	PIUS, NORMAN H		11 JUL 1985	12 MAR 1927		
329	C10	PIVNICK, ANNA		8 APR 1987	1901		IRVING
121	I 4	PIVNICK, FRED		13 JUN 1984	11 NOV 1902		

Cem	Row	Name	Maiden Name	DOD	DOB	Parents	Spouse
101	C23	PIVNICK, IDA		20 JAN 1945	1867		SAMUEL
329	C 9	PIVNICK, IRVING		29 OCT 1970	1897		ANNA
101	D28	PIVNICK, LENA		13 FEB 1951	1874		MICHAEL
101	D29	PIVNICK, MICHAEL		23 OCT 1955	1865		LENA
121	I 3	PIVNICK, RONALD PAUL		1 SEP 1971	28 DEC 1932	FRED	
101	C24	PIVNICK, SAMUEL		20 JAN 1933	1861		IDA
329	C11	PIVNICK, SEYMOUR		14 APR 1991	30 SEP 1926	IRVING & ANNA	
125	R161	PIZER, ABRAHAM		7 FEB 1944	1875	AZER & GITTEL	LEAH
125	L124	PIZER, HELEN	KATZ	15 FEB 1931	1909	ISAAC & JENNIE (STIGLITZ)	
125	S192	PIZER, LEAH	DANZIG	28 NOV 1960	1873		ABRAHAM
125	ZB172	PIZER, LOUIS R		1991	1909		MARTHA
125	ZB173	PIZER, MARTHA K		NDD	1905		LOUIS
102	Z210	PLATT, MARVIN W		1984	1924		
119	J45	PLATT, MIRIAM		23 AUG 1990	30 MAR 1912		
119	J46	PLATT, MITCHEL		23 JAN 1982	29 JAN 1908		
391	N32	PLATTUS, ROSE		17 AUG 1945			SIMON
391	I28	PLATTUS, SIMON		9 JUN 1927	1864	LEV	ROSE
372	E21	PLAUT, (BOY)					
372	E18	PLAUT, ABRAHAM		21 DEC 1898	10 AUG 1833		SARAH
372	D13	PLAUT, ARTHUR					
372	E23	PLAUT, DINA		21 APR 1934	20 FEB 1857		ISAAC
372	D23	PLAUT, GABIE		1877	1869		LOUIS
372	D14	PLAUT, HUGO					
372	E22	PLAUT, ISAAC		19 JAN 1905	27 AUG 1845		DINA
372	D16	PLAUT, JEROME		1935	1870		SADIE
372	E34	PLAUT, JOSEPH		1905	1837		ROSALIE
372	D22	PLAUT, LOUIS		1942	1870		GABIE
372	E36	PLAUT, ROSA		1954	1863		
372	E35	PLAUT, ROSALIE	STRAUSS	1886	1843		JOSEPH
372	E20	PLAUT, RUTHERFORD C		13 JAN 1943	15 MAR 1877	ABRAHAM & SARAH	
372	D15	PLAUT, SADIE		1957	1874		JEROME
372	E19	PLAUT, SARA	CADDEN	2 OCT 1918	9 JUL 1853		ABARAHAM
372	E37	PLAUT, SARA		1927	1865		
110	B 4	PLOTKIN, DVEIRA		16 SEP 1956	1870		REUBEN
248	G48	PLOTKIN, NATHAN		1 DEC 1977	1913		
391	D20	PLOTKIN, PHILIP		12 DEC 1934	1887	MESHELEM	
392	J11	PLOTKIN, REBECCA		26 DEC 1985	16 FEB 1890	NACHEM	
110	B 5	PLOTKIN, REUBEN		7 FEB 1943	5618		DVEIRA
433	I14	PLOTNICK, BETTY	SONDAK	18 FEB 1969	1880	CHAIM DAVID	
433	G22	PLOTNICK, ELIAS		21 APR 1956	1872	REUBEN	
373	F 2	PLOTNICK, ESTHER		1958	1904		LOUIS
373	F 1	PLOTNICK, LOUIS		1980	1895		ESTHER
102	AA154	POCH, MAURICE		7 MAY 1977	5 OCT 1910		
248	J13	PODBERESKY, ABRAHAM		1956	1871		ESTHER
248	J10	PODBERESKY, BETTY		1971	1908		
248	J12	PODBERESKY, ESTHER		1951	1868		ABRAHAM
328	A10	PODBERESKY, ROSE D		29 JAN 1981	5 JUL 1908		
102	AB181	PODNETSKY, CHARLES		16 FEB 1976			DORA
102	AB180	PODNETSKY, DORA		15 AUG 1972			CHARLES
113	L58	PODROVE, ABRAHAM		23 APR 1988	19 JUL 1892		GERTRUDE
113	L57	PODROVE, GERTRUDE		6 SEP 1967	18 MAR 1899		ABRAHAM
113	L56	PODROVE, LEON		24 MAY 1978	16 FEB 1924	ABRAHAM & GERTRUDE	
330	AD 5	POGOLOFSKY, DAVID RUBEN		29 JUN 1970	1903		
371	J35	POGOLOWITZ, ROSE		NDD			SAMUEL
371	J34	POGOLOWITZ, SAMUEL		2 AUG 1956			ROSE
331		POKEWITZ, ISAAC		8 MAY 1912	1867		
370	J 5	POLDMAN, HINDE RASHE				DAVID	
249	N10	POLEINSKI, OLGA		28 JUL 1984	17 JUN 1901		
222	L10	POLENS, ABRAHAM J		9 OCT 1952	1891		REBECCA
222	L 9	POLENS, REBECCA		4 SEP 1984	1891		ABRAHAM
116	BL120	POLES, BERTHA I		30 APR 1972	1900		ISAAC
116	BL121	POLES, ISAAC		27 DEC 1968	1895		BERTHA
751	K17	POLETSKY, SOPHIE		10 DEC 1940	1883		
447	D 9	POLINER, GEORGE FRANKLIN		1993	1934		
447	D14	POLINER, GOLDIE F		18 APR 1930	1867		JACOB
446	A73	POLINER, GUSTA H		26 FEB 1928	1866		HEIMAN

Cem	Row	Name	Maiden Name	DOD	DOB	Parents	Spouse
447	D12	POLINER, HARRY		18 JUN 1949	1891	JACOB & GOLDIE	
446	A72	POLINER, HEIMAN		1 FEB 1936	1869		GUSTA
447	I13	POLINER, IDA		1969	1879		MORRIS
447	Z25	POLINER, ISRAEL		27 AUG 1980	31 OCT 1898		
447	D13	POLINER, JACOB		7 DEC 1933	1863		GOLDIE
447	I14	POLINER, MORRIS		1969	1878		IDA
447	D11	POLINER, MORRIS		20 DEC 1978	28 OCT 1903	JACOB & GOLDIE	
446	C71	POLINER, PENY					
446	C79	POLINER, PESHE		18 AUG 1890	1863		HEIMAN
446	C70	POLINER, SAMUEL		9 JUL 1954	1883		
446	A74	POLINER, SAMUEL M		18 OCT 1915	19 MAR 1894	HEIMAN & GUSTA	
116	BH71	POLINSKY, BERNARD		2 APR 1990	19 DEC 1925		
391	G 4	POLINSKY, EDWARD		25 JUL 1928	1898	CHAIM	
371	AK 1	POLINSKY, MARC PETER		17 JUL 1988	30 DEC 1963		
371	AJ 2	POLINSKY, PAULINE GLADYS		21 AUG 1986	29 JUL 1905		SAMUEL
371	AJ 1	POLINSKY, SAMUEL		17 JUL 1988	9 AUG 1899		PAULINE
751	C34	POLKOF, IDA		9 NOV 1908	1843		
751	M25	POLLACK, BENJAMIN DAVID		24 MAR 1985	17 JUN 1908		
101	G 5	POLLACK, ELSIE	RIBEN	17 JUL 1991	24 MAR 1905		
125	A 10	POLLACK, ENACH		4 SEP 1917	1885	HERSHEL & RACHEL	
101	M31	POLLACK, ESTHER		18 JUN 1943	1876		JACOB
249	Q10	POLLACK, ESTHER	REINER	22 OCT 1975	31 MAR 1908		
101	M33	POLLACK, GEORGE		12 OCT 1972	1911	JACOB & ESTHER	
374	B 6	POLLACK, ISIDOR		26 OCT 1990	9 MAY 1917		
101	M32	POLLACK, JACOB		3 JUL 1946	1871		ESTHER
374	C10	POLLACK, PAULINE		21 MAY 1981			SAMUEL
371	N19	POLLACK, ROBERT L		31 JAN 1990	26 JAN 1914		
374	C 9	POLLACK, SAMUEL		25 SEP 1943	1890		PAULINE
119	K33	POLLACK, SAMUEL		28 JAN 1992	9 SEP 1907		
392	H15	POLLOCK, ALEXANDER		26 MAR 1963	1895	EFRRAIM FALIK	
371	AD 4	POLLOCK, ESTHER		14 FEB 1976	14 MAR 1894		LOUIS
125	N141	POLLOCK, JACOB		27 JUN 1968	15 FEB 1888		
370	L13	POLLOCK, LENA		8 MAR 1920	1880		
371	AD 5	POLLOCK, LOUIS		11 DEC 1982	5 SEP 1887		ESTHER
751	K19	POLLOCK, REBECCA		21 FEB 1936	1866		
392	H16	POLLOCK, ROSE		9 JUN 1951	1890	NACHEM FALIK	
116	W19	POLMAN, IDA	LASCHEVER	2 JUL 1980	1899		
751	A38	POLOKOF, MOSHE		25 NOV 1919			
372	K 9	POLSBY, DANIEL II		15 MAY 1946	2 AUG 1909	DANIEL & SARAH	
372	H 3	POLSBY, HINDA		NDD	28 MAY 1894		ISIDORE
372	I 6	POLSBY, IDA	MARKS	NDD	1 OCT 1888		JOSEPH
372	H 1	POLSBY, ISADORE		12 DEC 1962	12 OCT 1879		HINDA
372	I 5	POLSBY, JOSEPH W		11 OCT 1966	12 OCT 1879		IDA
372	H 2	POLSBY, RUTH		NDD	15 AUG 1918	ISADORE & HINDA	
372	K 8	POLSBY, SARAH K		1960	1880		
104	O33	POLSKAYA, ITA		1991	1910		
391	G 5	POLSKY, ABRAHAM		5 MAY 1919	1861	TZVI HIRSH	
370	J 4	POLSKY, CHIA LEBA		10 MAY 1930	1849		MAX
372	I 3	POLSKY, DANIEL		1957	1888		DINAH
372	I 2	POLSKY, DINAH	BERKOWITZ	1962	1888		DANIEL
371	K 6	POLSKY, ESTHER		1980	1895		MAX
371	K 7	POLSKY, MAX		1970	1889		ESTHER
370	B 7	POLSKY, MAX MORDECHAI		8 MAY 1925	1850	RACHEL	CHIA
370	A58	POLSKY, RACHEL		15 SEP 1911	1826		
433	G16	POLSTEIN, GUSSIE		6 JAN 1952	1874	SHRUGA FIVAL	SAMUEL
433	H 6	POLSTEIN, IDA		10 OCT 1941	1887	ZION LEV	
433	C12	POLSTEIN, ISADORE		24 JUN 1969	12 AUG 1887	YOSEF DAVID	JEAN
433	C13	POLSTEIN, JEAN		13 SEP 1969	24 MAR 1901	WOLF	ISADORE
433	G15	POLSTEIN, SAMUEL		9 APR 1951	1870	YOSEF DAVID	GUSSIE
433	K11	POLSTEIN, SIMON		20 MAR 1956	1878	YOSEF DAVID	TILLIE
433	K12	POLSTEIN, TILLIE		12 SEP 1964	1886	TOVA BEAR	SIMON
330	G63	POMERANTZ, ADELE		29 OCT 1921	1861		
103	C15	POMERANTZ, ISRAEL		13 MAR 1989	1904		
751	M32	POMERANTZ, JOSEPH		1991	1905		
222	AA25	POMERANTZ, MAX		22 SEP 1934	1862		REBECCA
222	K 2	POMERANTZ, MINNA		17 JUL 1962			NATHAN

Cem	Row	Name	Maiden Name	DOD	DOB	Parents	Spouse
751	M31	POMERANTZ, MIRIAM		1983	1910		
222	K 1	POMERANTZ, NATHAN JOSEPH		20 JAN 1952	1905		
222	AA26	POMERANTZ, REBECCA		23 JAN 1959	1873		MINNA
102	AA157	POMERANTZ, WILLIAM M		27 NOV 1979	1907	YETTA	MAX
102	AA156	POMERANTZ, YETTA		1 OCT 1973	1883		
118	D 9	POPKIN, OSCAR		1 JUN 1979			
112	E 6	POPPER, FELIX		23 JAN 1989	5 OCT 1919		
377	T17	PORDES, FRITZ		1961	1912		OLGA
377	T18	PORDES, OLGA		1977	1890		FRITZ
102	AG75	PORISS, ANNA G		9 JUN 1981	1894		HYMAN
102	M10	PORISS, BENJAMIN I		26 NOV 1958	18 NOV 1900		FANNY
104	K 9	PORISS, CELIA	LUTIN	15 DEC 1980	10 SEP 1894		
102	M11	PORISS, FANNY A		16 AUG 1980	12 MAR 1903		BENJAMIN
102	AG74	PORISS, HYMAN R		22 OCT 1952	1892		ANNA
102	AD80	PORISS, ISRAEL		11 DEC 1938	1882		
102	J39	PORISS, MAE		10 SEP 1956	27 MAR 1896		
102	A67	PORISS, PHILIP P		24 DEC 1941	1884		
102	AC69	PORISS, REUBERN		1935	1858		RACHEL
391	M30	POROUS, JOSEPH		13 NOV 1903	1860	MORDECHAI	
102	AC70	PORRIS, RACHEL	SHILANSKY	1924	1856		REUBEN
105	I38	PORTNER, ABRAHAM		30 APR 1958	1890		LEAH
105	I39	PORTNER, LEAH		26 MAR 1986	1894		ABRAHAM
101	C38	PORTNOY, ALEX		7 NOV 1938	1903	DAVID & IDA	
101	C37	PORTNOY, DAVID		7 MAY 1943	1872		IDA
101	C39	PORTNOY, IDA		31 DEC 1960	1873		DAVID
370	F 2	POSNER, HAROLD		24 AUG 1916	25 MAY 1911		
114	F 6	POSNER, STEVEN M		1 JAN 1982	16 MAY 1947		
377	ZA 8	POST, ESTHER		14 AUG 1983	15 JUL 1906	MOSHE BARUCH	
105	E24	POST, HARRY		17 JAN 1965	17 FEB 1901		MINNIE
121	D 9	POST, IRWIN		29 APR 1989	9 MAY 1914		
105	E23	POST, MINNIE COHN	TONKAN	24 JUL 1950	10 JUN 1881		HARRY
105	P47	POST, PEARL O		5 JUL 1982	29 OCT 1910		
222	AE11	POSTMAN, ESTA	OSCAR	4 OCT 1937	1894		
374	H36	POTNICK, DOROTHY	JENNES	1946	1902		
116	AU23	POTOFF, HARRIET	GOLD	16 JAN 1972	12 MAR 1917		WILLIAM
116	AU24	POTOFF, WILLIAM		21 NOV 1991	30 OCT 1916		HARRIET
125	K 66	POUZZNER, ABRAHAM		10 OCT 1918	1893	ISRAEL & FREIDA	
125	F 22	POUZZNER, EDITH		21 FEB 1925	1896	ISRAEL & FREIDA	
125	F 24	POUZZNER, FREDA YENTA		18 NOV 1940	1860		ISRAEL
125	F 23	POUZZNER, ISRAEL		26 APR 1927	1860		FREIDA
125	L 52	POUZZNER, JENNIE		28 DEC 1918	OCT 1896	ISRAEL & FREIDA	
125	L112	POVERMAN, ANN ELKY		26 NOV 1929	1858		SAMUEL
102	AJ22	POVERMAN, CHARLES		4 JUL 1944	1884		GOLDIE
125	M176	POVERMAN, DOROTHY R		15 MAR 1968	1901		
125	I 78	POVERMAN, ELIZABETH		2 AUG 1970	1920		
102	AJ21	POVERMAN, GOLDIE		4 APR 1962	1879		CHARLES
125	M 83	POVERMAN, SAMUEL		7 APR 1919	DEC 1863	ISAAC & SHINDEL	ANN
248	A53	PRAGUE, BENJAMIN		24 DEC 1954	1891		DOROTHY
248	A54	PRAGUE, DOROTHY		20 MAR 1961	1896		BENJAMIN
248	J80	PRAGUE, EDWARD		16 DEC 1954	9 DEC 1954		
248	E30	PRAGUE, MAURICE		31 MAY 1978	29 OCT 1922		
102	R 9	PRANT, FREIDA	BLAUZVERW	2 DEC 1954	1882		HARRY
102	R10	PRANT, HARRY		12 MAY 1928	1874		FREIDA
119	E37	PRANT, ROSE		17 OCT 1979	1909		
102	W44	PRAWDA, MOLLIE	CLIMAN	11 DEC 1960	9 SEP 1890		PHILIP
102	W43	PRAWDA, PHILIP		17 MAY 1961	15 MAR 1887	ISRAEL & LEAH	MOLLIE
121	L10	PREBLUD, REBA		26 OCT 1974	1898		
102	Z183	PRENSKY, EDITH	FELDMAN	20 JAN 1975	3 JUN 1918		JOSEPH
102	Z182	PRENSKY, JOSEPH LEVI		4 APR 1990	29 AUG 1920		EDITH
125	ZA181	PRENSKY, SHIRLIE	HORWITZ	25 MAY 1991	9 JAN 1925		
446	B18	PRESS, ANTOINETTE		30 JUL 1917	12 JUL 1913		
447	V17	PRESS, BERNARD		7 MAY 1940	1875		ROSA
447	L20	PRESS, BESSIE		27 OCT 1978	1 JUL 1897		
447	X 6	PRESS, CELIA		14 AUG 1977	1907		GEORGE
447	X 5	PRESS, ETHEL		19 MAR 1974	1904		
447	X 9	PRESS, GEORGE		24 MAY 1967	1909		CELIA

Cem	Row	Name	Maiden Name	DOD	DOB	Parents	Spouse
113	B22	PRESS, GERALD	LEVY	28 JUL 1983	6 JUN 1919		
102	BG19	PRESS, LOUIS		17 MAR 1992			
447	V15	PRESS, MAMIE		8 DEC 1949	1876		MAX
447	V16	PRESS, MAX		19 OCT 1969	1876		MAMIE
447	AD34	PRESS, PAULINE		1993	1913		
447	V18	PRESS, ROSA		7 AUG 1929	1877		BERNARD
447	D40	PRESSMAN, ARTHUR	11 JAN 1963*	31 DEC 1963*	1886	ISRAEL & MARISSA	
447	D39	PRESSMAN, ISRAEL JOSEPH		16 JAN 1980	1886		MARISSA
447	D38	PRESSMAN, MARISA					ISRAEL
116	BK 4	PRESTRIDGE, AARON		24 NOV 1988	16 JUN 1924		
101	L23	PREWEER, SAMUEL		2 AUG 1915	1843		
125	J186	PRICE, BENJAMIN M		26 MAR 1984	1912		
125	Z181	PRICE, JOE Z		17 JUN 1987	17 NOV 1912		
127	G	PRICE, OSCAR R		28 JAN 1981	19 SEP 1900		
110	D 2	PRIMACK, FRUMA BEILA		11 FEB 1945	1872		JACOB
110	D 1	PRIMACK, JACOB		28 AUG 1950	1871		FRUMA
116	O25	PRINCE, FRANCES		29 JAN 1984	3 SEP 1930		
102	N51	PRINCE, MOLLIE	GREENBERG	1970	1899		NATHAN
102	N52	PRINCE, NATHAN		1955	1892		MOLLIE
447	AB35	PRINS, SAL A MD		13 JAN 1883	1902		
106	F15	PRIZANT, JACK		17 MAR 1974	28 NOV 1903		MILLIE
106	F16	PRIZANT, MILLIE	LERNER	10 MAR 1992	28 SEP 1908		JACK
102	G44	PROLLER, CHARLES H		28 JUL 1979			IDA
102	G45	PROLLER, IDA	SHIKES	3 NOV 1968			CHARLES
102	G43	PROLLER, MOLLY		27 JAN 1987			
125	K 45	PROLLER, NATHAN		11 OCT 1912	1886		
125	E 42	PROTASS, BENJAMIN L		25 APR 1979	1890		
125	D 52	PROTASS, CLARICE		11 MAY 1979	1902		HARRY
125	F 42	PROTASS, DORA		11 DEC 1984	1894	LEON & REBECCA	
125	D 53	PROTASS, HARRY DR		22 APR 1980	1899		CLARICE
391	H28	PROTASS, ISAAC		25 MAR 1926	1860	SAMUEL	
125	F 41	PROTASS, LEON		10 FEB 1923	1868	BENZION & REBECCA	REBECCA
125	F 40	PROTASS, REBECCA		19 OCT 1919	1869	SIMON & DORA	LEON
371	G 5	PROTTAS, ABRAHAM AARON		16 JUN 1984	11 OCT 1897		SADIE
391	L28	PROTTAS, ARTHUR		21 APR 1904	1 MAR 1888	HAICAH & C	
391	I29	PROTTAS, HERMAN		11 NOV 1927	1866	SAMUEL	
391	K40	PROTTAS, IDA		25 APR 1941	1862	ISAAC	
391	P52	PROTTAS, LILLIAN S		8 JUN 1983	1895	SAMUEL	
371	G 6	PROTTAS, SADIE J		25 JAN 1991	19 MAR 1904		ABRAHAM
391	K39	PROTTAS, SARAH		31 OCT 1938	1865	ABRAHAM	
104	F25	PROVERMAN, NANCY	LACKER	8 MAY 1990	3 NOV 1945		
125	E 18	PROZOWSKY, H		25 OCT 1928	1928	HARRY	
102	AJ139	PRUDINS, JEANNETTE A		12 NOV 1971	1902		
125	S151	PRUSHONE, AARON		3 NOV 1940	1878	ABRAHAM YITZCHAK	PAULINE
125	S152	PRUSHONE, PAULINE		23 JUL 1962	1887		AARON
125	L180	PRUZANSKY, HARRY		5 JUL 1971	1891		MARCIA
125	L181	PRUZANSKY, MARCIA		23 JUL 1978			HARRY
377	U42	PTASHEW, DEBBIE		1991	1921	ARYEH	
377	U41	PTASHEW, SAMUEL		1984	1911	ARYEH	
125	M170	PUDLIN, JESSIE		14 JAN 1968	1880		
433	D20	PUKOFF, ADOLF		1970	1884	MOSHE AARON	ROSE
433	D19	PUKOFF, ROSE		1978	1887	ISAAC	ADOLPH
104	J30	PULVER, GLADYS		1980	1906		PAUL
104	J31	PULVER, PAUL		1959	1904		GLADYS
392	E33	PUMERANTZ, BENJAMIN		27 JUL 1958	1896	JACOB HIRSH	
392	E34	PUMERANTZ, GOLDIE		10 NOV 1951	1866	JACOB	
392	D37	PUMERANTZ, HARRY		9 AUG 1950	1889	JACOB TZVI	
377	Q17	PUMERANTZ, IDA	ROSEN	1970	1905		
392	C36	PUMERANTZ, LILLIAN		27 SEP 1967	1888		
392	E35	PUMERANTZ, NATHAN		30 NOV 1945	1884	JACOB TZVI	
392	C37	PUMERANTZ, PAULINE		23 SEP 1984	1896		
125	P192	PUTTERMAN, CHARLES		15 JUN 1963	1878		LENA
125	L116	PUTTERMAN, HARRIS		20 OCT 1935	1877	YAKOV & CHANA	
125	L170	PUTTERMAN, JACK		1971	1901		THELMA
125	P191	PUTTERMAN, LENA		20 AUG 1965	1899		CHARLES
125	Y177	PUTTERMAN, MAX		21 FEB 1984	18 DEC 1915		

Cem	Row	Name	Maiden Name	DOD	DOB	Parents	Spouse
125	O106	PUTTERMAN, SARAH		1 OCT 1928	1 DEC 1905	HARRY & LENA	
125	L171	PUTTERMAN, THELMA		1990	1909		JACK
102	CB33	QUINN, MOLLIE	GREENBERG	22 MAY 1984	15 AUG 1900		
106	A14	QUINT, EDNA	GERSTEIN	1 MAY 1986	25 JUL 1906		JULES
102	J49	QUINT, ELIZABETH W		1985	1889		HENRY
102	J50	QUINT, HENRY F		1961	1886		ELIZABETH
106	A15	QUINT, JULES V		22 FEB 1982	29 MAY 1904		EDNA
433	I15	RAAB, BERNARD B		24 MAY 1929	1928	JACOB	
433	G 2	RAAB, ISADORE		2 NOV 1945	28 JUN 1892	YESHYUA	MARTHA
112	C14	RAAB, JOZEFA		28 APR 1984	5 MAY 1910		
433	G 1	RAAB, MARTHA C		1985	1900	LEV	ISADORE
447	N10	RABINOFF, JENNIE	LUNTZ	28 APR 1986	9 MAR 1893	SAUL & ANNIE	
105	F12	RABINOVICH, MORRIS		28 DEC 1941	1887		SOPHIE
105	F11	RABINOVICH, SOPHIE		10 JAN 1976	1894		MORRIS
372	E 1	RABINOVITCH, ALEC		13 APR 1955	1896		
370	H18	RABINOVITCH, ANNA		1942	1872		
372	I 8	RABINOVITCH, ELIZABETH		13 OCT 1962	1879		MAX
370	O34	RABINOVITCH, HENRY		26 APR 1918			IDA
370	O35	RABINOVITCH, IDA		26 MAY 1927			HENRY
372	I10	RABINOVITCH, ISRAEL		27 AUG 1925	1879		LENA
372	I11	RABINOVITCH, LENA		18 AUG 1977	1885		ISRAEL
372	I 7	RABINOVITCH, MAX		18 OCT 1938	1876		ELIZABETH
372	I12	RABINOVITCH, SAMUEL				ISRAEL & LENA	
119	B31	RABINOVITZ, BESSIE		18 NOV 1992			
102	CA24	RABINOVITZ, DORA K		12 JAN 1990			SAMUEL
102	CA25	RABINOVITZ, SAMUEL		28 MAY 1973			DORA
119	B30	RABINOVITZ, SOLOMON		12 SEP 1992			
125	K124	RABINOW, HARRY		28 DEC 1934	15 AUG 1888		
125	K189	RABINOW, LOUIS		17 JAN 1974	1893		REBECCA
125	K190	RABINOW, REBECCA		12 NOV 1974	1896		LOUIS
125	O 82	RABINOWITZ, ABRAHAM M		25 JAN 1919	1871	SAUL	SADIE
102	K20	RABINOWITZ, ARTHUR		23 JAN 1972	1895		THERESA
330	B35	RABINOWITZ, BARNET		6 MAY 1962	1874		MINNIE
102	E13	RABINOWITZ, CORA	GOODMAN	14 AUG 1977	30 JUL 1901		
125	C 73	RABINOWITZ, DEWOSHA		27 MAY 1916	1893	ISAIAH & MARY LOU	
125	F 19	RABINOWITZ, FANNY	BELL	5 MAY 1976	1884		LOUIS
248	D30	RABINOWITZ, HYMAN		17 SEP 1964	1906	MAX & RACHEL	
125	F 20	RABINOWITZ, LOUIS		6 SEP 1976	1879	MENDEL & RIVKA	FANNY
248	D31	RABINOWITZ, MAX					RACHEL
370	B33	RABINOWITZ, MICHAEL		27 MAR 1926	1851		RIFKA
330	B34	RABINOWITZ, MINNIE		16 OCT 1954	1880		BARNET
125	E 20	RABINOWITZ, MORRIS		1989	1910		
248	D32	RABINOWITZ, RACHEL		11 MAY 1966	5 MAY 1884		MAX
370	J11	RABINOWITZ, RIFKA		27 DEC 1932			MICHAEL
125	O 81	RABINOWITZ, SAIDIE					ABRAHAM
102	K21	RABINOWITZ, THERESA		31 OCT 1966	1 NOV 1894		ARTHUR
125	O152	RACHER, MANUEL		19 DEC 1965	1923		
125	F158	RACHER, ROBERT		4 NOV 1981	1919		
125	O151	RACHER, SONIA	WASKOWITZ	7 MAR 1949	1895	SHAOUL	
110	E15	RACHLEFF, JACOB M		1 DEC 1982	6 DEC 1899		
125	K105	RACHLIN, BESSIE		15 FEB 1942	1870	SHIMSHON	DAVID
125	K104	RACHLIN, DAVID		15 MAR 1952	1868		BESSIE
125	J102	RACHLIN, IRVING I		4 NOV 1991	1894		
125	J101	RACHLIN, ROSE S		2 SEP 1992	1900		
113	N75	RADDING, MARTHA E		13 APR 1971	24 JAN 1922		
447	L40	RADEEN, ESTHER S		21 AUG 1971	1888		
105	G22	RADEEN, MINNIE		1 JAN 1984	1893		MORRIS
105	G21	RADEEN, MORRIS		27 JAN 1973	1893		MINNIE
371	AJ 7	RADIN, ARTHUR		27 JAN 1964	12 AUG 1923	SAMUEL & PEARL	
371	AP24	RADIN, MICHAEL Z		2 FEB 1965	23 APR 1954		
371	AJ 6	RADIN, PEARL		8 OCT 1972	23 MAR 1895		SAMUEL
371	AJ 8	RADIN, SAMUEL		11 NOV 1967	22 DEC 1895		PEARL
102	AI183	RADIN, SAMUEL		19 MAR 1970	23 AUG 1900		
751	M34	RADLER, ESTHER		8 MAR 1984	19 NOV 1899		
751	M35	RADLER, MORRIS		9 MAR 1986	29 DEC 1890		
222	M12	RADOM, CLARA	LIBBY	12 OCT 1960	1893		LEO

Cem	Row	Name	Maiden Name	DOD	DOB	Parents	Spouse
222	M13	RADOM, LEO		8 NOV 1965	1890		
494	C11	RADOM, ROBERT A		1964	1895		CLARA
331		RADUS, ABRAHAM		22 JUL 1904	1897		
102	AB171	RADVILLE, GUSSIE O		15 DEC 1971	17 NOV 1889		JOSEPH
102	AB170	RADVILLE, JOSEPH		10 MAR 1978	24 JAN 1885		GUSSIE
222	AJ11	RADZIVILOW, GOLDIE		15 DEC 1940	1861		JACOB
222	AJ10	RADZIVILOW, JACOB MORDECHAI		30 NOV 1945	1861		GOLDIE
118	A5	RAFFEL, MITCHELL		12 DEC 1987			
447	N30	RAFIND, A BENJAMIN MD		13 NOV 1990	12 OCT 1909		
446	B 1	RAFKIND, BELLA		14 MAR 1931	1882		ISAAC
446	A11	RAFKIND, ISAAC		6 APR 1929	1880		BELLE
102	F43	RAGATSKY, LENA	KRAUSS	24 OCT 1957	12 DEC 1887		
125	G729	RAGIN, ANNA		5 APR 1950	1864		
391	O57	RAGIN, HENRY		28 FEB 1954	1887	NATAN NATTA	
391	O60	RAGIN, ROSE ESTHER		18 FEB 1966	1889	YESHIYAHU	
104	B33	RAHN, CHARLES H		5 NOV 1965	2 MAY 1895		
377	Q28	RAKOFF, FRANK B		1976	1921		
377	F 8	RAKOSKY, ABRAHAM AARON		2 AUG 1958	12 FEB 1887		SARAH
377	F 9	RAKOSKY, RALPH R		17 JUL 1975		ABRAHAM & SARAH	
377	F 7	RAKOSKY, SARAH	PROTTAS	18 AUG 1975	19 AUG 1890		ABRAHAM
102	AA88	RANDALL, ANN	HEILPERN	5 DEC 1961	19 JUL 1908		
102	R14	RAPAPORT, BARNEY		16 JAN 1961	1885		VICTORIA
102	R12	RAPAPORT, ELLA	TUDOR	5 SEP 1977	1895		
117	D 4	RAPAPORT, LEONARD J		1989	1919		
102	R13	RAPAPORT, VICTORIA	TUDOR	19 NOV 1968	1890		BARNEY
102	AJ93	RAPHAEL, AARON		20 JUL 1941	1877		JENNIE
372	F 5	RAPHAEL, AGNES		1941	1863		
102	X13	RAPHAEL, BENJAMIN		23 MAR 1972	1883		ROSE
116	BU61	RAPHAEL, EDWARD		15 JUN 1965	1900		
372	E26	RAPHAEL, ELLIS		8 NOV 1912	11 JUN 1824		ROSETTA
372	D19	RAPHAEL, F					
372	E29	RAPHAEL, F (BABY)					
372	E28	RAPHAEL, FANNIE		14 APR 1889	1804		
102	W17	RAPHAEL, FANNY	KATZ	1975	1883		WILLIAM
372	D20	RAPHAEL, I					
102	N27	RAPHAEL, IDA		1974	1897	ISAAC & MINNIE	
102	N28	RAPHAEL, ISAAC		1936	1872		MINNIE
102	AJ92	RAPHAEL, JENNIE	SIEGEL	18 APR 1949	1878		AARON
372	G21	RAPHAEL, LENA	MARKS	1956	1872		REUBEN
125	ZB178	RAPHAEL, LEONARD		10 SEP 1993			
125	F 35	RAPHAEL, LILLIAN	KLEEBER	25 MAY 1941	1877	ISRAEL	MORRIS
102	U45	RAPHAEL, LOUIS		11 MAR 1945	1900		
125	F 34	RAPHAEL, LOUIS RALPH		28 MAY 1955	26 APR 1890		
102	N29	RAPHAEL, MINNIE		1928	1873		ISAAC
125	N130	RAPHAEL, MOLLIE A		1993	1906		WILLIAM
125	F 36	RAPHAEL, MORRIS		12 JUN 1921	10 MAY 1865	RAFAEL & REBECCA	LILLIAN
107	C1	RAPHAEL, REUBEN		15 JAN 1991	2 SEP 1901		
372	G22	RAPHAEL, REUBEN		1948	1868		LENA
372	H13	RAPHAEL, ROBERT MILTON		1958	1899		
125	P198	RAPHAEL, ROSE	KOMISS	22 JUL 1964	1895		
102	X14	RAPHAEL, ROSE B		5 JUL 1945	1889		BENJAMIN
102	K35	RAPHAEL, ROSE Z		1 AUG 1980	5 OCT 1898		
372	E27	RAPHAEL, ROSETTA		16 JUL 1896	7 OCT 1825		ELLIS
372	D17	RAPHAEL, S					
102	W16	RAPHAEL, WILLIAM		1964	1882		FANNY
125	N129	RAPHAEL, WILLIAM R		24 MAR 1972	1906		MOLLIE
119	I 8	RAPOPORT, HAROLD		15 DEC 1988	17 FEB 1911		
119	I 9	RAPOPORT, ROSE	ROBBINS	30 JUN 1992	8 MAY 1910		
126		RAPP, LOUIS W		25 JAN 1928	1 AUG 1898		
370	I69	RAPPAPORT, BESSIE		17 NOV 1952	1900		HYMAN
391	O30	RAPPAPORT, HAYIM MORRIS		15 MAR 1906		YEHUDA LEV	
370	I70	RAPPAPORT, HYMAN		27 AUG 1957	1894	LOUIS & MAMIE	BESSIE
370	E 9	RAPPAPORT, LOUIS		1940	1878		MAMIE
370	H 9	RAPPAPORT, MAMIE		1955	1878		LOUIS
392	J24	RAPPAPORT, PAULINE		24 MAY 1931	1876	JOSEPH TZVI	
222	M 4	RASHALL, ARNOLD MARK		5 SEP 1976	16 MAY 1946		

Cem	Row	Name	Maiden Name	DOD	DOB	Parents	Spouse
222	K 4	RASHALL, HYMAN		25 JUN 1985	1890		IMMA
222	K 3	RASHALL, IMMA	CANTOR	7 APR 1971	1896		HYMAN
125	M 91	RASHKOW, ABRAHAM		5 APR 1924	1873	NATAN DAVID & BECKI	THELIA
125	I145	RASHKOW, ANNA	GOURSON	18 JUN 1971	1903		DAVID
125	I144	RASHKOW, DAVID A		20 NOV 1944	19 APR 1898	ABRAHAM & TANIA	ANNA
125	K 30	RASHKOW, NATHAN		22 MAR 1916	AUG 1914	ABRAHAM	
125	M 92	RASHKOW, THELIA		6 NOV 1953	1879		ABRAHAM
376	A17	RASIN, KALMAN		28 APR 1969	1887		SARAH
376	A16	RASIN, SARAH		28 DEC 1981	1888		KALMAN
331		RASKIN, MOSES		19 NOV 1902	1845		
102	M44	RATNER, ESTHER		15 AUG 1978	1898		JACOB
101	J18	RATNER, FANNIE		11 MAR 1927	1893		
102	M45	RATNER, JACOB		4 DEC 1974	1898		ESTHER
125	J157	RATNER, SAMUEL		25 JUL 1967	1882		SARAH
125	J158	RATNER, SARAH	LIPMAN	30 MAY 1958	1888	SHIMON	SAM
330	F12	RATTNER, LASSIER		11 JUL 1924	1854		
370	R30	RAUCHER, BEATRICE		21 OCT 1957	1929	CHAYA	
370	R31	RAUCHER, CHAYE ROSE	PEARL	1 JAN 1970	1904		
370	T35	RAUCHER, HAROLD		19 APR 1928	20 MAR 1917	SAMUEL & JENNIE	
370	T37	RAUCHER, JENNIE S		11 JAN 1976	6 JAN 1895		SAMUEL
370	T36	RAUCHER, SAMUEL		21 JUL 1971	29 MAY 1890		JENNIE
110	C31	RAVICYH, MOLLIE	SHULSKY	23 MAR 1973	1910		
447	T14	RAVITCH, ABRAHAM		25 APR 1957	1886		SHAIVA
447	T12	RAVITCH, JOSEPH	4 JAN 1991*	25 DEC 1991*	1922	ABRAHAM & SHAIVA	
447	T13	RAVITCH, SHAIVA		27 MAR 1966	1889		ABRAHAM
377	S30	RAVITZ, SIDNEY		14 FEB 1970	25 AUG 1913		
371	AN17	RAYMOND, EDYTHE	KREIGER	7 MAR 1963	17 APR 1906		
493	E35	RAYMOND, GERTRUDE		21 JUN 1993			
493	E33	RAYMOND, MYRNA D		15 SEP 1987	14 FEB 1941		
108	C20	REDAK, SAUL		23 JUN 1985	14 APR 1910		
106	A34	REDD, JASON STUART		26 FEB 1979	27 JUL 1973		
105	O22	REDER, MAX		30 APR 1976	21 JUN 1908		
751	O27	REIBMAN, CLAIRE	KABACHNICK	1967	1927		
114	C11	REIBMAN, HAROLD M		3 JAN 1981	4 JAN 1924		
123		REICH, ALBERT A		13 OCT 1949	1906		
331		REICH, IDA		13 JUL 1913	20 MAY 1900		
123		REICH, JEANETTE N		2 NOV 1988	28 MAY 1908		
125	S157	REICHER, ISAAC		30 APR 1945	1879	SHLOMO & RACHEL	REBECCA
125	S156	REICHER, REBECCA	SCHLAFER	29 APR 1941	1882	JACOB	ISAAC
125	M 32	REICHER, S L					
222	L 7	REICHLIN, DAVID A		4 OCT 1975	18 APR 1958		
102	R44	REICHLIN, MAY		29 MAY 1973	8 MAY 1895		NATHAN
102	R43	REICHLIN, NATHAN		6 JUN 1964	15 JAN 1891		MAY
101	E 1	REILAND, ROBERTA	OKEN	30 MAR 1975	1936		
249	K 2	REINSTEIN, ABRAHAM		30 SEP 1937	1877		IDA
107	G13	REINSTEIN, ANNA		28 JUL 1984	5 AUG 1898		
249	K 3	REINSTEIN, IDA	DEMBOWITZ	28 DEC 1938	1889		ABRAHAM
248	M75	REINSTEIN, SAMUEL		25 JAN 1967	15 DEC 1905		
391	C33	REISER, HARRY		28 FEB 1951	1944	MOSHE	
377	X48	REISER, RHODA		8 JAN 1984	29 MAR 1918	YEHUDA LEV	
102	AJ65	REISLER, JACOB		13 JUL 1973	10 APR 1898		LOUISA
102	AJ66	REISLER, LOUISA	SILVER	19 JUL 1987	13 JUN 1899		JACOB
101	K 1	REISMAN, MORRIS		13 FEB 1969	1923		
371	G 4	REISMAN, OSHER ZEV RABBI		8 MAR 1980	31 DEC 1891		
101	E35	REITZFELD, MOSES		14 MAR 1970	1901		
116	L17	RENARD, HELENE D		20 APR 1989	25 DEC 1931		
110	C19	RENERT, SYLVIA		22 SEP 1964	1910		
121	A 4	RENNER, FRANCES		19 NOV 1976	18 MAY 1895		
391	C41	RESNEK, (BABY)		26 DEC 1926			
377	M34	RESNEK, BERTHA E		2 OCT 1988	23 AUG 1902		BERTHA
377	M33	RESNEK, SAMUEL H		7 MAR 1961	7 JAN 1896		SAMUEL
118	E16	RESNICK, HELEN		11 MAR 1988			
222	AI13	RESNICK, IDA	MASKEL	13 FEB 1978	18 DEC 1909		
125	E143	RESNICK, IRVING		31 MAY 1936	1892	ABRAHAM	
118	A14	RESNICK, JUDITH ANN		8 NOV 1981			
116	T 7	RESNICK, LESTER		19 JAN 1982	1920		

Cem	Row	Name	Maiden Name	DOD	DOB	Parents	Spouse
125	W178	RESNICK, LUCILLE JOAN		9 NOV 1992	1930		
392	G11	RESNIKOFF, FANNY S		7 MAY 1974	1891	ELIEZER BER	
392	F16	RESNIKOFF, HARRY		16 OCT 1943	1885	MORDECHAI	
392	G12	RESNIKOFF, ISAAC		30 MAR 1945	1880	EZRAEL MORDECHAI	
392	H10	RESNIKOFF, JOY H		9 NOV 1980	26 OCT 1925	ISAAC	
392	H11	RESNIKOFF, REBECCA ANNA		22 OCT 1957	1923	ISAAC	
433	F 3	REUTER, STEPHANIE R		12 AUG 1973	18 APR 1938		
101	C12	REVITCH, DORA		1 NOV 1943	1872		
125	M187	REVZON, HERMAN		30 SEP 1968			
125	N120	REVZON, IRVING		21 DEC 1971	1918		
125	P149	REVZON, LOUIS		29 FEB 1948	6 JAN 1881	MOSHE & HADASSAH	ROSE
125	P150	REVZON, ROSE		1 AUG 1963	1882		LOUIS
110	F 2	REYNGOLD, ANATOLY		4 MAR 1990	14 MAY 1929		
113	L36	REZNICK, CLARA	KANTOR	11 MAR 1982	29 MAR 1915		IRWIN
113	L35	REZNICK, IRWIN		31 JUL 1969	12 OCT 1912		CLARA
125	N147	REZNICK, MAX		25 JUN 1955	1895		
125	T145	REZNIK, PAULINE		13 FEB 1939	1899	JOSHUA & SHINA	
371	AH23	REZNITZKI, ISRAEL		14 NOV 1964	1904		
108	B29	RHODES, HARRIET R		3 APR 1987	12 APR 1916		PHILIP
108	B11	RHODES, LOUIS		21 JUL 1962	4 FEB 1907		SARAH
108	B28	RHODES, PHILIP J		20 AUG 1980	20 OCT 1917		HARRIET
108	B12	RHODES, SARAH		14 AUG 1986	4 APR 1912		LOUIS
108	A20	RHODES, STEVEN S		3 SEP 1983	22 FEB 1952	PHILIP & HARRIET	
392	I35	RIBCHINSKY, ABRAHAM DAVID		30 JUN 1949	1888	NACHEM	
392	I36	RIBCHINSKY, ANNA	BLUM	15 APR 1960	1891	ABRAHAM & GITEL (STEINBACH)	ABRAHAM
392	I37	RIBCHINSKY, LOUIS		15 JUL 1984	20 MAR 1922	ABRAHAM & ANNA (BLUM)	
101	M 4	RIBEN, HARRY		4 FEB 1949	1896	MAX & MARY	PAULINE
101	M 3	RIBEN, MARY		17 DEC 1945	1870		MAX
101	M 2	RIBEN, MAX		21 DEC 1943	1868		MARY
101	M 1	RIBEN, PAULINE		16 FEB 1983	1917		HARRY
104	D30	RIBICOFF, HILDA		15 NOV 1975	1904	SAMUEL & ROSE	
104	D28	RIBICOFF, ROSE		2 MAY 1959	1885		ROSE
102	AF92	RIBICOFF, RUTH		12 APR 1972	17 NOV 1908		
102	AE94	RIBICOFF, RUTH ROSE		16 JUL 1965	24 MAY 1965		
104	D29	RIBICOFF, SAMUEL		24 NOV 1969	1882		SAMUEL
392	J21	RIBNER, ANNA		30 JAN 1935	1854	MORDECHIA	
370	O20	RIBNER, BELLA		1935	1905	DAVID & ESTHER	
370	O22	RIBNER, DAVID		1952	1879		ESTHER
370	O25	RIBNER, ESTHER	KAPLAN	2 AUG 1966	10 APR 1880		DAVID
392	B50	RIBNER, ISIDOR		10 APR 1975	21 NOV 1890		
391	O31	RIBNER, ISRAEL		3 JUL 1921	1849	JACOB	
370	O21	RIBNER, MARGARET		1932	1913	DAVID & ESTHER	
392	E44	RIBNER, PAULINE	KAHN	17 MAY 1948	1889	JOSHUA JOSEPH	
372	D12	RICE, M WILFRED		1968	1909		
446	C26	RICH, HANNAH		1909	1905		
392	I43	RICH, MEYER		24 OCT 1968			
392	I44	RICH, MIRIAM		17 JUL 1990		MEYER & SARAH	
119	J29	RICH, MORRIS		13 MAR 1987	20 JUN 1895		
392	I42	RICH, SARAH		19 JUN 1957			
102	A61	RICHIE, DOROTHY	BORDON	27 MAR 1948	1902		
377	W22	RICHMAN, BERNARD		7 APR 1957	1910	MOSHE	
125	D111	RICHMAN, EMANUEL		25 DEC 1964	1884		ROSE
125	D112	RICHMAN, ROSE	MILKOWITZ	24 OCT 1978	1894		EMANUEL
391	J29	RICHMANN, SAMUEL		5 MAY 1924	1882		
377	T19	RICHMOND, ARTHUR		4 JUL 1967	1 JUN 1910	YESHIA	
377	D35	RICHMOND, CHARLES		14 MAY 1965	15 NOV 1879	ARYEH LEV	IDA
377	C34	RICHMOND, DOROTHY E		29 JUL 1993	15 NOV 1907	YESHAI	MAXWELL
391	H43	RICHMOND, FANNIE P		24 MAY 1944			
377	D34	RICHMOND, IDA	ELION	8 SEP 1955	15 JUL 1880	JACOB	CHARLES
377	C33	RICHMOND, MAXWELL E		22 OCT 1971	21 NOV 1913	YESHAI	DOROTHY
391	J28	RICHMOND, NATHAN I		25 JAN 1922		ISRAEL	
377	D33	RICHMOND, ROBERT S		20 NOV 1962	18 FEB 1920	CHARLES & IDA	
101	J 3	RIEMER, ROSE		11 DEC 1963	1894		
121	P19	RIFKIN, CECILE		29 SEP 1986	1922	SIEGFRIED & SOPHIE	
101	E21	RIFKIN, MORRIS S		17 SEP 1975	8 JAN 1900		
121	P16	RIFKIN, SAUNDER		28 NOV 1974	12 MAY 1918	SIEGFRIED & SOPHIE	

Cem	Row	Name	Maiden Name	DOD	DOB	Parents	Spouse
121	P17	RIFKIN, SIEGFRIED		18 APR 1966	1894		
121	P18	RIFKIN, SOPHIE		9 APR 1992			
391	N53	RIFKIND, HANNAH SARAH		23 MAR 1961	31 MAR 1883	BARUCH	
391	N50	RIFKIND, LAWRENCE		21 OCT 1948	27 SEP 1918	MOSHE	
391	N52	RIFKIND, MORRIS		5 OCT 1966	6 JUN 1877	DOV BER	
391	I34	RIFKIND, SARAH		24 MAY 1922	10 OCT 1865	DAVID	
391	N51	RIFKIND, SIDNEY		31 MAR 1955	27 SEP 1916	MOSHE	
391	Q34	RIFKIND, ZELDE		22 JAN 1916		JOSHUA ZELIG	
392	H35	RINER, IDA E		3 JAN 1984	31 JAN 1893	AVIGDOR	
392	H34	RINER, SAMUEL S		9 DEC 1965	6 FEB 1891	ISAAC	
447	B33	RISEN, SARAH LEAH		15 JUN 1935	1896		
391	ZD56	RITCH, CELIA		NDD		MICHAEL	
391	ZD57	RITCH, FRANCES		NDD		MICHAEL	
391	N28	RITCH, HANNOCH		25 AUG 1915	1837	AARON	
391	O43	RITCH, MARY		1 DEC 1949	1864	SAMUEL	WOLF
391	H39	RITCH, RUTH		3 JAN 1932		ABRAHAM JACOB	
391	O44	RITCH, WOLF		22 SEP 1949	1861	HINOCH	MARY
391	H29	RITT, ASHER		21 AUG 1924	1861	JACOB YEHUDAH	
391	L31	RITT, HATTIE		31 OCT 1973	1877	NACHMAN ELIEZER	
391	M32	RITT, HYMAN E		28 OCT 1946	1878	JACOB JUDAH	
391	N29	RITT, JACOB L		14 MAR 1913	1834	YECHEZCHAL	
391	R28	RITT, NESSA GITTAH		17 SEP 1923	1836	AVER	
391	I40	RITT, TOBY REBECCA		1 OCT 1938	1867	ABRAHAM ELIYAHU	
433	F10	RITTER, IDA		22 MAR 1994	1904		NATHAN
433	F12	RITTER, NATHAN		14 MAY 1973	28 MAY 1894	BZALEL	IDA
121	W 6	RITVO, STACEY		1965			
125	L105	RIVKIN, ABRAHAM		17 JUL 1940	1870	WILLIAM & IDA	YETTA
116	S26	RIVKIN, ANNE	PALATNICK	5 APR 1978	22 DEC 1904		ROBERT
101	K12	RIVKIN, FANNIE		22 MAY 1917			
102	H16	RIVKIN, JOSEPH L		19 NOV 1951	19 MAR 1902	NATHAN & LENA	
102	H14	RIVKIN, LENA	COHEN	18 JAN 1963	19 OCT 1881		NATHAN
102	H15	RIVKIN, NATHAN F		11 JUN 1961	14 FEB 1881		LENA
116	S25	RIVKIN, ROBERT A		29 DEC 1981	17 FEB 1897		ANNE
222	AI 6	RIVKIN, SAMUEL		11 DEC 1968	12 FEB 1900		
125	L106	RIVKIN, YETTA		26 MAY 1932	1869		ABRAHAM
103	E17	RIVKIND, FANYA		1988	1909		
101	I37	RIVLIN, SAMUEL		26 JUL 1980	1900		
119	C36	ROBBIN, FLORENCE K		14 FEB 1981	3 NOV 1904		
116	BJ95	ROBBIN, HARRIET C		18 SEP 1989	17 FEB 1926		
119	C37	ROBBIN, JACOB		10 APR 1990	22 FEB 1909		
123		ROBBINS, DAVID M		13 APR 1958	1917		
113	K73	ROBBINS, FLORENCE	GOLDFARB	15 JUL 1977	29 DEC 1916		
125	F 18	ROBBINS, SEYMOUR A		20 MAR 1976	1917	LOUIS & FANNIE RABINOWITZ	
125	H 16	ROBEY, FANNY	KENNEDY	15 JAN 1944	28 DEC 1895	SIMON & SARAH	
121	J10	ROBIN, ESTHER	GOLDBERG	6 MAR 1990	6 JUN 1903		
121	J 9	ROBIN, HYMAN		25 FEB 1984	12 DEC 1903		
125	U150	ROBINS, BEN		2 APR 1990	11 APR 1911		
125	C 37	ROBINSON, BELLE TOBYE	GLASS	28 APR 1946	1916		
751	I32	ROBINSON, BENJAMIN		1968	1878		LENA
125	C 39	ROBINSON, DAVID		22 JAN 1977	1917		
115	M70	ROBINSON, ERICA					
125	N 98	ROBINSON, ETTA		22 NOV 1925	1873		
370	J10	ROBINSON, EVELYN R	FLORMAN	10 DEC 1932	4 NOV 1909		
125	C 38	ROBINSON, JOSEPH DR		17 SEP 1969	1912		
121	I34	ROBINSON, LAURA C		10 MAR 1986	12 NOV 1924		
751	I31	ROBINSON, LENA	DANZIGER	1966	1894		BENJAMIN
125	D 44	ROBINSON, MAMIE		29 JUN 1945	1885	ISAAC & ALTA	MARTIN
125	D 43	ROBINSON, MARTIN H		15 SEP 1959	1890		MAMIE
125	M115	ROBINSON, MOSHE ESAU		16 NOV 1928	1899	MOSHE HERSHEL	
125	L125	ROBINSON, NATHAN		24 FEB 1931	1874		
125	E516	ROBINSON, RACHEL		5 APR 1937	1875	YOSEF & YETAL	
125	R160	ROBINSON, REUBEN		04 NOV 1943	1878	YOSEF	
751	I30	ROBINSON, SEYMOUR		1940	1922	BENJAMIN & LENA	
116	G 1	ROCK, HARVEY R		28 OCT 1986	23 FEB 1923		
391	ZB68	ROCKETTO, SYLVIA R		18 NOV 1974	30 NOV 1918	JACOB	
125	W152	RODEN, ALAN J		14 JUL 1993	5 SEP 1941		

Cem	Row	Name	Maiden Name	DOD	DOB	Parents	Spouse
102	M31	RODENS, CHARLES N		25 DEC 1983	18 FEB 1906	ISADORE & ANNA	
392	H46	RODENSKY, ABRAHAM		6 FEB 1993			
102	M29	RODENSKY, ANNA		30 OCT 1949	1879		ISADORE
329	G28	RODENSKY, BEATRICE B		26 MAY 1990	7 JAN 1921		
392	H45	RODENSKY, EVELYN	RICH	NDD			
330	AA 5	RODENSKY, FAGEL S		2 APR 1975	15 JAN 1907		
102	M28	RODENSKY, ISADORE		2 NOV 1928	1868		ANNA
392	B16	RODENSKY, LOUIS		7 MAR 1930	29 JUN 1908		
392	B44	RODENSKY, MARY		14 JAN 1960	1881		RUBIN
377	Q 1	RODENSKY, MORRIS		29 DEC 1992	18 JAN 1911		ROSE
377	Q 2	RODENSKY, ROSE S		NDD	16 OCT 1912		MORRIS
392	B45	RODENSKY, RUBIN		21 MAR 1950	1871		MARY
375	C17	RODENSKY, SAMUEL		1975	1902	REUBEN	
125	P141	RODER, ETHEL	WELINSKY	12 NOV 1993	22 OCT 1904	FRANK & LENA (SILVERSTEIN)	HENRY
125	P140	RODER, HENRY	GINSBERG	10 DEC 1946	1 MAY 1902	ANNA	ETHEL
447	V20	RODNER, MINNIE		16 APR 1928			
125	I126	ROGIN, ANNA		5 APR 1950			SAMUEL
102	AJ100	ROGIN, BARBARA ANN		21 FEB 1942	20 SEP 1941	EDWARD & MATILDA	
125	I126	ROGIN, SAMUEL		15 JUN 1938	1864	MENACHEM & BASYA	ANNA
391	E42	ROGOFF, ANNIE	STERN	16 AUG 1942		JOSEPH	HARRIS
391	E43	ROGOFF, HARRIS		6 JAN 1956		JOSEPH	ANNIE
391	ZC79	ROGOFF, MAURICE		26 APR 1983	1909	AARON	
374	D48	ROGOVIN, HERMAN		23 JUL 1951	1867		ROSE
374	D50	ROGOVIN, ISRAEL		5 SEP 1968	9 AUG 1896	HERMAN & ROSE	TILLIE
391	GI 1	ROGOVIN, MAX		31 MAR 1961	1887	AARON LEV	
374	D47	ROGOVIN, ROSE		13 FEB 1949	1869		HERMAN
374	D51	ROGOVIN, TILLIE		5 DEC 1987	2 MAR 1901		ISRAEL
123		ROHOWSKY, ALBERT		24 JAN 1970	1887		
123		ROHOWSKY, MIRIAM	ROSEN	1978	1894		
119	A 2	ROHRLICK, LIBBY B		5 APR 1993			
101	L29	ROISMAN, ANNA		30 JUL 1921	1882		
105	C20	ROISMAN, ROSE		1954	1898		
123		ROITMAN, MICHAEL		13 JUL 1989	16 APR 1906		
371	O28	ROLIDER, ADAM		4 JUL 1954	1895		
377	H 6	ROLINSKY, SARA		1970	1903		WILLIAM
377	H 7	ROLINSKY, WILLIAM		1977	1893		SARAH
370	P35	ROLLBAND, ANNA		1938	1870		ANNA
371	A29	ROLLBAND, ARTHUR		19 SEP 1982	19 MAR 1907		LILLIAN
371	J31	ROLLBAND, BERTHA B		16 OCT 1966	31 MAR 1904		
370	P36	ROLLBAND, ISAAC S		1926	1871		ISAAC
371	A30	ROLLBAND, LILLIAN S		19 NOV 1983	20 MAR 1911		ARTHUR
376	A19	ROLLBAND, SAMUEL		31 JAN 1988	29 DEC 1911		
116	AW17	ROLLER, MONA		27 AUG 1965	19 DEC 1921		SIDNEY
116	AW18	ROLLER, SIDNEY		9 AUG 1983	30 MAY 1914		MONA
102	AH74	ROMANKSY, BENJAMIN		26 MAY 1960	1875		HENRIETTA
102	AH76	ROMANKSY, ROSELLA		7 NOV 1992	4 SEP 1900	BENJAMIN & HENRIETTA	
102	AH75	ROMANSKY, HENRIETTA		28 SEP 1958	1877		BENJAMIN
104	H44	ROME, ALBERT H		21 MAY 1960	1899		CELIA
104	H42	ROME, BESSIE RUTH	TOBER	11 SEP 1981	19 OCT 1891		LOUIS
104	H45	ROME, CELIA	SABOL	29 JAN 1980	7 FEB 1898		ALBERT
121	AA33	ROME, DAVID		20 MAY 1982	1920		
104	I38	ROME, GOLDIE		3 NOV 1976	14 DEC 1914		THOMAS
104	G45	ROME, ILENE BEVERLY		6 MAY 1974	22 DEC 1939		MERRILL
104	I41	ROME, JOHN J		15 JAN 1978	6 FEB 1894		
104	H43	ROME, LOUIS LEVI		8 AUG 1962	1890	LIPMAN & NELLIE (KATZ)	BESSIE
104	H41	ROME, MARION		11 SEP 1981	28 MAR 1912		
104	G46	ROME, MERRILL ARTHUR		2 MAY 1983	16 FEB 1923		ILENE
222	AH 3	ROME, MILTON		6 JAN 1990	22 FEB 1914		
104	H38	ROME, MYNNE		1 SEP 1992			SAMUEL
104	H37	ROME, SAMUEL S		16 OCT 1983	8 JUN 1908		MYNNE
102	AA23	ROME, SIDNEY ARON		10 DEC 1972	1910		
106	D3	ROME, SIDNEY C		31 JUL 1974	12 JUL 1908		
104	I40	ROME, THOMAS DAVID		31 DEC 1986	6 SEP 1917		GOLDIE
102	E40	RONNICK, MILDRED	FEIN	16 MAY 1946	27 MAY 1906		
377	ZA31	ROOK, VIVIAN R		15 JAN 1969	25 DEC 1923	ISREAL ELCHANON	
112	D24	ROOS, ELLA ROSA		12 DEC 1977	15 JUN 1897		PAUL

Cem	Row	Name	Maiden Name	DOD	DOB	Parents	Spouse
112	D25	ROOS, PAUL		20 JUL 1978	1 FEB 1896		ELLA
751	G35	ROSANSKY, EDITH		28 APR 1949	5 SEP 1879		
751	N35	ROSANSKY, ETHEL		26 FEB 1988	1912		
751	K 7	ROSANSKY, FLORENCE		NDD			
751	G38	ROSANSKY, HARRY		8 MAR 1941	1877		
751	N36	ROSANSKY, HERMAN		27 FEB 1977	1902		
751	J 1	ROSANSKY, LOUIS		3 JAN 1988	18 DEC 1910		
751	K 8	ROSANSKY, MEYER		13 NOV 1985	7 APR 1909		
125	O 91	ROSANSKY, VICTOR		26 APR 1920	1881		
125	T150	ROSE, ANNA		20 AUG 1939	1881		
102	AC175	ROSE, BERNICE		28 MAY 1975	4 MAY 1909		MORRIS
125		ROSE, BERTHA	DEEHAM	16 JAN 1923	OCT 1920	ABRAHAM & DORA	
102	AC174	ROSE, MORRIS		9 DEC 1968	27 MAY 1907		BERNICE
102	I 1	ROSE, R PHILIP		9 MAY 1982	17 MAR 1900		REBECCA
102	I 2	ROSE, REBECCA		3 OCT 1986	28 JUL 1896		PHILIP
106	D14	ROSE, REBECCA J		4 JUL 1990	23 MAY 1898		YALE
102	I 4	ROSE, SYLVIA HANNAH		3 NOV 1938	7 MAR 1923	PHILIP & REBECCA	
106	D13	ROSE, YALE		11 NOV 1971	31 AUG 1895		REBECCA
125	Y200	ROSEMAN, BERNARD		13 APR 1986			
125	N180	ROSEMAN, MINNIE		10 DEC 1976	1892		SAMUEL
125	N181	ROSEMAN, SAMUEL		8 FEB 1966	1890		MINNIE
125		ROSEN, (CHILD)		1 APR 1917	1917	SAMUEL & FANNIE	
371	O11	ROSEN, ABRAHAM		28 MAR 1964	4 MAY 1906		CELIA
392	C32	ROSEN, ALVIN		25 NOV 1986	25 MAY 1920		
371	AE20	ROSEN, ANN		1962	1908		BEN
330	AG17	ROSEN, ANNA	MAZER	26 APR 1971	4 JAN 1902		JACK
102	AA166	ROSEN, BELLA		9 SEP 1988	1891		HYMAN
371	AE19	ROSEN, BEN					ANN
248	E47	ROSEN, BENJAMIN		18 SEP 1972	28 MAY 1918		
248	D35	ROSEN, BERTHA		22 JUL 1962	1876		FRANK
371	O10	ROSEN, CELIA	FELDMAN	8 AUG 1976	6 SEP 1906		ABRAHAM
101	C32	ROSEN, CHAIM JOSEPH		28 APR 1933	1851		
330	G36	ROSEN, CHANIE		18 SEP 1908	1862		
125	I 25	ROSEN, CHARLES		5 MAR 1941	1900	SAMUEL & FANNIE	FANNIE
330	E42	ROSEN, DORA B		5 FEB 1939	1902		
392	J 2	ROSEN, EDNA		14 NOV 1921		JUDAH	
391	C 6	ROSEN, ELSIE		25 NOV 1934	10 AUG 1922	JACOB	
392	B21	ROSEN, ELSIE	BAUMAN	30 MAR 1966	14 DEC 1894		JACK
248	D33	ROSEN, EVA		3 NOV 1960	5 OCT 1893		HASKEL
125	I 26	ROSEN, FANNIE	LUTEN	11 JUN 1952	1881		CHARLES
392	B20	ROSEN, FLORA		19 MAY 1963	16 NOV 1893		
248	D36	ROSEN, FRANK		14 JUL 1936	1870		BERTHA
248	I73	ROSEN, GERALD JACOB		16 DEC 1927	5 APR 1927		
248	D34	ROSEN, HASKEL		25 NOV 1981	7 MAR 1894	FRANK & BERTHA	EVA
102	AA167	ROSEN, HYMAN		9 SEP 1974	1888		BELLA
248	F43	ROSEN, IDA K		17 DEC 1963	1887		MEYER
121	L 8	ROSEN, IDA S		14 NOV 1985	4 JUL 1900		
249	A 4	ROSEN, IKE		14 MAY 1958	13 OCT 1880		JENNIE
330	AG16	ROSEN, JACK		18 MAY 1979	20 NOV 1900		ANNA
392	B19	ROSEN, JACK		31 MAY 1966	1895		ELSIE
377	D 3	ROSEN, JACOB		1971	1884		KATIE
125	K183	ROSEN, JACOB		27 SEP 1973			
125	G 34	ROSEN, JACOB D		8 JUL 1948	1900		
105	L28	ROSEN, JEAN K		10 APR 1982	11 APR 1930		
108	B23	ROSEN, JEANE		26 AUG 1975	8 DEC 1915		
249	A 3	ROSEN, JENNIE	LEVINE	9 JUN 1952	10 MAY 1876		IKE
377	D 2	ROSEN, KATIE B		1978	1893		JACOB
125	L163	ROSEN, LOUIS B (CANTOR)		14 DEC 1981	1893		SARAH
125	E116	ROSEN, MARION		28 FEB 1959	5 MAR 1906	LOUIS & MASHA	MORRIS
125	M144	ROSEN, MARTIN		6 JAN 1952	1897		
330	H 7	ROSEN, MARVIN		1931	1928		
391	N39	ROSEN, MARY		17 MAR 1937	1900	REUBEN JOSEPH	
248	D12	ROSEN, MAURICE		8 MAR 1981	30 MAR 1904		
248	F42	ROSEN, MEYER		3 NOV 1943	1887		IDA
248	A49	ROSEN, MORRIS		14 SEP 1990	1911	WOLFE & ROSE	
125	E115	ROSEN, MORRIS		2 AUG 1960	25 SEP 1900		MARION

Cem	Row	Name	Maiden Name	DOD	DOB	Parents	Spouse
248	E46	ROSEN, MURRAY		1 MAR 1964			
377	C 3	ROSEN, NATHAN		1988	1917		SELMA
447	L23	ROSEN, ROSE		1958	1904		
248	A48	ROSEN, ROSE LILLIAN		5 JAN 1947	1880		WOLFE
391	D 4	ROSEN, RUBIN		7 FEB 1948	1873	DAVID	
125	I 27	ROSEN, SAMUEL I		18 AUG 1930	1876	SAMUEL	
121	L 9	ROSEN, SAMUEL J		1976	1893		
371	J43	ROSEN, SARAH	ZIEF	31 JUL 1953	1 MAR 1897		WILLIAM
125	L164	ROSEN, SARAH DINAH		29 DEC 1956	1895		LOUIS
377	C 2	ROSEN, SELMA	HART	1990	1920		NATHAN
371	J44	ROSEN, WILLIAM		23 FEB 1960	30 SEP 1895		SARAH
248	A47	ROSEN, WOLFE		11 OCT 1955	1880		ROSE
330	AG11	ROSENBAUM, ABRAHAM		4 JAN 1986	2 AUG 1901		EDYTHE
330	G52	ROSENBAUM, ANNA		26 JUL 1928	1873		
110	C18	ROSENBAUM, DAVID		15 FEB 1964	1905		LAURA
330	AG12	ROSENBAUM, EDYTHE		NDD			ABRAHAM
102	BE12	ROSENBAUM, JACOB		11 SEP 1990	7 AUG 1897		
110	C17	ROSENBAUM, LAURA		1 OCT 1987	1908		DAVID
119	H38	ROSENBAUM, LEONARD		25 JAN 1977	1909		
329	C47	ROSENBAUM, LILLIAN		10 DEC 1965	13 DEC 1905		
329	A28	ROSENBAUM, LUDWIG		9 APR 1966	1882		
125	V185	ROSENBAUM, ROSE CLAIRE		25 FEB 1978	1902		
330	F57	ROSENBAUM, SAMUEL		3 MAR 1931	1869		
101	J34	ROSENBERG, ABRAHAM		18 OCT 1978	1884		MINNIE
222	AE 9	ROSENBERG, ABRAHAM		29 MAR 1950	6 SEP 1888	SAMUEL & SHIFRA	LILLIAN
102	T35	ROSENBERG, ADA		24 NOV 1983	1893		WILLIAM
104	B21	ROSENBERG, ADRIENNE E		7 NOV 1952	3 SEP 1949		
112	D16	ROSENBERG, ALBERT		1976	1896		
102	E42	ROSENBERG, ALTER		15 SEP 1949	1886		MARY
125	E 90	ROSENBERG, ANNA		4 JAN 1983	3 MAR 1892		ISRAEL
222	AE 7	ROSENBERG, BARNEY M		17 MAY 1944	1877	SAMUEL & SHIFRA	FANNIE
102	BA 6	ROSENBERG, BEN D		2 AUG 1987	28 JAN 1913		
121	K 7	ROSENBERG, BENJAMIN		1988	1903		
371	AF 9	ROSENBERG, BERTHA	CURLAND	29 MAY 1963	1899		
370	V15	ROSENBERG, BETSY		1939	1877		LOUIS
125		ROSENBERG, CHARLES		6 FEB 1925	1879		
125	M 89	ROSENBERG, DAVID		11 MAR 1923	1851		
125	K130	ROSENBERG, DAVID		8 FEB 1938	1905	CHARLES & REBECCA	
222	AE 6	ROSENBERG, DOROTHY B		9 JAN 1920	9 JAN 1919	BARNEY & FANNIE	
125	J 59	ROSENBERG, EDITH		1907			WILLIAM
370	V17	ROSENBERG, EDITH PAULINE		1902		LOUIS & BETSY	
125	F 90	ROSENBERG, ELIAS		29 OCT 1926	1863		IDA
102	F32	ROSENBERG, ELIZABETH D		3 JAN 1984	1 SEP 1901		LEO
125	I 56	ROSENBERG, EVA		17 JAN 1915	1844		
102	AJ86	ROSENBERG, FANNIE		16 FEB 1965	1881		REUBEN
222	AE 8	ROSENBERG, FANNIE R		17 JAN 1974	1 SEP 1888		BARNEY
370	V12	ROSENBERG, GEORGE		1985	1903	LOUIS & BETSY	
102	U28	ROSENBERG, HAROLD		23 APR 1967	1914	NATHAN & MARY	
371	AF10	ROSENBERG, HARRY	10 JAN 1974*	30 DEC 1974*	1898		
370	V13	ROSENBERG, HARRY I		1964	1900	LOUIS & BETSY	
119	E 5	ROSENBERG, HERMAN		8 MAY 1976	27 JAN 1915		
125	F 89	ROSENBERG, IDA		1943	1864		ELIAS
222	AE 5	ROSENBERG, IDA ESTHER		1 JUN 1947	1907		
125	K114	ROSENBERG, IDA G		18 JUN 1934	1870	ISRAEL & CHASHA	LOUIS
330	G50	ROSENBERG, IDA RACHEL		8 FEB 1924	1856		
125	E 91	ROSENBERG, ISRAEL ELAN		11 SEP 1969	15 DEC 1902		ANNA
370	V16	ROSENBERG, JENNIE ESTHER		1905		LOUIS & BETSY	
370	G 3	ROSENBERG, JOSEPH N		22 NOV 1950			MARION
102	F33	ROSENBERG, LEO		30 DEC 1962	11 JUN 1897		ELIZABETH
222	AE10	ROSENBERG, LILLIAN	OSCAR	12 APR 1980	30 SEP 1889		ABRAHAM
125	K113	ROSENBERG, LOUIS		10 MAR 1942	1866	MOSHE & RACHEL	IDA
370	V14	ROSENBERG, LOUIS		1947	1876		BETSY
370	G 2	ROSENBERG, MARION J		28 MAR 1963			JOSEPH
102	E41	ROSENBERG, MARY		16 FEB 1972	1877		ALTER
102	U30	ROSENBERG, MARY E		22 JAN 1987	15 JUL 1888		NATHAN
125	D 90	ROSENBERG, MAURICE W		1 DEC 1981	1897		MAURICE

Cem	Row	Name	Maiden Name	DOD	DOB	Parents	Spouse
123		ROSENBERG, MAX		7 SEP 1954	1913		
123		ROSENBERG, MILTON		18 DEC 1944	1916		
105	A11	ROSENBERG, MINNIE		4 OCT 1951	1874		
101	J35	ROSENBERG, MINNIE	BAGGISH	30 MAY 1976	1887		
107	C2	ROSENBERG, NATHAN E		26 SEP 1978	1914		ABRAHAM
102	U29	ROSENBERG, NATHAN H		6 SEP 1970	18 JUN 1885		MARY
374	A19	ROSENBERG, PAUL		25 FEB 1922	31 MAY 1907		
125	D 91	ROSENBERG, RAE	SHUFRO	21 SEP 1983	1898		RAE
125	d2-e1	ROSENBERG, REBECCA		20 MAY 1935	1874		
102	AJ87	ROSENBERG, REUBEN F		12 DEC 1943	1879		FANNIE
119	B11	ROSENBERG, ROBERT S		2 OCT 1988	1913		
248	J76	ROSENBERG, ROSE		13 JUL 1921			
374	G11	ROSENBERG, ROSE		1918	1890		
222	AE 3	ROSENBERG, SAMUEL		17 JUL 1934	1852		SHIFRA
105	AA10	ROSENBERG, SARA		19 APR 1992			
222	AE 4	ROSENBERG, SHIFRA M		7 DEC 1935	1856		SAMUEL
125	J 60	ROSENBERG, WILLIAM		1908			EDITH
102	T36	ROSENBERG, WILLIAM		28 SEP 1963	1889		ADA
125	D 78	ROSENBLATT, ABRAHAM		4 APR 1971	1890		
751	E11	ROSENBLATT, BERIL		16 NOV 1947	15 OCT 1871		RACHEL
125	C 81	ROSENBLATT, ELLIOT		10 SEP 1963	1920		
751	K22	ROSENBLATT, HARRY		14 MAR 1932			
108	A 5	ROSENBLATT, HERMAN		5 DEC 1971	1910		
108	B 6	ROSENBLATT, IDA	CUTLER	14 JUN 1946	16 MAR 1887		SAMUEL
125	D 79	ROSENBLATT, ITZEL MARC		10 JAN 1961	1915		SARAH
125	D 82	ROSENBLATT, JACOB		1 APR 1968	10 FEB 1892		ROSE
102	AE68	ROSENBLATT, JOAN M		8 OCT 1974	19 SEP 1949		
105	C53	ROSENBLATT, JOSEPH		15 FEB 1958	1892		
105	L8	ROSENBLATT, MARY	MANDELL	6 DEC 1987	1893		REUBEN
102	T50	ROSENBLATT, PAULINE		13 FEB 1947	1861		
751	E12	ROSENBLATT, RACHEL		2 JUN 1960	15 OCT 1874		BERIL
105	L11	ROSENBLATT, REUBEN A		16 FEB 1966	1900	MAX & LIBBY ITKIN	MARY
125	D 83	ROSENBLATT, ROSE		22 MAY 1973	4 NOV 1904		JACOB
108	B 5	ROSENBLATT, SAMUEL		21 MAR 1950	18 APR 1880		IDA
125	D 80	ROSENBLATT, SARAH MINNIE		5 APR 1952	1914		ITSEL
102	AD178	ROSENBLUM, HARRY B		16 JUL 1963	1898		
493	H15	ROSENBLUM, MARK ANDREW		4 MAR 1986	26 JUN 1975		
102	AJ125	ROSENBLUM, MAX		4 AUG 1959	1908		
111	12	ROSENBLUTH, ALVIN		11 MAY 1985	6 DEC 1931		
111	12	ROSENBLUTH, EMANUEL		9 JUL 1985	4 APR 1901		
125		ROSENFELD, (BABY)		15 OCT 1948			
102	CA 2	ROSENFELD, DOROTHY K		1961	1893		
113	O43	ROSENFELD, GERTRUDE	BEERMAN	2 AUG 1987	18 OCT 1897		
102	S11	ROSENFELD, JOSEPH EUGENE		18 JUN 1975	26 MAY 1907		
330	AG 9	ROSENFELD, MARCI LYNN		1972	1958		
125	W199	ROSENFELD, ROSE	GREENBERG	24 SEP 1981	1889		
125	M110	ROSENFELD, SOLOMON		12 JUN 1935	1882	BENJAMIN & TZERRELL	
125	ZB171	ROSENFIELD, ABBA LABE		1991	1910		
123		ROSENFIELD, BESSIE		1970	1890		JOSEPH
751	B35	ROSENFIELD, BESSIE		22 APR 1916	15 DEC 1858		
119	E25	ROSENFIELD, DAVID E		3 JAN 1988	30 NOV 1942		
102	A17	ROSENFIELD, EDWARD		11 APR 1933	1914		
101	A10	ROSENFIELD, GERTRUDE		25 JAN 1929	1848		LIEB
119	H52	ROSENFIELD, HYMAN		11 FEB 1987	6 APR 1916		
116	AZ 7	ROSENFIELD, IRVING		13 FEB 1991	9 SEP 1912		
123		ROSENFIELD, JOSEPH		26 MAR 1943	1892		BESSIE
101	A11	ROSENFIELD, LEIB		28 FEB 1923	1842		GERTRUDE
102	AD114	ROSENGARD, CHARLES L		19 JAN 1957			JENNIE
102	AD115	ROSENGARD, JENNIE F		18 SEP 1985			CHARLES
123		ROSENHOLTZ, DAVE		18 APR 1966			EVA
123		ROSENHOLTZ, EVA		26 AUG 1988	15 APR 1902		DAVE
392	J 8	ROSENHOLTZ, HARRY		13 SEP 1928	1913	MEYER	
248	A45	ROSENSTEIN, BESSIE		1 FEB 1980	15 NOV 1887		ISIDORE
104	H 6	ROSENSTEIN, DAVID		23 SEP 1979	1914		
248	N78	ROSENSTEIN, FANNIE		21 OCT 1938	1894		
751	M26	ROSENSTEIN, HILDA		1978	1888		

Cem	Row	Name	Maiden Name	DOD	DOB	Parents	Spouse
248	A46	ROSENSTEIN, ISIDORE		26 MAY 1963	6 MAY 1887		BESSIE
751	M27	ROSENSTEIN, JACK		1966	1889		
104	H 7	ROSENSTEIN, MRS					DAVID
104	I30	ROSENSTEIN, MURIEL J		6 DEC 1981	23 JUN 1944		
104	K38	ROSENSTEIN, NATHAN		26 NOV 1971	3 JUN 1904		
102	AK236	ROSENSTOCK, RITA	NEUMAN	9 OCT 1977	9 APR 1919		SAMUEL
102	AK237	ROSENSTOCK, SAMUEL		22 DEC 1987	16 FEB 1909		RITA
371	J24	ROSENSTREICH, AARON L		11 MAY 1969	1943	MAX & LENA	
371	J23	ROSENSTREICH, LENA		NDD	1909		MAX
371	J22	ROSENSTREICH, MAX		1989	1912		LENA
104	A29	ROSENSWEIG, CELIA		24 NOV 1974			CHARLES
104	A30	ROSENSWEIG, CHARLES		26 DEC 1968			CELIA
125	P166	ROSENSWEIG, SOPHIE		16 FEB 1968	1893		ALEXANDER
329	B46	ROSENTHAL, (BABY)					
329	B47	ROSENTHAL, (BABY)					
101	A28	ROSENTHAL, ABRAHAM		1 MAR 1912	1832		
102	AJ153	ROSENTHAL, ABRAHAM		8 JAN 1966	1908		
101	C 1	ROSENTHAL, ABRAHAM		20 SEP 1967	13 FEB 1884		IDA
222	AP12	ROSENTHAL, ADOLPH		22 DEC 1967	1890	EMIL & BERTHA (FORST)	
102	AC100	ROSENTHAL, ANNIE	GREEN	20 JUN 1935	1868		NATHAN
121	J32	ROSENTHAL, ARTHUR		23 FEB 1991	26 AUG 1915		
102	AC96	ROSENTHAL, AUGUSTA G		23 AUG 1977	1 JAN 1895		
119	J36	ROSENTHAL, BENJAMIN		2 OCT 1981	12 MAR 1913		
447	S18	ROSENTHAL, BENJAMIN		22 JUN 1959	1901		
222	AP13	ROSENTHAL, BERTHA	FORST	1 MAY 1938	1857		EMIL
119	F11	ROSENTHAL, BESSIE		5 AUG 1989	1 FEB 1909		
102	AB191	ROSENTHAL, BESSIE H		24 APR 1976	10 MAR 1900		HARRY
372	K 4	ROSENTHAL, CHARLOTTE		1967	1881		JOSEF
447	AB12	ROSENTHAL, DAVID		1975	1921		
102	A40	ROSENTHAL, ELISE	BARASH	3 JUL 1941	1874		
121	T14	ROSENTHAL, ELIZABETH	FRISCH	17 FEB 1973	25 MAY 1889		
222	AP14	ROSENTHAL, EMIL	OF BONN GERMANY	13 DEC 1941	27 DEC 1857	JOSEPH & SOPHIE	BERTHA
119	F16	ROSENTHAL, FANNIE		23 FEB 1976	1911		
447	C38	ROSENTHAL, FANNIE MURIEL		8 SEP 1947	1869		HARRIS
125	ZA188	ROSENTHAL, FRIEDA		12 NOV 1992	11 DEC 1908		
105	A16	ROSENTHAL, GLADYS KLEIMAN	KALINSKY	1974	1900		
447	C37	ROSENTHAL, HARRIS		29 MAR 1936	1868		FANNIE
447	Q14	ROSENTHAL, HARRY		15 DEC 1935			REBECCA
102	AB190	ROSENTHAL, HARRY M		20 OCT 1985	26 AUG 1897		BESSIE
102	AC97	ROSENTHAL, HELENA SELMA		11 FEB 1966	4 DEC 1889		SAMUEL
330	AH20	ROSENTHAL, HYMAN ROBERT		30 SEP 1976	9 JUL 1910		
101	C 2	ROSENTHAL, IDA		27 AUG 1957	14 MAY 1887		ABRAHAM
447	Q 9	ROSENTHAL, ISIDORE		23 JUN 1977	10 MAY 1901		
102	AI154	ROSENTHAL, JACOB		23 NOV 1966	1904		ESTHER FRE
372	K 3	ROSENTHAL, JOSEF		1959	1880		CHARLOTTE
102	BB16	ROSENTHAL, JULIA	PEARL	6 JUN 1987	7 OCT 1907		
125	J116	ROSENTHAL, MALKA		27 SEP 1938	1872	GEORGE & MASHA	
125	J113	ROSENTHAL, MAX		14 FEB 1946	10 JAN 1871		
102	A71	ROSENTHAL, MIRIAM	BOYLAND	30 MAR 1942			
121	R 3	ROSENTHAL, MORRIS L		10 AUG 1988	18 DEC 1919		
102	AC101	ROSENTHAL, NATHAN		23 JUL 1931	25 JAN 1869		ANNIE
125	J112	ROSENTHAL, NATHAN JACOB		16 DEC 1938	1912	MORDECHAI & MALKA	
119	A44	ROSENTHAL, NATHAN W		31 JAN 1992	12 SEP 1915		
447	Q13	ROSENTHAL, REBECCA		14 DEC 1955			HARRY
119	J35	ROSENTHAL, SADIE		21 OCT 1988	1908		
102	AC99	ROSENTHAL, SAMUEL		1 MAR 1960	1891		HELENA
447	C39	ROSENTHAL, SARAH		14 DEC 1966	1898	HARRIS & FANNIE	
102	A35	ROSENTHAL, SIDNEY		14 FEB 1937	1899		
446	C25	ROSENWASSER, ESTHER M		1979	1899		
125	P165	ROSENZWEIG, ALEXANDER		12 OCT 1948	15 JAN 1886	ISRAEL & IDA	SOPHIE
125	L117	ROSENZWEIG, DAVID		22 JUN 1930	1882	ISRAEL & IDA	
105	C52	ROSETSKY, BENJAMIN		1958	1886		ZELDA
105	C51	ROSETSKY, ZELDA		1972	1906		BENJAMIN
116	AW15	ROSKIN, ANNA BRONSTEIN	KAMINS	17 FEB 1972	30 SEP 1915		
102	AB28	ROSKIN, DORIS S		1959	1902		SAMUEL
331		ROSKIN, ESTHER		8 NOV 1893	1837		

Cem	Row	Name	Maiden Name	DOD	DOB	Parents	Spouse
102	AB29	ROSKIN, SAMUEL		27 MAR 1974	1894		
102	CA48	ROSOFF, ESTHER K		25 MAY 1966	1889		DORIS
102	CA49	ROSOFF, ISRAEL		17 APR 1965	1890		ISRAEL
125	T146	ROSOFF, JOSEPH J		18 MAY 1939	1882	LOUIS & DORA	ESTHER
125	N187	ROSOFF, ROSE D		17 OCT 1966	1884		
391	Q42	ROSOFSKY, BENJAMIN		21 SEP 1955	1895	ABRAHAM MORDECHAI	
391	G36	ROSOFSKY, IDA		27 JUN 1931	1861	SHLOMO ELIEZER	
391	D28	ROSOFSKY, MAX		10 APR 1944	1859	SHRUGA DOV	
377	O20	ROSON, PHILIP I		23 NOV 1958	3 APR 1896		
102	Q 2	ROSOW, DAVID		17 OCT 1950	18 OCT 1870		RUTH
102	AB161	ROSOW, LILLIAN F	ZUCKERMAN	20 OCT 1963	1 JAN 1907		TOBIAS
116	AW12	ROSOW, MARILYN E		31 JUL 1966	16 MAR 1931		STANLEY
102	Q 1	ROSOW, RUTH		19 APR 1965	19 JAN 1889		DAVID
116	AW14	ROSOW, SCOTT D		31 JUL 1966	31 OCT 1961	STANLEY & MARILYN	
116	AW11	ROSOW, SHERYL		31 JUL 1966	3 MAR 1954	STANLEY & MARILYN	
116	AW13	ROSOW, STANLEY P		31 JUL 1966	29 JAN 1929		MARILYN
102	AB162	ROSOW, TOBIAS H		5 NOV 1980	24 MAR 1905		LILLIAN
447	N32	ROSS, ALBERT LEWIS		24 FEB 1991	24 JUL 1915		SHIRLEY
447	T16	ROSS, HAROLD L		10 JUN 1960	1904		
750	J24	ROSS, HYMAN		8 MAY 1961	1896		MIRIAM
106	G19	ROSS, JAMES		23 DEC 1975	7 SEP 1916		SUE
222	AR 5	ROSS, JOHN ALBERT		27 SEP 1984	14 DEC 1904		ROSE
222	AJ15	ROSS, LOTTIE LIBBY		17 NOV 1989	14 JUL 1903		MEYER
102	BE 3	ROSS, MELVIN M "BUTCH"		18 JUN 1987	11 JUN 1941		
222	AJ16	ROSS, MEYER M		1 FEB 1978	5 APR 1898		LOTTIE
750	J25	ROSS, MIRIAM		2 MAR 1970	1900		HYMAN
125	I602	ROSS, PAULINE		11 AUG 1965	1889		
222	AR 4	ROSS, ROSE RACHEL		30 AUG 1968	21 FEB 1912		JOHN
447	N31	ROSS, SHIRLEY	BERG	NDD	22 JAN 1923		ALBERT
127	B	ROSS, STEVEN L		28 DEC 1987	9 NOV 1940		
106	G20	ROSS, SUE	WHITE	12 SEP 1976			JAMES
116	R 1	ROSS, WALTER M		1974	1925		
248	J60	ROTBLAT, MAURICE		29 JAN 1923	1853		SARAH
248	J61	ROTBLAT, SARAH D		24 NOV 1936	1857		MAURICE
329	C31	ROTFUSS, ESTHER LILLIAN		1 JUN 1961	1889		MORRIS
329	C32	ROTFUSS, MORRIS		30 SEP 1963	1887		ESTHER
125		ROTH, (STILLBORN)		9 APR 1967			
102	BC16	ROTH, BESSIE	BAGGISH	5 OCT 1988	28 FEB 1910		SAMUEL
125	E123	ROTH, BESSIE		10 MAY 1950	1857		
125	O100	ROTH, CALMON		JAN 1922	1913		
249	L 3	ROTH, DAVID MORRIS		13 DEC 1985	22 AUG 1935		
125	M156	ROTH, ETTA	RACHLIN	15 NOV 1982	1891		JESSIE
104	J 5	ROTH, HAROLD E		15 JUL 1955	1909		
113	A37	ROTH, IRENE		9 JUN 1991	5 OCT 1927		
102	AK238	ROTH, IRVING K		12 NOV 1976	19 AUG 1903		
107	E10	ROTH, JACK		27 JUL 1984	12 JUN 1914		MATILDA
125	E125	ROTH, JENNIE	WINTZ	28 JUL 1971	1880	YECHIEL KALMAN	JOSEPH
125	M155	ROTH, JESSIE		13 MAY 1952	1892		ETTA
125	E124	ROTH, JOSEPH		11 AUG 1965	1879	SHNEAR ZALMAN & BESSIE	JENNIE
107	E9	ROTH, MATILDA		18 JUN 1983			JACK
113	O73	ROTH, MAY	SELTZER	7 MAR 1975	14 AUG 1906		
102	BC15	ROTH, SAMUEL		31 MAY 1990	27 JUL 1945		BESSIE
125	X184	ROTH, SAUL		12 JUL 1982	1921	JOSEPH JENNIE (WINTZ)	
119	C15	ROTHBERG, ALBERT M		3 SEP 1987	22 JUL 1912		
248	D46	ROTHBLAT, EVA B		9 JAN 1945	1876		HYMAN
248	D44	ROTHBLAT, HELEN		13 OCT 1989	17 MAY 1907		HENRY
248	D43	ROTHBLAT, HENRY		25 FEB 1988	18 JAN 1906		HELEN
248	D47	ROTHBLAT, HYMAN		20 JUN 1952	1869		EVA
248	D45	ROTHBLAT, MAX		12 NOV 1973	14 MAR 1894		
248	C46	ROTHBLATT, REUBEN MD		23 JAN 1985	18 JAN 1906		
101	L28	ROTHCHILD, EVA		2 OCT 1918	1875		
371	AK 8	ROTHENBERG, ALICE		27 JAN 1964	1895		HARRY
371	AK 9	ROTHENBERG, HARRY		11 NOV 1967	1891		ALICE
331		ROTHENBERG, SARAH		28 JAN 1901	1874		
447	U26	ROTHENSTEIN, YETTA		11 APR 1932	1895		
125	H 41	ROTHFEDER, ISAAC		29 MAY 1940	1860	SOLOMON	LEAH

Cem	Row	Name	Maiden Name	DOD	DOB	Parents	Spouse
125	H 42	ROTHFEDER, LEAH		19 MAR 1948	25 MAR 1867	MENACHEM MENDEL	ISAAC
125	A 16	ROTHFEDER, SADIE		9 JUN 1984	1892		
125	H 40	ROTHFEDER, SIDNEY N DR		22 MAY 1975	1899		
125	Y171	ROTHKOPF, LAWRENCE BRIAN		21 AUG 1983	5 FEB 1970		
371	AC14	ROTHMAN, ESTHER F		27 JAN 1976	1893		HYMAN
371	AC13	ROTHMAN, HARRY		2 JAN 1990	12 MAR 1916	HYMAN & ESTHER	
751	D 4	ROTHMAN, HARRY		1958	1900		
371	AC15	ROTHMAN, HYMAN		12 MAY 1961	1887		ESTHER
101	I39	ROTHSCHILD, ANDREW DAVID		3 OCT 1991	8 AUG 1991		
102	AC182	ROTHSTEIN, ALEXANDER		27 DEC 1964	6 NOV 1900		
371	K20	ROTHSTEIN, CHARLES		1964	1874		IDA
371	A 4	ROTHSTEIN, FRANK		1993	1906		STELLA
371	K18	ROTHSTEIN, HENRY		15 SEP 1966	15 MAY 1911	CHARLES & IDA	
371	K19	ROTHSTEIN, IDA		1976	1884		CHARLES
125	H142	ROTHSTEIN, MORRIS		19 DEC 1967	9 APR 1884	MORRIS & ROSE (SILVERSTEIN)	NETTIE
125	H143	ROTHSTEIN, NETTIE	GREENSTEIN	25 NOV 1975	23 DEC 1883	HARRY & BAILE (GOLDBERG)	MORRIS
371	J15	ROTHSTEIN, SAUL		7 FEB 1987	2 MAR 1903		
371	A 3	ROTHSTEIN, STELLA		1977	1916		FRANK
125	G143	ROTHSTEIN, SYLVIA	FEIGENBAUM	25 SEP 1962	1 AUG 1921	MAX & MINNIE (DUBOWY)	GEORGE
104	H 9	ROTMAN, DAVID		26 SEP 1980	20 JAN 1897		ROCHLA
104	H 8	ROTMAN, ROCHLA		26 JUL 1988	13 JUL 1895		DAVID
113	M22	ROTTNER, JOHN S		2 NOV 1986	19 MAR 1907		
377	B38	ROWLAND, VERA	MAIBRUNN	1 JAN 1990	31 MAR 1901		
751	C 7	ROYER, ANNA	DOLINSKY	20 JUL 1959	17 JAN 1903		
125	O 80	RUBACK, WILLIAM MORDECHAI	REEBACK	7 DEC 1918	1889	MORDECHAI & REBECCA (COHEN)	JENNIE
112	B17	RUBEL, LORE		10 MAR 1990	21 DEC 1918		
751	M12	RUBENS, ANNA R	TUCHMAN	15 DEC 1956	1878		
751	M10	RUBENS, HENRY LENS		9 OCT 1958			
751	M13	RUBENS, ISIDORE		16 DEC 1955	1872		
125	O154	RUBENSTEIN, BENJAMIN		24 MAY 1953	1886		ROSE
125	B 62	RUBENSTEIN, BERNARD A		24 NOV 1991	11 MAY 1913		
125	N117	RUBENSTEIN, DAVID		6 DEC 1971	8 MAY 1907		
102	H37	RUBENSTEIN, ESTHER		1943	1892		MORRIS
102	J36	RUBENSTEIN, EVELYN		22 JUL 1969	1906		JOSEPH
125	B 59	RUBENSTEIN, HARRY		25 OCT 1958	1875	MOSHE	JENNIE
125	M169	RUBENSTEIN, JACOB		10 MAR 1953	16 DEC 1905		
125	B 60	RUBENSTEIN, JENNIE K		10 MAY 1964	1880		HARRY
125	A 62	RUBENSTEIN, JOSEPH		1983	1902		MARY
102	J35	RUBENSTEIN, JOSEPH		22 FEB 1977	1906		EVELYN
125	A 61	RUBENSTEIN, MARY	PEARSON	20 SEP 1971	1904		JOSEPH
125	C125	RUBENSTEIN, MINNIE	RUTKIN	11 JAN 1979	1917		ROBERT
102	H38	RUBENSTEIN, MORRIS		1969	1888		ESTHER
125	C124	RUBENSTEIN, NANCY S		24 JUL 1958	1942	ROBERT & MINNIE	
127	G	RUBENSTEIN, PAUL ALBERT		22 FEB 1992	11 SEP 1928		
125	C126	RUBENSTEIN, ROBERT		4 NOV 1966	1909		MINNIE
125	M158	RUBENSTEIN, ROSE		19 SEP 1952	27 JAN 1906		
125	O153	RUBENSTEIN, ROSE		2 APR 1949	1891		BEN
125	B 56	RUBENSTEIN, SAMUEL		17 APR 1984	1904		
116	O19	RUBIN, ALBERT NATHAN		1985	1925		
248	D51	RUBIN, ALICE		2 DEC 1988	15 JUN 1903		
377	L 8	RUBIN, ANNA		10 JUL 1969	6 NOV 1892		MEYER
392	I33	RUBIN, BELLA		1983	1893		
447	T 5	RUBIN, BENJAMIN		10 DEC 1961	22 AUG 1899		SYLVIA
370	T22	RUBIN, CHARLES		15 APR 1990			FANNIE
374	B13	RUBIN, CHARLES LOUIS		1 JAN 1946			FANNY
392	F33	RUBIN, DORA		4 OCT 1920	1881		
110	D17	RUBIN, DOROTHY	RACHLEFF	20 NOV 1971	25 DEC 1901		
370	T21	RUBIN, FANNIE		4 NOV 1989			CHARLES
374	B14	RUBIN, FANNY		7 SEP 1932			CHARLES
377	U 4	RUBIN, FAY C		19 JUL 1991	25 JAN 1903	MESHELEM LEV	NATHAN
248	D49	RUBIN, GEORGE		13 APR 1961	1900		LILLIAN
377	R28	RUBIN, HARRY J		30 AUG 1969	5 JAN 1894		MARION
101	E32	RUBIN, IDA		10 OCT 1988	11 OCT 1912		LEOPOLD
249	H38	RUBIN, ISRAEL		4 DEC 1988	12 MAR 1915		
249	N43	RUBIN, JACOB		3 NOV 1955	5 DEC 1888		
125	M127	RUBIN, JOSEPH		1930	1867		PAULINE

Cem	Row	Name	Maiden Name	DOD	DOB	Parents	Spouse
392	I32	RUBIN, JULIUS		1948	1885		
101	E33	RUBIN, LEOPOLD		7 APR 1970	24 AUG 1907		
248	D50	RUBIN, LILLIAN	BATTALIN	2 JAN 1957	1901		IDA
377	ZA26	RUBIN, LOUIS		1983	1906	YECHIEL	GEORGE
377	R29	RUBIN, MARION		4 OCT 1969	22 APR 1894		SARAH
377	L 9	RUBIN, MEYER		15 MAY 1974	10 MAR 1889		HARRY
446	B12	RUBIN, MIRIAM L		1924	1903		ANNA
377	U 3	RUBIN, NATHAN C		10 FEB 1991	21 SEP 1899	MOSHE CHAIM	
113	J43	RUBIN, NATHAN F		13 JUN 1954	25 MAY 1883		FAY
125	M128	RUBIN, PAULINE		15 FEB 1961	1870		PAULINE
113	J42	RUBIN, PAULINE T		6 MAY 1975	25 OCT 1886		JOSEPH
113	L48	RUBIN, REBECCA		27 MAR 1964	29 APR 1892		NATHAN
373	K15	RUBIN, RUTH		2 OCT 1948	4 MAY 1900		WILLIAM
377	ZA25	RUBIN, SARA		1975	1908	SOLOMON	
370	A59	RUBIN, SARAH	LIEBERMAN	14 JUN 1912			LOUIS
447	T 4	RUBIN, SYLVIA K		13 JUL 1966	25 DEC 1898		
370	G39	RUBIN, VICTOR		31 MAR 1910			BENJAMIN
113	L47	RUBIN, WILLIAM		29 MAY 1981	1 MAR 1892		REBECCA
105	F10	RUBINOVE, HARRY M		16 NOV 1986	26 AUG 1915	MORRIS & SOPHIE RABINOVICH	
447	T20	RUBINOW, EDWARD		1983	1905		FAYE
447	T21	RUBINOW, FAYE		1958	1910		EDWARD
113	I20	RUBINOW, MARY	BRODSKY	12 MAY 1981	16 SEP 1887		WILLIAM
113	I21	RUBINOW, WILLIAM		19 JAN 1972	20 JUN 1883		MARY
370	B39	RUBINOWITCH, MORDECHAI		8 MAY 1952	1867	SHMUIEL ELIYAHU	
102	A26	RUBINSON, SAMUEL		6 AUG 1935	1891		
370	I57	RUBINSTEIN, BARNEY		1 MAR 1933	15 APR 1884		
119	E 8	RUBINSTEIN, BERTHA		19 SEP 1986	1909		
248	I77	RUBINSTEIN, JACOB		6 APR 1935	1905		
125	B 79	RUBINSTEIN, JOSEPH		30 JUL 1983	1903		
222	A 5	RUBINSTEIN, MAX		11 JUL 1950	23 OCT 1880		TILLIE
119	E 7	RUBINSTEIN, MILTON		6 MAR 1976	1913		
751	M11	RUBINSTEIN, SASCHA		1990	1908		
222	A 6	RUBINSTEIN, TILLIE		13 MAR 1949	25 DEC 1881		MAX
121	S 3	RUCHIN, CHARLES I		1979	1919		
121	K16	RUCHIN, JOSEPH		29 JAN 1970	1890		
121	K17	RUCHIN, MINNIE		14 SEP 1965	1892		
121	R 4	RUCHIN, SAMUEL M		3 MAY 1985	7 FEB 1926		
125	P179	RUDEN, BERTHA		30 NOV 1963	1879		
104	J 1	RUDENS, SAMUEL		26 MAR 1950	1878		
447	E 5	RUDERMAN, ALLEN J		24 FEB 1965	1910	ISAAC & SOPHIE	
447	E 8	RUDERMAN, ISAAC S		5 MAR 1932	1883		SOPHIE
446	B33	RUDERMAN, JACOB		5 MAR 1910	23 APR 1864		
446	A45	RUDERMAN, MEYER W		26 NOV 1930	1858		SARAH
446	A46	RUDERMAN, SARAH		22 AUG 1933	1869		MEYER
446	B21	RUDERMAN, SARAH F	BERNSTEIN	21 SEP 1917	1863		
447	E 7	RUDERMAN, SOPHIE E		26 MAY 1968	1889		ISAAC
377	R17	RUDICH, AMELIA	AMSTER	29 AUG 1988	23 SEP 1897		HARRY
377	R18	RUDICH, HARRY		3 APR 1964	6 JAN 1891		AMELIA
125	N113	RUDINSKY, ABRAHAM		26 APR 1929	1887	MOSHE & RACHEL	
125		RUDINSKY, EDITH	KATKIN	3 OCT 1939	1876	YALE & IDA	
125		RUDMAN, ANNA		6 NOV 1918	1886	WOLF & YETTA	
125	J118	RUDMAN, DORA		11 AUG 1938	1856	DAVID & ETHEL	
125	O150	RUDMAN, EDWARD		31 JAN 1957	1892		MAY
125	L179	RUDMAN, JACK J		26 JUN 1971	1896		SYLVIA
125	O149	RUDMAN, MAE		13 FEB 1949	1895	YITZCHAK & HANNAH	EDWARD
125	K191	RUDMAN, SIMON		29 NOV 1978	1888		
125	L178	RUDMAN, SYLVIA ALEX		23 NOV 1975	1905		JACK
102	S35	RUDNER, SONIA		29 JUN 1947	1870		
120	D 4	RUDNICK, MICHAEL L		1 OCT 1991			
120	D 3	RUDNICK, RUTH K		NDD			
102	A 1	RUDOF, MARCIA		14 SEP 1940	6 FEB 1927		
101	A20	RUDOLPH, HYMAN ISIDOR		11 JAN 1919	1834		
751	M 5	RUDY, BURTON MACY		28 OCT 1987	16 FEB 1920		
104	J28	RUDY, GEORGE		21 FEB 1982	1890		IDA
104	J29	RUDY, IDA		14 MAR 1961	1897		GEORGE
116	BY84	RUDY, IDA SOLOMON	KAPLAN	21 OCT 1973	22 FEB 1890	JOHN & SARAH	

Cem	Row	Name	Maiden Name	DOD	DOB	Parents	Spouse
125	S187	RUDY, ISADORE		18 MAR 1958	12 NOV 1903		
377	O 9	RUFF, FANNIE R		1948	1874		SAMUEL
377	O 8	RUFF, SAMUEL S		1962	1876		FANNIE
102	AI61	RULNICK, BETTY	SACK	31 AUG 1963	1906		HARRY
102	AI62	RULNICK, HARRY		25 FEB 1979	1902		BETTY
105	L20	RULNICK, LEAH	GERSHMAN	24 FEB 1987	25 DEC 1898		
101	D21	RULNICK, NATHAN		1988	1900		
101	I18	RULNICK, SAMUEL		4 DEC 1986	9 OCT 1895		SARAH
101	I17	RULNICK, SARAH		14 APR 1979	12 AUG 1896		SAMUEL
102	J34	RULNICK, WILLIAM		JUN 1936	APR 1873		
750	G20	RUSKEIN, JOSEPH		28 FEB 1962	1885		
377	N 6	RUSS, JACOB A		1951	1885		LILLIAN
377	N 7	RUSS, LILLIAN W		1975	1885		JACOB
116	AV12	RUSSELL, ELLA		18 OCT 1980	5 SEP 1896		SAMUEL
370	S49	RUSSELL, ROBERT		26 JUL 1962	22 FEB 1907		
116	AV13	RUSSELL, SAMUEL		11 AUG 1979	20 DEC 1893		ELLA
249	B 8	RUSSIAN, RUTH		NDD	8 JUL 1921		SAMUEL
249	B 7	RUSSIAN, SAMUEL S		NDD	7 MAR 1917		RUTH
447	M 2	RUSSMAN, ABRAHAM		20 MAY 1947	1867		
447	M 6	RUSSMAN, CHARLES		29 JUL 1937	1898	ABRAHAM	
392	C17	RUTBERG, ANNA SARAH		13 AUG 1989	1910		MEYER
392	G15	RUTBERG, EVA RACHEL		3 APR 1943	1869	SAMUEL	
392	D 9	RUTBERG, FANNIE		11 MAY 1965	1891	ISRAEL MOSHE	SAMUEL
392	D28	RUTBERG, IDA B		6 JAN 1982	1912	ABRHAM	JACOB
392	D27	RUTBERG, JACOB D		25 MAY 1975	1904	JOSEPH	IDA
392	G16	RUTBERG, JOSEPH		27 APR 1953	1867		
392	C16	RUTBERG, LOUIS		16 MAY 1945	26 MAY 1930	MEYER & ANNA	
392	C18	RUTBERG, MEYER		8 JAN 1961	1899		ANNA
392	D10	RUTBERG, SAMUEL		9 APR 1964	1891	JOSEPH	FANNIE
373	K 2	RUTCHICK, (BABY BOY)		24 NOV 1952			
330	AD 7	RUTCHICK, SAMUEL		2 APR 1970	25 NOV 1917		
370	K13	RUTCHIK, ANNA		31 DEC 1947	1874		JOSEPH
371	AF 5	RUTCHIK, ANNIE		20 SEP 1990	17 OCT 1904		
330	D39	RUTCHIK, ANTHONY		8 JAN 1962	1886		
371	AF 6	RUTCHIK, ELIAS		14 JUN 1982	11 APR 1902		
374	G47	RUTCHIK, IDA		1947	1888		SAMUEL
376	B10	RUTCHIK, ISRAEL		9 MAY 1935	1893		SARAH
370	L 6	RUTCHIK, JOSEPH		22 OCT 1943	1873		ANNA
374	E52	RUTCHIK, LOUIS P		26 FEB 1989	13 JUN 1918		
370	A62	RUTCHIK, MALLY		1920	1896	JOSEPH & ANNA	
374	G48	RUTCHIK, SAMUEL		1959	1885		IDA
376	B 9	RUTCHIK, SARAH		23 NOV 1960	1891		ISRAEL
373	E 5	RUTCHIK, SAUL		26 JAN 1982	10 SEP 1912		
392	D16	RUTMAN, BENJAMIN		30 MAR 1960	1881	AKIBA	MINNIE
392	J29	RUTMAN, CHARNA		7 NOV 1924		JOSEPH MEYER	
392	D30	RUTMAN, ELIZABETH		22 OCT 1976	1884	SAMUEL	HYMAN
377	Y 2	RUTMAN, HAROLD J		1975	1904	ABRAHAM	MABEL
392	D31	RUTMAN, HYMAN		7 AUG 1949	1879	AKIBA	ELIZABETH
377	Y 1	RUTMAN, MABEL C		17 JAN 1988		CHAIM	HAROLD
392	D15	RUTMAN, MINNIE		4 JAN 1959	1889	JOSEPH SIMON	BENJAMIN
116	B10	RUTSTEIN, OSCAR		1989	1921		
102	AC92	RUTT, ABRAHAM		29 AUG 1961	1888		DORA
102	AC93	RUTT, DORA	EPSTEIN	13 APR 1976	1890		ABRAHAM
104	G14	RUTTER, MILTON		16 OCT 1986			
105	C19	RUZANSKY, HARRY		1979	1898		
105	G20	RUZENSKY, IRENE		23 DEC 1990	14 NOV 1923		
105	G30	RUZENSKY, JOSEPH		10 NOV 1973	1889		ROSE
105	G29	RUZENSKY, ROSE		11 FEB 1968	1892		JOSEPH
372	I 1	RYACK, MARJORIE		4 DEC 1986	20 FEB 1930		
123		SABAT, JOHN A		2 FEB 1942	1906		
125		SABLE, (BABY)		21 NOV 1934	1934		
125	B137	SABLE, ALICE	BAGGISH	27 FEB 1977	11 MAY 1904		LOUIS
125	L174	SABLE, BESSIE	LISS	15 JUL 1972			SAMUEL
125	X198	SABLE, EVA		27 MAY 1991	1905		MORRIS
125	B136	SABLE, LOUIS		9 FEB 1969	15 FEB 1896		ALICE
125	X199	SABLE, MORRIS		30 OCT 1983	1899		EVA

Cem	Row	Name	Maiden Name	DOD	DOB	Parents	Spouse
125	L175	SABLE, SAMUEL		25 APR 1971	1893	SHAYA	BESSIE
125	D 74	SABLE, YALE		7 JUN 1958	1902	MICHAEL & TILLIE	
125	C 71	SABLOTSKY, ANNA	KALMANOWICZ	23 JUN 1964	1907	KALMON & DORA	SAMUEL
125	D 73	SABLOTSKY, MICHAEL		15 APR 1946	1867		TILLIE
125	C 72	SABLOTSKY, SAMUEL		1986	1900		ANNA
125	D 72	SABLOTSKY, TILLIE		29 OCT 1956	1872		MICHAEL
102	O31	SABOL, JENNIE	GREENBERG	1937	1887		NATHAN
102	O30	SABOL, NATHAN		1924	1883		JENNIE
119	F23	SACARTOFF, BEN		29 NOV 1973	14 FEB 1905		
119	F24	SACARTOFF, TODD		2 JUL 1989	27 DEC 1904		
102	AH157	SACHER, ABRAHAM A		14 APR 1976	27 NOV 1911		
370	I51	SACHNER, SARAH		1943	1902		
105	E11	SACK, BECKY		3 JAN 1981	1898		
222	AO 2	SACK, EVA RACHEL		1956	1954		
105	I20	SACK, FREIDA	COHN	18 JAN 1970	1894		MAX
119	I46	SACK, HAROLD L		20 APR 1986	15 NOV 1919		
101	B12	SACK, HARRY		7 JUN 1947	1868		SADIE
119	J57	SACK, KENNETH C		4 JAN 1985	18 FEB 1919		
105	I19	SACK, MAX		27 DEC 1937	1890		FREIDA
119	C56	SACK, PHILIP H		17 DEC 1987	19 NOV 1910		
370	B 2	SACK, PHILIP S		12 MAR 1920	1858		
119	D 2	SACK, RUTH G		13 MAR 1991	27 OCT 1918		
101	B11	SACK, SADIE		2 JUL 1941	1871		HARRY
222	AO 1	SACK, SOL HENRY		1959	1958		
374	C37	SACKOWITZ, BENJAMIN		10 OCT 1973	1907	CELIA	
374	C36	SACKOWITZ, CELIA		28 NOV 1963	1884		
377	Y56	SACKS, CHARLOTTE		25 OCT 1991	11 JUL 1930	ELIMELECH	
119	D43	SACKTER, DAVID		1990	1905		
119	D42	SACKTER, MILTON		1975	1909		
371	M17	SADINSKY, ABRAHAM M		NDD	1906		
370	F15	SADINSKY, BENJAMIN		1918	1886		
370	G13	SADINSKY, DAVID HERMAN		14 JUN 1941			ETTA
371	M14	SADINSKY, DAVID I		14 SEP 1991	24 SEP 1906		
377	H28	SADINSKY, ELIZABETH		9 SEP 1991	1901	ISAAC	GEORGE
371	M16	SADINSKY, EMMA		6 OCT 1967			LOUIS
370	G14	SADINSKY, ETTA HANNAH		21 MAR 1939			DAVID
377	H27	SADINSKY, GEORGE		1961	1904	DAVID	ELIZABETH
370	L29	SADINSKY, HELEN		8 APR 1916			
447	Z15	SADINSKY, IDA Z		5 MAR 1986	1910		
370	G12	SADINSKY, JACK I		25 DEC 1965	17 MAR 1896	DAVID & ETTA	
370	F 4	SADINSKY, JACOB		3 AUG 1928	24 JUN 1905		
371	L15	SADINSKY, JOSEPH		2 JUN 1993	28 NOV 1910		
371	L16	SADINSKY, LORI BETH		28 MAY 1960	27 NOV 1959		
371	M15	SADINSKY, LOUIS H		18 FEB 1956			EMMA
371	N15	SADINSKY, MAX		14 JAN 1953	1894		ROSE
370	D21	SADINSKY, MORRIS		18 JAN 1918			
370	F16	SADINSKY, NATHAN		1918	1887		
371	N16	SADINSKY, ROSE		15 JAN 1973	1894		MAX
371	L17	SADINSKY, SAMUEL		20 SEP 1968	29 DEC 1915		
391	ZG52	SADLER, BRIAN KEITH		15 APR 1992	8 SEP 1959	JOSEPH MASHA	
391	V65	SADLER, EZEKIEL JACK		6 DEC 1971	1886	JOSEPH	IDA
392	E46	SADLER, HELEN	PUMERANTZ	7 FEB 1953	1917	NATHAN	
391	V66	SADLER, IDA D		11 FEB 1969	1895	ISAAC	EZEKIEL
447	E10	SADOWSKY, IDA		1 FEB 1965	5 JAN 1893		
112	C27	SAFALOW, MARCIA L		7 JUN 1987	23 FEB 1940		
371	N27	SAFENOVITZ, HELEN		14 JUN 1991	20 JAN 1910		SAMUEL
370	D17	SAFENOVITZ, KALMAN		1948	1892	MOSES	MARY
370	H 5	SAFENOVITZ, MARY		1958	1893		KALMAN
370	D16	SAFENOVITZ, MOSES ISAAC		1938	1859		ROSE
370	K25	SAFENOVITZ, ROSE BELLE		1944	1865		MOSES
371	N26	SAFENOVITZ, SAMUEL		19 NOV 1980	1 MAY 1907		HELEN
371	K22	SAFENOWITZ, ETHEL Y		1976	1890		SAUL
371	K21	SAFENOWITZ, SAUL A		1959	1887		ETHEL
376	B18	SAFFIAN, FAY		23 SEP 1934	1902		
750	J30	SAFFIAN, ISADORE		3 MAY 1967	17 FEB 1902		
446	A80	SAGAL, LOUIS		30 AUG 1886	29 DEC 1885	ABE & TILLIE	

Cem	Row	Name	Maiden Name	DOD	DOB	Parents	Spouse
102	S 1	SAKOLOVE, ARTHUR EDWARD		16 JUN 1957	8 JAN 1893		
119	I 3	SAKOW, LEON		6 MAY 1986	13 APR 1909		
371	N 4	SAKOWITZ, DONALD		1965	1921	SAMUEL & IDA	
371	N 6	SAKOWITZ, IDA	SHABECOFF	1954	1884		SAMUEL
371	N 5	SAKOWITZ, SAMUEL		1974	1887		IDA
101	I19	SALAD, ADELE		23 JUL 1976	8 JUN 1920		
110	C 8	SALAD, FANNIE	YUGER	6 JAN 1966	1879		JACOB
108	A36	SALAD, GERTRUDE L		22 NOV 1991	18 DEC 1906		
110	C 9	SALAD, JACOB MAYER		14 JAN 1959	1878		FANNIE
108	A35	SALAD, MARK J		5 JAN 1984	3 JAN 1955		
125		SALAD, SARAH	GANS	21 FEB 1915	14 DEC 1861	PERETZ & SELE	
331		SALANAR, SARAH		10 JAN 1929	1857		
377	U20	SALCMAN, EDITH A		1973	1927	DAVID	
101	A35	SALKOWITZ, PHILIP		12 FEB 1909	1880		
395	B11	SALOMON, ABRAHAM		28 SEP 1888	11 NOV 1823	SHLOMO	
392	D52	SALOMON, ALFRED		12 SEP 1954	27 JAN 1870		
395	A 9	SALOMON, CAROLINE		12 FEB 1945	31 JAN 1860		MICHAEL
372	E12	SALOMON, CELIA	MACHOL	1944	1859		LOUIS
372	D 8	SALOMON, DONALD		1992	1901		
395	A10	SALOMON, ERNESTINE		14 JUL 1915	1839	ISAAC	ISIDORE
248	I60	SALOMON, GOTTLIEB		2 JUN 1925	1882		
248	J11	SALOMON, HAROLD LOUIS		8 JUN 1957	26 APR 1921		
395	B13	SALOMON, IRA		25 JUL 1895	14 OCT 1893		
395	B10	SALOMON, ISIDOR		20 SEP 1889	1833	SHLOMO	ERNESTINE
372	E13	SALOMON, JOSEPH		1942	1887		MARION
395	B12	SALOMON, LEO		1897			
395	A11	SALOMON, LOUIS		1940	1870	ABRAHAM	
372	E11	SALOMON, LOUIS		1941	1853		CELIA
372	E10	SALOMON, MARION		1972	1880		JOSEPH
395	A 8	SALOMON, MICHAEL		18 SEP 1925	31 DEC 1858	ABRAHAM	CAROLINE
372	D 7	SALOMON, SIDNEY		1910	1892		
391	P58	SALOWITZ, CELIA		23 AUG 1955	1887	JACOB DAVID	
125	B116	SALOWITZ, EVA	CHORCHES	13 NOV 1992	21 SEP 1906		SAMUEL
391	C17	SALOWITZ, HARRIS		19 MAR 1937	1863	MORDECHAI	
391	Y79	SALOWITZ, LOUIS		19 APR 1982	10 FEB 1915	TZVI HIRSH	
125	B117	SALOWITZ, MORTON J		9 MAY 1990	3 JUN 1936	SAMUEL & EVA	
125	B115	SALOWITZ, SAMUEL D		19 DEC 1991	30 JUN 1909		EVA
121	B14	SALTZ, KIRK		25 MAR 1986	5 JUL 1896		
121	B15	SALTZ, LEAH		18 MAY 1986	28 JUL 1901		
330	E 6	SALTZMAN, EVA		28 JUN 1934	1867		
248	E60	SALTZMAN, ISRAEL		1 SEP 1977	1895		SARAH
371	AN23	SALTZMAN, JOSEPH	8 JAN 1974*	28 DEC 1974*	1900		
248	E61	SALTZMAN, SARAH A		11 JUL 1983	1900		ISRAEL
121	H36	SALVIN, LEWIS		6 NOV 1988	2 APR 1922		
102	K46	SALZ, DAVID		21 JUN 1950	13 SEP 1893		MARY
102	K45	SALZ, MARY		22 JUN 1960	19 SEP 1893		DAVID
101	C16	SALZBERG, NATHAN		15 SEP 1941	1883	RAIZA	REBECCA
101	L15	SALZBERG, RAISA		7 MAY 1934	1860		
101	C17	SALZBERG, REBECCA		22 APR 1956	1884		NATHAN
102	AH199	SALZBURG, RIVILYN K		10 NOV 1984	4 JAN 1921		
370	B28	SALZMAN, HAROLD		30 JUN 1914	15 JAN 1907		
391	C32	SAMER, ABRAHAM		24 DEC 1923			
119	K59	SAMLER, LEO		3 AUG 1974	4 JUL 1919		
222	AC18	SAMONOVITZ, SAMUEL		26 OCT 1985	24 OCT 1910		
372	A 4	SAMUEL, HERMAN		1938	1852		
372	B13	SAMUEL, THEODORE		1937	1865		THERESA
372	B14	SAMUEL, THERESA		NDD			THEODORE
377	S33	SAMUELS, ESTELLE	NASSER	1987	1924		HAROLD
377	S32	SAMUELS, HAROLD		1969	1921		ESTELLE
494	E22	SAMUELS, HAROLD M DDS		1988	1910		
121	F23	SAMUELS, HAROLD ROBERTS		15 MAY 1984	28 MAY 1936		
330	F50	SAMUELS, ISRAEL		9 JUN 1929	1854		
494	A 2	SAMUELS, SADIE		28 JAN 1960	1872	ABRAHAM	SELICK
494	A 1	SAMUELS, SELICK		16 JAN 1952	1873	ISRAEL	SADIE
395	B 8	SAMUELSOHN, MICHAELIS		15 MAY 1890	1820	ELIYAHU	
248	K26	SAMWICK, ALLEN A		19 FEB 1987	15 MAY 1908		LILLIAN

Cem	Row	Name	Maiden Name	DOD	DOB	Parents	Spouse
248	K27	SAMWICK, LILLIAN S		NDD	29 OCT 1923		ALLEN
125	M 26	SANDALL, MARY		22 NOV 1914			
113	J34	SANDALS, GEORGE EUGENE		10 JUN 1989	14 FEB 1913	NATHAN & ROSE	
113	J36	SANDALS, NATHAN		15 MAY 1974	15 MAR 1888		ROSE
113	J35	SANDALS, ROSE		3 OCT 1955	15 DEC 1889		NATHAN
102	AH201	SANDER, IRENE	KERNESS	1980	1915		MORRIS
102	AH202	SANDER, MORRIS H		1983	1911		IRENE
125	K 41	SANDERS, ABRAHAM H		7 JAN 1914	1854		
116	N17	SANDERS, BENJAMIN		6 MAY 1987	15 MAY 1907		
102	X 6	SANDERS, GERALD		29 JUN 1939	29 JUL 1924	MAX & ROSE	NAOMI
116	BJ107	SANDERS, JENNIE		1972	1899		MYER
102	X 5	SANDERS, MAX		26 APR 1955	25 NOV 1892		ROSE
116	BJ108	SANDERS, MYER S		1973	1897		JENNIE
102	X 7	SANDERS, NAOMI		14 FEB 1958			GERALD
102	X 4	SANDERS, ROSE		20 MAR 1967	25 MAR 1899		MAX
102	AB150	SANDERSON, BEATRICE		17 SEP 1990	1 SEP 1918		PHILIP
102	AB149	SANDERSON, PHILIP MH		12 OCT 1961	8 MAY 1916		BEATRICE
373	I19	SANDLER, AARON		1966	1912		
121	H 1	SANDLER, ABRAHAM		20 JAN 1982	1900		
248	H43	SANDLER, ANNIE H		22 APR 1955	1 NOV 1898		
125	X190	SANDLER, BENJAMIN		5 JUN 1986	11 SEP 1902		RAE
102	L37	SANDLER, ESTHER		1 JUN 1955	1880		MAX
371	A18	SANDLER, HANNAH		24 AUG 1988	3 SEP 1909		HARRY
371	A17	SANDLER, HARRY		21 DEC 1980	16 MAY 1906		HANNAH
121	V17	SANDLER, JACK B		27 DEC 1983	2 APR 1935		
120	B 3	SANDLER, LORETTA B		2 OCT 1989	16 SEP 1914		
102	L36	SANDLER, MAX G		10 FEB 1930	1877		ESTHER
116	AZ22	SANDLER, PEARL B		12 OCT 1970	19 OCT 1914		
125	X189	SANDLER, RAE D		12 SEP 1982	15 OCT 1904		BENJAMIN
101	G11	SANDLER, SOPHIE		11 NOV 1983	2 NOV 1911		
125	J132	SANDLOWITZ, JANETTE		29 MAR 1937	1919	AARON & CHANA MINDEL	
102	AB198	SANOFSKY, NATHAN		1978	1917		
391	I42	SANTER, ANNIE		5 AUG 1945	1870	LIPADOT	RAPHAEL
392	B25	SANTER, BESSIE		20 AUG 1980	1901		NATHAN
392	A28	SANTER, MAYER		NDD	1933		SANDRA
392	B26	SANTER, NATHAN		18 JUN 1963	1902		BESSIE
391	F 3	SANTER, RAPHAEL	ALTER	20 APR 1942	1878	MOSHE	ANNIE
392	A27	SANTER, SANDRA J		1980	1938		MAYER
329	C29	SARINSKY, CELIA		18 AUG 1958	1889		
329	C30	SARINSKY, WILLIAM		27 JUN 1960	28 APR 1925	CELIA	
447	A26	SARITSKY, ESTHER		1985	1905		
447	A22	SARITSKY, LEO		30 DEC 1975	1911		
447	A25	SARITSKY, RACHEL		1979	1908		
119	H68	SATELL, MURRAY		12 DEC 1985	5 JUL 1902		
119	H67	SATELL, SALLY G		22 SEP 1990	20 MAR 1910		
114	J13	SATTER, RUTH L		3 AUG 1989	8 MAR 1923		
102	AD194	SATTIN, HAROLD D		29 MAR 1965	2 MAY 1909		
370	R24	SATZ, GEORGE		1940	1893	PAUL & MARIA	
370	R23	SATZ, MARIA		1960	1870		PAUL
370	R22	SATZ, PAUL		1906	1861		MARIA
370	R25	SATZ, PAUL		1930	1907	PAUL & MARIA	
102	O21	SAUNDERS, FREDA	LEBON	27 JUN 1945	10 MAY 1906	SAMUEL & FRIEDA	
446	A16	SAVAGE, ABRAHAM		22 JAN 1924	1871		
371	AQ11	SAVAGE, ANNIE		1965	1894		JACOB
371	AQ12	SAVAGE, JACOB		1965	1881		ANNIE
370	X18	SAVAGE, MARVIN		1 MAR 1936	11 NOV 1930		
370	K14	SAVANUCK, SOPHIA		16 JUL 1947			
102	AC105	SAVIN, ABRAHAM I		6 APR 1987	1 MAR 1902		ANNA
102	AC106	SAVIN, ANNA	DUNN	3 AUG 1979	4 JUL 1900		ABRAHAM
377	U13	SAVIN, EDITH		6 APR 1974	26 OCT 1901	ISRAEL	MOSES
116	BY82	SAVIN, ISADORE		19 JUN 1972	10 JUN 1909		
116	BY81	SAVIN, MICHAEL JAY		20 AUG 1986	9 JUN 1933	ISIDORE	
377	U12	SAVIN, MOSES A		28 MAR 1993	4 JUL 1900	JACOB	EDITH
391	ZD50	SAVIN, SAM		17 JUL 1963	1873	CHINOCH	
102	L34	SAVITT, DAVID HARRISON		26 AUG 1982	9 JUN 1951	SAMUEL	
102	N37	SAVITT, FRANK E		6 SEP 1953	21 FEB 1895		

Cem	Row	Name	Maiden Name	DOD	DOB	Parents	Spouse
102	M35	SAVITT, HARRY		14 AUG 1929	10 JAN 1873		HATTIE
102	M36	SAVITT, HATTIE		9 OCT 1966	10 JUL 1876		HARRY
125	N182	SAVITT, IDA		3 DEC 1969	1896		ISADORE
125	N183	SAVITT, ISADORE		13 MAR 1966	1887		IDA
102	M38	SAVITT, MAX M		19 JUL 1979	27 JUL 1903	HARRY & HATTIE	
102	L35	SAVITT, SAMUEL		28 MAR 1942	2 NOV 1892	HARRY	
371	I 6	SAVITZ, HELEN		1953	1893		
447	AB22	SAVO, JOHN DAVID		8 MAR 1991	12 FEB 1944		
377	X67	SAXE, EARL MD		14 JAN 1990	12 JUN 1908	ZELIG	
125	E 26	SAXE, FANNIE		21 AUG 1987	1886		MORRIS
125	E 25	SAXE, MORRIS DAVID		23 JAN 1964	1886		FANNIE
125	K 38	SAXON, ANNIE		27 NOV 1912	1887		
127	L	SAYET, MARTIN M		12 JUN 1988	2 MAY 1904		
391	D27	SCAGOWITZ, HYMAN G		5 JAN 1927	1858	ELKOS	
125		SCHACH, (CHILD)		9 JUN 1925	8 JUN 1925	ABRAHAM	
370	I41	SCHACHTER, O LOUIS		11 APR 1949			ROSE
370	I42	SCHACHTER, ROSE R		13 FEB 1965			LOUIS
103	D47	SCHACK, ANN	GOLDFARB	6 AUG 1991			
329	C26	SCHADICK, ALEX		19 FEB 1959	1876		GOLDA
329	B23	SCHADICK, GOLDA		19 AUG 1953	1884		ALEX
447	Y 2	SCHAECHTER, ARNOLD		14 MAR 1983	16 MAY 1893		
125	Z192	SCHAEFER, DOROTHY	PERLMUTTER	18 DEC 1988	16 OCT 1919		
125	a2-4	SCHAEFER, NAPHTOLIN		25 MAR 1941		ABRAHAM	
125	F 26	SCHAEFER, ROSE G		15 NOV 1932	1870		SIMON
125	F 25	SCHAEFER, SIMON		7 FEB 1933	1862		ROSE
391	P29	SCHAEFFER, BARNET		27 OCT 1921		ISRAEL ABRAHAM	
376	D 6	SCHAEFFER, BERTHA	SHALMAN	5 JAN 1945	1878		SAMUEL
391	S33	SCHAEFFER, ESTHER		21 MAR 1921	1851	SHIMON MOSHE	
391	P30	SCHAEFFER, HYMAN		11 OCT 1909	1852	ISRAEL ABRAHAM	
117	D 2	SCHAFFER, ANNIE		20 MAY 1986	22 SEP 1925		BERNARD
117	D 1	SCHAFFER, BERNARD		6 DEC 1989	23 NPV 1924		ANNIE
376	C 4	SCHAFFER, LAWALL (BABY)		16 OCT 1978			
102	L41	SCHALLER, GUSSIE		13 DEC 1961	10 OCT 1889		MORRIS
102	H51	SCHALLER, HELEN		17 JAN 1982	22 AUG 1909		REUBEN
102	L40	SCHALLER, MORRIS		16 MAR 1960	10 MAR 1882		GUSSIE
102	H50	SCHALLER, REUBEN		27 AUG 1977	26 APR 1910		HELEN
374	F 8	SCHANKER, ABRAHAM		11 MAR 1928			ROSE
374	F 7	SCHANKER, ROSE L		13 MAR 1925	9 OCT 1908		ABRAHAM
102	BB22	SCHANZER, RETA E		28 FEB 1988	23 AUG 1910		
392	C27	SCHAPEROW, JAMES HARRY		1949	1893		LEAH
392	C26	SCHAPEROW, LEAH CELIA		1983	1898		JAMES
116	R21	SCHARR, DAVID B		3 JUL 1981	5 APR 1910		
102	L11	SCHARR, NATHAN G		9 APR 1951	1894		SARAH
102	L10	SCHARR, SARAH	MALLEY	25 OCT 1961	1894		NATHAN
116	H 5	SCHATTEN, SIEGFRIED S		1989	1905		
102	AC60	SCHATZ, DORA	GOLDBERG	8 NOV 1974	16 JAN 1893		NATHAN
371	AE 1	SCHATZ, ESTHER R		3 SEP 1969	7 NOV 1894		HARRY
371	AD 1	SCHATZ, GERTRUDE		10 JUN 1991	5 MAR 1921		
371	AE 2	SCHATZ, HARRY JACOB		8 OCT 1977	18 FEB 1891		ESTHER
101	C15	SCHATZ, JACOB		24 MAR 1945			
102	AC53	SCHATZ, LOUIS M		22 OCT 1953	1894		
102	AC59	SCHATZ, NATHAN A		16 MAR 1956	27 APR 1892		DORA
446	C23	SCHATZ, SARAH		10 MAY 1921			
116	AC22	SCHAYES, RUTH	FRIEDMAN	5 NOV 1984	11 NOV 1906		
121	G16	SCHECHTMAN, SARAH		2 JAN 1982	12 APR 1896		
116	G 3	SCHECTER, DOROTHY E		30 SEP 1989	23 MAY 1910		
125	H102	SCHECTMAN, CHARLES T MD		1989	1901	REBECCA	
125	O146	SCHECTMAN, FLORENCE		4 JAN 1949	1921	PINCHAS ZALMAN & CHANA	
125	G103	SCHECTMAN, GERTRUDE		2 JAN 1983	1897		
125		SCHECTMAN, JACOB		18 SEP 1918	1878		
125	H103	SCHECTMAN, REBECCA	GORBACH	8 JAN 1938	1880	MYER & SARAH	
125	X182	SCHEIN, IDA D	MALAMUD	29 MAY 1982	1912		
105	I3	SCHEINBLUM, ANDREW L		25 JUN 1986	20 MAY 1969		
102	G 9	SCHEINBLUM, DAVID A		12 DEC 1988	16 NOV 1968		
248	H54	SCHEINMAN, BERTHA		20 OCT 1933	1891		
125	A110	SCHENCK, MAC		21 AUG 1964	30 MAY 1921		

Cem	Row	Name	Maiden Name	DOD	DOB	Parents	Spouse
125	B101	SCHENCK, ROBERT L CAPT		14 NOV 1952	1921		
377	S42	SCHENK, BELLE R		1990	1922		HERBERT
377	S41	SCHENK, HERBERT		1986	1925		BELLE
102	AJ72	SCHENKER, REBECCA		9 JUL 1962	1887		SAMUEL
102	AJ71	SCHENKER, SAMUEL		9 JAN 1955	1890		REBECCA
377	L16	SCHER, ABRAHAM S		1958	1874		SARAH
377	L15	SCHER, SARAH H		1954	1876		ABRAHAM
222	AH11	SCHERESCHEFSKY, MAX		26 MAY 1924	1859		MOLLY
222	AH12	SCHERESCHEFSKY, MOLLY		5 AUG 1940			MAX
392	B 5	SCHICKLER, BESSIE		1968	1907		
447	S14	SCHICKLER, SAM		22 MAR 1976	6 APR 1906		
112	C29	SCHIFF, PAUL		7 AUG 1987	21 JUL 1903		SELMA
112	C30	SCHIFF, SELMA	AAL	NDD	28 SEP 1906		PAUL
248	H61	SCHILBERG, BELLA		16 JAN 1956	1892		NATHAN
248	H60	SCHILBERG, NATHAN H		7 OCT 1955	1891		BELLA
248	F57	SCHILLER, JACOB M		11 AUG 1976	1894		YETTA
377	O44	SCHILLER, JOHN		1942	1872		
248	F56	SCHILLER, YETTA		9 JAN 1968	1895		JACOB
125	Q189	SCHIMEK, JULIUS		28 APR 1967	1887		NELLIE
125	Q190	SCHIMEK, NELLIE		13 NOV 1961	1884		JULIUS
110	D20	SCHIPPER, JOSEPH		25 FEB 1991	1894		PAULINE
110	D19	SCHIPPER, PAULINE		9 JAN 1972	1898		JOSEPH
125	L107	SCHLAFER, SAMUEL		5 JUN 1929	25 DEC 1882	ABRAHAM	
102	A78	SCHLAIN, REBECCA		1943	1888		
751	M28	SCHLAPAK, ARLINE	ROSANSKY	15 NOV 1986			
751	G36	SCHLAPAK, MARK CRAIG		14 JUN 1966	8 JUN 1966		
105	H14	SCHLAR, BESSIE		7 SEP 1948	1874		SAMUEL
105	H15	SCHLAR, SAMUEL		24 FEB 1944	1873		BESSIE
391	ZG54	SCHLEIFER, BARBARA LOUISE		18 MAR 1992	18 DEC 1919	TZVI	
370	O33	SCHLEIFER, DAVID		6 MAR 1950			KALE
371	M12	SCHLEIFER, JACOB		16 MAR 1958	1886		SARAH
370	Z 5	SCHLEIFER, KALE		8 JUN 1960	21 JUL 1871		DAVID
391	ZG55	SCHLEIFER, SAM		NDD	3 FEB 1906	JACOB	
371	M13	SCHLEIFER, SARAH		12 DEC 1975	1882		JACOB
126		SCHLENKER, ALBERT		1 AUG 1899	16 DEC 1880	SIMON & ETKA	
126		SCHLENKER, EMIL MORRIS		11 FEB 1907	16 MAR 1874	SIMON & ETKA	
126		SCHLENKER, ETKA		21 DEC 1897	9 AUG 1854		SIMON
126		SCHLENKER, SIMON		1927	1857		ETKA
751	E25	SCHLESINGER, SIDONIE		1 DEC 1950	1874		
370	B45	SCHLOSSBERG, DORA		11 JAN 1950	14 MAR 1879		SIMON
371	M21	SCHLOSSBERG, FLORENCE R		3 FEB 1964	7 DEC 1915		LEE
125	B 93	SCHLOSSBERG, IDA	MOHILL	19 APR 1957	1877		ISRAEL
125	B 94	SCHLOSSBERG, ISRAEL H		19 SEP 1954	1872		IDA
371	M22	SCHLOSSBERG, LEE R		12 FEB 1966	22 JUL 1917		FLORENCE
125	B316	SCHLOSSBERG, LEON		22 SEP 1977	1904		
125	A108	SCHLOSSBERG, MILTON		8 DEC 1979	1910		MINNIE
125	A109	SCHLOSSBERG, MINNIE		17 MAR 1987	3 APR 1913		MILTON
370	B44	SCHLOSSBERG, SIMON		26 DEC 1932	14 JUL 1875		DORA
330	G65	SCHMUCKLER, ESTHER		19 DEC 1937			
330	E28	SCHMUCKLER, ISAAC		19 AUG 1935	1862		
330	A39	SCHMUCKLER, ISRAEL		31 MAY 1967	1892		
330	D20	SCHMUCKLER, LOUIS		29 JUN 1949	1890		
330	A40	SCHMUCKLER, MEYER		19 NOV 1968	2 AUG 1898		
125	N122	SCHNEIDER, DAVID		17 SEP 1970	1891		
377	R41	SCHNEIDER, DAVID		19 APR 1994			
125	R157	SCHNEIDER, FANNIE EPSTEIN	NEISTAT	29 JUL 1970	1878		
125	G166	SCHNEIDER, JACOB		3 JUN 1992	29 OCT 1918		
391	R52	SCHNEIDER, JOHN		24 MAR 1966	20 OCT 1880	ABRHAM JACOB	
374	E36	SCHNEIDER, LOUIS		1942	1885		
125	S189	SCHNEIDER, SAMUEL		5 APR 1958	1885		
102	J42	SCHNELLER, HELEN EFROS	KLEIN	1978	1894		JULIUS
102	J43	SCHNELLER, JULIUS		1945	1884		HELEN
391	P39	SCHNIEDER, MOLLIE		19 MAR 1938	1886	DAVID LEB	
222	AT 6	SCHNIEDER, WILLIAM		30 SEP 1984	1905		
751	O10	SCHNIER, ANNE	PIVNICK	NDD			
751	O14	SCHNIER, JOSEPH		24 JUL 1970	10 SEP 1892		

Cem	Row	Name	Maiden Name	DOD	DOB	Parents	Spouse
751	O16	SCHNIER, LOUIS DAVID		31 AUG 1991	25 DEC 1923		
751	O11	SCHNIER, ROBERT		1960	1894		
751	O15	SCHNIER, ROSE		4 MAY 1959	25 DEC 1895		
248	C56	SCHOCHET, JEROME L		29 OCT 1981	7 JUL 1934		
112	D20	SCHOEN, SOL		26 FEB 1975	2 MAY 1896		
392	E49	SCHOENBACH, ANNA	LANN	22 MAY 1954	1879	JUDAH	
371	L28	SCHOENBERG, DAVID		3 APR 1958	16 JUL 1910		
370	F25	SCHOENBERG, IDA		13 APR 1963			SAM
371	L29	SCHOENBERG, MAURICE		16 JUN 1955	24 SEP 1915		
370	F26	SCHOENBERG, SAM A		9 SEP 1950			IDA
433	B36	SCHOENEMANN, SIEGFRIED		24 MAY 1941	1893		
106	E24	SCHOLNICK, RUTH		15 AUG 1971	15 JUL 1918		
101	F22	SCHOOLNICK, ABRAHAM		2 JAN 1988	27 MAY 1909		FANNIE
101	F21	SCHOOLNICK, FANNIE		5 FEB 1989	1 JUN 1912		ABRAHAM
116	BV28	SCHOOLNIK, EUGENIE		23 OCT 1983	1920	LOUIS & MAMIE	
116	BV31	SCHOOLNIK, LOUIS		13 JUN 1965	1885		MAMIE
116	BV30	SCHOOLNIK, MAMIE		7 JUN 1967	1890		LOUIS
330	AA18	SCHOONMAKER, EVA ROSE		23 JUN 1990	28 JAN 1905		
447	H14	SCHOR, HARRY L		21 NOV 1941	1882	SOPHIE	SOPHIE
447	H11	SCHOR, PAUL		10 JUN 1960	8 JUN 1903		
447	H13	SCHOR, SOPHIE		1 DEC 1936	1877		HARRY
447	H12	SCHOR, SOPHIE L		13 JAN 1932	1852		
127	B	SCHREIBER, MARC		15 NOV 1988	21 AUG 1971		
329	B21	SCHREIBER, ROSE		29 APR 1955	1888		
330	E21	SCHUFFMAN, JACOB B		17 JUL 1932	1909	SAMUEL & SARAH (GITLIN)	
370	K48	SCHULKIN, CELIA		1963	1890		
370	H15	SCHULMAN, DORA		27 MAR 1901			
104	G21	SCHULMAN, EVELYN	LEE	11 MAR 1963	12 MAR 1899		HOWARD
370	R26	SCHULMAN, FANNIE		1905	1868		
121	G28	SCHULMAN, GEORGE		18 JAN 1987	22 FEB 1913		
104	G20	SCHULMAN, HOWARD W		25 FEB 1965	6 OCT 1896		EVELYN
371	AD20	SCHULMAN, LUBA		16 JUN 1973	1902		JULIUS
447	J 5	SCHULMAN, MAX		15 MAR 1975	26 MAY 1912		
433	H19	SCHULMAN, MAX		1975	1910	MORRIS & SONIA	
433	H18	SCHULMAN, MORRIS		12 APR 1938	1874	MORDECHAI	SONIA
330	AF39	SCHULMAN, MORRIS		24 JUN 1987	22 JUN 1916		
433	D21	SCHULMAN, SARAH		4 NOV 1960	2 APR 1913	CHAIM DOV BEAR	
433	H17	SCHULMAN, SONIA		16 NOV 1950	1878	ISRAEL	MORRIS
113	A24	SCHULTZ, HARRY		14 MAR 1989	10 FEB 1907		
102	AA65	SCHULTZ, LOUIS		15 JAN 1956	1 DEC 1894		
102	Z73	SCHUMACHER, REBECCA	KOPPLEMAN	22 AUG 1945	1883	HENRY & JESSIE (MINTZ)	ADAM
391	W69	SCHUMAN, ABRAHAM		11 JAN 1972	29 SEP 1897	MENACHEM MENDEL	BETTY
377	Q38	SCHUMAN, ANNABEL		20 DEC 1990	10 MAY 1905		
391	W76	SCHUMAN, BETTY		10 JUN 1988	28 FEB 1904	YECHIEL	ABRAHAM
391	D 3	SCHUMAN, CHARLES E		12 MAR 1950		MAX	ESTHER
102	CB61	SCHUMAN, DAVID H		13 MAR 1980	1907		FAY
391	G 7	SCHUMAN, DORA		16 FEB 1946	1867	JACOB	HARRY
102	CB60	SCHUMAN, FAY		3 NOV 1976	1913		DAVID
391	G 6	SCHUMAN, HARRY		26 JUN 1932	1868	CHAIM SHALOM	DORA
377	ZA45	SCHUMAN, JOSEPH I		21 MAR 1979	20 JUL 1908	MENACHEM MENDEL	
111	12	SCHUMAN, LARRY L		20 MAR 1981	28 OCT 1927		
111	12	SCHUMAN, MARK S		15 NOV 1988	11 OCT 1958	LARRY	
391	D 2	SCHUMAN, MAX		30 JUN 1961	1867	BENJAMIN MOSHE	
391	D 1	SCHUMAN, RACHEL L		15 SEP 1966	1879	ABRAHAM	CHARLES
376	D13	SCHUMER, MARTHA		31 JAN 1980	11 DEC 1894	ABRAHAM	SAMUEL
107	F11	SCHUMER, MATILDA	BANNER	22 FEB 1980	22 AUG 1922		
376	D12	SCHUMER, SAMUEL		9 JUN 1973	7 APR 1889	SIMON	MARTHA
125	A101	SCHUPACK, ALMA A		23 DEC 1982	1915		EDWARD
125	N136	SCHUPACK, AUGUSTA	COHEN	16 DEC 1972	1900		GEORGE
125	P177	SCHUPACK, BERTHA		30 SEP 1969	1897		MAX
125	E 88	SCHUPACK, DOROTHY Z		24 OCT 1993	1899		SAMUEL
125	A100	SCHUPACK, EDWARD		1 SEP 1974	1906		ALMA
125	G162	SCHUPACK, EDWARD		18 FEB 1979	1920		
125	N137	SCHUPACK, GEORGE		31 MAR 1973	1901		AUGUSTA
125	Q178	SCHUPACK, HATTIE		26 MAR 1994			SAMUEL
125	F 86	SCHUPACK, HENRY		30 NOV 1980	1896		

Cem	Row	Name	Maiden Name	DOD	DOB	Parents	Spouse
125	F 88	SCHUPACK, LENA		14 JUN 1951	1866		
125	P178	SCHUPACK, MAX LOUIS		26 DEC 1962	1886		
125	K 77	SCHUPACK, MORRIS		14 DEC 1918	1861	MORDECHAI & CHASHA	BERTHA
125	G163	SCHUPACK, ROBERT SIDNEY		18 FEB 1985	1919		
125	Q179	SCHUPACK, SAMUEL		19 JUN 1961	1893		
125	E 87	SCHUPACK, SAMUEL D		26 MAR 1984	1897		HATTIE
433	E 8	SCHURR, ARNOLD J		20 MAR 1961	12 MAY 1922	ARTHUR	DOROTHY
433	E 9	SCHURR, ARTHUR DDS	8 JAN 1963*	27 DEC 1963*	1894	YOSEF	
391	G40	SCHUSS, GILDA RACHEL		8 MAY 1932		ELIYAHU	
373	F11	SCHUSTER, AARON		1984	1910		LIZA
330	D15	SCHUSTER, BESSIE		16 DEC 1971	11 JUL 1894		REUBEN
115	E10	SCHUSTER, HARRY MD		20 SEP 1992			
373	F10	SCHUSTER, LIZA		1984	1910		AARON
330	E33	SCHUSTER, MORRIS		4 APR 1937	13 MAY 1916		
330	D14	SCHUSTER, RUBEN		16 MAY 1942	1 APR 1894		BESSIE
113	M59	SCHWALB, NICHOLAS		17 FEB 1983	22 NOV 1903		
370	A43	SCHWARTZ, (BABY)				BERRISH	
330	G22	SCHWARTZ, AARON NATHAN		10 JAN 1956			
370	X 5	SCHWARTZ, ABNER		9 AUG 1950	1882	MAX & BETTY (GREENBERG)	LILLIAN
330	H 3	SCHWARTZ, ABRAHAM		17 DEC 1922	1908		
330	F49	SCHWARTZ, ABRAHAM S		24 MAY 1929	1854		
222	AP22	SCHWARTZ, ABRAM		1952	1878		
117	E11	SCHWARTZ, ANDREW N		27 APR 1989	11 APR 1950		
371	AN 6	SCHWARTZ, ANNA R	RABINOVICH	NDD	16 AUG 1922		
446	C15	SCHWARTZ, ANNIE	BIRNBAUM	9 MAY 1926	1891		HARRY
377	E26	SCHWARTZ, ARTHUR		28 JUL 1987	18 OCT 1908	ISRAEL	THERESE
107	G12	SCHWARTZ, BENJAMIN		19 DEC 1970	1905		
370	G40	SCHWARTZ, BERISCH		10 FEB 1905	1843		
371	A 7	SCHWARTZ, BESSIE		1972	1892		
119	I30	SCHWARTZ, BETTY	SHAKUN	11 APR 1988	5 MAR 1902		
370	W 2	SCHWARTZ, BETTY		26 OCT 1935	1865		MAX
222	AP21	SCHWARTZ, CHARLES		1943	1913	ABRAM	
104	A42	SCHWARTZ, CHARLES H		6 MAY 1950	1888		MAE
107	G14	SCHWARTZ, DAVID		18 OCT 1976	1 JAN 1942		
371	K23	SCHWARTZ, DAVID		1963	1893		ROSE
370	X 2	SCHWARTZ, DIANA		1940	1887		HYMAN
447	E27	SCHWARTZ, ERNEST I		12 JAN 1981	1896		THERESA
377	F29	SCHWARTZ, EVELYN		10 OCT 1991	29 DEC 1914	MICHAEL	
102	AJ134	SCHWARTZ, FRANK		6 NOV 1957			ROSE
447	D28	SCHWARTZ, GEORGE		19 NOV 1983	28 MAY 1919		
370	O 8	SCHWARTZ, GOLDIE		1928	1859		
377	F23	SCHWARTZ, HARRIET B		26 MAR 1993	17 MAR 1898	BENJAMIN	JOSEPH
371	AN 5	SCHWARTZ, HARRY		2 FEB 1963	12 AUG 1903	ABNER & JENNIE (BLUM)	ANNA
104	O52	SCHWARTZ, HARRY		9 NOV 1980	17 MAR 1903		RITA
330	AB 5	SCHWARTZ, HYMAN		3 MAR 1969	20 NOV 1913		
370	X 1	SCHWARTZ, HYMAN		1947	1888		DIANA
447	V32	SCHWARTZ, IDA		14 JUN 1946	1910		MORDECHAI
103	E33	SCHWARTZ, ISAAC		24 JUL 1992	2 MAY 1907		
370	W 5	SCHWARTZ, JENNIE	BLUM	3 NOV 1940	1 JAN 1883	ABRAHAM & GITEL (STEINBACH)	ABNER
102	AJ88	SCHWARTZ, JOSEPH LT		15 JUL 1944	14 MAR 1924	SAMUEL & MARY (RECHLIN)	
377	F22	SCHWARTZ, JOSEPH R		12 NOV 1970	25 FEB 1893	MENDEL	HARRIET
447	E22	SCHWARTZ, KARL		28 JAN 1959	1869		ROSA
371	AO 4	SCHWARTZ, LARISE		6 SEP 1938	29 AUG 1938	hARRY & ANNA (RABINOVICH	
107	C11	SCHWARTZ, LESLIE M		23 JUN 1991	7 MAR 1915		
102	AB67	SCHWARTZ, LILLIAN	COHEN	22 MAR 1980	23 AUG 1901		
370	X 6	SCHWARTZ, LILLIAN	KLIMPL	AUG 1971	26 MAR 1898	EMILE & FRANCIS (REICH)	ABNER
374	G45	SCHWARTZ, LOUIS		5 DEC 1976	1884		SADIE
370	X 8	SCHWARTZ, LOUIS		12 JUL 1917		ABNER & JENNIE	
377	F25	SCHWARTZ, LOUIS J		15 APR 1950	11 DEC 1882	MENACHEM MENDEL	ROSE
104	A43	SCHWARTZ, MAE M		26 JUN 1967	1888		CHARLES
102	P 9	SCHWARTZ, MAURICE		20 JAN 1978	12 FEB 1913	NATHAN & REBECCA	
330	G24	SCHWARTZ, MAX		10 JUL 1943	16 APR 1878		
370	W 1	SCHWARTZ, MAX		14 NOV 1930	7 JUN 1862		BETTY
377	F27	SCHWARTZ, MAX B		24 NOV 1968	10 DEC 1889	JACOB	
125	X196	SCHWARTZ, MAX E		23 OCT 1983	1896		
377	F28	SCHWARTZ, MICHAEL		24 AUG 1952	10 JUN 1884	MENACHEM MENDEL	

Cem	Row	Name	Maiden Name	DOD	DOB	Parents	Spouse
330	G23	SCHWARTZ, MINNIE		28 JUL 1944			
102	CA20	SCHWARTZ, MIRIAM	DUNN	3 AUG 1976	12 JUN 1898		MAURICE
370	W 4	SCHWARTZ, MISCHA LOUIS		6 SEP 1950	10 MAR 1918	ABNER & JENNIE (BLUM)	
447	V27	SCHWARTZ, MORDECHAI		14 NOV 1926	1 SEP 1891		IDA
102	P 8	SCHWARTZ, NATHAN		18 FEB 1955	15 APR 1884		REBECCA
391	M63	SCHWARTZ, NELLIE	KITTROSSER	31 MAR 1941	1882	ABRAHAM	
370	W 3	SCHWARTZ, PAUL ABEL		14 OCT 1956	4 SEP 1896	MAX & BETTY	
370	O11	SCHWARTZ, PERETZ		1929	1855		
447	AB14	SCHWARTZ, PHILIP EDWARD MD		6 AUG 1977	11 FEB 1906		
102	P 7	SCHWARTZ, REBECCA S		7 DEC 1958	16 JAN 1886		NATHAN
447	AB15	SCHWARTZ, RICHARD ANDREW		5 OCT 1990	2 MAY 1951		
104	O53	SCHWARTZ, RITA		22 MAR 1971	25 MAR 1904		HARRY
447	E23	SCHWARTZ, ROSA		27 AUG 1947	1871		KARL
371	K24	SCHWARTZ, ROSE		1973	1895		DAVID
102	AJ135	SCHWARTZ, ROSE		27 MAR 1976			FRANK
377	F26	SCHWARTZ, ROSE I		31 MAY 1977	2 JAN 1891	MENACHEM MENDEL	LOUIS
374	G46	SCHWARTZ, SADIE		16 DEC 1963	1892		LOUIS
433	H26	SCHWARTZ, SADIE	WEISS	24 JAN 1958	1898	ISRAEL	SOL
433	H25	SCHWARTZ, SOL		17 JUN 1944	1891	SHLOMO	SADIE
330	G25	SCHWARTZ, SOPHIE		22 MAR 1958	14 MAR 1882		
447	E26	SCHWARTZ, THERESA R		13 FEB 1986	1897		ERNEST
377	E25	SCHWARTZ, THERESE R		11 OCT 1992	28 DEC 1910	SAMUEL	ARTHUR
370	S10	SCHWARTZBERG, JOEL		29 MAR 1941	1843		RIFKA
370	S11	SCHWARTZBERG, RIFKA		25 AUG 1907			JOEL
110	A 7	SCHWARTZBERG, SOL		27 SEP 1949	1898		
125	W176	SCHWARTZMAN, IRWIN W DR		30 OCT 1976	5 APR 1921		
446	D28	SCHWARTZMAN, LENA		21 AUG 1896			
447	Q16	SCHWARZ, EVA		5 OCT 1952			FRED
447	Q15	SCHWARZ, FRED B		17 JUL 1973			EVA
329	B22	SCHWARZ, MORITZ		3 NOV 1953	2 AUG 1882		
222	AU15	SCHWEBEL, HENRIETTA		31 AUG 1972	1875		MORTON
222	AU13	SCHWEBEL, LEE K		4 MAY 1971	1907		LEE
222	AU14	SCHWEBEL, MORTON D		4 MAY 1971	1901	HENRIETTA	
125		SCHWECHNICK, MARK ALLEN		19 DEC 1947	17 FEB 1947	SIMI	
377	Y 9	SCHWEID, CARL		6 MAY 1978	1902	CHAIM	FANNIE
377	Y10	SCHWEID, FANNIE TILEY		23 MAR 1954	1902	AARON	CARL
121	AA20	SCHWEITZER, CHARLES		1988	1908		
222	AA 9	SCHWEITZER, JACOB		15 OCT 1911	1837		
222	I 2	SCHWEITZER, TILLIE		14 JAN 1990	12 SEP 1905		
374	I33	SCHWELL, ANNIE		1940	1880		IKE
374	I32	SCHWELL, IKE		1981	1877		ANNIE
374	I31	SCHWELL, JOANN		1951	1950		
374	J32	SCHWELL, LOUIS		21 NOV 1981	14 MAR 1905		
329	E24	SCHWIMMER, RUTH		15 JAN 1988	1895		
101	B14	SCHWINKEN, LOUIS					SARAH
101	B13	SCHWINKEN, SARAH		11 MAR 1948	1877		LOUIS
371	D 1	SCHWITZER, DAVID		4 SEP 1990	10 SEP 1918		
101	H13	SCHWOLL, LENA		15 AUG 1981	1895		
102	A47	SCHWOLSKY, BENJAMIN		23 MAY 1974	1887		HATTIE
102	A45	SCHWOLSKY, FAY		6 MAR 1962	1921		DAVID
102	AB84	SCHWOLSKY, GEORGE		6 MAY 1983	4 FEB 1901	LOUIS & RACHEL (MILLER)	
102	V 1	SCHWOLSKY, HARRY			4 SEP 1894	LOUIS & RACHEL (MILLER)	HELEN
102	A46	SCHWOLSKY, HATTIE	SISKIND	24 JUL 1938	1893		BENJAMIN
102	V 2	SCHWOLSKY, HELEN I			12 FEB 1907		HARRY
113	A 3	SCHWOLSKY, HELENE	FREEDMAN	24 JUL 1984	18 OCT 1928		
102	A38	SCHWOLSKY, HOPE NINA		4 JUN 1937	1922		
102	S18	SCHWOLSKY, IDA	UMANS	29 AUG 1978	1 JAN 1899		MYER
102	V 4	SCHWOLSKY, JACOB			27 NOV 1890	LOUIS & RACHEL (MILLER)	LYABELLE
102	V 6	SCHWOLSKY, LOUIS REV		29 JAN 1954	1869		RACHEL
102	V 3	SCHWOLSKY, LYABELLE M			24 MAR 1895		JACOB
102	S19	SCHWOLSKY, MYER		20 APR 1970	28 SEP 1892	LOUIS & RACHEL (MILLER)	IDA
102	V 5	SCHWOLSKY, RACHEL	MILLER	24 JUN 1947	1874		LOUIS
102	V 7	SCHWOLSKY, SAMUEL J		29 OCT 1981	22 AUG 1903	LOUIS & RACHEL (MILLER)	
102	A68	SCHWOLSKY, TILLIE	GOLDENBERG	1974	1895		
102	E33	SCOLER, BELLE		26 AUG 1948	1891		ELY
102	E34	SCOLER, ELY		14 DEC 1958	1890		BELLE

Cem	Row	Name	Maiden Name	DOD	DOB	Parents	Spouse
101	M27	SCOLL, CELIA		14 MAY 1914	1850		
330	AG 5	SCOTT, BEA	MUSKIN	MAY 1984	MAY 1906		SAMUEL
330	AB 4	SCOTT, MALVINA		6 JUN 1992	10 JUN 1905		
329	F18	SEARLE, LOUIS		10 AUG 1987	28 DEC 1908		
372	G 5	SEARS, EMMA		24 JUN 1967	3 JAN 1892		
370	I29	SEARS, FANNIE		2 JUN 1915	1891		HERMAN
372	G 6	SEARS, HERMAN S		5 DEC 1982	20 DEC 1887	JOHN & RACHEL	
370	T28	SEARS, JACOB		29 OCT 1953	1876		IRMA
370	A10	SEARS, JOHN		1892	1847		ROSE
370	U11	SEARS, JONATHAN		1946	1944		RACHEL
370	U10	SEARS, LOUIS		9 FEB 1986	12 JUN 1905		
370	I27	SEARS, RACHEL		1926	1850		
370	U12	SEARS, ROBERT I		1949	1947		JOHN
370	T27	SEARS, ROSE		1973	1881		JACOB
371	I 5	SECHTER, FANNIE	TUBER	1966	1879		
371	J45	SECHTER, HAKERE RAZEV		1955	1881		
371	H 3	SECHTER, HELEN		8 JUN 1973	30 SEP 1909		
371	H 1	SECHTER, LOUIS		14 SEP 1980	6 MAR 1915		SAMUEL
371	H 2	SECHTER, SAMUEL		27 APR 1978	10 AUG 1910		
102	A56	SECHTMAN, CHARLES		11 FEB 1948	10 OCT 1882		HELEN
102	P29	SECHTMAN, ROSE L		29 MAY 1987	1896		SOPHIE
102	A57	SECHTMAN, SOPHIE	HARRIS	29 AUG 1940	1884		
371	L 8	SEDER, ANNA		13 JAN 1973	1894		CHARLES
371	L 7	SEDER, CHARLES		17 JUL 1964	1889		CHARLES
127	J	SEEFER, CARL JOSEPH		2 DEC 1991	3 MAY 1969		ANNA
370	K31	SEELICK, JACOB		27 OCT 1919	1847		
104	I 9	SEER, RHODA	SPONGIN	21 OCT 1984	15 AUG 1915		
371	AH12	SEGAL, AARON		26 DEC 1991	11 MAR 1901		
371	O20	SEGAL, ABRAHAM		1985	1910	ISAAC & ANNA	
374	B40	SEGAL, ANN	ROSENWASSER	20 FEB 1982	17 JUN 1914	DAVID & DINA	
371	O22	SEGAL, ANNA		7 MAY 1952			MEYER
248	L68	SEGAL, ANNIE HANNAH		11 MAY 1963	1888		ISAAC
102	AB82	SEGAL, BARNET		9 DEC 1952	1869		MORRIS
125	I 49	SEGAL, BENJAMIN		20 FEB 1912	1868		SARAH
118	E5	SEGAL, CHARLES		20 MAY 1960			
374	B38	SEGAL, DAVID		22 JUL 1946	1945	MEYER & ANN (LEVY)	
125	O 66	SEGAL, DOROTHY		15 APR 1922	1918	AARON & FANNIE	
447	C10	SEGAL, ETHEL	EDELBERG	28 FEB 1979	1913	SIMON & HESSIE	
371	N22	SEGAL, FREDA	BURACK	7 JAN 1976			RUBIN
374	D 9	SEGAL, FREDA B		24 FEB 1977			MAX
391	N34	SEGAL, HANNAH LEAH		7 JUL 1902	1898		
125	N194	SEGAL, HERMAN		14 APR 1967	1874	NACHMAN ELIEZER	
371	O21	SEGAL, ISAAC		26 APR 1956	1898		
113	M24	SEGAL, JACOB ALDEN		7 APR 1970			ANNA
102	C22	SEGAL, KATE	GREENBERG	4 APR 1966	3 JAN 1903		
248	K56	SEGAL, LARRY J		8 MAR 1985	1881		SAMUEL
371	N23	SEGAL, MAX		1964	1949		
374	B39	SEGAL, MAYER		1 FEB 1974	1898		FREDA
248	L67	SEGAL, MORRIS		29 JUN 1970	6 MAY 1912		ANN
125	M116	SEGAL, MORRIS		5 JAN 1940	1883		ANNIE
370	E 2	SEGAL, MOSES MURRAY		1932	1870		SARAH
447	C11	SEGAL, RUBIN		13 FEB 1955	1895		
493	F 5	SEGAL, SAM		13 SEP 1979	1904		ETHEL
102	C21	SEGAL, SAMUEL M		21 AUG 1946			
102	A83	SEGAL, SAMUEL W		18 SEP 1944	1879		KATE
102	AB83	SEGAL, SARAH	COHEN	18 MAR 1957	1900		
125	M117	SEGAL, SARAH		8 JAN 1929	1877		BARNETT
102	AD71	SEGALL, ELSIE	DUBOWY	11 MAR 1962	1875	HERSHEL MORDECHAI & FREIDA	MORRIS
102	AD72	SEGALL, MORRIS		9 AUG 1968	1874		
370	R27	SEGEL, LIZZIE		1922	26 MAR 1900	ELSIE	
102	AB41	SEIDE, ISRAEL		1981	1844		
377	O28	SEIDMAN, BENJAMIN H		2 JAN 1956	1884		
106	D20	SEIDMAN, JANET S		4 OCT 1982	21 JAN 1899		
104	G17	SEIDNER, GERTRUDE	SCHWARTZ	31 MAY 1979	15 SEP 1953		
372	B 9	SEIDYL, HENRY		21 NOV 1895	24 OCT 1898		
102	K37	SEIGEL, CLARA		24 MAR 1936	1828		
					1886		CHARLES

Cem	Row	Name	Maiden Name	DOD	DOB	Parents	Spouse
374	C26	SEIGEL, ISRAEL		7 DEC 1947	1873		SARAH
374	C25	SEIGEL, MAX CLARENCE		13 AUG 1982	13 JAN 1908	ISRAEL & SARAH	
374	C27	SEIGEL, SARAH		16 FEB 1939	1878		ISRAEL
447	G17	SEIP, CARRIE G		22 NOV 1982			
391	J41	SELESNITSKY, SARAH		2 MAR 1939	1870	MOSHE GERSHON	
391	F36	SELESNITZKY, NATHAN L		18 APR 1901		CALEB	
116	R10	SELETSKY, MOLLY		11 JAN 1979	13 SEP 1909		WILLIAM
116	R 9	SELETSKY, WILLIAM		21 JAN 1987	2 OCT 1908		MOLLY
371	AE21	SELIGMAN, IDA	NATHAN	27 NOV 1980	1 MAR 1898		SIEGFRIED
371	AE22	SELIGMAN, SIEGFRIED		3 OCT 1962	5 AUG 1891		IDA
112	D23	SELIGMANN, ERICA		1976	1907		
222	AR11	SELIGSON, ROSE		4 DEC 1958	1895		SEYMOUR
222	AR12	SELIGSON, SAMUEL		15 AUG 1974	1888		
222	AR10	SELIGSON, SEYMOUR A		23 JUL 1951	1898		ROSE
116	BY46	SELITZKY, ROSE		18 MAR 1970			
376	A 9	SELKOWITZ, ISIDORE		29 OCT 1970	1891		LENA
376	A 8	SELKOWITZ, LENA	SMITH	30 JUL 1967	1891		ISADORE
377	J10	SELLECK, JENNIE RUTH		17 JAN 1972	22 JUL 1892		
112	C24	SELMAN, LEONARD		19 MAR 1987	5 APR 1924		
123		SELTERMAN, LILLIAN		19 MAR 1962	14 SEP 1896		MAURICE
123		SELTERMAN, MAURICE		22 AUG 1957	1894		LILLIAN
102	AI209	SELTZER, ALAN MARC		25 SEP 1973	14 JAN 1969	EDWARD	
102	AI207	SELTZER, EDWARD		3 JUL 1992			
123		SELTZER, GEORGE B		4 JAN 1960	1918		
102	S36	SELTZER, HELEN	RUDNER	6 JAN 1980	1895		ISADORE
102	S37	SELTZER, ISIDORE		7 OCT 1975	1895	MENDEL	HELEN
101	D30	SELTZER, MAXWELL		27 FEB 1950	1859		
102	S38	SELTZER, MENDEL		26 DEC 1946	1860		
102	S39	SELTZER, MILTON		20 MAR 1976	4 JAN 1924	ISADORE & HELEN	
105	H48	SELTZER, SARAH		10 AUG 1953	1902		
392	A 1	SELTZER, SOPHIE		NDD	15 OCT 1925		
114	J26	SELTZER, SYDELLE B		17 DEC 1985	11 AUG 1934		
101	M13	SELVIN, AMELIA		3 FEB 1913			ISAAC
119	F 6	SELWITZ, LIPMAN		30 APR 1974	14 SEP 1914		
248	L52	SEMEL, BERNARD		3 SEP 1971	5 APR 1911	WILLIAM & CELIA	
248	L53	SEMEL, CELIA		6 JAN 1965	14 MAR 1888		WILLIAM
248	L55	SEMEL, ELLIA		11 JAN 1929	12 APR 1922	WILLIAM & CELIA	
248	L54	SEMEL, WILLIAM		12 JAN 1964	17 APR 1888		CELIA
248	E33	SEPLOWITZ, HARRY		8 DEC 1961	19 OCT 1920	HYMAN & SOPHIE	
248	E35	SEPLOWITZ, HYMAN		25 APR 1945	1886		SOPHIE
248	E34	SEPLOWITZ, SOPHIE S		27 AUG 1969	1886		HYMAN
370	J29	SERBER, CHARLOTTE		11 JAN 1970	4 MAR 1907		
125	E 49	SERLIN, ANNA		30 AUG 1982	2 FEB 1898		ABRAHAM
125	J 65	SERLIN, GUSSIE G		19 FEB 1911	1858		
370	A 2	SERLING, CHAVA					
370	H 1	SERLING, LEAH		30 JAN 1913			
750	I17	SERVETNICK, RAE	GRABOW	3 JUN 1982	1899		
371	AD 9	SESERMAN, LEON F		14 JUL 1964	12 OCT 1894		LILLIAN
371	AD 8	SESERMAN, LILLIAN		26 JUN 1974	30 DEC 1898		LEON
370	O15	SHABECOFF, BESSIE		1933	1863		PHILLIP
370	O14	SHABECOFF, PHILLIP		1928	1852		BESSIE
370	O17	SHABECOFF, ROSE		1971	1891		WILLIAM
371	AJ14	SHABECOFF, SIDNEY		31 MAR 1988	1900		SYLVIA
371	AJ13	SHABECOFF, SYLVIA C		12 JUL 1968	1907		SIDNEY
370	O16	SHABECOFF, WILLIAM		1936	1888		ROSE
433	F16	SHACHTER, SARAH	PEAR	29 JAN 1957	1884	YOSEF DAVID	
392	A25	SHACTER, BENJAMIN I		28 JAN 1992			LEE
392	A26	SHACTER, LEE DEAN		25 NOV 1987			BENJAMIN
102	L42	SHAFER, ALEXANDER		4 MAR 1946	15 MAY 1893		PAULINE
391	K32	SHAFNER, ANNA	JURIN	11 OCT 1960	1904		
391	C27	SHAFNER, IRVING		23 MAY 1986	1901	SAMUEL & ROSE	
391	E10	SHAFNER, PERRY T		4 NOV 1976	1895	SAMUEL & ROSE	
391	K33	SHAFNER, PHILIP		24 NOV 1991	1900	SAMUEL MORDECHAI	
391	C29	SHAFNER, ROSE	GABRILOWITZ	26 MAR 1967	1877	ISRAEL JACOB	SAMUEL
391	C28	SHAFNER, SAMUEL		7 AUG 1941	1863	MOSHE	ROSE
392	B13	SHAGOWITZ, MARTIN		1 OCT 1918	25 APR 1915		

Cem	Row	Name	Maiden Name	DOD	DOB	Parents	Spouse
125	O 90	SHAIMMAN, (BABY)		20 MAR 1920	APR 1919		
102	M23	SHANE, JOSEPH		19 MAY 1960	1882		
102	M22	SHANE, ROSE		2 SEP 1952	1885		ROSE
222	AI 8	SHAPERA, CHARLES		11 FEB 1981	13 FEB 1886		JOSEPH
222	AI10	SHAPERA, JACOB DMD		NDD	21 OCT 1915		LENA
222	AI 9	SHAPERA, LENA		21 APR 1984	20 JAN 1895	CHARLES & LENA	
371	O 8	SHAPIRO, ABRAHAM		27 APR 1974	8 JUN 1893		CHARLES
392	E28	SHAPIRO, ABRAHAM		30 MAR 1946	1887		IDA
110	C30	SHAPIRO, ABRAHAM M		29 APR 1969	1898	SAMUEL	RACHEL
371	O 6	SHAPIRO, ALBERT		13 FEB 1983	9 JUN 1901		FANNY
116	C11	SHAPIRO, ANN	JAINCHILL	30 NOV 1991	27 NOV 1927		FAY
125	J162	SHAPIRO, ANNIE		1 JAN 1959	1891	ISAAC	
101	E13	SHAPIRO, ANTHONY C		21 SEP 1969	1951	LIONEL	JACOB
116	BW 9	SHAPIRO, BEATRICE		2 APR 1969	1882		MAX
125	J103	SHAPIRO, BESSIE	CANTER	8 DEC 1983	17 OCT 1895		MORRIS
494	B13	SHAPIRO, CARRIE	WILCOX	1965	1890		EDWARD
447	H19	SHAPIRO, CHARLES		31 MAY 1953	1877		SADIE
374	A18	SHAPIRO, DAVID		2 JAN 1921			
101	G30	SHAPIRO, DAVID ALLEN		1984	1957		
494	B12	SHAPIRO, EDWARD		1964	1897		CARRIE
110	B33	SHAPIRO, ELEANOR V		6 OCT 1968	1932		
125	W177	SHAPIRO, ELIOT M		19 APR 1978	1914		
370	O39	SHAPIRO, ESTHER		2 JUL 1923			
116	BW 5	SHAPIRO, ESTHER	PODOROWSKY	6 JAN 1971	1899		MILTON
110	C29	SHAPIRO, FANNY A		17 MAY 1987	1900		ABRAHAM
371	O 5	SHAPIRO, FAY G		14 APR 1990	12 FEB 1907		ALBERT
377	S12	SHAPIRO, FRANCES	BOWERS	1965	1892		SAMUEL
125	41 C	SHAPIRO, FRASHE		20 OCT 1920	30 SEP 1920	HYMAN & YUDIS	
392	J41	SHAPIRO, GERTRUDE		10 MAR 1937	1899	YESHIYAHU	
101	G23	SHAPIRO, HARRY		25 APR 1984	1916		
447	J12	SHAPIRO, HARRY LOUIS		4 FEB 1983	30 AUG 1888	JOSEPH & SARAH	ROSE
447	I10	SHAPIRO, HERMAN		1987	1897		MARGRET
125	J 98	SHAPIRO, HYMAN		30 JUN 1951	1882		JULIA
371	O 7	SHAPIRO, IDA	MEYER	2 APR 1961	1 MAR 1891		ABRAHAM
391	G 9	SHAPIRO, IDA		21 SEP 1932		ISRAEL	
102	A50	SHAPIRO, ISRAEL		29 APR 1939	1899		
125	J161	SHAPIRO, JACOB		19 MAR 1960	1890		ANNIE
370	S47	SHAPIRO, JACOB		26 NOV 1951	1900		RACHEL
447	K 2	SHAPIRO, JENNIFER LYNN		10 JUN 1984	10 MAY 1972		
222	J 5	SHAPIRO, JOSEPH		12 NOV 1952	1886		REBECCA
447	J14	SHAPIRO, JOSEPH A		16 AUG 1927	1857		SARAH
125	O199	SHAPIRO, JOSEPH DAVID		17 JUL 1965	19 MAR 1945		
329	B15	SHAPIRO, JOSEPH S		24 SEP 1958	1893		LENA
125	J 97	SHAPIRO, JULIA	MILCOWITZ	15 FEB 1975	1885		HYMAN
373	C 2	SHAPIRO, JULIUS		1958	1892		ROSE
374	F54	SHAPIRO, KATIE		29 AUG 1963	1897		MAX
125	I 45	SHAPIRO, LEAH					
110	B30	SHAPIRO, LEAH		14 NOV 1963	1875		MEYER
391	H45	SHAPIRO, LEE		1962	1911		
329	B14	SHAPIRO, LENA	SCHUCARD	31 MAY 1958	1893		JOSEPH
116	BW 7	SHAPIRO, LILLIAN P		26 DEC 1974	1925	MILTON & ESTHER	
101	E12	SHAPIRO, LIONEL		19 JUN 1991	25 OCT 1925		
374	A46	SHAPIRO, LOUIS		8 JAN 1959	1892		RACHEL
116	BW11	SHAPIRO, MAE AMALIE		19 JAN 1989	1910	MAX & BEATRICE	
391	F39	SHAPIRO, MANDEL		24 APR 1939		ALEXANDER	MARTHA
447	I 9	SHAPIRO, MARGRET		1987	1904		HERMAN
102	N45	SHAPIRO, MARION		3 JAN 1992	1899		
391	F40	SHAPIRO, MARTHA		9 JUN 1946	1876	ELIEZER	MANDEL
248	F22	SHAPIRO, MARTIN J		27 MAY 1973	18 FEB 1921		
446	A 7	SHAPIRO, MARY REBECCA		24 NOV 1946	1874		WILLIAM
447	D30	SHAPIRO, MAURICE L		27 AUG 1929	6 APR 1902		KATIE
374	F55	SHAPIRO, MAX		19 AUG 1984	12 OCT 1897		
125	F 95	SHAPIRO, MAX		29 JUN 1944	27 MAR 1869	ZALMAN & RACHEL ZAVIAH	
116	BW10	SHAPIRO, MAX DAVID		9 DEC 1963	1882		BEATRICE
377	H13	SHAPIRO, MAX M		29 APR 1992	1 MAR 1911		
110	B31	SHAPIRO, MEYER		6 NOV 1955	1873		LEAH

Cem	Row	Name	Maiden Name	DOD	DOB	Parents	Spouse
116	BW 6	SHAPIRO, MILTON F		17 AUG 1968	1899		ESTHER
447	H17	SHAPIRO, MILTON M		14 FEB 1943	1915	CHARLES & SADIE	
125	ZA189	SHAPIRO, MORRIS		7 OCT 1988	2 AUG 1915		
105	P20	SHAPIRO, MORRIS		17 MAR 1970	26 APR 1905		
125	J104	SHAPIRO, MORRIS		18 AUG 1956	17 FEB 1889		BESSIE
102	AH167	SHAPIRO, MORRIS S		11 JAN 1968	1897		
125	H149	SHAPIRO, PHILIP		1986	1904		
447	H16	SHAPIRO, PHILIP R		29 NOV 1980	1900	CHARLES & SADIE	
370	S48	SHAPIRO, RACHEL	SAKOWITZ	1 FEB 1981	1900		JACOB
374	A45	SHAPIRO, RACHEL		17 SEP 1951	1895		LOUIS
392	E27	SHAPIRO, RACHEL		25 JUL 1977	1888	MORDECHAI	ABRAHAM
222	J 6	SHAPIRO, REBECCA K		7 JAN 1950	1890		JOSEPH
447	J11	SHAPIRO, ROSE	SCHWARTZ	9 DEC 1963	6 APR 1889		HARRY
373	C 3	SHAPIRO, ROSE		1975	1899		JULIUS
371	AN27	SHAPIRO, RUBIN		9 APR 1951	1880		
391	Q65	SHAPIRO, SADIE		2 MAY 1967	17 JAN 1899		
374	D 5	SHAPIRO, SADIE		6 DEC 1931	1871		
447	H18	SHAPIRO, SADIE		18 FEB 1947	1880		CHARLES
377	S11	SHAPIRO, SAMUEL		1953	1893		FRANCES
391	GC 5	SHAPIRO, SAMUEL		2 JUL 1955	1880	ELIEZER	
446	A14	SHAPIRO, SAMUEL J		17 FEB 1925	1898	WILLIAM & MARY	SARAH
446	A 5	SHAPIRO, SARAH		24 MAY 1982	24 OCT 1916		SAMUEL
447	J13	SHAPIRO, SARAH S		26 MAY 1952	1865		JOSEPH
446	A 6	SHAPIRO, WILLIAM		14 MAR 1957	1870		MARY
371	L 9	SHAPIRO, WILLIAM		1965	1885		
222	J 7	SHAPIRO, WILLIAM BERNARD		19 FEB 1989	1927	JOSEPH & REBECCA	
377	T 3	SHARAF, AARON H		1988	1895	ISRAEL	
391	J31	SHARAF, FANNIE F		28 JUL 1933	1889	JACOB	
391	M37	SHARAF, GUSSIE D		18 OCT 1920	12 OCT 1891	JACOB	
391	D 7	SHARAF, HARRY J		1946	1884	JOSEPH	
377	R10	SHARAF, IDA	MILLER	13 DEC 1977	22 FEB 1891		LIEBERMAN
377	R 9	SHARAF, LIEBERMAN		16 APR 1972	15 MAY 1880		IDA
377	Q19	SHARAF, SADIE		13 MAR 1970	12 JAN 1897		
121	D12	SHARASHEFF, HOWARD A		12 AUG 1983	19 AUG 1952		
125	V146	SHARASHEFF, PHILIP I		22 SEP 1976	11 NOV 1921		
102	P23	SHARFMAN, ALBERT B		24 AUG 1937	9 SEP 1890	BARNETT & FANNIE	ROSE
102	P19	SHARFMAN, BARNETT		19 MAY 1936	1848		FANNIE
102	P25	SHARFMAN, ETTA		17 AUG 1979	11 FEB 1896		SAMUEL
102	P21	SHARFMAN, FANNIE		19 DEC 1927	14 JAN 1862		BARNETT
102	P22	SHARFMAN, MAURICE		2 DEC 1931	25 JUN 1894	BARNETT & FANNIE	
102	P24	SHARFMAN, ROSE		25 FEB 1979	3 AUG 1899		ALBERT
102	P20	SHARFMAN, SAMUEL S DMD		19 MAR 1925	1 FEB 1891	BARNETT & FANNIE	ETTA
102	AA39	SHARNIK, ROSE		7 NOV 1987	3 JAN 1901		SAMUEL
102	AA40	SHARNIK, SAMUEL PHILIP		20 JUN 1963	31 JAN 1896		ROSE
222	AH13	SHARR, ISAAC		10 JUN 1939	1892		
102	N20	SHATZ, ROSE	WEINSTEIN	13 JAN 1961	1873	REBECCA	
371	K 9	SHATZMAN, ARON		1962	1888		REBECCA
371	K 8	SHATZMAN, REBECCA		1968	1890		ARON
330	G45	SHEBITZ, MARY	WEINRIB	1919	1867		JACOB
105	I54	SHECHTMAN, ALLEN A		24 JUL 1956	5 DEC 1901		JEAN
102	Z192	SHECHTMAN, HARRY R		18 FEB 1976	12 MAR 1898		SADIE
105	I55	SHECHTMAN, JEAN B		20 NOV 1978	4 APR 1907		ALLAN
102	Z191	SHECHTMAN, SADIE V		23 JAN 1976	16 JUN 1905		HARRY
104	J17	SHECTMAN, HERBERT		11 AUG 1961	1925		
330	AG13	SHEDROFF, DAVID		29 AUG 1984	26 FEB 1908		
330	AF 6	SHEDROFF, EDWARD		12 AUG 1964	3 OCT 1904		ROSE
330	A19	SHEDROFF, JACOB		6 OCT 1960	31 AUG 1902		
330	AF 5	SHEDROFF, ROSE		28 MAR 1987	11 JUL 1905		EDWARD
392	J19	SHEDROFF, ROSE		31 OCT 1943	1877	ARYEH LEV	
447	Q30	SHEFTEL, ABRAHAM		11 MAY 1952	1928	SAMUEL & ANNA	
447	Q29	SHEFTEL, ANNA		24 JAN 1988	1896		SAMUEL
447	Q28	SHEFTEL, SAMUEL		7 NOV 1977	1885		ANNA
119	E29	SHEIN, JENNIE	SHOLKOWITZ	27 MAY 1990	29 JUN 1919	MORRIS & ROSE	
391	F35	SHEINBACK, MAYER		11 AUG 1909	1879	MORDECHAI	
125	B125	SHEINMAN, ELIAS		6 JAN 1994			
125	K143	SHEINMAN, RACHEL		22 OCT 1931	1863		

Cem	Row	Name	Maiden Name	DOD	DOB	Parents	Spouse
102	AF48	SHEKETOFF, CHARLES J		27 MAY 1971	1 MAR 1893		
102	AA203	SHEKETOFF, JOSEPH L		4 NOV 1983	11 SEP 1916		SADE
102	AF47	SHEKETOFF, SADE B		26 APR 1991	4 OCT 1898		CHARLES
751	B34	SHELKA, RIVKA LEAH		19 OCT 1910		RAFAEL	
102	AJ242	SHELLING, PEARL		8 MAR 1991	6 MAR 1911		
102	CA33	SHEMONSKY, IDA	ROGERS	3 AUG 1959	1882		ISAAC
123		SHEMONSKY, ISAAC		4 MAR 1955	1877		
102	CA32	SHEMONSKY, RACHEL L		22 DEC 1971		ISAAC & IDA (ROGERS)	
121	N 5	SHEMONSKY, RUTH		11 DEC 1983	10 MAR 1916		
377	T24	SHENFIELD, SAUL		8 MAT 1972	9 DEC 1918	SIMCHA	
447	U 8	SHENKER, BENJAMIN M MD			1913		EDNA
119	H49	SHENKER, E REUBEN		27 JUN 1981	27 OCT 1931		
447	U 7	SHENKER, EDNA ROSE		1992	1911		BENJAMIN
433	G10	SHENKMAN, BERNARD		16 MAR 1951	1876	MENACHEM MENDEL	FRANCES
433	G11	SHENKMAN, FRANCES		4 JUN 1976	1886	ABRAHAM MOSHE	BERNARD
433	G12	SHENKMAN, LOUIS J		21 MAY 1981	14 JUN 1917	FRANCES & DAVID	
377	W 5	SHEPATIN, EVA S		15 DEC 1986	13 SEP 1903	SAMUEL	JOSEPH
377	W 6	SHEPATIN, JOSEPH		7 APR 1961	30 JAN 1900	HIRSHEL	EVA
119	E 9	SHEPTOFF, MOLLY	EDELMAN	21 FEB 1976	21 MAR 1913		
391	K28	SHERB, BENJAMIN		4 FEB 1918	1869	JACOB LEV	
391	ZE75	SHERB, BESSIE		4 JUN 1992	1897	URI	JACOB
391	ZE76	SHERB, JACOB		1 JUL 1984	1895	TZVI DAVID	BESSIE
248	I70	SHERBILL, PHILIP		31 JUL 1917	1898		
330	F42	SHEREFSKY, MAX		20 APR 1922	1850		
377	K16	SHERER, LILLIAN D		1987	1902		
330	G26	SHERESEFSKY, IDA RACHEL		19 AUG 1928	1850		
370	P40	SHERESHEVSKY, AUGUSTA		1941	1901		
370	F19	SHERESHEVSKY, BENJAMIN		1912	1902	DAVID & REBECCA	
370	B 9	SHERESHEVSKY, DAVID		4 APR 1926	1868		REBECCA
370	P41	SHERESHEVSKY, ESTHER		1 AUG 1960			
372	J 1	SHERESHEVSKY, LOUIS		1957	1897		
370	C13	SHERESHEVSKY, MOSES AARON		24 MAY 1933			
370	I 1	SHERESHEVSKY, REBECCA DORA		27 NOV 1925	1866		DAVID
370	J35	SHERESHEVSKY, ZISEL LEAH		21 JUN 1941			
377	Z 6	SHERIFF, ANDREW KEITH		13 FEB 1977	12 JAN 1956	JOSEPH	
377	J31	SHERIFF, BERTHA	SOMACH	1984	1897	CHAIM SHALOM	JULIUS
392	E13	SHERIFF, FRANK		20 AUG 1952	1884	MOSHE LIPA	SOPHIE
377	ZA 7	SHERIFF, GEORGE		5 AUG 1978	20 MAY 1920	EFRAIM	
377	J32	SHERIFF, JULIUS LEWIS		1977	1890	MOSHE LIPA	BERTHA
377	J30	SHERIFF, MILTON I		1941	1917	JULIUS	
392	E14	SHERIFF, SOPHIE		18 APR 1966	1886	CHAIM AARON	FRANK
374	A29	SHERMAN, (BABY BOY)		14 MAR 1950			
125	H 23	SHERMAN, ALBERT		14 SEP 1946	8 AUG 1879	MOTEL & CHANA LEAH	ESTELLA
374	A28	SHERMAN, ARTHUR M		19 JAN 1938	1928		
248	K21	SHERMAN, BELLE S		16 SEP 1992	3 FEB 1912		HYMAN
374	B31	SHERMAN, BENJAMIN		1991	1905		
249	E41	SHERMAN, BESSIE		23 JUN 1967	15 SEP 1893		HYMAN
330	AG 2	SHERMAN, CLARA		3 APR 1992	18 SEP 1911		DAVID
330	AG 1	SHERMAN, DAVID		2 FEB 1982	15 SEP 1898		CLARA
125	H 24	SHERMAN, ELLIOT		20 MAY 1919	4 FEB 1917	ALBERT & ESTHELO	DAVID
125	H 22	SHERMAN, ESTELLA REBECCA		4 MAR 1954	DEC 1883		ALBERT
329	B34	SHERMAN, FANNY		22 NOV 1946	1865		SAM
248	C60	SHERMAN, HARRY LOUIS		2 JUN 1984	13 JUN 1911		ROSE
249	E40	SHERMAN, HYMAN A		28 MAY 1963	14 JUL 1888		BESSIE
248	K20	SHERMAN, HYMAN JACK		5 AUG 1987	9 OCT 1912		BELLE
125	B 54	SHERMAN, IDA K	KOTKIN	30 JAN 1968	1906		
125	A 54	SHERMAN, ISADORE		28 JAN 1977	1892		
751	L35	SHERMAN, JACLYN		6 AUG 1968			
102	AH33	SHERMAN, LOUIS B		26 MAR 1955	11 SEP 1889		MINDEL
329	C 3	SHERMAN, MAX		18 MAY 1974	5 MAY 1904		SHIRLEY
119	I 1	SHERMAN, MILTON		5 DEC 1979	13 FEB 1923		
102	AH34	SHERMAN, MINDEL		1 OCT 1964	18 AUG 1886		LOUIS
119	B33	SHERMAN, PHILIP		3 JUN 1991	23 OCT 1918		
374	C30	SHERMAN, PHILIP		7 APR 1987	1898		ROSE
102	AD35	SHERMAN, REBECCA F		19 JUL 1952	1877		
248	C61	SHERMAN, ROSE	WINTER	3 MAY 1992	20 JUN 1910		HARRY

Cem	Row	Name	Maiden Name	DOD	DOB	Parents	Spouse
374	C31	SHERMAN, ROSE S		10 MAR 1967	1900		PHILIP
329	B33	SHERMAN, SAM		26 AUG 1944	1862		FANNY
329	C 4	SHERMAN, SHIRLEY		15 JUN 1982	25 JUL 1913		MAX
248	I21	SHERMANN, MOLLY		NDD	27 JUL 1912		
119	J23	SHERRY, BESSIE PAT		16 DEC 1984	31 MAY 1905		
119	J22	SHERRY, ISRAEL MOSES		14 NOV 1986	28 AUG 1905		
101	B 8	SHERRY, MEYER		9 AUG 1936	1876		SARAH
102	N18	SHERRY, REBECCA	MERIDY	15 JUL 1973	31 JUL 1889	MORRIS	
102	AE59	SHERRY, SAMUEL		30 SEP 1948	1894		
101	B 7	SHERRY, SARAH J		30 AUG 1960	1881		MEYER
392	D25	SHIFREEN, ANNA		26 APR 1980	1894	SAMUEL	SIMON
392	C10	SHIFREEN, BERTHA	NAISTAT	30 MAR 1952	1886		SAMUEL
392	C13	SHIFREEN, CELIA		12 JUL 1972	1893		
392	C12	SHIFREEN, DORA		1 APR 1943	1886		
392	D 4	SHIFREEN, MINNIE B		30 DEC 1991	29 SEP 1907	GERSHON & ETTA	
392	C11	SHIFREEN, SAMUEL C		24 DEC 1961	1886		BERTHA
392	D26	SHIFREEN, SIMON		30 APR 1964	1887	EZIEKEL	ANNA
248	G34	SHIFRIN, BARNET		29 FEB 1972	1898		MOLLIE
248	G33	SHIFRIN, MOLLIE	BRETTSCHNEIDER	21 SEP 1978	1900	ESTHER	BARNET
248	G24	SHIFRIN, NATALIE		25 FEB 1980	1924		
125	S180	SHIMANSKY, NATHAN		26 OCT 1959	1889		REBECCA
125	S181	SHIMANSKY, REBECCA		18 OCT 1957	1889		NATHAN
125	T181	SHIMANSKY, SHIRLEY	HORN	1985	1926		
751	K20	SHIMBLER, ISRAEL B		3 JUN 1935	1876		
248	K70	SHIMEK, CHARLES		11 JAN 1938	21 DEC 1872		
102	S32	SHIMELMAN, ABRAHAM		1944	1881		BESSIE
102	S33	SHIMELMAN, BESSIE G		1989	1890		ABRAHAM
102	S31	SHIMELMAN, ERICA MARCY		16 DEC 1974	18 SEP 1970		
102	S34	SHIMELMAN, MORTON		4 DEC 1992			
103	A32	SHIMKOWITZ, SANDRA	FISHBERG	25 JUN 1989	24 JAN 1947	ABRAHAM & SYLVIA (ZIEKY)	
392	D32	SHINE, BERUCH TZVI A LEVINE		1950	1882	JUDAH	
127	J	SHIROKI, BESSIE		4 SEP 1991	8 DEC 1912		LOUIS
127	J	SHIROKI, LOUIS		24 JAN 1985	1 JAN 1905		BESSIE
127	J	SHIROKI, POLA		14 OCT 1980	7 SEP 1909		
104	O30	SHKOLNIK, MIKHAIL		1992	1927		
104	M49	SHLAIFER, DAVID		6 FEB 1957	25 MAR 1887		SADIE
104	M48	SHLAIFER, SADIE		9 AUG 1951	28 DEC 1883		DAVID
447	Y14	SHLEIN, HAROLD DAVID		25 MAY 1967	21 MAY 1926		
446	C36	SHLEIN, MORRIS		18 DEC 1913	1855		IDA
447	U31	SHLIEN, ABRAHAM		6 JUN 1985	15 APR 1893		ETHEL
447	D17	SHLIEN, BESSIE		30 MAY 1944			MORRIS
447	U30	SHLIEN, ETHEL G		9 JUL 1978	1 JAN 1900		ABRAHAM
447	R20	SHLIEN, ETTA		6 OCT 1957	1890		LOUIS
447	P27	SHLIEN, HYMAN		18 JUL 1949	1886		ROSE
446	B10	SHLIEN, IDA		5 NOV 1941			MORRIS
447	R21	SHLIEN, LOUIS		30 DEC 1967	1888		ETTA
447	V33	SHLIEN, MARION		17 JUN 1985	24 AUG 1926		MARTIN
447	V34	SHLIEN, MARTIN		29 NOV 1986	30 SEP 1922		MARION
447	D16	SHLIEN, MORRIS		13 DEC 1960			BESSIE
447	P28	SHLIEN, ROSE		5 JUL 1949	1890		HYMAN
125	K128	SHLOMBERG, SARAH	COHEN	30 JAN 1933			
110	B20	SHLOSKY, ISADORE		27 OCT 1943	1858		LEAH
110	B19	SHLOSKY, LEAH		20 AUG 1927	1862		ISADORE
372	K 2	SHMAUK, BENJAMIN		1928	1841		PAULINE
372	K 1	SHMAUK, PAULINE		1931	1855		BENJAMIN
750	I21	SHNAEROF, SAM		25 NOV 1961	1884		
750	E22	SHNAEROF, SARAH		27 SEP 1962	1894		
446	A15	SHNEIR, MORRIS		22 DEC 1924	1859		
391	GF 2	SHNITKIN, (BOY)					
391	GF 5	SHNITKIN, (BOY)					
391	GF 4	SHNITKIN, ANYA					
112	E24	SHOHAM, SAMUEL A		17 FEB 1982	24 AUG 1892		SARAH
112	E23	SHOHAM, SARAH	STONE	17 JAN 1985	24 OCT 1897		SAMUEL
125		SHOOLER, N		27 JAN 1928	26 JAN 1928	NATHAN & REBECCA	
110	D18	SHOOR, ANNA	GLASS	14 JUN 1972			
102	AJ37	SHOOR, BESSIE	NEWHOFF	10 MAR 1961	10 MAR 1879		JACOB

Cem	Row	Name	Maiden Name	DOD	DOB	Parents	Spouse
115	A32	SHOOR, ERNEST J		21 MAY 1959	12 OCT 1907		
102	AJ38	SHOOR, JACOB		29 MAY 1942	15 DEC 1874		
121	D38	SHORE, ANN	MARON	28 NOV 1979	11 JUL 1913		BESSIE
123		SHORT, MAX		11 NOV 1944	1911		
248	J16	SHOSSNOK, HANNAH		10 JUN 1918	1834		
116	R25	SHOTTEN, THEODORE		10 AUG 1977	23 DEC 1909		
391	F32	SHRAGOWITZ, ALFRED		25 JUL 1925	20 JUN 1912		
391	H40	SHRAGOWITZ, FANNIE		12 MAR 1935	1860	MOSHE	
391	G33	SHRAGOWITZ, GUSSIE E		15 NOV 1931	1895	CHAIM GADLI	
392	B49	SHRAGOWITZ, MAX		5 JAN 1962	1899		
377	Q23	SHRAGOWITZ, MORTIMER		22 APR 1993	5 MAR 1911		
377	Q42	SHRAGOWITZ, REBECCA	RIBNER	14 JUL 1988	23 DEC 1888		
391	L27	SHRAGOWITZ, WILLIAM		26 APR 1926	19 DEC 1883	CHAIM GEDALIAH	
102	BG15	SHTERGAS, ROSE M					
103	D29	SHUCH, FRANK M		11 FEB 1992	27 AUG 1951	MORRIS	
103	C29	SHUCH, MORRIS		25 JAN 1984	7 SEP 1919		
102	P16	SHULANSKY, LIBBY		3 FEB 1977	1886		SAMUEL
102	P17	SHULANSKY, SAMUEL A		26 MAR 1965	1881		LIBBY
102	P18	SHULANSKY, SAUL		19 JUL 1984	5 MAR 1904		EDITH
102	A87	SHULANSKY, WILLIAM E		8 FEB 1945	1896	SAMUEL & LIBBY	
374	C32	SHULMAN, BENJAMIN		16 FEB 1991	12 SEP 1905	MAX & JENNIE	
330	B28	SHULMAN, ESTHER	NEIDEL	27 SEP 1954	1886		SAMUEL
374	C33	SHULMAN, JENNIE		5 NOV 1940	1863		MAX
125	G 35	SHULMAN, LAWRENCE S		22 FEB 1984	1926		
370	W25	SHULMAN, MARK ALLEN		19 JAN 1944	1 JAN 1944		
374	B 4	SHULMAN, MARTHA		15 APR 1933	1890		
374	C34	SHULMAN, MAX		13 OCT 1954	1860		JENNIE
125	S160	SHULMAN, ROSE	TEPPER	14 DEC 1942	1882	HYMAN & REBECCA	
330	B29	SHULMAN, SAMUEL		19 FEB 1973			ESTHER
110	C15	SHULSKY, BEATRICE		19 JUL 1975	1904		LOUIS
110	C14	SHULSKY, LOUIS		29 AUG 1960	1893		BEATRICE
125	F136	SHULTZ, FREDA		4 JUN 1967	1900		JOSEPH
125	F135	SHULTZ, JOSEPH		19 JAN 1956	1890		FREIDA
119	D18	SHUMAN, ALLAN SAUL		21 JUN 1978	13 SEP 1919		
105	D22	SHUMAN, DORA		8 JUL 1974	1894		MAX
101	B21	SHUMAN, FRUMA		18 NOV 1951	1869		JACOB
374	A13	SHUMAN, HERMAN		28 JUN 1966	12 FEB 1905		
101	H15	SHUMAN, JACK		27 JUN 1980	28 MAR 1917		
101	B20	SHUMAN, JACOB		1 NOV 1940	1859		FRUMA
392	F37	SHUMAN, LOUIS		29 JUN 1909	1888	TZVI HIRSH	
105	D21	SHUMAN, MAX		17 APR 1951	1892		DORA
125	Y179	SHURBERG, ANNA	WEINSTEIN	7 MAR 1984	15 JUL 1903		
125	F 66	SHURBERG, JOSEPH E		27 JAN 1965	28 MAR 1903		
125	R180	SHURBERG, MARY		13 SEP 1959	17 JUL 1898		MEYER
125	R179	SHURBERG, MEYER		8 JAN 1970	3 JAN 1901		MARY
125	Y189	SHURBERG, MICHAEL ISIAH BEH		15 OCT 1984	15 MAR 1934		
125	E 73	SHURBERG, MORRIS		21 MAY 1987	22 JUN 1898		SADIE
125	F 68	SHURBERG, RACHEL		8 AUG 1937	13 OCT 1873	HIRSH YONA & GITTA	SOLOMON
125	E 72	SHURBERG, SADIE		5 JAN 1981	16 APR 1908		MORRIS
125	F 67	SHURBERG, SOLOMON		20 JAN 1953	15 APR 1868		RACHEL
105	A23	SHUSTERMAN, MORRIS		19 MAR 1979	1890		ROSE
105	A22	SHUSTERMAN, ROSE MARIE		15 JUN 1970	1894		MORRIS
125	Z185	SHYEV, IRA		3 NOV 1987	28 DEC 1904		
125	C116	SICKLICK, ADELE	DWORIN	23 JUL 1992	5 MAY 1923		SHERMAN
125	D106	SICKLICK, GRACE		19 SEP 1991	30 JAN 1895		MENDEL
125	D115	SICKLICK, JACOB		5 JAN 1970	15 JUN 1887		MARTHA
125	D116	SICKLICK, MARTHA	ROGIN	11 OCT 1978	7 APR 1887		JACOB
125	D105	SICKLICK, MENDEL		16 JAN 1973	13 JUL 1883		GRACE
125	C117	SICKLICK, SHERMAN		29 OCT 1986	27 JAN 1922		ADELE
125	F 46	SIDEROWF, ALEX EDWARD	SIDEROWFSKY	15 FEB 1941	3 JAN 1895	MORRIS & ROSE (GORDON)	
125	E 47	SIDEROWF, ROBERT ISRAEL	SIDEROWFSKY	18 JUL 1947	3 MAR 1900	MORRIS & ROSE (GORDON)	
125	E 35	SIDEROWF, SARAH C		1988	1903		
125	F 47	SIDEROWFSKY, MORRIS W		19 JAN 1933	1873		ROSE
125	G 48	SIDEROWFSKY, NATHANIEL HARR		21 JAN 1923	AUG 1895	MORRIS & ROSE (GORDON)	
125	F 48	SIDEROWFSKY, ROSE	GORDON	1 JUN 1956	1877		MORRIS
123		SIDRANE, BENJAMIN		8 NOV 1945	1895		

Cem	Row	Name	Maiden Name	DOD	DOB	Parents	Spouse
102	AI165	SIDRANSKY, FANNIE R		24 OCT 1986	3 DEC 1887		
751	D 3	SIEDMAN, JACOB I		29 NOV 1955	27 NOV 1896		
125	O182	SIEDMAN, REUBEN		16 OCT 1968	1893		SARAH
125	O183	SIEDMAN, SARAH		6 NOV 1964	1889		REUBEN
102	CB50	SIEGAL, FRANCIS		23 OCT 1986	31 AUG 1914		
105	J46	SIEGAL, HARRY		15 NOV 1961	1895		ROSE
102	M13	SIEGAL, IDA	DUBROW	9 DEC 1961			LOUIS
102	M14	SIEGAL, LOUIS R		5 AUG 1955	1893		IDA
105	J45	SIEGAL, ROSE		6 SEP 1973	1896		HARRY
116	G 4	SIEGALL, PHYLLIS S		29 JUL 1989	10 MAR 1916		
102	AD52	SIEGEL, ABRAHAM		4 MAR 1971	21 APR 1881		REBECCA
371	N25	SIEGEL, ABRAHAM		1969	1893		LEAH
330	H44	SIEGEL, ABRAHAM		25 SEP 1940	1896		
370	J14	SIEGEL, BLUME ROSA	BLOOM	1 MAY 1934	1865	SHMUEL & HELEN (TEPPER)	DAVID
370	A29	SIEGEL, DAVID		17 NOV 1908	1862		BLUME
101	J21	SIEGEL, DORA		18 NOV 1930	1888		
102	AE92	SIEGEL, FLORENCE		1956	1883		JACOB
370	L11	SIEGEL, HENRY		11 FEB 1940			
374	B 8	SIEGEL, JACOB		10 APR 1935	1866		
222	AN 2	SIEGEL, JACOB		13 FEB 1971	3 JAN 1898		ROSE
370	A21	SIEGEL, JACOB		15 DEC 1907			
102	AE93	SIEGEL, JACOB		1939	1885		FLORENCE
113	B67	SIEGEL, JAMES		15 OCT 1989	18 OCT 1922		
374	G 4	SIEGEL, JOCI HINDA		8 NOV 1916	1832		
371	I 7	SIEGEL, LEAH B		1988	1905		ABRAHAM
121	R17	SIEGEL, MARY		7 APR 1987	4 APR 1921		
330	H47	SIEGEL, MAX		1 MAR 1947	1872		
117	D 7	SIEGEL, MAX		6 DEC 1987	27 JUL 1924		
370	I 7	SIEGEL, MINNIE		23 MAY 1921			
330	G43	SIEGEL, MOLLIE		12 FEB 1915	1874		
391	GN 7	SIEGEL, MORRIS L		12 FEB 1926	1867	AARON	
102	AE138	SIEGEL, NEAL R		3 JUN 1982	7 AUG 1956		
102	AD56	SIEGEL, REBECCA	GOLDBERG	18 JUL 1964	24 JAN 1884		ABRAHAM
222	AN 1	SIEGEL, ROSE	KAUFMAN	1 FEB 1973	28 FEB 1900		JACOB
102	AD57	SIEGEL, SAUL MAURICE		21 FEB 1925	1 MAY 1923	ABRAHAM & REBECCA	
370	F 7	SIEGEL, SIGMOND		1 AUG 1922	12 DEC 1891		
330	AC 1	SIEGEL, SUSAN GAIL		5 APR 1983	13 DEC 1940		
370	J42	SIEGEL, TOBY	SOLOMON	14 MAR 1956			
248	H56	SIEGELBAUM, ANNIE		8 SEP 1927	1860		
248	J70	SIEGELBAUM, DAVID		7 MAR 1923	1860		
391	M26	SIFF, OSCAR		15 OCT 1922	1866	NATHAN	
391	F41	SIFF, TILLIE TOBA		30 NOV 1951	1868	JACOB	
330	F54	SIGAL, ABRAHAM L		6 MAY 1930	1916	MORRIS	
105	J32	SIGAL, ABRAHAM N		31 AUG 1975	1896		ALICE
105	J33	SIGAL, ALICE E		17 APR 1985	1908		ABRAHAM
372	C 9	SIGAL, ANNA HELEN	LAND	1941	1904		
105	M15	SIGAL, EILEEN		11 AUG 1988	1913		MORRIS
125	A 72	SIGAL, IRVING M		21 MAY 1983	31 JUL 1920		LEONA
105	J31	SIGAL, IRVING N		6 DEC 1949	1905		
105	H31	SIGAL, ISRAEL		3 JUL 1949	1893		ROSE
105	J37	SIGAL, ISRAEL MAX		22 APR 1952		NAFTALI	ROSE
102	AJ172	SIGAL, JACOB B MD		9 MAY 1966	17 FEB 1897		
125	A 72	SIGAL, LEONA	HORWITZ	18 MAR 1965	1923		IRVING
105	I33	SIGAL, LEONARD IRWIN		24 SEP 1938	16 APR 1938		
107	G19	SIGAL, MATHILDA	KAUFMANN	8 OCT 1987	30 JAN 1907		
105	M14	SIGAL, MORRIS		1992			EILEEN
102	V 9	SIGAL, MORRIS		26 FEB 1937	1872		
330	F55	SIGAL, MORRIS N		30 SEP 1930	1888		
102	V10	SIGAL, NATHAN		19 OCT 1933	1892		
105	H30	SIGAL, ROSE		29 DEC 1954	1894		ISRAEL
105	J38	SIGAL, ROSE	PORTNER	3 SEP 1944	1883		ISRAEL
370	Q45	SIGEL, SIMON					
117	C12	SIKORA, JENNIFER LYNN		18 SEP 1983	17 SEP 1983		
126		SILBERG, JOSEPH		14 JUL 1899	6 JAN 1899		
116	BL124	SILBERMAN, DOROTHY	MOLSTEIN	11 APR 1978	13 MAY 1923		SALO
331		SILBERMAN, HARRY		9 JAN 1902	1878		

Cem	Row	Name	Maiden Name	DOD	DOB	Parents	Spouse
222	AE17	SILBERMAN, ISRAEL		6 NOV 1940	1882		
222	AE16	SILBERMAN, ROSE		4 JAN 1950	1884		ROSE
116	BL125	SILBERMAN, SALO JOSEF		30 JUN 1975	8 DEC 1911		ISRAEL
750	I23	SILLER, GEORGE		2 OCT 1968	7 FEB 1918		DOROTHY
248	B19	SILLMAN, JEANETTE L	MANDELL	18 NOV 1967	1903	MAX & CELIA	
121	S12	SILLMAN, MIRIAM B	STROH	26 JUN 1977	21 MAR 1928	LOUIS & ROSE	
447	E 9	SILOWITZ, REBECCA		14 JUN 1966			
432		SILTERMAN, IDA		26 JUL 1897			
751	C11	SILVER, AARON		23 NOV 1954	1885		MARY
125	V148	SILVER, ABRAHAM		1 JAN 1977	25 JUL 1915		
125	K 68	SILVER, ADOLPH H		20 OCT 1918	18 JUL 1887		
125	E128	SILVER, BARBARA ELLEN		17 APR 1947	5 JAN 1947	ABRAHAM	
104	G11	SILVER, BEN		6 NOV 1985			
125	K140	SILVER, CELIA	HARLEM	27 OCT 1981	1894		MORRIS
116	M23	SILVER, EMANUEL M		24 JUN 1983	1919		
102	R 6	SILVER, FRANCINE	ETELIS	10 MAR 1983	9 MAY 1956		
102	U25	SILVER, HANNAH	SPIEGEL	11 JUN 1956	13 MAY 1878		JACOB
102	U26	SILVER, HENRY L		22 MAR 1982	1 FEB 1904	JACOB & HANNAH (SPIEGEL)	
328	A24	SILVER, ILSA	MAYER	22 MAR 1979		ALFRED	
110	F 1	SILVER, IRENE 'IDA'		25 JUN 1992	7 JUN 1902		
102	U24	SILVER, JACOB	OF HOMSK, GRODN	2 DEC 1940	25 JUN 1875	MORDECHAI & ESTHER	HANNAH
118	D19	SILVER, JACOB A		16 FEB 1964			ROSE
102	AB87	SILVER, JENNIE M		13 SEP 1965	29 DEC 1878		WOLF
118	D15	SILVER, LORA		12 JUL 1963			SAUL
125		SILVER, M		5 MAY 1930	1930	MORRIS & CELIA	
751	C10	SILVER, MARY		21 JUL 1976	1887		AARON
248	M74	SILVER, MEYER		1966	1892		
125	K141	SILVER, MORRIS		8 JUN 1964	1892		CELIA
104	G12	SILVER, MRS					BEN
102	AE65	SILVER, ROSALIND	GLANZ	2 FEB 1980	27 MAY 1914		SIDNEY
118	D19	SILVER, ROSE		1 MAY 1972			JACOB
248	N77	SILVER, SARAH		9 FEB 1925	1847		
118	D15	SILVER, SAUL		22 OCT 1987			LORA
102	AE64	SILVER, SIDNEY		26 MAR 1972	4 JUN 1910		ROSLIND
119	C34	SILVER, WILLIAM		24 JUN 1981	10 JAN 1916		
118	D20	SILVER, WILLIAM C		20 MAR 1991			
102	AB86	SILVER, WOLF		1 SEP 1951	26 APR 1873		JENNIE
370	S41	SILVERBERG, ABRAHAM					SARAH
370	S37	SILVERBERG, GERSON		29 JUL 1990	1 SEP 1918		
370	S40	SILVERBERG, ORIN		20 AUG 1981	14 MAY 1929		
110	D33	SILVERBERG, SAMUEL		24 APR 1978	27 AUG 1904		
370	S42	SILVERBERG, SARAH RACHEL					ABRAHAM
102	AJ196	SILVERGLEID, DORIS	DAVIDSON	1970	1899		SAM
222	AK 3	SILVERHERZ, HANNAH		28 OCT 1985	10 AUG 1902		
222	AK 1	SILVERHERZ, JOSEPH		10 APR 1987	21 NOV 1908	MORRIS & REBECCA	
222	AJ 1	SILVERHERZ, MORRIS	OF ROMANIA	8 FEB 1943	15 MAY 1872		REBECCA
222	AJ 2	SILVERHERZ, REBECCA	MARGOSHES	1957	1876		MORRIS
222	AK 2	SILVERHERZ, SAM		24 OCT 1989	2 APR 1900	MORRIS & REBECCA	HANNAH
370	J66	SILVERLIEB, OSCAR		1968	1880		REBECCA
370	J65	SILVERLIEB, REBECCA		1944	1887		OSCAR
222	AN 9	SILVERMAN, AARON		27 MAR 1950	1924	WILLIAM	
370	G11	SILVERMAN, ALECK		1959	1888		LENA
102	Z127	SILVERMAN, ALTHEA O		29 AUG 1977	20 APR 1897		MORRIS
370	D 9	SILVERMAN, ANNA B	6 JAN 1961*	25 DEC 1961*	1903		MORRIS
125	K 31	SILVERMAN, ANNIE	BERKOWITZ	8 SEP 1915	1892	MORRIS & ESTHER (GREENSTEIN)	
371	K 1	SILVERMAN, ARYEH ZEV		26 JAN 1966	23 JAN 1930		
102	BG30	SILVERMAN, BEATRICE	PEARL	31 JUL 1990	6 OCT 1915		
102	Z125	SILVERMAN, BEN-AMI		26 DEC 1923	14 JUL 1921	RABBI MORRIS & ALTHEA	
222	AN10	SILVERMAN, BORIS		14 DEC 1960	1914	WILLIAM	GLORIA
114	B 1	SILVERMAN, BRET REUBEN		21 OCT 1991	20 OCT 1991	JAY & EVELYN	
371	N24	SILVERMAN, CALVIN		7 FEB 1969	22 FEB 1921		
750	G24	SILVERMAN, CLARA		9 MAR 1969	25 JUN 1904		HARRY
114	B 3	SILVERMAN, CORY DANIEL		16 OCT 1991	16 OCT 1991	JAY & EVELYN	
116	BI38	SILVERMAN, DOROTHY		29 MAY 1989	6 JUL 1904		
370	C28	SILVERMAN, DVORAH LEAH		30 NOV 1933	19 JAN 1930	MORRIS	
102	Z128	SILVERMAN, ELIHU O		3 MAR 1952	20 APR 1928	RABBI MORRIS & ALTHEA	

Cem	Row	Name	Maiden Name	DOD	DOB	Parents	Spouse
222	AN11	SILVERMAN, GLORIA		7 JUN 1979	1910		BORIS
125	M141	SILVERMAN, HARRIET MIRIAM		13 AUG 1969	16 JUN 1913		WILLIAM
750	G25	SILVERMAN, HARRY		19 SEP 1972	10 MAR 1900		CLARA
494	A20	SILVERMAN, HARRY		28 AUG 1971	22 JUL 1890	KIBA	RUTH
123		SILVERMAN, HARRY P		29 JAN 1949	1920		
248	I68	SILVERMAN, HENRY		30 MAY 1916	1890		
374	A42	SILVERMAN, JOSEPH		1951	1863		
751	B18	SILVERMAN, JOSEPH		20 DEC 1956	1892		LILLY
370	G10	SILVERMAN, LENA EDITH		1965	1893		ALECK
494	B17	SILVERMAN, LEONARD JOSEPH D		5 OCT 1987	21 FEB 1923	MAURICE	
751	B17	SILVERMAN, LILY	SMITH	1968	1896		JOSEPH
114	B 2	SILVERMAN, LIOR ADINA		21 OCT 1991	20 OCT 1991	JAY & EVELYN	
392	B28	SILVERMAN, MATILDA		31 AUG 1993	1912		
494	B19	SILVERMAN, MAURICE		1957	1900	KIBA	MIRIAM
370	C27	SILVERMAN, MAYER MISHA		1 AUG 1930	16 MAR 1925	MORRIS	
222	AO 9	SILVERMAN, MEYER		10 DEC 1982	3 JAN 1925		
127	B	SILVERMAN, MITZI		31 JUL 1989	15 MAY 1920		ANNA
370	B16	SILVERMAN, MORRIS		3 AUG 1981	27 MAR 1897		ALTHEA
102	Z126	SILVERMAN, MORRIS RABBI		3 MAR 1972	19 NOV 1894		
370	Q34	SILVERMAN, OSCAR		1964	1897		REBECCA
370	G 9	SILVERMAN, PHILIP		1957	1891		
370	P39	SILVERMAN, RACHEL		12 NOV 1930	1841		PHILIP
370	G 8	SILVERMAN, REBECCA		1984	1896		HARRY
494	A19	SILVERMAN, RUTH	SAMUELS	23 DEC 1958	12 JUL 1898	SELICK & SADIE	
101	B42	SILVERMAN, SAMUEL		7 JUL 1912	1840		
125	L134	SILVERMAN, SAMUEL		17 NOV 1931	1886		
125	ZA184	SILVERMAN, SAMUEL L		8 JAN 1992			
392	B29	SILVERMAN, SHELDON		24 AUG 1970	1947	MATILDA	
330	F45	SILVERMAN, SIMON		26 APR 1926	1856		
125	M142	SILVERMAN, WILLIAM		12 DEC 1974	23 MAY 1906		HARRIET
222	AN 8	SILVERMAN, WILLIAM		1939	1893		MOLLIE
109	C10	SILVERSMITH, L FISHER		18 DEC 1952	1888		MOLLIE
248	D17	SILVERSTEIN, ABRAHAM		14 SEP 1957	5 JUN 1896		JACOB
377	Y 3	SILVERSTEIN, ANNA C		24 JAN 1984	21 JUN 1893	ZALMAN	
391	X65	SILVERSTEIN, BEATRICE R		NDD	1910	IRVING	
248	G59	SILVERSTEIN, BELLE		25 APR 1990	24 OCT 1913		
371	AC 6	SILVERSTEIN, BENJAMIN		16 AUG 1982			
374	B15	SILVERSTEIN, BESSIE		1 APR 1942	1860		IRVING
371	AC10	SILVERSTEIN, BESSIE		29 OCT 1962			DAVID
371	AC 7	SILVERSTEIN, CHARLOTTE		11 AUG 1982			
113	K25	SILVERSTEIN, DORIS C		15 AUG 1976	23 NOV 1931	SAUL & REBECCA	
374	E38	SILVERSTEIN, DOROTHY M		1959	1899		ISAAC
248	G58	SILVERSTEIN, ESTHER SARAH	SIEGELBAUM	28 FEB 1969	25 NOV 1891	DAVID & ANNIE	
371	AC 9	SILVERSTEIN, HENRY		2 JUL 1960	19 JAN 1887		MOLLIE
391	X67	SILVERSTEIN, IRVING		5 JUN 1981	1909	ELEIZER	DOROTHY
374	E37	SILVERSTEIN, ISAAC		1945	1889		
371	AC 5	SILVERSTEIN, ISIDOR		16 MAR 1984			CHARLOTTE
371	AC 8	SILVERSTEIN, J DAVID		2 NOV 1980			
248	K71	SILVERSTEIN, JACOB M		16 AUG 1937	19 JUL 1912		ANNA
377	Y 4	SILVERSTEIN, JACOB S		17 AUG 1972	17 FEB 1883	DAVID	
391	D 8	SILVERSTEIN, LOUIS		4 MAY 1944	1878	ISRAEL MOSHE	
391	H33	SILVERSTEIN, MARY		16 JUL 1924			IRVING
391	X66	SILVERSTEIN, MOLLIE		4 APR 1972	1884	SAMUEL	ABRAHAM
248	D16	SILVERSTEIN, MOLLIE	HOLIN	21 DEC 1969	5 JAN 1901		
391	X57	SILVERSTEIN, MORRIS		18 MAR 1959	1884	ISAAC	
248	J71	SILVERSTEIN, MORRIS		20 FEB 1924	1866		SAUL
113	K27	SILVERSTEIN, REBECCA B		24 APR 1970	6 JUN 1905		
751	O32	SILVERSTEIN, RUBY	ZAGOREN	9 JUN 1974	9 DEC 1922		REBECCA
113	K26	SILVERSTEIN, SAUL M		17 MAY 1972	25 AUG 1900		
248	J77	SILVERSTEIN, SILVIA		11 SEP 1921	8 JUL 1921		
102	S 2	SILVERSTEIN, SOPHIE	WHITE	30 JUL 1982	28 FEB 1893		
391	G22	SILVERSTEIN, THERESA		26 AUG 1916			
370	H32	SILVERSWEIG, MIRIAM ESTHER		18 JUN 1913			
392	H26	SILVERSWEIG, REBECCA	SHAPIRO	8 FEB 1933	1867	ARI LEV	
114	K18	SILVERWATCH, JOHN		20 NOV 1990	6 AUG 1913		
447	AA31	SILVERZAHN, GERTRUDE		17 OCT 1990	18 JAN 1920		

Cem	Row	Name	Maiden Name	DOD	DOB	Parents	Spouse
447	V10	SILVERZAHN, LENA			1890		
447	V 9	SILVERZAHN, MEYER		4 OCT 1979			MEYER
391	F22	SIMENOWITZ, MEYER W		12 JUN 1983	1889		LENA
125	C 47	SIMMONS, MONROE		27 NOV 1927	1859	ISAAC	
330	F56	SIMON, ABRAHAM		24 JAN 1981	1897		
377	W18	SIMON, ALBERT ABRAHAM		18 OCT 1930			
391	ZG51	SIMON, ALEX		29 APR 1965	25 NOV 1913	SAMUEL	
330	AC 2	SIMON, BEATRICE		29 NOV 1991	21 JUN 1905	SAMUEL	
372	G 4	SIMON, CHARLES		1970	1926		
331		SIMON, ESTHER FREDA		1960	1897		MITCHELL
330	G61	SIMON, FLORA					
391	ZE61	SIMON, GUSSIE		9 JUN 1935			
330	AB10	SIMON, HANNAH ANNA		12 JUN 1992	1 MAY 1911	CHINACH	
391	ZE60	SIMON, JACK		25 JUN 1967	1 APR 1896		JACK
391	P51	SIMON, JENNIE MARYU		18 SEP 1966	6 JUL 1908	SENDER	
330	AD 8	SIMON, LION		8 OCT 1947		BARUCH ABRAHAM	GUSSIE
329	A 5	SIMON, MALCHEN		26 NOV 1970	7 MAY 1897		SAMUEL
433	A10	SIMON, MAX		14 OCT 1959	3 APR 1880		
330	AC 3	SIMON, MITCHELL		20 JAN 1990	2 SEP 1911		
102	B 3	SIMON, MURRAY		13 APR 1986	24 NOV 1921	HANNAH ANNA	
433	B10	SIMON, PAUL DAVID		27 APR 1959	1908		BEATRICE
102	AI46	SIMON, PHILIP L		1978	1955		
102	AI47	SIMON, RUBIN		23 MAR 1974	12 JUN 1922	RUBIN & YETTA	
391	P50	SIMON, SAMUEL		4 APR 1952	4 JUL 1892		YETTA
330	AF14	SIMON, TILLIE		11 JAN 1956		MOSHE	JENNIE
102	AI48	SIMON, YETTA		24 DEC 1970			
370	F31	SIMONER, DAVID		26 DEC 1979	25 JUL 1894		RUBIN
371	G 3	SIMONER, TSIPA	GELBEIN	1977	1889		
371	AF22	SIMONOWITZ, ABRAHAM A		27 MAR 1980	25 JUL 1898		
370	A63	SIMONOWITZ, DAVID		30 OCT 1962	1883		
370	A51	SIMONOWITZ, ELI		27 JUL 1936	1889	ELI & IDA	
371	AG22	SIMONOWITZ, GEORGE		14 OCT 1942	1848		IDA
370	A50	SIMONOWITZ, IDA LENA		21 NOV 1967	1914		MARY
371	AG21	SIMONOWITZ, MARY		3 JAN 1922	1852		ELI
371	AF21	SIMONOWITZ, MINNIE	4 JAN 1975*	6 AUG 1979	1915		GEORGE
102	I44	SIMONS, BENJAMIN C		25 DEC 1975*	1892		
119	H20	SIMONS, HARRY "BUZZ"		17 JUN 1955	1888		SADIE
102	I43	SIMONS, SADIE	RUFFKESS	14 JUL 1991	3 JUL 1911		
446	A 3	SIMONSON, ABRAHAM		21 AUG 1977	28 MAY 1895		BENJAMIN
446	A42	SIMONSON, FANNY		1928	1864		JENNIE
446	A 1	SIMONSON, HARRIS		MAR/APR 1920	1860		
446	A 2	SIMONSON, JENNIE	ISUKOFF	1922	1897	ABRAHAM & JENNIE	
121	V20	SIMPSON, GEORGE		1923	1865		ABRAHAM
121	U 8	SIMPSON, RITA		20 OCT 1989	5 MAR 1908		
433	Q 3	SIMSON, NATHAN		1982	1907		
125	B131	SINAY, SHIRLEY	SLATER	27 APR 1988	1 APR 1906	ZALMAN	
125	K144	SIND, BEN		4 FEB 1980	1925		
102	AJ168	SIND, H GEORGE		10 OCT 1986	5 FEB 1912		HILDA
102	AJ169	SIND, HANNAH	DOBKIN	10 OCT 1986	23 APR 1905		HANNAH
125	K145	SIND, HILDA		2 JUL 1988	25 DEC 1904		GEORGE
249	F32	SINDER, SOLOMON		11 MAR 1992	29 JAN 1913		BEN
371	L11	SINE, BESSIE	LAHN	20 JAN 1982	16 NOV 1910		
102	AB192	SINGER, ALBERT		NDD	26 MAY 1898		
102	AC164	SINGER, BETTY		18 JAN 1980	26 MAR 1909		TILLIE
102	AJ60	SINGER, HENRY		12 DEC 1962	1902		
107	H22	SINGER, HERSCHEL HARRY		28 SEP 1958	26 APR 1908		
391	M39	SINGER, IDA		7 AUG 1987	17 MAR 1908		
329	A 7	SINGER, JENNIE		8 APR 1935	25 DEC 1873	ELCHANA YECHIEL	
102	AI34	SINGER, JOSEPH		1981	1888		JENNIE
329	A38	SINGER, JULIUS		18 JAN 1967	14 JAN 1904		SARAH
102	AC161	SINGER, KATE	FEINBERG	1980	1915	SAMUEL & JENNIE	
102	AC160	SINGER, LOUIS B		11 AUG 1977	7 NOV 1895		LOUIS
391	I26	SINGER, MAX		12 DEC 1971	15 OCT 1890		KATE
329	A 6	SINGER, SAMUEL		11 SEP 1925	1870	MEYER	
750	G28	SINGER, SARA RACHEL		26 JUN 1960	1882		SAMUEL
102	AI33	SINGER, SARAH	GABERMAN	17 MAR 1985	15 OCT 1894		JOSEPH
				15 OCT 1973	5 JUN 1907		

Cem	Row	Name	Maiden Name	DOD	DOB	Parents	Spouse
102	AB193	SINGER, TILLIE		18 OCT 1973	27 JUN 1907		ALBERT
102	AI32	SINGER, WALTER VICTOR		29 MAY 1967	30 MAY 1929	JOSEPH & SARAH	
104	L43	SINGER, WILLIAM		13 FEB 1989	1913		
125	W172	SIRKIN, ARTHUR A		16 FEB 1978	29 SEP 1918		RUTH
370	F12	SIRKIN, DAVID H		15 JAN 1919	1898		
125	J 54	SIRKIN, F		2 NOV 1916	1849		LOUIS
125	J 53	SIRKIN, LOUIS		25 JAN 1904	15 MAR 1879		F
125	O 94	SIRKIN, SAMUEL		9 AUG 1920	1844	DOV & BEILA	
125	E 48	SIRLIN, ABRAHAM JOSEPH		8 MAR 1951	1886		ANNA
125		SIRLIN, CASSIE		1911	1852		
125	L 21	SIRLIN, HIRSHEL		14 APR 1918	1848		
125	M126	SIROT, JENNIE		25 JUL 1930			
102	AE39	SISK, DAVID		7 OCT 1979	1892		
119	D52	SISKEN, ROSE		23 MAY 1992	6 SEP 1909		
119	D53	SISKEN, SIMON		15 JUN 1977	14 FEB 1909		
107	G10	SITCOVSKY, LOUIS		4 APR 1983	14 APR 1907		
371	L23	SITKER, HYMAN		18 MAY 1968	1908		NORMA
371	L24	SITKER, NORMA		7 NOV 1971	1907		HYMAN
121	L18	SKAL, ARTHUR MORRIS		1 FEB 1973	4 SEP 1920		
391	G26	SKALOWSKY, ALICE		20 FEB 1914	7 JUN 1912	J & A	
391	O61	SKLAR, BETTY		7 JAN 1973	14 JUL 1911	SAMUEL	
121	E 1	SKLAR, DAVID		5 MAR 1985	23 SEP 1924		
103	C26	SKLAR, FLORENCE		17 JUN 1982			
371	AK20	SKLAREW, FANNY C		1986	1900		LOUIS
371	AK19	SKLAREW, LOUIS I		16 JUN 1973	1898		FANNIE
751	F38	SKOLNICK, IDA		20 OCT 1925	1870		
751	G39	SKOLNICK, LOUIS		20 NOV 1946	1873		
222	AT15	SKOLNICK, SADIE		24 NOV 1949	1889		
102	CB38	SKOLNICK, WILLIAM H		30 JUN 1981	1 JUN 1905		
391	I39	SLADE, ANNIE		18 JAN 1936		ISAAC	
391	R67	SLADE, BESSIE		24 SEP 1973	2 JAN 1899	JOSEPH	
391	R26	SLADE, JOSEPH		30 JAN 1919	1873	ISAAC	
391	D 6	SLADE, LOUIS		23 APR 1946	1905	JOSEPH	
101	K18	SLASNEY, SARAH					
102	L 1	SLATER, ANNA F		15 JAN 1992	3 FEB 1899		FRANK
102	L 2	SLATER, FRANK H		10 AUG 1970	1893		ANNA
102	L 3	SLATER, JULIAN	TOBIAS	16 OCT 1934	12 JAN 1925	FRANK & ANNA	
391	O40	SLAVEN, ELLEN H		1 DEC 1940	20 SEP 1863	ZEV WOLF	
391	F25	SLAVIN, (SON)		31 MAY 1895	1882	H & R	
377	O 4	SLAVIN, GREGORY		1945	1868		ILANA
377	O 5	SLAVIN, ILLANA		1940	1866		GREGORY
121	J 5	SLAVKIN, ANNE L		12 SEP 1986	28 AUG 1934		
330	E 1	SLAVKIN, BESSIE		17 FEB 1950	1866		
112	E17	SLAVKIN, HYMAN		13 DEC 1973	23 NOV 1904		
330	AI24	SLAVKIN, LILLIAN		15 JAN 1990	14 MAY 1901		SAMUEL
121	J 7	SLAVKIN, LOUIS		28 FEB 1971	25 DEC 1901		
123		SLAVKIN, MARSHALL P		29 JAN 1968	16 SEP 1936		
330	F 7	SLAVKIN, MORRIS		29 JAN 1937			
330	AI23	SLAVKIN, SAMUEL		24 APR 1977	15 JUL 1900		LILLIAN
121	E 3	SLESS, SIMON J		14 FEB 1986	20 MAY 1902		
108	C21	SLIPCHINSKY, EDWARD		27 NOV 1987	22 SEP 1912		
119	E 1	SLITT, AARON M		10 JUL 1986	29 SEP 1922		
104	E32	SLITT, EDWARD		15 DEC 1968	21 MAR 1913		
102	A52	SLITT, LOUIS		3 MAR 1940	1890		YETTA
119	E 2	SLITT, RHODA	DANEN	7 JUN 1979	26 MAR 1926		
102	A53	SLITT, YETTA		5 FEB 1959	1894		LOUIS
105	H46	SLOAN, ANNA		25 NOV 1963	1890		
391	L40	SLOAN, BESSIE	NOVITCH	25 SEP 1934	1900	MOSHE	
750	H18	SLOANE, PERRY J		1983	1915		
102	AH140	SLOAT, JACK		30 MAY 1977	5 JUL 1902		
222	AH15	SLOBIN, AARON		8 FEB 1945	1873		RUTH
222	AH14	SLOBIN, ABRAHAM		4 AUG 1922	1902	AARON & RUTH	
222	AH16	SLOBIN, RUTH		8 OCT 1959	1878		AARON
102	AE116	SLOBODIEN, ALICE	HOROWITZ	15 OCT 1967	3 MAY 1909		
374	A10	SLOM, HYMAN		18 JUL 1914			
116	V24	SLONIM, EDNA		23 OCT 1989	17 FEB 1907		JOSEPH

Cem	Row	Name	Maiden Name	DOD	DOB	Parents	Spouse
102	AB 4	SLONIM, FANNIE	COOPER	10 NOV 1935	1895		MAX
116	V23	SLONIM, JOSEPH		29 SEP 1979	28 APR 1904		EDNA
110	C22	SLONIM, LOIS	KAPLAN	8 MAY 1989	7 AUG 1931		
102	AB 3	SLONIM, MAX P		13 OCT 1959	1885		FANNIE
102	AB202	SLONIM, NATHAN M		18 JAN 1988	1 JUL 1923		
330	G53	SLOPAK, ADELE		19 SEP 1928	1906		
330	H49	SLOPAK, FISHEL		28 JUN 1961	1879		ODES
330	H50	SLOPAK, ODES		26 DEC 1949	1879		FISCHEL
330	AH23	SLOPAK, SARA LINDA		5 SEP 1972	1942		
370	C22	SLOSBERG, BENNIE		1896	13 OCT 1895		
370	G 1	SLOSBERG, CHARLES		4 JAN 1963	1869		
371	AQ 2	SLOSBERG, FANNIE	STROM	20 FEB 1978	10 SEP 1891	MOSES & GUTE LIEBA (SHAPIRO)	SAMUEL
370	H28	SLOSBERG, MIRIAM B		29 MAY 1911			
370	I18	SLOSBERG, RACHEL L		22 MAR 1920	1828		
371	AQ 1	SLOSBERG, SAMUEL		31 JAN 1969	13 OCT 1895		FANNIE
370	I 8	SLOSBERG, SARAH		17 NOV 1920			
370	C21	SLOSBERG, WILLIAM		1896	12 SEP 1894		
370	O19	SLOSSBERG, BENJAMIN		31 JUL 1978	9 MAY 1896		LENA
370	F28	SLOSSBERG, ETHEL		1905	1 FEB 1905		
370	K 6	SLOSSBERG, GUSSIE		2 OCT 1949	1885		CHARLES
370	B43	SLOSSBERG, HATTIE		1967	1888		JACOB
370	B42	SLOSSBERG, JACOB R		1974	1881		HATTIE
370	C 1	SLOSSBERG, JAMES		25 JUN 1932			
370	O18	SLOSSBERG, LENA S		1983	1897		BENJAMIN
370	A 4	SLOSSBERG, MICHAEL O		20 FEB 1911			
392	B31	SLOTNECK, FREDA		22 MAR 1923			
391	V55	SLOTNICK, FREIDA		11 FEB 1954	1872	TZVI JACOB	
392	E31	SLOTSKY, RUBIN		17 OCT 1933	1860		
104	L33	SLUSKY, MARTHA		26 APR 1985	23 JUL 1923		
392	J33	SLUTSKY, ABRAHAM					
104	M34	SLUTSKY, IDA		15 NOV 1975	5 DEC 1898		JACK
104	M33	SLUTSKY, JACK		1 SEP 1985	12 AUG 1896		IDA
102	AJ239	SLUTSKY, LEONARD		9 AUG 1990	15 JUL 1913		
446	A20	SLUTSKY, MYER		29 JAN 1921	1873		
447	N19	SLUTZKY, HARRY		5 SEP 1943	1874		
447	U25	SLUTZKY, TAMARA		17 MAY 1935	1871		
330	E51	SLUTZMAN, BESSIE		3 OCT 1941			
330	F65	SLUTZMAN, LAZER		25 APR 1940			
330	E46	SMALL, ANNIE		25 SEP 1940	1876		
101	G 1	SMALL, SANDRA C		8 JUN 1983	23 MAR 1956		
392	B35	SMETTER, LILLIAN		3 JUN 1967	1903		WILLIAM
392	B34	SMETTER, WILLIAM		15 NOV 1963	1905		LILLIAN
101	B36	SMILOVITZ, NATHAN		9 SEP 1913	1877		
751	L37	SMITH, (BABY BOY)		8 JAN 1958			
751	B 1	SMITH, (BABY GIRL)		15 SEP 1956		PAUL & KAYWIN	
751	J32	SMITH, ABRAHAM		1 AUG 1931			
751	E29	SMITH, BENJAMIN		29 DEC 1963	7 JAN 1879		ABRAHAM
101	D 3	SMITH, BENJAMIN E		9 APR 1973	1900		RAE
102	U22	SMITH, BESSIE	KELMAN	4 MAY 1945	1887		SADIE
751	J25	SMITH, DAVID		1 NOV 1936	1896		SAMUEL
751	E35	SMITH, EPHREM		6 MAY 1972	1882		
751	E32	SMITH, FLORENCE		1949	1908		
377	Z30	SMITH, GABRIELLE H		27 SEP 1977	12 JUN 1973	SOLOMON	
102	AE97	SMITH, HAROLD M		16 MAR 1990	1909	HYMAN BANKS	
391	ZA69	SMITH, HARRY J		27 JAN 1975		CHAIM	
102	AE96	SMITH, HYMAN		27 NOV 1954	1879		
391	C18	SMITH, HYMAN		28 DEC 1936	1866	AARON	
751	E31	SMITH, ISIDORE		15 DEC 1968			
101	K10	SMITH, LADA		5 MAR 1933	1873		ROSE
374	G14	SMITH, LOUIS		4 JAN 1918			
125	F 7	SMITH, MARTHA	ALEXANDER	8 MAY 1975	1900		SAMUEL
751	J30	SMITH, MORRIS		17 JUN 1939	1876		
102	N47	SMITH, MORRIS		29 FEB 1952	1875		REBECCA
751	M17	SMITH, MORRIS W		19 MAY 1959			
751	J 8	SMITH, PAUL		18 DEC 1986	6 SEP 1926		
391	G37	SMITH, RACHEL		26 MAR 1931	1863	ELCHANA MOSHE	

Cem	Row	Name	Maiden Name	DOD	DOB	Parents	Spouse
751	E28	SMITH, RAE	BELKIN	29 JUN 1988	12 MAR 1892		BENJAMIN
102	N46	SMITH, REBECCA		8 JUN 1958	1876		MORRIS
116	BJ50	SMITH, ROBERT		15 SEP 1971	19 MAY 1927		
751	J24	SMITH, ROBERT		26 JUN 1978	25 MAR 1894		
116	D 2	SMITH, RONALD P		6 OCT 1987	22 MAY 1958		
751	E30	SMITH, ROSE	WELINSKY	NDD		FRANK & LENA (SILVERSTEIN)	ISIDORE
751	J14	SMITH, ROSE MOSS		1965	1904		VICTOR
101	D 2	SMITH, SADIE K		26 FEB 1982	1901		BENJAMIN
125	F 8	SMITH, SAMUEL		30 OCT 1955	1893		MARTHA
102	U23	SMITH, SAMUEL D		14 FEB 1965	1882		BESSIE
101	H 4	SMITH, SEYMOUR		10 JAN 1987	1911		
751	J15	SMITH, VICTOR		26 JUN 1966	10 FEB 1890		ROSE
102	R25	SMITH, ZELDA LEAH	APTER	23 JUN 1983	1934	MORRIS & BESSIE	
751	J31	SMITH, ZIPA		3 APR 1933			ZIPA
392	E15	SMITHLINE, BENJAMIN		29 JUN 1949	1886	JACOB	MINNIE
391	O37	SMITHLINE, GUSSIE		11 NOV 1914		SIMON ASHER	
392	E16	SMITHLINE, MINNIE		4 DEC 1955	1892	BENJAMIN	BENJAMIN
377	U37	SMITHLINE, SEYMOUR J		29 AUG 1982	6 AUG 1915	PINCUS	
446	C75	SMOLANSKY, FLORA		1885	1884	ROSE	
446	C76	SMOLANSKY, HARRY		1884	1881	ROSE	
446	C78	SMOLANSKY, HAYMAN		1888	1888	ROSE	
446	C77	SMOLANSKY, ROSE		1890	1867		
371	A37	SMOLOWITZ, SAMUEL		24 MAY 1949			WIFE
371	A38	SMOLOWITZ, WIFE		4 JUN 1949			SAMUEL
373	K 1	SMOTRICH, (BABY BOY)		18 JUL 1953			
374	C19	SMOTRICH, BASHA		23 MAR 1952	1875		LEIBISH
373	K 6	SMOTRICH, FRED		NDD	11 MAY 1927		HELEN
373	K 5	SMOTRICH, HELEN	CRAMER	12 OCT 1991	18 NOV 1929		FRED
370	K44	SMOTRICH, HERMAN W		6 JUL 1964	21 APR 1929	MAX & IDA	
370	K43	SMOTRICH, IDA		30 DEC 1992	17 JUN 1906		MAX
373	J 1	SMOTRICH, IDA M		1962	1900		JOSEPH
373	J 2	SMOTRICH, JOSEPH		1968	1899		IDA
374	C18	SMOTRICH, LEIBISH		18 NOV 1956	1875		BASHA
370	K42	SMOTRICH, MAX		19 JAN 1986	10 AUG 1904		IDA
371	AA 6	SMOTRICH, SAM		1973	1902		SARAH
371	AA 7	SMOTRICH, SARAH		1971	1910		SAM
125	R181	SNEIDEMAN, ABRAHAM		26 JUL 1980	1879		BESSIE
125	R182	SNEIDEMAN, BESSIE HANNAH	MARK	30 JAN 1960	1877		ABRAHAM
125	Z180	SNEIDEMAN, ESTELLE		24 SEP 1991	1905		ROBERT
125	M136	SNEIDEMAN, MYER		22 OCT 1973	1 NOV 1902	ABRAHAM	PAULINE
125	M135	SNEIDEMAN, PAULINE	WEINER	4 NOV 1983	7 JUL 1909		MYER
125	Z179	SNEIDEMAN, ROBERT		6 MAR 1987	1905	ABRAHAM	ESTELLE
125	ZA186	SNEIDEMAN, RUTH		1992	1910		
330	G40	SNITCOFSKY, FRAIDA		1 OCT 1910	1840		
391	B 4	SNITKIN, (BABY GIRL)		1940	1940	HERMAN & LILLIAN	
391	B 5	SNITKIN, (BABY GIRL)		1940	1940	HERMAN & LILLIAN	
392	F42	SNITKIN, BEN ZION		27 OCT 1920		SAMUEL	
391	O52	SNITKIN, DORA REBECCA		16 NOV 1951	1876	ISAAC	MAX
391	O56	SNITKIN, HERMAN		10 JUN 1952	1915	MORDECHAI	
371	AC11	SNITKIN, IRVING M		14 NOV 1962			BESSIE
392	F41	SNITKIN, ISAAC		9 AUG 1920		SAMUEL	
391	Y77	SNITKIN, LOUIS		16 JAN 1991	18 AUG 1909	MORDECHAI	
391	O53	SNITKIN, MAX		20 APR 1948	1872	ISAAC MEYER	DORA
392	F35	SNITKIN, REBECCA		22 FEB 1920	1889	CHAIM LEV	
391	Z65	SNITKIN, SAMUEL M		2 DEC 1989	2 JUN 1905	MORDECHAI	
222	I16	SNYDER, AARON		28 SEP 1935	1867		
113	M62	SNYDER, ADOLPH CARL		9 FEB 1973	24 NOV 1915	FRANK & JANET (BROWNSTEIN)	
114	J22	SNYDER, ANNA	ADLER	19 OCT 1980	7 JUL 1909		
101	M35	SNYDER, BESSIE		31 MAR 1951	1904		
113	M61	SNYDER, FRANK		30 NOV 1974	18 JAN 1895		JANET
113	M60	SNYDER, JANET	BROWNSTEIN	21 DEC 1981	13 SEP 1894		FRANK
113	J58	SNYDER, KATHLEEN ANNE		7 MAR 1985	29 SEP 1950	LILLIAN	
113	J61	SNYDER, LILLIAN		16 DEC 1979	20 JUL 1920		
112	B 9	SNYDER, MALCOLM M		28 NOV 1990	26 AUG 1932		
222	I15	SNYDER, RISA PEARL	SPITZ	25 AUG 1958	1890		
248	J79	SNYDER, RIVKAH		1 NOV 1964			

Cem	Row	Name	Maiden Name	DOD	DOB	Parents	Spouse
121	D32	SOBEL, HYMAN		10 MAY 1979	29 DEC 1913		
750	K30	SOBEL, JOSEPH		14 DEC 1982			
102	AI177	SOBEL, RUTH	DOLGORUCK	16 SEP 1973	18 JUL 1920		
102	AI41	SOBOL, DAVID		17 DEC 1988	26 JAN 1907		
102	AI42	SOBOL, EDWARD A DDS		16 MAR 1989	20 APR 1904		
102	U36	SOBOL, FANNIE S		21 SEP 1973	20 SEP 1887		HARRY
102	U35	SOBOL, HARRY E		16 JUN 1973	17 MAR 1882		FANNIE
102	U37	SOBOL, JOSEPHINE		15 SEP 1948	30 APR 1909	HARRY & FANNIE	
102	AI43	SOBOL, MAURICE		2 JUN 1966	7 FEB 1901		
110	H27	SOBOLDOFSKY, MOLLY		30 MAY 1926	15 JUN 1925		
101	J26	SOBOLEVSKY, ESTHER	LANSING	22 MAY 1942	1850		
101	C14	SOBOLEVSKY, PINCHAS RABBI		26 MAR 1940	1871		SARAH
101	C13	SOBOLEVSKY, SARAH		9 MAR 1947	1871		PINCHAS
125	P193	SOCHRIN, JOSEPH		5 MAY 1975	18 MAR 1888		SARAH
125	P194	SOCHRIN, SARAH		16 JUL 1963	25 JAN 1893		JOSEPH
125	R195	SOCKUT, SADIE	TRESKY	19 FEB 1961	1896		
392	F30	SOCOL, AARON		16 APR 1920	1876	MOSHE MORDECHAI	
392	H19	SOCOL, EVA		20 JUN 1944	1875	MOSHE	
116	BK111	SODAFSKY, IRVING		27 MAY 1965	8 DEC 1898		SADY
116	BU12	SODAFSKY, MILTON M		5 AUG 1976	9 MAY 1904		
116	BK110	SODAFSKY, SADY	ACKERMAN	17 DEC 1980	13 OCT 1901		IRVING
371	I 4	SOFFER, DORA		25 MAY 1957	1887		
371	AK15	SOGOLOW, IDA ROSE		9 FEB 1964	1 OCT 1895		MAX
371	AK16	SOGOLOW, MAX		12 JUL 1968	1 JAN 1894		IDA
125	Z173	SOHN, DAVID R		22 FEB 1988	25 DEC 1901		
370	Z 3	SOHN, DINAH		26 JAN 1947	1883		ISAAC
370	I66	SOHN, ISAAC		20 APR 1947	1882		DINAH
125	K176	SOHN, JOSEPH		6 MAY 1973			
370	Z 9	SOHN, JUDITH DR		4 JAN 1977			MORRIS
370	Z 8	SOHN, MORRIS DR		2 SEP 1968			JUDITH
392	H31	SOHN, ROSE	ORDANSKY	18 NOV 1964	1882	ELCHANON	
125	Z176	SOHN, SAMUEL D		19 SEP 1986	16 SEP 1911		
101	J24	SOICHER, GERTRUDE		14 DEC 1953			
101	C29	SOICHER, MORDECHAI		5 JUN 1923	1853		
106	A28	SOIFER, DAVID		25 JUN 1986	1 SEP 1934		
392	H18	SOKARL, ETHEL		10 OCT 1944	1880	ELIEZER	
392	D36	SOKARL, MAX W		1954	1908	MOSHE	
392	G22	SOKARL, MORRIS		7 JUL 1932	1876	NACHEM	
112	E20	SOKOL, BETTY		19 JUN 1970	26 MAR 1894		
125		SOKOL, DORIS		26 MAR 1928	1928	DAVID & CHANA	
392	E22	SOKOL, HARRY		12 JAN 1952	1883	NACHEM	ROSE
125	P144	SOKOL, HERMAN		23 APR 1947	18 DEC 1929	MORDECHAI	
377	W46	SOKOL, LOUIS G		1 MAR 1953	5 OCT 1908	TZVI	
125	I189	SOKOL, MORTIMER		4 AUG 1969			SADIE
392	E23	SOKOL, ROSE	ROWINSKY	25 JUN 1969	1887		HARRY
125	I190	SOKOL, SADIE		2 MAR 1990	22 JUL 1906		MORTIMER
125	I188	SOKOL, SOL		7 OCT 1993	10 NOV 1900		
119	A56	SOKOLOFF, BERNARD		10 JUN 1986	27 NOV 1912		
222	AL19	SOKOLOV, FREIDA W		13 JUN 1964	12 FEB 1884		SAM
222	AL18	SOKOLOV, LOUIS		12 AUG 1971	20 OCT 1915	SAM & FREIDA	
222	AL20	SOKOLOV, SAM		17 OCT 1946	25 OCT 1884		FREIDA
125	N 91	SOKOLOWSKY, ZUNDEL		28 OCT 1924	1890		
119	K53	SOKOLSKY, JACK		25 JUL 1979	16 NOV 1895		
248	I30	SOLATAROFF, SAMUEL K		29 AUG 1985	11 JUN 1905	SAMUEL & HINDA	
370	J25	SOLEVEITZIK, BUNIA		1937	1879		HARRY
370	A14	SOLEVEITZIK, HARRY A		29 MAY 1950	1885		BUNIA
370	I14	SOLEVEITZIK, MALCA		18 OCT 1918			
370	B23	SOLEVEITZIK, MORRIS		28 APR 1924			
370	B21	SOLEVEITZIK, SANDER ZEV		5 JAN 1918		SAMUEL DAVID	
370	I22	SOLEVEITZIK, SLATA		29 JUL 1926			
370	B22	SOLEVEITZIK, SOLOMON		28 JUL 1936	1868		
103	D18	SOLODOVNIK, GRIGORY		5 AUG 1984	31 JAN 1918		
374	A 2	SOLOFF, BESSIE	BRUCKNER	8 APR 1991	31 JUL 1907		SIMON
374	A 3	SOLOFF, SIMON KING		24 OCT 1977	8 APR 1904		BESSIE
101	B19	SOLOMKIN, HARRY		31 JAN 1944			
115	B35	SOLOMKIN, MARK MD		20 MAY 1974	13 MAR 1912		

Cem	Row	Name	Maiden Name	DOD	DOB	Parents	Spouse
330	AI14	SOLOMON, ALYCE		13 SEP 1985	1914		
125	H132	SOLOMON, ANNA	DOLBER	5 MAY 1943	28 JAN 1878	ALEXANDER	BENJAMIN
101	H19	SOLOMON, ANNABELLE LEE		24 AUG 1979	27 MAR 1914		LOUIS
330	AI13	SOLOMON, ARBY		23 MAR 1979	1912		SAMUEL
370	O57	SOLOMON, BELLE	SERLING	4 OCT 1974	8 MAR 1900		SIMON
125	H133	SOLOMON, BENJAMIN		1 JUN 1957	1872		ANNA
447	L37	SOLOMON, BENJAMIN		1973	1904		CELIA
377	B22	SOLOMON, BESSIE	SHAFNER	1 AUG 1984	16 JAN 1898	SAMUEL	NATHAN
370	S 2	SOLOMON, BESSIE		11 SEP 1971	1 OCT 1896		HARRY
447	L36	SOLOMON, CELIA		1990	1903		BENJAMIN
447	W34	SOLOMON, CELIA R		JAN 1960			
370	U26	SOLOMON, CHALRES W		20 AUG 1984	8 SEP 1901		
102	M52	SOLOMON, DORA K		17 APR 1983	1897		DORA
114	J12	SOLOMON, E KING		13 OCT 1988	22 MAR 1897		FRANCES
101	A29	SOLOMON, ELIYAHU		26 OCT 1931			
125	M160	SOLOMON, ESTHER		1986	1902		MORRIS
114	J11	SOLOMON, FRANCES L		19 APR 1982	28 MAR 1900		KING
125	O 62	SOLOMON, GERALD ROBERT		28 APR 1930	JUN 1928	MORRIS & ESTHER	
370	S 3	SOLOMON, HARRY		4 FEB 1970	1 MAY 1887		BESSIE
330	B 2	SOLOMON, HARRY		26 NOV 1950	1883	JONAH	MINNIE
113	K45	SOLOMON, HELEN	BAYER	20 NOV 1990	19 APR 1911		
101	K20	SOLOMON, IDA		19 NOV 1925	1875		
391	E25	SOLOMON, IDA HATTIE		29 MAR 1951	19 JUN 1882	ARI TZVI	JACOB
330	E40	SOLOMON, IDA S		9 MAR 1943	1873		
330	B 7	SOLOMON, ISAAC		5 MAR 1940	1897	JONAH	REBECCA
222	L 6	SOLOMON, ISIDORE		9 JUN 1965	1887		LIBBY
330	H18	SOLOMON, IVAN MYLES		18 NOV 1942	18 DEC 1940		
123		SOLOMON, JACK		14 JUN 1944	1910		
330	AA 4	SOLOMON, JACK		22 APR 1909	10 JUL 1907		
391	E26	SOLOMON, JACOB		21 DEC 1955	20 JUL 1875	SAMUEL YEHUDA	IDA
370	U27	SOLOMON, JAMES MURRAY		3 DEC 1940	MAR 1940		
330	B 3	SOLOMON, JONAH		18 AUG 1938	1856		
102	AF40	SOLOMON, KATIE	MAISLEN	19 NOV 1973	24 FEB 1872		WILLIAM
370	H30	SOLOMON, LEAH		20 SEP 1953	31 OCT 1901	MOSHE	LEWIS
102	AJ47	SOLOMON, LENA	WEINER	10 NOV 1967	1905	JACOB & IDA	MINNIE
391	E16	SOLOMON, LEON HAROLD		6 JAN 1988	4 JUL 1901		LENA
102	AJ48	SOLOMON, LEWIS		8 OCT 1961	1894		ISIDORE
222	L 5	SOLOMON, LIBBY		7 NOV 1981	4 MAR 1900		SARAH
102	AJ166	SOLOMON, LOUIS		30 SEP 1931	1877		
330	F20	SOLOMON, LOUIS		9 SEP 1984	12 JUN 1905		ANNABELLE
101	H20	SOLOMON, LOUIS CALVIN		24 JUL 1956	1882		LOUIS
102	M50	SOLOMON, LOUIS H		1968	1884		SOPHIE
447	U39	SOLOMON, MAX		11 DEC 1964	30 JAN 1930	LOUIS & SARAH	
102	AJ165	SOLOMON, MELVIN S		11 JAN 1966			HARRY
330	B 1	SOLOMON, MINNIE		21 MAY 1984	23 MAY 1913	JACOB & IDA	LEON
391	E18	SOLOMON, MINNIE		19 MAY 1964	28 MAR 1876		SADYE
102	F11	SOLOMON, MORRIS		6 OCT 1952	1898		ESTHER
125	M159	SOLOMON, MORRIS		26 JAN 1925	24 DEC 1880		
370	B26	SOLOMON, MOSES J		23 DEC 1968	15 MAY 1887	SAMUEL	BESSIE
377	B21	SOLOMON, NATHAN MAX		8 JUN 1950	1901	BEN	
125	H134	SOLOMON, NELLIE MIRIAM		7 FEB 1966	1890		ISAAC
330	B 8	SOLOMON, REBECCA		30 MAR 1986	23 JUL 1936		
102	BB21	SOLOMON, RODELLE	SCHANZER	21 FEB 1961	15 MAY 1887		MORRIS
102	F10	SOLOMON, SADYE	NEWMAN	24 APR 1978	2 DEC 1909		ARBY
330	AI12	SOLOMON, SAMUEL		25 FEB 1926	1851	DAVID	
391	H30	SOLOMON, SAMUEL L		23 OCT 1970	10 MAR 1914	MORRIS & SADYE	
102	F12	SOLOMON, SANFORD E		20 JUN 1954			
125	I155	SOLOMON, SARAH		25 AUG 1907	DEC 1906	JACOB & IDA	
391	A 4	SOLOMON, SARAH		1912	1856		
370	H29	SOLOMON, SARAH L		2 SEP 1986	23 SEP 1903		LOUIS
102	AJ167	SOLOMON, SARAH M		16 JAN 1924	1847		
330	G49	SOLOMON, SHENA MUSAH		29 SEP 1929		MOSHE	
370	C 2	SOLOMON, SHMARYAHU		27 JAN 1956	27 MAR 1883		BELLE
370	O56	SOLOMON, SIMON		19 APR 1984	21 APR 1898		
370	U 8	SOLOMON, SOPHIE		1971	1886		MAX
447	U38	SOLOMON, SOPHIE					

Cem	Row	Name	Maiden Name	DOD	DOB	Parents	Spouse
102	AF42	SOLOMON, SYLVIA	CLARK	13 MAR 1980	12 OCT 1906		
371	A10	SOLOMON, SYLVIA		29 APR 1973	15 APR 1900		
102	AF39	SOLOMON, WILLIAM		1 SEP 1948	28 FEB 1870		KATIE
103	A17	SOLOMONSON, SADIE		13 DEC 1988	11 OCT 1913		
104	L27	SOLONCHE, DAVID JOSHUA		18 NOV 1991	10 APR 1945		DEBRA
392	F12	SOLOTAROFF, HERMAN		25 JUL 1946	1893	ZEV WOLF	
248	I27	SOLOTAROFF, HINDA	GOSH	20 OCT 1968	20 JUN 1871		SAMUEL
392	F13	SOLOTAROFF, MINNIE		21 MAR 1960	1873	JACOB	
248	I28	SOLOTAROFF, SAMUEL		30 NOV 1942	15 SEP 1870		HINDA
392	F14	SOLOTAROFF, WOLF		8 JAN 1945	1868	NATHAN ALTER	
371	AB15	SOLOVEITZIK, ELLA		1983	1915		SAMUEL
371	AB13	SOLOVEITZIK, FLORENCE		1982	1904		
371	AB14	SOLOVEITZIK, SAMUEL		1983	1912		ELLA
371	AO 3	SOLOVEITZIK, SARAH		7 NOV 1955	1883	MENDEL	
222	AA13	SOLOW, SIMA	DOBKIN	14 FEB 1933	1881	JACOB & REBECCA	
391	I27	SOLSONITSKY, CALEB		2 JUN 1927	1899	YEKOTEL	
391	D 9	SOLTZ, CHARLES		29 APR 1943		ISAAC	
377	Q14	SOLTZ, DAVID		27 DEC 1971	10 NOV 1887		
391	X54	SOLTZ, HATTIE		7 MAY 1974	1883	MORDECHAI	MAX
377	Q34	SOLTZ, HERMAN H		4 MAY 1977	7 DEC 1896		
391	ZG60	SOLTZ, HOWARD		23 FEB 1995	15 MAR 1947		
391	D12	SOLTZ, JOSEPH		5 MAR 1940	1869	TZVI HIRSH	
377	O17	SOLTZ, KATHEREN G		1959	1912		THOMAS
391	H31	SOLTZ, KOLOFF		10 JAN 1931	1847	ELIYAHU TZVI	
391	H41	SOLTZ, LIBBE F		3 DEC 1936	1845	JOSEPH	
391	X53	SOLTZ, MAX		28 DEC 1956	1877	CALEB	HATTIE
391	K29	SOLTZ, RUFFUS		19 NOV 1917	1880	CALEB	
391	G44	SOLTZ, RUTH A		20 JUN 1965	5 JAN 1879	ISRAEL ISAAC	
447	D10	SOLTZ, SOPHIA	POLINER	6 MAY 1965	27 MAY 1893		KATHERN
377	O16	SOLTZ, THOMAS		19 OCT 1962	11 MAY 1889		RUFFES
391	L34	SOLTZ, TILLIE		8 SEP 1967		MEYER	HERMAN
447	R39	SONDAK, ELIZABETH L		1 AUG 1969	1897		ELIZABETH
447	R40	SONDAK, HERMAN		3 MAY 1965	1908		
433	I20	SONDAK, LESTER		1918	1826		
433	I13	SONDAK, SAMUEL		5 JAN 1940	1876	DAVID	
447	N26	SONDAK, WILLIAM		25 JUL 1930	24 JUN 1907		
116	BV43	SONDIK, DORA	MOHILL	2 JUN 1970	1889		PHILIP
329	C45	SONDIK, HYMAN		31 JAN 1991			
121	G 4	SONDIK, LEONA		27 JAN 1967	1885		DORA
116	BV44	SONDIK, PHILIP		20 MAR 1943	1899		FREDA
105	L18	SONIN, M SAUL		9 OCT 1929			
110	A12	SONN, ELIAHU		6 FEB 1948		MOSHE BEN ZION & GOLDIE	
110	A14	SONN, GOLDIE		21 JUN 1949	1872	ABRAHAM	MOSHE
392	I34	SONN, LOUIS		29 AUG 1937			GOLDIE
110	A13	SONN, MOISHE BENZION		21 SEP 1973	1883		SARAH
102	B11	SONN, SAMUEL		13 APR 1973	1885		SAMUEL
102	B10	SONN, SARAH	LIPONICK	30 DEC 1951	1862		
392	B46	SONN, ZLATA		2 JUL 1905	7 DEC 1902		
375	D50	SONNENBLICK, JOSEPH		18 MAY 1931	10 MAR 1889		SHLOMO
447	U27	SOOBITSKY, REBECCA		18 NOV 1948	1947		
447	W19	SOOBITSKY, RUSSEL M		17 OCT 1956	10 NOV 1881		REBECCA
447	U28	SOOBITSKY, SHLOMO		17 JUN 1986	1907		REBECCA
447	AB 9	SOREFF, LOUIS MD		30 AUG 1992	1908		LOUIS
447	AB 8	SOREFF, REBECCA	ZOKEN	5 FEB 1941	1889	GETZEL	
125	S153	SOROKER, ROBERT		13 OCT 1982	4 JUN 1924		
102	E10	SOROKIN, BERNARD		30 JUN 1969			
125	B 78	SORTMAN, JULIUS		1992			DORA
105	M18	SOSIN,		19 APR 1981	31 OCT 1906		
105	M19	SOSIN, DORA		25 MAR 1955	1881		SAMUEL
105	C16	SOSIN, FANNIE		13 SEP 1955	1904		M SAUL
105	L19	SOSIN, FREDA T		13 NOV 1936	1864		
105	L15	SOSIN, IDA		20 MAR 1956	1874		
105	J12	SOSIN, KAILA	ROUJANSKY	27 FEB 1967	20 JUL 1890		YETTA
105	C34	SOSIN, SAMUEL		29 SEP 1963	1891		FANNIE
105	C17	SOSIN, SAMUEL		26 JUN 1987	28 DEC 1891		SAMUEL
105	C35	SOSIN, YETTA					

Cem	Row	Name	Maiden Name	DOD	DOB	Parents	Spouse
105	I16	SOSIS, ISRAEL		22 APR 1940	1870		
374	A14	SOVNER, CHAIM YITZCHAK		5 FEB 1916		MEYER ARYEH	
125	D138	SPALTER, PAUL F		13 JUL 1980	1886		SONIA
125	D137	SPALTER, SONIA	BUSHER	10 NOV 1970	1889		PAUL
370	Z 6	SPANDORF, ESTHER		25 JAN 1982	25 DEC 1908		FRANK
370	Z 7	SPANDORF, FRANK		29 AUG 1979	22 MAR 1901		ESTHER
112	B32	SPANIER, EDWIN ERWIN		1988	1910		
370	O40	SPANIER, HANTY		14 AUG 1900	1865		
125	L185	SPARBER, BESSIE	ABRAHAMSON	14 AUG 1971	1899		
125	E107	SPECTOR, (BABY)		25 DEC 1933	1933	DAVID & REBECCA	
125	AA108	SPECTOR, BEATRICE		18 JAN 1992	24 MAR 1913	DAVID & REBECCA	
125	AA109	SPECTOR, BERTHA		10 JUN 1973	18 MAY 1906		SAMUEL
125	B 55	SPECTOR, BESSIE		2 JAN 1989	19 OCT 1913		
125	AA103	SPECTOR, BESSIE B		14 MAY 1974	29 JUN 1902		
107	C20	SPECTOR, CHARLES B		1984	1894		
125	AA107	SPECTOR, DAVID		12 JUL 1961	10 OCT 1886		REBECCA
125	AA105	SPECTOR, IDA		9 NOV 1988	10 OCT 1919		MAX
125	T149	SPECTOR, IDA		19 JUL 1939	1866		
119	F22	SPECTOR, IRVING		16 MAR 1974	14 MAR 1923		
125	M105	SPECTOR, ISAAC		9 NOV 1927	1857		
125	AB108	SPECTOR, LEE PAUL		23 MAR 1969	14 JAN 1969		
102	AJ111	SPECTOR, LILLIAN	WYNICK	4 JAN 1969	22 OCT 1894		
248	L50	SPECTOR, MAURICE BENJAMIN		20 FEB 1972	10 MAR 1899		
125	AA104	SPECTOR, MAX		27 NOV 1975	1 JAN 1897		IDA
125	AB107	SPECTOR, MAX		30 AUG 1983	13 SEP 1916		
113	A10	SPECTOR, MORRIS		27 AUG 1987	15 JUN 1911		
113	I44	SPECTOR, NORMAN		21 SEP 1971	23 OCT 1916		
125	AA106	SPECTOR, REBECCA		17 APR 1955	4 JUL 1892		DAVID
125	AA111	SPECTOR, SAMSON		3 JAN 1990	1 MAR 1902		
125	AA110	SPECTOR, SAMUEL		4 JAN 1992	17 JUL 1904		BERTHA
248	I63	SPECTOR, SAMUEL		20 DEC 1932	1872		
125	L 22	SPERRY, ALEX		7 OCT 1918	1897	JACOB	
125	O 76	SPERRY, ALIA		18 SEP 1915	24 MAY 1915	JACOB & BASHA	
125	P159	SPERRY, BESSIE		5 JUL 1948	30 AUG 1879		JACOB
125	Z169	SPERRY, EDWARD		15 JAN 1981	1903		
125	P158	SPERRY, JACOB		9 MAY 1951	1871		BESSIE
125	O136	SPERRY, MEYER		22 APR 1976	10 MAR 1901		
101	C11	SPIEGELMAN, LEAH	GOLD	23 APR 1948	1873		
110	C32	SPIELER, ESTHER		6 DEC 1978	1893		
372	D21	SPIER, JULIUS		12 NOV 1891	9 APR 1860		
372	E30	SPIER, LIPPMAN		8 JUL 1870	1827		REGINA
372	E31	SPIER, REGINA		12 OCT 1900	1833		LIPPMAN
113	L52	SPIES, IDA		26 JUL 1986	6 JUN 1896		JOSEPH
113	L51	SPIES, JOSEPH S		17 MAR 1972	7 OCT 1893		IDA
222	B 2	SPITELNIK, MORRIS		19 OCT 1935	12 JUL 1889		REBECCA
377	B27	SPITZ, EZEKIEL		13 JAN 1968	11 JAN 1891	HILLEL	SADIE
377	B29	SPITZ, LORRETTA O		26 MAY 1983	13 FEB 1894	ISAAC	
377	A28	SPITZ, NATHANIEL		31 MAY 1979	16 JUN 1922		
377	B28	SPITZ, SADIE J		7 MAR 1938	15 APR 1889		EZIEKEL
104	C37	SPITZER, HENRY I		4 APR 1954	6 FEB 1897		
125	N133	SPIVAK, JOSEPH		28 AUG 1972	1911		
125	P176	SPIVAK, SARAH ROSE	CHOTINER	2 NOV 1962	1902		
392	B15	SPOLAN, ALEX		3 JUN 1950	1869		
392	F22	SPOLAN, JACOB		28 JUL 1930	1845	JOEL	JENNIE
392	J20	SPOLAN, JENNIE		2 JUL 1935	1848	CHAIM	JACOB
433	E 4	SPRECHER, ABRAHAM JOSEPH		8 DEC 1960	1 JAN 1916	MOSHE ELIEZER	S.R.
446	C27	SPRECHER, BENJAMIN		17 AUG 1910	1852		
433	E 7	SPRECHER, BENJAMIN L		25 NOV 1992	23 JAN 1912		MARION
433	F 4	SPRECHER, ELIZABETH		12 APR 1949	1880	SHALOM	MORRIS
433	E 6	SPRECHER, MARION		22 JUL 1991	7 MAR 1912		BENJAMIN
433	F 5	SPRECHER, MORRIS L		5 OCT 1954	6 JUN 1877	BENJAMIN	ELIZABETH
433	E 5	SPRECHER, S R					ABRAHAM
371	G 7	SPREJREGEN, ISRAEL		15 JUL 1973	1 APR 1930		
121	AA21	SPRINCZELES, ANNA		10 DEC 1977	26 AUG 1904		
105	J16	SPRINGEL, EDITH K		28 DEC 1972	1924		
121	G12	SPRINZELES, BERNARD		8 MAY 1966	14 SEP 1893		

Cem	Row	Name	Maiden Name	DOD	DOB	Parents	Spouse
119	A 1	SPRYNGER, REGINA		26 APR 1982	1908		
121	I18	SPUNGIN, ALEXANDER		12 AUG 1973	10 DEC 1902		
121	I19	SPUNGIN, ANNA		29 JAN 1980	20 OCT 1900		
104	I 8	SPUNGIN, JACK		21 DEC 1968	27 MAR 1907		
392	J25	SQUIRE, FANNIE		1 MAR 1929	1864	MORDECHAI	
330	AB11	SQUIRE, MARY		8 AUG 1971	10 JUL 1903		
392	J46	SQUIRE, MAX		24 NOV 1944	1893	MOSHE	
370	P45	STAMM, ISRAEL		1984	1906	MAX & LEAH	
102	AJ175	STAMM, JULIUS		29 DEC 1966	18 SEP 1892		REBECCA
370	P43	STAMM, LEAH		1980	1876		MAX
370	P44	STAMM, MAX RABBI		1937	1875		LEAH
102	AJ174	STAMM, REBECCA W		26 MAY 1970	12 AUG 1899		JULIUS
248	G55	STARGER, JOSEPH		11 FEB 1987	1901		
248	N69	STARR, CELIA		9 OCT 1918	1902		
494	A 8	STARR, ESTHER		1972	1908		JULIUS
391	K42	STARR, FANNY		17 DEC 1959	1897	ISAAC	
370	G41	STARR, ISAAC		2 APR 1906	1858		
494	A 9	STARR, JULIUS		1983	1903		ESTHER
116	AC12	STAVIS, HAROLD J		10 MAY 1988	11 AUG 1909		
125	L160	STAVNEZER, LOUIS		16 JAN 1956	1915		
125	ZA167	STAVNEZER, MAX		10 AUG 1984	1913		
125	K127	STAVNEZER, MORRIS		31 MAR 1933	1889		RACHEL
125	K126	STAVNEZER, RACHEL		29 MAR 1964	1884		MORRIS
330	AF15	STEG, EDITH K		19 OCT 1970			
330	AH22	STEG, STEPHEN		7 APR 1991	5 JUL 1902		
493	B 3	STEIGLITZ, ESTHER H		30 NOV 1990	15 OCT 1912	ABRAHAM	IRVING
493	B 4	STEIGLITZ, IRVING		15 JAN 1991	10 JUN 1903	MOSHE	ESTHER
330	F36	STEIN, ADOLPH		1 AUG 1918	1870		
494	B 5	STEIN, ANNA		15 JAN 1958	4 NOV 1890		JOSEPH
248	I75	STEIN, BARACH		8 DEC 1921		MOSHE ZIBLER	
125	N131	STEIN, BENJAMIN		28 JUL 1972	1887		FREDA
125	H141	STEIN, BERNARD		8 MAR 1974	16 FEB 1882		
104	M42	STEIN, EDWARD		30 OCT 1978	1 NOV 1892		
104	B22	STEIN, ERICA BETH		15 APR 1967	8 MAR 1967		
125	N132	STEIN, FREDA	ELINOVITCH	8 JUN 1981	1891		BERNARD
370	I49	STEIN, GITEL		22 MAY 1935			SAMUEL
494	B 4	STEIN, JOSEPH		14 MAY 1957	28 AUG 1890		ANNA
125	M125	STEIN, M MATHEW		1930	1915		
102	K32	STEIN, MICHAEL		NDD	29 OCT 1899		
101	K21	STEIN, MOLLIE		14 MAY 1929	1849		
433	H20	STEIN, NATHAN		12 JAN 1938	1848	YSHYAHU	SARAH
119	D10	STEIN, RAYMOND		7 NOV 1982	10 FEB 1909		
370	I50	STEIN, SAMUEL		31 MAY 1938			GITEL
433	H21	STEIN, SARAH		23 JAN 1942	1861	ABRAHAM	NATHAN
125	H139	STEIN, SARAH G		14 JAN 1966	16 FEB 1882		
751	K27	STEIN, YETTA		17 JUN 1926	1898		
392	B23	STEINBERG, ALEX		21 APR 1962	10 FEB 1890		FANNIE
125	R188	STEINBERG, BENJAMIN		7 AUG 1960	1899		EVA
125	R187	STEINBERG, EVA	HERSHOWITZ	7 OCT 1981	1900		ALEX
392	B24	STEINBERG, FANNIE		22 JUN 1973	12 JUL 1891		
101	I 7	STEINBERG, FLORENCE		24 AUG 1972			WILLIAM
330	H31	STEINBERG, HARRY ALEX		29 OCT 1950	12 JAN 1896		ROSE
222	AJ20	STEINBERG, IDA		17 JUL 1943	1876		
104	D33	STEINBERG, IRENE	LEBON				MORRIS
104	C20	STEINBERG, ISAAC		20 APR 1962			
119	H62	STEINBERG, JOSEPH		28 FEB 1990	25 JUL 1909		
121	V18	STEINBERG, LESTER ALFRED		12 AUG 1984	13 NOV 1914		
119	A63	STEINBERG, LOUIS		27 JUN 1982	18 MAR 1907.		
433	B14	STEINBERG, LOUIS		31 OCT 1982	28 OCT 1900		TILLIE
123		STEINBERG, MAX		30 NOV 1984	26 NOV 1909		
104	D34	STEINBERG, MORRIS WILLIAM		27 MAR 1982	27 OCT		IRENE
330	H30	STEINBERG, ROSE		10 MAR 1983	15 FEB 1900		HARRY
121	U13	STEINBERG, ROSE		1968	1898		
121	AA29	STEINBERG, SADIE	ROME	17 APR 1971	13 AUG 1916		
391	GN 1	STEINBERG, SADIE		22 FEB 1937		NACHEL	MICHAEL
433	B13	STEINBERG, TILLIE	SCHEPS	25 APR 1981	14 MAR 1898		LOUIS

Cem	Row	Name	Maiden Name	DOD	DOB	Parents	Spouse
101	I 8	STEINBERG, WILLIAM		30 SEP 1976			
101	L19	STEINHAUS, MATHILDA		11 APR 1914	1852		FLORENCE
101	C26	STEINHAUS, OSHER		15 SEP 1925	1855		USHER
112	C 1	STEINHAUSER, DAVID		29 NOV 1987	12 MAY 1909		
371	AL11	STEINMAN, AARON JOSEPH		14 SEP 1959	1886	RUBIN	
371	AM 3	STEINMAN, ALLAN A		2 FEB 1969	1943	SAUL & AUGUSTA	SADIE
371	AM 1	STEINMAN, AUGUSTA		12 APR 1966	1910		SAUL
222	I 1	STEINMAN, HARRIET		30 NOV 1982	23 OCT 1930		
125	B105	STEINMAN, HARRY		1 JAN 1968	1905		
373	J15	STEINMAN, ISAAC		26 JUN 1963	1883		SADIE
373	J16	STEINMAN, ISRAEL CHARLES		1987	1906	ISAAC & SADIE	
371	AL 6	STEINMAN, MARY	SMOLOWITZ	20 MAY 1954	1893		SAMUEL
371	AL 4	STEINMAN, MAURICE		25 FEB 1984	1905	RUBIN	TESSIE
371	AM 5	STEINMAN, MAX		25 MAY 1989	5 MAY 1900		
371	AL 5	STEINMAN, RUBIN		21 APR 1952	1860		
373	J14	STEINMAN, SADIE		24 JUL 1949	1885		ISAAC
371	AL10	STEINMAN, SADIE	FEINER	28 JUL 1963	1894		AARON
371	AL 8	STEINMAN, SAMUEL		12 SEP 1980	1908	REUBIN	MARY
371	AM 2	STEINMAN, SAUL		27 MAR 1976	1904		AUGUSTA
371	AL 3	STEINMAN, TESSIE		8 MAY 1964	4 JUL 1905		MAURICE
373	G 3	STENGEL, ANNA	SHAPIRO	15 JUL 1990	1923		
125	O134	STENSCH, ELSBETH		1989	1907		HEINZ
125	O135	STENSCH, HEINZ I		1986	1906		ELSBETH
123		STERLING, ALBERT M		26 MAY 1958	1912		
110	C 5	STERN, ABRAHAM		19 OCT 1953	1880		CLARA
372	D10	STERN, ANNA		1934	1855	FRED & HATTIE	
377	R34	STERN, CARL		25 DEC 1968	9 JAN 1916		
110	C 6	STERN, CLARA	KAPLAN	2 DEC 1962	1890		ABRAHAM
110	B 8	STERN, EVA		19 FEB 1944	1882		MAX
372	D 9	STERN, FRED A		1936	1879		HATTIE
112	B36	STERN, GERTRUDE		22 NOV 1991	13 FEB 1909		
447	N15	STERN, HARRY		11 NOV 1927	1879		
372	D11	STERN, HATTIE	KRONIG	1963	1883		FRED
447	Y 6	STERN, JOHN A		1969	1927		
330	F 1	STERN, LENA		22 SEP 1978			SAMUEL
330	AD 4	STERN, NELSON		10 APR 1966	31 MAR 1906		
110	B 9	STERN, REV MAX		27 SEP 1955	1880		EVA
330	F 2	STERN, SAMUEL L		29 APR 1954			LENA
116	BL27	STERN, STEVEN IRA		9 SEP 1960	28 MAY 1948	SIDNEY & RUTH (YOLEN)	
372	A 9	STERN, VERONICA		24 JUN 1878	30 AUG 1873	JACOB & ANNA	
112	D26	STERN, WALTER		1978	1910		
104	G 1	STERNBACH, SYLVIA G		5 FEB 1958	1915		
370	Y 4	STERNFIELD, FANNY		11 MAY 1923			SAMUEL
370	Y 2	STERNFIELD, SAMUEL		26 AUG 1893	1870		FANNY
370	Y 3	STERNFIELD, SOLOMON		26 AUG 1893		SAMUEL & FANNIE	
370	S 4	STERNLIEB, ELSIE		22 NOV 1957	1900		JACOB
370	S 5	STERNLIEB, JACOB		18 MAY 1922	1903	LOUIS	ELSIE
370	S 8	STERNLIEB, LOUIS		1960	1887		
249	C 2	STERNLIEB, LOUIS		24 JUL 1944	1884		SADIE
370	S 6	STERNLIEB, MAX		25 MAR 1929	1867		TYTTE
249	C 3	STERNLIEB, SADIE		11 JUN 1969	1893		LOUIS
370	S 7	STERNLIEB, TYTTE		11 NOV 1939	1863		MAX
101	G35	STERSTEIN, RAURIE	MELODY	21 FEB 1990	22 APR 1950		
102	I 7	STICKLOR, JACOB		2 FEB 1952	30 JUL 1894		REBECCA
116	AV 9	STICKLOR, JERALD WARREN		22 DEC 1978	21 MAR 1949		
102	I 8	STICKLOR, REBECCA F		23 OCT 1990	27 OCT 1900		JACOB
330	E52	STOCK, DORA		18 NOV 1949	1886		
372	D24	STOCK, EMANUEL A		30 APR 1933			HATTIE
372	D25	STOCK, HATTIE	PLAUT	1956	1878		EMANUEL
331		STOCK, MAX		13 NOV 1912	1881		
751	J18	STOCKMAN, ANNA		20 MAR 1944	1874		HERMAN
751	J17	STOCKMAN, HERMAN		1956	1881		ANNA
222	E 1	STOCKSER, ABRAHAM		4 AUG 1958	1885		GUSSIE
222	E 2	STOCKSER, GUSSIE		9 JUL 1965	1887		ABRAHAM
222	E 3	STOCKSER, PAUL		5 NOV 1939	25 JUN 1910	ABRAHAM & GUSSIE	
433	U 1	STOCKTON, ERIC P		14 APR 1986	2 JAN 1949	LEBAN	

Cem	Row	Name	Maiden Name	DOD	DOB	Parents	Spouse
751	O30	STOGATZ, MIMI		23 MAY 1974	1924		
330	AI25	STOLLMAN, MOLLIE		9 JAN 1980	1905		
330	E36	STOLLMAN, SOLOMON		31 AUG 1938	1858		
330	E39	STOLLMAN, SOPHIE		4 MAR 1943	1868		
222	M 9	STOLOFF, KATHRYN		27 MAY 1984	12 AUG 1914		WILLIAM
222	M 8	STOLOFF, WILLIAM		25 OCT 1985	6 AUG 1915		KATHRYN
104	K17	STOLTZ, CELIA		1 SEP 1984	29 AUG 1908		
103	D21	STOLTZ, SYLVIA		1990	1913		
113	M45	STONE, ABRAHAM		12 DEC 1958	8 MAR 1891		ANNA
113	M44	STONE, ANNA	MORRIS	29 MAR 1977	9 DEC 1888		ABRAHAM
222	AI 5	STONE, ANNA	BRONSTEIN	29 OCT 1990	29 OCT 1898		HENRY
222	AN21	STONE, ANNIE		11 FEB 1960	1884		HYMAN
104	J41	STONE, BARBARA R		29 MAR 1976	8 JUL 1922		FRANK
104	J40	STONE, BRADFORD J		4 JUL 1978	13 DEC 1957	FRANK & BARBARA	
377	R20	STONE, CARL		18 APR 1974	8 MAY 1896		MINNIE
112	D22	STONE, ETTA		26 APR 1975	31 DEC 1903		
116	L12	STONE, FAY	BECKENSTEIN	1 NOV 1985	15 SEP 1906		SAMUEL
102	H47	STONE, FRANK		7 FEB 1950	1896		SADIE
249	C 6	STONE, GERTRUDE	CHUS	22 MAY 1965	1915		
222	AI 4	STONE, HENRY L		14 MAY 1973	1895		ANNA
222	AN20	STONE, HYMAN		28 JUL 1937	1880		ANNIE
391	K41	STONE, IDA EDEL		1943	1894		
248	E28	STONE, JOSEPH		1 AUG 1969			
102	CA11	STONE, JOSEPH H		28 MAY 1958	1900		
102	G29	STONE, JOSHUA		18 JAN 1936	16 FEB 1907	PAUL & SARAH	
330	Z8	STONE, JULIUS		7 JAN 1924	4 NOV 1923		
125	ZC155	STONE, KATE	SOLOWAY	3 SEP 1980	14 AUG 1909		
222	AN22	STONE, LEO H		21 DEC 1970	1911	HYMAN & ANNIE	
329	B 8	STONE, LOUIS R		3 JAN 1954	7 AUG 1914		MARY ANN
329	E17	STONE, MARY ANNE		27 APR 1972	2 MAR 1929		LOUIS
377	R21	STONE, MINNIE	ROSENBLUM	29 JUL 1991	8 JUL 1904		CARL
391	ZC54	STONE, MOES		28 FEB 1964	1900	GICHEL	
102	G27	STONE, PAUL		16 SEP 1957	1877		SARAH
222	AN23	STONE, RICHARD S		23 FEB 1980	1948	LEO	
102	H46	STONE, SADIE	WHITE	5 FEB 1954	1905		FRANK
222	AO12	STONE, SAMUEL S DDS		23 APR 1980	1904		
116	L11	STONE, SAMUEL SANFORD		6 MAR 1989	24 JUL 1904		FAY
102	G28	STONE, SARAH		17 FEB 1945	1887		PAUL
102	CB44	STONER, AUDREY	LUBIN	1 OCT 1989	17 DEC 1929		
102	CB46	STONER, DAVID		27 NOV 1980	7 DEC 1898		DOROTHY
102	CB47	STONER, DOROTHY	GOLDSTEIN	17 FEB 1980	5 APR 1905		DAVID
377	E10	STONER, EVA	RAKOVSKY	23 OCT 1961	15 SEP 1861		
392	G34	STONER, HARRY		28 MAR 1983	1 JUL 1889	MOSHE	REBECCA
392	H32	STONER, REBECCA	MERIMS	12 AUG 1963	25 DEC 1894	YERACHMIEL	HARRY
104	I17	STOTLAND, JEAN	WOLPER	28 JUL 1979	1911		
104	J 9	STOTLAND, SAMUEL		10 JUN 1959	1906		
374	F44	STRACHMAN, MAX		1958	1904		
102	AJ201	STRAUCH, FRANCES	TULIN	10 MAY 1971	20 OCT 1906		
446	A68	STRAUSS, ALBERT L SUTHERLAN		21 FEB 1911	4 MAR 1861	LEOPOLD & JOHANNA	
446	A67	STRAUSS, BENJAMIN F		1 MAY 1944	28 SEP 1868	LEOPOLD & JOHANNA	
249	F38	STRAUSS, ERNA		18 SEP 1977	20 FEB 1911		SIEGMUND
446	A66	STRAUSS, JOHANNA		19 AUG 1887	2 JUN 1835		LEOPOLD
248	J64	STRAUSS, LAZER		8 MAY 1930	1855		
446	A65	STRAUSS, LEOPOLD		8 JUL 1888	1 JUN 1831		JOHANNA
446	A75	STRAUSS, MAY		20 JUN 1979	16 MAY 1875	MAX & RAY	
446	B68	STRAUSS, SARAH		15 JAN 1882	2 JAN 1867		
329	B43	STRAUSS, SAUL		1 MAY 1955	1895		
249	F37	STRAUSS, SIEGMUND		2 FEB 1983	19 AUG 1906		ERNA
121	E33	STRELSER, FANNY	BRYNIN	1946	1897		
121	E34	STRELSER, ISRAEL		7 NOV 1977	15 AUG 1895		
371	J 8	STRICK, BERNARD		11 SEP 1965	17 NOV 1918	MORRIS	
330	G 3	STRICK, MOLLIE		29 NOV 1943			
371	J 9	STRICK, MORRIS		25 MAY 1963	1883		
116	I 2	STROGATZ, GERTRUDE	HERLANDS	12 NOV 1990	25 JUN 1922		
121	S10	STROH, LOUIS		12 SEP 1964	1902		
121	S11	STROH, ROSE		18 DEC 1974	1906		

Cem	Row	Name	Maiden Name	DOD	DOB	Parents	Spouse
370	D18	STROM, ALFRED H		21 DEC 1920	15 NOV 1916	ABRAHAM & BESSIE (LIPSHUTZ)	
433	D17	STROM, BENJAMIN		1 AUG 1962	4 MAY 1874	TZVI HIRSH	
370	K27	STROM, GUTE LIEBE	SHAPIRO	30 DEC 1943	1855	GABRIEL & SARAH	MOSES
433	E12	STROM, IRVING		25 OCT 1961	25 DEC 1916	BENJAMIN	
370	L 9	STROM, JACOB		12 MAR 1941	1874	MOSES & GUTE LIEBA	SARAH
371	O27	STROM, LOUIS		29 SEP 1949	1884	MOSES & GUTE LIEBA	
370	B 5	STROM, MOSES P		11 JUL 1923	1852	TZVI HIRSCH	GUTE LIEBA
371	AM22	STROM, SARAH H		4 OCT 1967	1883		JACOB
391	N58	STROSSBERG, HARRY		18 FEB 1955	3 JAN 1896	MORDECHAI	
391	B 6	STROSSBERG, IRWIN		21 JUN 1933	13 MAR 1930	HARRY & MARY	
391	N59	STROSSBERG, MARY		19 NOV 1974	21 DEC 1901	MORDECHAI	
116	W 3	STROUCH, CHARLES C		17 JUN 1989	16 JUL 1910		
370	G49	STUDD, ABRAHAM		8 SEP 1929	1849		
376	J 7	STUDD, ESTHER		7 FEB 1939		MICHALE	
371	J47	STUDD, MORRIS		13 MAY 1952	1877		SARAH
371	J46	STUDD, SARAH		28 AUG 1956	1877		MORRIS
125	L189	STUHLMAN, ELIZABETH	KRAVITZ	17 SEP 1971	1912	MAX & EDITH (GORFAIN)	
101	D25	STURM, HERMAN N		13 MAY 1968	1913	SAMUEL & SARAH	
101	D26	STURM, SAMUEL		1 FEB 1955	1885		SARAH
101	D27	STURM, SARAH		23 JUN 1952	1883		SAMUEL
493	G 7	STUTZ, MURRAY		1984	1906		
751	E13	SUCHECKI, ALYCE	WEITZEN	1953	1909		
102	X 9	SUDARSKY, CHARLES		21 JAN 1966	5 OCT 1885		DORA
102	X 8	SUDARSKY, DORA	LUBIN	11 FEB 1956	5 OCT 1893		CHARLES
102	AE48	SUDARSKY, ELIZABETH	KEMLER	21 JUL 1991	4 APR 1893		ISADORE
102	D20	SUDARSKY, ETHEL		9 AUG 1982	5 OCT 1906		
102	AE49	SUDARSKY, ISIDORE W		1978	1895		ELIZABETH
102	X12	SUDARSKY, JOHN		1960	1888		MINERVA
102	AE50	SUDARSKY, MATILDA		19 DEC 1981	3 JUL 1896		
102	X11	SUDARSKY, MINERVA S		1992	1899		JOHN
102	X10	SUDARSKY, SYLVIANN		1988	1934	CHARLES & DORA	
376	J 4	SUGARMAN, EVA S		10 NOV 1969	12 OCT 1906	YOSEF CHAIM	
222	AL16	SUGARMAN, JULIUS		11 NOV 1928	1869		MOLLY
248	I23	SUGARMAN, MINNIE		15 MAR 1949	7 AUG 1907		
222	AL15	SUGARMAN, MOLLIE		8 MAY 1927	1869		JULIUS
376	D20	SUGARMAN, SAMUEL		28 APR 1954		YEHUDA LEV	
102	T 1	SUISMAN, EDWARD		14 DEC 1991			
102	T29	SUISMAN, HELEN	KATZ	16 AUG 1981	1 MAR 1900		SAMUEL
102	T30	SUISMAN, SAMUEL CHARLES		24 MAY 1970	7 AUG 1900		HELEN
391	Q40	SUISMAN, SARAH		26 JUN 1935	1880	HILLEL	
391	F11	SUISMAN, SAUL		30 OCT 1933	1876	NATHAN	
446	D30	SUKOFF, RUTH EVA					
248	J78	SULLIVAN, BETH		18 MAY 1964			
377	Y40	SULMAN, DORIS	LEAR	24 SEP 1992	1919	JOSEPH	
391	Q43	SULMAN, ESTHER	ROSOFSKY	8 APR 1971	1886	ABRAHAM MORDECHAI	SIMON
391	R45	SULMAN, ESTHER E		5 JUN 1987	18 MAR 1913	SENDER	
391	R44	SULMAN, IDA R		5 MAR 1982	10 SEP 1892	CHAIM	
391	R43	SULMAN, SIDNEY M		2 JUN 1943	1887	MOSHE	
391	Q44	SULMAN, SIMON		2 MAY 1945	1880	MOSHE	ESTHER
331		SULTAN, ANNIE		2 JAN 1905	1844		
330	D33	SULTAN, IDA		1 OCT 1956			
330	H42	SULTAN, JULIUS		7 AUG 1940	1864		
125	P146	SULTON, ANNIE		9 MAY 1947	1870		BEN
125	P145	SULTON, BEN		14 JUN 1949	1867	YEHUDA KALIK	ANNIE
125	AA140	SULTON, SCOTT ALAN		11 APR 1964	9 MAY 1960		
102	AF110	SUMMERS, BENJAMIN		16 MAR 1988	20 NOV 1894		EVA
102	AF109	SUMMERS, EVA	ROSENBLATT	11 OCT 1986	1 SEP 1902		BENJAMIN
248	K65	SUMMERS, LOUIS		3 MAR 1950	1875		
750	H20	SUMMIT, FANNIE		27 OCT 1980	1894		FRANK
750	H21	SUMMIT, FRANK		15 JUL 1963	1894		FANNIE
750	F14	SUNDEL, LILLIAN		19 JUL 1973	8 JUN 1907		
102	L14	SUNDERLAND, FANNIE	EICHELMAN	20 JUL 1972	1889		GEORGE
102	L13	SUNDERLAND, GEORGE A		29 JUN 1967	1885		FANNIE
121	A21	SUNDILSON, ELLA O		22 AUG 1973	4 MAR 1915		
121	A20	SUNDILSON, HENRY M		28 DEC 1985	31 MAY 1910		
117	I 1	SUNENSHINE, CAROLINE		26 MAR 1992	10 JUL 1901		

Cem	Row	Name	Maiden Name	DOD	DOB	Parents	Spouse
330	F13	SUPER, ABRAHAM		7 FEB 1919	1865		
330	G31	SUPER, ANNIE F		30 JUL 1917	1854		
446	A29	SUPOVE, IDA		9 APR 1914	20 JAN 1882		JACOB
446	A28	SUPOVE, JACOB		15 APR 1954	12 JUL 1876		IDA
446	C44	SURASKY, GOLDIE		8 JAN 1903	1860		BENJAMIN
446	C80	SUSMAN, ALEXANDER					
102	W38	SUSMAN, ESTELLE	HOFFMAN	16 AUG 1991	10 JUN 1902		
102	W40	SUSMAN, SAMUEL		30 APR 1927	1878		SARAH
102	W39	SUSMAN, SARAH	SOLOMON	21 APR 1956	1881		SAMUEL
101	J25	SUSSELMAN, GITEL	KLAZ	9 APR 1942	1876		
372	K21	SUSSLER, DAVID MD		13 OCT 1992	2 NOV 1891		LIBBY
372	K20	SUSSLER, LIBBY	LEVIN	10 APR 1971	9 JUN 1903		DAVID
248	N63	SUSSMAN, ABRAHAM I		13 DEC 1969	1888		
370	P18	SUSSMAN, ALFRED		17 AUG 1926	12 JUL 1908	MORRIS & ROSE	ROSE
751	C 2	SUSSMAN, ARTHUR		3 FEB 1967	1895		
370	P16	SUSSMAN, BESSIE PAULINE		14 DEC 1965	4 JAN 1885		
248	N65	SUSSMAN, ESTHER R		8 FEB 1978	14 OCT 1907		MORRIS
370	Z 1	SUSSMAN, ETHEL		15 NOV 1941	1906		JULIUS
370	P14	SUSSMAN, FRANCIS ELON		16 OCT 1952	9 OCT 1905		
125	B 80	SUSSMAN, HAROLD MAX		9 NOV 1985	19 DEC 1922	MORRIS & BESSIE	
370	A19	SUSSMAN, JULIUS		27 OCT 1904	1854		
125	K137	SUSSMAN, JULIUS BERNARD		2 JUN 1932	15 DEC 1893		
248	N66	SUSSMAN, JULIUS L		6 MAR 1979	29 APR 1909		
125	B 81	SUSSMAN, LENA		6 MAR 1959	1899	ABRAHAM & ROSE	ESTHER
248	I71	SUSSMAN, MAX		6 OCT 1918	1888	CHAYA	
248	N61	SUSSMAN, MORRIS		12 MAR 1964			
370	P15	SUSSMAN, MORRIS SOLOMON		16 JUL 1958	7 FEB 1878		ROSE
370	P12	SUSSMAN, NAOMI RACHEL		1927	1852		BESSIE
248	N60	SUSSMAN, ROSE		4 DEC 1931	1861		SAMUEL
248	N62	SUSSMAN, ROSE HELEN		11 AUG 1956			MORRIS
125	B 82	SUSSMAN, ROSLYNN LEE		20 MAR 1970	1960		ABRAHAM
370	F33	SUSSMAN, SAM		20 NOV 1903	MAY 1891		
370	P11	SUSSMAN, SAMUEL		1921	1849		NAOMI
125	D 32	SUSSMAN, SAUL		1989	1910		
371	M29	SUTTON, FANNY		8 FEB 1976	1879		MOSHE
371	M28	SUTTON, JACK MD		21 SEP 1957	1918		
371	M30	SUTTON, MOSHE G		15 MAY 1954	1878	MOSHE & FANNY	FANNY
371	M27	SUTTON, PAUL MD		16 FEB 1986	1912		
330	G 5	SUTTON, YETTA		8 MAR 1950	1864	MOSHE & FANNY	
105	H10	SWADOSH, RUTH		4 NOV 1990	5 JUN 1919		
125	H 56	SWARSKY, IDA	HOROWITZ	6 NOV 1960	1881		ISAAC
125	H 57	SWARSKY, ISAAC		4 DEC 1926	1870		IDA
125	H 58	SWARSKY, MAE BELLE		29 JUN 1973	1903		
125	G 56	SWARSKY, ROSE		6 DEC 1980	1908	ISAAC & IDA	
370	H14	SWARTS, SARAH		13 APR 1908			
370	S13	SWATZBERG, KINE		19 JAN 1935			MARY
370	S14	SWATZBERG, MARY		28 MAR 1946	1868		KINE
370	P25	SWATZBERG, NATHAN		1943	1870		SOPHIE
370	P26	SWATZBERG, SOPHIE		1956	1866		NATHAN
370	J47	SWATZBURG, ESTHER D		1910	1906	JOSEPH & ROSE	NATHAN
374	H39	SWATZBURG, FANNIE		1935	1877		
374	J42	SWATZBURG, JENNIE		1980	1901		
370	J49	SWATZBURG, JOSEPH		1936	1877		ROSE
370	J48	SWATZBURG, LOUIS H		1933	1900	JOSEPH & ROSE	
374	G39	SWATZBURG, LOUIS M		1961	1899		
370	A 5	SWATZBURG, MYER		1947	1882		
370	J50	SWATZBURG, ROSE		14 AUG 1912	1867		JOSEPH
370	J51	SWATZBURG, RUTHERFORD		25 JAN 1992	3 MAR 1910	JOSEPH & ROSE	
370	S27	SWATZBURG, SAMUEL		20 DEC 1983	25 SEP 1893		SARAH
370	S26	SWATZBURG, SARAH		7 JAN 1965	12 APR 1891		SAMUEL
374	F39	SWATZBURG, TILLIE		1962	1901		SAMUEL
222	AH20	SWAYE, DANIEL		12 MAY 1943	1863		ELIZABETH
222	AH21	SWAYE, ELIZABETH		22 JUN 1955	1872		DANIEL
116	M 8	SWEEDLER, NATHAN B		15 OCT 1982	12 JUN 1914		
370	A16	SWEET, ABRAHAM DAVID		25 APR 1884	1870		ANNA
370	O32	SWEET, ANNA SARAH		27 MAR 1927	27 AUG 1893		ABRAHAM

Cem	Row	Name	Maiden Name	DOD	DOB	Parents	Spouse
125	U152	SWEIG, ARNOLD		23 OCT 1990	21 DEC 1913		MARION
125	U153	SWEIG, MARION		21 DEC 1986	18 MAY 1911		ARNOLD
125	P182	SWEIG, MOLLIE R		24 MAR 1968	15 SEP 1889		SAMUEL
125	P181	SWEIG, SAMUEL S		12 FEB 1963	18 JAN 1886		MOLLIE
125	D 96	SWETCHNICK, MEYER		1986	1891		SARAH
125	D 95	SWETCHNICK, SARAH	WEINER	9 OCT 1978	1897		MEYER
374	B25	SWETT, FLORENCE	KENIG	10 OCT 1956	1929		
125	D 94	SWETT, LEONARD L		7 SEP 1960	1926	MEYER & SARAH	
125	C 96	SWETT, SIDNEY		10 NOV 1969	1919	SARAH	
121	V11	SWILLING, ELLEN JOY		4 NOV 1963	3 DEC 1962		
121	V16	SWILLING, WILLIAM		22 SEP 1971	1902		
102	E20	SWIRSKY, DAVID		12 SEP 1954	1893		MAE
102	E19	SWIRSKY, MAE	KEMLER	8 JAN 1971			DAVID
750	E19	SWIRSKY, MORRIS		24 JUN 1966	30 OCT 1887		SARAH
750	E17	SWIRSKY, SARAH		21 FEB 1980	20 DEC 1897		MORRIS
372	H10	SYMON, MINNIE	GREENBERGER	1977	1893		SYDNEY
372	H 9	SYMON, SYDNEY		1970	1891		MINNIE
113	J53	SYMONDS, FRANK		2 NOV 1981	23 JAN 1918		
249	O10	SZAJNBERG, (BABY GIRL)		2 FEB 1983			
115	A22	TABANSKY, MORRIS		1 JUL 1991	23 JUL 1908		
113	N20	TABATSKY, ISRAEL (CANTOR)		1 JUN 1987	17 FEB 1922		
374	E34	TAFFEL, FANNIE		1953	1885		JOSEPH
374	E35	TAFFEL, JOSEPH		1947	1876		FANNIE
373	B 6	TAFFEL, ROSE		1981	1905	JOSEPH	
373	B 5	TAFFEL, SARAH M		1970	1912	JOSEPH	
373	B 7	TAFFEL, WILLIAM		11 MAY 1990	1 JUL 1907	JOSEPH	
102	AC79	TAGER, THEODORA	JOSEPH	19 APR 1982			
102	BD 1	TALAN, HYMAN		23 AUG 1991	7 DEC 1913		
101	L20	TALBER, ITA BAILA		5 MAY 1935			
330	F47	TALIS, ABRAHAM		8 NOV 1927	1850		
113	J22	TAMAREN, BERNARD		22 JAN 1971	15 OCT 1900		LEE
113	J23	TAMAREN, LEE	YULES	14 DEC 1987	14 MAR 1912	SAMUEL & MARSHA (KUTTEN)	BERNARD
119	B49	TAMAREN, LORRAINE G	GRINBLATT	29 FEB 1992	27 JUL 1921		MORRIS
110	A27	TAMKIN, MEYER		29 APR 1954			
447	R27	TANE, ANDREW H		31 MAR 1955	1 FEB 1955		
447	R31	TANENBAUM, ABE		1984	1883		
447	R34	TANENBAUM, IDA		1969	1869		SAMUEL
391	GC 6	TANENBAUM, ISAAC		16 FEB 1952	2 APR 1877	YESHIYAHU	
447	R35	TANENBAUM, SAMUEL		3 JUN 1949	1869		IDA
391	GM 7	TANENBAUM, SAUL		25 DEC 1929	6 SEP 1910	ISAAC	
392	B42	TANER, LOUIS		1943	1869		SARAH
392	B43	TANER, SARAH F		1939	1874		LOUIS
121	U14	TANKLE, NORTON		19 FEB 1969	22 MAY 1920		
249	C31	TANNENBAUM, ABRAHAM		9 DEC 1957	15 OCT 1879		MOLLY
391	GA 1	TANNENBAUM, ANNA		17 JAN 1986	15 JUN 1886	ABA ABRAHAM	
249	F34	TANNENBAUM, FRANCES W		3 FEB 1979	13 MAY 1924		
249	C30	TANNENBAUM, MOLLY		25 JAN 1975	15 MAR 1892		ABRAHAM
102	AI189	TARANTUL, BARNET S		15 MAY 1970	28 JUL 1901	BARUCH & ROSE (SPOLENSKY)	RHODA
102	AI190	TARANTUL, RHODA M	MATHOG	11 JAN 1989	1903		BARNET
377	S 1	TARNAPOL, DAVID D		1977	1904		
377	J16	TARNAPOL, HELEN S		3 JUL 1965	16 MAY 1901		ISADORE
377	J15	TARNAPOL, ISADORE		7 OCT 1989	6 SEP 1900		HELEN
392	B39	TARNAPOL, ROSE		30 OCT 1934	15 NOV 1865		ZALMAN
392	B38	TARNAPOL, ZALMAN F		18 FEB 1950	30 MAY 1863		ROSE
391	N35	TARNAPOLSKY, ANNIE		11 JAN 1908	15 AUG 1886	JACOB	
391	S31	TARNOPOL, EVA MASHA		21 OCT 1928	1840	ZALMAN	
249	E32	TASHLIK, JOSEPH		29 JAN 1972	1891		
751	B12	TASHMAN, BERTHA		31 OCT 1984	15 MAR 1900		MORRIS
751	B13	TASHMAN, MORRIS		5 AUG 1973	25 DEC 1897		BERTHA
370	X17	TASSISON, KALMAN MEYER		14 JUN 1935	23 NOV 1932	CHAIM	
392	D48	TAUBER, BENJAMIN		8 JAN 1958	1882	JACOB	MARY
391	GD 5	TAUBER, MARY		28 AUG 1951	1889	MOSHE	BENJAMIN
447	I17	TAVEL, HELEN		24 JUN 1941	1917		
447	S36	TAVEL, JOSEPH		27 MAR 1948	12 MAR 1878		
447	I18	TAVEL, MARY		4 APR 1962	1885		
110	A24	TAXSAR, SADIE	MEDNICK	28 SEP 1960	1892		

Cem	Row	Name	Maiden Name	DOD	DOB	Parents	Spouse
371	AE 9	TAYLOR, CHARLOTTE		1994	1923		
102	X18	TAYLOR, ESTELLE K		18 NOV 1961	9 MAR 1890		MAURICE
121	A 3	TAYLOR, EVA J		31 OCT 1968	6 MAR 1897		MORRIS
105	I13	TAYLOR, FLORENCE S		28 FEB 1992	1905		
105	I12	TAYLOR, HERMAN D		15 JAN 1965	1900		
102	X15	TAYLOR, HILDA REVA		12 MAR 1931	22 AUG 1911		
371	AG 3	TAYLOR, IDA		18 NOV 1961	1870		WILLIAM
371	AE10	TAYLOR, MAURICE T		4 APR 1993	25 DEC 1911		CHARLOTTE
102	AJ152	TAYLOR, MINNIE	LEVI	7 DEC 1965	5 JUN 1883		
102	X17	TAYLOR, MORRIS M		30 JAN 1956	10 JUL 1882		ESTELLE
371	AF 3	TAYLOR, ROSE S		22 NOV 1968	1892		
371	AF 4	TAYLOR, SAMUEL		17 APR 1952	1886		
102	X16	TAYLOR, WILLIAM COLEMAN		8 MAY 1981	10 DEC 1915	MORRIS & ESTELLE	HILDA
123		TEICHER, BENJAMIN H		4 JUN 1952	1898		
391	T63	TEICHER, HANNAH R		1994	1907		
114	N20	TEITELBAUM, ANNA		21 APR 1982	15 FEB 1907		SIDNEY
114	N19	TEITELBAUM, SIDNEY S		1 AUG 1948	1 SEP 1906		ANNA
104	K45	TELLER, JACOB		12 SEP 1976	17 DEC 1907		
102	CA35	TELLER, LOUIS		19 JUN 1959	1911		
374	F11	TELZONSKY, IDA MOLLY		17 JAN 1967			MORDECHAI
374	F10	TELZONSKY, MORDECHAI LEIB		27 APR 1956			IDA
374	F 6	TELZONSKY, SAMUEL C		25 APR 1977			
121	AA23	TEMKIN, CELIA		20 JAN 1982	1900		
751	O23	TEMKIN, LOUIS		16 FEB 1967	10 OCT 1889		MOLLIE
751	O22	TEMKIN, MOLLIE		23 SEP 1975	15 JAN 1895		LOUIS
121	AA24	TEMKIN, NATHAN		20 OCT 1983	1896		
125	X174	TEMPLE, EARL		1988	1928		NAOMI
125	X173	TEMPLE, NAOMI	BLACKMAN	6 JUL 1981	1921		EARL
248	N70	TENENBAUM, SCHEINE F		11 JAN 1919	1881		
371	M35	TEPOROFSKY, SARAH		24 DEC 1967	1 MAY 1865		
125	E144	TEPPER, HANNAH		1 JUN 1936	1886	VELVEL	
102	AD162	TEPPER, MOLLIE F		26 NOV 1984	4 NOV 1898		PETER
102	AD161	TEPPER, PETER D		23 DEC 1963	1896		MOLLIE
102	S21	TERRY, ALBERT B		1989	1911		JEANETTE
102	S20	TERRY, JEANNETTE		1972	1914		ALBERT
125	I136	TERTES, HYMAN		25 AUG 1941	1880	ELI	
377	N36	THALL, MORRIS		28 JAN 1968	5 JUL 1901	JOSEPH	PHYLIS
377	N37	THALL, PHYLIS	COHEN	19 FEB 1983	17 MAR 1904	SAMUEL	MORRIS
112	C17	THEISE, BERNARD		1984	1892		HENRIETTE
112	C16	THEISE, HENRIETTE	THEISEBACH	1985	1888		BERNARD
125	H166	THEODORE, JULIUS		15 MAR 1945		KITREAL	
112	C12	THIERFELD, WALTER		1 MAR 1984	20 SEP 1920		
377	ZA47	THOMPSON, ROBERT J		12 DEC 1986		ABRAHAM	SARAH
377	ZA46	THOMPSON, SARAH		6 OCT 1978		MORDECHAI	ROBERT
249	O12	THRONE, ROGER C		4 JAN 1972	1929		
447	B 1	THUMIM, MARK DR		1993	1909		
222	AI 3	TICK, EUGENE E		26 MAR 1989	5 NOV 1933		
493	H 3	TICOTSKY, ISRAEL		28 AUG 1982	1907		MARY
493	H 4	TICOTSKY, MARY	NOUMAN	8 FEB 1988	15 APR 1917		ISRAEL
123		TIETZE, SAMUEL		9 JUN 1949	1884		
751	.15	TILLES, ABRAHAM		8 NOV 1950	23 MAY 1912		
371	C 1	TINTORIN, TOWIA		20 MAR 1994	18 JUN 1907		
330	C18	TIRSCHLER, LOUIS		12 MAR 1940	1869		
370	A46	TISCHLER, GERTRUDE		2 DEC 1975	18 DEC 1899		HARRY
370	A47	TISCHLER, HARRY		8 AUG 1954	10 MAY 1892		GERTUDE
391	I43	TISHKOFF, ALICE		5 MAY 1948	1871	SAMUEL	
391	G 8	TISHKOV, BESSIE		18 JUN 1933	10 JUL 1880	NATHAN	
391	L45	TISHKOV, HARRY		27 AUG 1953	1886	MEYER	SOPHIE
391	R69	TISHKOV, HERMAN		7 AUG 1968	1909	TZVI HIRSH	
391	L43	TISHKOV, MARY		17 MAR 1953	1864	ISAAC JACOB	
391	F 6	TISHKOV, MELVIN		29 AUG 1938	DEC 1911	ISAAC TZVI	
391	L44	TISHKOV, SOPHIE		31 JAN 1946	1894	MENACHEM MENDEL	HARRY
105	G23	TISHLER, ARTHUR D		8 AUG 1954	1900		
101	K 3	TISHLER, MURIEL		4 NOV 1989	3 SEP 1927		
102	AG103	TISHLER, PAUL MORTON		29 JUN 1981	6 OCT 1916		
125	A104	TISHLER, PHILIP		1 JUL 1974	11 NOV 1909		

Cem	Row	Name	Maiden Name	DOD	DOB	Parents	Spouse
106	C4	TISHLER, ROSALIE G		19 JAN 1977	20 MAR 1935		
101	J 4	TISLER, DAVID I		18 SEP 1963	1901		
101	J 6	TISLER, MORRIS		26 FEB 1960	1894		FLORA
119	C 8	TITLEBAUM, JOSEPHINE	KATZ	20 DEC 1987	11 JUN 1904		
119	C 9	TITLEBAUM, PHILIP		22 SEP 1988	4 FEB 1900		
102	U31	TIVEN, BARBARA R		10 NOV 1971	17 MAY 1922		
376	A13	TIVEN, JUDITH W		NDD	1926		ROBERT
102	U27	TIVEN, PHILIP MARK		4 NOV 1971	17 AUG 1953	BARBARA	
376	A12	TIVEN, ROBERT PETER		1981	1927		JUDITH
105	AA20	TOBACK, (BABY)		19 MAY 1971	19 MAY 1971		
105	N46	TOBACK, IRVING		30 NOV 1979	24 JAN 1907		
102	AE75	TOBER, MEYER E		18 JUN 1964	1882		RACHEL
102	AE74	TOBER, RACHEL H	BECKER	25 DEC 1937	17 JUL 1888		MEYER
102	AE73	TOBER, SIDNEY B		6 MAY 1983	16 JUL 1917	MEYER & RACHEL	
125	Z174	TOBEY, BURTON D		3 AUG 1986	26 AUG 1916		
446	C18	TOBEY, JENNIE		12 JUL 1923			
112	C22	TOBIAS, HUGO		13 MAR 1987	6 MAY 1897		
112	D40	TOBIAS, LEAH E		13 JUN 1981	23 FEB 1923		
391	Z78	TOBIN, BLANCHE	GREENBLATT	28 SEP 1981	29 JUN 1923	MATTISYAHU	
102	M40	TOBOCO, ABRAHAM I		1951	1875		MINNIE
102	M39	TOBOCO, MINNIE	SEIGALL	1929	1876		ABRAHAM
125	O 68	TOBY, MYRNA LEE		29 DEC 1947	18 MAY 1945		
118	D17	TOLPIN, ADELAIDE		20 SEP 1962			
118	D17	TOLPIN, ESTHER		16 SEP 1953			
118	D17	TOLPIN, HELEN		25 FEB 1992			
447	I 7	TOMBANK, JEAN		12 AUG 1974	15 SEP 1913		NATHAN
447	I 8	TOMBANK, NATHAN		9 FEB 1979	30 OCT 1905		JEAN
101	L21	TOMCHIN, REBECCA		11 APR 1915	1867		
391	B 9	TOMSKY, DAVID JASON		29 AUG 1980	15 AUG 1980	WAYNE & SYLVIA	
105	E22	TONKAN, IDA		14 SEP 1944	1872		
105	D24	TONKEN, BESSIE		9 JUL 1967	1883		NATHAN
105	D23	TONKEN, NATHAN		13 DEC 1954	1888		BESSIE
105	P18	TONKEN, SONIA		1966	1887		
371	AC22	TOPKIN, IRVING W		1962	1900		
751	N20	TOPLITZ, MARY		10 APR 1964	1892		
751	N19	TOPLITZ, SAM		26 OCT 1969	1888		
102	AI157	TORCHINSKY, ABRAHAM E		1984	1895		ANNA
102	AI158	TORCHINSKY, ANNA S		1985	1896		ABRAHAM
102	S22	TORETSKY, BARNEY		1968	1888		MINIE
102	S23	TORETSKY, MINNIE	DAVIS	1971	1890		BARNEY
102	S40	TORETSKY, MYN		14 FEB 1966	21 JAN 1896		
102	AD97	TOUBMAN, BELLE	EPSTEIN	8 OCT 1981	13 APR 1900		
107	D19	TOUBMAN, JOSEPH W DDS		14 JAN 1973	2 MAR 1910		MARTHA
107	D18	TOUBMAN, MARTHA R		14 JAN 1982	22 JUN 1912		JOSEPH
121	U 3	TRACHTENBERG, ISRAEL		21 MAR 1983	4 JAN 1904		
370	Q21	TRACHTENBERG, NATHAN		1947	1895	WILLIAM & REBECCA	
370	Q20	TRACHTENBERG, REBECCA		1944	1867		WILLIAM
372	A 5	TRACHTENBERG, ROBERT A		1990	1920		
370	Q19	TRACHTENBERG, WILLIAM		1934	1865		REBECCA
372	C10	TRACTENBERG, DAVID		1969	1897		
372	A 8	TRACTENBERG, LOUIS		1971	1890		
372	A 7	TRACTENBERG, SARAH		1987	1898		
116	AU 3	TRAUB, IRVING		5 MAR 1981	17 SEP 1905		JOYCE
116	AU 2	TRAUB, JOYCE	SACHER	15 MAR 1971	14 SEP 1916		IRVING
391	V69	TRAUB, RIVKO		3 DEC 1971		RABBI JACOB	
105	N23	TRAUB, SADIE	COHEN	1 MAY 1991	15 MAR 1898		SAMUEL
105	N22	TRAUB, SAMUEL		22 FEB 1987	19 MAY 1897		SADIE
447	J38	TRAVERSE, I ROBERT		13 MAY 1969	1906		
125	O129	TRAVIS, IRVING		1986	1903		RUTH
125	O130	TRAVIS, RUTH	SHERMAN	5 NOV 1975	1906		IRVING
392	F24	TRAYSTMAN, HARRY		21 NOV 1924	1904	NATHAN & SADIE	
392	G10	TRAYSTMAN, ISADORE		30 JAN 1954	1915	NATHAN & SADIE	
392	F 9	TRAYSTMAN, NATHAN		20 OCT 1953	1881	CHAIM ELIYAHU	NATHAN
392	F 8	TRAYSTMAN, SADIE		26 APR 1956	1884	SAMUEL ZEV	SADIE
125	J 50	TRESKE, ANNIE		16 APR 1905	1863		
125	K 26	TRESKE, JACOB		13 JAN 1918	1856	LEIZER AARON & SALAVE	

Cem	Row	Name	Maiden Name	DOD	DOB	Parents	Spouse
125		TRESKY,		APR 1919			
125	T147	TRESKY, JACOB		20 JUN 1939	DEC 1928	MAX & RACHEL	
125	I 71	TRESKY, JESSIE		14 JAN 1968	1881		
371	AA 8	TRESKY, LESTER		16 MAY 1977	1913		ROSE
125	S161	TRESKY, MAX		30 AUG 1941	1883	JACOB	
125	N 93	TRESKY, ROSE		20 JAN 1925	1887	SAMUEL & YETTA	
371	AA 9	TRESKY, ROSE S		16 NOV 1983	1903		LESTER
121	G24	TRESTMAN, LOUIS		1985	1923		
113	J49	TRESTON, ANITA	KARP	7 AUG 1978	15 JUN 1949		
376	J 5	TRONER, IDA GERTRUDE		24 APR 1974	5 MAY 1904	ISRAEL	PINCUS
376	J 6	TRONER, PINCUS		13 DEC 1965	1 JUL 1899	ALEXANDER ZISKIN	IDA
447	N18	TROUB, JULIUS SIDNEY		7 NOV 1941	1896	MOSES & DORA	
371	AP12	TUBER, BENJAMIN MICHAEL		26 DEC 1991	28 FEB 1901		SADIE
370	K21	TUBER, ETHEL R		22 AUG 1945			SAMUEL
371	AP11	TUBER, SADIE PEARL		17 MAR 1992	13 JUN 1908		BENJAMIN
370	B25	TUBER, SAMUEL ISAAC		1924	1871		ETHEL
123		TUBIN, ALLIE		10 JUN 1951	25 JUN 1891		SAMUEL
751	E37	TUBIN, LOUIS		11 DEC 1923	1869		
123		TUBIN, SAMUEL		3 JUN 1960	1898		ALLIE
372	B11	TUCH, ERNESTINE		1937	1856		LOUIS
102	I37	TUCH, FANNIE	COHEN	30 AUG 1935	1886		MORRIS
372	B12	TUCH, HELEN		1944	1890	LOUIS & ERNESTINE	
395	C11	TUCH, LEAH FLORENCE		30 MAY 1882	15 NOV 1880	LOUIS & HENRIETTA	
102	V11	TUCH, LILLIAN	SIGAL	28 JUL 1965	1898		
372	B10	TUCH, LOUIS		1925	1850		ERNESTINE
102	I36	TUCH, MORRIS MD		2 OCT 1969	1882		FANNIE
102	X25	TUCK, BETTY	LEIKIND	6 JUN 1980	4 JUL 1896		
123		TUCK, LOUIS S		24 FEB 1940	1895		
102	W21	TUCKEL, BLUMA	WELSON	26 JAN 1946	1877		
102	AJ176	TUCKEL, DAVID M		23 DEC 1966	15 APR 1902		
102	Q22	TUCKER, ABRAHAM H		5 MAR 1976	10 OCT 1884		ALICE
102	Q20	TUCKER, ALICE		23 JUL 1972	5 JUN 1895		ABRAHAM
105	D30	TUCKER, DAVID		15 APR 1978	27 MAR 1908		RUTH
222	AS 6	TUCKER, DORA		1959	1886		JOSEPH
222	AP10	TUCKER, HYMAN		1949	1874		PAULINE
222	AT12	TUCKER, HYMAN		1983	1913		
222	AS 5	TUCKER, JOSEPH		1956	1883		DORA
222	AP11	TUCKER, PAULINE		1960	1875		HYMAN
105	D29	TUCKER, RUTH		10 SEP 1967	3 JUL 1914		DAVID
102	Z30	TUCKER, SOPHIE	ABUZA	9 FEB 1966	13 JAN 1887	CHARLES & JENNIE (LENZ)	LOUIS
101	L25	TUDOR, YETTA	BARONESS	1918	1893		
105	B17	TULIN, AARON		9 FEB 1950	1886		ANNA
102	E24	TULIN, ABRAHAM N		4 JAN 1974	30 MAY 1883		MARY
105	B16	TULIN, ANNA R		28 APR 1989	1898		AARON
102	AJ202	TULIN, BESSIE	LANSING	28 APR 1972	12 MAR 1888		
116	U 8	TULIN, ELEANOR	KOVITSKY	30 JUN 1987	5 DEC 1920		MORRIS
102	K25	TULIN, EMMA L	LERNER	1936	1873		SAMUEL
222	L 2	TULIN, ESTHER		15 JUN 1953			SAMUEL
101	A13	TULIN, EVA		10 JUN 1924	1852		NATHAN
101	E10	TULIN, FAYE		27 FEB 1987	1903		MORRIS
102	I35	TULIN, FRANCES S		1 AUG 1941	11 JUN 1941		
102	K12	TULIN, HARRY		19 JUL 1906	19 JUL 1906		
102	K26	TULIN, LEON		1932	1901	SAMUEL & EMMA	
102	E23	TULIN, MARY		12 DEC 1980	4 JUL 1896		ABRAHAM
101	E11	TULIN, MORRIS		22 DEC 1973	1893		FAYE
116	U 7	TULIN, MORRIS		29 AUG 1979	13 APR 1915		ELEANOR
101	A12	TULIN, NATHAN		10 AUG 1924	1841		EVA
116	AW10	TULIN, NORMAN L		27 MAR 1988	7 FEB 1922		
102	K24	TULIN, SAMUEL S	HOMSK, RUSSIA	30 JUN 1938	1869	SHAIA & BASIA	EMMA
222	L 1	TULIN, SAMUEL V		27 DEC 1961			ESTHER
751	H23	TUNICK, LOUIS		2 DEC 1963	1 MAY 1942		
751	I23	TUNICK, LOUIS		1938	1878		ROSE
751	I22	TUNICK, ROSE		1957	1883		LOUIS
392	F38	TURETZKY, ANNA		28 AUG 1944	1884	ZACHARIAH	
370	Q38	TURETZKY, BARNETT		12 JUL 1929	1866		FANNIE
370	Q37	TURETZKY, FANNIE		16 FEB 1931	1870		BARNETT

Cem	Row	Name	Maiden Name	DOD	DOB	Parents	Spouse
377	Q20	TURETZKY, HELEN		4 APR 1969	24 MAR 1909		
371	A25	TURETZKY, ISADORE		3 AUG 1972	15 APR 1902		
377	R19	TURETZKY, MEYER		2 FEB 1975	20 DEC 1880		
248	L63	TUROFF, JAY L		1966	1956		
119	C43	TURTZ, BENJAMIN		23 DEC 1985	30 JAN 1896		
119	C44	TURTZ, RAE		26 FEB 1982	10 NOV 1898		
371	A47	TYLES, LEJZER		27 OCT 1988	16 JAN 1909		
377	Q27	TYLO, ERNEST		8 FEB 1977	16 MAR 1897		
125	E 23	UBERSTEIN, HARRY L		11 SEP 1956	1894		
328	A38	UDIN, JOSEPH J		7 MAY 1976	1 MAY 1918		SONIA
328	A39	UDIN, SONIA		21 NOV 1990	15 MAY 1923		JOSEPH
391	G35	UHRMAN, SYLVIA		16 OCT 1931	1862	AARON DAVID	
112	B19	ULLMANN, IVAN		7 JUL 1989	21 NOV 1906		
125	I137	ULMAN, EVA	TERTES	21 SEP 1981	1882		
447	K39	UNGER, LENA		1 MAY 1992	1906		SIDNEY
751	E 4	UNGER, MARY		27 FEB 1991	10 OCT 1915		
447	K40	UNGER, SIDNEY		8 JUN 1971	1907		LENA
117	I 4	UNGER, ZELDA		25 JAN 1993			
392	C 9	UNSDORFER, ESTHER I		11 MAR 1949	1869		
101	A26	URICH, ABRAHAM		21 AUG 1930			SHEINA
101	L18	URICH, SHEINA					ABRAHAM
751	I 3	UTLEY, LINDA	ROSANSKY	3 MAY 1991	4 FEB 1944		
112	B23	VALFER, SIEGFRIED		4 MAY 1989	16 JAN 1920		
330	B41	VALINSKY, ANNA		24 JAN 1956	1876		MORRIS
330	H39	VALINSKY, MORRIS		28 DEC 1945	1862		ANNA
374	I40	VALLOWITZ, CELIA		13 OCT 1941			SAM
374	I42	VALLOWITZ, IDA		22 DEC 1968	30 MAY 1908		
374	I41	VALLOWITZ, SAM		18 FEB 1955			CELIA
392	C21	VERLINSKY, CLARA		6 JUN 1948	1868		
248	D14	VERNORN, ROSALIE		4 OCT 1983	18 APR 1919		
377	S65	VICTOR, ALVIN		28 SEP 1987	12 FEB 1908		
377	R65	VICTOR, NORMAN D		9 APR 1989	19 APR 1932	ALVIN	
222	AT10	VILKOMERSON, IDA		12 JUN 1965	1887		
370	R18	VINCENT, SARAH	BENDETT	1983	1897		
110	A30	VINETSKY, JENNIE		17 MAR 1957			
110	A11	VINETSKY, WILLIAM		8 NOV 1941	1882		
104	J 2	VINICK, ESTHER		24 JUN 1953	1882		
102	W 3	VINICK, HELEN	BAILYN	3 APR 1987	5 SEP 1918	CHARLES & ESTHER	
249	K 6	VINOGRAD, MORRIS		20 SEP 1938	1866		
102	CB21	VIRSHUP, HENRIETTA	NASSAU	11 JUN 1979	19 APR 1896		HYMAN
102	CB22	VIRSHUP, HYMAN		31 OCT 1985	19 FEB 1889		HENRIETTA
493	G10	VISELTEAR, ARTHUR J		7 JAN 1990	19 MAR 1938	HARRY & LENA	
493	F10	VISELTEAR, HARRY		1990	1911	MORDECHAI	LENA
493	F11	VISELTEAR, LENA		1986	1912	ELIYAHU	HARRY
102	BF 7	VISNER, MARJORIE S		1 AUG 1988	29 MAR 1918		
113	N18	VITRIOL, IDA		20 JUL 1974	8 JUL 1887		MILTON
113	N17	VITRIOL, MILTON J		22 APR 1985	8 DEC 1910		IDA
121	F16	VOGEL, DAVID L		29 JAN 1992	6 JUL 1920		
121	T16	VOGEL, HYMAN A		23 MAY 1967	23 SEP 1903		
102	AJ108	VOGEL, NATHAN		4 AUG 1961	21 MAR 1899	WILLIAM & IDA (BRENNER)	RUTH
102	AJ109	VOGEL, RUTH	KLEIN	6 JAN 1985	22 NOV 1902		NATHAN
222	AP20	VOGEL, RUTH	ALLEN	24 JUL 1960	1918		
115	L45	VOGEL, STANLEY W		1989	1917		
370	K47	VOGELSON, RACHEL		1960	1884		SOLOMON
370	K46	VOGELSON, SOLOMON		1965	1882		RACHEL
104	G36	WACHTEL, SADIE		7 AUG 1989	24 JUL 1902		
391	C 1	WACHTER, CELIA S		14 DEC 1953	1899	ISRAEL	
121	R9	WAGNER, JENNIFER SUE		14 FEB 1991			
121	R10	WAGNER, JORDAN ZACHARY		11 MAR 1992			
222	AF17	WAINER, ANNA		1945	1861		
102	U39	WAINGROW, BENJAMIN		15 OCT 1964	31 JAN 1889	DAVID & ADA	BESSIE
102	U38	WAINGROW, BESSIE	JENNES	19 AUG 1973	1885		BENJAMIN
102	U40	WAINGROW, SIDNEY		18 AUG 1992		BENJAMIN & BESSIE (JENNES)	
103	B5	WAISMAN, ZELDA		26 SEP 1935	1854		
433	R 1	WALD, LILLIAN		19 JUN 1982	1915	MOSHE	
248	H57	WALD, ROSIE		2 FEB 1915	1884		

Cem	Row	Name	Maiden Name	DOD	DOB	Parents	Spouse
494	B 1	WALDINGER, EMANUEL		30 JUN 1956	18 APR 1899	DAVID MYER	REGINA
494	B 2	WALDINGER, REGINA		26 NOV 1985	27 MAY 1895		EMANUEL
113	A 6	WALDMAN, BERNARD		17 JUN 1985	6 FEB 1911		
751	E39	WALDMAN, ROCHEL LEAH		17 APR 1923	1846		
447	Q18	WALDMANN, EMANUEL		27 AUG 1953	1904		
125	Q162	WALKER, HARRY		9 JUL 1946	3 MAR 1892	MOSHE	
102	U33	WALKER, HENRIETTA		19 JUL 1951	1886		MAX
102	U32	WALKER, MAX		17 MAY 1952	1884		HENRIETTA
222	AG 4	WALL, FANNIE	DOBKIN	17 MAY 1979	26 MAR 1895		JOSEPH
222	AG 3	WALL, JOSEPH		25 OCT 1982	29 JAN 1892		FANNIE
116	BL13	WALLACE, LEWIS D		15 FEB 1967			MARY
116	BL12	WALLACE, MARY		27 JAN 1967			LEWIS
102	AJ 8	WALLACH, FRANCHANE	WEISMAN	16 OCT 1984	1889		ISADORE
102	AJ 7	WALLACH, ISADORE		14 MAY 1953	1886	MANUEL & ESSA	FRANCHANE
330	E18	WALLACH, JULIUS		8 SEP 1930	1878		DORA
222	AD 3	WALLACK, ANNETTE G		29 MAY 1991	3 DEC 1904		EDWARD
330	AH24	WALLACK, DORA		28 DEC 1977	1874		JULIUS
222	AD 2	WALLACK, EDWARD H		NDD	17 NOV 1902		ANNETTE
102	A29	WALLACK, MORRIS		1936	1882		
121	A22	WALLANS, SAMUEL		26 NOV 1974	22 JUL 1912		
391	F15	WALLEN, HYMAN		23 JUL 1931	1868	KALMONOS	
116	BL87	WALLET, ANNABELLE		21 JUN 1974	9 JAN 1906		
102	AH87	WALMAN, HILDA	MARMER	28 AUG 1978	25 DEC 1903		JOSEPH
102	AA207	WALTER, FRANK		7 NOV 1985	1 MAY 1903		
447	R26	WALTI, LEONIE JEANNE		5 APR 1955	1870		
447	R25	WALTI, MARGUERITE		22 JAN 1983	21 NOV 1898		
102	AH179	WALTMAN, DAVID		13 JUN 1986	1885		MATILDA
102	AH180	WALTMAN, MATILDA		24 MAR 1970	1890		DAVID
104	O45	WARD, IDA B		3 JUL 1967	1900		NATHAN
104	O44	WARD, NATHAN		13 MAY 1972	1898		IDA
101	L 8	WARNER, FREDA	OLER	12 NOV 1967			
102	AH204	WARNER, SAMUEL		6 OCT 1982	1885		SARAH
102	AH205	WARNER, SARAH	MISSAL	5 MAY 1973	1888		SAMUEL
222	AH 4	WARSCHAVSKY, ABE		13 OCT 1918	1889		
222	AH 5	WARSCHAVSKY, HARRY		29 SEP 1918	1879		ROSE
222	AH 6	WARSCHAVSKY, ROSE		3 OCT 1958	1881		HARRY
447	D23	WARSHAUER, LENORE		8 NOV 1967	3 AUG 1900		WILLIAM
447	D24	WARSHAUER, WILLIAM		15 FEB 1970	21 SEP 1898		LENORE
119	H46	WARSHAVSKY, ALAN J		3 DEC 1987	4 AUG 1902		
119	H45	WARSHAVSKY, SARAH	SOKOLL	12 SEP 1976	23 DEC 1904		
105	L7	WARSHAWSKY, ELSIE R		2 MAR 1965			
433	D 8	WARTEL, MATHEW		3 OUT 1964	24 FEB 1913		
392	J16	WASHTON, SAMUEL		12 DEC 1971	1903	AARON TZVI	
102	AE91	WASKOWITZ, ANNA	SIEGEL	1960	1887		MAX
125	AA114	WASKOWITZ, BETSY ANN	RIDER	14 NOV 1963	1934		
125	AA113	WASKOWITZ, DAVID		17 DEC 1972	1897		RUTH
102	SR90	WASKOWITZ, MAX		1960	1884		ANNA
125	H107	WASKOWITZ, REBECCA	BERKOWITZ	24 OCT 1942	1876	DAVID & MASHA	SAMUEL
125	AA112	WASKOWITZ, RUTH	NOACK	4 OCT 1979	1902		DAVID
125	H106	WASKOWITZ, SAMUEL		6 MAR 1949	1874	JOSEPH & CHANAH	REBECCA
102	AD175	WASSERMAN, BERNADINE		1963	1889		JULIUS
222	AP17	WASSERMAN, BERTHA		1975	1894		DAVID
222	AP16	WASSERMAN, DAVID		1978	1888		BERTHA
370	H 2	WASSERMAN, DORA		15 APR 1891		MAYER JACOB	
222	AP15	WASSERMAN, FRED		1989	1918	DAVID & BERTHA	
102	AD174	WASSERMAN, JULIUS		1972	1886		BERNADINE
106	B4	WASSERMAN, SIDNEY		1 AUG 1992	2 JUL 1917		
102	AI163	WATASH, JEAN		NDD			
392	G29	WATCHINKSY, JOSEPH		17 JUL 1927	1869	DAVID & CHAYA	
392	G26	WATCHINSKY, AARON HARRY		26 SEP 1934	1878	DAVID & CHAYA	BESSIE
392	G27	WATCHINSKY, BESSIE		4 JAN 1957	1881	JACOB JOSEPH	AARON
392	F27	WATCHINSKY, CHAYEH		21 JAN 1924	1843		DAVID
392	F26	WATCHINSKY, DAVID		19 SEP 1927	1825	SAMUEL	CHAYA
392	H27	WATCHINSKY, FANNIE		12 AUG 1935		ISAAC	ZELEK
392	F28	WATCHINSKY, ZELEK		20 OCT 1920		ABRAHAM	FANNIE
102	AD190	WAX, IDA	FRIEDLAND	25 MAR 1968	11 JUN 1895		SAMUEL

Cem	Row	Name	Maiden Name	DOD	DOB	Parents	Spouse
102	AD191	WAX, SAMUEL		7 MAR 1984	15 FEB 1899		IDA
102	L20	WAXMAN, FRIEDA G		17 MAR 1978	2 APR 1922		
102	G26	WAXMAN, JACOB		14 DEC 1932			
102	AH86	WAXMAN, JOSEPH		15 MAR 1973	10 MAR 1893	KALMAN & FANNIE (BROOCH)	HILDA
102	G25	WAXMAN, LOUIS		16 OCT 1941	1877	KALMAN & FANNIE (BROOCH)	
119	J28	WAXMAN, MEYER CASEY		18 OCT 1981	15 SEP 1910		
125	K161	WAXMAN, RUBEN		13 FEB 1960	1877		
119	D 8	WAYNE, SYLVIA		22 DEC 1990	14 JUN 1905		
101	L37	WEBBER, GLORIA SONDRA		23 JAN 1936	1928		
116	R11	WEBBER, LOUIS W		20 MAR 1989	11 NOV 1909		
106	D25	WEBER, BARNETT		1 JAN 1991	1 JUN 1914		
371	K35	WEBER, LOUIS		22 APR 1973			MINNIE
371	K36	WEBER, MINNIE		12 MAY 1966			LOUIS
102	Z35	WEBER, S CHOPSEY		9 SEP 1963	1890		SAMUEL
102	Z36	WEBER, SAMUEL		1945	1886		S CHOPSEY
433	I19	WEBER, YETTA S		7 APR 1927	1866	EFFRAIM	
370	J64	WECHSLER, FANNIE		16 APR 1939			SOLOMON
370	J67	WECHSLER, JACOB		1934	1883		
370	J68	WECHSLER, RUTH		26 MAR 1908	20 FEB 1907	JACOB	
370	J63	WECHSLER, SOLOMON		22 JUN 1934			FANNIE
119	D61	WEIDMAN, LOUIS		22 JUL 1982	13 APR 1911		
125	AA100	WEIL, BEATRICE	MAXEN	10 JUL 1975	1915		
113	O18	WEIL, CARL K		4 NOV 1988	31 OCT 1902		
391	GI 3	WEIL, EMIL		2 OCT 1950	1873	MOSHE	RIVKA
119	C55	WEIL, JEFFREY D		12 MAR 1989	11 NOV 1949		
121	J30	WEIL, MORRIS		7 DEC 1966	7 JUL 1920		
121	J31	WEIL, PAULINE		3 JAN 1977	14 MAR 1921		
391	GI 2	WEIL, RIVKA		3 JAN 1969	1881	EFRAIM	EMIL
392	E 6	WEIN, ABE		4 MAY 1975	12 OCT 1907	ZION	
392	G32	WEIN, BENJAMIN		7 APR 1926	1874	MOSHE YEHUDA	
392	E 4	WEIN, DANIEL		22 DEC 1980	1908	ZION	SARAH
101	K 4	WEIN, HYMAN		11 JAN 1977	1899		MINNIE
392	E 3	WEIN, JULIUS		28 MAY 1982	15 JUL 1911	ZION	
392	E10	WEIN, JULIUS		31 JUL 1971	1914	NACHEM	
392	E12	WEIN, MAURICE		26 JAN 1957	1904	ZION	SALLY
392	E29	WEIN, MINNIE		5 APR 1955	1882	JUDAH	NATHAN
101	K 5	WEIN, MINNIE		15 JAN 1967	1896		HYMAN
392	B30	WEIN, MORRIS M		29 OCT 1966	14 MAR 1905		
392	E30	WEIN, NATHAN		31 MAR 1944	1878	MOSHE LEV	MINNIE
392	E11	WEIN, SALLY		20 JUL 1971	1899	ZALMAN	MAURICE
392	E 5	WEIN, SARAH		7 NOV 1986	1906	ISAAC	DANIEL
392	G18	WEIN, SEME		9 OCT 1946	1869	NACHEM	ZALMAN
392	G19	WEIN, ZALMAN		6 JUN 1939	1867	MOSHE YEHUDA	SEME
392	G33	WEIN, ZELDA		14 AUG 1956	1878	PINCUS	
104	K28	WEINBAUM, BEATRICE		1980	1907		BEATRICE
104	K29	WEINBAUM, GABRIEL		1986	1904		GABRIEL
106	C8	WEINBAUM, GOLDINE		2 JUL 1992			WILLIAM
102	AD202	WEINBAUM, MAURICE		8 FEB 1972	22 FEB 1896		
106	C9	WEINBAUM, WILLIAM		17 FEB 1972	10 DEC 1903		GOLDINE
125		WEINBERG, (CHILD)		5 JUL 1922	1922	ISIDORE	
391	C 2	WEINBERG, ANNA		6 JUN 1953	1885	CHAIM WOLF	MORRIS
116	L 8	WEINBERG, BLANCHE		24 JUL 1984	24 DEC 1898		
125	A 32	WEINBERG, DAVID		3 SEP 1966	1895		MARY
391	E 3	WEINBERG, DORIS M		8 JUL 1961	1936	SAMUEL	
102	C12	WEINBERG, ETHEL IDA		3 MAR 1988			
125	J 58	WEINBERG, ETTA		23 SEP 1908	25 MAR 1822		
125	I 54	WEINBERG, GUSSY		8 JAN 1906	17 MAR 1869		
104	J33	WEINBERG, HETTY		23 MAR 1963	1888		MARK
125	G161	WEINBERG, ISADORE		4 MAR 1978	12 FEB 1892		RACHEL
392	A12	WEINBERG, LILLIAN		4 SEP 1993	11 MAR 1906		WOLFE
391	X60	WEINBERG, LOUIS		18 MAR 1972	1905	MOSHE	SARA
104	J32	WEINBERG, MARK S		6 NOV 1958	1883		HETTY
125	A 33	WEINBERG, MARY E		10 JAN 1979			DAVID
391	F10	WEINBERG, MORRIS		5 NOV 1935	1876	SAMUEL	ANNA
102	Z101	WEINBERG, NATALIE	GILSTON	16 APR 1990	1924	MORRIS & LEAH	
125	K 76	WEINBERG, PHILIP		23 MAR 1926	22 APR 1863	SHLOMO MATHEW	

Cem	Row	Name	Maiden Name	DOD	DOB	Parents	Spouse
125	B 34	WEINBERG, RACHEL	KRONSON	5 SEP 1975	1891		ISIDORE
391	X61	WEINBERG, SARA		27 AUG 1987	1912	BENJAMIN	LOUIS
125	K 75	WEINBERG, SHLOMO MATHEW		14 MAR 1916	1835	PESACH & RACHEL	
392	A11	WEINBERG, WOLFE		13 MAY 1981	9 SEP 1902		
392	C20	WEINBERGER, SAMUEL		1948	1884		LILLIAN
102	AJ118	WEINER, ABRAHAM		11 DEC 1943	1893		LENA
102	AD184	WEINER, ABRAHAM D		1988	1894	MAX & ANNA (KOHN)	BERTHA
102	D31	WEINER, ANNA	KOHN	29 APR 1961	1872	ABRAHAM & RACHEL	MAX
102	AD185	WEINER, BERTHA L		6 FEB 1984	12 JAN 1894		ABRAHAM
125	W153	WEINER, CHARLES J		18 APR 1984	1914		
374	G53	WEINER, DIANA R		19 FEB 1990	10 AUG 1910		JOSEPH
125	D4 E1	WEINER, FLORENCE		1 MAY 1935	1914	LOUIS & MENA	
101	A21	WEINER, H		15 MAY 1917	1889		
125	DB 12	WEINER, HARRY		25 JAN 1966	1910		
374	G54	WEINER, JOSEPH D		12 DEC 1988	2 NOV 1904		DIANA
125	H158	WEINER, KOPPEL H		24 JAN 1966	1909		
102	AJ117	WEINER, LENA	KATZ	6 JAN 1956	1894		ABRAHAM
125	P162	WEINER, LOUIS		8 MAR 1951	1883		MINNIE
102	E43	WEINER, MAURICE		17 SEP 1968	19 APR 1896	MAX & ANNA (KOHN)	RUTH
102	D30	WEINER, MAX	OF MINSK	5 DEC 1962	27 SEP 1866	SIMON & SARAH (COLEDESKY)	ANNA
433	C 4	WEINER, MILTON HAROLD		20 JUN 1965	1 SEP 1917	ELIEZER	PEARL
125	P161	WEINER, MINNIE		7 AUG 1948	1884	WILLIAM	LOUIS
125	X175	WEINER, MORRIS		28 NOV 1981	1909		
116	AU20	WEINER, NATHAN		11 DEC 1963	1922		
433	C 5	WEINER, PEARL RUTH		26 DEC 1964	12 SEP 1922	YOSEPH MICHAEL	MILTON
374	K32	WEINER, WILLIAM		24 FEB 1986	9 FEB 1921		
102	Q17	WEINERMAN, ANNA	SCHWARTZ	1971	1893		MORRIS
102	Q15	WEINERMAN, ANNIE		1964	1886		DAVID
102	Q16	WEINERMAN, DAVID T		1979	1888		ANNIE
102	Q14	WEINERMAN, MORRIS W		27 DEC 1947	19 OCT 1896		ANNA
494	C 5	WEINGART, HARRY		8 AUG 1983	29 JAN 1906	DAVID	
377	ZA 5	WEINGARTEN, BRUNO		24 SEP 1978	31 JAN 1911	MESHALEM	
249	E43	WEINGRAD, MINNIE		23 DEC 1961	10 MAY 1878		SAMUEL
249	E42	WEINGRAD, SAMUEL		9 MAY 1965	9 AUG 1882		MINNIE
123		WEINICK, FRANK M		24 MAY 1940	1897		
329	F30	WEINKOFF, IRVING		15 FEB 1988	23 SEP 1901		REGINA
329	F31	WEINKOFF, REGINA		15 FEB 1988	13 SEP 1907		IRVING
330	A12	WEINSTEIN, AARON		13 NOV 1959	1867		
377	Q24	WEINSTEIN, ALBERT		12 DEC 1975	29 MAR 1895		RACHEL
121	G26	WEINSTEIN, ANNA A		29 JAN 1987	23 FEB 1901		
446	A43	WEINSTEIN, BENJAMIN		21 APR 1919	14 JUL 1890		
119	A31	WEINSTEIN, BETTY		17 JUL 1992	24 APR 1909		
125	P189	WEINSTEIN, CECILIA		28 NOV 1990	23 MAR 1911		MORRIS
116	BZ40	WEINSTEIN, DORA	PELZEL	9 MAR 1969	10 SEP 1887		MORRIS
109	C 2	WEINSTEIN, EDWARD		11 MAR 1992	15 NOV 1905		MAY
101	I16	WEINSTEIN, ESTHER		11 AUG 1980	19 JUL 1916		MORRIS
125	K162	WEINSTEIN, ESTHER		6 APR 1984			ISIDORE
392	C42	WEINSTEIN, FANNIE	LUBCHANSKY	6 APR 1964	1888		
125	H153	WEINSTEIN, FANNIE	KRIM	18 FEB 1975	26 JAN 1892		LOUIS
750	J20	WEINSTEIN, HANNAH		27 DEC 1972			PAUL
433	L 1	WEINSTEIN, HARRY		1985	1902	JACOB	
123		WEINSTEIN, HARRY		20 MAY 1952	1897		
370	J 1	WEINSTEIN, IDA FANNIE		29 MAY 1929	1871		
370	D 5	WEINSTEIN, ISAAC		23 AUG 1935	1851		
102	AD204	WEINSTEIN, ISADORE		1 JUL 1968	1911		
392	F29	WEINSTEIN, ISADORE		13 NOV 1919	1907		
125	K163	WEINSTEIN, ISADORE		20 AUG 1962	1899		ESTHER
391	H27	WEINSTEIN, ISRAEL MOSHE		22 APR 1926		REUBEN DAVID	
370	F 5	WEINSTEIN, JACOB		1920	1900		
102	AB148	WEINSTEIN, JULIUS		12 MAR 1965	1888		
102	N21	WEINSTEIN, LENA		12 DEC 1965	1888		MAX
222	A 2	WEINSTEIN, LOUIS		3 APR 1961	1892		ROSE
125	H154	WEINSTEIN, LOUIS		3 JUN 1979	4 AUG 1894		FANNY
102	E32	WEINSTEIN, MAURICE H		1 APR 1971	15 APR 1891		ROSE
102	AA159	WEINSTEIN, MAX		1974	1914		
102	N22	WEINSTEIN, MAX WILLIAM		10 DEC 1960	1885	REBBECCA	LENA

Cem	Row	Name	Maiden Name	DOD	DOB	Parents	Spouse
125	L120	WEINSTEIN, MICHAEL		25 NOV 1930	25 JAN 1876	ELIYAHU	TILLIE
101	I15	WEINSTEIN, MORRIS		7 MAR 1982	6 APR 1914		ESTHER
125	P190	WEINSTEIN, MORRIS		12 JUN 1963	19 APR 1908		CECELIA
116	BZ41	WEINSTEIN, MORRIS J		28 JAN 1958	15 JAN 1881		DORA
377	U18	WEINSTEIN, NANCY ANNE		13 OCT 1973	24 JAN 1930	ABRAHAM	
116	BZ42	WEINSTEIN, NATHAN HART		26 DEC 1974	10 DEC 1906	MORRIS & DORA	
750	J21	WEINSTEIN, PAUL		26 SEP 1967			HANNAH
433	D15	WEINSTEIN, PAULINE	BERWICK	19 SEP 1964	13 NOV 1887		
377	Q25	WEINSTEIN, RACHEL		24 JAN 1977	1 APR 1900		ALBERT
102	N19	WEINSTEIN, REBECCA		9 OCT 1930	1846		
102	E31	WEINSTEIN, ROSE	HERSHENOW	12 MAY 1961	2 NOV 1894	SHALOM & BESSIE	MAURICE
222	A 1	WEINSTEIN, ROSE P		22 APR 1979	1894		LOUIS
121	G25	WEINSTEIN, SAMUEL		29 DEC 1984	27 JUN 1903		
222	A 3	WEINSTEIN, SAUL		15 JUL 1991	1918	LOUIS & ROSE	
125	L121	WEINSTEIN, TILLIE	DADONY	7 AUG 1931	10 APR 1875	LOUIS & SARAH	MICHAEL
101	A16	WEINSTOCK, UDEL		1 MAY 1937	1847		
751	J35	WEINTRAUB, CLARA		10 SEP 1949	1870		
249	J 2	WEINTRAUB, ELIZABETH		14 MAY 1937	1882		LOUIS
249	J 3	WEINTRAUB, LOUIS		10 SEP 1945	1875		ELIZABETH
102	A60	WEINTRAUB, MINNIE		20 FEB 1941	1882		
125		WEIS, MAX		25 MAY 1925	22 MAY 1925	BENNY & SARAH	
108	B 7	WEISBERG, ALBERT		9 MAY 1962	18 AUG 1896		ROSE
125		WEISBERG, ELICK		21 JUL 1918	1876	ROSE	
108	B 8	WEISBERG, ROSE	CUTLER	9 JAN 1982	9 SEP 1896		ALBERT
121	U12	WEISBURD, WILLIAM		8 JUN 1986	8 JAN 1916		
119	K56	WEISE, ISRAEL J		6 FEB 1993			
370	L10	WEISENBERG, ABRAHAM		1941	1853		FLORENCE
116	T23	WEISENBERG, CYNTHIA T		2 AUG 1992	4 OCT 1954		
116	T19	WEISENBERG, EDWARD JOSEPH		30 MAY 1977	1918		HARRIET
370	K26	WEISENBERG, FLORENCE		1944	1853		ABRAHAM
116	T20	WEISENBERG, HARRIET ETHYL	KURTZ	25 JUL 1989	13 JAN 1924		EDWARD
119	I38	WEISENBERG, JACK		26 JUN 1984	19 AUG 1904		
493	C21	WEISER, FAYE		1992	1919		WILLIAM
493	D22	WEISER, WILLIAM		1979	1918		FAYE
370	J34	WEISINGER, LENA		14 NOV 1940	25 MAY 1860		NATHAN
374	G 5	WEISINGER, MATILDA		13 SEP 1917	13 SEP 1866		
370	M 4	WEISINGER, NATHAN		2 AUG 1947	30 MAY 1861		LENA
370	A31	WEISMAN, ESTHER		16 JUN 1971	17 MAR 1886		SOLOMON
110	E18	WEISMAN, GORDON H		17 JUL 1987	4 NOV 1965		
125	O121	WEISMAN, HELEN	HOCHMAN	21 OCT 1978	4 JAN 1903		JOSEPH
119	H29	WEISMAN, JENNIE		9 MAY 1992	10 MAY 1900		
125	O122	WEISMAN, JOSEPH		22 OCT 1974	15 APR 1893		HELEN
110	E33	WEISMAN, LEO		29 SEP 1986	4 JUL 1906		
119	J38	WEISMAN, LOUIS		9 DEC 1981	1899		
119	H28	WEISMAN, MAX		25 MAY 1987	10 JUL 1905		
123		WEISMAN, MORRIS	IN FRANCE	WW I			
750	J31	WEISMAN, NORMAN		18 FEB 1983	24 OCT 1902		
370	A32	WEISMAN, SOLOMON		9 MAR 1974	13 MAY 1884		ESTHER
371	I 2	WEISMAN, YETTA		1973	1888		
374	B49	WEISS, ABRAHAM		5 FEB 1960	1882		SARAH
125	J163	WEISS, BENJAMIN		1 SEP 1973	6 JAN 1900		SABINA
102	T46	WEISS, BENJAMIN C		21 MAY 1982	1909		
330	F15	WEISS, BERNARD		3 SEP 1920	1844		
102	E37	WEISS, BURT		1977	1891		ESTHER
447	AA19	WEISS, CLAIRE A		22 APR 1985	1924		COLEMAN
125	O 57	WEISS, CLAIRE M		24 JUN 1934	11 JUL 1932		
447	AA20	WEISS, COLEMAN C		21 SEP 1985	1920		CLAIRE
113	O76	WEISS, EDWARD		18 JUN 1982	6 AUG 1896		
102	E38	WEISS, ESTHER	HOROWITZ	31 MAY 1984			BURT
125	M 23	WEISS, ETHEL ADELLE		9 JUL 1915	1853	RUSEL SAMUEL & HANA CHANA	
113	K47	WEISS, JACK		17 JUL 1977	7 APR 1903		
125	ZA178	WEISS, JEROME V		19 JUN 1990	17 NOV 1918		
125	L127	WEISS, KALA	MISTAU	6 APR 1931	1931	SAMUEL	
121	T 6	WEISS, PAULINE	RAVINTSKY	1986	1898		
391	ZD70	WEISS, ROSE	DELATIZKY	19 AUG 1992	28 AUG 1913	CHAIM	
125	J164	WEISS, SABINA	ROSEN	25 DEC 1978	6 APR 1900		BENJAMIN

Cem	Row	Name	Maiden Name	DOD	DOB	Parents	Spouse
374	B48	WEISS, SARAH		14 FEB 1959	1880		ABRAHAM
330	G42	WEISSBERG, ANNA		14 AUG 1914	1824		
222	AQ 5	WEISSMAN, STEVEN B		18 JUL 1985	12 AUG 1942		
751	K24	WEITZEN, BERNARD		8 OCT 1929	1872		
391	M29	WEITZEN, CHAIM		31 JUL 1905		ISAAC	
751	J19	WEITZEN, ESTHER	STURCZ	1946	1873		
447	G24	WEITZMAN, BENJAMIN		1993	1897		FAYE
447	G22	WEITZMAN, CHARLES L		2 DEC 1952	1874		IDA
447	G25	WEITZMAN, FAYE		1992	1908		BENJAMIN
447	G23	WEITZMAN, IDA		22 APR 1950	1876		CHARLES
119	L37	WELENSKY, RALPH B		8 JUN 1987	2 DEC 1926		
125		WELINSKY, (BABY GIRL)		14 MAR 1908	13 MAR 1908	SAMUEL & ANNA (SMITH)	
125	I122	WELINSKY, ANNA	SMITH	24 JUN 1936	1862	ABRAHAM & MALKA (DUSKYN)	SAMUEL
125	I 70	WELINSKY, DINAH MERYL	WINTZ	29 NOV 1906	3 APR 1844	ARYEH LEV	MAX
125	J128	WELINSKY, FRANK		12 OCT 1936	1872	MENACHEM MENDEL & DINA MERYL	LENA
125	K 56	WELINSKY, GRACE		7 SEP 1912	AUG 1911	MICHAEL & SARAH (FINKELSTEIN)	
125	J 51	WELINSKY, HARRY		17 JUN 1905	10 SEP 1868	MENACHEM MENDEL & DINA MERYL	FANNIE
125	E136	WELINSKY, JACOB		25 MAR 1962	27 NOV 1885	MENACHEM MENDEL & DINA MERYL	
125	J129	WELINSKY, LENA	SILVERSTEIN	31 DEC 1946	8 SEP 1872	YERRACHMEAL MOSHE & CHANA SARA	FRANK
125		WELINSKY, LIBBIE		29 SEP 1903	6 JUL 1901	FRANK & LENA (SILVERSTEIN)	
125	M192	WELINSKY, MICHAEL		17 NOV 1969	11 APR 1883	MENACHEM MENDEL & DINA MERYL	SARAH
125	S177	WELINSKY, MILTON S		22 JUN 1957	22 JAN 1894	SAMUEL & ANNA (SMITH)	
125	K 57	WELINSKY, RUTH		10 SEP 1912	AUG 1911	MICHAEL & SARAH (FINKELSTEIN)	
125	I123	WELINSKY, SAMUEL		23 MAR 1947	JUN 1867	MENACHEM MENDEL & DINA MERYL	ANNA
372	G20	WELLING, MOLLIE L		1990	1891		ROBERT
372	G19	WELLING, ROBERT		1963	1894		MOLLIE
125	K 73	WELLINS, EDWARD		11 FEB 1920	1884	MENACHEM MENDEL & DINA MERYL	DOROTHY
125	I191	WELLINS, EDWARD		11 JAN 1974	18 OCT 1901	SAMUEL & ANNA (SMITH)	HELEN
121	G14	WELLINS, FLORENCE S		10 JUN 1984			
115	A13	WELLINS, GERALD A		1991	1926	MICKEY WELINSKY	
125	T152	WELLINS, HARRY ROBERT		21 OCT 1939	16 NOV 1899	SAMUEL & ANNA (SMITH)	ESTELLE
125	J140	WELLINS, HELEN	KOMINSKY	7 JUN 1951	27 DEC 1907		EDWARD
116	N25	WELLINS, HOWARD A		13 OCT 1989	31 AUG 1946	MILTON	
125	A142	WELLINS, LOUIS		1 JUL 1982	29 MAY 1906	FRANK & LENA (SILVERSTEIN)	MARION
125	A143	WELLINS, MARION	COHEN	14 SEP 1981	20 MAY 1913		LOUIS
116	N27	WELLINS, MILTON		13 SEP 1980	7 JUL 1909		
330	AD14	WELLISCH, HUGO		18 MAY 1972	8 MAR 1895		
374	F47	WENER, ANNIE		16 JUN 1954	3 FEB 1888		
371	AA19	WENER, ELINOR NANCY		5 NOV 1952	14 FEB 1941		
377	W 2	WENER, MABEL	LEVINSON	11 MAR 1985	3 JUN 1904	ABRAHAM JACOB	WILLIAM
374	F48	WENER, SALAMAN		9 MAY 1956	23 SEP 1876		
377	W 1	WENER, WILLIAM V MD		11 JUL 1981	28 OCT 1904	MICHAEL	MABEL
121	O17	WENICK, ELEANOR L		29 APR 1981	11 FEB 1924		
121	O18	WENICK, RAYMOND		12 OCT 1968	5 OCT 1921		
377	T39	WENICK, SHEAL S		9 JAN 1990	15 SEP 1912	SHLOMO	
102	AD177	WERBA, ELIZABETH		17 DEC 1984	1889		MARCUS
102	AD176	WERBA, MARCUS		25 JAN 1979	1886		ELIZABETH
113	N40	WERBNER, DAVID		27 FEB 1962	1 MAY 1893		EDNA
113	N41	WERBNER, EDNA		4 NOV 1987	18 FEB 1904		DAVID
447	S40	WERNER, IRWIN P		1961	1895		
127	C	WERNIKOFF, BARNEY		20 JUL 1978	13 APR 1906		
494	C 2	WERSHOW, PAULINE	PAPISH	25 APR 1975	10 AUG 1897		
101	A30	WESHLER, HARRY		23 APR 1911	1882		
125	B 16	WESKER, IDA H	JAFFE	15 MAR 1931	1874	MORRIS & SOPHIE (KOSIS)	MAX
125	B 15	WESKER, MAX		1 APR 1938	1875	PINKUS & DORA	IDA
127	D	WESTERFIELD, LILLY	LEHMAN	7 DEC 1982	14 MAR 1889		
751	M14	WESTERMAN, LILLIAN NELKIN	KAPLAN	1989	1922		
119	A54	WESTON, BELLE A	KALLER	3 NOV 1990	9 FEB 1923		
119	A55	WESTON, HOWARD J		12 MAR 1992	18 MAR 1921		
222	AD 5	WETSTONE, BENJAMIN		19 OCT 1945	3 DEC 1891		ESTHER
102	T44	WETSTONE, BERTHA	WEINER	27 MAY 1943	1872		LOUIS
222	AD 6	WETSTONE, ESTHER LOIS	HALPERIN	13 NOV 1974	23 JUL 1889		BENJAMIN
102	T23	WETSTONE, EVELYN		30 NOV 1974	27 APR 1908		HARRY
102	T24	WETSTONE, HARRY		1 JUL 1991	18 APR 1901		EVELYN
102	T45	WETSTONE, JOHN B		8 MAY 1949	15 AUG 1893	LOUIS & BERTHA (WEINER)	
102	T25	WETSTONE, JULIUS		1 DEC 1973	1903		RHEA

Cem	Row	Name	Maiden Name	DOD	DOB	Parents	Spouse
102	T43	WETSTONE, LOUIS		16 JUL 1959	1870	DAVID & RODEL	BERTHA
102	AC185	WETSTONE, MURRAY		1971	1896	LOUIS & BERTHA (WEINER)	NATALIE
102	AC184	WETSTONE, NATALIE		1976	1901		MURRAY
102	T26	WETSTONE, REA K		21 JAN 1968	1902		JULIUS
104	G22	WEXELSTEIN, FREDA		4 JAN 1971	6 MAR 1913		
121	C37	WEXLER, ABRAHAM J DR		21 NOV 1980	23 SEP 1952	NAOMI	
125	F134	WEXLER, ISRAEL R		3 JUN 1976	1883	KATY	LILLIAN
125	F132	WEXLER, KATY		31 MAY 1951	1857		
125	F133	WEXLER, LILLIAN DORA		9 APR 1954	1886		ISRAEL
121	C38	WEXLER, NAOMI	CHIDEKEL	2 DEC 1988			
371	O 1	WHILEFISH, MORRIS		3 FEB 1970	24 SEP 1886		
102	AF30	WHITE, BRUCE HOWARD		26 SEP 1982	1 AUG 1951		
102	L16	WHITE, ESTHER	EICHELMAN	14 JUL 1986	1899		SAMUEL
102	AB46	WHITE, EVA	KATZ	1970	1898		MORRIS
102	AD 5	WHITE, HYMAN		8 JUN 1972	1882	MEYER ISAAC & IDA (ISAACSON)	JESSIE
102	AD 4	WHITE, JESSIE		4 APR 1938	1889		HYMAN
102	S 3	WHITE, LOUIS		10 APR 1971	25 APR 1887	MEYER ISAAC & IDA (ISAACSON)	
102	S 4	WHITE, MARSHALL IRVING		1984	1925	LOUIS	
106	D21	WHITE, MINNIE		18 AUG 1979	16 JUN 1929		
102	AB45	WHITE, MORRIS J		1972	1894	MEYER ISAAC & IDA (ISAACSON)	EVA
102	L15	WHITE, SAMUEL		20 APR 1965	1892	MEYER ISAAC & IDA (ISAACSON)	ESTHER
102	AC29	WHITE, WILLIAM		1 JAN 1968	1898	MEYER ISAAC & IDA (ISAACSON)	
102	AJ145	WHITESTONE, CLAIRE F		20 JAN 1959	4 AUG 1906		ERVING
102	AJ144	WHITESTONE, ERVING		2 MAY 1975	8 AUG 1906		CLAIRE
249	N12	WHITMAN, BENJAMIN		21 JUL 1971	15 OCT 1885		
377	S55	WHITTEMORE, DEE A		1953	1920		
377	S56	WHITTEMORE, RUTH B		1989	1917		
125	H124	WHOLL, ANNA		26 NOV 1941	1863		
125	H123	WHOLL, ISADORE		3 DEC 1956	1889		REBECCA
125	H125	WHOLL, REBECCA		15 OCT 1961	1882		ISADORE
119	A53	WICE, DEBORAH D		15 NOV 1990	11 OCT 1928		
125	M109	WICE, SAMUEL		21 OCT 1935	15 SEP 1889	AKIVA & ESTHER	
113	O44	WICHMAN, SUSAN	COHEN	10 JUN 1990	29 JUL 1943		
101	H25	WIDAM, HARRY		2 JAN 1983	1908		SHIRLEY
110	B28	WIDAM, LIBBY		24 OCT 1947	1882		
110	A25	WIDAM, MEYER		10 NOV 1958	1873		
101	H26	WIDAM, SHIRLEY		5 MAY 1990	1906		HARRY
371	G 1	WIDROW, IDA G		3 MAY 1991	23 MAY 1904		
371	A24	WIDROWITZ, IDA		10 APR 1987	10 OCT 1906		SAL
370	M 1	WIDROWITZ, MAX		23 JAN 1949	1870		
371	J28	WIDROWITZ, REBECCA		24 MAR 1967	26 JUL 1872		
371	J27	WIDROWITZ, SAL		8 NOV 1973	5 JAN 1897	REBECCA	IDA
102	AC151	WIEBER, EVELYN	BASS	1961	1904		
123		WIEBER, GEORGE J		25 DEC 1951	1912		HARRIET
123		WIEBER, HARRIET R		26 AUG 1993			GEORGE
111	2	WIEDER, CARRIE	BIRCH	23 SEP 1949	24 JUN 1875		MILTON
111	2	WIEDER, MILTON		27 JUN 1958	10 JUN 1874		CARRIE
102	F24	WIEGEL, YETTA	SINGER	26 SEP 1974	28 NOV 1882		
125	L 45	WIENER, ABRAHAM		1 OCT 1909	1885		
125	L108	WIENER, ANSHAL		1 AUG 1929	1870		GERTRUDE
392	C15	WIENER, BERNARD		12 SEP 1949			CELIA
125	O118	WIENER, BETH K		20 MAY 1974	1902		
125	I 93	WIENER, CATHY LYNN		24 APR 1973	1959		
392	C14	WIENER, CELIA		22 FEB 1944			BERNARD
125	K165	WIENER, EDWARD H		12 OCT 1967	1901		FRIEDA
125	P185	WIENER, ERICH P		8 NOV 1975	1898		SALKA
125	N151	WIENER, ETTA		25 FEB 1951	1891		ISRAEL
125	K164	WIENER, FREIDA R		1993	1905		EDWARD
125	L109	WIENER, GERTRUDE		4 JUL 1955	1873		ANSHEL
125	R150	WIENER, HYMAN		6 JUN 1964	1877		RACHEL
102	AD210	WIENER, IRVING		17 SEP 1975	5 APR 1916		
125	K171	WIENER, ISADORE		17 MAR 1973			KATHY
125	N152	WIENER, ISRAEL J		27 OCT 1977	1891		ETTA
125	K172	WIENER, KATHIE LYNNE		24 APR 1973	8 JUL 1958		ISADORE
102	AB168	WIENER, LOUIS A		17 DEC 1986	13 NOV 1912		SALLY
125	N153	WIENER, MORRIS		5 SEP 1951	1907	ISRAEL & ETTA	

Cem	Row	Name	Maiden Name	DOD	DOB	Parents	Spouse
330	G41	WIENER, PEARL L		20 JUN 1911	1839		
125	R149	WIENER, RACHEL		11 JAN 1943	1880	ABRAHAM JACOB	HYMAN
125	X192	WIENER, ROSE		7 JAN 1987	29 OCT 1897		SAMUEL
125	X185	WIENER, ROSE		1994	1910		
125	P186	WIENER, SALKA	FUCKS	5 MAR 1963	1901		EHRICH
102	AB169	WIENER, SALLY		8 JUN 1984	12 NOV 1914		LOUIS
125	X191	WIENER, SAMUEL E		13 NOV 1982	31 JAN 1895		ROSE
125	E 95	WIENER, SEYMOUR LEON		23 DEC 1932	12 AUG 1927		
446	A18	WIERNIKOFF, BENJAMIN		20 SEP 1923	1910		
391	L36	WIESNIEWSKI, ALICE	CURRAN	19 JAN 1978	1911	JOSHUA	
116	BK28	WILDER, DANIEL		27 FEB 1978	1892		NETTIE
116	BK27	WILDER, NETTIE	KORSHINSKY	13 MAR 1981	1 JUN 1901		DANIEL
101	L33	WILDFEUER, CAROLYN		14 MAY 1934	1873		
750	B19	WILENCHIK, MORRIS		6 APR 1988	8 MAY 1919		
377	H16	WILENSKY, ANNA ROCHEL		1950	1880		
377	T59	WILENSKY, ESTELLE F		NDD	1 FEB 1925		LEO
392	I41	WILENSKY, ETHEL		20 OCT 1967		ZALMAN	MAX
248	I54	WILENSKY, FRANCES		22 JUL 1982	15 FEB 1896	ISRAEL & REBECCA	
377	U50	WILENSKY, HYMAN		19 APR 1990	1913	MENACHEM MENDEL	
248	H52	WILENSKY, ISRAEL		27 SEP 1952	APR 1865	SAMUEL & ESTHER FAGEL	REBECCA
377	T58	WILENSKY, LEO		NDD	7 NOV 1919		ESTELLE
392	I40	WILENSKY, MAX (MENDEL)		29 AUG 1955		REUBEN	ETHEL
248	H53	WILENSKY, REBECCA	SAMKOFF	4 NOV 1950	OCT 1875	JULIUS & LEAH	ISRAEL
248	I51	WILENSKY, SEYMOUR		25 MAY 1983	22 JUL 1910	ISRAEL & REBECCA	
377	Q51	WILINSKY, MAX		1990	1912	ABRAHAM & ANNA	
104	D35	WILLENS, LENA		3 JUN 1982	1898		LEO
104	D36	WILLENS, LEO		29 NOV 1966	1895		LENA
114	N14	WILLIAMS, ABRAHAM S		21 MAY 1992	12 APR 1912		
392	B22	WILLIAMS, DOROTHY B		12 DEC 1959	1924		
125	S173	WILLIAMS, LOUIS I		2 FEB 1957	1883		MAUDE
125	S172	WILLIAMS, MAUDE	SAXE	25 JAN 1982	1893		LOUIS
329	F34	WILLMANN, EUGENE		9 MAY 1989	18 FEB 1935		
392	A51	WILNER, MAURICE A		25 NOV 1975	20 JAN 1909		
105	C11	WILSON, ABRAHAM		5 OCT 1947	1874		ROSE
105	C12	WILSON, ROSE JUDITH		19 APR 1937	1879		ABRAHAM
373	D 1	WINAKER, JOSEPH		26 FEB 1960	1887		
373	E 3	WINAKER, LEO L		1973	1909	SAMUEL & LENA	
329	E22	WINAKER, SIDNEY		1983	1914		
373	E 2	WINAKOR, LENA		16 JUL 1954	1875		SAMUEL
375	E37	WINAKOR, OSIAS		4 JUL 1904	1844		
391	G14	WINAKOR, SADIE		12 NOV 1928	1895	NAFTALI	
373	E 1	WINAKOR, SAMUEL		10 MAY 1954	1875		LENA
222	G 7	WIND, MAURICE		1979	1897		SARA
222	G 8	WIND, SARA	MILLER	NDD	1906		MAURICE
125	L111	WINEFSKY, SARAH		20 NOV 1929	1895		
447	P39	WINER, ALICE	BATTALIN	24 SEP 1977	17 JUN 1906	HENRY & RACHEL	
104	O50	WINER, FRIEDA		2 DEC 1969	1893		
104	O51	WINER, LOIS		7 JAN 1981	1892		
104	I28	WINICK, GUSSIE		23 JUL 1977	1900		SAMUEL
110	C 3	WINICK, HASIA		10 MAR 1933	1863		JULIUS
110	C 4	WINICK, JULIUS		13 DEC 1940	1858		HASIA
102	AI193	WINICK, NATHAN MAX MD		13 OCT 1971	22 MAY 1914	WILLIAM & SARAH	
104	I29	WINICK, SAMUEL		10 NOV 1987	1892		GUSSIE
102	AI194	WINICK, SARAH	WAGMAN	7 JUN 1987	15 JUL 1896		WILLIAM
102	AI195	WINICK, WILLIAM		10 MAY 1910	15 APR 1889		SARAH
125	I 39	WINKLE, ABRAHAM		19 SEP 1950		FRED & GITEL	
125	K 72	WINKLE, ADA CLARA		6 JUL 1931	SEP 1878		
125	I 40	WINKLE, FRED		20 NOV 1946	1868	MORDECHAI	GUSSIE
125	I 41	WINKLE, GUSSIE		29 JAN 1916	1867	ABRAHAM & MALKE	FRED
125	H161	WINKLE, JACOB		27 AUG 1958	1890		
125	M 86	WINKLE, LOUIS		17 SEP 1921	1869		
119	D47	WINKLER, GABRIEL		24 JUL 1991	30 DEC 1928		
125	O170	WINN, AARON B		6 FEB 1971	1892		ETTA
125	L128	WINN, BENJAMIN		31 MAY 1931	1859		
125	O171	WINN, ETTA	GOLDSTEIN	19 AUG 1964	1895	ISRAEL & SOPHIE	AARON
125	O105	WINN, SHIRLEY LEAH		10 AUG 1927	25 APR 1920	AARON B & ETTA (GOLDSTEIN)	

Cem	Row	Name	Maiden Name	DOD	DOB	Parents	Spouse
125		WINNICK, (CHILD)		20 JAN 1923	1923	ISAAC & ROSE	
101	D41	WINOKUR, GITEL		4 OCT 1960	1888		
101	E37	WINOKUR, MOSCHKO		24 MAY 1962	1882		MOSCHKO
249	G40	WINSTEN, EDWARD ABRAHAM MD		1983	1910		GITEL
751	J 9	WINTER, CLAIRE R		28 DEC 1984	24 MAY 1924		
102	M43	WINTON, BERL P		13 MAY 1972	1903		
102	AH216	WINTON, JULIUS	OF VILNA	26 JUL 1976	14 OCT 1904		
102	N43	WINTON, MURRAY		1 DEC 1991	1897		MYRA
102	N44	WINTON, MYRA	MOKIL	18 AUG 1939			MURRAY
125	J135	WINTZ, ALICE	STEIN	17 APR 1935	1885	JL & LM (AXELROD)	ABRAHAM
105	C14	WISE, ANNA		17 JAN 1955	1887		JACOB
102	AJ113	WISE, HERMAN H		17 OCT 1981	2 SEP 1907		
105	C15	WISE, JACOB		21 JAN 1965	1886		ANNA
111	12	WISE, WILLIAM	SPATZ	1981	1895		
377	N16	WISEMAN, ESTHER H		2 SEP 1963	16 AUG 1894		HYMAN
377	N15	WISEMAN, HYMAN		21 DEC 1966	10 AUG 1893		ESTHER
222	AL 5	WISEMAN, KATE	LEVIN	1966	1886		
447	V11	WITENBERG, GOLDIE		8 JUN 1963	1891		NATHAN
447	V12	WITENBERG, NATHAN		16 OCT 1965	1885		GOLDIE
446	A41	WITENBERG, STUART		1924	1921		
125		WITKIN, DAVID LAWRENCE		26 APR 1957	16 FEB 1957		-
371	M20	WITKIN, ESTHER		8 FEB 1964	20 MAR 1882		HENRY
125	N155	WITKIN, ESTHER	ANTHONE	8 JAN 1985	1887		FRANK
125	N154	WITKIN, FRANK J		13 MAR 1951	1884		ESTHER
125	K100	WITKIN, HARRY A		13 FEB 1972	1891		IDA
371	M19	WITKIN, HENRY		23 JAN 1963	22 OCT 1876		ESTHER
125	K101	WITKIN, IDA G		4 JUL 1982	1896		HARRY
125	N102	WITKIN, LENA		29 JUL 1927	1857		MORRIS
125	N186	WITKIN, MARTHA	ROSOFF	9 JUL 1966	1904		
125	N103	WITKIN, MORRIS		4 MAR 1942	1851	ABRAHAM & CHANA	LENA
125	J176	WITKIN, RITA	PRUZANSKY	4 MAR 1976	1921		
116	BV50	WITKOWER, ISRAEL		2 SEP 1968	27 MAR 1889		ROSE
116	BV49	WITKOWER, ROSE	ROSENBLATT	15 NOV 1982	24 SEP 1889		ISRAEL
102	T49	WITKOWER, SARAH		1928	1853		USHER
374	C 4	WITLIN, JEFFREY J		14 JUL 1942	7 JAN 1942		
249	L14	WITRYOL, SHANDEL	POKORT	1972	1932		
328	B15	WITTENBERG, ALFRED		26 AUG 1972			RHODA
328	B16	WITTENBERG, CHAIM MEYER		27 JUN 1962		ALFRED & RHODA	ALFRED
328	B17	WITTENBERG, RHODA		23 AUG 1972			ALFRED
371	AA16	WOHL, BETTY	BUDNICK	24 DEC 1973	11 SEP 1897		
125	L 93	WOHL, ELIAS		6 MAY 1926	1859		
330	D25	WOLF, EDITH		2 AUG 1960	29 SEP 1901		
391	R39	WOLF, HARRY		3 APR 1941	1871	JOSEPH	
105	C43	WOLF, IDA		4 APR 1969	1889		
751	O 3	WOLF, JENNIE	BAKER	10 AUG 1989	18 APR 1906		
125	Q153	WOLF, JENNIE	ABERBACK	6 FEB 1948	1886	ISRAEL & RACHEL	SAMUEL
751	O 4	WOLF, LOUIS		3 JUL 1964	14 JAN 1906		
391	K26	WOLF, LOUIS		24 APR 1919	1877	CHAIM	
330	C26	WOLF, MAX		6 APR 1952	29 APR 1897		
125	Q152	WOLF, SAMUEL		22 DEC 1944	1885	MYER & ROSE	JENNIE
372	D 1	WOLF, SUSAN		30 MAY 1986	7 FEB 1931		
391	R38	WOLF, ZELDA		16 FEB 1958	1880	SANDER	
370	B12	WOLFE, JOSEPH		16 FEB 1920		YISRAEL	
112	D17	WOLFF, EUGENE		8 FEB 1990	6 SEP 1896		HELENE
112	D18	WOLFF, HELENE		2 SEP 1975	22 APR 1903		EUGENE
376	D19	WOLFMAN, CLARA		17 SEP 1954	21 OCT 1896	EPHRIAM	MAX
376	D18	WOLFMAN, MAX		8 JUL 1958	11 MAY 1891	MOSHE YITZCHAK	CLARA
377	T 5	WOLFMAN, MEYER M		1992	1917	MICHAEL	
112	E26	WOLFSON, JOSEPH		3 JUN 1991	14 FEB 1917		
248	N73	WOLFSON, REBA MALKA		19 NOV 1931			
750	J22	WOLK, CLARENCE		10 AUG 1962	23 OCT 1904		ROSE
750	C26	WOLK, ROSE		5 NOV 1987			SAMUEL
750	J23	WOLK, ROSE S		6 AUG 1980	23 FEB 1908		CLARANCE
750	C25	WOLK, SAMUEL		18 FEB 1975			ROSE
330	G44	WOLLACK, EVA		16 JAN 1916	1862		
123		WOLLMAN, GUSSIE		1968	1896		SAMUEL

Cem	Row	Name	Maiden Name	DOD	DOB	Parents	Spouse
123		WOLLMAN, SAMUEL		1976	1893		GUSSIE
370	H33	WOLLOCK, JACOB		6 AUG 1913		REUBEN	
125	K 60	WOLOWITZ, ANNIE		2 MAR 1913			HIRSH
125	K 59	WOLOWITZ, HIRSH		22 NOV 1922			ANNIE
446	B34	WOLPERT, DAVID H		1978	1893		HATTIE
446	B35	WOLPERT, HATTIE M		1989	1897		DAVID
104	L37	WOLPOE, HARRY		25 SEP 1988	3 NOV 1909		
118	E10	WOLSHEN, SAMUEL		18 MAR 1974			
374	H42	WOOD, EUGENE J		12 NOV 1962	1896		LEONA
374	H43	WOOD, LEONA		9 NOV 1984	1905		EUGENE
392	D14	WOOL, DAVID		16 FEB 1963	1886	JUDAH LEV	JENNIE
392	D13	WOOL, JENNIE	RUTMAN	17 FEB 1968	1890	AKIBA	DAVID
370	S45	WOOLMAN, MORRIS		1945	1885		
106	A17	WORGAFTIK, ALEX		1979	1917		
102	BG27	WORTMAN, SZLAMA DAVID		10 FEB 1991	25 MAY 1904		
123		WRIGHT, OSCAR		24 MAY 1944	1921		
447	H26	WRUBEL, ANNIE		9 MAR 1991	1907		DAVID
446	A 9	WRUBEL, BENJAMIN		15 OCT 1932	1864		
446	A 8	WRUBEL, BERNARD		13 NOV 1940	1902	BENJAMIN	
447	H25	WRUBEL, DAVID A		16 SEP 1952	1903	MEYER & FREDA	ANNIE
447	W32	WRUBEL, DEBRA JOYCE		26 AUG 1957	1955		
447	S26	WRUBEL, FANNIE	BECKER	27 JAN 1956	1897		SAMUEL
447	H23	WRUBEL, FREDA	8 JAN 1952*	28 DEC 1952*	1880		MEYER
446	C11	WRUBEL, IDA	LERER	8 NOV 1930	1875		LOUIS
447	N16	WRUBEL, ISAAC		1 MAY 1937	1885		
447	Z10	WRUBEL, LEWIS A		17 MAR 1974	1920		
447	H22	WRUBEL, LILLIAN		7 JUN 1945	1912		MORRIS
446	B22	WRUBEL, LOUIS		1917	1868		IDA
447	H24	WRUBEL, MEYER S		23 JUL 1950	1875		FREDA
447	H21	WRUBEL, MORRIS H	4 JAN 1955*	25 DEC 1955*	1901	MEYER & FREDA	LILLIAN
447	S25	WRUBEL, SAMUEL H		14 FEB 1961	1896		FANNIE
102	Z198	WRUBEL, SANDRA D		20 JUL 1984	31 JUL 1932		
125	O 58	WURTZBERGER, CHARLES		5 DEC 1933	2 SEP 1925		
125	O 59	WURTZBERGER, CHARLES M		4 OCT 1924	31 DEC 1922		
125	A103	WURTZENBERG, OLGA V		15 JUN 1967			YENO
125	A102	WURTZENBERG, YENO		31 MAR 1968	1882		OLGA
102	AD164	WYNN, BETTY	ABRAHAMS	2 OCT 1964	4 NOV 1909		
102	AF22	WYNN, CELIA	GOULD	21 MAR 1968	1890		HARRY
102	AF21	WYNN, HARRY		17 MAR 1961	1888		CELIA
105	E26	WYNN, WILLIAM M		21 APR 1977			
377	T38	YAFFE, ELEANOR R		3 DEC 1989	17 FEB 1917	ARYEH LEV	
102	AH40	YAFFO, ANNE		25 JUL 1966		SAMUEL & SARAH	
123		YAFFO, MARCUS W	IN FRANCE	WWI			
102	AH41	YAFFO, SAMUEL BENJAMIN	HOMSK, RUSSIA	14 JUL 1967	16 MAR 1890	TOBIAS & SARAH (TELECHANSKY)	SARAH
102	AH42	YAFFO, SARAH RUTH	NEWMARK	5 JUL 1962			SAMUEL
119	A51	YALEN, DANIEL		2 OCT 1992			
119	A50	YALEN, SEYMOUR		13 NOV 1978			
103	C28	YALOW, HENRY		1 JUN 1983	1908		
392	G28	YAMPOLSKY, ABRAHAM		17 AUG 1928	15 MAY 1912	ISARAEL	
370	G15	YANAVOR, ESTHER GUSSIE		8 NOV 1936			
125	G157	YANKOWITZ, ABRAHAM		27 MAY 1971	1902		
125	T143	YANKOWITZ, GOLDIE		19 SEP 1937	1885	ABRAHAM & GITTLE	
125	O 78	YANKOWITZ, HARRY		18 OCT 1918	1916	SIGMOND	
102	U49	YANOWETZ, BEATRICE	RUBIN	1 SEP 1969	1911	GEORGE & FRANCES (BENNETT)	FRANK
102	G50	YANOWETZ, CELIA		12 JUL 1965		FRANCES	
102	U48	YANOWETZ, FRANK		30 MAY 1991		SAMUEL & ROSE	BEATRICE
102	G51	YANOWETZ, MAE		11 JUL 1964		FRANK & BEATRICE	
102	U46	YANOWETZ, ROSE R	RAPHAEL	1 AUG 1965	1886		SAMUEL
102	U47	YANOWETZ, SAMUEL		30 JUN 1955	12 JUL 1883	FRANCES	ROSE
371	M34	YANOWICH, LOUIS		25 MAY 1952	1884		
392	H25	YANOWSKY, MINNIE		7 DEC 1935	1872	MOSHE TZVI	
392	F21	YANOWSKY, MUNISH		13 APR 1931	1871	TZVI YEHUDA	
123		YANUSHEWETZ, LOUIS		22 FEB 1971	1899		
391	GL 6	YARDUSKY, JACOB		1907	1855	ZEV DAVID	
392	A 8	YAVNER, MAX E		23 OCT 1986	16 APR 1905		
116	BI117	YELLIN, MICHAEL P		13 AUG 1992	15 MAR 1950		

Cem	Row	Name	Maiden Name	DOD	DOB	Parents	Spouse
102	AE52	YESSNER, JACOB		25 MAY 1948	15 APR 1899		
116	BL24	YOLEN, ESTHER B		20 MAY 1988	10 FEB 1917		
123		YOLISH, MIRIAM	KATZ	16 OCT 1979	22 NOV 1906		SIMON
123		YOLISH, SIMON		1 MAY 1966	1893		MIRIAM
102	E 6	YORKER, MURRAY B		26 SEP 1985	26 MAY 1898		
102	E 8	YORKER, ROBIN LEWIS		6 DEC 1946	3 DEC 1946	MURRAY	
374	B21	YOSELEVSKY, ABRAHAM		12 NOV 1974	12 MAY 1901		ANNA
374	B22	YOSELEVSKY, ANNA		4 AUG 1972	4 JUL 1901		ABRAHAM
374	A26	YOSELEVSKY, BENJAMIN		9 SEP 1959	1882		ETHEL
374	A27	YOSELEVSKY, ETHEL		29 JAN 1949	1883		BENJAMIN
374	A23	YOSELEVSKY, MAX		30 JAN 1927	9 SEP 1902		
374	A25	YOSELEVSKY, MORRIS		24 MAR 1964	1875		ROSE
374	A24	YOSELEVSKY, ROSE		19 FEB 1962	1879		MORRIS
371	J38	YOSER, BETTY		1992	1902		HYMAN
371	J37	YOSER, HYMAN		1970	1896		BETTY
105	J 9	YOULOVSKY, BENJAMIN		24 DEC 1959	1883	ETTA LEAH	YETTA
105	J13	YOULOVSKY, ETTA LEA		21 OCT 1938	1863		
105	J 8	YOULOVSKY, YETTA	ITKIN	25 AUG 1969	15 JUL 1886	JACOB & SARAH	BENJAMIN
392	B47	YOUNG, CHARLES		1953	1886		
433	D22	YOUNG, JENNIE		5 OCT 1959	1883	BENJAMIN ELIEZER	
377	O10	YOUNG, WILLIAM		1949	1892		
123		YOUSMAN, PETER		15 MAY 1954	1906		
494	B14	YUDKIN, EDWARD LOUIS		1969	1896		
102	AB155	YUDOWITCH, ESTHER		1 SEP 1972	1 MAY 1895		MAX
102	AB156	YUDOWITCH, MAX		8 NOV 1975	4 JUL 1892		ESTHER
113	J24	YULES, MARSHA	KUTTEN	8 DEC 1958	SEP 1889		SAMUEL
113	J25	YULES, SAMUEL		5 JAN 1982	15 APR 1890		MARSHA
123		YUSH, DAVID E		4 JUL 1944	1917		
116	BH63	YUSH, LEONARD		18 APR 1988	24 DEC 1921		
119	C 3	YUSH, LILLIAN	GERE	14 APR 1991	15 SEP 1911		
377	T16	ZABARSKY, MARY		1973	1898		SAMUEL
377	T15	ZABARSKY, SAMUEL		1961	1894		MARY
370	N11	ZABIN, MARY		5 AUG 1968			WILLIAM
370	N12	ZABIN, WILLIAM		3 OCT 1974			MARY
125	M 25	ZABINSKY, ANNA		10 APR 1915	1873		
376	J 8	ZACHEM, JACOB		7 DEC 1973	1922	LIBA	
376	J 9	ZACHEM, RALPH		21 MAR 1985	1920	LIBA	
116	BI134	ZACHS, EDWARD		25 DEC 1975			
494	A13	ZACK, BESSIE RACHEL		23 OCT 1983	1899	MOSHE CHAIM	HARRY
494	A12	ZACK, HARRY JACOB		15 NOV 1981	1898	ABRAHAM	BESSIE
119	H36	ZACK, JEAN		11 FEB 1977	1929		
125	M134	ZACKIN, DORIS R		10 MAR 1969	21 MAR 1916		
125		ZACKIN, MIRIAM		15 MAY 1915	13 JAN 1914	WILLIAM & LEAH	
125	V178	ZAGER, SAMUEL W		9 NOV 1976	1904		
370	J23	ZAGER, SUSIE		1936	1866		
329	D 7	ZAGOR, CLARA		5 AUG 1973	1901		SAMUEL
329	D 8	ZAGOR, SAMUEL		9 JUL 1982	1901		CLARA
447	Q39	ZAGOREN, LOUIS S		29 JUL 1964	23 NOV 1890		MARIE
447	Q40	ZAGOREN, MARIE M		10 APR 1985	1 JUN 1897		LOUIS
447	AD37	ZAGOREN, MILTON M		22 FEB 1981	24 MAY 1910		
432		ZAGORSKI, LILLIE		5 JUL 1897			
116	AX18	ZAIDMAN, MORRIS		5 FEB 1976	1905		
125	D114	ZAKIN, SYLVIA	SICKLICK	25 SEP 1952	3 DEC 1913		
125		ZAKOWITZ, M		1 NOV 1926	AUG 1926		
374	J51	ZALFAS, GUSSIE		21 NOV 1984	3 MAR 1908		
370	R28	ZALINGER, PEARL		1943	1862		SIMON
370	R29	ZALINGER, SIMON		1949	1855		PEARL
391	G30	ZAMKOW, FRANK		14 JAN 1928	1910	NAFTALI ARI	
391	E20	ZAMKOW, HARRY		30 SEP 1967	1882	ELIEZER	LENA
391	E19	ZAMKOW, LENA		17 NOV 1970	1888	MOSHE	HARRY
102	K53	ZARCHEN, LOUIS H		2 JUN 1958	1903	MAX & MYRTLE (LEVANT)	MYRTICE
102	K52	ZARCHEN, MYRTICE H	KURLANSKY	18 JUL 1987	1909		LOUIS
104	H 4	ZARETSKY, HAROLD S		8 JAN 1978	9 APR 1915		
330	G34	ZASLOVSKY, BERTHA		3 NOV 1902			
391	J37	ZASLOW, ANNIE	OWAROFF	19 OCT 1963	1885	ELCHANA	LEON
392	I31	ZASLOW, MORRIS		22 APR 1948	1883	YONAH	

Cem	Row	Name	Maiden Name	DOD	DOB	Parents	Spouse
392	A46	ZASLOW, SAMUEL		1982	1897		
391	ZE55	ZAUSMER, ANNETTE		25 APR 1969	30 JAN 1898	DAVID	
433	D 4	ZAVODNICK, BARNET		16 AUG 1962	12 JUN 1905		
433	G 9	ZAVONICK, MAX		19 DEC 1952	1873	ZEV WOLF	ROSE
433	G 8	ZAVONICK, ROSE		8 FEB 1951	1879	JACOB	MAX
125	T141	ZEIDMAN, LOUIS		16 DEC 1942	1857		SARAH
125	T140	ZEIDMAN, SARAH D		16 MAY 1937	1853	YAKOV MEYER & BASYA	LOUIS
750	D26	ZEIMAN, ESTHER		26 DEC 1971			SOLL
750	D27	ZEIMAN, SOLL		25 APR 1973			ESTHER
125	Q200	ZELDES, BEATRICE	BOWMAN	22 JUN 1962	1933		
125	J174	ZELDES, GERTRUDE	FALK	3 NOV 1974	1898		LOUIS
125	G160	ZELDES, HARRY		1986	1919		
125	J175	ZELDES, LOUIS		27 MAR 1981	1892		GITEL
121	J11	ZELDIS, GEORGE		22 FEB 1992	16 AUG 1924		
103	D10	ZELDNER, CLARA		27 APR 1984	12 AUG 1895		
391	G21	ZELIGSON, ANNIE		6 DEC 1919	1889	ISAAC MEYER	HYMAN
391	GK 2	ZELIGSON, HYMAN		1 DEC 1948	1890	JOEL	ANNIE
370	B37	ZELINESKY, LENA		29 MAR 1973	1895		SAMUEL
371	E 3	ZELINSKY, FREIDA		1985	1919		
370	A54	ZELINSKY, GITEL		30 JAN 1924			SAMUEL
370	B36	ZELINSKY, SAMUEL V		3 SEP 1950	1891		LENA, GITE
433	I 6	ZELVIN, DORA		3 DEC 1935	1874	DAVID	LOUIS
433	D29	ZELVIN, GOLDIE B		18 AUG 1990	24 SEP 1908	JOSHUA	MORRIS
433	I 7	ZELVIN, LOUIS		18 AUG 1932	1889	DOV BEAR	DORA
433	D28	ZELVIN, MORRIS D		5 OCT 1976	16 APR 1913	ELEASER	GOLDIE
371	A14	ZELVIN, SAMUEL A		1978	1927		
248	I66	ZENCHOFF, ABRAHAM		23 SEP 1915			ROSE
249	B 5	ZENCHOFF, CARL		23 APR 1956	1890		PAULINE
249	B 6	ZENCHOFF, PAULINE		2 MAR 1987	1892		CARL
248	M72	ZENCHOFF, ROSE D		10 JUL 1940	1862		ABRAHAM
248	N72	ZENOVITZ, MIRIAM		26 JAN 1921	1913	VICTOR	
248	K72	ZENOWITZ, VICTOR		11 SEP 1937	1870		
102	AH215	ZERWITZ, KATHERINE		28 NOV 1985	8 JUN 1891		
433	G27	ZETLIN, ANNA		3 OCT 1954	1881		WOLF
433	G26	ZETLIN, WOLF		2 JUN 1948	1878		ANNA
125	H 60	ZEVIN, ABRAHAM		10 NOV 1926	1872		CELIA
125	H 59	ZEVIN, CELIA		5 OCT 1949	1883		ABRAHAM
125	H 32	ZEVIN, FANNIE		5 OCT 1954	15 APR 1877		HARRY
125	H 33'	ZEVIN, HARRY		31 JAN 1952	27 DEC 1864		FANNIE
125	G 32	ZEVIN, ISRAEL		4 OCT 1990	19 JAN 1914	HARRY & FANNIE	
125	H 31	ZEVIN, LIZZIE		2 SEP 1947	1882	ISRAEL	
125	H 37	ZEVIN, LOUIS		18 APR 1918	16 FEB 1865		
125	H 34	ZEVIN, NATHANIEL		18 FEB 1968	1912	HARRY & FANNIE	
328	B22	ZHEUTLIN, BEREL		5 APR 1981	1911		
371	J42	ZIEF, JENNIE		1951	1869		
370	A25	ZIEF, LOUIS		30 JAN 1912	1896		
370	C14	ZIEF, MOSES HYMAN		1 SEP 1934			
114	D14	ZIEGLER, ANDREW M		13 MAR 1992	20 APR 1962		
371	N18	ZIEGLER, LENA					MORDECHAI
371	N17	ZIEGLER, MORDECHAI E		23 OCT 1986	15 OCT 1889		LENA
103	A29	ZIEKY, ANNA	MARKMAN	2 MAY 1968	1900		MAX
116	BI140	ZIEKY, HARRY C		11 MAY 1988	29 MAR 1905		NELLIE
103	A28	ZIEKY, MAX		13 DEC 1963	1890	SAMUEL & FREDA	ANNA
116	BI139	ZIEKY, NELLIE	SHUMAN	21 JUL 1971	10 SEP 1907		HARRY
119	D14	ZIEKY, PAUL LESTER		27 SEP 1979	5 MAY 1919		
373	D 4	ZIERLER, DOROTHY		6 APR 1974	12 SEP 1915		JACK
374	F40	ZIERLER, FREDA		5 JAN 1946	1891		HYMAN
373	D 3	ZIERLER, HAROLD GEORGE		8 FEB 1953	24 JAN 1938	JACK & DOROTHY	
374	F41	ZIERLER, HYMAN		14 OCT 1972	1886		FREDA
373	D 5	ZIERLER, JACK		NDD	8 NOV 1913		DOROTHY
374	F36	ZIERLER, LOUIS		1980	1912		
371	K31	ZIERLER, MEYER		29 JUL 1965	14 NOV 1919	MORDECHAI & LENA	SHIRLEY
371	K32	ZIERLER, SHIRLEY		20 MAR 1969	28 AUG 1921		MEYER
374	F 1	ZIERLER, TILLIE		10 OCT 1918	1888		
116	BL31	ZIETZ, LEON		25 FEB 1969	1922		
125	O148	ZIGMAN, ANNA	GOLD	12 JAN 1982	1893		PHILIP

Cem	Row	Name	Maiden Name	DOD	DOB	Parents	Spouse
125	O147	ZIGMAN, PHILIP		18 MAY 1969	1889		ANNA
101	A 6	ZIMMERMAN, ABRAHAM		7 JAN 1922	1826		
102	K 5	ZIMMERMAN, BARBARA P		29 NOV 1945	1922		
102	J 5	ZIMMERMAN, EVA	GOLDSTEIN	31 AUG 1974	25 DEC 1895		MAURICE
125	U158	ZIMMERMAN, HANNA	WISENHOLTZ	4 NOV 1979	1900		ISIDORE
101	A 7	ZIMMERMAN, HARRY		18 AUG 1957	1875		IDA
447	W 5	ZIMMERMAN, HERBERT I		1968	1912		
101	A 8	ZIMMERMAN, IDA		15 OCT 1951	1869		HARRY
116	U15	ZIMMERMAN, IRVING		15 MAY 1977	3 SEP 1913		SYLVIA
125	U157	ZIMMERMAN, ISADORE		13 JUL 1982	1891		HANNAH
370	G43	ZIMMERMAN, JULIUS		23 AUG 1917			
493	G 5	ZIMMERMAN, LEO M		1983	1898		
374	B 1	ZIMMERMAN, LOUIS		13 JAN 1938			ROSE
102	J 4	ZIMMERMAN, MAURICE J		1975	1895		EVA
103	B29	ZIMMERMAN, MIRIAM		1986	1924		GERALD
101	A18	ZIMMERMAN, MOSES		17 JUN 1919	1844		
374	B 2	ZIMMERMAN, ROSE		16 OCT 1937			LOUIS
101	E17	ZIMMERMAN, ROSE	KATZ	17 AUG 1978	1895		
102	K 6	ZIMMERMAN, SARAH F		3 JUN 1946	1887	SARAH	
101	J23	ZIMMERMAN, SOPHIE		1 NOV 1940	1868		
116	U16	ZIMMERMAN, SYLVIA		23 FEB 1989	3 NOV 1914		IRVING
493	G 3	ZIMMERMAN, TOBY F		1992	1925		
101	J11	ZIMMERMAN, TRENNE		14 OCT 1935			
102	AI162	ZINKERMAN, FRANK		17 NOV 1972	16 MAR 1912		
125	O 88	ZINMAN, BASSE		29 APR 1919	30 MAY 1863		
125	O172	ZINMAN, GUSSIE		22 MAY 1965	1892		HARRY
125	O173	ZINMAN, HARRY		3 JAN 1964	1890		GUSSIE
125	D 21	ZINMAN, HYMAN A		5 DEC 1936	1880	SIMON DAVID & BASHE	
125	O133	ZINMAN, ISRAEL		29 MAR 1973	22 APR 1913		
125	M121	ZINMAN, MAIME	FEIN	31 MAR 1929	1881	ELI	
125	M122	ZINMAN, MYER		24 DEC 1942	1877		REBECCA
125	D 20	ZINMAN, REBECCA	WITKIN	16 NOV 1967	1885		MYER
125	ZA170	ZINMAN, SAMUEL L		17 MAY 1989	22 OCT 1923		
102	AG27	ZIONTS, ABRAHAM P		6 APR 1957	5 MAY 1895	DAVID & CLARA	GERTRUDE
102	AG28	ZIONTS, GERTRUDE G	GARR	20 JAN 1987	1897		ABRAHAM
222	AG 7	ZIPKIN, JENNIE		12 MAR 1914	1865		
222	AC12	ZIPKIN, SAMUEL		24 DEC 1940	1857		
104	K30	ZIPLOW, RAYMOND		20 JUN 1988	15 FEB 1902		
102	AB200'	ZISKIN, LOUIS		1979	1900		
102	J 2	ZITSER, ABRAHAM A		8 DEC 1951	30 DEC 1883	SAMUEL & RHODA (ABRAMSON)	EDITH
102	J 1	ZITSER, EDITH	DWORKIN	1945	1885		ABRAHAM
102	K56	ZITSER, HARRY		26 FEB 1975	24 DEC 1908	ABRAHAM & EDITH (DWORKIN)	
102	K54	ZITSER, ROBERT M		11 APR 1958	15 JUN 1932	HARRY	
391	ZF68	ZIVYAK, BESSIE		28 NOV 1988	3 SEP 1903	ELIYAHU	
102	A74	ZLOCHIVER, BERTHA P		23 AUG 1942	1892		HARRY
121	S19	ZLOCHIVER, EVELYN H		23 MAY 1977	18 APR 1921		
102	A73	ZLOCHIVER, HARRY L		25 AUG 1958	1885		BERTHA
121	S18	ZLOCHIVER, ISAAC M		23 AUG 1983	16 FEB 1912		
104	J18	ZLOCHIVER, TILLIE ARONSON	SCHECTMAN	20 SEP 1984	15 APR 1896		
447	I37	ZLOKOWER, ABRAHAM		23 JUL 1950	1879		ROSE
447	I36	ZLOKOWER, ROSE LEAH		11 MAR 1930	1885		ABRAHAM
119	E12	ZLOTNICK, MARION S		13 FEB 1983	1909		
119	E11	ZLOTNICK, SIDNEY B		4 NOV 1975	1907		
370	A44	ZOLA, ROSALIND	MANDEL	11 NOV 1980	9 NOV 1909		
249	O 6	ZOLLER, DORA	HELLER	1984	1899		
391	G11	ZOZLIN, ROSE		12 FEB 1930	15 AUG 1895	NACHEM	
374	A51	ZUBOV, BENJAMIN		9 DEC 1931	1892		
105	M24	ZUBROW, BESSIE		10 MAR 1971	1878		HARRY
105	M25	ZUBROW, HARRY		25 MAR 1962	1877		BESSIE
121	T18	ZUCH, LOUIS		28 SEP 1969	20 SEP 1888		
121	T19	ZUCH, RICHARD		3 OCT 1990	21 FEB 1936	LOUIS & RUTH	
121	T17	ZUCH, RUTH		6 AUG 1967	6 MAY 1909		
125		ZUCKER, (BABY)		11 APR 1918	1918	ABRAHAM	
125	K111	ZUCKER, ABRAHAM		10 NOV 1939	1878	PESACH & YEHUDIS	FREIDA
125	H 26	ZUCKER, ABRAHAM		13 SEP 1928	1875		TILLIE
125	E 81	ZUCKER, BENJAMIN		25 OCT 1924	1877		

Cem	Row	Name	Maiden Name	DOD	DOB	Parents	Spouse
248	B50	ZUCKER, DORA		17 NOV 1971	15 OCT 1898		SAMUEL
125	G 27	ZUCKER, EVELYN		13 JUL 1988	18 JUL 1905	MAX & PAULINE	
125	K112	ZUCKER, FREIDA		29 JUN 1934	6 JUL 1875		ABRAHAM
125	K134	ZUCKER, GUSSIE		22 DEC 1936	1878		
112	A36	ZUCKER, JOHN		27 APR 1992			
125	G 26	ZUCKER, MAX		20 AUG 1951	17 MAY 1877		PAULINE
125	G 25	ZUCKER, PAULINE		6 OCT 1958	24 MAR 1884	YAKOV	MAX
248	H72	ZUCKER, ROSE		29 SEP 1963	1877		
248	B49	ZUCKER, SAMUEL		30 JAN 1959	5 MAR 1895		DORA
125	W191	ZUCKER, SIDNEY		17 FEB 1980	1902		
116	M 6	ZUCKER, STANLEY A		4 MAR 1988	28 SEP 1934		
125	H 27	ZUCKER, TILLIE		23 SEP 1948	1872	LIPPA	ABRAHAM
371	AK 5	ZUCKERBRAUN, HENRIETTA		21 AUG 1986	24 DEC 1892		ISAAC
371	AK 6	ZUCKERBRAUN, ISAAC		8 OCT 1972	22 DEC 1888		HENRIETTA
370	J28	ZUCKERMAN, ANNA G		7 JUN 1938	24 OCT 1891		
377	Q13	ZUCKERMAN, BEATRICE IRENE		23 APR 1987	7 NOV 1905		MURRAY
102	AH169	ZUCKERMAN, IRVING I		13 AUG 1968	10 JAN 1922		
248	K73	ZUCKERMAN, MORRIS		7 FEB 1943	1873		
377	O19	ZUCKERMAN, MURRAY JOSEPH		11 APR 1948	28 MAR 1889		BEATRICE
116	BX70	ZUKERMAN, MINNIE		2 SEP 1958	1873		
329	A39	ZUPNIK, RUTH G		30 AUG 1982	2 OCT 1910		
370	Q22	ZURLIN, JENNIE		1991	1908		WILLIAM
370	Q23	ZURLIN, WILLIAM		1993	1908		JENNIE
377	S44	ZUSMAN, FLORENCE G		1982	1923		
377	Z53	ZUTLOWSKY, LOREN		31 AUG 1993	25 FEB 1955	KOPEL BER	
125	J 95	ZWELLING, HARRY Z		5 AUG 1987	2 JUN 1906		
125		ZWENGA, (BABY)		14 MAY 1929	FEB 1929	SAM & REBECCA	
121	O 1	ZWERDLING, FRITZI		13 JAN 1985	26 NOV 1910		
102	J30	ZWICKER, ABRAHAM H		6 JAN 1946	27 NOV 1894	SAMUEL & ANNA (AVIS)	MINNIE
102	J31	ZWICKER, GEORGE S SGT		2 SEP 1944	30 JAN 1924	ABRAHAM & MINNIE	
102	J29	ZWICKER, MINNIE	SOLOMON	17 DEC 1988	30 NOV 1893		ABRAHAM
370	P62	ZWIEG, DAVID		1960			
101	J14	____,		22 FEB 1919	1893		
101	J16	____,		26 DEC 1919	1850		
370	A42	____, (BABY)					
377	P 4	____, (BABY)		1 NOV 1965			
370	E 7	____, (GIRL)				YITZCHAK	
374	A31	____, (GIRL)					
101	K36	____, (GIRL)		31 JAN 1937			
370	B29	____, (SON)				MEYER	
370	D10	____, AARON				DAVID	
432		____, ADELE		27 JUN 1895		ISAR	
101	L13	____, BITULAH DEVORAH		8 DEC 1933		CHAIM	
374	C 2	____, CELIA		3 MAY 1924			
375	E45	____, CHAIM AARON		30 DEC 1894		JOSEPH	
370	C23	____, CHANA		7 JUN 1894		YISRAEL MEYER	
391	R30	____, CHANA BAYLA		1915			
248	H59	____, CHAYA					
391	L35	____, DEBORAH		12 NOV 1900	5 OCT 1891	SHMARYAHU	
101	L27	____, DEBRA				BENJAMIN	
101	A33	____, EFFRAIM RABBI		21 MAR 1940			
125	K 37	____, ELIZABETH		1914			MEYER
370	E 5	____, ESTHER				ABRAHAM	
370	H10	____, ETTA		23 FEB 1894		ABBA	
370	H22	____, FAIGA		27 APR 1906		YISRAEL MEYER	
330	G27	____, FRUME LEAH		21 APR 1928		SHLOMO SHMUEL	
446	C45	____, HAYA LEAH				YECHESKEL	
370	L33	____, HILLEL					
101	M23	____, ITAH		28 JUL 1932		CHAIM	
392	J 1	____, JACOB (BABY)					
370	I31	____, JACOB BENJAMIN		9 SEP 1932		MOSHE SHMARYAHU	MEYER
370	H12	____, JENNIE		14 APR 1922		YEHOSHUA	
446	C43	____, JOSEPH		2 JUN 1904	1898	DAVID	
391	J38	____, JOSEPH		8 AUG 1913		SHMARYAHU CHAIM	
370	A26	____, JUDAH		21 NOV 1931		JOSEPH	
370	H20	____, MALCAH		6 JUL 1904		NAFTALI SHIFRA	

Cem	Row	Name	Maiden Name	DOD	DOB	Parents	Spouse
370	Y 6	____, MALKA		23 MAY 1908		AKIVA	
370	E 6	____, MICHAEL		8 OCT 1918		JACOB REUBEN	
370	A24	____, MORDECHAI LEV		15 JUL 1914		TZVI	
370	L30	____, PEARL		13 JUN 1918			
370	C30	____, PINCAS		10 JAN 1899	20 DEC 1898		
370	B30	____, RACHEL		8 AUG 1914		ELIYAHU BER	
125	K 42	____, RACHEL LEAH		8 JAN 1904		MOSHE	
447	W33	____, RISKA		5 NOV 1945	2 APR 1945	SHIMON JOSEPH	
101	M16	____, RIVKAH		5 MAY 1929		MOSHE	
370	C29	____, SAMPSON		17 SEP 1900	1896		
101	K38	____, SHIRLEY EVELYN		27 JUN 1913	4 FEB		
392	J31	____, SIVA BROCHA		11 FEB 1923		GABREAL YEHUDA	
751	K26	____, SVIYA RACHEL		3 MAY 1926		BENJAMIN	
330	G54	____, TOVYA		1 FEB 1929		YAKOV	
391	M31	____, TZVI HIRSH		1920	1840	SAMUEL	
751	E40	____, ZVIYA		11 JUN 1921		ARI LEV	

CEM NUM	CEMETERY NAME	DATE COMPLETED	EARLIEST GRAVE	NUMBER OF GRAVES	TOWN	COUNTY/ STATE
3	OLD NORTH CEMETERY	6/92	1909	25	HARTFORD	HARTFORD
7	BETH ISRAEL	8/92	1852	1614	HARTFORD	HARTFORD
14	CHEVRY LOMDAY MESHNAYES	12/91	1921	398	HARTFORD	HARTFORD
15	AGUDAS ACHIM	5/92	1924	410	HARTFORD	HARTFORD
16	HEBREW MERCHANTS PROTECTIVE	12/91	1923	289	HARTFORD	HARTFORD
17	AARON ASSOCIATION	12/91	1929	97	HARTFORD	HARTFORD
18	FIRST LUDMIR BENEVOLENT	5/92	1926	175	HARTFORD	HARTFORD
19	HOPE OF ZION	4/92	1924	64	HARTFORD	HARTFORD
20	ATERES ISRAEL	4/92	1923	193	HARTFORD	HARTFORD
21	WORKMEN'S CIRCLE NO 326	4/92	1923	92	HARTFORD	HARTFORD
22	FARBAND LABOR ZIONISTS	4/92	1927	196	HARTFORD	HARTFORD
23	BESS ISRAEL	4/92	1929	289	HARTFORD	HARTFORD
24	JOHN HAY MEMORIAL PARK	5/92	1949	446	HARTFORD	HARTFORD
25	TEFERES ISRAEL	4/92	1942	24	HARTFORD	HARTFORD
26	BRAHILOVER BENEVELENT	1/92	1931	125	HARTFORD	HARTFORD
27	BETH EL	5/92	1933	154	HARTFORD	HARTFORD
28	HTFD MUTUAL/WORKERS CIRCLE 15	1/92	1938	572	HARTFORD	HARTFORD
29	JEWISH WAR VETS/B'NAI YISRAEL	5/92	194	129	HARTFORD	HARTFORD
30	CAPITAL CITY LODGE	6/92	1895	418	HARTFORD	HARTFORD
31	HTFD WORKINGMENS SICK BENEFIT	6/92	1900	349	HARTFORD	HARTFORD
32	MOSES MONTIFNER LODGE	6/92	1898	369	HARTFORD	HARTFORD
33	HARTFORD CITY LODGE	7/92	1902	370	HARTFORD	HARTFORD
34	DREYFUS LODGE	6/92	1902	136	HARTFORD	HARTFORD
35	AGUDAS ACHIM	7/92	1890	290	HARTFORD	HARTFORD
36	HTFD LDGE #108 SONS OF BENJ	7/92	1901	134	HARTFORD	HARTFORD
37	ADAS ISRAEL	7/92	1867	639	HARTFORD	HARTFORD
38	SHAREE TORAH	7/92	1896	217	HARTFORD	HARTFORD
39	ROTHCHILDS PLOT	7/92	1878	17	HARTFORD	HARTFORD
40	HTFD HEBREW BENEFIT ASSOC	7/92	1906	106	HARTFORD	HARTFORD
41	WORKERS CIRCLE #610	6/92	1921	127	HARTFORD	HARTFORD
42	WORKMENS CIRCLE #936	6/92	1915	100	HARTFORD	HARTFORD
43	WORKMENS CIRCLE #184	6/92	1914	200	HARTFORD	HARTFORD
44	BETH MIDRASH HAGADOL	6/92	1915	262	HARTFORD	HARTFORD
45	ATERES ISRAEL (HTFD MUTUAL)	6/92	1920	124	HARTFORD	HARTFORD
46	ATERES ISRAEL (HTFD PEDDLERS)	6/92	1912	236	HARTFORD	HARTFORD
47	HTFD FREE BURIAL ASSOCIATION	6/92	1913	328	HARTFORD	HARTFORD
48	AUSTRIAN HEBREW CONGREGATION	6/92	1909	276	HARTFORD	HARTFORD
49	ALL JEWS	6/92	1906	224	HARTFORD	HARTFORD
54	YOUNG FRIENDS PROGRESSIVE	4/92	1908	106	HARTFORD	HARTFORD
55	JONATHAN WELFARE LODGE	5/92	1936	381	HARTFORD	HARTFORD
57	WOLKOWYSKER CEM ASSOCIATION	5/92	1937	203	HARTFORD	HARTFORD
58	ALBANY JEWISH COMM	4/92	1900	248	HARTFORD	HARTFORD
59	HTFD SICK BENEFIT ASSOCIATION	5/92	1948	63	HARTFORD	HARTFORD
60	YOUNG LUDMIR BENEVELENT	2/92	1935	90	HARTFORD	HARTFORD
61	YOUNG ISRAEL	4/92	1925	33	HARTFORD	HARTFORD
62	BETH MIDRASH HAGADOL	4/92	1957	115	HARTFORD	HARTFORD
63	ADOS ISRAEL	5/92	1945	325	HARTFORD	HARTFORD
64	TIKVOH CHADOSHAH	5/92	1944	167	HARTFORD	HARTFORD
65	SHARAI TORAH	5/92	1940	103	HARTFORD	HARTFORD
66	HARTFORD CITY LODGE	6/92	1943	169	HARTFORD	HARTFORD
101	TEFERES ISRAEL	11/92	1900	377	WEST HARTFORD	HARTFORD
102	EMANUEL	10/92	1920	1830	WETHERSFIELD	HARTFORD
103	UNITED SYNAGOGUES	9/92	1928	76	WETHERSFIELD	HARTFORD
104	BETH DAVID	9/92	1951	242	WETHERSFIELD	HARTFORD
105	PIATER VEREIN	9/92	1935	318	WETHERSFIELD	HARTFORD
106	BETH TEFILAH/B'NAI SHALOM	9/92	1971	58	WETHERSFIELD	HARTFORD
107	TEMPLE BETH TORAH	9/92	1972	57	WETHERSFIELD	HARTFORD
108	CUTLER FAMILY PLOT	11/92	1942	36	WEST HARTFORD	HARTFORD
109	KOENIG FAMILY PLOT	11/92	1949	8	WEST HARTFORD	HARTFORD
110	BETH JACOB	11/92	1922	157	WEST HARTFORD	HARTFORD
111	FAIRVIEW CEMETERY (MIXED)	11/92	1934	33	WEST HARTFORD	HARTFORD
112	BETH AHM	11/92	1968	93	WINDSOR	HARTFORD
113	BETH SHALOM	9/92	1954	177	MANCHESTER	HARTFORD
114	TEMPLE SINAI	11/92	1980	56	NEWINGTON	HARTFORD
115	BETH ISRAEL	10/92	1987	25	AVON	HARTFORD
116	BETH EL	5/93	1958	354	AVON	HARTFORD

CEM NUM	CEMETERY NAME	DATE COMPLETED	EARLIEST GRAVE	NUMBER OF GRAVES	TOWN	COUNTY/ STATE
117	FARMINGTON VALLEY	5/93	1983	24	AVON	HARTFORD
118	BETH ISRAEL	7/94	1954	34	BRISTOL	HARTFORD
119	HARTFORD MUTUAL	4/93	1973	277	EAST GRANBY	HARTFORD
120	TEFERES ISRAEL	3/93	1989	6	EAST GRANBY	HARTFORD
121	BETH HILLEL	3/93	1962	240	EAST GRANBY	HARTFORD
123	VETERANS CEMETERY (MIXED)	5/94	1938	120	WINDSOR	HARTFORD
125	BETH ALOM	6/94	1897	2051	NEW BRITAIN	HARTFORD
126	BETH MISHKIN	1985	1891	12	NEW BRITAIN	HARTFORD
127	BETH ALOM	1/93	1974	39	SOUTH WINDSOR	HARTFORD
222	KNESSETH ISRAEL	3/93	1910	465	ELLINGTON	TOLLAND
248	SONS OF ISRAEL	5/93	1901	323	MANSFIELD	TOLLAND
249	AGUDAS ACHICH	5/93	1937	134	MANSFIELD	TOLLAND
328	CONGREGATION OF LEBANON	5/93	1957	35	COLCHESTER	NEW LONDON
329	HEBREW AID	5/93	1914	160	COLCHESTER	NEW LONDON
330	AHAVAS ACHI	5/93	1902	511	COLCHESTER	NEW LONDON
331	OLD CEMETERY	5/93	1893	21	COLCHESTER	NEW LONDON
370	NORWICH HEBREW BENEFIT	7/94	1879	884	PRESTON	NEW LONDON
371	BROTHERS OF JOSEPH	9/93	1932	539	PRESTON	NEW LONDON
372	FIRST HEBREW BENEFIT	7/94	1870	194	PRESTON	NEW LONDON
373	NORWICH BURIAL SOCIETY	7/94	1927	65	NORWICH	NEW LONDON
374	BROTHERS OF JOSEPH	7/94	1913	299	NORWICH	NEW LONDON
375	NEW LONDON SICK BENEFIT	7/94	1893	24	MONTVILLE	NEW LONDON
376	HEBREW SOCIETY	7/94	1921	67	MONTVILLE	NEW LONDON
377	CONGREGATION BETH EL	7/94	1910	474	GROTON	NEW LONDON
391	AHAVATH CHESED	5/95	1893	814	WATERFORD	NEW LONDON
392	OHAVE SHALOM	10/94	1909	376	WATERFORD	NEW LONDON
395	CEDAR GROVE (JEWISH SECTION)	10/94	1882	22	NEW LONDON	NEW LONDON
432	PORTLAND JEWISH	3/93	1895	9	PORTLAND	MIDDLESEX
433	EAST HADDAM	7/94	1923	173	MOODUS	MIDDLESEX
446	INDIAN HILL (JEWISH SECTION)	5/93	1881	174	MIDDLETOWN	MIDDLESEX
447	AHAVAS ACHIM	5/93	1878	559	MIDDLETOWN	MIDDLESEX
493	BEAVERBROOK (JEWISH SECTION)	8/94	1978	34	CLINTON	MIDDLESEX
494	CONGREGATION BETH SHALOM	11/94	1952	41	DEEP RIVER	MIDDLESEX
500	JEWISH PEOPLES	12/94	1944	89	EAST HAVEN	NEW HAVEN
501	YOUNG ISRAEL OF NEW HAVEN	6/94	1963	48	EAST HAVEN	NEW HAVEN
502	WARSHAVER	6/94	1960	99	EAST HAVEN	NEW HAVEN
503	VILNER MEMORIAL	12/94	1963	43	EAST HAVEN	NEW HAVEN
504	SHEVET ACHIM	12/94	1860	952	EAST HAVEN	NEW HAVEN
505	BIKOR CHOLIM	7/94	1879	595	EAST HAVEN	NEW HAVEN
506	HEBREW FREE BURIAL	7/94	1864	617	EAST HAVEN	NEW HAVEN
507	INDEP RAMBAM LODGE	9/94	1921	275	EAST HAVEN	NEW HAVEN
508	NEW HAVEN LODGE	9/94	1924	215	EAST HAVEN	NEW HAVEN
509	BETH MIDRASH HAGADOL	12/94	1888	482	EAST HAVEN	NEW HAVEN
510	B'NAI SHALOM	7/94	1856	523	HAMDEN	NEW HAVEN
511	B'NAI ISRAEL	5/95	1848	1152	HAMDEN	NEW HAVEN
512	WALLINGFORD	7/94	1915	197	WALLINGFORD	NEW HAVEN
534	MERIDEN HEBREW	12/96	1882	880	MERIDEN	NEW HAVEN
538	MALCHE TZEDEK	7/93	1881	225	WATERBURY	NEW HAVEN
539	WORKERS CIRCLE	7/93	1906	426	WATERBURY	NEW HAVEN
540	CONGREGATION SHARAI ISRAEL	4/94	1914	283	WATERBURY	NEW HAVEN
541	FARBAND	9/93	1927	53	WATERBURY	NEW HAVEN
542	BRASS CITY	9/93	1901	436	WATERBURY	NEW HAVEN
543	HEBREW BENEFIT ASSOCIATION	9/93	1860	845	WATERBURY	NEW HAVEN
544	STAR LODGE	9/93	1877	357	WATERBURY	NEW HAVEN
545	BETH EL	9/93	1951	94	WATERBURY	NEW HAVEN
550	MISHKAN ISRAEL	2/97	1849	2231	NEW HAVEN	NEW HAVEN
551	B'NAI JACOB	2/97	1888	1281	NEW HAVEN	NEW HAVEN
552	AHAVAS ACHIM	6/96	1920	208	NEW HAVEN	NEW HAVEN
554	HERZEL	6/96	1900	415	NEW HAVEN	NEW HAVEN
555	CONGREGATION BETH ISRAEL	6/96	1919	299	NEW HAVEN	NEW HAVEN
556	INDEPENDENT WILNER	6/96	1921	288	NEW HAVEN	NEW HAVEN
557	WASHAVER RELIEF	3/96	1920	286	NEW HAVEN	NEW HAVEN
558	INDEPENDENT ADAS ISRAEL	5/96	1896	592	NEW HAVEN	NEW HAVEN
559	MOUNT SINAI	1/97	1929	1836	NEW HAVEN	NEW HAVEN
560	UNITED INDEPENDENT	7/96	1922	503	NEW HAVEN	NEW HAVEN
580	ORSHALOM	7/93	1925	92	WEST HAVEN	NEW HAVEN

CEM NUM	CEMETERY NAME	DATE COMPLETED	EARLIEST GRAVE	NUMBER OF GRAVES	TOWN	COUNTY/ STATE
581	WORKERS CIRCLE	5/95	1896	495	WEST HAVEN	NEW HAVEN
582	CONGREGATION SHARAI TORAH	7/95	1899	185	WEST HAVEN	NEW HAVEN
583	CONGREGATION SINAI	7/95	1934	256	WEST HAVEN	NEW HAVEN
584	B'NAI JESHRUN	7/95	1901	112	WEST HAVEN	NEW HAVEN
585	KESSER ISRAEL	7/95	1896	288	WEST HAVEN	NEW HAVEN
586	BETH EL	7/95	1898	715	ORANGE	NEW HAVEN
591	INDEPENDENT LODGE I	10/94	1945	204	NEW HAVEN	NEW HAVEN
592	INDEPENDENT LODGE II	6/95	1925	407	NEW HAVEN	NEW HAVEN
593	INDEPENDENT LODGE III	12/94	1879	532	NEW HAVEN	NEW HAVEN
594	INDEPENDENT LODGE IV	6/96	1899	337	NEW HAVEN	NEW HAVEN
595	BEAVERBROOK (JEWISH SECTION)	7/96	1926	334	NEW HAVEN	NEW HAVEN
596	BETH JACOB	6/97	1936	1066	NEW HAVEN	NEW HAVEN
598	UNITED ISRAEL	5/96	1923	560	NEW HAVEN	NEW HAVEN
599	FITCH STREET	5/96	1942	107	NEW HAVEN	NEW HAVEN
600	JEWISH	6/95	1960	274	BROOKFIELD	FAIRFIELD
601	CHILDREN OF ISRAEL	5/95	1911	215	DANBURY	FAIRFIELD
602	UNITED JEWISH	5/95	1932	212	DANBURY	FAIRFIELD
603	CONGREGATION ADOTH ISRAEL	7/97	1898	638	DARIEN	FAIRFIELD
604	HEBREW HOME CEMETERY	7/97	1907	128	DARIEN	FAIRFIELD
605	HEBREW SICK BENEFIT	7/97		969		FAIRFIELD
606	RODEPH SHALOM	9/96	1983	5	EASTON	FAIRFIELD
607	B'NAI ISRAEL	9/96	1855	631	FAIRFIELD	FAIRFIELD
608	LOYALTY LODGE	1934	1907	69	FAIRFIELD	FAIRFIELD
609	RODEPH SHALOM	6/97		199	FAIRFIELD	FAIRFIELD
610	EINTRACT SICK BENEFIT	6/97		311	FAIRFIELD	FAIRFIELD
611	WORKERS CIRCLE	1934		300	GREENWICH	FAIRFIELD
612	BETH EL	N		209	GREENWICH	FAIRFIELD
613	TEMPLE BETH SHALOM	N		23	NORWALK	FAIRFIELD
620	AHAVAS ACHIM	5/96	1943	188	NORWALK	FAIRFIELD
622		N		8	NORWALK	FAIRFIELD
631	WESTCHESTER WORKERS ALLIANCE	5/96	1897	542	NORWALK	FAIRFIELD
632	GREENWICH HEBREW INSTITUTE	N			SHELTON	FAIRFIELD
633	HEBREW MUTUAL	N			SHELTON	FAIRFIELD
634	KENES TIFERETH ISRAEL	N			STAMFORD	FAIRFIELD
643	NEW JEWISH CEMETERY	N		7	STAMFORD	FAIRFIELD
644	OLD JEWISH CEMETERY	N			STAMFORD	FAIRFIELD
650	PARK CEMETERY SECTION 4	N		35	TRUMBULL	FAIRFIELD
750	MORRIS	5/95	1961	79	MORRIS	LITCHFIELD
751	TORRINGTON	5/95	1899	303	TORRINGTON	LITCHFIELD
900	KADIMAH	11/96	1928	1027	WEST SPRINGFIELD	MASSACHUSETTS
901	BETH JACOB	5/96	1893	1015	WEST PRINGFIELD	MASSACHUSETTS
902	BETH EL	7/96	1917	730	WEST SPRINGFIELD	MASSACHUSETTS
903	BETH ISRAEL	5/96	1894	1865	WEST SPRINGFIELD	MASSACHUSETTS
904	BETH EL II	6/96	1942	433	WEST SPRINGFIELD	MASSACHUSETTS
905	CITY OF HOMES 1	11/96	1918	840	SPRINGFIELD	MASSACHUSETTS
906	CITY OF HOMES 2	1/97	1906	584	SPRINGFIELD	MASSACHUSETTS
907	CITY OF HOMES 3	2/97	1927	313	SPRINGFIELD	MASSACHUSETTS
908	SINAI TEMPLE	4/97	1951	513	SPRINGFIELD	MASSACHUSETTS
909	RODOLPHE SHALOM	5/97	1928	316	CHICKAPEE	MASSACHUSETTS
910	SONS OF ZION	6/97	1895	163	CHICKAPEE	MASSACHUSETTS
920	HEBREW CEMETERY	5/97	1895	49	NORTHHAMAMPTON	MASSACHUSETTS
921	B'NAI ISRAEL	5/97	1926	55	PITTSFIELD	MASSACHUSETTS

www.ingramcontent.com/pod-product-compliance
Lightning Source LLC
Chambersburg PA
CBHW080237270326
41926CB00020B/4277